The Battle of the Dnepr: The Red Army's Forcing of the East Wall, August-December 1943, details a critical period in the Red Army's advance along the southwest strategic direction during the general offensive that followed the fighting in the area of the Kursk salient in July-August 1943. The Germans, who were now on the strategic defensive in the East, sought to fall back and consolidate their front along the line of the Dnepr River. The Red Army's success in overturning these expectations along this particularly important sector is the subject of this study.

This is a composite work based upon three studies carried out by the Red Army General Staff's military-historical directorate, which was charged with collecting and analyzing the war's experience. The first is a lengthy internal document, dating from 1946, which was eventually published in Russia in 2007, although heavily supplemented by commentary and other information not contained in the original. The present work omits these additions, while supplying its own commentary in places deemed necessary. Two short articles from another publication round out the collection.

The book is divided into two parts. The first deals with the efforts by General N.F. Vatutin's Voronezh (later renamed First Ukrainian) Front to exploit the Soviet victory during the battle of Kursk and to carry the war to the Dnepr River and beyond. This involved pursuing the retreating Germans and attempting to seize crossings over the Dnepr in the Kiev area before the Germans could get across and consolidate their position. Although they were able to seize several small footholds, the Soviets were unable at first to expand them to bridgeheads of operational significance. By shifting their efforts to the bridgehead north of Kiev, the Soviets were eventually able to break out and capture Kiev, although a German counterattack from the Zhitomir area threw them back somewhat. Nevertheless, by the end of the year the Red Army in this area was ready to resume the offensive to retake the Ukrainian right bank.

The two articles which comprise the second part cover the combat operations of General I.S. Konev's Steppe (later renamed Second Ukrainian) Front through Poltava and Kremenchug and across the Dnepr and to seize bridgeheads south of Kiev. These are more narrowly focused tactical-operational studies, dealing with the efforts of the *front's* 37th and 52nd armies to expand their positions on the Ukrainian right bank into operational bridgeheads capable of supporting a larger offensive to the west in 1944.

Richard W. Harrison earned his undergraduate and master's degrees from Georgetown University, where he specialized in Russian area studies. In 1994 he earned his doctorate in War Studies from King's College London. He also was an exchange student in the former Soviet Union and spent several years living and working in post-communist Russia.

Dr Harrison has worked for the US Department of Defense as an investigator in Russia, dealing with cases involving POWs and MIAs. He has also taught Russian history and military history at college and university level, most recently at the US Military Academy at West Point.

Harrison is the author of two books dealing with the Red Army's theoretical development during the interwar period: *The Russian Way of War: Operational Art, 1904–1940* (2001), and *Architect of Soviet Victory in World War II: The Life and Theories of G.S. Isserson* (2010). He has also authored a number of articles on topics in Soviet military history. He is currently working on a history of the Red Army's high commands during the Second World War and afterwards.

Dr Harrison currently lives with his family near Carlisle, Pennsylvania.

THE BATTLE OF THE DNEPR

The Red Army's Forcing of the East Wall, September-December 1943

Soviet General Staff

Edited and Translated by Richard W. Harrison

Helion & Company
Published in cooperation with the Association of the United States Army

Helion & Company Limited
Unit 8 Amherst Business Centre
Budbrooke Road
Warwick
CV34 5WE
England
Tel. 01926 499619
Email: info@helion.co.uk
Website: www.helion.co.uk
X (formerly Twitter): @Helionbooks
Facebook: @HelionBooks
Visit our blog at https://helionbooks.wordpress.com/

Published by Helion & Company 2018, in cooperation with the Association of the United States Army.
This new edition 2025
Designed and typeset by Mach 3 Solutions (www.mach3solutions.co.uk)
Cover designed by Paul Hewitt, Battlefield Design (www.battlefield-design.co.uk)
Text and maps © Association of the United States Army 2017. English edition translated and edited by Richard W. Harrison. Maps drawn by David M. Glantz

Every reasonable effort has been made to trace copyright holders and to obtain their permission for the use of copyright material. The author and publisher apologise for any errors or omissions in this work, and would be grateful if notified of any corrections that should be incorporated in future reprints or editions of this book.

ISBN 978-1-806720-65-1

British Library Cataloguing-in-Publication Data.
A catalogue record for this book is available from the British Library.

All rights reserved. No part of this publication may be reproduced, stored in a retrieval system, or transmitted, in any form, or by any means, electronic, mechanical, photocopying, recording or otherwise, without the express written consent of Helion & Company Limited.

For details of other military history titles published by Helion & Company Limited, contact the above address, or visit our website: http://www.helion.co.uk

We always welcome receiving book proposals from prospective authors.

Contents

List of Maps	vii
List of Tables	viii
Preface to the English-Language Edition	ix

Part I
The First Ukrainian Front's Offensive along the Kiev Axis in 1943   11

Introduction   13
    A Brief Military-Geographical Description of the Area of Combat Activities   16
    The Operational Situation in the Voronezh Front's Sector   23

1   **The Forcing of the Dnepr and the Seizure of Bridgeheads Along the River's Right Bank. The Voronezh Front's Offensive Operation in October 1943**   26
    The Forcing of the Dnepr and the Seizure of Bridgeheads Along the River's Right Bank (22-29 September)   26
    The Voronezh Front's First Offensive on the Right Bank of the Dnepr in October 1943   48
    The Voronezh Front's Second Offensive Along the Right Bank of the Dnepr in October 1943   70
    The Organization of Communications and Troop Control During the *Front's* First and Second Offensives in October 1943   73
    Results and Conclusions   74

2   **The First Ukrainian Front's November Offensive Operation**   80
    The Planning and Preparation of the Operation   80
    The Breakthrough of the German Defense North of Kiev and the Liberation of Kiev (3-6 November). The Fighting Along the *Front's* Left Wing on the Bukrin Bridgehead   109
    Overall Results and Conclusions from the First Ukrainian Front's November Offensive Operation   140

3   **The First Ukrainian Front's Defensive Battles in the Areas of Kornin, Zhitomir and Brusilov During 13-30 November. The Offensive by the *Front's* Right Flank Along the Korosten' and Ovruch Axes**   144
    The First Ukrainian Front's Defensive Battles in the Area of Kornin, Zhitomir and Brusilov   144
    The Offensive by the 60th Army's Right Wing Along the Korosten' Axis   157
    The 13th Army's Offensive Along the Ovruch Axis   158
    Rear Organization and Materiel Support   159
    Results and Conclusions From the First Ukrainian Front's Defensive Fighting During the Second Half of November 1943   162

Conclusions   170

Part II
The Second Ukrainian Front's Operations in September-December 1943   241

1 **The Forcing of the Dnepr by the 37th Army in the Kremenchug Area (September-October 1943)**   243
   - Introduction   243
   - The Training of the 37th Army's Forces for Forcing the Dnepr   247
   - The Forcing of the Dnepr and the Seizure of Bridgeheads Along its Right Bank   264
   - Brief Results and Conclusions   284

2 **The Forcing of the Dnepr by the 52nd Army in the Cherkassy Area (November-December 1943)**   290
   - Introduction   290
   - The Operation's Preparation   295
   - The Conduct of the Operation   309
   - The Operation's Results and Brief Conclusions   333

Index   340

List of Maps

1 The Battle for the Dnepr, 25 August-23 December 1943.   28
2 The Kiev Operation, 3 November-22 December 1943.   81
3 The Steppe (2nd Ukrainian) Front's Operations along the Krivoi Rog Axis,
   15 October-3 November 1943.   244

List of Tables

Part I

1.1	The Overall Correlation of Forces Along the Voronezh Front	31
1.2	The Voronezh Front's Ammunition Supply Situation (In Combat Loads)	32
1.3	The Overall Correlation of Forces Along the Rzhishchev—Kanev Sector	53
1.4	The Correlation of Forces Along the 38th and 60th Armies' Front	60
1.5	The Voronezh Front's Materiel Provisioning	61
1.6	The Voronezh Front's Ammunition Provisioning	63
2.1	The Saturation of the First Ukrainian Front's Armies with Artillery by the Start of the November Offensive	95
2.2	Planned Artillery Expenditure	97
2.3	Artillery Supplies (in Combat Loads)	98
2.4	The First Ukrainian Front's Bridge Capacity	101
2.5	The Correlation of Forces Along the First Ukrainian Front	105
2.6	The Correlation of Forces Along the 38th Army's Offensive Sector	106
2.7	The Correlation of Forces Along the 60th Army's Offensive Sector	106
2.8	The Correlation of Forces Along the 40th and 27th Armies' Offensive Sector	106
2.9	The 38th and 60th Armies' Ammunition Supply	122
2.10	The Maximum Advance of the *Front's* Forces During 7-9 November (in km)	130
3.1	The Distribution of the *Front's* Forces By Axes and Sectors	164
3.2	The Saturation of the 38th, 60th and 3rd Guards Tank Armies' Combat Formations with Artillery Along the Front Zhitomir—Kornin During the Defensive Fighting in the Second Half of November 1943	166
3.3	The Tank Formations' Provisioning With Combat Equipment in the Second Half of November 1943	167
	Supplement to Part I	
	1.1 The Voronezh Front's Combat Strength by 20 September 1943	173
	1.2 The Voronezh Front's Combat Strength by 10 October 1943	190
	1.3 The Voronezh Front's Combat Strength by 31 October 1943	209
	1.4 The Voronezh Front's Combat Strength by 15 November 1943	224

Part II

1.1	The 37th Army's Strength as of 25 September 1943	249
1.2	The 37th Army's Artillery Strength on 27 September 1943	254
1.3	The Presence of Artillery and Mortars in the First-Echelon Rifle Divisions and in the Army Artillery Group by the Start of the Forcing	255
1.4	Crossing Equipment with the 37th Army	258
1.5	The Correlation of Forces Opposite the 37th Army's Front on 10 October	284
	Supplement to Chapter 1	
	1.1 The Arrival of Crossing Equipment to the 37th Army in September-October 1943	289
	1.2 The Crossing of the 37th Army's Forces From 28 September To 11 October 1943	289
2.1	The Combat Strength of the 52nd Army's Artillery	298
2.2	The Types of Crossing Equipment and Their Capabilities	300
2.3	The Distribution of Crossing Equipment by Rifle Corps y the Start of the Operation	301
2.4	The Distribution of Crossing Equipment by Crossing Points	301
2.5	The Correlation of Men and Materiel in the 52nd Army's Sector by the Start of the Operation	308
2.6	The Correlation of Men and Materiel in the 52nd Army's Sector on 25 November 1943	324
	Supplement to Chapter 2	
	2.1 The 52nd Army's Combat and Numerical Strength as of 5 November 1943	337

Preface to the English-Language Edition

This book represents a detailed study and two articles, all united by the common theme of the Red Army's approach to and crossing of the Dnepr River during the fall of 1943. The first is a lengthy study entitled "The First Ukrainian Front's Offensive Along the Kiev Axis in 1943," which was produced by the Soviet army General Staff's military-scientific directorate in 1946. This study covers the Kiev offensive and defensive operations, as the forces of the First Ukrainian Front sought to secure and expand their bridgeheads over the Dnepr River and to then defend these gains against German counteroffensives.

The second contains two articles that deal with similar efforts by the Second Ukrainian Front during September-December 1943. The first article is "The Forcing of the Dnepr by the 37th Army in the Kremenchug Area (September-October 1943)" and appeared in the *Sbornik Voenno-Istoricheskikh Materialov Velikoi Otechestvennoi Voiny*, No. 12, 1953. The second article, entitled "The Forcing of the Dnepr by the 52nd Army in the Cherkassy Area (November-December 1943)," appeared in the same issue.

The study contains a number of terms that may not be readily understandable to the casual reader in military history. Therefore, I have adopted a number of conventions designed to ease this task. For example, major Soviet formations (i.e., Voronezh Front) are spelled out in full, as are similar German formations (i.e., Army Group South). Soviet armies are designated using the shortened form (i.e., 38th Army). German armies, on the other hand, are spelled out in full (i.e., Second Army). In the same vein, Soviet corps are designated by Arabic numerals (1st Guards Cavalry Corps), while the same German units are denoted by Roman numerals (e.g., VII Army Corps). Smaller units (divisions, brigades, etc.) on both sides are denoted by Arabic numerals only (7th Guards Cavalry Division, 255th Infantry Division, etc.).

Given the large number of units involved in the operation, I have adopted certain other conventions in order to better distinguish them. For example, Soviet armored units are called tank corps, brigades, etc., while the corresponding German units are denoted by the popular term *panzer*. Likewise, Soviet infantry units are designated by the term rifle, while the corresponding German units are simply referred to as infantry.

Many of the place names in this study are hyphenated, such as Korsun'-Shevchenkovskii and Pereyaslav-Khmelnitskii. In these cases, the names are separated by a single hyphen, which is to distinguish them from a number of such locales along a particular line, such as Velizh—Dorogobuzh—Bryansk—Sumy. In the latter case, the individual villages and towns are separated by double hyphens.

The work subscribes to no particular transliteration scheme, because no entirely satisfactory one exists. I have adopted a mixed system that uses the Latin letters ya and yu to denote their Cyrillic counterparts, as opposed to the ia and iu employed by the Library of Congress, which tends to distort proper pronunciation. Conversely, I have retained the Library of Congress's ii ending (i.e., Chernyakhovskii), as opposed to the commonly-used y ending. I have also retained the apostrophe to denote the Cyrillic soft sign.

The original work contains a number of footnotes inserted by the authors, in order to explain this or that technical question. These have been retained as endnotes and have been supplemented by a number of appropriately identified editorial notes, which have been inserted as an explanatory guide for a number of terms that might not be readily understandable to the foreign reader.

Elsewhere, I have taken some small liberties as regards the book's overall organization, although there is nothing here that deviates in a major way from the original. These liberties primarily involve leaving out some maps, copies of orders, and tables, the inclusion of which would have made the final product too long. On the other hand, I do not take issue with some of the claims made in the text, and any errors or interpretations should be disputed after examining the relevant documents in the two countries' military archives. Nor have I attempted to make the language more "literary," and have striven throughout to preserve the military-bureaucratic flavor of the original.

Part I

The First Ukrainian Front's Offensive along the Kiev Axis in 1943

Introduction

The offensive by the forces of the First Ukrainian (Voronezh)[1] Front along the Kiev axis in September –October 1943, which was conducted under the command of General N.F. Vatutin,[2] occupies an important place in the Soviet army's historic battle for the Dnepr.

The chief military event of the 1943 summer campaign was the grandiose battle of Kursk. This battle, which lasted from 5 July through 23 August, concluded with the defeat of the Hitlerite army's main shock group of forces. Following the rout of the enemy around Kursk the German-Fascist command could no longer consider resuming the offensive against the Soviet army. The counteroffensive by Soviet forces around Kursk in August 1943 grew into a general offensive along an enormous front from Velikie Luki to the Black Sea.

In September-October the Soviet Supreme High Command set about carrying out major offensive operations for the purpose of inflicting a defeat on the German-Fascist forces operating along the western and southwestern strategic directions. The depth of the tasks facing the Soviet forces in this grandiose offensive reached 250-300 kilometers against an overall front of combat operations stretching 1,000-1,200 kilometers.

The Hitlerite command attempted to halt the further offensive by the Soviet army along the line Velizh—Dorogobuzh—Bryansk—Sumy—the rivers Severskii Donets and Mius through a stubborn defense. Simultaneously, he was carrying out defensive works along the western banks of the Desna, Sozh, Dnepr, and Molochnaya rivers, calculating that he could employ them for defense in the event of a breakthrough by Soviet forces. These lines had major operational significance, because they intercepted the lines of the Soviet army's offensive to the west. The fascist command attached particular importance to the line of the Dnepr. The broad and deep Dnepr is difficult for crossing, and its high right bank, with steep and precipitous banks commands the left bank and enables one to organize a powerful defense. The left bank is gently sloping and, for the most part, open and unfavorable for the approach and concentration of troops attacking from the east.

Following the unsuccessful outcome of the battles around Orel, Belgorod and Khar'kov for the Hitlerites, the fascist propagandists loudly proclaimed the fortifications along the Dnepr to be an impregnable line. Despite the harsh lessons received along the Soviet-German front in the campaigns of 1941, 1942 and 1943, the Hitlerites believed that the Soviet army would not be able to carry out a large offensive in summer conditions. The fascist command's plans for 1943 proved to be adventuristic. They, as before, were based upon an overestimation of their own forces and an underestimation of the enemy's forces.

The battle for the Dnepr consisted of a series of *front* and multi-*front* operations, unified by the overall design of the High Command. In accordance with the course of unfolding events and the sequence of carrying out the tasks, the battle for the Dnepr can be divided into three stages.

---

1 By a *Stavka* directive of 20 October the Voronezh Front was renamed the First Ukrainian Front and the Steppe Front the Second Ukrainian Front.
2 Editor's note. Nikolai Fedorovich Vatutin (1901-44) joined the Red Army in 1920. During the Great Patriotic War he served as chief of the General Staff's operational directorate, deputy chief of staff and a *Stavka* representative. From 1942 he commanded a number of *fronts* along the southwestern strategic direction. Vatutin died from wounds received in a partisan attack.

The first stage (August-September 1943) is characterized by the rout of the German-Fascist armies along the left bank of the Dnepr and in the Donbass,[3] the arrival of our forces at the Dnepr, the forcing of the Dnepr and the seizure of the first bridgeheads along its right bank. Simultaneously, Soviet forces along the western strategic direction inflicted a defeat on the central group of German-Fascist forces and captured Smolensk and Roslavl'.

The second stage embraces October-December 1943. During this time there was bitter fighting along the right bank of the Dnepr southeast of Kremenchug and in the areas of Dnepropetrovsk, Kiev and Rechitsa. It concluded with the formation of major bridgeheads, which had important strategic significance for the unfolding of the Soviet forces' subsequent offensive operations. The enemy's defense was also routed in the area of Zaporozh'ye and along the Molochnaya River, the German and Romanian Crimean group of forces was isolated from the land, and the entire southern part of the Ukrainian left bank was liberated as far as the mouth of the Dnepr, with the exception of the sector in the Nikopol' area, where the Germans held a small bridgehead. At the same time the Soviet army was concentrating its reserves along the Dnepr's right-bank bridgeheads and was preparing for a decisive offensive from these bridgeheads. Along the western strategic direction, Soviet forces were fighting along the approaches to Vitebsk and Orsha.

The third stage (the end of 1943-March 1944) is characterized by the Soviet forces' successful operations along the Ukrainian right bank. The Germans, having suffered a cruel defeat, were thrown back from the Dnepr along an enormous front from the mouth of the Berezina River to Kherson. Soviet forces continued to successfully develop the offensive toward the Soviet Union's state border. The Korsun'-Shevchenkovskii operation was conducted during this stage, during which the second largest enemy group of forces after Stalingrad was routed. Throughout the course of the entire battle for the Dnepr and the Ukrainian right bank, the forces of the Voronezh (First Ukrainian) Front operated along the main axis.

Further on, the entire course of the *front's* battle in the Kiev area is divided into the following stages:

1. The forcing of the Dnepr and the seizure of bridgeheads along the river's right bank in the second half of September 1943. The *front's* offensive operation in October 1943.
2. The *front's* November offensive operation and the liberation of Kiev (the first half of November 1943).
3. The *front's* defensive operation in the second half of November 1943 in the areas of Zhitomir and Brusilov. The development of the offensive by the *front's* right flank along the Ovruch and Korosten' axes.

From the end of August 1943 (that is, from the moment the battle of Kursk ended) the Voronezh Front's forces, in close coordination with the Central Front's left wing (attacking along the Chernigov axis) and the Steppe Front's forces (attacking along the Kremenchug axis) conducted an uninterrupted offensive. By 22-24 September 1943 they had reached the Dnepr south of the town of Pereyaslav-Khmelnitskii and north of Kiev, forced the river from the march and seized bridgeheads in these two areas.

With their arrival at the Dnepr, the forces of the Voronezh Front faced an extremely grand and responsible task. It was necessary to broaden the captured bridgeheads and through a decisive attack rout the enemy's Kiev group of forces and liberate Kiev—the capital of Soviet Ukraine. The formation of a major bridgehead in the Kiev area would place the Soviet forces in a favorable situation facing the enemy and would create the prerequisites for the successful development of the fighting along the Ukrainian right bank. The Kiev bridgehead hung from the north over the entire

---

3   Editor's note. Donbass ("Donets Basin") is a major industrial area in eastern Ukraine.

southern wing of the German armies and enabled us to carry out an offensive along three important axes: to Rovno and L'vov to the west and leading to the southern areas of Volhynia[4] and to the lower course of the Vistula River, to the southwest toward Mogilev-Podol'skii, and to the south along the right bank of the Dnepr. These axes would put the Soviet forces on the enemy's communications and would place the German-Fascist armies in a position of semi-encirclement. Besides this, the first two axes would secure our forces' arrival at the Carpathians and would enable us to split the German front into two parts and complicate the cooperation of two major enemy groups of forces—central and southern.

The *Stavka*[5] of the Supreme High Command attached great significance to the Kiev area for its forthcoming operations. Comrade Stalin[6] indicated twice during the course of the Voronezh (First Ukrainian) Front's offensive that the Kiev bridgehead is the most important and most favorable bridgehead along the right bank of the Dnepr.

Despite several failures by the *front's* forces in October, during the fighting on the Bukrin bridgehead, the Kiev operation was completed brilliantly.

Following the liberation of Kiev by Soviet forces the German command concentrated significant forces along this sector and undertook a counteroffensive in the second half of November 1943 for the purpose of halting the Soviet army's advance and then to destroy our Kiev group of forces and to eliminate the bridgehead along the right bank of the Dnepr in the Kiev area. For this purpose the enemy removed forces from various sectors of the Soviet-German front and dispatched them to the Kiev area, and also shifted reserves here from the occupied countries of Europe—Norway and France. Troops were also removed from Italy, despite the fact that at this time the Anglo-American armies had landed in the south of the country and were fighting there.

However, having expended enormous forces and equipment, the Germans were unable to achieve their goals and to eliminate the Kiev bridgehead.

At the end of December 1943 and the beginning of 1944 the forces of the First Ukrainian Front conducted successful offensive operations along the Zhitomir—Berdichev, Rovno and Chernovtsy axes, which played an important role in developing the second Stalinist blow's[7] operations.

Our forces' combat operations along the Kiev axis in the fall of 1943 have a great practical and theoretical interest, thanks to their extreme dynamism and rapid alternation of the forms of struggle in very complex combat situations.

In studying the *front's* offensive operations, the most important questions are the forcing of a major water barrier from the march, the capture of bridgeheads and subsequent actions from these bridgeheads. If the offensive by the main group of forces from the Bukrin bridgehead in October failed to yield positive results, then the November offensive from the Lyutezh bridgehead, which

---

4 Editor's note. Volhynia is a historic region along the Polish-Ukrainian-Belarusian frontier.
5 Editor's note. The *Stavka* of the Supreme High Command/*Stavka* of the Supreme Commander-in-Chief (*Stavka Verkhovnogo Glavnokomanduyushchego*) was the highest Soviet military body during the Second World War. It was formed on 23 June 1941 and disbanded following the war with Japan in 1945.
6 Editor's note. Iosif Vissarionovich Stalin (Dzhugashvili) (1879-1953) joined the Russian Social Democratic Worker's Party as a young man and soon aligned himself with the Bolshevik faction under V.I. Lenin. Following the Bolshevik coup, Stalin was appointed people's commissar for nationalities and was a political commissar during the civil war. In 1922 Stalin was appointed general secretary of the party and used this position to increase his power and eliminate his rivals. During the Great Patriotic War he was simultaneously general secretary of the Communist Party, chairman of the Council of People's Commissars, people's commissar of defense, supreme commander-in-chief, and chairman of the State Defense Committee. Following Stalin's death, his successors denounced him as a mass murderer.
7 Editor's note. The ten Stalinist blows were a series of major offensive operations conducted by the Red Army during 1944.

was conducted on the basis of a new operational design, which was indicated in a directive by the *Stavka* of the Supreme High Command, was crowned with success.

Of great interest are the regrouping of the *front's* forces from the Bukrin bridgehead to the Lyutezh bridgehead, which was carried out according to a compressed schedule and in very difficult conditions, by our forces' smooth crossing over the Dnepr and Desna rivers.

The choice of the axis of the main attack in the November offensive operation and its development is instructive, as well as the skillful operations of the *front's* forces in repelling the counteroffensive by a major enemy tank group of forces in the second half of November.

A decisive condition for the success of the *front's* combat operations was the firm and constant leadership by the *Stavka* of the Supreme High Command, which directed the *front's* activities, rendering the necessary assistance with men and materiel in the decisive moments.

The Voronezh (First Ukrainian) Front's offensive during the battle for the Dnepr unfolded in conditions of close operational and strategic cooperation, which were organized by the *Stavka* of the Supreme High Command, with the Central (Belorussian) and Steppe (Second Ukrainian) fronts.

The Steppe (Second Ukrainian) Front's forces, having seized bridgeheads along the right bank of the Dnepr southeast of Kremenchug at the end of September, launched powerful attacks against the enemy along the Krivoi Rog and Kirovograd axes in October and November. As a result of these attacks by the forces of the Steppe Front, the major railroad junction of Pyatikhatka was liberated. Following the liberation of the cities of Dneprodzerzhinsk and Dnepropetrovsk by the Southwestern (Third Ukrainian) Front in this area a bridgehead of major operational significance was formed in this area, just as in the Kiev area.

The forces of the Central (Belorussian) Front forced the Dnepr in the Loyev area, routed the enemy in the areas of Gomel' and Rechitsa, and also formed major bridgeheads along the right bank of the Dnepr and Berezina rivers.

The successful realization of the *Stavka* of the Supreme High Command's plan for routing the Kiev group of German-Fascist forces, the liberation of the capital of Soviet Ukraine—Kiev and the creation of major strategic bridgehead on the right bank of the Dnepr was linked with the name of the commander of the First Ukrainian Front, General Nikolai Fedorovich Vatutin—one of the most talented young commanders who advanced during the course of the Great Patriotic War.

N.F. Vatutin's talent as a commander manifested itself during the defense of Voronezh in the summer of 1942, in the rout of the German-Fascist forces around Stalingrad, in the swift offensive by Soviet forces from the Don bend to the Donbass, and in the rout of the Hitlerite hordes in the battle of Kursk.

The successful operations of the forces commanded by General N.F. Vatutin were noted several times in the orders of the Supreme Commander-in-Chief.

General N.F. Vatutin died on the night of 14-15 April 1944, after being seriously wounded, and was buried in Kiev, the liberation of which is indelibly linked with his name. According to a decree by the Soviet government a monument has been erected on General Vatutin's grave. On the day of N.F. Vatutin's funeral, the Supreme Commander-in-Chief, Generalissimo of the Soviet Union, comrade Stalin noted in his order that the Soviet Union's army and navy lower their combat banners before N.F. Vatutin's grave and salute one of the Soviet army's best commanders.

A Brief Military-Geographical Description of the Area of Combat Activities

The area of the First Ukrainian (Voronezh) Front's combat activities in the Kiev operation is bounded from the north by the line Chernigov—Yel'sk, from the west by the Yel'sk—Ovruch—Korosten'—Zhitomir—Berdichev railroad, from the south by the line Cherkassy—Belaya Tserkov'—Berdichev, and from the east by the line Chernigov—Nezhin—Priluki—Piryatin—Cherkassy.

The overall size of the area was 65,000 square kilometers. Combat activities took place in the territory of the Kiev and Zhitomir oblasts of the Ukrainian SSR and the southern areas of the Belorussian SSR's Poles'ye Oblast'.

The Structure of the Surface

The Ukrainian left bank represents a flat forest-steppe plain. The soil in this area is loamy. Following rains the dirt roads and the terrain off the roads is covered with a deep and viscous mud and becomes difficult of passage. The rivers' flood plains are for the most part swampy.

The right bank of the Dnepr in this area embraces part of the southern Poles'ye[8] and the Dnepr Highlands.

Southern Poles'ye is a flat lowland with low sandy hillocks. The rivers flow along low-lying banks. The soil is sandy and in places is sandy loam. In dry weather the loose sands become difficult of passage. There are a large number of small, primarily peat, marshes, overgrown with trees, particularly in the rivers' flood plains. The area's tree cover and degree of swampiness increase sharply to the north of the Uzh River (Ush on some maps).

The Dnepr Highlands are a plain cut by a thick network of deep river valleys, gullies and hollows. The heights usually do not exceed 200 meters above sea level. In the Dnepr bend and along its right bank south of Pereyaslav-Khmel'nitskii, the terrain sharply differs from the remaining area. This sector is deeply cut by deep gullies and valleys with steep precipices. The terrain here does not allow for the employment of any kind of large mobile forces (especially tanks) and makes an offensive by all combat arms more difficult.

Rivers

The majority of rivers flow north to south, or close to it and cross all paths leading from east to west. The majority of rivers have swampy valleys difficult of access. All of this complicates the troops' offensive operations to the west and creates favorable conditions for defense.

The Dnepr River. The sector from the mouth of the Pripyat' River to the mouth of the Desna River. The river valley as far as the mouth of the Irpen' River is more than 20 kilometers wide and lower down narrows to 4-8 kilometers. The valley's right slopes, reaching a height of 60-95 meters, are at the same time the river bank. The flood plain, deeply cut by channels and lakes is swampy in places and is everywhere more than three kilometers wide (up to 12 kilometers near the mouth of the Desna River). Movement along the flood plain off the roads is difficult: the river bed is winding and often breaks up into branches. The river's width is 400-500 meters and in some places is up to 1,000 meters; the predominant depth is 1.7-2.0 meters. The average speed of the current is 0.8-0.9 meters per second. The river's bottom and banks are sandy, while loamy in the Vyshgorod area.

The sector from the mouth of the Desna to Osokorka. The river flows in a broad valley, hugging the right bank, while the latter's height near Kiev reaches 70 meters. The river's flood plain is from two to 18 kilometers wide and sharply cut by channels, old beds and lakes. The river bed is twisting and changeable; its width is 170-2,000 meters, predominantly 300-400 meters; the depth is 4-5 meters; the bottom is sandy; the speed of the current is 0.7-0.8 meters per second.

The sector from Osokorka to Rzhishchev. The valley is 6-30 kilometers wide. The right bank commands along almost the entire length of the sector and is particularly high near Tripol'ye (50 meters); from Vitachev the right bank is a high ridge, cut by ravines. The left bank is lower and

---

8   Editor's note. The Poles'ye is a large forested and swampy area extending from the Western Bug River to the Dnepr River and covering 130,000 square kilometers.

gently sloping and gradually falls to the end of the sector. The flood plain is 2-11 kilometers wide. The flood plain is heavily cut by channels, lakes and swamps, making it difficult of passage. The river is winding and often splits up into branches, among which it is difficult to find the main branch. The river's width is 500-600 meters, the depth 4-5 meters, the speed of the current is 0.8 meters per second, and the bottom is sandy. The height of the river's banks is 1-2 meters and in some places reaches five meters.

The sector from Rzhishchev to Cherkassy. The river valley is wide. The right bank commands, with a height of 60-80 meters and 150 meters near Grigorovka; the banks steeply fall down to the river along almost the entire length of the sector. The left bank is low. The flood plain is 1-15 kilometers wide and is overgrown with bushes and cut by lakes and old beds. The soil is a sandy loam and in some places there are sectors of open and loose sands. The river bed is winding and divides into branches, forming a large number of islands. The river's width is 500-600 meters and the depth is 4-6 meters; the speed of the current is 0.7-0.8 meters per second.

The Dnepr's Tributaries

The Teterev River. The river valley widens toward the mouth to three kilometers. The height of the valley's banks is 10-20 meters and in some places reaches 25-40 meters; the left bank is higher than the right one; sandy and loamy slopes are cut by gullies. The river's wide flood plain is covered with glades and swampy in places and cut by lakes and old channels in its lower areas.

The river bed is winding, contains rapids along its middle course, and abounds in lakes, coves and channels. The predominant width of the river is 30-40 meters and up to 70 meters along its lower course. The depth along the upper course is 0.6-1.0 and 1.5-3.0 meters along the lower course. The river's banks are 1.5-2.0 meters high and 3-4 meters in places and are predominantly steep and precipitous. The speed of the current is 0.2-0.5 meters per second; the bottom is sandy.

There are fords from Korostyshev to the river's mouth on an average of every five kilometers and 0.2-1.0 meters deep. The river's banks are sandy and the slopes are mostly accessible.

The Irpen' River. The valley is 0.5-1.5 kilometers wide; the height of the banks is 4-20 meters and in places reaches 40-60 meters; the commanding heights are on both sides. The river's flood plain is swampy, for the most part, and difficult to traverse; the river bed is winding. The river is 2-15 meters wide along its upper course and 0.7-1.5 meters deep; the river is 10-20 meters wide along its middle course and 70-100 meters in places, with a depth of 1.5-3.0 meters, while along its lower course it is 9-15 meters wide and 2-3 meters deep. The bottom is sandy and silted. Fords are encountered on the average every 8-9 kilometers and their depth is 0.3-0.7 meters.

The Irpen' River, due to its swampy flood plain and silted bottom is a significant barrier for crossing troops along its upper and lower course. The river's banks serve as good defensive lines facing west and east.

The lower course of the Pripyat' River. The valley is wide and low. The right bank is high (8-30 meters) and steep, and precipitous in places; the left bank is low and gently sloping. The flood plain is 2-10 kilometers wide and swampy and is overgrown with bushes in places; it is cut by channels and old river beds. The river's depth along some stretches is 3-8 kilometers and one kilometer along the shoals. The speed of the current is 0.4-0.7 meters per second. The river bottom is sandy and clogged with rocks. The approaches to the river are made difficult by a large number of coves and channels.

The Uzh River. The river valley is 1-6 kilometers wide and swampy and overgrown with trees in places and difficult of passage. The river bed is changeable and often forms new channels. The river's width is 15-30 meters and at its greatest is up to 80 meters; its depth is 0.8-2.0 meters, and going as deep as five meters. The river's banks along the Kaganovich—Zamosh'ye sector are low and marshy in places and dry along the remainder of its length. The speed of the current is 0.1-0.8 meters per second. The bottom is sandy and hard. The fords are 0.2-1.0 meters deep.

Woods

The most heavily wooded area is to the north of the Kiev—Zhitomir line, where large wooded areas are located. The woods are primarily untouched, with a thick network of cuttings, which have been cleared to a significant degree and are easily traversed by infantry and cavalry. Large wooded areas are rarely encountered south of this line. There are thickets of bushes and small trees along the swamps.

Inhabited locales

Rural inhabited areas vary quite a lot according to size. Alongside very small ones, consisting of 10-20 homesteads, there are large ones, numbering 300-600 homesteads. There are only two large cities—Kiev, the capital of the Ukrainian SSR, and Zhitomir. The structures in the rural inhabited locales and small towns are primarily made of wood.

Communications Means

Railroads. While temporarily occupying the territory, the Germans changed over all the main railroads to the European gauge. They significantly destroyed them during their withdrawal: they blew up bridges, particularly destroying all the bridges over the Dnepr (three near Kiev and one near Kanev), upon which the area's entire railroad network depends, burned depots and stations, destroyed the roadbed, destroyed communications, and burned or sent to Germany the rolling stock.

There were the following railroads in the area under study: Nezhin—Kiev (double-track main line), Lubny—Kiev (single-track), Kiev—Korosten' (double-track), Kiev—Fastov—Kazatin (double-track main line), Fastov—Zhitomir (double-track), and Zolotonosha—Kanev—Fastov (single-track along the Zolotonosha—Mironovka sector and from then on double-track). All of these lines run from east to west.

There were the following lateral lines: Nezhin—Priluki—Grebenka—Cherkassy (single-track) and Ovruch—Korosten'—Zhitomir—Berdichev—Kazatin (single and double-track).

Among the important railroad junctions are Bakhmach, Grebenka, Darnitsa, and Nezhin along the left bank and Kiev, Fastov I and II, Zhitomir, Korosten', Ovruch, Berdichev, Kazatin, and Mironovka along the Dnepr's right bank.

The capacity of these lines for the enemy was low and was far from prewar norms. On the territory liberated from the enemy by Soviet forces the capacity depended upon the degree to which the railroads had been restored, particularly the railroad junctions and bridges.

Vehicular roads. The left bank of the Dnepr is supplied with dirt and improved roads. The thickness of the road network enabled us to select one through road for every 5-6 kilometers of front. There were improved dirt roads every 12-17 kilometers. There was one Kiev—Chernigov highway.

In the area's right-bank part there were only two hard-surfaced roads: Kiev—Zhitomir and Kiev—Belaya Tserkov'. There was one through route every 4-6 kilometers and an improved dirt road every 10-14 kilometers of front. The roads were difficult of passage in bad weather.

The Dnepr could be used for river navigation. However, due to the destruction of the Dneproges[9] dams in 1941 the conditions for navigating the river had sharply worsened. The Desna River could be employed for navigation along the sector from the town of Oster to where it flows into the Dnepr.

---

9   Editor's note. The Dneproges (Dnepr hydroelectric station) was constructed near Zaporozh'ye in 1927-32. The Soviets destroyed it in 1941 to prevent its capture by the Germans. It was rebuilt in 1944-50.

Communications

The area's territory is covered by a sufficiently dense and developed network of permanent communications lines, primarily telephone. However, as a result of the destruction carried out by the Germans during their withdrawal, major restoration work was required.

The Airfield Network

The nature of the terrain, with the exception of the Poles'ye, is generally favorable for developing an airfield network. There were first and second-class airfields (airports and permanent airfields) on the left bank in Priluki, Lubny, Oster, Brovary, and Borispol' and along the right bank in Kiev, Korosten', Zhitomir, Berdichev, Vasil'kov, and Belaya Tserkov'. There was also a dense network of field airfields, although in the conditions of the autumn rains it was difficult to employ the latter.

Weather

The weather in the area of military activities in the second half of September was predominantly dry and clear. Rains fell rarely and the average temperature varied from 6-8 degrees Celsius above freezing at night and 15-20 degrees during the day.

In October the weather continued dry, with good visibility, with the exception of 16-19 October, when a light rain fell, which sharply worsened visibility and ruined the roads. The temperature at the beginning of the month was comparatively high: 8-12 degrees above freezing at night and 18-20 degrees during the day. The temperature fell somewhat during the second half of October, going down to 0 at night, and even lower, and 8-10 degrees during the day. In the last days of the month the daytime temperature did not exceed 2-4 degrees. There was fog throughout the month, which sharply limited visibility.

November was overcast, with frequent precipitation (rain, wet snow, drizzle). The average daytime temperature at the beginning of the month ranged from +10 to -3 degrees and by the end of the month from +2 to -4 degrees; the nighttime temperature wavered between +6 to -5 degrees. There were only two clear days, with the remainder overcast, with cloudiness from 100 to 400 meters; there was fog at night and in the mornings, and often during the day. There was precipitation for 17 days. Visibility varied from 4-10 kilometers, and 1-2 kilometers and less in the fog. The dirt roads were difficult of passage for all kinds of vehicles, especially toward the end of the month.

The Germans loudly advertised the fortifications which they called the "Eastern Wall" (*Ostwall*), or "the 1943 defensive line." They considered the first and most powerful barrier of the "wall" to be the line along the Dnepr River, west of which they had outfitted intermediate defensive lines, chiefly along the western banks of the water barriers. The Germans refitted and also employed the old fortifications built by the Soviet Union in this area even before the war.

In general, the area enabled us to conduct wide-ranging maneuver operations by all the combat arms. However, it is necessary to take into account that the organization of the tactical breakthrough of the enemy's defense in the October and November offensive operations took place in the least favorable, in the military-geographical sense, sectors. The Dnepr bend south of the town of Pereyaslav-Khmel'nitskii represented a sector that was very much cut by deep gullies, which almost excluded the possibility of the mass employment of tank troops in the offensive and created very favorable conditions for the defense. The sector north of Kiev, which was heavily wooded, also created significant difficulties for the offensive activities of all the combat arms.

If in September and October the weather favored the conduct of combat operations, then it sharply worsened in November, the roads were ruined, and visibility was significantly reduced, all of which limited the combat activities of the ground and air forces.

Upon reaching the Dnepr the Voronezh Front's forces operated simultaneously along several operational axes. The Ovruch and Korosten' operational axes, which ran along the wooded and swampy part of the southern Poles'ye, remained auxiliary throughout this entire time. These axes had no roads with a stone surface, which made the operations of mobile forces (tanks and cavalry) more difficult. On the other hand, the partisan movement was widespread in this area and to a significant degree the partisans tied down the German forces. The Voronezh Front's objectives along these axes were the major railroad junctions of Ovruch and Korosten', which were located along the Nevel'—Vitebsk—Zhlobin—Kazatin—Zhmerinka strategic lateral railroad, which was very important for the Germans.

The Zhitomir operational axis, the axis of which was the Kiev—Zhitomir—Rovno highway, enabled us to deploy major forces and widely employ mobile troops. This axis was one of the main ones for the front, because it led to the major railroad junction of Zhitomir and, further, in attacking along the southern boundary of the Poles'ye, to western Ukraine and southern Poland.

The Fastov—Kazatin operational axis was very important, because following the capture of Kiev it led Soviet forces to a number of major railroad junctions along the Ukrainian right bank (Fastov, Kazatin, Zhmerinka, and Proskurov), which, in turn, cut the German forces' front and created a threat to the entire enemy group of forces in southern Ukraine. This axis enabled us to widely employ all the combat arms.

The Belaya Tserkov' operational axis, given operations by the front's forces from the Dnepr bend south of Pereyaslav-Khmel'nitskii, enabled us to bypass Kiev from the south and also led to the important areas of Fastov and Kazatin. This axis, which was the main one at the start of the operation, later acquired secondary significance. The terrain conditions did not enable us to effectively employ mobile forces and eased the Germans' defensive activities.

The Overall Strategic Situation

During the summer and fall of 1943 the events of the Second World War developed in conditions in which the main forces of the German-Fascist army and the armies of Germany's satellites were, as before, concentrated in the east. In 1943 the Soviet army once again had to bear on its shoulders the entire weight of the fight against the German-Fascist aggressors. In May 1943 the Anglo-American forces completed their combat operations in Tunisia and completely eliminated the German-Italian forces in North Africa. Nothing interfered with the opening of the second front in Europe by an invasion of the main British and American forces into the continent. However, once again, as in 1942 the governments of the USA and Great Britain continued to put off carrying out their responsibilities in the common fight against German fascism. Guided not so much by the interests of the most rapid defeat of fascist Germany as the desire to prolong the war and thus maximally weaken the Soviet Union and also to forestall the Soviet army in reaching the Balkans and Central Europe, Churchill was able to cancel the invasion of northern France in the summer of 1943. Instead of a decisive attack along the shortest and most favorable direction against Germany's vital centers, the Anglo-American command adopted a plan for operations in the south of Europe, beginning with an invasion of the island of Sicily, and then of the Apennine peninsula. Naturally, this could not draw any kind of significant German forces from the east and led to a prolongation of the war.

In 1943, when the Soviet army was waging a gigantic struggle around the Kursk bulge, which concluded with the crushing of the German forces along a broad front, the Anglo-American armies and navy were engaged in operations of secondary significance, which in no way altered the overall strategic situation in Europe. For example, in June they easily seized the islands of Pantelleria and Lampedusa and in July carried out a landing on the island of Sicily, and in August cleared this island of German and Italian forces. In September the Anglo-American forces forced the narrow

Strait of Messina and landed on the Apennine peninsula on the sock of the Italian "boot" and at Salerno.

All that the Anglo-American strategists were capable of was the slow and methodical pushing out of the Germans from Italy. Having begun combat activities in the far south of the country, the Anglo-American command allowed the Germans to consolidate in its central and northern parts. Following the capture of Naples in October 1943, the Anglo-American forces' operations in Italy quieted down and the fight here took on a prolonged character until almost the very end of the war.

As concerns the distribution of the German army's forces between the fronts, on 1 October 1943, at a time when the Soviet army had achieved major strategic results and had reached the middle course of the Dnepr along an enormous front, more than two-thirds of the German-Fascist army was engaged in combat on the Soviet-German front. At this time there were only 12 divisions in Italy, or little more than four percent of the Germans' total forces, particularly as only a few divisions were directly engaged in fighting the Anglo-American forces in southern Italy. Taking advantage of this, in the fall of 1943 the German command transferred a significant number of forces from Italy to the Soviet-German front.

Alongside this along the war's eastern front the Soviet army's majestic struggle unfolded, which yielded major strategic successes in 1943. Following the crushing defeat of the German armies around Stalingrad in the winter of 1942-43, the German command attempted to take the initiative in its hands and began a major offensive in the summer of 1943 around Kursk. As is known, this offensive failed as early as its beginning stage and the subsequent mighty blows by the Soviet army, which had gone over to the offensive, shook the Germans' front along an enormous expanse from Velikie Luki to the shores of the Sea of Azov and the Black Sea. Combat operations were conducted simultaneously along the western, southwestern and southern strategic directions. The Soviet army advanced vigorously to the west, routed tens of the enemy's pick divisions and destroying and capturing large amounts of his military equipment.

The enemy resisted furiously, clinging to favorable lines and terrain, while mainly employing for this purpose water barriers. In a number of cases, the enemy launched brief but powerful counterblows with his operational reserves. In this way, the Germans calculated on disrupting the Soviet command's plans and in the final analysis prevent it from fully employing the strategic success, which had taken shape following the rout of the enemy's main groups of forces in July and August in the area of Orel, Belgorod, and Khar'kov and in the Donbass.

The Soviet Supreme High Command, while skillfully organizing operational-strategic coordination and uninterruptedly guiding the fronts' combat activities, prevented the enemy from stabilizing the front along the Kiev axis. In the second half of September 1943 Soviet forces reached the Dnepr's middle course and seized bridgeheads along its right bank. Along the western strategic direction, there was fighting on the approaches to Smolensk and Roslavl', while along the southern strategic direction Soviet forces reached the Germans' fortified line along the Molochnaya River.

The German command began to feverishly bring up forces to the Dnepr and to develop along its right bank the previously begun defensive works for the purpose of sitting it out behind this powerful obstacle and to prolong the war in the hopes of a change in the political situation and the breakup of the anti-Hitlerite bloc of freedom-loving peoples. Goebbels'[10] agency constantly declared in all languages over the radio and in the press the impregnability of the defensive "wall"

---

10 Editor's note. Paul Joseph Goebbels (1897-1945) joined the Nazi Party in 1924 and soon became part of Hitler's inner circle. He served as Reich minister of propaganda from 1933 until 1945. Goebbels and his wife committed suicide, after poisoning their children.

along the Dnepr. In this way he was attempting to raise the troops' spirits and to fool world public opinion as to the true state of affairs on the Soviet-German front.

By the close of the 1943 summer campaign the Soviet army was faced with a new task: employing the captured bridgeheads, to rout the enemy, deprive the German army of a favorable and powerful defensive line, as was the Dnepr, and to thus create favorable prerequisites for the final expulsion of the fascist aggressors from the Soviet land.

The Operational Situation in the Voronezh Front's Sector

In September 1943 the Central, Voronezh and Steppe fronts were developing the offensive along the southwestern strategic direction with the task of reaching the Dnepr's middle course. The offensive developed most successfully along the Kiev axis, involving the left wing of the Central Front and the right wing of the Voronezh Front. The forces of the Voronezh Front's left wing and the Steppe Front advanced more slowly, while waging a fierce battle with the Germans' Poltava group of forces. The overall situation demanded the all-round development of the success along the Kiev axis in order to destroy the German forces falling back to the west before they could organize a defense along the right bank of the Dnepr. It was necessary to force the Dnepr from the march and to seize on its right bank bridgeheads that would enable us to deploy major shock groups of the front's forces for the subsequent development of the offensive along the Ukrainian right bank.

Having captured the town of Sumy in the beginning of September, the Voronezh Front's forces, consisting of the 38th, 40th, 47th, 52nd, 27th, 4th Guards, 6th Guards, and 2nd Air armies, were developing the offensive in the general direction of Romny and Pereyaslav-Khmel'nitskii. In the middle of September the *Stavka* of the Supreme High Command reinforced the front with powerful mobile formations—the 3rd Guards Tank Army and the 1st Guards Cavalry Corps.

By 9-10 September the troops of the front's right wing were approaching the Khorol River, and the troops in the center the Psyol River; that is, they were 190-240 kilometers from the Dnepr.

By this time the *front* headquarters, in accordance with instructions from the *Stavka* of the Supreme High Command, had drawn up a plan for an offensive operation for the purpose of reaching the Dnepr River.

The overall goal of the operation was the destruction of the enemy along the Ukrainian left bank, the arrival at the Dnepr River and the seizure by mobile formations of bridgeheads along its right bank along the Rzhishchev—Cherkassy sector and to subsequently continue the offensive on the Ukrainian right bank.

It was planned that the mobile formations would reach the Dnepr by 26-27 September and the main forces of the combined-arms armies by 1-5 October.

The enemy did not have any operational reserves along the Kiev axis. The German command could operate only with those forces that by this time were already tied down in fighting with the attacking Soviet army, or with forces brought in from other sectors of the Soviet-German front, or transferred from Western Europe—to which the Germans were forced to turn. When it became clear that the Germans were not strong enough to halt the Soviet army's offensive on the Ukrainian left bank, the enemy, while striving to maximally maintain the combat capability of its forces, began to pull them back to the right bank of the Dnepr for the purpose of employing them primarily for defending the river.

The Voronezh Front's Offensive, 9-22 September

Up to the moment they reached the river, the offensive by the forces of the Voronezh Front unfolded in the following manner.

The Central Front's 13th and 60th armies, taking advantage of the weak resistance by the beaten enemy, were developing the offensive south of the Desna River along the Bakhmach—Nezhin railroad and throwing the Germans to the south of the road into the sector of the Voronezh Front's 38th Army, which was operating along its right flank.

An enemy group of forces, consisting of eight divisions,[11] was falling back with open flanks in the direction of Romny, Priluki and Kiev. Both of this group's flanks were exposed.

On 15 September yet another isolated group of German forces, consisting of one motorized and four infantry divisions,[12] was noted falling back opposite the 40th and 47th armies toward the Dnepr to the Kanev—Cherkassy sector. This group's flanks were also exposed.

The group of armies along the Voronezh Front's right flank and center (38th, 40th, 47th, and 52nd armies), while developing the offensive to the Dnepr, were up to 15 September fighting with the enemy who was attempting to hold our offensive along lines favorable to the defense, particularly along the Psyol, Khorol, Sula and Romen rivers.

By the close of 15 September the front's forces had reached the line Lipovoe—the eastern outskirts of Romny—Zalatykha—Lutsenki—Sencha—Rashivka—Bol'shaya Obukhovka—Oposhnya—Konstantinovka. The Central Front's left wing—the 13th and 60th armies—had by this time captured Nezhin; that is, they were already 60-90 kilometers west of the line reached by the 38th Army.

On 16 September the commander of the Voronezh Front issued an order to pull back the 27th Army, which up to this time had been attacking with the front's left-wing armies—into the front's second echelon in the Lokhvitsy area. The purpose of this measure was to reinforce the front's group of forces which had the task of forcing the Dnepr along the Rzhishchev—Cherkassy sector.

From 16 September the enemy's resistance weakened sharply. Having lost any hope of holding the pressure by the Soviet forces along the Kiev axis, he began to hurriedly pull back his forces to the Dnepr for the purpose of occupying in an organized fashion a defense along the river's right bank. This was undoubtedly facilitated by the overall operational-strategic situation along the Ukrainian left bank, particularly the success by the Central Front's left wing along the Nezhin axis, as well as that of the Southwestern and Southern fronts in the Donbass and along the Dnepropetrovsk axis. The forces of the Voronezh Front's right wing and center, upon going over to a pursuit of the enemy, advanced 30-35 kilometers and more per day.

Up to 22 September the 38th and 47th armies pursued the enemy who was falling back opposite the 38th Army to the Kiev crossing and, opposite the 47th Army—the Kanev crossing. The 40th Army, as it approached the Dnepr, experienced less and less resistance from the enemy, who was pulling his forces to the above-named crossings. The left-wing armies (4th and 6th guards and 52nd) attacked slowly, while continuing to engage in intense fighting with the Germans' Poltava group of forces and turning their front to the southwest and south.

The front's mobile forces were to decide the success of the operation to force the Dnepr and to seize bridgeheads. The 3rd Guards Tank Army, which up to now had been in the reserve of the *Stavka* of the Supreme High Command in the Kursk and Tula areas, was moving by combined march to the area east of Sumy. With the advance of the front's forces to the west, by 19 September the army had concentrated in the area west of Romny. The slow pace of the army's concentration is explained by the low capacity of the railroad, which was being restored, along which the army's echelons were moving with combat materiel. By 19 September the army's rear establishments had also failed to move. At this time the army fuel depots were located 300 kilometers from the army's concentration area.

---

11 183rd, 340th, 327th, 208th, 68th, 88th, 75th, and 82nd infantry divisions.
12 10th Motorized and 57th, 255th, 112th, and 24th infantry divisions.

The 1st Guards Cavalry Corps, while following on the march from the area east of Sumy, by 19 September had concentrated in the Romny area and was operationally subordinated to the commander of the 3rd Guards Tank Army.

As early as 16 September the front commander ordered the 3rd Guards Tank Army, along with the 1st Guards Cavalry Corps,[13] to speed up the gathering and concentration of their units and, while moving in the general direction of Priluki and Yagotin, to reach the Pereyaslav-Khmel'nitskii area and be ready to immediately force the Dnepr River (the front commander's directive No. 0036/op).

By 19 September the 38th and 40th armies had already reached the line Makeevka—Rudovka—Krutoyarovka—Grebenka—Lubny and were continuing to pursue the enemy who was falling back to the Dnepr.

The movement of the tank army from its concentration area west of Romny began on the night of 19-20 September. It was only on 21 September that the 6th Guards Tank Corps' forward detachment began fighting with enemy units along the Supoi River (east of Pereyaslav-Khmel'nitskii). The pace of the army's advance over three days to a depth of 180-200 kilometers (until its arrival at the Dnepr) averaged 60-70 kilometers per day).

On 22 September the front's forces reached the line Letki—Gogolev—Baryshevka—the Dnepr's left bank from Kal'ne to Grigorovka—Chepilki—Zolotonosha—Brigadirovka—Stepanovka—Fedun'ki. The 3rd Guards Tank Army's forward detachments forced the Dnepr south of Pereyaslav-Khmel'nitskii and captured the area of Zarubentsy and Grigorovka. At this time the enemy did not have a continuous front. There were gaps between the armies' flanks and even between the formations' flanks. On 22 September the 6th Guards Army was pulled into the *Stavka* of the Supreme High Command reserve. The front's second echelon—the 27th Army—was moving into the area west of Lubny.

As early as the end of August the Central Front broke through the German Second Army's defense in the Sevsk area and was attacking toward the Desna River. The greatest success was noted along the front's left flank, and by 15th September the 13th and 60th armies had occupied Nezhin. The enemy tried to halt our offensive along the Desna; however the forces of the Central and Bryansk fronts forced the river and, having crushed the enemy's resistance, on 16-17 September captured the towns of Novgorod-Severskii, Bryansk and Bezhitsa. On 21 September our forces liberated Chernigov.

Following the capture of Novgorod-Severskii the Central Front's right wing developed the offensive along the Gomel' axis and its left wing (13th and 60th armies) forced the lower course of the Desna south of Chernigov and reached the eastern bank of the Dnepr and on 21 September began to force it north of Kiev, along the Chernobyl' axis.

Throughout September the Steppe Front was engaged in fighting with the stubbornly resisting Poltava group of the German Eighth Army. By 22 September the front's forces had arrived immediately at Poltava along the eastern bank of the Vorskla River and further to the line Maloye Pereshchepino—Mayachka. The German forces, which were defending the Poltava salient, were under the threat of flank attacks by the armies of the Voronezh Front's left flank and the Steppe Front's right flank.

---

13 The corps included the 1st, 2nd and 7th guards cavalry divisions.

1

The Forcing of the Dnepr and the Seizure of Bridgeheads Along the River's Right Bank. The Voronezh Front's Offensive Operation in October 1943

The Forcing of the Dnepr and the Seizure of Bridgeheads Along the River's Right Bank (22-29 September)

The Troops' Situation by 22 September 1943 and the Correlation of Forces

The enemy's group of forces. The right-flank formations of the German Fourth Panzer Army and the left-flank formations of the Eighth Army (Army Group South) were falling back in the Voronezh Front's offensive sector. The panzer army's main group of forces was falling back on Kiev, where there were two bridges.

Because the enemy was unable to rapidly transfer all of his forces, combat equipment and materiel supplies to the right bank of the Dnepr, his resistance grew as he fell back. If before 22 September this group of forces was falling back in the direction of Romny, Priluki and Kiev, with open flanks, and could have been easily outflanked from the north and south, then by the close of that day the enemy's flanks were covered from the north by the Desna River and from the south by the Dnepr River.

The enemy was strongly covering the Kiev crossing, while striving to transfer all his forces to the right bank of the river in an organized manner. Along the Pukhovka—Gogolev—Borispol'—Kailov line the 213th Security and 68th, 88th and 75th infantry divisions, and part of the Germans' 82nd and 327th infantry divisions were engaged in holding actions. The 291st Infantry Division was occupying Brovary. On this day the 183rd and 340th infantry divisions were crossing the Dnepr in the Kiev area, while the 95th and 339th infantry divisions were arriving from other sectors of the front. The 208th Infantry Division, which had earlier crossed the river, was occupying defensive positions along the right bank of the Dnepr north of Kiev, while there were no German forces to the south. Thus in all the enemy had 12 infantry divisions in the Kiev area, of which six were covering the crossings, while the remainder were crossing over the Dnepr and occupying defensive positions along its right bank. The German forces in the Kiev area were part of the VII and XIII army corps.

The German Eighth Army's left-flank formations were falling back to the crossing near Kanev. By the close of 22 September the XXIV Panzer Corps, which consisted of the 10th Motorized, the 57th, 255th, 112th, and 34th infantry divisions, and the 12th Assault Brigade (a brigade of assault guns), was engaged in defensive fighting along the line Liplyavo—Glemyazovo—excluding Korobovka and was hurriedly crossing its units to the right bank of the Dnepr near Kanev. There were no enemy forces along the left bank of the Dnepr on the sector of the front from Kailov to Liplyavo. Individual units of the German 11th and 3rd panzer divisions were moving along the

THE VORONEZH FRONT'S OFFENSIVE OPERATION, OCTOBER 1943

left bank of the Dnepr on Zolotonosha, which on that day had been occupied by the 47th Army's forces. The Germans had no organized defense along the right bank of the Dnepr.

The 19th Panzer Division, which had earlier been pulled out of the fighting and which had crossed the Dnepr near Kiev, was moving out of Kiev through Kagarlyk toward the bend of the Dnepr south of Pereyaslav-Khmel'nitskii. In the second half of 22 September this division's lead elements and units of the 34th Infantry Division, which had managed to cross the Dnepr near Kanev in strength of no more than a regiment, appeared in the Dnepr bend near the inhabited locales of Grigorovka and Zarubentsy and got into a fight with the 3rd Guards Tank Army's motorized infantry, which was crossing here. The Germans' 7th Panzer and 72nd Infantry divisions were moving along the right bank of the Dnepr from the southeast, in the direction of Kanev. By the close of 22 September the head of these divisions' column was approaching Cherkassy. The bridges over the Dnepr near Cherkassy were being covered by composite units in strength up to a regiment. In all, the Germans had more than five infantry divisions, a motorized and three panzer divisions along the sector of the front from Rzhishchev to Cherkassy, of which four infantry and one motorized divisions were directly involved in the fighting.

The German Eighth Army's main group of forces, which consisted of the III and XLVII panzer and XI Army corps, while engaged in stubborn fighting in the Poltava area, was falling back slowly toward the crossings over the Dnepr near Kremenchug. The III Panzer Corps, consisting of the *Wiking* Panzer Division, the 6th Panzer Division and the "D" group of forces, as well as the SS *Totenkopf* Division and the 223rd Infantry Division from the XLVII Panzer Corps, was operating in the Voronezh Front's sector, opposite its left wing. All of these forces were fighting facing north and were falling back slowly to the south toward Kremenchug. Thus the enemy had one and a half infantry and three panzer divisions opposite the Voronezh Front's left wing.

In all, by the close of 22 September the enemy had about 26 divisions, of which there were up to 19 infantry, one motorized and six panzer divisions, facing the Voronezh Front. All of these divisions had suffered heavy losses in the previous fighting.

The Germans were carrying out defensive works along the right bank of the Dnepr using the local population and prisoners of war and were digging trenches with open platforms for heavy infantry weapons. However, by the time the Soviet forces arrived at the Dnepr these works had not been completed. There were no continuous trenches and along individual sectors the Germans had only begun to carry out defensive works in depth, building second and third trenches. The work was being carried out most intensively in the Kanev area and in the Dnepr bend south of Pereyaslav-Khmel'nitskii. The enemy had previously prepared a bridgehead for defense along the left bank of the Dnepr near Kiev. Trenches had been dug and minefields prepared here.

The Voronezh Front's group of forces. The Voronezh Front was attacking along three axes. The front's right wing, the 38th Army, was attacking directly on Kiev. The front's center and main group of forces, consisting of the 40th and 47th armies and the 3rd Guards Tank Army, along with the 1st Guards Cavalry Corps, was attacking toward Pereyaslav-Khmel'nitskii and was approaching the Dnepr along the Rzhishchev—Kanev sector. The front's left-wing forces, the 52nd and 4th Guards armies, were fighting along the line Brigadirovka—Kuzubeevka—Stepanovka—Volok—Dikan'ka and, in conjunction with the Steppe Front, were attacking to the south.

The 38th Army consisted of the 50th and 51st rifle corps[1] and the 3rd Guards Tank Corps. By the close of 22 September the army was engaged in fighting a major enemy group of forces, consisting of the 213th Security, 68th, 88th, 75th, 82nd, 327th, and 291st infantry divisions,

---

1 The 50th Rifle Corps included the 163rd, 136th, 232nd, and 71st rifle divisions, and the 51st Rifle Corps included the 240th, 167th, 180th, and 340th rifle divisions.

28 THE BATTLE OF THE DNEPR

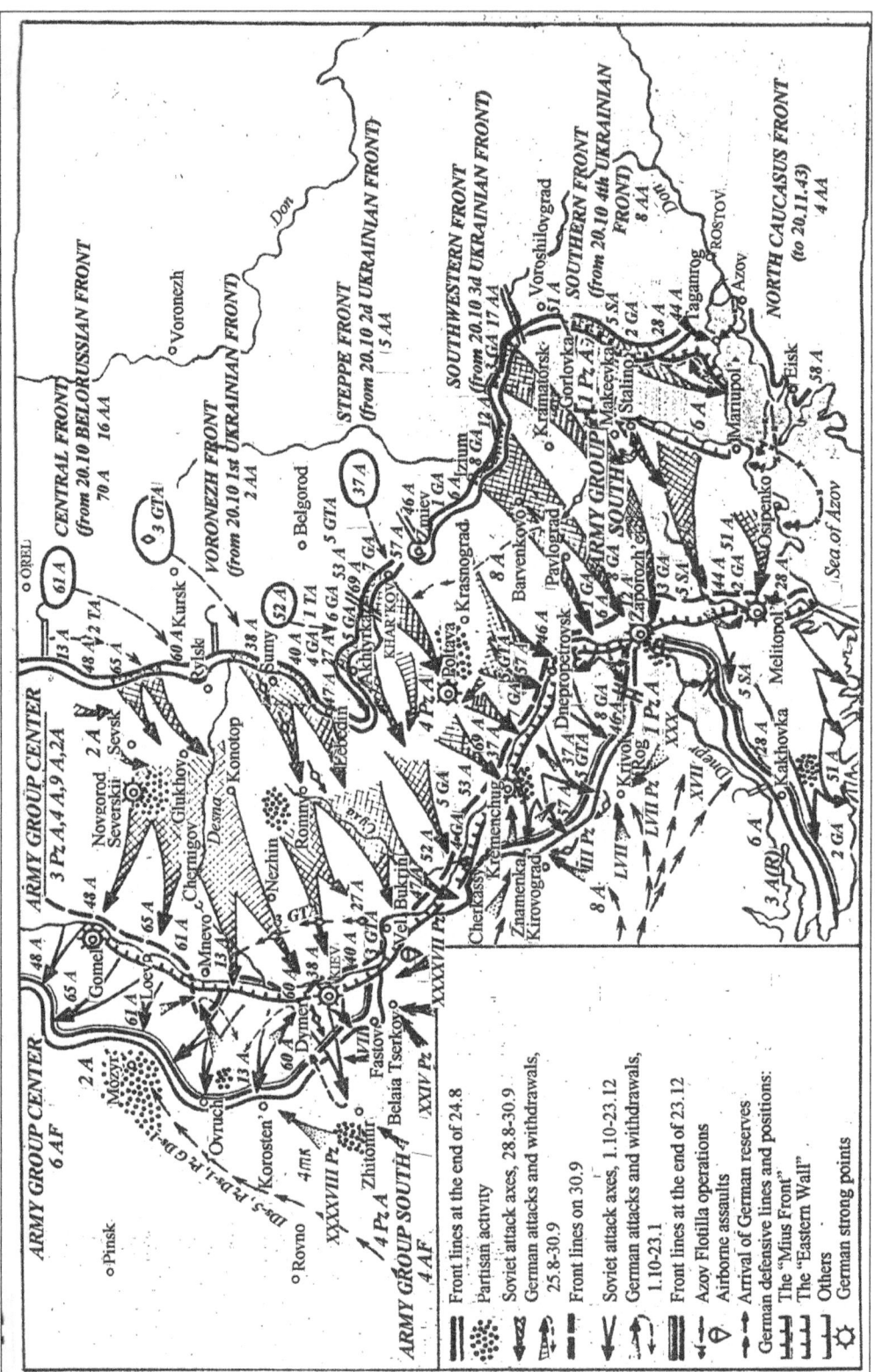

Map 1 The Battle for the Dnepr, 25 August–23 December 1943.

which were covering the Kiev crossings. However, only two and a half of the army's rifle divisions (163rd, 232nd and part of the 167th rifle divisions) were directly engaged with the enemy.

By the close of 22 September the 240th and main forces of the 167th rifle divisions had arrived at the left bank of the Desna River along the Letki—Rozhny sector and set about crossing this river. The division lacked crossing equipment and, despite the fact that there was no enemy facing them, were crossing over on materials at hand very slowly. The army's remaining divisions (180th, 340th, 136th, and 71st rifle) were carrying out a march, while regrouping to the north. As early as the previous evening the 3rd Guards Tank Corps had reached the operational sector of its neighbor to the right, in the area of the town of Oster (50 kilometers north of Brovary). Neither the front nor army headquarters had communications with the corps. A total of 12 German infantry divisions faced the 38th Army's eight rifle divisions. The correlation of forces along this sector of the front was 1:1.5 in favor of the enemy.[2]

On 22 September 1943 the central group of the *front's* forces reached the Dnepr in the Pereyaslav-Khmel'nitskii area.

Units of the 3rd Guards Tank Army were the first to reach the Dnepr. As early as the close of 21 September, reconnaissance elements of the 9th Mechanized Corps' 69th Mechanized Brigade arrived at the left bank of the Dnepr in the Zarubentsy area. Throughout the night the scouts raised and repaired the half-sunken peasant ferry and at dawn on 22 September a battalion of motorized infantry from the 9th Mechanized Corps' 69th Mechanized Brigade crossed the Dnepr and occupied Zarubentsy. At 1500 on 22 September a motorized rifle battalion from the 6th Guards Tank Corps' 51st Guards Tank Brigade also forced the Dnepr and occupied Grigorovka. The battalion's crossing was accompanied by a 15-minute artillery fire onslaught against the heights on the right bank of the river. The partisans operating here rendered significant assistance to the tank army's forward units, leading them to the places most convenient for forcing and helping them to gather materials at hand for the crossings.

By the close of the day the main forces of the 9th Mechanized Corps were approaching the river bank along the Andrushi—Kozintsy—V'yunishche sector and the main forces of the 6th Guards Tank Corps to the Gorodishche area. the 7th Guards Tank Corps was concentrating in Pereyaslav-Khmel'nitskii and the 1st Guards Cavalry Corps was on the march to the north and northwest of Priluki.

By the close of 22 September the 40th Army, consisting of the 52nd Rifle Corps,[3] the 47th Rifle Corps[4] and the 10th and 8th Guards tank corps, had reached the Dnepr River with its forward detachments along the Kal'ne—Gusentsy—Andrushi sector. The 52nd Rifle Corps' main forces reached the line Staroye—Kovalin and those of the 47th Rifle Corps the line Stovpyagi—Tsybli—excluding Khotski. The 10th Tank Corps arrived directly at the Dnepr in the Yashniki area (the corps on 20 September had only 19 tanks and self-propelled guns available). The 8th Guards Tank Corps was concentrating in Pereyaslav-Khmel'nitskii.

By the Close of 22 September the 47th Army, consisting of the 23rd Rifle Corps,[5] the 21st Rifle Corps[6] and the 3rd Guards Mechanized Corps reached the line Chepilki—Bogdany—Kovrai-Bezborodkov—Ashanovka with the forces of the 30th, 23rd and 206th rifle divisions, having lost contact with the enemy covering the crossing in the Kanev area. Only the 23rd Rifle Division's forward detachment was approaching the Supoi River near Glemyazovo and was fighting units of

---

2   In calculating the correlation of forces, the 38th Army's 3rd Guards Tank Corps, which left for the north to its neighbor's sector, is not counted as it did not take part in the fighting in the Kiev area during this period.
3   42nd Guards, 237th, 309th, and 68th Guards divisions.
4   253rd, 161st, 337th, and 38th divisions.
5   23rd and 30th divisions.
6   206th and 218th divisions.

the Germans' 255th Infantry Division. The 3rd Guards Mechanized Corps and the 218th Rifle Division occupied Zolotonosha.

The 27th Army, consisting of four rifle divisions,[7] was in the *front's* second echelon and carrying out a march to the Pereyaslav-Khmel'nitskii area. By the close of 22 September the army's formations had reached the line Karsakovka—Khorunzhiev—Nesenov.

In all, 16 rifle and three cavalry divisions, two mechanized and four tank corps from the Voronezh Front were operating along the Rzhishchev—Cherkassy sector. The correlation of forces was 3:1 in rifle troops, 2:1 in motorized troops, and 1.3:1 in tank troops in favor of the Voronezh Front. Besides this, Soviet forces included cavalry, of which the Germans had none.

By the close of 22 September on the front's left wing the 52nd Army, consisting of five rifle divisions,[8] and the 4th Guards Army,[9] consisting of six divisions, were fighting with their front facing to the south. The 52nd Army reached the line Brigadirovka—Kuzubeevka—Pushkarevo—Velikaya Bogachka, with four divisions in the first echelon and one (373rd), minus a regiment, in the second. The 4th Guards Army also had one rifle division (166th) in the second echelon. The remaining five first-echelon divisions reached the line Mezeny—Volok—Dikan'ka. The correlation of forces in rifle troops along this sector was 7:1 in favor of the Voronezh Front. However, the 52nd and 4th Guards armies had no tanks and the Germans, with three panzer divisions, had an absolute superiority in tanks here.

The 2nd Air Army consisted of the 202nd Bomber Division (Pe-2s[10]), the 208th Night Bomber Division, the 5th Assault Air Corps (Il-2s[11]), the 5th Fighter Corps (La-5s,[12] Yak-7s,[13] Yak-9s[14]), and the 10th Fighter Corps (Yak-7s, La-7s[15]).

The front had in reserve powerful artillery formations: the 7th Breakthrough Artillery Corps and the 3rd Guards Mortar Division (RS).

The front's overall correlation of forces was as follows:

---

7   100th, 147th, 155th, and 241st divisions (the army did not have rifle corps headquarters).
8   93rd, 138th, 254th, 294th, and 373rd divisions.
9   69th, 80th and 166th rifle divisions and the 5th, 7th and 8th guards airborne divisions.
10 Editor's note. The Pe-2 was a twin-engine bomber that appeared in 1936. It had a three-man crew and a maximum speed of 450 kilometers per hour. Its armament consisted of four 7.62mm machine guns, while it could carry six 100 kilogram bombs in its bomb bay and two 250 kilogram bombs on its wings.
11 Editor's note. The Il2 ("Sturmovik") ground attack aircraft first appeared in 1941. It carried a crew of two and had a top speed of 414 kilometers per hour. Its armament consisted of two 23mm cannons, two 7.62mm machine guns, and one 12.7mm machine gun and it could carry up to 600 kilograms of bombs.
12 Editor's note. The La-5 was a Soviet fighter that first appeared in 1942. One model had a crew of one and a maximum speed of 648 kilometers per hour. It was armed with two 20mm cannons and could carry up to two 100-kilogram bombs.
13 Editor's note. The Yak-7 was a Soviet fighter that first appeared in 1940. One model had a crew of one and a maximum speed of 571 kilometers per hour. It was armed with one 20mm cannon and two 7.62mm machine guns.
14 Editor's note. The Yak-9 was a Soviet fighter that first appeared in 1942. One model had a crew of one and a maximum speed of 591 kilometers per hour. It was armed with a 20mm cannon and one 12.7mm machine gun.
15 Editor's note. The La-7 was a Soviet fighter that first appeared in 1944. One model carried a crew of one and had a maximum speed of 661 kilometers per hour. It was armed with two 20mm cannons and could carry 200 kilograms of bombs.

THE VORONEZH FRONT'S OFFENSIVE OPERATION, OCTOBER 1943

Table 1.1 The Overall Correlation of Forces Along the Voronezh Front

Soviet Forces	Total	Correlation	Total	German Forces
Rifle Divisions	35	1.8:1	19 (approximately)	Infantry Divisions
Cavalry Divisions	3	–	–	Cavalry Divisions
Mechanized Corps	2	2:1	1	Motorized Divisions
Tank Corps	4	1:1.5	6	Panzer Divisions
Tanks	908	2.1:1	422	Tanks and Assault Guns
Guns and Mortars (76mm and larger)	2,960	1.3:1	2,229	Guns and Mortars
Planes	733	1.6:1	445	Planes

Note: The number of planes is as of 1 October 1943.

The overall superiority was in favor of the Voronezh Front. However, it is necessary to take into account that the Germans, in falling back behind the Dnepr, enjoyed freedom of maneuver for regrouping their forces in any direction along a good road network. The Voronezh Front's forces, upon seizing the bridgeheads, had behind them the broad Dnepr, which constrained any kind of maneuver. Nor could the more than one and a half-fold superiority in planes during the first stage of the fighting for the bridgeheads be employed. Only part of the 2nd Air Army managed to rebase to the Priluki, Piryatin and Lubny airfields; that is, 85-110 kilometers to the east of the Dnepr. At the same time, by this time the enemy's aviation had been able to rebase to a dense network of well prepared airfields along the right bank of the Dnepr, very close to their ground forces (Kiev, Vasil'kov, Belaya Tserkov', Mironovka, and others). Soviet aviation carried out flights to the maximum extent of their range.

The Organization of Communications

During the course of the offensive to the Dnepr, the *front* headquarters became separated from the troops by a significant distance and did not always have reliable communications with the armies. On the date of the troops' arrival at the Dnepr south of Pereyaslav-Khmel'nitskii; that is, on 22 September 1943, the *front* headquarters moved from Lebedin to Grievy Yuskovtsy and was 185-190 kilometers from the troops. Such a remove by the headquarters at an important stage of the operation made troop control more difficult. Wire communications had been laid to the 38th Army's headquarters only as far as Borshna (six kilometers east of Priluki), although this army's forces were located 100 kilometers to the west and the army headquarters was in the Yaroslavka area. There was direct wire communications with the 40th Army's headquarters in Khar'kivtsy. There were no wire communications with the headquarters of the 47th Army (Belousovka) and the 3rd Guards Tank Army (Velikaya Karatul'). Wire communications were maintained with the headquarters of the 52nd Army (Zubovka) and the 4th Guards Army (Pokorvskoe) through the communications center of the front's old command post in Lebedin. The main means of communications for headquarters at all levels was radio and communications officers. A great deal of attention was devoted to the command's personal interaction. The front commander and the army commanders visited the troops and laid down tasks on the spot.

Coordination communications was poorly organized. The communications of the 3rd Guards Tank Army's headquarters worked unsatisfactorily with the headquarters of the combined-arms armies; the 2nd Air Army's headquarters did not have its own representatives at the headquarters of the ground forces, even along the main axis, and poorly understood the ground situation.

Rear Organization and Materiel Supply

As the troops' offensive to the west developed, the *front* and army rear services became greatly extended in depth. By 3 September the army bases had moved and deployed along the Belopol'e—Sumy—Bogodukhov—Merchik railroad sector. However, as early as the middle of September the gap between the army bases and the attacking troops once again reached 100-150 kilometers, causing an overload in the work of automobile transport, which was already experiencing a shortage of fuel. By 22 September this gap had increased even further and had reached 275-300 kilometers.

On 19 September, in accordance with front directive No. 0038/op, which sought to define the troops' tasks for arriving at the Dnepr River, a plan for the materiel supply of the operation was drawn up and confirmed by the *front* commander.

The armies' basing was to remain as before until the restoration of the Nezhin—Priluki—Piryatin—Grebenka—Zolotonosha railroad sector. At the same time, the plan did not foresee any kind of deadlines for restoring the railroad and, thus the approach of the army bases and *front* depots to the line of the Dnepr River.

The plan called for the creation by 22 September of supplies of five refills each of fuels and lubricants in the 3rd Guards Tank Army and in individual tank corps, and, four refills in the 38th, 40th and 27th armies, and an average of three refills in the remaining armies. Besides this, it was planned in this deadline to create a 400-ton supply of fuel for the commander of the *front's* artillery, and 100 tons for the chief of the *front's* engineer troops in connection with the planned major maneuver of artillery equipment and engineer troops with crossing materials.

However, due to the fact that the planned railroad transports with fuels and lubricants were arriving late, the above-listed supplies were not created and the troops experienced a severe shortage of fuel. By the close of 21 September the overall supply of gasoline with the *front* consisted of only two refills (0.6 refills with the troops and 0.1 at the army bases, with the rest en route to the armies).

The troops were supplied with munitions upon their approach to the Dnepr. However, in a number of cases this provisioning was insufficient. A lack of equality in their distribution among the armies was observed. The provisioning with munitions in combat loads by 19 September is as follows:

Table 1.2 The Voronezh Front's Ammunition Supply Situation (In Combat Loads)

Types of Munitions	38th Army	40th Army	27th Army	52nd Army	4th Guards Army	3rd Guards Tank Army
Rifle Rounds	1.0	2.1	4.15	1.9	3.8	3.27
82mm Mortars	1.8	3.5	0.9	2.1	3.5	3.0
120mm Mortars	0.9	0.55	0.4	1.9	0.3	2.77
76mm Shells for Regimental Artillery	1.7	1.3	1.2	2.0	4.0	–
76mm Shells for Divisional Artillery	2.0	1.75	0.86	1.3	1.96	3.77
122mm Shells (Howitzer)	0.9	0.4	0.8	2.1	1.25	4.15

In order to supply food and forage, it was decided to immediately deploy a reserve *front* food depot in Romny, which would significantly ease the delivery of food to the troops. Particular attention was paid to the procurement of food and forage from local supplies. The rich agricultural area in which the *front* was conducting combat operations, and the favorable time of year enabled us to significantly count on local food and forage resources which reduced the strain on deliveries in conditions of extended communications. The Germans did not have time to take advantage of the harvest in the summer of 1943 along the Ukrainian left bank. Nor were they able to destroy the unharvested wheat in the field and in stacks by burning it. However, the Germans inflicted a great loss to Ukraine's animal husbandry. The number of heads of livestock fell sharply during the period of their occupation.

The *front* had an auto transportation regiment and five independent auto transport battalions, which numbered overall 1,050 available vehicles of various makes with an overall carrying capacity of 1,943 tons. Such an amount of vehicles in conditions of *front* and army basing lagging behind was clearly insufficient.

The presence of the *front's* and armies' hospital establishments fully met the *front's* requirements. It was necessary to bring the hospitals closer to the line of the Dnepr and to maximally relieve them of wounded who required prolonged treatment. The area of the *front's* combat operations was favorable from the medical point of view. There were only individual cases of infectious diseases (typhus and diphtheria) among the troops and the local population.

The Operational Plans

As the *front's* forces approached the Dnepr, the enemy sought to break away from the pursuing Soviet forces as quickly as possible and get behind the river.

The German command had the goal of getting all of its men and materiel across to the right bank of the Dnepr in good condition and, by taking advantage of the river's favorable natural conditions, to take up a solid defense here and to halt the Soviet army's further advance to the west.

As early as the offensive to the river, a plan for the *front's* actions along the right bank of the river, following the seizure of bridgeheads, gradually arose. The *front's* initial plan of 9 September had in mind only the seizure of bridgeheads, "depending on the situation." The *front's* operational directive No. 0038/op of 18 September demanded that the 38th and 47th armies throw their forward units to the Dnepr's eastern bank. The 40th and 3rd Guards Tank armies were warned of the necessity to be ready to force the Dnepr. It was only on 22 September, when the troops were actually arriving at the Dnepr, that their tasks along the right bank were defined.

The troops were assigned the following tasks through oral and written orders.

By the close of 26 September the 40th and 47th armies were to reach the front excluding Yushki—Yanivka—Shandra—Sinyavka—Gamarnya—Khmel'na.

The 38th Army was ordered to force the Dnepr and the Irpen' north of Kiev with the forces of five rifle divisions by 27 September and to reach the line Demidovo—Ozery—Bucha station—the northern outskirts of Priorka. The *front* commander subsequently planned to capture Kiev through a concentric attack by the 38th Army from the north and the 40th Army from the south and to reach the Zdvizh River. The 3rd Guards Tank Army was to attack toward Kagarlyk and Belaya Tserkov'.

However, following the development of the fighting to seize and broaden the bridgeheads, the plan underwent a number of changes. Subsequently, a final plan for the offensive operation was adopted, which was carried out from 12 October 1943.

The Course of Combat Operations by the Front's Main Group of Forces Along the Bukrin Axis

As was mentioned above, by the close of 22 September the 40th Army's forward detachments had reached the left bank of the Dnepr along the Kal'ne—Andrushi sector. At the same time, the 3rd Guards Tank Army's forward units (the motorized infantry of the 9th Mechanized and

6th Guards Tank corps) and were crossing to the Dnepr's right bank on materials at hand in the Zarubentsy—Grigorovka area.

The 47th Army was approaching the Glemyazovo area and had captured the town of Zolotoshna, while the 27th Army—the *front's* second echelon, was moving into the Pereyaslav-Khmel'nitskii area and by the close of 22 September was 25-30 kilometers west of the town of Lubny. The 1st Guards Cavalry Corps, which comprised the 3rd Guards Tank Army's second echelon, was on the march north and northwest of the town of Priluki.

In his first report to the *Stavka* about the forcing of the Dnepr, the *front* commander on 22 September reported that the following measures would be adopted for consolidating and developing the first success:

1. To cross over to the right bank of the Dnepr River on the night of 22-23.9.43 as many troops as possible from Rybalko's[16] 3rd Guards Tank Army and Moskalenko's[17] 40th Army.
2. During the day and night of 23.9.43 the *front's* aviation will assist the units that have crossed and which are crossing, putting a ring around them and preventing the enemy's arrival. It will simultaneously cover our forces in the area of the crossings.
3. Artillery fire is being organized for supporting the troops that have crossed.

During 22-23 September the Germans' situation in the Bukrin area was critical. Units of the enemy's 19th Panzer and 34th Infantry divisions, upon reaching the Dnepr's bank and not knowing the situation, were getting pulled into the fighting from the march with the units of the 3rd Guards Tank and 40th armies that had crossed.

However, despite this 22 and 23 September were the most favorable for seizing bridgeheads. It was only on 24 September that the situation changed sharply. On this day the enemy pulled into the Bukrin area the troops that had crossed from the left bank near Kanev. By the close of 24 September units of the 10th Motorized and the 112th and 255th infantry divisions had appeared here. The 34th Infantry Division's main forces had reached the Dnepr along the Rzhishchev—Shchuchinka sector. The 57th Infantry Division was detected near Kanev. Units of the 72nd Infantry and 7th Panzer divisions, which have been mentioned earlier, were approaching the area of the fighting.

On 26 September units of the 20th Motorized Division appeared on 26 September, and on 27-28 September units of the SS *Das Reich* Panzer Division began to arrive. Simultaneously, the enemy was putting in order his control of the troops waging defensive fighting in the Dnepr bend. As a result, from 24 September all of the German units near Bukrin had been consolidated under an overall command and the headquarters of the XXIV and, from 26 September, the XLVIII panzer corps had been created.

Throughout 22-23 September the army commanders, in accordance with the *front's* instructions, issued combat orders to force the Dnepr and to seize bridgeheads along its right bank. The commander of the 3rd Guards Tank Army issued orders to his corps to reach the line Makedony—Shandra—Sinyavka—Stepantsy—Khmel'na by the close of 23 September. According to the

---

16 Editor's note. . Pavel Semyonovich Rybalko (1894-1948) joined the Russian imperial army in 1915 and the Red Army in 1919. During the interwar period he served mainly in the cavalry and intelligence branches. During the Great Patriotic War he served in the General Staff apparatus and the tank troops, becoming commander of the 3rd Tank Army in 1943. Following the war, Rybalko commanded the Red Army's armored forces.
17 Editor's note. Kirill Semyonovich Moskalenko (1902-85) joined the Red Army in 1920 and fought in the civil war. During the Great Patriotic War he commanded a motorized anti-tank artillery brigade, a rifle corps and a number of armies. Following the war, he held a number of positions in the central military apparatus.

army commander's decision, the 40th Army was to reach by the close of 25 September the line Yushki—Kuz'mintsy—Yanivka—Makedony—Shandra, while the 47th Army was to reach the line Shandra—Gamarnya—Khmel'na by the close of 25 September.

The *front* commander demanded that the 3rd Guards Tank Army set aside part of its forces for launching an attack along the river's left bank in the direction of Kanev, in order to prevent the enemy's withdrawal over the Dnepr and to clear it of his units on the river's left bank. The army commander entrusted this task to two brigades from the 6th Guards Tank Corps, which, however, were unable to carry it out. The enemy, by taking advantage of the weak pressure along the 47th Army's front, repelled these tank brigades' attacks and on 24 September completed the withdrawal of its units to the right bank of the Dnepr, having destroyed all of the crossings behind him.

All of the decisions and orders by the *front* and army commanders during these days (22-23 September) were infused by the categorical demand that the troops reach the Dnepr as soon as possible, that they immediately force it and that they seize and broaden their bridgeheads. The troops were accorded broad initiative for this. Particularly typical in this regard were combat orders nos. 897 and 898 by the commander of the 40th Army on 23 September, which were addressed to the commanders of the 47th and 52nd rifle corps. Having indicated the tasks of each rifle division, the army commander wrote in conclusion: "The Dnepr River must be forced in the most favorable places, without regard for boundary lines and available crossing equipment." On that same day the commander of the 3rd Guards Tank Army issued fragmentary field order No. 0010/op to the commander of the 1st Guards Cavalry Corps, in which he demanded of the latter that "The forces of one cavalry division, mounted on the best horses, are to concentrate by 0300 on 24.9 in the Gusentsy—Yashniki—Kovalin area and at dawn on 24.9 are to force the Dnepr River along the sector excluding Rzhishchev—excluding Khodorov, employing materials at hand for crossing."

The affording of broad initiative to the troops in the developing situation was correct and completely justified. However, the *front* and armies were unable to supply the troops with crossing equipment, to cover them against enemy aviation and, having a poor knowledge of the situation, relied only on the broad initiative and resourcefulness of the division and regiment commanders.

The tasks set by the armies' forces, were not only not fulfilled by the appointed deadlines, but were not fulfilled throughout the entire operation.

On 23 September the 3rd Guards Tank Army had its corps' main forces, which were extended to a great depth into the bargain, on the approaches to the Dnepr. Small elements of motorized infantry continued to fight along the Dnepr's right bank near the villages of Zarubentsy and Grigorovka. The enemy stubbornly counterattacked with tanks and infantry in strength up to a battalion and supported by aviation, which concentrated its efforts in the Bukrin bend.

On this day the 40th Army began to force the Dnepr on materials at hand along a comparatively broad front: units of the 52nd Rifle Corps were crossing northwest and southeast of Rzhishchev near Staiki, Grebeni and Shchuchinka, while the 47th Rifle Corps was crossing near the villages of Traktomirov, Zarubentsy and Grigorovka. However, only the infantry was crossing, without reinforcements, and slowly.

On this day the 47th Army was slowly moving to the right bank of the Dnepr along the Kanev and Cherkassy axes. The enemy resisted stubbornly, covering his crossings in these areas and securing the organized withdrawal of his forces to the right bank.

The initial plan for the offensive by the *front's* forces to the Dnepr, which was drawn up as early as 9 September, called for employing airborne troops to support the seizure of bridgeheads. The *front* commander had at his disposal three airborne brigades for this purpose. However, despite the fact that two weeks passed from the moment the decision was adopted to the start of the forcing, the operation was badly organized. It was planned to carry out the nighttime drop of three airborne brigades during the course of two nights. Such a complex operation required scrupulous preparation. However, an intolerable improvisation, which expressed itself, first of all, in the hurried collection of transport aircraft with poorly-trained crews, was the result.

The dropping of two airborne brigades during the first night was to have taken place in the areas of Pii—Grushevo—Potantsy and Trostinets—Litvinets—Kopani (10-20 kilometers from the line of the Dnepr), with the task of preventing the arrival of enemy units at the Bukrin bend from the west and southwest. The *front* headquarters believed that there were no enemy forces in the landing areas. Actually, units of the 19th Panzer Division were already here and units of the Germans' 10th Motorized, 112th and 255th infantry divisions were arriving on the day of the landing.

During the night of 23-24 September the 3rd and units of the 5th airborne brigades were dropped. However, the landing's poor technical preparation led to a situation in which the parachutists were dropped over a very broad area. Part of them was dropped on their own forces' positions, part right into the Dnepr, and part even on its left bank. The main body of paratroopers, which landed in the planned areas, unexpectedly ended up in the center of the German forces' position. As a result, the landing suffered significant losses and was unable to carry out the tasks assigned to it.

The surviving airborne elements fell back into the woods in the Cherkassy area and subsequently operated in the enemy rear, carrying out small diversions. The *Stavka* of the Supreme High Command pulled the remaining unemployed brigade and a half into its reserve.

On 24 September the situation did not change appreciably. Stubborn fighting continued with the counterattacking enemy in all the areas of the landing. The 3rd Guards Tank Army hardly increased the number of its forces on the river's right bank and a noticeable success was achieved only near Traktomirov: on this day the 40th Army's 161st Rifle Division crossed in full. One rifle regiment of the same army's 38th Rifle Division also crossed near Grigorovka. The 1st Guards Cavalry Division reached the left bank of the Dnepr with its forward elements near Gusentsy and Yashniki. The 47th Army also reached the left bank of the river in its sector, having failed, however, to disrupt the crossing of the German forces to the right bank. Small reconnaissance groups from the army's 206th and 218th rifle divisions forced the Dnepr southeast of Kanev.

On 25 September the slow augmentation of forces on the right bank continued in all armies. The 337th Rifle Division crossed near Zarubentsy and the 38th Rifle Division's second regiment crossed near Grigorovka. The 161st Rifle Division, which crossed the previous evening, together with the 69th Mechanized Brigade, which had only ten tanks which had been crossed over on a ferry boat, on this day began an attack to the south and captured the villages of Velikii Bukrin and Malyi Bukrin. Although Malyi Bukrin was soon lost as the result of an enemy counterattack, one may consider, however, that on this day the Bukrin bridgehead, which was more than six kilometers in depth and 10-12 kilometers in width, was created. The 47th Army crossed part of the 206th and 218th rifle divisions' forces (up to three rifle regiments) to the right bank. Besides this, a small bridgehead was formed near Selishche (north of Kanev) by the forces of the 23rd and 30th rifle divisions.

On 26 September the crossing of the 40th Army's infantry was basically completed. The 3rd Guards Tank Army had three mechanized brigades (the 22nd and 23rd guards and 69th) on the Bukrin bridgehead and four motorized battalions from various tank brigades. As before, the crossing of the artillery and tanks was exceedingly slow. By the close of the day there were only 27 76mm guns 29 120mm mortars, 13 tanks from the 40th Army, and 13 tanks from the 3rd Guards Tank Army on the Bukrin bridgehead. During all these days only five of the 10th Tank Corps' tanks were crossed over in the Shchuchinka area.

On 27-29 September fierce fighting was being waged on the bridgeheads along the right bank along the sector Staiki—Rzhishchev—Khodorov—Velikii Bukrin—Grigorovka—Selishche—Kanev—the mouth of the Ross' River. Both sides were pursuing active aims: the Voronezh Front's forces were striving to crush the enemy's resistance and reach the line Yushki—Makedony—Khmel'na and thus broaden their bridgehead up to 30 kilometers in depth and up to 75 kilometers in width, which would enable them to deploy the main forces of the *front's* central group of forces and go over to a decisive offensive to the west.

In his telegram No. 2/k of 28 September to the commanders of the 27th, 40th, 47th, and 3rd Guards Tank armies, the *front* commander assigned them the task: "The common immediate task for all troops is to pulverize as many enemy forces as possible along the right bank of the Dnepr River and to prepare the necessary conditions for a further offensive."

The Germans, having guessed the axis along which the Voronezh Front was placing its main efforts, augmented its forces here and were seeking to throw the Soviet troops that had crossed, back into the Dnepr and securely consolidate along its right bank, through active infantry and tank counterattacks, supported by aviation. The slow augmentation of forces by the 40th, 47th and 3rd Guards Tank armies along the captured bridgeheads, and especially the slow movement of artillery and tanks to the bridgeheads, along with a shortage of ammunition, prevented these armies from combining into one bridgehead during these days (25-26 September) all of the individual sectors seized along the right bank.

On 27 September the *front* commander made the decision to commit the 27th Army, which had concentrated on 25 September in the Pereyaslav-Khmel'nitskii area, into the fighting. The army received orders to cross to the Bukrin bridgehead by the morning of 29 September and on 30 September to relieve units of the 40th Army along the Yanivka—Shandra sector. It was planned that if the 40th, 47th and 3rd Guards Tank armies were unable to crush the enemy's resistance and reach their designated line, then the 27th Army's forces would enter the fighting before the designate deadline. The *front* commander's directive to the 27th Army is cited in full below.

> To the commander of the 27th Army
> Copy to: the commander of the 40th Army,
> the commander of the 47th Army,
> the chief of the Red Army General Staff
> Operational directive No. 0041/op
> Headquarters of the Voronezh Front, 27.9.43
> 200,000:1 map

The 40th and 47th armies, along with the 3rd Guards Tank Army, have the immediate task of seizing a bridgehead on the right bank of the Dnepr River and reaching the line: Khalen'e—Stritovka—Shandra—Rzhavets—Gamarnya—the mouth of the Ross' River.

I order:

1. The commander of the 27th Army is to immediately begin crossing over the Dnepr River along the 3rd Guards Tank Army's sector and that of the left flank of the 40th Army.

    The crossing of the troops is to be completed by the morning of 29.9.43.

    Following the crossing, the army is to advance immediately to the line excluding Yanivka—Shankra, where it is to arrive no later than 30.9.43 and relieve here the units of the 40th Army.

    You are to be ready to attack from the aforementioned line. In case of necessity, you are also to be ready, on my special orders, to deploy and enter the fighting before reaching the line in question.

    You are to pay special attention to organizing anti-air and anti-tank defense.

    From the moment you enter the fighting you are to observe the following boundary: with the 40th Army on the right, excluding Kulazhentsy—Kozintsy—Malyi

Bukrin—excluding Yanivka—excluding Grebenki—excluding Bertniki; with the 47th Army on the left, Svechkova—excluding Khotski—Buchak—Troshchin—Shandra—excluding Lubyanka—Rakitno—excluding Volodarka.
2. Confirm receipt and report on the plan for the crossings and the completion of the task.

No. 18702/code
Vatutin, Khrushchev,[18] Ivanov[19]

The 27th Army's forces crossed slowly, and only its infantry, without artillery. On 28 September the 147th Rifle Division crossed near Grigorovka, and on 29 September part of the forces of the 100th and 155th rifle divisions. Due to the fact that the enemy counterattacked uninterruptedly, the army's crossings units were immediately committed into the fighting.

On 27 September the *front* commander made another important decision: the 1st Guards Cavalry Corps was removed from operational subordination to the 3rd Guards Tank Army to the *front's* reserve, while remaining in its previous position.[20] The crossing of the corps' main forces to the right bank was halted. The crossing of no more than one mixed cavalry regiment was authorized. The latter fought for several days on the bridgehead near Shchuchinka, in the sector of the 40th Army's 52nd Rifle Corps. This decision was prompted by the fact that the open terrain along the right bank of the Dnepr in the Rzhishchev area could place the cavalry corps under enemy air attack.

As a result of the fighting during 22-29 September, the central group of the *front's* forces failed to carry out the *front's* main task—the seizure of such a bridgehead on the right bank of the Dnepr, which by its size would enable us to deploy on it our main forces for a subsequent offensive. We only managed to seize seven small and separate bridgeheads along the sector Staiki—the mouth of the Ross' River. The largest of them was the Bukrin bridgehead. Here were concentrated both sides' main efforts.

The *front's* forces were unable to hinder the crossing of the enemy's Kanev group of forces, which was pressed against the Dnepr. The numerically weak 47th Army scattered its forces along two axes—Kanev and Cherkassy, while the army's most mobile formation—the 3rd Guards Mechanized Corps—was fighting along its left-wing neighbor's sector. The army itself operated slowly and indecisively. The attempt to employ part of the 3rd Guards Tank Army's forces to destroy the enemy's Kanev group of forces while still on the left bank proved unsuccessful. The army commander, considering the Kanev axis to be secondary to his purposes, allotted insufficient forces for operating here. As a result, the Germans managed to get away over the Kanev crossing to the Dnepr's right bank and to employ all of their forces for a subsequent active defense of the Bukrin bridgehead.

---

18 Editor's note. Nikita Sergeevich Khrushchev (1894-1971) joined the Communist Party in 1918 and served as a political commissar during the civil war. He later gained Stalin's favor and rose rapidly through the party's ranks. During the Great Patriotic War he served as a political commissar with various *fronts*. Following the war, he was party boss in Ukraine in Moscow. After Stalin's death he gradually pushed aside his rivals and occupied the top posts in the party and government. Khrushchev was removed from his offices in 1964 and sent into retirement, where he wrote his clandestine memoirs.
19 Editor's note. Semyon Pavlovich Ivanov (1907-93) joined the Red Army in 1926 and held a number of command and staff positions. During the Great Patriotic War he served in a number of staff assignments at the army and *front* level, along the Soviet-German front and in Manchuria. Following the war, Ivanov served as chief of staff of several military districts and chief of the General Staff Academy.
20 By this time the 1st Guards Cavalry Corps' main forces were completing their concentration in the Gusentsy—Yashniki—Voitovtsy—Rogozov—Staroye area.

THE VORONEZH FRONT'S OFFENSIVE OPERATION, OCTOBER 1943

The sides' situation by the close of 29 September along the front Tripol'ye—Rzhishchev—Kanev—Cherkassy was as follows.

The 40th Army's 52nd Rifle Corps was fighting to expand two bridgeheads northwest and southeast of Rzhishchev. The first of them, in the Yushki—Grebeni area, was 16 kilometers across and four kilometers deep, while the second bridgehead in the Shchuchinka area was 11 kilometers across and four kilometers in depth.

The 47th Rifle Corps (minus the 38th Rifle Division) and the 40th Army's 8th Guards Tank Corps, the 27th Army's 100th and 147th rifle divisions, and the motorized infantry of the 3rd Guards Tank Army's 7th Guards Tank and 9th Mechanized corps were fighting on the Bukrin bridgehead, which was 11 kilometers across and six kilometers deep.

The 40th Army's 38th Rifle Division, one regiment from the 27th Army's 155th Rifle Division, and a motorized rifle battalion and a tank battalion from the 3rd Guards Tank Army's 6th Guards Tank Corps were fighting on the bridgehead near Grigorovka, which was 5-6 kilometers wide and up to two kilometers deep.

The 47th Army's 23rd Rifle Corps and units of the 3rd Guards Mechanized Corps' 7th Guards Mechanized Brigade, which had just begun to cross, were fighting on the bridgehead in the Selishche area, which was 5-6 kilometers wide and up to two kilometers deep, with the task of expanding the bridgehead and linking up with the forces of the 40th Army's left wing.

The 47th Army's 21st Rifle Corps captured two insignificant shoreline sectors southeast of Kanev. Two of the 3rd Guards Mechanized Corps' brigades continued fighting along the army's left boundary south of Zolotonosha.

The enemy was holding the Soviet forces' offensive from the bridgehead near Yushki and Grebeni with the main forces of the 34th Infantry Division. By the close of 29 September units of the SS *Das Reich* Panzer Division were approaching this area. The 10th Motorized Division was fighting southeast of Rzhishchev. The densest group of German forces was in the Velikii Bukrin and Grigorovka area. Here two-thirds of the 72nd Infantry Division's forces, the 19th Panzer and 20th Motorized divisions, and combat groups from the 112th and 255th infantry divisions (in all, five divisions along an 18-20 kilometer front) were operating here. In the Pii area the enemy was holding the 7th Panzer Division in reserve. A combat group from the 3rd Panzer Division was concentrating in the Bobritsy area. In all, the German forces had three and two-thirds infantry, two motorized and three and one-half panzer divisions along this sector of the front.[21]

The overall correlation of forces by the close of the fighting to seize bridgeheads on the right bank of the Dnepr; that is, by 29 September, was moving in favor of the Soviet forces by 3.2:1 in rifle formations, 1:1 in motorized infantry, and 1.3:1 in tank formations. However, it is necessary to take into account the fact that the 3rd Guards Tank Army still had all of its tanks on the Dnepr's left bank. In striving to destroy the Soviet forces along the captured bridgeheads, the German command at the same time was hurriedly carrying out defensive works, while attempting to develop them in depth.

The *front's* forces, following a vigorous offensive to the Dnepr throughout September, had achieved a great operational success, while at the same time they were in very complex and difficult conditions, which had arisen, caused by shortages in materiel supply (first of all, a shortage of fuel and ammunition), the lagging behind of the artillery and crossing equipment and the air force's airfield rebasing. During the fighting for the first bridgeheads (22-29 September), the *front* and army commanders and their staffs had done a great deal to overcome all the difficulties which arose during the course of the offensive to the Dnepr. However, these difficulties still made

---

21 In calculating the strength of the German forces, a division's combat group is counted as numbering one half of the strength of a fully-outfitted German division.

themselves felt and it required further energetic measures to ensure success in the troops' activities on the bridgeheads.

It should be noted that the *front* and army staffs had poorly studied the enemy group of forces and were completely unaware of his plans and intentions. All intelligence means worked insufficiently effectively. The *front's* headquarters mostly made use of that data on the enemy which the troops gathered during the course of the fighting, while capturing prisoners and enemy documents. As a result, the headquarters proceeded from a prejudiced notion about the equal distribution of the enemy's forces along the right bank of the Dnepr. In reality, the enemy did not employ such a cordon distribution of his forces and was concentrating major forces in those areas where Soviet forces were most active. The Germans occupied defensive positions along a broad front with their weakest units along the remaining sectors.

The enormous extension of all the artillery led to a situation in which our forces, which had crossed over to the Dnepr's right bank during the first days of the fighting, were deprived of efficacious support with artillery fire.

Taking into account the importance of support by powerful artillery fire for the formations forcing the Dnepr and fighting to seize bridgeheads along the right bank, the *front* commander, in his directive No. 0038/op of 18 September, which defined the tasks of the troops for reaching the Dnepr River, demanded of the *front's* artillery commander the creation of a powerful artillery grouping in the offensive sector of the *front's* main forces, and especially the movement of the 7th Breakthrough Artillery Corps into the 40th Army's sector.

On the instructions of the *front* commander, by 19 September the 13th Artillery Division was to concentrate in the Lubny area and to the west (100-110 kilometers east of Pereyaslav-Khmel'nitskii) and the 17th Artillery Division in the Piryatin area and to the east (90-100 kilometers east of Pereyaslav-Khmel'nitskii). By the close of 22 September the 3rd Guards Mortar Division was also to concentrate in the area east of Piryatin (110-120 kilometers east of Pereyaslav-Khmel'nitskii). The artillery reconnaissance of both divisions had the task of beginning its work in combat conditions in the combat formations of the 40th and 47th armies' attacking forces on the morning of 23 September. The artillery divisions were to move at a distance of no more than 8-12 kilometers from the forward detachments of these armies. However, the shortage of towing equipment and fuel immediately disrupted the plan. By the close of 25 September, when the forces of the 40th and 3rd Guards Tank armies were engaged in fierce fighting on the bridgeheads, the 7th Breakthrough Artillery Corps was only approaching the Dnepr, while stretching 150-220 kilometers to the east.

Both troop and army artillery were moved to the right bank slowly due to the shortage of crossing equipment and its main body fired from maximum distances from their firing positions on the river's left bank. By the close of 28 September almost all of the 40th Army's army artillery (two howitzer and two cannon regiments, four mortar regiments, two anti-tank brigades, and four anti-tank regiments) were still on the Dnepr's left bank. Only part of the 27th Anti-Tank Artillery Brigade had been moved to the Zarubentsy area and eight mortars from the 493rd Mortar Regiment to the Shchuchinka area. By the close of 29 September two of the 3rd Guards Tank Army's anti-tank artillery regiments were still on the left bank, with one mortar regiment even in the Yagotin area. Only the army's 272nd Mortar Regiment had been moved to the Grigorovka area. The troop artillery that had been shifted to the bridgeheads experienced a serious shortage of ammunition.

Artillery fire during this period was unsatisfactorily organized. Part of the division and all of the army artillery failed to fire, while waiting in line at the crossings. The artillery chiefs had few observation posts on the bridgeheads. On 28 September the *front* commander was forced to personally intervene in this matter. He demanded that all of the artillery that had been concentrated near the crossings be positioned in firing positions for waging fire along the left bank, while emplacing observation posts on the bridgeheads within the combat formations of the troops that had crossed. The *front's* artillery commander was ordered to organize a centralized and massed artillery fire opposite our troops' *front* on the Bukrin bridgehead and in the Shchuchinka area.

Despite the fact that the front's aviation outnumbered the enemy's by one and one-half times, its employment during the forcing of the river and the fighting to seize and expand the bridgeheads was unsatisfactory. Air reconnaissance uncovered the regrouping of the enemy's forces along the line of the Dnepr too late, proof of which, in particular, was the dropping of an airborne landing in the combat formations of the German forces on the night of 23-24 September. Our forces' air cover was also poor, and one should note that the German air force's activity increased significantly. On 24 September 683 overflights by German aviation were noted, 528 on 25 September, 1,061 on 27 September, and 544 on 28 September. The enemy, in groups of 40-50 planes, launched powerful air strikes against the crossings and the crossing troops and also supported the counterattacks of its ground forces.

The reasons behind our aviation's unsatisfactory work were the slow rebasing of the 2nd Air Army to forward airfields, the insufficient provisioning of the armies with fuel and ammunition and, finally, the separation of the air headquarters from the headquarters of the ground forces, the poor knowledge of the ground situation, and the absence of proper cooperation, so that even the army headquarters had no aviation representatives during this period.

The anti-aircraft defense in the areas of the crossings in the fighting of the first days was essentially absent. There were three anti-aircraft artillery divisions and eight army anti-aircraft artillery regiments as part of the 40th, 47th, 27th armies and the 3rd Guards Tank Army. However, the anti-aircraft units fell behind and arrived at the Dnepr quite late. Their transfer to the bridgeheads, due to the shortage of crossing equipment, proceeded very slowly. The employment of masking smoke for covering the crossings was supposed to have played an important role; however, the chemical units also fell behind and there were no reserves of smoke equipment with the *front*. On 23 September the *front* chief of staff responded as follows to a request by the commander of the 40th Army: "I can't supply you with subunits for releasing smoke, smoke charges or smoke hand grenades, because there are none with the *front*." On 24 September the *front* headquarters reported to the Red Army's Main Military-Chemical Administration that the existing 30,000 smoke charges and 74 tons of smoke mixture at the disposal of the *front* were en route in the deep rear and that the approach of smoke equipment to the front line was extremely difficult due to operational shipments.

The chief reason behind the lack of success in the fighting to expand the bridgeheads is the delay in bringing up crossing equipment to the Dnepr. The width of the river bed near the Bukrin bridgehead reaches 600 meters. The 40th, 47th and 27th armies and the 3rd Guards Tank Army had been directed at this bridgehead, along with major cavalry and artillery formations. The situation demanded that they be transferred to the bridgehead rapidly in order to deny the enemy the opportunity to organize a defense along the right bank of the river. In these conditions crossing equipment should have literally followed behind the attacking forces' first echelons, without getting held up along intermediate and comparatively small water lines along this axis. In his 24 September report, the headquarters of the *front's* engineer forces noted: "*Front* pontoon units had been regrouped and were approaching the Dnepr River according to the schedule called for in the directive by the Voronezh Front's military council. However, in light of the fact that the actual speed of our forces' advance proved to be higher than planned, the troops reached the Dnepr River without crossing equipment."

Crossing equipment was held up for a long time along intermediate water lines (the Psyol, Khorol, Udoi and other rivers), while the engineer troops, which were busy repairing roads were not relieved in time by road units. As early as 10 September the *front* commander issued an order to rapidly advance behind the crossing parks' troops; however, this order was not carried out and the *front* headquarters did not verify it and did not insist that it be carried out.

The headquarters of the *front's* engineer troops drew up a plan for the engineer support of the forcing of the Dnepr River in accordance with the *front* commander's instructions. This plan called for the preparation before 23 September of 50 sapper wooden boats or rafts for each rifle divisions crossing the river, the preparation of 21 pairs of ferries with a carrying capacity of 30 tons apiece in the 40th and 47th armies, and seven pairs of ferries with a carrying capacity of 16 tons, 36 pairs with a carrying capacity of nine tons, as well as the preparation of parts for three bridges with a carrying capacity of 30 tons and two with a carrying capacity of six tons each. The plan failed to take into account the 3rd Guards Tank Army's demands.

However, this plan was drawn up late and was not carried out. Upon arriving at the Dnepr on 22-23 September, the 3rd Guards Tank and 40th armies' forces had no crossing equipment. The crossing of units was carried out only using means at hand and which were gathered upon the initiative of the units' commanders.

The situation with crossing equipment as of 25 September was as follows.

In the 40th Army two and one-thirds of an bow half-pontoon park, two NA-3 parks, 31 collapsible wooden boats boats, ten A-3 boats, three sets of flotation equipment, and one park of light pneumatic pontoons arrived at the crossing points and were partially used.

By this time the 3rd Guards Tank Army had two ferries operating, one of 60 tons and one of 30 tons, three pontoon bridges, two cutters, and two assault boats.

By 27 September the 47th Army had 19 A-3 boats.

The 27th Army, having begun the crossing on 28 September, employed the 40th and 3rd Guards Tank armies' crossing equipment, which created great difficulties for the latter.

All of this available crossing equipment could in no way secure the timely crossing of the troops and their combat equipment and their supply with ammunition, fuel and food. Up to 29 September the armies did not have a single pontoon bridge.

The Course of Combat Activities in the 38th Army's Sector Along the Kiev Axis

The 38th Army, while attacking from 9 September along the Kiev axis, was preparing to force the Dnepr immediately south of Kiev, and in accordance with this, it had its main forces along its left wing. However, when the army's forces were already only two to three marches from the Dnepr, the *front* commander ordered it to regroup its forces to the right wing during the course of its offensive, with the task of forcing the Dnepr north of Kiev. In this regard, on 22 September the army was forced to carry out a lateral maneuver by its main forces along the front from south to north. Only two of the army's divisions were fighting the enemy defending the Darnitsa bridgehead along the Dnepr's left bank. The army's 3rd Guards Tank Corps also did not take part in the fighting, because by this time it had moved to the north to its right-flank neighbor's sector. The enemy, not experiencing serious pressure from the attacking 38th Army, was hurriedly consolidating along the line Pukhovka—Gogolev—Borispol'—Kailov and was simultaneously crossing its men and materiel to the Dnepr's right bank.

The 38th Army had the following tasks: first, to force the Dnepr north of Kiev and upon reaching the Irpen' River to form a bridgehead on the right bank of the Dnepr; second, to destroy the enemy's Darnitsa left-bank group of forces. In the evaluation of the situation and decision by both the *front* and army commander, particular attention was devoted to the first task—the immediate forcing of the Dnepr and the seizure of a bridgehead north of Kiev. However, the presence of major enemy forces along the Darnitsa bridgehead position led to a situation in which the army's forces were essentially divided equally. Four of the 51st Rifle Corps' rifle divisions (240th, 180th, 167th, and 340th) were supposed to force the Dnepr north of Kiev. The 232nd Rifle Division, which was also part of the corps, covered its left flank, defending with its front facing south along the line Pukhovka—Bol'shaya Dymerka. Three of the 50th Rifle Corps' rifle divisions (163rd, 71st

THE VORONEZH FRONT'S OFFENSIVE OPERATION, OCTOBER 1943

and 136th) had the task of destroying the Darnitsa enemy group of forces and clearing the left bank of the Dnepr of him in the immediate Kiev area.

On 22 September the *front* commander ordered the commander of the 3rd Guards Tank Army to allot one tank brigade with the task of launching an attack from the Yerkovtsy area in the direction of Brovary and Predmostnaya Slobodka in order to prevent the enemy's withdrawal over the Dnepr in this area and to clear him from the river's left bank.

On 23 September all of the 50th Corps' divisions were committed into the fighting. The 3rd Guards Tank Army's 56th Guards Tank Brigade also arrived in the Borispol' area. The enemy was thrown out of Gogolev and Borispol'. However, the further advance by our forces was halted by the enemy, who resisted stubbornly and who often launched counterattacks.

Up to 28 September inclusively, the 50th Corps and the 56th Guards Tank Brigade were engaged in stubborn fighting with the Germans in the area of Brovary and Darnitsa, although they were unable to break through directly to the bank of the Dnepr and disrupt the crossing of the enemy forces. The 2nd Air Army, having concentrated its forces for operations in the sector of the *front's* central group of forces, did not render meaningful support to the 38th Army. Thus by the close of 28 September the enemy was able to complete the transfer of his forces to the right bank of the Dnepr and destroyed all the crossings behind him. During this time the 50th Corps reached the bank of the Dnepr near Kiev with all of its forces.

Events along the right wing of the 38th Army developed just as slowly while forcing the Desna and Dnepr by units of the 51st Corps. As has already been shown, by the close of 22 September the 240th and the main forces of the 167th rifle divisions reached the Desna River along the Letki—Rozhny sector, with no enemy in front of them. On this day units of the Germans' 208th Infantry Division were approaching the right bank of the Dnepr from the mouth of the Irpen' River as far as Kiev. Naturally, the task of the 240th and 167th rifle divisions was to force the Desna as quickly as possible and to seize bridgeheads along the right bank of the Dnepr before the enemy had time to organize a solid defense there.

The 38th Army also reached the Desna and Dnepr without crossing equipment. The 240th and 167th rifle divisions required two days to force the river and arrive at the eastern bank of the Dnepr (a distance of 15-16 kilometers), even given the absence of the enemy. It was only by the close of 24 September that the 240th Rifle Division reached the Svarom'ye area and the 167th Rifle Division the Starosel'ye area. By this time the enemy had managed to reinforce his troops and had organized a fire system and was entrenching. The German 208th Infantry Division was defending along the Kozarovichi—Lyutezh sector, with part of the forces of the 82nd and 327th infantry divisions, which had been pulled back from the Darnitsa bridgehead, were to the south as far as the mouth of the Desna.

The 51st Corps was slowly approaching the rivers' eastern bank. The 180th Rifle Division reached the Dnepr on 25 September and the 340th Rifle Division even later, while the troops were only able to make use of materials at hand for crossing, which enabled them to cross only rifle elements, in limited numbers and without artillery. Their organic crossing equipment remained far behind in the rear.

The situation with crossing equipment on 25 September was as follows. The crossing over the Desna in the Letki area (the only crossing) was conducted using local crossing materials (50 local boats and seven ferries, one of which had a carrying capacity of up to 12 tons and the remainder of 1.5-2.5 tons). By the close of 26 September a bridge for horse-drawn and auto transport had been built over the Desna near Letki. For the forcing of the Dnepr, half a park (16 half pontoons) could be used from the 108th Pontoon-Bridge Battalion, which left Semipolki (34 kilometers east of Svarom'ye) at 1740 on 26 September. For this purpose, local boats were dragged to the Dnepr from the Letki area. Boats, barrels and other materials were gathered in inhabited locales along the eastern bank of the Dnepr. The army's available crossing park—62 A-3 boats, 16 Hungarian half-pontoons and the second half of the 108th Pontoon-Bridge Battalion's park lagged behind. It was only on 26 September that the army's motor vehicles were sent for part of this equipment at Belopol'e station (250 kilometers east of the Dnepr).

The army's artillery was also stretched out and by no means was all of it ready for action. By 0800 on 27 September the artillery's situation was as follows. The artillery regiments of the 240th, 180th and 167th rifle divisions, the 491st and 492nd mortar regiments, a battalion apiece from the 16th and 6th guards mortar regiments (RS) and the 868th Anti-Tank Artillery Regiment had crossed over the Desna and occupied firing positions. As a result of the absence of fuel, part of the battalions from the 16th and 6th guards mortar regiments (RS), the 1950th Artillery Regiment, the 895th Howitzer Regiment, and the 1244th, 1660th and 222nd anti-tank artillery regiments remained east of the Desna.

The crossing over the Desna was covered by the 978th and part of the batteries of the 848th anti-aircraft artillery regiments (light anti-aircraft artillery). The 1065th and part of the batteries of the 848th anti-aircraft artillery regiments remained east of the Desna due to a fuel shortage.

There were insufficient artillery shells. By the morning of 27 September there were about 0.7 combat loads of 76mm shells and 0.24 combat loads of 122mm shells in the 51st Rifle Corps' division artillery; there was 0.55 of a combat load of 120mm mortar rounds in the 491st and 492nd mortar regiments, 0.6 of a combat load in the 868th Anti-Tank Artillery Regiment, and 2.3 salvos of rocket rounds.

By this time the army and troop rear services were much extended and were unable to supply the troops with the important things for fighting. On 26 September the corps commanders reported that people were being fed from local stores and it was organized in an unsatisfactory manner.

The organization of the forcing of the Dnepr by units of the 51st Rifle Corps, with the help of materials at hand, proceeded slowly. The enemy was feverishly regrouping his forces that had been pulled back from the left bank, was organizing a fire system, deploying engineer defensive works, and was organizing troop control.

On the night of 25-26 September the 38th Army's forces undertook their first attempt to force the Dnepr, but it was repulsed by the enemy's artillery and infantry fire. Nevertheless, by the close of 26 September they managed to cross over the 180th Rifle Division's reconnaissance company to the northern outskirts of Novo-Petrovtsy. One battalion from the 167th Rifle Division crossed over to an island east of Vyshgorod. On 27 September a company from the 240th Rifle Division crossed over to the right bank near Svarom'ye.

While slowly augmenting efforts and broadening the forcing front and fending off fierce enemy counterattacks on the captured bridgeheads, by the close of 29 September the 51st Rifle Corps occupied the following position:

The 240th Rifle Division, while occupying Svarom'ye with its main forces, had up to three rifle battalions on the right bank and was beating off enemy counterattacks from the area of Lyutezh;

Two of the 180th Rifle Division's companies were fighting along the northeastern outskirts of the village of Novo-Petrovtsy and two battalions along its southeastern outskirts;

One of the 167th Rifle Division's regiments was fighting along the northeastern outskirts of Vyshgorod and the division was occupying the islands east and southeast of Vyshgorod;

The 340th Rifle Division was concentrated in the woods east of Svarom'ye and was beginning to cross its lead elements over in the Svarom'ye area;

The 232nd Rifle Division was still on the eastern bank of the Desna in the Pukhovka area.

The enemy group of forces in the 38th Army's operational sector on 29 September was as follows. The 208th Infantry Division continued to defend along the Kozarovichi—Lyutezh sector. The enemy had increased his forces from Lyutezh to Priorka; here the 82nd, 327th and 68th infantry divisions were defending. The 75th Infantry Division was directly defending Kiev. The 213th Security and 88th Infantry divisions occupied defensive positions south of Kiev as far as Tripol'ye.

Thus four German infantry divisions were defending against four divisions of the 51st Rifle Corps; one German division was defending against three divisions from the 51st Rifle Corps. In all, on 29 September seven enemy infantry divisions, which had been falling back in front of the 38th Army all of September, were operating against eight rifle divisions from the 38th Army. The German divisions had been weakened in the preceding fighting and numbered on average from 2,000 to 4,200 men. The 38th Army's rifle divisions each numbered from 5,000 to 8,500 men, except for the 71st Rifle Division, which numbered 3,750 men. The 3rd Guards Tank Corps had only six tanks and by 29 September had been pulled back into the Bol'shaya Dynmerka area.

The 38th Army's right-hand neighbor—the Central Front's 60th Army—was fighting to seize and widen bridgeheads on the right bank of the Dnepr in the Dymera area and to the north.

Despite the insistent and numerous demands from the *front* command to quickly carry out the assigned objectives of forcing the Dnepr River north of Kiev and destroying the enemy's Darnitsa group of forces on the left bank of the Dnepr, the 38th Army had not carried out these tasks by 29 September. The Germans were able to pull back their main group of forces, which had been falling back through Romny and Priluki on Kiev, across the Dnepr, occupy a defense along the right bank of the river and prevent Soviet forces from creating any kind of significant bridgeheads.

The Course of Combat Activities on the Front's Left Wing

The 52nd and 4th Guards armies were attacking with their front facing south, pursuing the retreating enemy along this axis. Continuing the offensive, the 52nd Army could reach the Dnepr along the Gradizhsk—Kremenchug sector, while the 4th Guards Army's forces, upon reaching the line Reshetilovka—Poltava, would inevitably get mixed up with the formations of the Steppe Front's right wing. The 52nd and 4th Guards armies' offensive to the south would have led to a large gap between these armies and the 47th Army. By 22 September the gap between the flanks of the 47th and 52nd armies had already reached 70 kilometers. At the same time, it was quite clear that the 52nd Army's energetic offensive in the direction of Semenovka, Gradizhsk and Kremenchug would create the threat of encirclement for the enemy's Poltava group of forces, because it would deprive it of prepared crossings over the Dnepr near Kremenchug. The interests of the Steppe Front's and the Voronezh Front's left wing undoubtedly demanded the acceleration of the 52nd Army's offensive.

The *front* commander repeatedly demanded the acceleration of the 52nd Army's offensive on Gradizhsk, although it developed slowly. The enemy was stubbornly holding on to favorable lines and often counterattacked. On 22 September the *front* commander demanded that the 52nd Army capture Gradizhsk by the close of 23 September, and ordered the 47th Army to launch an attack with part of its forces in the direction of Zolotonosha and Cherkassy.

On 23 September the enemy, while continuing to pull back his forces from the Poltava area, was putting up stubborn resistance along both his flanks. The 52nd Army, enjoyed insignificant success that day while attacking to the south. The *front* commander ordered the 52nd Army to continue the offensive on Gradizhsk with the forces of one corps, while the remaining forces were to be moved to the west, into their own zone. At 1000 on 24 September the *front* commander completely cancelled his order to attack on Gradizhsk and demanded the acceleration of the entire army's arrival at the Dnepr in its own sector.

On 24 September all of the army's forces turned to the west, losing contact with the enemy. On this day the 4th Guards Army, having reached the *front's* left boundary near Reshetilovka, met up with the forces of the Steppe Front's right wing, lost contact with the enemy and began a march to the southwest toward the Dnepr, in its own sector.

On 25 September the Germans, not feeling any pressure from the north, fell back directly on Gradizhsk and Kremenchug, for the purpose of covering the crossing of their forces remaining on the left bank.

On 27 September the 52nd Army reached the left bank of the Dnepr River in its own sector, and on 28 September the 4th Guards Army carried out this task. The enemy, having completed the crossing of its forces to the right bank of the Dnepr, on 29 September still continued to hold the city of Kremenchug.

On 27 September the *front* commander issued an order to turn over the 52nd Army's sector along the Dnepr to the 4th Guards Army and ordered the 52nd Army's main forces to be crossed over to the right bank of the river in the 47th and 3rd Guards Tank armies' sector, employing their crossing equipment. Actually, the 52nd Army's task was not carried out due to the shortage of crossing equipment. Only insignificant units of the army were crossed in the 47th Army's sector southeast of Kanev. The 4th Guards Army was had to temporarily go over to the defense along the left bank of the Dnepr River.

By the close of 29 September the situation of the *front's* left-wing forces was as follows.

All of the 52nd Army's formations had regrouped to the boundary with the 47th Army along the Kaleberda—Prokhorovka—Bubnovo—Domantov sector and were preparing to cross the Dnepr. The 4th Guards Army's formations had reached the Dnepr along the front Domantov—Vasyutintsy—Lyalintsy—Gradizhsk exclusively. The Steppe Front was fighting along the approaches to Kremenchug.

The Germans were organizing a defense along the Dnepr's right bank from Kanev to Novo-Georgievsk with the forces of the *Wiking* Panzer Division and the combat groups of the 11th and 6th panzer and 168th, 223rd, 167th, and 320th infantry divisions. Thus the Germans had two calculated panzer and two infantry divisions overall along this sector.

Results of the Fighting to Force the Dnepr and the Seizure of Bridgeheads

During 22-29 September there was fighting to seize individual bridgeheads along the right bank of the Dnepr and to clear the left bank of the river of the enemy's remaining units. The overall situation insistently demanded the troops' skillful maneuver and cooperation for the purpose of destroying the enemy's forces pressed against the Dnepr crossings. This should have resulted in the significant weakening of the enemy's defense along the right bank of the Dnepr, because the Germans did not dispose of free operational reserves.

The Voronezh Front's forces achieved a major success in the September 1943 operation. An enormous territory on the Ukrainian left bank was cleared of the enemy; the Germans were deprived of the opportunity to make use of the gathered harvest from the fields of the Ukraine's rich agricultural oblasts: Sumy, Khar'kov, Poltava, Chernigov, and part of the Kiev Oblast'. The enemy's defensive system on the Dnepr's right bank was disrupted. The *front's* forces had seized nine bridgeheads along a 170-kilometer sector north and south of Kiev, and although they were small in size, they had not only a great tactical, but operational significance as well.

However, the Voronezh Front failed to take full advantage of the overall favorable conditions of the situation and its undoubtedly major success was insufficiently complete and did not make full use of all the available opportunities. The following may be included among those unexploited opportunities:

a) the unsuccessful rout of the German-Fascist forces near the Kiev and Kanev crossings, and although the Germans suffered significant losses here they were able to cross their forces over the Dnepr and take up defensive positions along its right bank;

b) the slow forcing of the Dnepr and widening of the initial bridgeheads, which led to a weakening of the factor of operational surprise, which had been earlier achieved by the *front* as a result of its vigorous arrival at the Dnepr and its forcing along many sectors from the march.

The situation in the Voronezh Front's sector in the final days of September was characterized by the enemy's growing resistance and the fierceness of the fighting in all the areas of the Dnepr's forcing by Soviet forces. In these conditions each day and each hour of delay in beginning our offensive along the right bank of the Dnepr gave the enemy additional time for organizing a defense. Taking advantage of this, the Germans strengthened their defense and did not cease in their attempts to eliminate through local counterattacks the bridgeheads seized by us. Simultaneously, the enemy was preparing more powerful counterblows against the crossing Soviet forces, gathering up forces for this purpose.

The *front's* initial plan to create significant bridgeheads by the end of September by the 38th Army's forces reaching the line of the Irpen' River and the advance of the 3rd Guards Tank and 40th and 47th armies to the line Yushki—Shandra—Sinyavka—Khmel'na was not carried out, due to the reasons enumerated.

The German command, having determined that the Soviet forces were striving to secure the bridgeheads along the right bank of the Dnepr south of Pereyaslav-Khmel'nitskii and north of Kiev, created their densest group of forces here. In all, by 29 September 12 infantry, two motorized and five and a half panzer divisions were operating in the Voronezh Front's sector. Compared to the day the *front's* forces reached the Dnepr, the overall number of German decreased by seven infantry divisions, due to the fact that the enemy's formations operating opposite the *front's* left wing had fallen back to the Kremenchug area, into the Steppe Front's sector.

The operational situation in the *front's* sector continued to be favorable and demanded the acceleration of the crossing over the Dnepr of the *front's* main forces and the expansion of the bridgeheads. The rapid bringing up of crossing equipment and the construction of crossings over the Dnepr, the rebasing of our aviation and the bringing up of the rear services and the troops' supply with ammunition and fuel should have secured the success of the forthcoming operations by the *front's* forces along the right bank of the Dnepr in the Kiev area.

The Organization of Communications

The significant distance of the *front's* headquarters from the troops demanded the adoption of immediate measures to improve the entire system of communications with subordinate forces. From 26 September 1943 the *front* headquarters was located in the inhabited locale of Lozovyi Yar (16 kilometers northeast of Yagotin), 70 kilometers from the front line, from which control over the forces' combat operations was organized. The *front* commander, General N.F. Vatutin, and the member of the *front's* military council, Lieutenant General N.S. Khrushchev, often went out to the troops, became acquainted with the situation and issued orders on the spot.

The *front* headquarters and the lower headquarters at all levels did not always have reliable technical communications with subordinate forces and widely practiced the dispatch of staff officers to the front to gather information on the situation and to relay orders. Because the formation and army headquarters during the first days of forcing the Dnepr continued to remain on the left bank, and telephone communications over the river was being organized slowly, and radio communications was also working unreliably, they often lacked exact data on the actual situation on the captured bridgeheads.

Cooperation communications between the combat arms were poorly organized, particularly between the armies and *front* aviation. During the entire period from 22 through 29 September the headquarters of the 2nd Air Army did not have its representatives with the headquarters of the combined-arms armies and were poorly informed of the ground situation.

Communications with the airborne detachment, which was unsuccessfully dropped in the Bukrin bend of the Dnepr, was absent altogether. Of the 20 radio sets dropped with the landing detachment, only one worked, and it was designate for communications among the landing troops and also lacked call signs for communicating with *front* headquarters.

Rear Organization and Materiel Support

At the moment of the Soviet forces' arrival at the Dnepr and the seizure of bridgeheads on its right bank, the rear-area situation was characterized by the slow restoration of the railroads, the low capacity of the restored railroad sectors, a shortage of supplies of fuel and lubricants and ammunition. Despite the fact that during 22-29 September the front line did not move to the west and remained stable, the elimination of these shortcomings occurred slowly. The rear services were not able to support the troops' needs in their operation. The shortage of fuel led to the artillery's falling behind, the overextension of tank formations, the slow bringing up of crossing equipment, and to delays in delivering munitions.

Matters were particularly bad with supplying munitions and food to the troops who had crossed over the Dnepr and were engaged in heavy fighting on the bridgeheads.

By 29 September the armies continued to be based on the Vorozhba—Khar'kov railroad. Thus the supply bases were separated from the troops by the following distances: 275 kilometers for the 40th Army; 325 kilometers for the 27th Army; 300 kilometers for the 3rd Guards Tank Army, and; 320 kilometers for the 47th Army.

By this time only the 38th Army's supply base had moved to the area south of Nezhin and was located 130 kilometers from its forces.

In the territory liberated from the enemy in the offensive sector of the Voronezh Front and the Central Front's left wing in September there were 1,247 kilometers of railroad and among them the important L'gov—Vorozhba—Bakhmach—Nezhin—Kiev trunk line. Even before the arrival of the *front's* railroad restoration troops, the local railroad workers and engineer-technical personnel were taking measures to restore the destruction. With the arrival of the railroad troops, the local population was also conscripted. The restoration of the railroads was carried out at an average pace of 24.3 kilometers per day. Overall, in September 730 kilometers of main railroad sectors and branches and 124 kilometers of narrow-gauge branches were restored.

Two rail lines ran from east to west toward Kiev on the Ukrainian left bank: Vorozhba—Nezhin—Kiev and Khar'kov—Poltava—Lubny—Kiev. All means were concentrated on the quickest restoration of the first railroad and the Nezhin—Zolotonosha lateral railroad, which enable us to more favorably deploy our army supply bases during the fighting along the Dnepr. The large amount of destruction of the railroads, which was carried out by the enemy during his retreat, the weakness of the *front's* railroad restoration units, and the shortage of construction materials, which had to be delivered from the country's deep rear, were the reasons for the slow pace of railroad restoration and the low capacity along the restored sectors.

The Voronezh Front's First Offensive on the Right Bank of the Dnepr in October 1943

The *front* commander, in the developing situation by 29 September, considered it possible to begin an offensive in the next few days with the troops of the central group of forces from the line Rzhishchev—Kanev and the *front* headquarters was drawing up just such an offensive plan.

THE VORONEZH FRONT'S OFFENSIVE OPERATION, OCTOBER 1943

Measures were simultaneously being taken to bring up crossing equipment, to create a sufficient number of crossings, and to bring up the *front's* artillery and rear establishments.

Instructions by the Stavka of the Supreme High Command

The *Stavka* of the Supreme High Command, in its directive No. 30197 of 28 September, assigned the *front's* forces the task of preparing and launching an attack in the direction of Kagarlyk, Fastov and Brusilov, in conjunction with the Central Front's left wing (13th and 60th armies) and to reach the line Stavishche—Brusilov—Fastov—Belaya Tserkov'. This directive informed the *front* that on 10 October it would incorporate the Central Front's 13th and 60th armies.

On 29 September the *Stavka* issued a second directive, No. 30203, which significantly expanded the *front's* tasks on the Ukrainian right bank. The overall direction of the offensive was to be Zhitomir—Berdichev—Mogilev-Podol'skii. The *front's* immediate task was to reach the line Ovruch—Korosten'—Zhitomir—Berdichev—Kazatin, with a subsequent arrival at the line Sarny—Slavuta—Proskurov—Mogilev-Podol'skii. The directive indicated that the Central Front's 13th and 60th armies would be transferred to the Voronezh Front and the 52nd and 4th Guards armies to the Steppe Front.

The Front's Operational Plan

The operation's overall goal was the rout of the enemy on the right bank of the Dnepr by means of launching the main attack in the direction of Kagarlyk, Fastov and Brusilov and a supporting one in the direction of Svarom'ye and Svyatoshino. In this way, Kiev would be enveloped from the north, west and south. It was subsequently planned to launch the main attack in the direction of Berdichev, Zhmerinka and Mogilev-Podol'skii, while reliably securing it from the Rovno area. In carrying out the Supreme High Command's instructions, the *front's* forces were supposed to capture the very important railroad junctions of Ovruch, Zhitomir, Berdichev, and Kazatin and, while continuing the offensive, to get into the deep rear of the enemy's entire southern army group, to cut all of his main communications and to reach the line Sarny—Slavuta—Proskurov—Mogilev-Podol'skii.

The operation was planned to a depth of 320 kilometers, scheduled to last 30-35 days and was to be carried out in three stages.

It was planned to accomplish the first stage from 3 to 9-12 October; that is, over 7-10 days. During this time the *front's* forces were to capture Kiev and reach the line Radomyshl'—Fastov—Belaya Tserkov'—Boguslav. The army's tasks during this stage were as follows.

The 38th Army, consisting of eight rifle divisions, one tank and one cavalry corps, had the task of launching its main attack north of Kiev, with the forces of five rifle divisions, one tank and one cavalry corps, to the southwest toward Svyatoshino, and a supporting attack with the forces of three rifle divisions south of Kiev toward Zhulyany. The army was to capture Kiev on 7 October and reach the line Radomyshl'—Brusilov with its mobile formations by 9 October and with its main forces by 12 October.

The 40th Army, consisting of six rifle divisions and two tank corps, was to attack toward Vasil'kov and also reach the line excluding Brusilov—excluding Fastov with its mobile formations by 9 October and with its main forces by 12 October.

The 27th Army, consisting of five rifle divisions, had the task of attacking toward Kagarlyk and Fastov and by 12 October reaching the line Fastov—Belaya Tserkov'.

The 3rd Guards Tank Army (two tank and one mechanized corps) was to develop the success in the 27th Army's sector and reach the Brusilov area by 9 October.

The 47th Army, consisting of four rifle divisions and one mechanized corps, had the task of launching an attack in the direction of Kanev and Mironovka and by 10 October reaching the front excluding Belaya Tserkov'—Rakitno—Boguslav, securing the *front's* left flank.

The 13th and 60th armies, which were operating along the Korosten' axis, were to attack during this period according to the Central Front's plan from the line of the Pripyat' and Dnepr rivers.

It was planned to bring the artillery density along the 40th, 27th and 47th armies' attack sectors to 200 tubes per kilometer of front. Due to the troops' lack of readiness for immediate operations and the overextension of the rear establishments, the slow arrival of transport with munitions, fuel and crossing equipment, the start of the offensive was set for 3-4 October.

It was planned to carry out the second stage during 12-20 October. During this time the troops were to carry out the *front's* immediate objective, contained in *Stavka* directive No. 30203; that is, to reach the line Ovruch—Korosten'—Zhitomir—Berdichev—Kazatin. The operations of the 13th and 60th armies, which by this time were already supposed to be part of the Voronezh Front, were planned for this stage.

It was planned to carry out the third stage before 1-5 November, during the course of which the *front's* forces were supposed to carry out the immediate objective, assigned in the *Stavka* of the Supreme High Command's directive No. 30203—to reach the line Sarny—Proskurov—Mogilev-Podol'skii. The armies' main forces where to reach the indicated front by 1-5 November, and the mobile formations by 27-30 October. The possibility of pulling the 47th Army into the *front's* second echelon was envisaged during this stage.

In his directive No. 0043/op, issued on 29 September, the *front* commander demanded of all armies operating along the front Rzhishchev—Kanev to attack on 30 September with the objective of uniting all the individual bridgeheads along this front by the end of the day, and from 1 October to prepare a new offensive and during 2-3 October reach the front Yushki—Shandra—the mouth of the Ross' River; that is, that line which the *front's* forces should have reached as a result of the 23-26 September fighting. It was planned to launch the general offensive from this front on 3-4 October, in accordance with the plan laid out above. The 3rd Guards Tank Army was given the following task: "To completely cross your tanks to the right bank of the Dnepr River by the morning of 3 October, with the idea of attacking in the 27th Army's sector, without awaiting the army's complete concentration." Up to 1 October the army, in conjunction with the 40th and 47th armies, was to continue its offensive fighting on the Bukrin bridgehead with the forces available there.

The 38th Army was given the task of capturing Kiev through concentric attacks from the north and south.

The 38th Army was reinforced with the 5th Guards Tank Corps, which up until this time was being refitting in the *front's* rear, as well as the 1st Guards Cavalry Corps. However, neither of these corps was employed in the operation before 5 October.

The Course of Combat Operations South of Kiev from 30 September through 11 October and the Preparation of the October Offensive from the Bukrin Bridgehead

On the Bukrin bridgehead on 30 September the forces of the 40th, 3rd Guards Tank and 47th armies went over to the offensive in accordance with the *front's* operational directive No. 0043/op. They encountered fierce resistance from the enemy, who was striving to halt our forces' offensive through organized fire and counterattacks. By the close of the day the *front's* forces had not only not carried out their assigned tasks, but in some places were themselves pushed back somewhat by the enemy. We only managed to link up the bridgehead in the Grigorovka area with the main bridgehead in the Bukrin bend.

This may be explained, first of all, by the lack of readiness of the *front's* forces for the offensive, as well as the absence of the necessary organization and control of the fighting, particularly in the Bukrin bend. The following formations fought here: the 40th Army's 47th Rifle Corps (253rd, 161st, 337th, and 38th rifle divisions), the 27th Army's 100th, 147th and part of the 155th rifle divisions, and units of all of the 3rd Guards Tank Army's corps (69th, 23rd Guards, 70th, 71st and 22nd Guards motorized brigades, motorized battalions from the 54th and 55th guards tank brigades, and a tank battalion from the 21st Guards Tank Brigade). All of these formations and units, which were not united under overall leadership, got mixed up and fought in a disorganized manner. Many formation headquarters were on the left bank of the Dnepr. In the 3rd Guards Tank Army there was created a so-called "combat sector" of the 3rd Guards Tank Army on the right bank of the Dnepr, headed by a sector chief and his chief of staff, although the army did not have an independent sector on the Bukrin bridgehead, but was mixed up with the forces of the 40th and 27th armies. The army commander himself and his staff remained on the left bank of the river. The chief of the "combat sector" issued written orders to the corps, parallel with the army commander, although there was no shortage of such orders signed by the army commander. Such a form of control only confused the organization of the tank army's fighting and caused significant harm to the cause.

At 0330 on 30 September the *front* commander sent a telegram to the commanders of the 40th and 3rd Guards Tank armies, in which he sharply pointed out the weak organization of the fighting and its control, which had been observed during the days following the forcing of the Dnepr, and demanded:

> You must eliminate shortcomings in troop control. The headquarters of the corps, divisions, and brigades, the troops of which are located on the Bukrin bridgehead, are to be immediately shifted to the right bank of the Dnepr. The commanders of the 40th and 3rd Guards Tank armies on the right bank of the Dnepr are to organize their own auxiliary command posts for observing the battle and controlling it.

Despite the *front* commander's intervention twice in the organization and control of the battle on the Bukrin bridgehead, order was established slowly here. It was only during the night of 1-2 October that the Bukrin bridgehead was divided into two parts. Its eastern part was occupied by the forces of the 27th Army (241st, 100th and 155th rifle divisions), while the western part was reserved for the 40th Army. The 40th Army's 38th Rifle Division continued to fight in the Grigorovka area and had been transferred along with its sector to the 27th Army. However, as before, the 3rd Guards Tank Army's motorized rifle brigades and battalions were among the 40th and 27th armies' formations and were mixed up with them, while remaining subordinated to their own commanders.

On 2 October the enemy launched an attack with the forces of the 34th Infantry Division and the *Das Reich* Panzer Division against the bridgehead northwest of Rzhishchev, which was occupied by the 237th and 42nd Guards rifle divisions. By 5 October this sizeable (ten kilometers in width and four kilometers in depth) and important bridgehead had essentially been abandoned by our forces. Only a single rifle regiment from the 237th Rifle Division was holding a small shoreline sector northwest of Grebeni and one rifle battalion from the 42nd Guards Rifle Division was holding near the bank southeast of Grebeni. The 237th Rifle Division had taken up defensive positions along the left bank of the Dnepr, while the 42nd Guards Rifle Division concentrated in the Pidsinne area.

On 2 and 3 October the Germans carried out insistent attacks with infantry and tanks along all sectors of the 40th, 27th, 3rd Guards Tank, and 47th armies, and on 4 and 5 October the German-Fascist troops' offensive impulse weakened and there was fighting only along individual sectors.

During these days the *front's* forces lost the bridgehead northwest of Rzhishchev and, as was shown earlier, the 68th Guards Rifle Division was pushed back somewhat on the bridgehead in the Shchuchinka area. The remaining units held their positions. During the course of the fighting the enemy suffered significant losses in both tanks and men.

Despite the heavily broken terrain in the Bukrin bend of the Dnepr, the Germans attempted to employ their tanks *en masse*. The attacking tanks' combat formations were organized in the following manner: three to five heavy tanks were in the front, and behind them medium and light tanks and, finally, the infantry advanced on armored personnel carriers behind the tanks, in order to consolidate the captured line. The enemy often deployed 150 tanks for an attack along a five-kilometer front, along with 2-3 regiments of infantry, while paying no attention to heavy losses from our artillery fire.

During 6-11 October a period of quiet settled over the entire front from Rzhishchev to Kanev, which was sometimes interrupted by fighting between reconnaissance detachments. The enemy was feverishly entrenching, while our forces were preparing for an offensive. However, it did not begin as planned, due to the troops' lack of readiness and the shortage of ammunition, and also due to enemy counterattacks. On 2 October the 52nd Army's 294th and 254th rifle divisions relieved the 47th Army's units on several small bridgeheads southeast of Kanev. The relieved 206th and 218th rifle divisions were shifted to the 47th Army's bridgehead north of Kanev.

Due to the transfer of the 52nd and 4th Guards armies to the Steppe Front, the left boundary line with the latter was established at 2400 on 2 October along the line Bogodukhov—Romodan—Zolotonosha—the mouth of the Ross' River—Zhashkov—Nemirov—Mogilev-Podol'skii, with all locales, except for Romodan, for the Voronezh Front.

One of the reasons for the delay in preparing the troops for the offensive continued to be the slow construction of crossings over the Dnepr. On 10 October; that is, two and a half weeks following the start of the forcing of the Dnepr, the number of crossings finally enabled us to cross forces and their equipment.

On this day the small bridgeheads northwest of Rzhishchev were being supported with weak crossings; there were two ferry (eight and 30 tons) and three landing crossings on the bridgehead in the Shchuchinka area southeast of Rzhishchev; besides this, a bridge was being built. Two ferry and two landing crossings were working on the Bukrin bridgehead in the Traktomirov area; there were two heavy ferry crossings of up to 60 tons in the area of Monastyrek village (west of Traktomirov); there were three ferry (16 and 30 tons) and three landing crossings in the Zarubentsy area, and a bridge was also being built here; there was a bridge with a capacity of 16 tons, three ferry (with a capacity of 16 tons apiece) and two landing crossings in the Grigorovka area. On the 47th Army's Studenets bridgehead one ferry (30 tons) and three landing crossings were working and a bridge was being built.

By the start of the offensive the *front's* aviation had managed to rebase and was in significantly better conditions than during the first days of the troops' arrival at the Dnepr. Fighter aviation airfields were 10-30 kilometers from the Dnepr.

The enemy group of forces along the front Tripol'ye—Kanev by the close of 11 October is as follows.

The 34th Infantry Division was defending along a 30-kilometer front from Tripol'ye to Rzhishchev. Following the nearly complete loss of the 52nd Rifle Corps' bridgehead in the Yushki—Grebeni area, this was a comparatively quiet sector.

The 10th Motorized Division was operating along a 6-kilometer front and the SS *Das Reich* Panzer Division along a 10-kilometer front against 52nd Rifle Corps' Shchuchinka bridgehead.

The 72nd Infantry, 19th Panzer, 20th Motorized, 112th and 255th infantry divisions were operating in the Bukrin bend along a 22-kilometer front. On average, each division defended a 4-5 kilometer front.

THE VORONEZH FRONT'S OFFENSIVE OPERATION, OCTOBER 1943

The 3rd Panzer Division, and to the south the 57th Infantry Division, with one regiment from the 88th Infantry Division, were operating against the 47th Army's Studenets bridgehead.

Thus the enemy had more than five infantry, two motorized and three panzer divisions, or more than ten divisions, along a 100-kilometer front. He did not dispose of any tactical or operational reserves along this axis. All of the Germans' forces had been pulled into the fighting. All of the above-named divisions were part of the Eighth Army's XXIV and XLVIII panzer corps, the left boundary of which ran through the Tripol'ye area.

Although German radio and press propaganda actively broadcast the "strength" and "might" of their "eastern wall," which had been created by them along the Dnepr, nevertheless the main strength of their defensive line chiefly consisted of the natural features and qualities of such a large river as the Dnepr. The defensive structures along the Dnepr consisted of a hurriedly built field defensive position, which included 2-3 lines of trenches, which were not continuous along all sectors. The defensive works along the right bank of the Dnepr River were being carried out primarily through the efforts of prisoners of war and the local population. With the arrival of Soviet forces at the Dnepr and the withdrawal of the Germans to the right bank, the intensity of the enemy's defensive works increased significantly, particularly along those sectors where the enemy had been pushed bank from the bank. Alongside active measures having the purpose of throwing back our crossed forces into the Dnepr, the Germans were strengthening their defense: they dug trenches, put up barbed wire obstacles and mine fields. It is necessary to note that the enemy employed the large number of tanks which he had along this sector in the first line of defense. This can be explained by the enormous manpower losses which the Germans had suffered in the summer campaign and, as a result, the sharply felt lack of infantry. At this time their infantry divisions numbered 2-3,000 men and panzer divisions up to 80 tanks.

The overall correlation of forces along the sector from Rzhishchev to Kanev, where on 12 October the main combat activities unfolded, was as follows:

Table 1.3 The Overall Correlation of Forces Along the Rzhishchev—Kanev Sector

Combat Arm	Our Forces		The Enemy	
	Number	Correlation of Forces	Number	Combat Arm
Rifle Divisions	16	5.3:1	3	Infantry Divisions
Mechanized Corps	2	1:1	2	Motorized Divisions
Tanks and Self-Propelled Guns	694	3.5:1	200	Tanks and Assault Guns
Artillery Guns and Mortars 76mm and greater	1,673	1.3:1	1,243	Artillery Guns and Mortars
Aircraft	More than 600	1.2:1	500	Aircraft

Thus the overall superiority in forces was in favor of the Voronezh Front.

During the course of the 30 September-11 October fighting the deadlines for the start of the offensive changed several times. Naturally, the plan also changed. In its final form, the plan for the *front's* offensive operation was as follows.

The 40th Army was to launch its main attack along the left flank with the forces of the 47th Rifle Corps and by the close of the offensive's first day capture the line Staiki—Zikrachi—Yanivka, and by the close of the second day the rifle formations were to reach the line Khalep'ye—Verem'ye—Chernyakhov—excluding Kagarlyk, while the tank corps (8th Guards and 10th) were to reach the Dolina—Gusachevka—Germanovskaya Sloboda—Antonovka area. the 52nd Rifle Corps' 237th Division was to defend along the left bank of the Dnepr along a broad front from Kailov to

Rzhishchev; the corps' 309th and 68th Guards rifle divisions received orders to attack to the south and southeast on the operation's first day, assisting the 47th Rifle Corps in defeating the enemy in the Khodorov area, while throughout the second day to develop the offensive to the northwest, rolling up the Germans' defensive front along the right bank of the Dnepr River. The 47th Rifle Corps was supposed to attack, having in its first echelon the 253rd Division, with 12 of the 10th Tank Corps' tanks, the 161st Division, with 12 tanks from the 8th Guards Tank Corps, and the 337th Division. The 42nd Guards Rifle Division comprised the corps' second echelon. The 10th and 8th Guards tank corps were ordered to develop the offensive following the rifle units' breakthrough of the enemy's defense to a depth of 2-3 kilometers, and by the close of the operation's second day reach the area indicated above.

The 27th Army had the task, in close cooperation with the 40th Army's 47th Rifle Corps, of launching its main attack along the right flank in the direction of Malyi Bukrin. By the close of the operation's first day the army's forces were supposed to reach the front excluding Yanivka—Shandra, and by the close of the second day the front Kagarlyk—Lipovets. It was planned to organize its combat formation in two echelons: the 241st, 100th, 155th, and 38th rifle divisions in the first echelon, and the 147th rifle division in the second.

The 47th Army received orders to launch an attack to the southwest and by the close of the operation's first day reach the front excluding Shandra—Stepanin, and by the close of the second day the rifle formations were to reach the front Zelenki—Yemchikha, and the mobile forces the Rossava—Mironovka area. The army had the task of solidly securing the left wing of the *front's* shock group. All of the army's forces were supposed to attack from the Studenets bridgehead (six kilometers in width and two kilometers in depth) in a single echelon. The 21st Rifle Corps (206th and 218th rifle divisions) was on the right flank, and the 23rd Rifle Corps (30th and 23rd rifle divisions) on the left flank. The 3rd Guards Mechanized Corps was to also attack in the first echelon, in cooperation with the 21st Rifle Corps.

The 3rd Guards Tank Army, which comprised the *front's* mobile group, received orders to attack with its main forces in the 27th Army's sector and to enter the breach upon the rifle formations taking Malyi Bukrin (that is, upon their advance to a depth of 5-6 kilometers). By the close of the operation's first day the army was supposed to reach the Nikolaevka—Potok area; the Stavy—Shpendovka—Vintsentovka area by the close of the second day; the Grebenki—Belaya Tserkov' area by the close of the third day; the Fastov area by the close of the fourth day, and, finally; the Stavishche—Brusilov—Khomutets—Gruzkoye area by the close of the fifth day. The army was supposed to enter the breach in a single echelon: the 7th Guards Tank Corps in the 161st and 337th rifle divisions' (40th Army) sector and the 27th Army's 241st Rifle Division's sector; the 9th Mechanized Corps would enter the sector of the 27th Army's 241st and 100th Rifle Divisions and the 6th Guards Tank Corps in the same army's 155th Rifle Division.

Within 15 minutes following the start of the infantry attack, the forward detachments of the tank corps were to begin their movement and, behind them, depending on the situation, the corps' main forces. However, the order of the tank army's movement was quite conditional, because up until the last day not all of its units had been moved behind the infantry's combat formations and thus continued to remain in contact with the enemy. Besides this, it should be noted that the depth of the troops' organization on the Bukrin bridgehead was so insignificant that the beginning of the movement of the army's forward detachments, and the entire army behind them, within 15 minutes following the beginning of the infantry attack, essentially meant that the army would be dragged into the fighting long before the rifle units reached the bypass line. Thus there was the risk of employing the army not so much for developing the breakthrough as for direct infantry support in completing the breakthrough of the depth of the enemy's tactical defense. As a result, the army was threatened with the danger of expending its tanks in a way not designated. Such a prospect was particularly dangerous in conditions of exceptionally difficult terrain for tanks in the Bukrin bend of the Dnepr.

It should be noted that the assigning of such an infantry bypass line as the Malyi Bukrin line, along with the adjacent heights, in no way changed the situation and did not render the conditions for the tank army's operations any easier. The terrain along this line was the same as to the north of Malyi Bukrin. The commitment of the tank army was expedient only after the infantry's arrival at the Yanivka—Shandra line; that is, following the breakthrough of the enemy's defense to a depth of 20-25 kilometers.

The plan for employing the 2nd Air Army was as follows. Upon the beginning of the infantry attack, the 5th Assault Air Corps (264th and 4th Guards assault air divisions), along with the 235th Fighter and 292nd Assault Air divisions, were to launch consecutive attacks in assault groups of 6-8 and 12-16 planes against the enemy's artillery, tanks and personnel in the areas of Khodorov, Velikii Bukrin and Kolesishche; that is, opposite the front of the 40th Army's 47th Rifle Corps and the 27th Army. The readiness of the groups for repeat sorties was established at two hours after landing. Subsequently, the 5th Assault Air Corps was supposed to assist the 3rd Guards Tank Army and the 291st Assault Air Division the 27th Army. The intensity of the corps' combat activity was set at 3-3.5 sorties per day for each combat-ready plane. The 202nd Bomber Division, along with one fighter regiment, had the task of launching three bombing strikes against the enemy's artillery and strong points opposite the 27th Army's left flank. The readiness for repeat sorties was set at 2.5 hours following landing, with an intensity of three sorties per day per combat-ready plane.

During the night of 11-12 October the 208th Night Bomber Division was to exhaust the enemy's personnel, disrupt his command and control, suppress his artillery, and destroy his depots through bombing raids in the immediate tactical depth of his defense. The intensity of its combat activity was 140 sorties per night.

The 10th Fighter Corps had the task of covering the *front's* main group of forces in the Dnepr's Bukrin bend against enemy air activity. Particular attention was to be paid to covering the 3rd Guards Tank Army. The 5th Fighter Corps was supposed to cover the 38th and 60th armies' combat formations north of Kiev, as well as to be ready to reinforce the coverage of the *front's* forces south of Pereyaslav-Khmel'nitskii. The intensity of its combat activity was set at four sorties per combat-ready plane.

For cooperation with the ground forces and more precise command and control of their units' actions, the air corps and air division commanders were supposed to be at the observation posts of the combined-arms and tank formations: the commanders of the 5th Assault Air Corps and the 291st Assault Air and 202nd Bomber divisions at the observation post of the commander of the 27th Army (northeast of Grigorovka, along the left bank of the Dnepr); the commander of the 10th Fighter Corps at the observation post of the commander of the 3rd Guards Tank Army (south of Zarubentsy). The observation post of the commander of the 2nd Air Army was organized together with the observation post of the commander of the 27th Army.

The density of the forces designated for the attack from the Bukrin bridgehead (the 40th Army's 47th Rifle Corps, 27th Army and 3rd Guards Tank Army), given a breakthrough front of 16 kilometers, was 162 artillery pieces and mortars and 38.5 tanks and self-propelled guns per kilometer of front. A rifle division was to attack in a sector of about 1.8 kilometers, on the average.

The pace of the attack by the infantry and tanks was planned as follows: on the first day the 40th Army's 47th Rifle Corps was to advance 18 kilometers and 20 kilometers on the second day; the 27th Army was to advance 22 kilometers each on the first and second days; the 47th Army was to advance 18 kilometers on the first day and 20 on the second; the 3rd Guards Tank Army was to advance 26-28 kilometers on the first day and 30-35 on the second. The planned pace of the offensive should be viewed as quite intense, particularly when taking into account the terrain conditions in which the troops were to operate in the first two days of the operation.

In the final variant of the plan, the beginning of the artillery preparation on 12 October was set at 0700; the attack by the infantry and infantry-support tanks was set for 0740, as was the first strike by assault aircraft, and then in continuous waves. The bombing strikes were to follow thusly: the first at 0800, the second at 1100, and the third at 1500. The artillery preparation was planned as follows: a three-minute fire onslaught at maximum intensity; deliberate fire against the enemy's firing positions and observation posts for 30 minutes, and intensified fire for seven minutes.

The *front* commander, in his instructions on planning the artillery preparation, particularly stressed that the first three-minute fire onslaught be extremely strong and powerful, for the purpose of rapidly paralyzing the enemy's defense and inflicting maximum losses on him.

The *front* commander demanded not only the full exertion of fire, but personally laid down the norms of the number of rounds during this period: 36 rounds for 82mm mortars, 18 for 120mm mortars, 30 for 45mm guns, 24 for 76mm guns, 12 for 122mm and 107mm guns, and nine for 152mm guns. Intensive fire from all types of infantry weapons was also to be waged during this period. In particular, each heavy machine gun was to expend two belts of ammunition and each light machine gun and machine gun pistol two disks each, and each rifle 20 rounds.

The guns that were set aside for firing over open sights were supposed to have definite targets and were to wage deliberate fire throughout the entire period of the artillery preparation.

A major role in the destruction of the enemy's defensive structures personnel was entrusted to mortar fire. The *front* commander ordered the movement to the right bank of the Dnepr the mortar brigades of the 13th and 17th artillery divisions. The commanders of these brigades were instructed to plan a massive mortar fire by employing all mortars from the army mortar regiments and the mortars of the 40th and 27th armies' rifle regiments.

Attention was also paid to the scrupulous reconnaissance and study of the enemy's artillery and mortar fire system and to the organization of counterbattery fire.

A significant part of the artillery, particularly the 7th Breakthrough Artillery Corps' artillery, occupied firing positions along the left bank of the Dnepr, due to the small capacity of the bridgeheads on the right bank. The *front* commander demanded the maximum approach of this artillery's firing positions to the Dnepr for the purpose of fully employing the range of its fire. Throughout the first day of fighting, the 7th Breakthrough Artillery Corps' artillery was to fire without changing its firing positions. It was subsequently planned to cross the 13th Artillery Division to the right bank of the Dnepr over the 27th Army's crossings, and the 17th Artillery Division over the 40th Army's crossings. The planning and organization of the crossing was entrusted to the commander of the 7th Breakthrough Artillery Corps and the chief of the *front's* engineer troops.

The *front* commander demanded the scrupulous verification of fire readiness and the presence of ammunition for each battery and gun designated for firing over open sights.

The *front* headquarters had information that the enemy was listening in to our telephone conversations. On 9 October the *front* commander demanded an increase in the secret command and control of troops.

Insofar as there was reason to assume that the enemy was expecting our offensive from the Bukrin bridgehead, the same orders demanded of the commanders of the 40th, 27th, 47th, and 3rd Guards Tank armies that they take measures to deceive the Germans. However, only the 27th Army's headquarters compiled a specific plan for deceiving the enemy for the purpose of concealing the army's preparations for the offensive and to create the impression with the enemy that we had decided not to attack along the Belaya Tserkov' axis and that the 27th Army's forces were moving laterally to the south. This plan called for the following measures: a) the movement of the forces along the left bank of the Dnepr along the route Tsybli—Khotski—Glemyazovo; b) the

THE VORONEZH FRONT'S OFFENSIVE OPERATION, OCTOBER 1943

movement along this same route of the army's radio station as far as Zolotonosha (ten kilometers southeast of Glemyazovo); c) telephone conversations between the army headquarters and division headquarters, as well as between the division and regimental headquarters on crossing troops from the bridgehead to the left bank of the Dnepr.

However, this measure did not achieve its goal. The enemy was not fooled and knew that the Soviet forces' attack was being prepared from the bridgeheads they had seized. This was evident if only from the fact that the enemy in no way changed his behavior and, in turn, was preparing for decisive fighting for the bridgeheads. The disposition of German forces along the front Rzhishchev—Kanev during 9-12 October remained without any changes.

The Course of Combat Activities North of Kiev from 30 September through 10 October and the Preparation of the October Offensive from the Lyutezh Bridgehead

On 30 September the commander of the 38th Army presented to the *front* headquarters his plan for the capture of Kiev through concentric attacks by the 51st Rifle Corps from the north and the 50th Rifle Corps from the south. Simultaneously, the commander of the 50th Rifle Corps was ordered to concentrate the 163rd and 136th rifle divisions in the Bortnichi—Vishenki area and to force the Dnepr with their forward detachments on the night of 30 September-1 October in the direction of Pirogovo. It was subsequently planned to widen the bridgehead near Pirogovo, to concentrate the corps' three divisions there and to begin the attack simultaneously north and south of Kiev for the purpose of capturing the city. The defense along the left bank of the Dnepr in the immediate Kiev area was entrusted to army screening detachments.

On 2 and 3 October elements of the 136th, and then of the 163rd rifle divisions forced the Dnepr in the direction of Pirogovo, they did not have success during subsequent days. The reason for this was first of all the fact that the 50th Rifle Corps had been insufficiently reinforced and had very little ammunition and little crossing equipment.

North of Kiev, the 51st Rifle Corps was engaged in intensive fighting to expand the bridgehead, while leaving little success. The 1st Guards Cavalry and 5th Guards Tank corps were still only concentrating in the area between the Desna and Dnepr. Thus the *front's* initial plan to capture Kiev by 7 October with the forces of the 38th Army and one tank and one cavalry corps was not fulfilled, while in essence its realization had not even begun.

From 2400 on 5 October the 13th Army, which consisted of eight rifle divisions,[22] and the 60th Army, consisting of 12 rifle divisions,[23] was transferred to the Voronezh Front by a directive from the *Stavka* of the Supreme High Command.

The new boundary line with the Central Front from this time was established as follows: Snagost'—the Seim River—the Desna River—Chernigov—Mozyr'—the Pripyat' River—Pinsk; all points (except for Pinsk) were for the Voronezh Front. The 13th and 60th armies were fighting with all their forces against the enemy along the right bank of the Dnepr. This enabled the *front* command to more closely and purposefully organize the cooperation of the armies, which had been transferred to the *front*, with the 38th Army and to direct the efforts of these armies (especially of the 38th and 60th armies) for an attack against the Germans' Kiev group of forces from the north. As a result of this, a new plan for an offensive by the *front's* right-flank armies was drawn up. On 6 October the *front* commander assigned these armies the following objectives.

---

22 181st, 211th, 74th, 8th, 148th, and 322nd rifle divisions and the 6th and 70th guards rifle divisions.
23 2nd, 3rd and 4th guards airborne divisions, 132nd, 141st, 143rd, and 280th rifle divisions, the 248th Rifle Brigade, the 226th and 112th rifle divisions, the 75th Guards Rifle Division, and the 121st Rifle Division.

At 2400 on 6 October the 13th Army's left-flank 17th Guards Rifle Corps, consisting of the 6th and 70th guards rifle divisions, was to be transferred to the 60th Army along with the sectors they occupied, while its remaining forces were to go over to the defensive along the line Kolyban'—Krivaya Gora—the mouth of the Uzh River. The boundary line on the left was the Pripyat' River as far as the mouth of the Uzh River, and then along the Uzh River.

At 2400 on 6 October the 60th Army was to incorporate the 17th Guards Rifle Corps and the 1st Guards Cavalry Corps. Throughout 6 and 7 October the army was to clear the enemy from the south bank of the Uzh River along the right flank and seize a bridgehead along the southern bank of the Teterev River along the Pilyava—Zatonsk sector. On the night of 7-8 October the 1st Guards Cavalry Corps was to cross the Dnepr River in the Okuninovo area; besides this, it was necessary to cross one cavalry division, with tanks, over the Teterev River to its southern (right) bank. Upon completing the enumerated preparatory measures, the army had the task of launching its main attack to the southwest, between the Zdvizh and Irpen' rivers, rolling up the enemy's front, and also a supporting attack toward Ivankov. By the close of the fifth day of the operation the army's main forces were to reach the front Fillipovichi—Vorzel'. As the army moved south, it was to organize a defense along the Zdvizh River. The 1st Guards Cavalry Corps was ordered to operate between the Zdvizh and Irpen' rivers in the direction of the main attack, and by the close of the operation's fourth day reach the Gavronshchina—Makarov—Yurov—Kopylov—Vyshegrad area. The army's boundary on the left was set at the mouth of the Irpen' River—the Irpen' River as far as Demidovo—Vorzel'—Buzova (all locales, except for Buzova, were for the 60th Army).

The army commander decided to launch his main attack with the forces of the 1st Guards Cavalry Corps and the 77th Rifle Corps in the direction of Manuil'sk and Litvinovka; simultaneously, the 24th and 30th rifle corps were to launch an attack from the line Yasnogorodka—Kozarovichi in the direction of Dymer. However, in drawing up the objectives for the corps, the decision's idea did not hold up, because the 77th Rifle Corps was to attack strictly to the west along the northern and southern banks of the Teterev River, while the main attack along the main axis, toward Filippovichi, was essentially to be launched by only the 1st Guards Cavalry Corps.

The 38th Army was ordered to broaden its bridgehead during 6-7 October as far as the line Guta Mezhigorskaya—Lyutezh—Novo-Petrovtsy, to gather no less than five rifle divisions to its left flank and on the night of 7-8 October cross the 5th Guards Tank Corps to the Lyutezh bridgehead. In launching the main attack along both banks of the Irpen' River and outflanking Kiev from the northwest and west, the army had the task of reaching the front Svyatoshino—Syrets—Priorka with its rifle formations by the close of the operation's third day and by the close of the fourth day to capture the city of Kiev. It was planned to employ the 5th Guards Tank Corps to develop the success along the western bank of the Irpen' River, with the task of cutting the Kiev—Zhitomir highway by the close of the fourth day. To the south of Darnitsa, along the sector Osokorki—excluding Kailov, the army was to defend with the forces of one rifle division and continue to demonstrate a crossing in the Vishenki area. The boundary line to the left was set at Zhuravka—Yagotin—Kailov (all locales, except for Zhuravka, were for the 38th Army).

It was planned to complete the regrouping of forces by the close of 8 October. By 9-11 October the Lyutezh bridgehead was to be expanded. For this purpose, the 5th Guards Tank Corps was ordered, with the assistance of part of the 340th Rifle Division's forces, to force the Irpen' River in the Demidovo—Guta Mezhigorskaya area and reach the Dymer—Litvinovka—Demidovo area, after which it was to turn south to operate along the western bank of the Irpen' River in the direction of Shpitki. The 50th and 51st rifle corps had the task of attacking to the south between the Irpen' and Dnepr rivers.

The beginning of the offensive by the army's right flank was set for 9 October, but due to the troops' lack of readiness it was moved to 11 October. Active operations along the front of all the right-wing armies continued without letup until their attack.

THE VORONEZH FRONT'S OFFENSIVE OPERATION, OCTOBER 1943

On 6 October the enemy in the Gornostaipol' area attacked with the forces of the 7th Panzer and 339th Infantry divisions and part of the 217th Infantry Division's forces. Throughout 6-7 October the 60th Army's forces were engaged in intensive fighting here. The enemy, having launched a powerful attack, immediately pulled the 7th Panzer Division into the reserve in the Ivanovka area.

On 8 October the 60th Army's forces seized the initiative in the Gornostaipol' area and themselves took up the attack. On 9 October fighting began south of Chernobyl', where the Germans also attacked our units. On 10 October the enemy, with the forces of the 4th Panzer Division, began attacks against the 13th Army's 8th and 148th rifle divisions west of Karpilovka, while attempting to eliminate our bridgehead on the western bank of the Pripyat'.

On 7 October the 1st Guards Cavalry Corps began to cross the Dnepr, and on 9 October its 7th Guards Cavalry Division forced the Teterev River and captured Zatonsk. On 10 October the 2nd and 7th guards cavalry divisions completely crossed to the southern bank of the Teterev River and began a successful attack to the south, having advanced seven kilometers in a day of fighting. The enemy threw units of the 7th and 8th panzer divisions into a counterattack and thus the 1st Guards Cavalry Corps was immediately drawn into the fighting against German tanks in difficult and wooded terrain, without coordination with our infantry.

During the time until 10 October the 38th Army enjoyed small success and only slightly expanded the Lyutezh bridgehead. On 9 October the 5th Guards Tank Corps began to cross over the Dnepr near Svarom'ye.

The 13th and 60th armies were better supplied with crossings over the Dnepr than the *front's* remaining forces. For example, by 10 October the 60th Army had the following operating in its sector: a low-water bridge with a capacity of up to 30 tons in the Okuninovo area, four ferry crossings of 30 tons each, about 12 ferry crossings from two to 12 tons, and a landing crossing southwest of Okuninovo. The 38th Army did not have a single bridge ready. The construction of a bridge in the Svarom'ye area was moving ahead slowly. Here there were two ferry crossings of 50 and 30 tons and several smaller ferries.

The German Fourth Panzer Army was operating opposite the 60th and 38th armies' front along a sector 150 kilometers wide. The 291st and 339th infantry divisions, as well as part of the forces of the 8th Panzer and 217th Infantry divisions were operating between the Uzh and Teterev rivers. The following were operating along the southern bank of the Teterev River against the attacking units of the 1st Guards Cavalry Corps: the 7th Panzer and part of the 8th Panzer division's forces, while to the south as far as the Dymer area were the 183rd, 340th and part of the 327th infantry divisions, and the 208th Infantry Division from Dymer to the Irpen' River. The 68th, 82nd, 327th, 323rd infantry divisions and one regiment from the 340th Infantry Division were opposite the 38th Army on the Lyutezh bridgehead. The 75th Infantry Division was immediately defending Kiev. The 213th Security and the main forces of the 88th Infantry divisions were defending south of Kiev, as far as Tripol'ye.

In all, the enemy had in the first line along this front 12 infantry and two panzer divisions. He could employ the 454th Security Division, which was guarding the rear along the Korosten' axis, as a reserve, as well as the Hungarian 201st Light Infantry Division, which also had the task of guarding the rear in the Berdichev area. The headquarters of the German Fourth Panzer Army was located in Makarov. All of these formations were part of the LIX, XIII and VII army corps. The enemy divisions were short of men and numbered from 2,000 to 4,000 men; the 7th Panzer Division had only 60 tanks. The Germans, aside from active operations aimed at throwing our forces behind the Dnepr, were also heavily engaged in constructing defensive works; they were digging trenches with light shelters and were laying barbed wire obstacles and mine fields along individual sectors.

The correlation of the sides' forces along the 60th and 38th armies' fronts by 11 October is as follows:

Table 1.4 The Correlation of Forces Along the 38th and 60th Armies' Front

Combat Arm	Our Forces		The Enemy	
	Number	Correlation of Forces	Overall	Combat Arm
Rifle and Cavalry Divisions	25	2.1:1	12	Infantry Divisions
Tank Corps	1	0.5:1	2	Panzer Divisions
Tanks and Self-Propelled Guns	228	0.7:1	323	Tanks and Assault Guns
Artillery Guns and Mortars 76mm and greater	1,329	0.9:1	1,450	Artillery Guns and Mortars

Thus our forces in this area had a 2:1 superiority in rifle formations, almost an equal number of artillery pieces and mortars, and were somewhat inferior in the number of tanks.

The 60th Army's overall offensive front in the sector between the Zdvizh and Irpen' rivers reached 25 kilometers. Here three cavalry and five rifle divisions and one rifle brigade were supposed to attack, which comprised 2.8 kilometers per division. In the 38th Army the offensive front between the Irpen' and Dnepr rivers was first narrow, about ten kilometers wide, and only following the arrival in the Kiev area would the width of the offensive sector broaden and reach 20 kilometers. The density of rifle troops in this army was 1.5 kilometers per division. The number of direct infantry support tanks was insignificant and reached about five tanks and self-propelled guns in the 60th Army and 11-12 tanks and self-propelled guns in the 38th Army per kilometer of front. In the 60th Army the artillery density reached about 80 and in the 38th Army 96.5 guns and mortars per kilometer of offensive front.

The pace of the offensive was planned at 8-9 kilometers per day for the 60th Army's rifle formations, six kilometers for the 38th Army's rifle formations, and up to 15 kilometers per day for the cavalry corps.

The Front's Organization of Communications and Command and Control of the Troops

By the start of the October offensive the headquarters of the Voronezh Front's armies were located in the following locales: 13th Army in Khotilova Guta, 60th in Vypolzovo, 38th in Letki, 40th in Soshnikov, 27th in Vinnitsy, 47th in Glemyazovo, and the 3rd Guards Tank in Malaya Karatul'. Despite the comparative nearness of the armies' headquarters to the front line, stable and reliable communications with the forces, which were engaged in intense fighting immediately on the bridgeheads, was organized slowly and was completed only by the start of the offensive; that is, by 11-12 October.

From 3 October an auxiliary *front* control center was organized in Yerkovtsy with direct communications with the 40th, 27th and 3rd Guards Tank armies. Communications were maintained with the remaining armies through the *front* headquarters' communications center. The latter was deployed during 6-7 October in Trebukhovo (23 kilometers east of Kiev). The central location of the *front's* headquarters and the organization of an auxiliary control center along the *front's* left wing increased the stability of communications and improved the conditions for troop control.

The *front's* communications troops did a great deal of work in organizing communications over the Dnepr. By the start of the offensive there were a sufficient number of lines linking the *front* headquarters with all of the bridgeheads. In all, 30 communications crossings were constructed over the Dnepr, of which nine were cable and four were mast ones with spaces between the poles up to 330-500 meters above the river, although the mast lines were often damaged by the enemy's artillery fire. The cable crossings secured more reliable communications and were laid down by armored river cable and telegraph cable, which had been previously greased with artillery grease.

The *front* headquarters' radio communications with the armies were reliable, except for with the 47th Army, where there were frequent breaks. The commanders and headquarters of the troop formations resorted to employing radio equipment in all situations when wire communications equipment over the Dnepr worked unreliably. However, a serious shortcoming of the troop and artillery radio networks was the insufficient provisioning of the communications units with anode batteries and small radio bulbs. Radio communications with the neighboring *fronts*—Central and Steppe—worked with significant breaks.

By the start of the offensive by the *front's* forces all types of communications had been organized and supported reliable communications of both the *front* and army headquarters, as well as of the troop formations. Coordination communications worked precisely and reliably, particularly the communications of the combined-arms armies with the tank and air armies.

Rear Area Organization and Materiel Support by the Start of the Operation

The lagging behind of the rear organs and the insufficient provisioning of the troops operating on the bridgeheads with ammunition, fuel and food made the situation more complex and was one of the chief reasons for the stretching out of the deadlines for the start of the offensive by the *front's* forces on the right bank of the Dnepr.

The availability of the main types of supply by the morning of 2 October is as follows:

Table 1.5 The Voronezh Front's Materiel Provisioning

Item	With the Troops and in Army Depots	En Route to Army Bases	At Front Depots	Total
Ammunitions (in combat loads)				
37mm Anti-Aircraft Shells	2.1	0.4	1.9	4.4
76mm Regimental Gun Shells	1.9	0.2	0.7	2.8
76mm Divisional Gun Shells	1.3	0.4	0.1	2.0
85mm Anti-Aircraft Shells	1.4	0.3	0.7	2.4
122mm Howitzer Shells	0.8	0.8	0.2	1.8
152mm Gun and Howitzer Shells	0.8	0.5	0.5	1.8
82mm Mortar Rounds	1.0	0.4	0.5	1.9
120mm Mortar Rounds	0.5	0.3	0.1	0.9
Rifle Rounds	1.7	--	0.4	2.1
Sub Machine Gun Rounds	1.4	0.3	0.2	1.9
Hand Grenades	1.6	0.1	0.3	2.0
Fuels and Lubricants (in refills)				
Automobile Fuel	0.85	No information available		
Food and Forage (in daily rations)				
Flour, bread, rusks	13.1	–	1.6	14.7
Groats	23.6	–	3.1	26.7
Meat	10.2	–	1.7	11.9
Fats	15.2	–	1.5	16.7
Sugar	3.4	–	1.7	5.1

Item	With the Troops and in Army Depots	En Route to Army Bases	At Front Depots	Total
Tobacco	14.4	–	0.5	14.9
Oats	30.8	–	5.6	36.4
Hay	20.5	–	2.9	23.4
Salt	61.1	–	0.9	62.0

Note: There was no tobacco at all in the 27th and 47th armies.

Thus the *front* was supplied satisfactorily with ammunition and well supplied with food and forage. However, these figures do not represent a complete picture of the situation. Part of these supplies were at the *front* and army depots, while among the troops there was a serious shortage of all kinds of supplies. Matters stood poorly with fuels and lubricants.

Before 11 October the armies were based, as before, on the Vorozhba—Bogodukhov railroad and only the 38th Army had shifted its depots to the Nezhin—Priluki railroad sector. Only on 11 October; that is, on the eve of the front's offensive from the Bukrin bridgehead, was *front* rear services directive No. 001107 issued, which finally defined organization of the rear services in connection with the troops' arrival at the Dnepr.

The *front's* rear area boundary was established along the line Lokinskaya—Sudzha—Krasnopol'e—Bol'shaya Pisarevka—Bogodukhov, and the armies rear area boundary along the line Baturin—Bakhmach—Sribnoye—Melekhi—Bereznyaki.

The *front's* regulating stations were located as follows: No. 9 in Vorozhba and No. 10 in Bakhmach. The front's railroad sectors were: a) Bakhmach—Vorozhba—Gaponovo; b) Vorozhba—Krasnopol'e; c) Basy—Bogodukhov; d) Bakhmach—Romny—Lokhvitsa—Romodan, with the branch line Likhvitsa—Gadyach. The number of trains allotted to the *front* along the Vorozhba—Bakhmach sector was 11 trains per day.

The armies were supposed to be based on the following sectors: Chernigov—Nezhin, with a supply station in Anisovo, for the 13th Army; Nezhin—Bobrik, with a supply station in Zavorichi, for the 60th Army; Yagotin—Pereyaslavskaya, with a supply station in Yagotin, for the 40th Army; Priluki—Grebenka, with a supply station in Grebenka, for the 27th Army; a supply station in Priluki, with emergency trains at Yagotin station and the Chernyakhovka passing track, for the 3rd Guards Tank Army, and; Grebenka—Zolotonosha, with a supply station in Drabovo-Baryatinskaya, for the 47th Army.

The *front* had two military-automobile roads: No. 21, Priluki—Zgurovka—Novaya Basan'—Yadlovka—Brovary, and No. 8, Piryatin—Yagotin—Pereyaslav-Khmel'nitskii.

Dirt roads for the armies' supply and evacuation were established as follows: Anisovo—Chernigov—Kuibyshev—Pakul'—Gden', with an overall length of 75 kilometers, for the 13th Army; Nezhin—Nosovka—Kozary—Kozelets—Oster—Okuninovo, with an overall length of 120 kilometers, for the 60th Army; the directive established the 38th Army's supply and evacuation route of Bobrik—Brovary—Predmostnaya Slobodka. However, due to the fact that all of the army's main forces were fighting on the Lyutezh bridgehead, north of Kiev, the 50-kilometer supply route actually ran along the direction Bobrik—Letki—Svarom'ye. The 40th Army had the 50-kilometer Yagotin—Pereyaslav-Khmel'nitsii—Andrushi route; the 27th Army had 80-kilometer Grebenka—Svechkovka—Tashan'—Vypolzki—Tsybli route, and; the 47th Army had the 70-kilometer Drabovo-Baryatinskaya—Drabov—Sofievka—Glemyazovo route. The 3rd Guards Tank Army had two supply routes: a) Priluki—Yablonevka—Lizoguboba—Sloboda—Yagotin—Studeniki—Pereyaslav-Khmel'nitskii—Dem'yantsy, stretching 100 kilometers, and b) Yagotin—Studenish—Tsybli—Gorodishche, which was 60 kilometers long.

THE VORONEZH FRONT'S OFFENSIVE OPERATION, OCTOBER 1943

The location of the rear services, in accordance with *front* directive No. 001107, although it made the organization of supply significantly easier, nevertheless was unable to positively tell upon the offensive that began on 11-12 October, because time was required for such a shift.

The accumulation of munitions went slowly. The depots were slowly brought up to the Dnepr, the crossings were overloaded due to the movements of people, equipment and ammunition, the expenditure of which was quite significant due to the intense fighting. The *front* commander repeatedly pointed to the poor organization of the ammunition supply and demanded its accumulation as quickly as possible. For example, on 7 October the following order was issued.

> To the Commanders of the 40th, 27th, 47th, and 3rd Guards Tank Armies
> No. 21-K
> 7.10.43, 0510

The delivery of munitions is going quite slowly. That which has already been delivered to the armies has not yet reached the troops. Very little has been delivered to the right bank of the Dnepr and not enough attention is being paid to this.

I order:

1. To strengthen the delivery of ammunition in all possible ways. Adopt all measures so that all batteries, including those located on the right bank of the Dnepr, will have delivered to the no less than 1-1 1/3 combat loads by the close of 8.10.43.
2. Report on fulfillment.

Vatutin
Khrushchev

The provisioning of ammunition by the close of 11 October; that is, by the start of the offensive, was as follows (in combat loads).

Table 1.6 The Voronezh Front's Ammunition Provisioning

Item	With the Troops and in Army Depots	En Route to Army Bases	At Front Depots	Total
37mm Anti-Aircraft Shells	2.4	0.3	1.6	4.3
76mm Regimental Gun Shells	1.2	0.2	0.7	2.1
76mm Divisional Gun Shells	1.6	0.1	0.2	1.9
85mm Anti-Aircraft Shells	1.4	0.2	0.7	2.3
122mm Howitzer Shells	0.7	0.1	0.2	1.0
152mm Howitzer Shells	2.5	0.2	1.1	3.8
152mm Gun-Howitzer Shells	0.7	0.6	0.3	1.6
82mm Mortar Rounds	1.0	0.2	0.5	1.7
120mm Mortar Rounds	0.4	0.2	0.4	1.0

Thus the provisioning of ammunition, compared to the beginning of October, remained almost unchanged, with the exception of 152mm shells.

The *front's* supply of automobile fuel consisted of two refills, while in the armies its availability varied between 0.4 and 0.7 refills, while the 40th Army had only 0.1 of a refill.

The Course of Combat Activities on the Front's Left Wing, 12-15 October 1943

An aviation preparation by light bomber aviation was carried out on the night of 11-12 October. Po-2[24] aircraft carried out 226 sorties for the purposes of destroying the enemy's personnel, equipment and firing positions in the areas of Velikii Bukrin, Malyi Bukrin and the western outskirts of Kanev. In all, 1,086 demolition and fragmentation bombs were dropped, with 40 percent of them weighing 100 and 50 kilograms.

The artillery preparation began at 0700 and the attack by infantry and direct infantry support tanks at 0740. Units of the 52nd Rifle Corps began their attack from the Shchuchinka bridgehead at 1100. Assault air and bomber strikes by the 2nd Air Army began with the start of the infantry attack.

Despite the powerful artillery and air attacks (the 2nd Air Army carried out 1,054 sorties in the day's fighting), from the very beginning of the attack the enemy put up stubborn resistance. The reason for this was our headquarters' poor knowledge of the enemy's defensive system, particularly his fire system, because the targets had been poorly reconnoitered. As a result of this, the artillery and air preparation proved insufficiently effective.

Throughout the entire day there was fierce fighting along the front from Rzhishchev to Kanev. The enemy, feeling the great threat of a breakthrough of his defense on the Bukrin bridgehead, committed all of his available forces, particularly his tank units, into the fighting. By the close of the day the enemy removed part of the forces of the SS *Das Reich* Panzer Division from the area of the Shchuchinka bridgehead, where the 40th Army's attack was weak, and shifted them to the fighting along the boundary between the 27th and 47th armies north of Buchak, for the purpose of preventing the development of the success by the 27th Army's left wing and the uniting of the Bukrin and Studenets bridgeheads. Moreover, the Germans began to transfer the 11th Panzer Division from the south, from the Steppe Front's sector; its lead units were approaching the Tulintsy area by the close of 12 October. During the offensive a second enemy defensive line was uncovered, which had been prepared along the front Romashki—height 205.6—height 206.9—the woods north of Buchak.

In the day's fighting, the 40th Army's 47th Rifle Corps and the forces of the 27th and 3rd Guards Tank armies advanced eight kilometers along the main axis. The advance was insignificant along the secondary axes. The 40th Army's' 52nd Rifle Corps on the Shchuchinka bridgehead advanced no more than a kilometer to the south and southeast. Despite the capture of the village of Khodorov by units of the 47th Rifle Corps, we were not able to unite the Shchuchinka and Bukrin bridgeheads. The 47th Army's formations on the Studenets bridgehead advanced up to two kilometers to the west and southwest, but were also unable to link up with units of the 27th Army on the Bukrin bridgehead.

The 3rd Guards Tank Army, without awaiting the infantry's arrival at the bypass line called for in the plan, was immediately committed into the fighting. The forward detachments of the army's corps began their movement at 0755, and the main forces at 0930. Because the organization of our forces on the bridgehead was shallow, due to its small capacity, the tank army essentially was immediately drawn into the fighting to break through the enemy's first and sector defensive sectors. The tank corps were supposed to overcome the enemy's unsuppressed artillery and anti-tank defense, and also to fight off powerful counterattacks by his tanks. Due to the difficult terrain conditions the movement and deployment of the tank units took place slowly.

---

24 Editor's note. The Po-2 (also known as the U-2) was a general purpose Soviet biplane that first appeard in 1929. One model had a crew of one and a maximum speed of 152 kilometers per hour. It was armed with one 7.62mm machine gun and could carry six 50-kilogram bombs.

Thus the instructions to commit the tank army into the fighting only after the breakthrough of the tactical depth of the enemy's defense remained unfulfilled.

As a result of the operation's first day of fighting, the forces of the *front's* left wing did not carry out their assigned tasks. The enemy's defense had not been penetrated and, all the more so, he was quite active and counterattacked along all axes. The enemy's aviation concentrated its efforts against our forces' crossings over the Dnepr, carrying out 650 sorties during the day's fighting along the Bukrin bridgehead. Fierce fighting also continued during the night of 12-13 October. Nor did the units of the 3rd Guards Tank Army, which were operating at night, enjoy any success.

At 1700 on 12 October the *front* commander issued an order to continue the offensive from 0800 on 13 October. The 40th Army was ordered to capture Rzhishchev and its main forces to reach the front Rzhishchev—Yanivka, and its main forces the Chernyakhov—Yuzefovka—Stritovka area. The 27th Army was to reach the front excluding Yanivka—Shandra with its main forces, and its forward detachments the area Nikolaevka—Potok. The 47th Army received orders to reach the front excluding Shandra—Stepantsy—Gamarnya and to firmly secure the left flank of the *front's* shock group. The 3rd Guards Tank Army, while vigorously developing the success, was to reach the Kagarlyk—Savovka—Zelenki area, while securing itself from the south.

A 15-minute fire onslaught was to precede the infantry and tank attack. The army commanders and the commander of the 7th Breakthrough Artillery Corps were ordered to cross over to the bridgeheads on the night of 12-13 October their artillery, bring up ammunition and fuel, bring up their headquarters, lay down communications, and to organize troops cooperation and anti-tank and anti-aircraft defense.

During the night of 12-13 October our night aviation continued to operate against the enemy's combat formations and immediate rear and carried out 300 sorties. At 0930, following a 15-minute fire onslaught, the *front's* forces resumed the offensive, although they had no success along the entire front from Rzhishchev to Kanev. Our units even fell back somewhat along individual sectors; for example, the 27th Army's 241st Rifle Division and the 7th Guards Tank Corps abandoned Romashki.

The Germans' resistance during the operation's second day increased noticeably. As early as 0730 enemy infantry and tank counterattacks, supported by aviation, began along our forces' entire offensive front. His aviation's activity was greater than during the preceding day. Its air activity was increased by the German command's bringing in air power from neighboring sectors of the front. The German aviation carried out 1,000 sorties in the day's fighting. The 3rd Guards Tank Army was particularly subjected to powerful air strikes.

Our artillery was unable to render the attacking troops the same support as in the operation's first day, because the majority of it continued to be located in firing positions along the left bank of the Dnepr. Our forces' advance of 5-8 kilometers on the operation's first day made firing on the enemy more difficult. It was necessary to shift our firing positions to the bridgeheads, which is what the *front* commander demanded in his 12 October order. However, it was impossible to accomplish this in one night. Moreover, the availability of ammunition fell sharply on the second day.

In his report to comrade Stalin, the *front* commander noted that the troops had not been successful during the day's fighting and that to achieve success the commitment of the armies' second echelons was being prepared and that the regrouping of the 3rd Guards Tank Army was being carried out for an attack along a narrower sector of the front.

Despite the fact that the *front* commander's report and the orders by the representative of the *Stavka* of the Supreme High Command spoke of decisive actions for the purpose of breaking through the enemy's defense along a narrow front, the actual events of 14 October were distinguished by the troops' uncoordinated activities. The offensive carried out on this day at dawn by the forces of the 9th Mechanized Corps in the Malyi Bukrin area was not successful. Along another sector and at another time the 42nd Guards Rifle Division, which previously had been in the 47th Rifle Corps' second echelon, was committed into the fighting. This division's actions were also unsuccessful. The activity of the 2nd Air Army's planes fell sharply and it carried out only 183 sorties during the day. At the same time, the enemy's aviation carried out 500 sorties against our forces' combat formations and the crossings.

During 12-14 October the air cover of our forces along the Bukrin bridgehead was organized unsatisfactorily. The aircraft of the 8th Fighter Division, which were on duty at their airfields, were summoned into the air and appeared over the battlefield only when single enemy aircraft were flying. Following the withdrawal of our fighters, groups of German bombers would immediately appear.

On 15 October several attempts were made to continue the offensive at different times from 0700 to 1100 along the entire front from Rzhishchev to Kanev. However, only the 47th Rifle Corps' 42nd Guards Rifle Division enjoyed an insignificant local success, while the *front's* forces failed to advance along the remaining sectors of the front. The *front's* aviation carried out only 103 sorties for reconnaissance purpose and troop cover during the day. The enemy continued to actively oppose the Soviet forces' offensive with powerful artillery and mortar fire, the actions of his aviation and infantry and tank counterattacks. The disposition of the enemy's forces remained unchanged. On this day the 11th Panzer Division was completing its concentration in the Tulintsy area. The SS *Das Reich* Panzer Division had been concentrated toward Potaptsy.

At 1910 on 15 October the *front* commander issued an order to continue the offensive on 16 October. Limited tasks were set for the day's fighting for the armies. The forces of the 40th Army and the right wing of the 27th Army had the task of advancing 4-6 kilometers and the 47th Army 1-2 kilometers; the 3rd Guards Tank Army was to entrench part of its tanks behind the infantry's combat formations and be ready to develop the 40th and 27th armies' success, depending upon the situation.

It was planned to resolve these tasks by our forces through the method of consecutively destroying the enemy's strong points. The artillery preparation was planned as follows: 60 minutes of deliberate fire for destroying individual targets, particularly the enemy's tanks entrenched in the ground, and three minutes for a fire onslaught. It was planned to accompany the infantry and tank attack through the method of augmented fire over 22 minutes. Our aviation was to assist the infantry in launching bomber and assault air strikes against the enemy's combat formations. The *front* commander pointed to the presence of the necessary amount of artillery ordnance for repelling the enemy's tank and infantry counterattacks. Each 76mm gun was supposed to have 0.5 combat loads for this purpose and the large caliber guns 40 shells each. It was planned to launch the attack at 1400.

Following four days of our forces' unsuccessful attack, it became clear that the plan for the 16 October offensive was obviously unrealistic. The offensive's scope and the strength of the attack fell more and more each day. Although the artillery preparation was scheduled to last 63 minutes, the artillery fire proved to be insufficiently powerful due to a shortage of shells. Thus the *Stavka* of the Supreme High Command cancelled the offensive by the *front's* left-wing forces that had been planned for 16 October and demanded the more complete and careful preparation of the offensive.

At 0040 on 16 October the *front* commander cancelled his order for an offensive on 16 October, in order to carry out the *Stavka's* decision.

Thus the first October offensive by the *front's* left-wing forces ended unsuccessfully. Only an insignificant broadening of the Bukrin bridgehead had been achieved as the result of fierce fighting.

THE VORONEZH FRONT'S OFFENSIVE OPERATION, OCTOBER 1943

The Course of Combat Activities North of Kiev, 11-17 October 1943

The 60th and 38th armies combat activities had been planned in such a way that over the course of two days before the start of the decisive offensive on Kiev these armies' forces were to carry out an objective to expand the bridgeheads seized on the right bank of the Dnepr. As a result of this, on 11 October, before the start of the general offensive, the 60th and 38th armies' forces were involved in stubborn fighting on the right bank of the Dnepr north of Kiev, particularly in the area of the 1st Guards Cavalry Corps, which had forced the Teterev River and which was attacking to the south.

At 1230 on 10 October the *front* commander ordered the 60th and 38th armies to simultaneously launch a decisive offensive along their sectors on the morning of 11 October. The *front* commander demanded that the armies' mobile formations be committed into the breach, having carefully organized cooperation with them. The *front* commander demanded decisive actions from the mobile formations, for the 1st Guards Cavalry and 5th Guards Tank corps to reach the Kiev—Zhitomir highway. The cavalry corps was ordered to attack at night, in order to reduce losses from enemy aviation.

At 1200 on 11 October the 60th and 38th armies attacked along all sectors in accordance with the plan. The enemy simultaneously began active counterattacks along a number of sectors. The Germans' 4th Panzer Division attacked with the task of eliminating the bridgehead on the western bank of the Pripyat' River in the Karpilovka area, which had been occupied by the 13th Army's 8th and 148th rifle divisions.

The 60th Army's 17th and 18th guards rifle corps, which were attacking along the secondary axis between the Pripyat' and Teterev rivers, did not have any success. The enemy launched attacks along both banks of the Teterev River against the 77th Rifle Corps' units. A particularly powerful attack was launched south of the Teterev River, where units of the German 7th and 8th panzer divisions were operating. A group of enemy tanks with automatic riflemen broke through into the rear of the 1st Guards Cavalry Corps, occupied Zatonsk and basically cut the cavalry corps off from the crossings over the Teterev River. At the same time the enemy's aviation destroyed the bridge over the Teterev near Rotichi.

The 1st Guards Cavalry Corps, while fighting off the enemy's attacks, had no success in its attempts to go over to the offensive. The offensive by the 24th and 30th rifle corps was also unsuccessful, and only on the right flank of the 24th Rifle Corps did the 248th Rifle Brigade capture the inhabited locale of Tolokun. The 38th Army, having begun the offensive along the Lyutezh bridgehead, enjoyed insignificant success. Part of the 340th Rifle Division's forces and the 5th Guards Tank Corps' motorized infantry forced the Irpen' River in the Sinyak area. Units of the 50th Rifle Corps advanced two kilometers to the southwest and captured the inhabited locale of Guta Mezhigorskaya. Thus the first day of the offensive brought no great success, which can be explained to a certain degree by the German aviation's active operations. In the 60th Army's sector alone 700 enemy sorties were noted during the day's fighting.

On 12 October fierce fighting continued along the 13th Army's Karpilovka bridgehead and along the entire front from the Teterev River to Lyutezh. The 1st Guards Cavalry Corps did not manage to completely eliminate the enemy's group of forces that had broken through to its rear the evening before along the southern bank of the Teterev River. The cavalry also had to beat off the Germans' fierce attacks from the front. The 38th Army expanded its bridgehead insignificantly along the western bank of the Irpen' River in the Sinyak area. The second day of offensive fighting north of Kiev also failed to yield success.

The fighting on 13 October was unsuccessful. Only the 5th Guards Tank Corps advanced to the south along the western bank of the Irpen' River as far as Gostomel'. However, the absence of success along the 50th and 51st rifle corps' front deprived the tank corps of the opportunity of further developing its success along the western bank of the Irpen' River, and the commander of the 38th Army issued an order for its withdrawal to the eastern bank of the river for joint operations with the infantry. The enemy's activity did not decrease. As a result of powerful counterattacks, the Germans on this day managed to break through to Lyutezh, from which they were expelled only on 14 October.

It was clear that the 60th and 38th armies' offensive operations to capture Kiev had suffered a setback. However, the *front* commander demanded that the troops continue the offensive.

At 1200 on 14 October the armies renewed the offensive, but had no luck this time either. On this day the enemy began to pull back into the reserve the 7th Panzer and 339th Infantry divisions, which had been operating opposite the 77th Rifle and 1st Guards Cavalry corps.

On the night of 14-15 October the *front* commander demanded in a series of orders that the armies carry out their assignments. In a telegram addressed to the commander of the 38th Army, which was signed at 0150 on 15 October, he instructed the following:

> The army's actions are slow and insufficiently organized. The designated deadlines for the offensive have been changed several times and reassigned without any particular reason and without the permission of the *front's* military council.
>
> I order that the offensive be continued with all forces on the morning of 15.10.1943 and to avoid the shortcomings listed above.
>
> Commit Kravchenko[25] rapidly and in an organized manner into the fighting and, together with the rifle divisions; defeat the enemy along the approaches to Kiev. Kiev is to be subsequently taken by a vigorous attack.

In his telegram addressed to the commander of the 60th Army, the *front* commander wrote:

> The army's forces are unsuccessful along almost all sectors and are standing in place. The chief reason for this is the dispersion of men and materiel, instead of concentrating a superiority of forces along each attacking formation's sector along the main axes and creating a large density of artillery and mortar fire along the sector of the main attack.
>
> If you do not adopt decisive measures for pushing the 1st Guards Cavalry Corps forward into the enemy's depth, then there is a danger that the cavalry corps will be transformed into a typical rifle formation and will be exhausted in fruitless frontal attacks and will completely lose its role as a mobile-maneuver formation.
>
> I order:
> 1. To plan and organize the breakthrough of the enemy's front along a narrow sector, by creating an artillery density of no less than 150 tubes per kilometer of front. Tanks are to be employed *en masse* along this sector and are to break through the enemy's defense at all costs and to allow the 1st Guards Cavalry Corps to develop the success.
> 2. You must precisely define the sector and axis of the main attack in all of the attacking formations and ensure a superiority of forces and a great density of fire in them.
> 3. Report on completion and the measures taken.

In another telegram, which was addressed to the commander of the 60th Army, the *front* commander emphasized the extremely important significance of uniting the 60th and 38th armies' bridgeheads along the western bank of the Dnepr River. The *front* commander demanded that this circumstance should be considered by the operational plan and the fulfillment of this task be secured by the left-flank rifle corps.

---

[25] Geneal Kravchenko was the commander of the 5th Guards Tank Corps.

On 15 October the offensive was renewed at 1400. The 60th Army enjoyed an insignificant success and occupied the inhabited locale of Rovy. The 38th Army advanced somewhat along the eastern bank of the Irpen' River toward Moshchun. The enemy along the 13th Army's sector cut off our forces along the Karpilovka bridgehead, reached the crossings over the Pripyat' River and surrounded part of the 8th and 148th rifle divisions' forces northwest of Karpilovka. The Germans' 7th Panzer Division was thrown in from the reserve into the fighting against the 24th Rifle Corps in the Rovy area in order to hinder the development of the *front's* success. The enemy threw an infantry regiment from the 75th Infantry Division, which comprised the Kiev garrison, to the Moshchun area.

On 16 October the attempts to continue the offensive were carried out by only part of the 60th and 38th armies' forces in the areas of Rovy and Moshchun, although they once again did not yield success.

The 1st Guards Cavalry Corps suffered heavy losses in its attempts to independently break through the enemy's defense. In five days of fighting, from 11-15 October, the corps lost more than 2,000 men, including many officers. The command understood perfectly the order of employing a fully outfitted and well trained cavalry corps for developing the success. However, the situation developed in such a way that the cavalry, having forced the Teterev River and having achieved some success in the first two days, could not be supported by the rifle troops. Nonetheless, measures to pull the corps out of the fighting in a timely manner were not taken and its relief by units of the 77th Rifle Corps began only on the night of 17-18 October.

On the night of 16-17 October the *front* commander issued operational directive No. 0049/op, in which he assigned his forces tasks for preparing them for a new offensive. According to this directive, the 60th Army was to go over to the defensive from 17 October and pull the 1st Guards Cavalry Corps into the second echelon. The 38th Army was ordered to continue the offensive throughout 17 October and by the close of the day reach the front Moshchun—Staro-Petrovtsy and, upon consolidating along this line, began preparing for a new operation.

On 17 October the Germans' 7th Panzer Division broke through the 24th Rifle Corps' front as the result of repeated attacks and penetrated deeply into its combat formations. The 24th Rifle and 1st Guards Cavalry Corps were engaged in fierce fighting with the enemy all day. As a result of this fighting, two German regiments were encircled, although by evening they had broken out in the direction of Manuil'sk, suffering heavy losses in the process.

The 38th Army, while continuing to attack along the Lyutezh bridgehead, achieved some success, advancing 3-5 kilometers to the south, and significantly expanded this bridgehead. The northern part of Moshchun and Staro-Petrovtsy and Novo-Petrovtsy were occupied by the army's forces.

Thus the offensive operation by the *front's* right wing, which had the objective of destroying the enemy's Kiev group of forces and taking Kiev, ended unsuccessfully. Only a certain expansion of the bridgeheads south of the mouth of the Teterev and Irpen' rivers was achieved.

As a result of the offensive by the Voronezh Front's forces during 12-15 October 1943 along the Bukrin bridgehead and during 11-17 October 1943 north of Kiev, they failed to carry out their assigned tasks. The enemy's defense was not broken through and he continued to stubbornly resist, while actively counterattacking our forces along a number of axes. The *front's* forces achieved only an insignificant expansion of the bridgeheads along the right bank of the Dnepr River north of Dymer on the 60th Army's front, and in the Lyutezh area directly north of Kiev along the 38th Army's front, and in the area of the Bukrin bridgehead along the *front's* left wing.

The Voronezh Front's Second Offensive Along the Right Bank of the Dnepr in October 1943

Throughout 16-17 October the commander of the Voronezh Front issued instructions defining the armies' objectives in the forthcoming operation. According to the commander's decision, the overall idea and plan of action remained as before. Following the breakthrough of the enemy's defense north of Kiev for developing the success to the south and southwest, it was planned to employ the 1st Guards Cavalry and 5th Guards Tank corps.

The *front's* right-wing forces were to assume the offensive on 20 October. However, on the evening of 18 October the *front* commander issued a new order. According to the latter, the 1st Guards Cavalry Corps was to be transferred from the 60th Army to the 38th, for which purpose it was to cross to the left bank of the Dnepr, move south, and once again cross the Dnepr to the Lyutezh bridgehead. This regrouping of forces demanded a change in the deadline for starting the offensive from 20 to 23 October.

During 18-23 October the 60th Army was engaged in intensive fighting with the enemy, who repeatedly counterattacked along the southern bank of the Teterev River. The German attacks were particularly insistent along the 24th Rifle Corps' sector in the Dmitrievka area, where the army's forces had previously enjoyed their greatest success. During 18-19 October the 38th Army was engaged in unsuccessful offensive fighting and during 20-22 October the army's forces fought off powerful enemy attacks. Both of the *front's* right-wing armies had been poorly supplied with munitions. The enemy's high level of activity made it necessary to expend a great deal of ammunition and prevented us from accumulating it for the forthcoming offensive. All of this led to a situation in which the 60th and 38th armies' offensive on 23 October did not take place.

The plan for the offensive by the *front's* left wing called for breaking through the enemy front along the narrow Khodorov—Romashki sector, while the 27th Army was supposed to capture the enemy's powerful strong point of Romashki on the eve of the overall offensive. It was ordered to concentrate 250 artillery pieces and mortars per kilometer of front to break through the enemy's defense and to carry out an artillery preparation over the course of two hours. The armies were given more limited assignments than in the previous offensive for the first three days of the operation. The 40th Army was to advance 30 kilometers and reach the front Khalep'ye—Kagarlykskaya settlement; the 27th Army received orders to advance 40 kilometers and reach the front Kagarlyk—Mironovka. The 47th Army was to advance only 15 kilometers and reach the Rossava River. It was ordered to commit the 3rd Guards Tank Army into the breach on the first day of the operation following the infantry's breakthrough of the enemy's defense to a depth of five kilometers. During the first day the army was to advance 15 kilometers and 60 kilometers by the close of the third day, and reach the front Makeevka—Uzin—Rakitno (16 kilometers east of Belaya Tserkov').

In his operational directive for the *front's* left-wing armies, the *front* commander gave detailed instructions for the artillery offensive and the order of carrying out tasks by the armies. Aside from the two-hour artillery preparation, an artillery accompaniment for the infantry and tank attack was also planned for 40 minutes. However, this plan was not carried out due to a shortage of munitions and the offensive began following the artillery preparation, which lasted one hour.

As early as 11 October communications were established with a group from a 600-man landing force, which had gathered in the woods south of Kanev following the unsuccessful airborne landing on 24 September. The commander of the 5th Airborne Brigade was ordered to unite this group under his command, to get in touch with the local partisans, and during 20-25 October disrupt the work of the enemy's rear in the area north of Korsun'-Shevchenkovskii, interfering with the possible movement of the enemy's units from the south in the direction of Rzhishchev.[26]

Throughout 18-19 October quiet reigned along the *front's* left wing. The troops were preparing for the offensive. On 20 October a reconnaissance in force was conducted along all sectors of the forthcoming offensive from Khodorov to Kanev by reconnaissance detachments, varying in strength from a company to a battalion. Naturally, this measure put the enemy on his guard. The Germans were defending in their previous group of forces, with the SS *Das Reich* and 11th panzer divisions in reserve. They continued to carry out intensive defensive work, entrenching and increasing the number of engineer obstacles.

One should note that by the start of the second October offensive the situation with munitions and fuel in the *front* had not improved, because the intensive combat along almost all sectors of the front demanded a large expenditure of munitions. At times the *front's* forces would get into a critical situation due to a shortage of ammunition. For example, in the middle October the enemy's insistent and powerful counterattacks in the 60th Army's sector were creating the serious threat that our forces would lose the bridgehead south of the Teterev River. This army's munitions had almost been exhausted. On instructions from the *Stavka* of the Supreme High Command, on 18 October a transport column was dispatched directly from Moscow, consisting of 300 motor vehicles with munitions, and delivered to the 60th Army 12,000 120mm mortar rounds and 5,000 122mm howitzer shells.

On 21 October, following an hour-long artillery preparation, the *front's* left-wing forces went over to the attack at 0830. At 0900 the 3rd Guards Tank Army, which, as had been the case in the previous offensive, was to carry out the task of breaking through the tactical depth of the enemy's defense in the role of direct infantry-support tanks, was committed into the fighting. The 40th Army's 47th Rifle Corps, which was operating along the main axis, penetrated three kilometers into the enemy's defense and linked up with units of the 52nd Rifle Corps, which was operating along the Shchuchinka bridgehead. By the close of the day the 3rd Guards Tank Army's 6th and 7th guards tank corps were fighting along the approaches to Ul'yaniki and Lipovyi Rog, having advanced five kilometers in the day's fighting. The 27th Army's right-flank formations captured Romashki and, just as was the case with the 47th Army, had no success on the remaining sectors of the front. The enemy committed the SS *Das Reich* Panzer Division into the fighting in the Ul'yaniki—Lipovyi Rog area. By this time the German 11th Panzer Division had been shifted to the south, where the Steppe Front was developing the offensive along the Kirovograd and Krivoi Rog axes.

Aside from emergency reports and bulletins dispatched to the *Stavka* and General Staff, at 2110 on this day the *front's* military council sent I.V. Stalin a report in which it evaluated the results of the first day of fighting in the following manner: "As a result of the difficult character of the terrain, which allows us to employ tanks in an offensive only on the roads, and also due to the enemy's organized defense along a prepared line, we were not able to fully develop the success on the first day of the offensive."

It should be said that this was the first report in which the *front's* military council indicated the impossibility of deploying the tank army for battle. The 3rd Guards Tank Army's lack of success can also be explained by the fact that the corps' commanders and headquarters controlled the battle poorly and did not always know the true situation of their own units.

At 0050 on 22 October the *front* command issued an order to continue the offensive from the morning of 22 October, following a 15-minute fire onslaught. The *front* commander demanded

---

26 This airborne group was subsequently subordinated to the Second Ukrainian Front and in November-December 1943 cooperated with the 52nd Army during the conduct of the Cherkassy offensive operation.

from the army commanders "… the most energetic offensive and maneuver on the battlefield and an excellent organization of cooperation, and from comrade Rybalko the vigorous development of the success. If intelligence and the forward detachments establish the presence of gaps in the enemy's defensive line during the night or morning up until 1030, then they are to be immediately exploited for developing the success."

The offensive resumed at 1030. The 3rd Guards Tank Army's tank corps along the main axis attacked the Germans at the same time as did the 40th Army's infantry. During the night the enemy reinforced his forces with part of the 34th Infantry Division, which he removed from the passive Tripol'ye—Rzhishchev sector. Contrary to the statements by the *front's* headquarters that the enemy's defense had been penetrated during the course of the 21 October fighting, the *front's* attacking forces ran into the enemy's unsuppressed system of artillery and mortar fire and his anti-tank defense. The Germans did not only put up stubborn fire resistance, but throughout the day actively counterattacked our forces for the purpose of eliminating the successes achieved the previous day and to throw them back to their jumping-off positions. The Germans accompanied their counterattacks with powerful artillery and aviation support. Groups of German bombers, numbering 25-30 planes, uninterruptedly appeared above the battlefield. By the close of the day the 40th and 3rd Guards Tank armies had not only not advanced, but had even been forced to abandon several tactically important heights. The 27th and 47th armies also failed to advance.

The *front's* artillery and air offensive was weak on this day and did not offer effective support to the rifle troops and tanks. The 15-minute artillery preparation proved to be insufficient. The *front's* aviation carried out only 574 sorties during the day (along with sorties for covering our forces), as opposed to 1,099 sorties during the first day's fighting.

By the morning of 23 October the *front* commander reached a new decision. The idea of this decision was that the *front* should renounce the offensive along secondary axes and should concentrate all of its efforts in the sector of the 40th Army and the right flank of the 27th Army along the Bukrin bridgehead. It was planned during 23-25 October to carry out the appropriate troop regrouping and to accumulate munitions. A new and third attempt at an offensive was planned for 26 October.

By this time the extended preparation for an offensive north of Kiev by the 38th Army was supposed to be completed. During 23-25 October the commander of the 47th Army was supposed to remove the 23rd Rifle Corps (30th and 23rd rifle divisions) from the Studenets bridgehead and transfer it to the 40th Army. It was ordered to pull the corps out after the army captured the village of Buchak and linked up with the 27th Army's left flank. At the same time, it was necessary for the 27th Army to carry out a number of local attacks to improve its jumping-off position and in order to link up with the 47th Army's right flank, thus uniting the Bukrin and Studenets bridgeheads. After this the army was to pull the 38th Rifle Division into the second echelon behind its right flank and to prepare for a decisive offensive.

Along with this, the artillery was to be regrouped—the 40th Army was to be reinforced with the 13th Breakthrough Artillery Division. Thus it was planned to employ all of the 7th Breakthrough Artillery Corps in the 40th Army's narrow attack sector. The 47th Army's 33rd Artillery Brigade was to be transferred from the Studenets bridgehead and transferred to the 27th Army.

The 3rd Guards Tank Army was to pull the main forces of the 6th and 7th guards tank corps behind the infantry's combat formation, leaving behind forward and rearguard units for the direct infantry support of the 40th Army's rifle units. The army was ordered to be ready by 26 October for decisive offensive operations in the 40th Army's sector.

In the meantime, on the morning of 23 October the enemy carried out a reconnaissance in force along the 40th Army's entire front and at 1630 attacked in the direction of Khodorov. A regiment from the 34th Infantry Division, part of the SS *Das Reich* Panzer Division and the 72nd Infantry Division took part in the offensive. The Germans pushed back units of the 47th Rifle Corps insignificantly after a fierce battle. The 27th and 47th armies' forces attacked the 112th Infantry Division at different times (at 1400 and 1540) in the area of the village of Buchak, for the purpose of uniting the occupied bridgeheads, but were unsuccessful.

On 24 October the enemy unsuccessfully attacked our units along the entire front of the 27th Army, in up to a battalion in strength and supported by tanks.

The *Stavka* of the Supreme High Command, in its directive No. 30232, canceled the *front's* offensive scheduled for 26 October, and offered an evaluation of the reasons for the *front's* unsuccessful activities in October. The *Stavka* of the Supreme High Command pointed out that the failure of the offensive along the Bukrin bridgehead came about because the terrain conditions, which made more difficult the troops' offensive operations, particularly those of the tank army, were not taken into account in time.

The Organization of Communications and Troop Control During the *Front's* First and Second Offensives in October 1943

By the start of the *front's* offensive along the Bukrin bridgehead and north of Kiev and to the conclusion of the offensive fighting the wire communications of the *front's* headquarters and the armies' headquarters worked uninterruptedly and secured reliable troop control. Due to the fact that the front line throughout October did not undergo any significant changes, the wire communications network continued to develop and improve.

From 14 October the *front's* auxiliary command post (VPU) began to work in the Monastyrek on the Bukrin bridgehead. The *front* commander, the member of the *front's* military council, and an operational group from the *front* headquarters were at this post during the offensive. The VPU was provided with direct communications with the 40th, 27th and 3rd Guards Tank armies, and with the remaining armies through the *front's* headquarters.

Throughout the entire 11-25 October period wire communications were reliable. The breaks in its work along individual lines that did take place were not reflected in the unbroken communications, because it was realized through second channels and bypass lines, which had been laid down in sufficient numbers by this time. The reliability of wire communications was achieved as a result of carrying out the following measures:

a) the improvement of the lines' technical condition, an increase in their capacity and the construction of bypass lines;
b) a more expedient allocation of men and materiel servicing the lines and centers;
c) the significant increase in the number of control-testing posts.

The communications troops carried out a great deal of work in building and restoring telephone-telegraph lines within the *front's* operational sector. Overall, 353.3 kilometers of new lines were built in October, 1,633 kilometers of wire hung from them, 806 kilometers of wire hung along existing lines, and 1,017 kilometers of line restored, with another 5,201 kilometers hung from them.

During the fighting of 11-25 October radio communications at all levels of the *front* worked in a restricted manner, due to the reliable work of wire communications. In the majority of situations, radio networks worked only to receive, along with a regular communications check. As a rule, radio networks in regiments were closed. Radio equipment, which had been allotted for linking the crossings with fighter aviation airfields, worked actively. Reliable radio communications with the airborne detachment, which was in the enemy's rear from 24 September, were established only from 20 October, when a radio operator was dropped there with a radio set.

Mobile communications equipment, particularly communications planes, worked intensively. The *front* and armies' headquarters' communications planes experienced a great shortage of automobile transport for serving their information gathering posts and of communications officers.

With the start of the offensive, the communications of the army headquarters' communications with the *front's* aviation formations, the representatives of which were located at the armies' observation posts, along with their radio equipment, were organized satisfactorily. The tank and combined-arms formations' communications were also organized satisfactorily.

Results and Conclusions

During the Great Patriotic War the Soviet army repeatedly resolved the most difficult tasks while attacking with one or several *fronts*, and which were linked to forcing major river barriers. The enemy always placed great hopes on such water barriers and sought to employ them in order to halt our forces' offensive, to achieve a more or less lengthy operational pause and to get the opportunity for a breathing space and putting his forces in order.

In a number of cases, the Germans, while falling back to the west under the Soviet forces' blows, tried to hold along the eastern bank of major rivers bridgeheads, which could be convenient jumping-off areas for launching serious counterblows against our forces. Such were the Germans' Zaporozh'ye and Nikopol' bridgeheads along the Dnepr and along the eastern bank of the Oder, in the areas of Kustrin and Frankfurt. The German strategists proceeded from the fact that in past wars the attacking armies were always forced to halt before major river lines and make an extended pause in order to bring up their forces and ready themselves for the next stage of the offensive, which must begin with the forcing of the river.

The Soviet Supreme High Command in the past war found a new method of resolving this complex task. This new thing was that the attacking troops were to force river barriers from the march and secure one or more major bridgeheads on the opposite bank of the river. The seizure of such bridgeheads on the Dnepr, Prut, Vistula, Danube, and Oder made it much easier for the Soviet command to organize subsequent offensive operations, created complete confidence in these operations' success and, finally, reduced personnel and equipment losses. An offensive operation, during the final stages of which the troops reached a major river line, was considered to have been successfully completed only in that case where we managed to secure one or several operationally important bridgeheads on the opposite bank.

The Dnepr River, which Soviet forces reached in the fall of 1943, as a result of their successful summer offensive, was the first such major obstacle (if you don't count a number of small rivers east of the Dnepr). It was precisely on the Dnepr that Soviet forces for the first time had to carry out the Supreme High Command's new idea on a strategic scale.

The Voronezh Front's forces, upon arriving at the Dnepr along the Kiev axis, successfully carried out the seizure of tactical bridgeheads on the right bank of the river south of Pereyaslav-Khmel'nitskii. During the course of the operation the enemy suffered serious losses in personnel and combat equipment. Operational surprise was achieved by the vigorous drive to the Dnepr and its forcing from the march. However, the *front* command was unable to creatively realize the Supreme High Command's idea along its sector. During the first stage of the Kiev operation the *front's* forces were unable to carry out the objective assigned them. The *front* command was unable to take advantage of the favorably developing situation and overcome the difficulties that inevitably arise in such cases. The forcing of the Dnepr in the Voronezh Front's sector went on slowly and in an unorganized fashion, which led to a delay in carrying out the important task assigned by the *Stavka* of the Supreme High Command. The fulfillment of this objective became drawn out and was successfully accomplished only in November on the basis of the *Stavka's* new operational plan.

THE VORONEZH FRONT'S OFFENSIVE OPERATION, OCTOBER 1943

In developing the offensive to the Dnepr River during 9-22 September, the *front* headquarters failed to fully study the enemy's group of forces, its condition and the German command's intentions. The enemy, while falling back from one line to another, was able to, despite the losses he suffered, pull back his main forces behind the Dnepr and take up defensive positions on its right bank.

The *front's* offensive operation on the left bank of the Dnepr unfolded in complex conditions and in the face of constantly increasing difficulties. Among these difficulties were the overextension of the troops and the lagging behind of the supply bases, breakdowns in fuel and ammunition, and the lagging behind of the rebasing of the *front's* aviation. However, alongside this there were also increased favorable conditions which made the fulfillment of their task easier. The enemy was falling back hurriedly, gaps appeared in his front and the flanks of individual groups of forces became exposed. The Germans were in a critical situation upon approaching the Dnepr crossings, because the limited number of crossings led to the pileup of a large number of troops along the small bridgehead sectors. The enemy was in this situation for three days near the Kanev crossing and an entire seven days near the Kiev one.

The insufficiently correct employment of the available mobile forces in the beginning of the operation, their dispersal along various sectors of the front (the 3rd and 8th guards tank corps, 10th Tank Corps and the 3rd Guards Mechanized Corps), as well as the late commitment of the tank army and the cavalry corps, the combined-arms armies' (38th, 40th and 47th) excessively "methodological" offensive from one line to another, the absence of pressure on the enemy's open flanks, the 38th Army's fruitless maneuver on the approach to the Dnepr, and *front* aviation's insufficiently precise assignment all made it easier for the enemy to fall back to the right bank of the Dnepr without serious losses.

The incorrect choice of the sector for forcing the river by the *front's* main shock group in the Bukrin bend failed to give us the opportunity to fully and effectively employ the tank army and the cavalry corps. The difficult terrain created serious obstacles for the mobile forces' offensive and made it much easier for the enemy to organize a defense.

The late deployment of significant infantry, artillery and tank forces on the Bukrin bridgehead and the poor organization of the airborne landing enabled the enemy to bring up to the area of the bridgehead major forces, to dig into the ground and to strengthen his defense with wire obstacles and mine fields. Because of the enthusiasm for the plan of a double envelopment and encirclement of the enemy's Kiev group of forces on the right bank of the Dnepr, the Voronezh Front's forces began to be jerked around between the Bukrin bridgehead and the sector north of Kiev (the removal to the north of the 5th Guards Tank and 1st Guards Cavalry corps, the dispersal of existing stocks of fuel and ammunition and the jerking around of the air army's efforts). All of this taken together led to a situation in which our forces' offensive fighting in the beginning of October was unsuccessful.

The *front* commander, while striving to begin the offensive as soon as possible from the captured bridgeheads on the right bank of the Dnepr, excessively reduced the preparation time for the offensive without taking into account the developing situation. Initially the troops were assigned the task of occupying a favorable jumping-off position for the offensive along the Rzhishchev—Kanev sector by 25-26 September, and north of Kiev by 27 September. However, the *front* commander was forced to shift the beginning of the offensive to 3-4 October, although by this time the troops were not yet ready to attack. As a result, it began only on 11-12 October. The beginning of the second offensive from the Bukrin bridgehead was also postponed from 19 to 21 October. North of Kiev, the offensive planned for 20 October was not carried out altogether as a result of the troops' lack of readiness. The *front* command, while correctly striving to take advantage of the surprise achieved as a result of its vigorous advance to the Dnepr, was nevertheless unable to bring about the organized preparation of the troops for the offensive in a short period.

The repeated and fruitless attacks from the Bukrin bridgehead and the incorrect employment of the tank army, its commitment into the fighting simultaneously with the infantry attack, essentially as direct infantry-support tanks, the continuing dispersal of the *front's* forces between two axes, and the refusal to adopt in a timely manner a new and bold decision led to a situation in which the *front's* October offensive operation was a failure.

After the adoption of the decision by *front* commander on 16 October to repeat the offensive along the previous axes, with its previous forces and previous tasks, there was no chance of surprise. In carrying out such a decision, it was necessary to rely only on acquiring a decisive superiority in men and materiel along the axis of the main attack for the purpose of breaking through the enemy's defense throughout the entire tactical depth and the commitment of our mobile forces into the resulting breach. However, the *front* commander, in planning the operation, did not secure its successful realization, because, as before, he dispersed his forces along various axes and set such deadlines for preparing for the offensive that could not guarantee the troops' readiness.

Throughout all of October the *front* command attempted to resolve the task of breaking through the tactical depth of the enemy's defense with a brief and powerful attack along the Rzhishchev—Kanev front. However, the equal distribution of forces on the Bukrin, as well as the Shchuchinka and Students bridgeheads, the unsatisfactory organization of the offensive and the shortage of ammunition sharply reduced the strength of this attack, and the deep organization of the enemy's defense and the difficult terrain for attacking led to the offensive's insignificant results. On the offensive's second day, as a rule, there was already an obvious shortage of forces and the troops' offensive possibilities were quickly exhausted. The breadth of the breakthrough front and the troops' tasks in depth were gradually reduced.

The *front's* headquarters, in its combat report and operational summary of 12 October, noted that the tank army had been committed into the fighting following the breakthrough of the forward edge of the enemy's defense, but that did not yet mean that the entire main zone of the enemy's defense had been penetrated. By this time there already existed in the Soviet army developed principles for employing major tank formations, as laid out in the instructions by the Supreme High Command and confirmed by the experience of the war. These instructions forbade throwing the tanks against the enemy's unsuppressed artillery and anti-tank defense or to employ them for fighting counterattacking enemy tanks, as was the case on 12 October in the area of the village of Romashki, when the 7th Guards Tank Corps engaged 100 enemy tanks in fighting. The violation of this principle was not engendered by any kind of special conditions for operating on the Bukrin bridgehead. Just the opposite; the conditions of the situation demanded the commitment of the tank army into the fighting only following the completion of the breakthrough of the enemy defense.

The Germans' air and ground reconnaissance during the September fighting did not sufficiently completely reveal the composition and strength of the Voronezh Front's forces designated for attacking along the front Rzhishchev—Kanev. It was only on 25 September that the enemy's intelligence determined the operational area of the 3rd Guards Tank Army's 69th Mechanized Brigade and the 21st Guards Tank Brigade on 28 September.

The overall correlation of forces throughout the operation was in favor of the Voronezh Front, although it was only by 12 October that the *front* completed the movement and concentration of its forces (tanks and artillery) to the Bukrin bridgehead and the rebasing of its aviation. Before 12 October the Germans enjoyed a superiority in forces on the bridgeheads, especially in tanks and artillery.

A typical feature of the October fighting in the Voronezh Front's sector was that both sides in the fighting for the Dnepr pursued decisive aims. If our forces strove to break through the front and defeat the enemy's Kiev group of forces, then the Germans, in turn, pursued the task of defeating the Soviet forces on the bridgeheads and restoring a sound defense along the right bank of the Dnepr. This led to the extreme fierceness of the fighting.

THE VORONEZH FRONT'S OFFENSIVE OPERATION, OCTOBER 1943

Throughout the Voronezh Front's entire offensive to the Dnepr and during the October fighting, the situation along the *front's* flanks was favorable and made the achievement of the front's immediate tasks by its forces easier. The neighbor on the right—the Central Front—was successfully developing the offensive with its left-wing armies (13th and 60th) along the Bakhmach—Nezhin—Kiev main rail line and was echeloned forward the whole time. During 18-21 September this *front's* forces reached the Dnepr and seized bridgeheads along its right bank from Chernobyl' to Dymer.

Following the transfer of the 13th and 60th armies to the Voronezh Front, the Central Front continued to develop the offensive along the Gomel' axis, forced the Sozh River along its lower course and reached the Dnepr. On 15 October the Central Front's forces forced the Dnepr near Loyev and the mouth of the Sozh River, and developed the offensive along the Mozyr' axis until the end of the month.

The Central Front's active operations deprived the commander of the German Second Army of the opportunity to transfer his forces to the Chernobyl' area and he limited himself here to local counterattacks against the Voronezh Front's 13th Army.

The neighbor to the left—the Steppe Front—reached the Dnepr by 26 September and by the beginning of October had seized its first bridgeheads on the river's right bank southeast of Kremenchug. From the middle of October the *front's* forces began a successful offensive from the captured bridgeheads along the Krivoi Rog and Kirovograd axes and captured the major rail junction of Pyatikhatka. Further south, the Southwestern Front had eliminated the Germans' Zaporozh'ye bridgehead and occupied the cities of Dneprodzerzhinsk and Dnepropetrovsk on the right bank of the Dnepr. As a result, the situation in October for the enemy in Ukraine became more and more difficult and kept him from transferring his reserves to the Kiev area from other sectors of the front. Moreover, the Germans were forced to remove the 11th Panzer Division, which was in reserve behind the Bukrin bridgehead, and transfer it to the south.

The *front* command failed to manifest sufficient foresight in the organization of an extremely complex offensive operation to a depth of 200 kilometers, with the subsequent forcing of a large river barrier from the march. All of its calculations were built on a low offensive pace (up to ten kilometers per day), and when events overtook the planning presumptions, the rapid reorganization in accordance with the demands of the changing situation was not carried out. Crossing equipment fell behind and the limited materiel resources and transport equipment were employed equally along the entire front.

Having arrived at the Dnepr, the *front's* forces failed to take advantage of the weakness of an enemy who had not yet managed to consolidate along the Rzhishchev—Kanev sector and, due to the absence of crossings, until October was essentially unable to engage in major offensive operations. The infantry, which crossed without artillery and with poor aviation support, was unable to develop the success. The construction of crossings proceeded slowly.

The main shortcoming in the employment of artillery was its lateness in arriving at the Dnepr and transfer to the bridgeheads. The organization of artillery fire during the first days of the forcing was unsatisfactory and failed to secure the sufficient support of the rifle formations in the intensive fighting to broaden the bridgeheads.

Nor was the sufficient density of artillery fire along the axis of the main attack during the 12 October offensive secured. The increase in the artillery's density during the following days did not enable us to resolve our tasks, as there was a shortage of munitions.

Artillery reconnaissance failed to fully uncover the entire system of the enemy's artillery and mortar fire and failed to sufficiently employ for this purpose data from the headquarters of the combined-arms and tank formations and our aviation; thus the artillery preparation was not always effective. The shortage of munitions led to a situation in which we could wage intensive artillery fire only on the first day of the offensive (12 and 21 October) and were forced during the succeeding days to limit ourselves to weak fire onslaughts and did not help the troops to carry out their tasks.

The *front's* aviation in the first days of forcing the Dnepr, and during the fighting to expand the bridgeheads, did not achieve its objectives either for covering our forces and the crossings or for aerial reconnaissance due to its slow rebasing. During 22-28 September our aviation was not tasked with destroying the enemy's crossings near Kiev and Kanev and defeating the German forces which had grouped along the left bank of the Dnepr near these crossings.

Having rebased to new airfields and established contact with the ground forces, the 2nd Air Army, as before, poorly covered the ground forces on the bridgeheads against the enemy's aviation, particularly during 12-14 October during the first offensive along the Bukrin bridgehead. Assault air and bomber strikes against the enemy's main centers of defense and his counterattacking troops were conducted only during the first days (12 and 21 October) of the offensive on the Bukrin bridgehead and were insufficiently effective. During the following days, due to the shortage of fuel and munitions, the activity of the *front's* aviation fell sharply.

The anti-aircraft defense of the crossings over the Dnepr and the combat formations of the forces on the bridgeheads were also unsatisfactory, due to the lagging behind of the anti-aircraft divisions, their slow transfer to the bridgeheads and the limited stocks of munitions.

It should be admitted that the employment of smoke equipment while forcing the Dnepr was completely unsatisfactory. This very valuable means in this situation was not employed. Only from the middle of October, when the *front* had brought up its chemical units and smoke equipment did the latter play a significant role in covering the crossings over the Dnepr against enemy air strikes. Masking smoke was employed very rarely and with insufficient skill during the offensive fighting on the bridgeheads and did not yield the desired effect even at the tactical level.

Shortcomings in troop control during the operation at all levels, from *front* to division headquarters, significantly worsened all the other shortcomings and miscalculations. The frequent change of the *front's* plans and orders and the systematic non-fulfillment of these plans and orders was a typical feature in the operations of the *front's* forces at the end of September and in October. The authority and undisputed force of an order were undermined and this was reflected poorly on the entire course of the operation.

The formation's headquarters remained for an extended time (until 1-2 October) on the left bank of the Dnepr, had poor communications with their subordinate forces fighting on the bridgeheads, and had a poor knowledge of the real situation. It was only by the start of the first offensive on 11-12 October that the headquarters at all levels organized reliable communications. However, during the days when there was the most intensive fighting, communications from the corps level down were disrupted once again and the headquarters did not know the troops' situation. This is particularly true of the 3rd Guards Tank Army during the second offensive (21-23 October).

As a rule, attempts to mislead the enemy and to distract his attention from the sectors of the front where the main attacks were being prepared and were launched did not yield the desired results: we were unable to fool the Germans. The reason for this was first of all that the proper scope was not attached to disinformation measures and insufficient means were devoted to their conduct. The *front* headquarters did not combine the efforts of all the armies in this regard and limited itself to laying out goals and determining the time in which the false measures were to be carried out. The armies' headquarters drew up and carried out these measures independently and without the proper coordination among themselves. If the 27th Army's headquarters tried to organize the display of false measures as fully as possible and allotted means for this purpose and appointed responsible organizers and executors, then the headquarters of the 40th and 38th armies limited themselves to merely compiling a plan and subsequently did nothing to see that it was carried out. All disinformation measures failed to attract the enemy's attention and did not bring about material changes in the disposition of his forces.

By the time they arrived at the Dnepr the strength of the rifle divisions ranged from 3,600 to 6,500 men, and it was only in the 38th Army by 10 October that the average strength of a division was 8,500 men. The troops were mainly reinforced by the call up of the male population of the liberated areas.

At the same time, it is necessary to take into account that the called up reinforcements required a lot of work, both in questions of political education, due to the extended time they spent under German-Fascist occupation, and in matters of combat training, due to the acceptance by the army of new kinds of combat equipment during the war, changes in tactics and the introduction of new manuals. On the whole, those divisions which received local reinforcements were reliable in combat and could carry out any tasks. A serious shortcoming was the fact due to the poor work of the rear services the called up reinforcements could not be outfitted in a timely manner, which extended the time required to move it from the reserve regiments to the divisions.

Due to the slow restoration of the railroads, the *front* and army depots fell a considerable distance behind. The 11 October *front* directive regarding the new supply basing was carried out slowly and the rebasing had not been fully completed by the end of the offensive fighting in October. The troops on the bridgeheads not only experienced a constant shortage in munitions, fuels and lubricants, but also in food, which must be ascribed fully to the inefficiency of the rear services.

2

The First Ukrainian Front's November Offensive Operation

The Planning and Preparation of the Operation

Instructions of the Stavka of the Supreme High Command

In its directive No. 30232, which was signed at 2300 on 24 October, the *Stavka* of the Supreme High Command, having evaluated the reasons for the October offensive's lack of success, pointed out a new path for the operations by the *front's* main shock group, defined it strength, dates for the preparation and beginning of the operation and, finally, the date for committing the *front's* mobile forces—the tank army and cavalry corps—into the battle.

The necessity of a new decision sprang from the fact that the *front's* forces did not achieve a success in the October offensive operation along the right bank of the Dnepr and that the overall strategic situation along the southern wing of the Soviet-German front demanded the immediate creation of a major bridgehead in the Kiev area. Throughout October the forces of the Steppe (Second Ukrainian) Front broke through the enemy's defense along the right bank of the Dnepr southeast of Kremenchug and formed a major bridgehead of operational significance, reaching the approaches to Krivoi Rog captured the major railroad junction of Pyatikhatka. Further south, the Germans' Zaporozh'ye bridgehead on the left bank of the Dnepr was eliminated and the Soviet forces' successful development of the offensive in the Melitopol' area had begun. Thus the necessary prerequisites had been created for the realization of a major offensive operation on the Ukrainian right bank in the winter of 1943-44. It followed that it was necessary to create before the onset of winter a major bridgehead in the Kiev area along the right bank of the Dnepr, which could serve as a convenient jumping-off area for the deployment of a powerful shock group of Soviet forces in the forthcoming winter campaign. Beside this, the creation of a major bridgehead in the Kiev area would place the German forces in an unfavorable position, significantly worsening their strategic situation along the entire front from the Poles'ye to the Black Sea.

Featured below is the 24 October 1943 directive from the *Stavka* of the Supreme High Command to the First Ukrainian Front, in which the basic idea of the operation is laid out and the most important instructions for preparing it are indicated.

FIRST UKRAINIAN FRONT'S NOVEMBER OFFENSIVE OPERATION

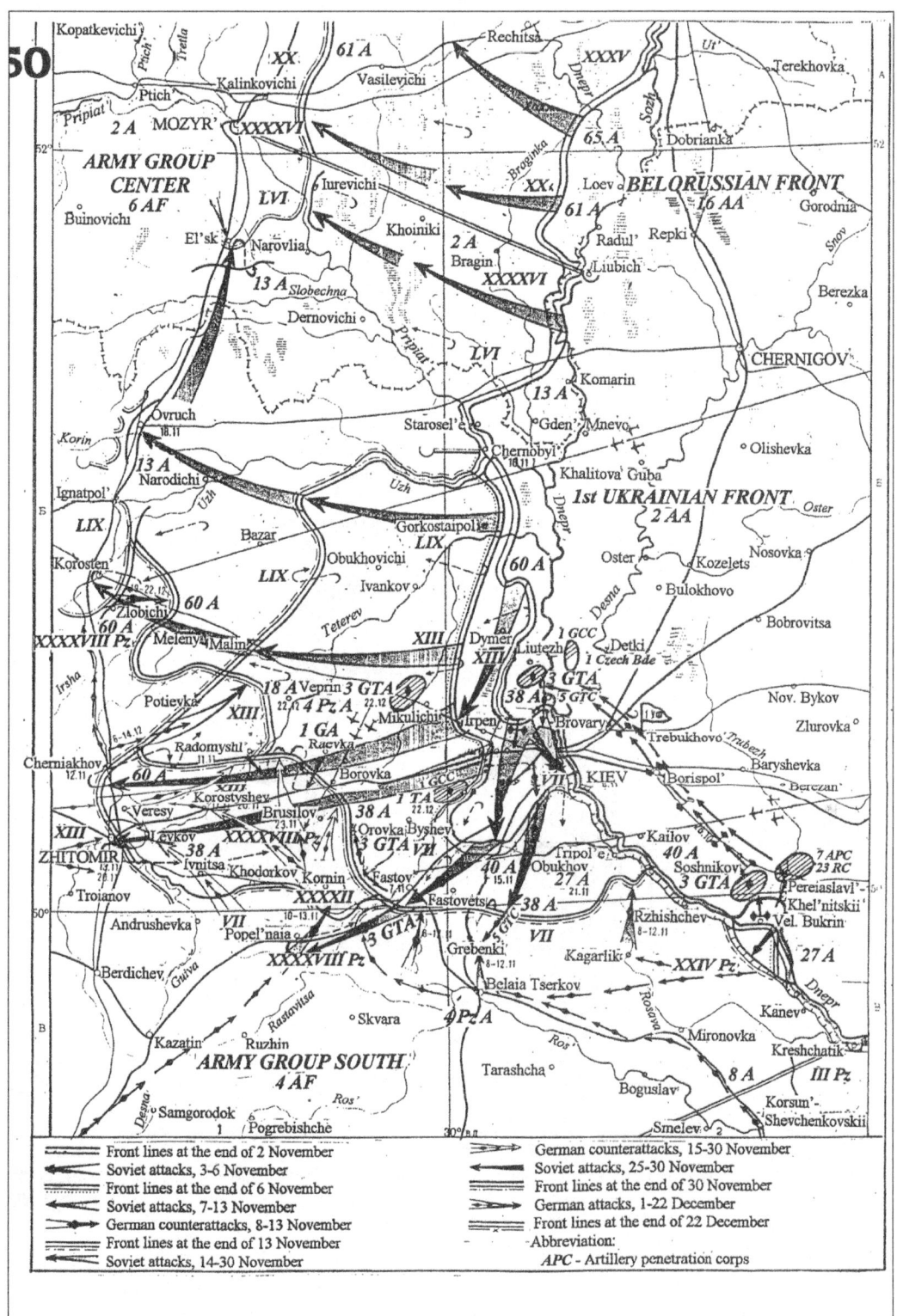

Map 2 The Kiev Operation, 3 November–22 December 1943.

Very Important
24.10.43, 2300
No. 30232

Comrade Zhukov[1]
Comrade Vatutin
Comrade Khrushchev

In reference to your message No. 21223/sh of 24.10

1. The *Stavka* of the Supreme High Command points out that the failure of the offensive on the Bukrin bridgehead occurred because not all of the terrain conditions, which hinder offensive operations here, especially of the tank army, were not taken into account. References to a lack of munitions are without foundation, because Konev,[2] who has no more munitions than Vatutin, but who properly employing his forces and operating in somewhat more favorable terrain, is successfully carrying out his assignment.

2. The *Stavka* orders you to regroup the First Ukrainian Front's forces for the purpose of strengthening the *front's* right wing, with the immediate task of defeating the enemy's Kiev group of forces and capturing Kiev.
   For this, it is necessary:
   a) to shift Rybalko's 3rd Guards Tank Army to the sector of the front north of Kiev and employed it here in conjunction with the 1st Guards Cavalry Corps. Rybalko's worn out tanks should remain to be replenished by the 8th Guards and 10th tank corps. The tanks arriving at the *front* should be used, first of all, for fleshing out Rybal'ko's tank corps.
   b) to reinforce the *front's* right wing with 3-4 rifle divisions from the *front's* left wing.
   c) to also employ the 135th and 202nd rifle divisions, being transferred to you from the 70th Army in the *Stavka* reserve, to reinforce the right wing.
   d) to bring the 60th, 38th and 3rd Guards Tank armies to take part in the offensive on Kiev.

3. To wage offensive operations on the Bukrin bridgehead with the remaining forces here, including tank units, with the task of attracting to itself as many enemy forces as possible and, under favorable conditions, to break through his front and advance.

4. Rybalko's transfer is to be carried out so that it takes place unnoticed by the enemy, employing dummy tanks.

5. Rybalko's transfer and that of 3-4 rifle divisions from the left wing is to be begun immediately and their completion on the right wing completed by 1-2.11.43.

---

1   Editor's note. Georgii Konstantinovich Zhukov (1896-1974) joined the Russian imperial army in 1915 and the Red Army in 1918. He defeated the Japanese at the Khalkhin-Gol River in 1939 and at the beginning of the Great Patriotic War was Red Army chief of staff. During the war he commanded a number of *fronts* and also served as deputy supreme commander-in-chief, immediately under Stalin. The dictator turned against him in 1946 and Zhukov returned to power only after his death. Zhukov was appointed defense minister in 1955, but was dismissed two years later by Nikita Sergeevich Khrushchev.

2   Editor's note. Ivan Stepanovich Konev (1897-1973) joined the Russian imperial army in 1916 and the Red Army in 1918. During the Great Patriotic War he commanded an army and a number of *fronts*, including the Steppe Front during the Battle of Kursk. Following the war, Konev was the commander-in-chief of the Central Group of Forces, the USSR Ground Forces and commander-in-chief of the Warsaw Pact Forces.

6. The right wing's offensive is to begin on 1-2.11.43, so that the 3rd Guards Tank Army can begin operations on 3-4.11.43. The left wing is to begin its offensive no later than 2.11.43.
7. The boundary line between the Belorussian and First Ukrainian fronts is to be as before. At 2400 on 25.10.43 two left-flank divisions from the Belorussian Front's 61st Army are to be transferred to the First Ukrainian Front's 13th Army.
8. Report on fulfillment.

Stavka of the Supreme High Command
   I. Stalin
   Antonov[3]

As was shown earlier, throughout 24 October the *front* was still continuing to prepare for an offensive from the Bukrin bridgehead, which was scheduled for 26 October. At the same time, it was decided to begin the 60th and 38th armies' offensive north of Kiev on the morning of 25 October.

On the night of 24-25 October, three to four hours after the receipt of directive No. 30232, the *front* headquarters received new telegraphic instructions from the *Stavka* of the Supreme High Command, according to which the offensive planned for 25-26 October was to be cancelled. Here is the text of this telegram.

                                   Very Important
Personally to the Commander of the First Ukrainian Front
                        In reference to your No. 21305/sh
                                   25.10.43, 0250
                                         No. 30233

The *Stavka* of the Supreme High Command orders:
1. The offensive by Chernyakhovskii[4] and Chibisov,[5] planned by you for 25.10.43, is to be cancelled and you are to be guided by *Stavka* directive No. 30232.
2. In the future, do not order any kind of offensive without the *Stavka's* approval.

The *Stavka* of the Supreme High Command.
   I. Stalin
   Antonov

---

3 Editor's note. Aleksei Innokent'evich Antonov (1896-1962) served as a junior officer in the Russian imperial army during World War I. He joined the Red Army in 1918 and took part in the civil war. During the Great Patriotic War he served in various front-line staff assignments, before being appointed chief of the General Staff's operational directorate in 1942 and deputy chief of staff the following year. Antonov was appointed chief of the General Staff in 1945, although he held that post for less than a year. Following the war, Antonov commanded a military district and served as chief of staff of the Warsaw Pact forces.
4 Editor's note. Ivan Danilovich Chernyakhovskii (1906-45) joined the Red Army in 1924 and served in various command capacities before the war. During the Great Patriotic War he advanced from the command of a division to that of a corps and army, and in 1944 was appointed to command the Third Belorussian Front. He was killed during the East Prussian operation in February 1945.
5 Editor's note. Nikandr Yevlampievich Chibisov (1892-1959) joined the Russian imperial army in 1913 and the Red Army in 1918. During the Great Patriotic War he commanded a military district, a *front* and a number of armies, including the 38th Army during the Battle of Kursk. Following the war, Chibisov headed the Frunze Military Academy and was deputy military district commander.

The Troops' Regrouping

From the moment the *front* received these directives from the *Stavka* of the Supreme High Command, all of the *front* commander's attention and that of his staff was concentrated on organizing the regrouping of the troops and drawing up a plan for the forthcoming operation. Throughout 25 October all of the orders were issued for regrouping from the *front's* left flank to the north the 3rd Guards Tank Army, the artillery and the rifle forces. The troops were to begin crossing from the Bukrin bridgehead to the left bank of the Dnepr as early as the night of 25-26 October.

The *front's* headquarters did not manage to draw up a general plan for regrouping the troops and all instructions in this regard were issued as individual orders. This made the organized transfer of the troops more difficult, because the tight deadlines and the complexity of the maneuver, which involved three river crossings (twice across the Dnepr and once across the Desna), as well as a shortage of towing equipment in the 7th Breakthrough Artillery Corps required a very high degree of precision and control of the troops' march. The crossings were under enemy air and, in some cases, artillery fire.

During 25 October-1 November the following troop regroupings were carried out. The 3rd Guards Tank Army moved from the south to the north. The 38th Army received the following reinforcements: the 23rd Rifle Corps, consisting of the 23rd, 30th and 218th rifle divisions, the headquarters of the 21st Rifle Corps, the 83rd Guards Mortar Regiment (RS), the 9th Anti-Tank Artillery Brigade, and the 21st Anti-Aircraft Artillery Division from the 47th Army; the 3rd Guards Mortar Division (RS) (minus one brigade) and the 7th Breakthrough Artillery Corps from the 40th Army, and; the 235th Motorized Engineer Battalion from the 3rd Guards Tank Army. The 7th Guards Anti-Tank Artillery Brigade was to be transferred from the 47th Army to the 60th Army.

The following were to be transferred from north to south: the 74th Rifle Division, transferred from the 13th Army to the 38th Army; the 322nd Rifle Division and the 129th Tank Brigade, to be transferred from the 13th Army to the 60th Army, and the 1488th Anti-Aircraft Artillery Regiment, to be transferred from the 38th Army to the 47th Army.

Four main routes were chosen for moving the troops from the area of the Bukrin bridgehead to the 38th Army's sector:

a) Khotski, Yadlovka, Rudnya, Semipolki, Letki, and Svarom'ye—a distance of 190 kilometers;
b) Leplyavo, Pereyaslav-Khmel'nitskii, Voitovtsy, Ivan'kovo, Gogolev, Bol'shaya Dymerka, Letki, Svarom'ye—a distance of 165 kilometers;
c) Pereyaslav-Khmel'nitskii, Borispol', Brovary, Kalinovka, Rozhny, Svarom'ye—a distance of 130 kilometers;
d) Koshary, Yerkovtsy, Voronkov, Knyazhichi, Brovary, Rozhny, Svarom'ye—a distance of 130 kilometers.

The movement of forces from the south to the 60th Army's sector was to be carried out along the route, Khotski, Yagotin, Novyi Bykov, Kobyzhcha, Kozelets, Oster, Staro-Karpilovskaya Guta—a distance of 225 kilometers.

It was planned to carry out the troops' movement only at night. The enemy was carrying out air attacks against the crossings over the Dnepr day and night. During 20-25 October the Germans carried out 20 air attacks against the Bukrin bridgehead's crossings. Aside from cases of direct hits, the damaging and destruction of individual bridge spans and the explosions of heavy high-explosive bombs on the banks of the river had an influence on the stability of the latter.

Some crossings were located close to the enemy's defensive line and were subject to deliberate artillery bombardment. For example, for this reason it was impossible to employ the bridge near Grigorovka on the Bukrin bridgehead to withdraw the 3rd Guards Tank Army to the left bank of the Dnepr, so it was disassembled and used to build ferry crossings in other sectors. The enemy's air and artillery attacks made the crossing of our troops difficult and demanded a great deal of work by our engineer units, which were servicing the crossings. The 7th Breakthrough Artillery Corps, which was forced because of a lack of towing equipment to cross its equipment in 2-3 trips, was in difficult conditions.

The daily pace of the rifle formation's movements was 22-28 kilometers, with 32-33 kilometers per day for the tank and artillery formations.

Despite all of these difficulties, the lateral movement of a significant part of the *front's* forces from its left wing to the area north of Kiev was essentially carried out according to schedule.

Smoke screens were broadly employed for masking purposes in carrying out the regrouping.

The *front's* chemical troops employed smoke on the crossings over the Dnepr, and smoke screens were laid down in those areas where troop crossings were not actually carried out, in order to fool the enemy. The smoke cover of the crossing areas and smoke screens at false crossings had a significant effect. For example, on 28 October 14 enemy planes bombed the crossings near Traktomirov (the Bukrin bridgehead) and on 31 October up to 30 planes bombed the crossings near Tolokunskaya Rudnya (the 60th Army's area). However, as a result of the fact that at the moment of the enemy's air attacks both crossings were wreathed in smoke, there were no direct hits on the bridges. In all (according to incomplete information), in October the enemy air force dropped up to 1,000 high explosive bombs on smoke-wreathed crossings over the Dnepr in the *front's* sector, with only six direct hits recorded against the bridges.

In order to disguise the movement of the tank army and a large number of artillery to the north from the 40th, 27th and 47th armies' sector, a large number of dummy tanks and guns were built and dispersed on the Bukrin bridgehead. Here some of the tank army's radio stations continued working and the former artillery and mortar fire regime was maintained. Only a limited number of people were brought in for the operation's planning in the headquarters during the first stage. Alongside the preparations for the offensive, orders were also issued to go over to the defensive and to increase defensive work. False concentration areas for troops, tanks and artillery were created in the 13th Army's sector; rumors were launched among the local population that the army was going to attack, although the 13th Army's sector was to remain passive, according to the operational plan.

All of these measures enabled us to hide the beginning of the regrouping of the First Ukrainian Front's forces from the enemy. It was only on 30 October that the enemy understood that an intensive movement of forces was taking place on the left bank of the Dnepr, although the goal and meaning of this movement were not clear to him. Due to this, the Germans increased their reconnaissance measures. On 29 October they carried out a major reconnaissance in force in the area south and southwest of Khodorov with up to an infantry division in strength, supported by tanks. The Germans' attack was beaten off and quiet set in on the bridgehead up to 1 November. For reconnaissance purposes, the enemy began to throw over the river landings of automatic riflemen, in up to company strength, over the river in the Kailov area and in the immediate Kiev area. By the start of the offensive by the *front's* forces north of Kiev; that is, by 3 November, the Germans had basically established the direction of our troops' regrouping and began to expect an attack north of Kiev. However, the data at the enemy's disposal were out of date and he was subjected to an attack a few days earlier than he had expected. This is clear from the fact that General Rybalko's tank corps had been noted by the Germans at the close of 3 November only at the approaches to the crossings over the Dnepr at Svarom'ye, when they actually had already been concentrated on the Lyutezh bridgehead and entered the fighting on 4 November.

The headquarters of the 47th Army was pulled into the *Stavka* of the Supreme High Command reserve during the regrouping. As was mentioned earlier, the 23rd Rifle Corps, consisting of three divisions, and the headquarters of the 21st Rifle Corps, were transferred to the 38th Army. Only the 206th Rifle Division, which had been transferred to the 27th Army, remained on the Studenets bridgehead.

The Enemy's Group of Forces and a Description of his Defense

Following stubborn fighting in the First Ukrainian Front's sector, by 1 November the enemy's forces were distributed unequally. The seizure by our forces of bridgeheads on the right bank of the Dnepr, their offensive battles from these bridgeheads, and also the Germans' insistent attempts to eliminate these bridgeheads, resulted in the creation of powerful groups of German forces north and south of Kiev in the areas of the bridgeheads, while at the same time the remainder of the front was covered by only insignificant forces.

The enemy had concentrated up to seven divisions opposite the 60th Army. The 291st Infantry Division was defending along a 28-kilometer front between the Uzh and Teterev rivers; the 339th Infantry Division, with the 65th Artillery Battalion from the High Command Reserve, the 183rd and 217th infantry divisions, with a regiment of chemical mortars, and the 327th and 340th infantry divisions, with the 276th Assault Gun Battalion, were operating along a 36-kilometer front from the Teterev River to Kozarovichi. Thus the density of the enemy's group of forces along the sector opposite the 60th Army was comparatively high; each division occupied an average of seven kilometers of defensive front.

Seven infantry and two panzer divisions were operating against the 38th Army. The 208th Infantry Division, with the 611th Heavy Artillery Battalion, was defending along the 22-kilometer sector Borki—excluding Gostomel'. The 8th Panzer Division was concentrated in the Mikulichi area. The 18-kilometer sector excluding Gostomel'—the southern outskirts of Vyshgorod was the most densely occupied. The following units were defending here: the 68th Infantry Division, along with a regiment from the 75th and a regiment from the 88th infantry divisions, and with two battalions of six-barreled mortars, the 388th and 323rd infantry divisions, along with the 109th Artillery Regiment from the High Command Reserve, and the 618th Anti-Tank Battalion, which yielded 4-5 kilometers per division. The 7th Panzer Division was concentrated along the northwestern outskirts of Kiev and its 25th Panzer Regiment had been moved to the Goryanka—Dachi Pushcha-Voditsa area and the woods to the east. Each division was defending along a front up to five kilometers. The 75th Infantry Division (minus the 172nd Regiment), the 213th Security and 82nd Infantry divisions were defending along the 60-kilometer front excluding Vyshgorod—excluding Tripol'ye, along the right bank of the Dnepr. This was a quiet sector and the Germans here had only individual strong points and patrolled between them. Each division occupied more than 20 kilometers of defensive front.

The 40th and 27th armies, which had their main forces on the Bukrin bridgehead and which also occupied the Shchuchinka (40th Army) and Studenets (27th Army) bridgeheads, were operating along a 96-kilometer front, with the 40th Army along a 44-kilometer front and the 27th Army along a 52-kilometer front. The enemy had along a 45-kilometer front opposite the Shchuchinka, Bukrin and Studenets bridgeheads four infantry, three panzer and one motorized division, which yielded 5.6 kilometers per division. The 34th Infantry Division, along with the 70th Artillery Regiment from the High Command Reserve, the 10th Motorized Division, along with the 159th Anti-Tank Artillery Battalion, the *Das Reich* SS Panzer Division, with the 52nd Mortar Regiment from the High Command Reserve, and the 861st Light Artillery Battalion from the High Command Reserve were opposite the 40th Army along the front Tripol'ye—Kanada. The 72nd Infantry Division, the 19th Panzer Division, along with the 100th and 241st artillery regiments from the High Command Reserve, the 112th Infantry Division and the 255th Infantry Division, along with the 723rd Sapper Battalion and the 165th Mortar Regiment from the High Command Reserve, the 3rd Panzer Division, along with the 55th Mortar Regiment, and the 57th Infantry Division were defending opposite the 27th Army along the front excluding Kanada—Kreshchatik.

The 34th Infantry Division opposite the 40th Army's right flank was defending along a 25-kilometer front, while the 57th Infantry Division opposite the 27th Army's left flank was defending along a 20-kilometer front.

Besides the 7th and 8th panzer divisions, which were in reserve in the Kiev area, the Germans also disposed of the following reserves. The 20th Motorized Division had been dispersed in detail between Kiev and Kagarlyk in the Glevakha—Obukhov—Potok area and could be employed both against the Bukrin and the Lyutezh bridgeheads at any time. The 454th Security Division was located in the enemy's immediate rear opposite the 60th Army in the Ivankov—Stanishevka area. Up to two regiments of infantry, with tanks, were stationed in the area of Tolstyi Les station and the town of Kaganovich. Concentrations of troops of unknown number were noted in the areas of Korosten' and Skvir. The 147th Infantry Division was concentrated in Novograd-Volynskii. The headquarters of the Hungarian VII Army Corps was located in Zhitomir. Four Hungarian light divisions were located as follows: the 18th Division in Yel'sk, the 19th in Ovruch, the 201st in Berdichev, and the 21st in Shepetovka. The Hungarian units were employed by the Germans for fighting partisans and guarding the railroads.

The enemy aviation operating against the First Ukrainian Front included the 3rd, 27th, 51st, 53rd, and 60th bomber squadrons, the 77th Dive Bomber Squadron, and a fighter group from the High Command Reserve, which was part of the city of Kiev's anti-aircraft defense.

The German aviation's basing was as follows.

The enemy aviation had 30 planes in Ovruch, 20 in Kaganovich, 30 in Korosten', 50 in Kiev, 100 in Zhitomir, 80 in Skomorokhi (southeast of Zhitomir), 40 in Vasil'kovo, 30 in Uzino (15 kilometers east of Belaya Tserkov'), 60 in Belaya Tserkov', 100 in Kalinovka, 100 in Vinnitsa, and 25 in Zhashkov. In all, 665 planes had been noted, of which 400 were bombers, 205 were fighters, 30 reconnaissance aircraft, and 30 night bombers. Besides this, the enemy had about 120 transport aircraft.

In all, the enemy had opposite the First Ukrainian Front 27 divisions in the first defensive line, of which 21 were infantry (34th, 57th, 68th, 75th, 82nd, 86th, 88th, 112th, 168th, 183rd, 208th, 217th, 255th, 291st, 323rd, 327th, 339th, 344th, and 388th infantry and the 213th Security divisions), one motorized division (10th), five panzer divisions (3rd, 4th, 5th, 19th, and *Das Reich* SS). There were up to three German infantry divisions and four Hungarian light infantry divisions in reserve, as well as two panzer and one motorized divisions (147th Infantry and 454th Security divisions, 20th Motorized, 7th and 8th panzer, and the 18th, 19th, 21st, and 201st Hungarian light infantry divisions).

The enemy had his densest groups of forces along the sector excluding Gornostaipol'—Gostemel'—Vyshgorod (up to 14 divisions, of which two were panzer), and along the sector Shchuchinka—Kiev (up to eight divisions with reinforcements, of which three were panzer divisions). The enemy's artillery density opposite the 38th Army along the sector for the planned offensive (Moshchun—Vyshgorod) was 37 guns and mortars 75mm and greater per kilometer of front.

All of the enemy's forces had taken part in the October fighting and had suffered significant losses. The strongest (numbering more than 4,000 men) were the 291st and 340th infantry divisions. The 213th Security, 323rd and 82nd infantry divisions numbered less than 2,000 men. The remaining divisions had from 2,000 to 3,000 men.

All of the German forces operating opposite the First Ukrainian Front were part of the Second Army, the headquarters of which was located in Mozyr', and the Fourth Panzer Army, the headquarters of which was located in Makarov. The Uzh River was the boundary line between the armies. The Fourth Panzer Army's boundary line on the right coincided approximately with the First Ukrainian Front's left boundary and ran south of Kanev. The 57th Infantry Division alone formed part of the Eighth Army, which was operating opposite the Second Ukrainian Front.

The construction of the enemy's engineer defensive structures on the right bank of the Dnepr had not been completed by the time our troops reached the river. The hue and cry of the Goebbels propaganda machine about the invincibility of the Germans' defensive wall along the Dnepr was not founded on real, powerful fortified structures, but on the natural might of this line and the calculation of the weakness of the Soviet army's tactical skill. The Germans did not believe in the possibility that the Soviet forces could force the Dnepr and did not hurry to organize a defense along its right bank. And here the German command also revealed the limitations of its thinking and an inability to correctly evaluate the Soviet army's qualities. When the Germans became convinced that the Soviet army's units had seized a number of bridgeheads on the right bank of the Dnepr and all attempts to eliminate the latter remained uncrowned with success, feverish work began to engineer outfit the defense.

In going over to a static defense along the entire front, the enemy began to reinforce his units with anti-tank weapons, to strengthen his positions with engineer works, to develop a defensive system in depth, and to replenish his troops with men and materiel, while striving to maximally compress his defense and to prevent the expansion of our bridgeheads along the right bank of the Dnepr.

The Germans' defensive line north of Kiev represented the simplest kind of hastily erected and unfinished field fortification structures. This line consisted of three positions with an overall depth up to 14 kilometers in the sector of the 38th Army's forthcoming offensive. The first position ran from the mouth of an unnamed creek west of Moshchun, along the southern bank of this creek, to height 158.7, and then further as far as the central part of Vyshgorod. The forward edge of the second position ran along the line Dachi Pushcha-Voditsa—the children's sanitarium, the edge of the woods one kilometer north of a rest home. The forward line of the third position ran along the line Belichi—Berkovets—the northern outskirts of Priorka, and then to Vyshgorod. An anti-tank ditch, which had been built as early as 1941, ran immediately north of Kiev.

The Germans' defensive positions consisted of trenches, communications trenches, covered machine gun and mortar emplacements and a comparatively small number of wood and earthen firing positions. The sector of the Lyutezh—Kiev paved road contained the greatest density of defensive structures. The first position consisted of two trenches. The trenches had offshoots ("mustaches"), single and double foxholes and emplacements for machine guns and mortars. The foxholes were outfitted with niches for ammunition. Overhead covers for living quarters had been built in gullies behind the trenches and were covered by anti-tank obstacles and were connected with the trenches by communications trenches. There were anti-tank minefields in front of the first trench along its entire length at a distance of 80-100 meters. T-42 metal mines were distributed in three rows, chessboard style; the distances between the rows of mines reached three meters and four meters between them in the rows. The density of the mining reached 600-700 mines per kilometer of front. In some places remote-controlled charges had been placed at a distance of 25-30 meters in front of the trench. There were no wire obstacles.

The second and third positions consisted of one trench, abutted by machine gun and mortar emplacements. There were unknown wire obstacles of the German fence type in front of the trenches and unfinished overhead covers for quarters were also located in the gullies behind the trench. There were no minefields in front of the second and third positions.

A defensive line was also being prepared along the left bank of the Irpen' River. The towns of Fastov and Vasil'kov were being hurriedly transformed into strong points.

FIRST UKRAINIAN FRONT'S NOVEMBER OFFENSIVE OPERATION

The Operational Plan and its General Idea

On 24 October the *front* commander issued directive No. 0050/op, in which he assigned the armies their overall tasks in preparing for the offensive. This directive was a guideline for the army commanders in preparing for the offensive before receiving specific assignments.

According to the directive, the *front's* forces were to consolidate along the lines occupied and immediately set about studying the enemy's defense from all sides, employing all intelligence means. Local attacks were authorized for the purpose of improving the jumping-off position for the offensive.

It was ordered to carry out a number of exercises in all the formations designated to take part in the offensive in the first echelon, for the purpose of training the troops in attacking along broken terrain and instilling habits of organizing the cooperation of the combat arms. The infantry was to train in moving to the attack immediately behind the explosions of its own artillery shells. The troops designated for attacking in the first echelon were ordered pulled back for rest and replenishment. It was ordered to bring the strength of the rifle companies to 70-80 men. A large reserve of ordnance of no less than two combat loads was to be accumulated in the artillery positions. Command and observation posts were to be outfitted in time. All the offensive preparation measures were to be scrupulously masked. The work of radio stations was categorically forbidden.

This directive set the troops' readiness at 1 November. On 27 October the *front* commander signed directives nos. 0052, 0053 and 0054/op, in which he assigned all the armies specific offensive tasks.

The overall idea of the operation consisted of the following.

The 38th Army was to launch an attack from the Lyutezh bridgehead to the south, to outflank Kiev from the west and to capture it.

The *front's* mobile formations (3rd Guards Tank Army and the 1st Guards Cavalry Corps) were to enter into the breach in the 38th Army's sector and to develop the offensive to the southwest, with the mission of reaching the Fastov—Belaya Tserkov'—Grebenki area.

The 60th Army was to launch an attack in the direction of Rovy and Dymer and then to the south, between the Zdvizh and Irpen' rivers, securing the 38th Army's operations in the Kiev area.

The 40th and 27th armies had the mission of breaking through the enemy's front opposite the Bukrin bridgehead and to develop the offensive in the general direction of Pii, Kagarlyk and Belaya Tserkov', for the purpose of tying down enemy forces located along the front Rzhishchev—Kanev and to deny the Germans the opportunity of employing these forces for countering the *front's* main group of forces attacking north of Kiev.

The *front's* forces were to subsequently develop the offensive to the west and southwest and by the fourteenth day of the operation by the combined-arms armies to reach the line Korosten'—Zhitomir—Berdichev—Rakitno, while the mobile forces were to reach the line Korosten'—Vinnitsa—Zhmerinka.

Thus the Germans' Fourth Panzer Army in the Kiev area was to be routed as early as the beginning stage of the operation through attacks by the *front's* main group of forces from the bridgeheads north of Kiev and an auxiliary group of forces along the *front's* left flank from the Bukrin bridgehead.

The Armies' Tasks

The 38th Army, along with the 5th Guards Tank and 7th Breakthrough Artillery corps, had the task, upon securing itself from the west along the Irpen' River with two rifle divisions, it was to launch the main attack with its remaining forces along the front Moshchun—Vyshgorod in the direction of Dachi Pushcha-Voditsa, Belichi and Vasil'kov and secure the commitment into the breach of the 3rd Guards Tank Army and the 1st Guards Cavalry Corps. By the close of the operation's first day the army's forces were to reach the front Mostishche—the northern outskirts of Priorka; Sofievka—Borshchagovka by the close of the second day; Buzova—Budaevka—Kremenishche and encircle Kiev by the close of the third day, and; Motyzhin—Perevoz—Plesetskoye—Vasil'kov—Bezradichi by the close of the fourth day. The army was ordered to force the Dnepr south of Kiev with the forces of one rifle division during the night of the operation's second day, with the mission of cutting the roads leading from Kiev from the south.

The 60th Army was to launch its main attack in the direction of Rovy with no less than nine rifle divisions and then to the south, along the left bank of the Irpen' River. Supporting attacks were to be launched as follows: the first in the direction of Sychevka and Manuil'sk and then along the right bank of the Zdvizh, and the second toward Kozarovichi, for the purpose of tying down the enemy in the Dymer area. By the close of the operation's first day the army was to reach the front Sychevka—Manuil'sk, Dymer—Kozarovichi, and the front Sychevka—Manuil'sk—Katyuzhanka—Kozintsy by the close of the fourth day.

The 3rd Guards Tank Army, along with the 1st Guards Cavalry Corps, comprised the *front's* mobile group. By the start of the operation the tank army had the mission of occupying a jumping-off position on the Lyutezh bridgehead, and the cavalry corps one on the eastern bank of the Dnepr in the Svarom'ye area and the woods to the east. The tank army was to be committed into the fighting following the breakthrough of the enemy's defense to a depth of eight kilometers; that is, the breakthrough of his first and second defensive positions. Developing the success, by the close of the operation's second day the army was to capture the Zabor'ye—Glevakha—Khotov—Sofievka area; the Plesetskoye—Vasil'kov—Glevakha area by the close of the third day, and; to reach the Fastov—Belaya Tserkov—Grebenki area by the close of the fourth day. The 1st Guards Cavalry Corps was to be committed into the breach behind the tank corps, with the mission of attacking through the wooded sectors along the right bank of the Irpen' River toward Fastov. The plan foresaw the possible employment of the corps to the west for attacking along the Kiev—Zhitomir paved road.

The 13th Army received orders to continue defending in its sector, developing the engineer work of its positions, and conducting uninterrupted reconnaissance of the enemy. At the same time, it was ordered to begin preparations for an offensive. The general direction of the offensive by the 13th Army's left wing, along with developing the 60th and 38th armies' success, was the town of Ovruch. To prepare for the offensive, it was ordered to pull back two rifle divisions into the second echelon by broadening the defense sectors of the other formations and to refit them and conduct the corresponding tactical exercises with them.

The 40th Army, upon breaking through the enemy's defense opposite the Bukrin bridgehead, was to reach the front Yushki—Burty by the close of the fourth day, while the mobile formations were to reach the area Stavy—Vintsentovka—Kagarlyk.

The 27th Army, while launching an attack from the Bukrin bridgehead in the direction of Potaptsy, was to reach the front Nikolaevka—Grushentsy by the close of the fourth day.

The Decisions by the Army Commanders

The decision by the 38th Army commander. The newly appointed commander of the 38th Army, Colonel General K.S. Moskalenko, adopted the following decision for the army's offensive.

It was planned to carry out the breakthrough of the German defense along the 14-kilometer Moshchun—Vyshgorod sector with the forces of the 50th Rifle Corps (163rd, 232nd and 167th rifle divisions), the 51st Rifle Corps (136th, 240th and 180th rifle divisions) and the 5th Guards Tank Corps. The main attack was to be launched by the internal flanks of the 50th and 51st rifle corps along a 6-kilometer front with the forces of four rifle divisions (232nd, 167th, 136th, and 240th).

The 50th Rifle Corps, reinforced by the 39th Tank Regiment, had the task of launching its main attack along the left flank with the forces of two rifle divisions (232nd and 167th) in the direction of Dachi Pushcha-Voditsa and Berkovets and by the close of the first day of the offensive to reach the line Belichi station—Berkovets, while employing one rifle division for covering the right flank of the army's shock group along the bank of the Irpen' River. Subsequently, while developing the attack toward the village of Svyatoshino and Pirogovo, the corps was to reach the line Dal'nii Yar farm, Kostopal'naya by the close of the second day and the line Veta Pochtovaya—Lesniki by the close of the fourth day. The corps' left boundary ran along the line Staro-Petrovtsy—height 158.7—Dachi Pushcha-Voditsa—the village of Svyatoshino—the village of Chokolovka—Myshelovka (all locales, except for Dachi Pushcha-Voditsa and Svyatoshino, were exclusively for the 50th Rifle Corps).

The 51st Rifle Corps, supported by two of the 5th Guards Tank Corps' tank brigades, was to launch its main attack along the right wing in the direction of the children's sanitarium and Syrets, and by the close of the first day of the offensive it was to reach the front excluding Berkovets—the northern outskirts of Priorka; subsequently, by the close of the third day of the offensive the corps was to completely capture Kiev. The corps was to be reinforced by the Czechoslovak Brigade, transferred from the army reserve, during the course of the offensive.[6]

The 23rd Rifle Corps, consisting of the 23rd, 30th and 218th rifle divisions, was ordered to be in the army's second echelon, and on the morning of the offensive's third day to attack the enemy along the front Mostishche—Goryanka and by the close of the day reach the line of the mouth of the Bucha River—Zabucha—Lychanka—Negrashi, ready to repel the Germans' counterattacks from the west and to continue the offensive along the Zhitomir paved road to the west. The corps was to be reinforced during the course of the offensive with the 50th Rifle Corps' 74th Rifle Division. The corps' boundary line on the left was established from the Zhitomir paved road to the south along the left bank of the Irpen' River.

The 21st Rifle Corps, consisting of the 135th and 202nd rifle divisions, which was also in the army's second echelon, had the task of deploying along the line Bobritsa—Boyarka-Budaevka by the close of the offensive's third day, in readiness to attack to the southwest. The boundary line on the left was the village of Svyatoshino—the Bol'shevik State Farm—Yurovka—Yankovichi (all locales exclusively for the 21st Rifle Corps).

As the 60th Army's offensive developed, the corps was to be reinforced with the 340th and 71st rifle divisions, which were defending along the right bank of the Irpen' River on the 38th Army's right wing.

By the close of the offensive's fourth day, the army's forces were to reach the following fronts: Nikolaevka farm—Motyzhin—Yablonovka for the 23rd Rifle Corps; Perevoz—Plesetskoye for the 21st Rifle Corps, and; Vasil'kov—Nikolenki for the 50th Rifle Corps.

The 5th Guards Tank Corps received orders to attach two tank brigades to the 51st Rifle Corps for joint operations with the infantry as direct infantry-support tanks, while its remaining forces (one tank and one motorized rifle brigades) were to develop the 50th Rifle Corps' success in the direction of the village of Svyatoshino.

The decision by the 60th Army commander. The army's units that were occupying defensive positions between the Pripyat' and Teterev rivers received no offensive tasks. The army's forces were to attack along the front Sychevka—excluding Yasnogorodka. Six rifle divisions, a rifle brigade, a tank brigade, and a tank regiment were detailed to the army's first echelon of attacking forces; the second echelon consisted of three rifle divisions and a tank brigade.

---

6 This corps' 74th Division, which was defending along the right bank of the Irpen' River north of Moshchun, was to be subordinated to the commander of the 23rd Rifle Corps on the first day of the offensive.

The main attack was to be launched along the sector Rovy—excluding Yasnogorodka in the direction of Dymer, Litvinovka and Gavrilovka by the forces of the 24th and 30th rifle corps, and a supporting attack along the Sychevka—Manuil'sk—Buda sector by the forces of the 77th Rifle Corps. The overall attack front was 20 kilometers.

The 77th Rifle Corps had the task, while securely defending with units of the 280th Rifle Division along its right flank, to launch an attack with the forces of the 143rd and 132nd divisions in the direction of Sychevka, Manuil'sk and Andreevka, with the immediate task of capturing Sychevka and Manuil'sk.

The 24th Rifle Corps (248th Rifle Brigade, the 226th and 112th rifle divisions, and the 150th Tank Brigade), which had the immediate task of capturing Rostesno and, while developing the success to the southwest, was to reach the front Alekseevka—height 150.8—height 143.7 by the close of the operation's first day, and by the close of the third day the right bank of the Zdvizh River along the sector Vladimirovka farm—Guta Katyuzhanskaya—Dudki farm, where it was to firmly consolidate, while preventing enemy counterattacks in the direction of Katyuzhanka and Dymer. By this time the corps' forward detachment was to capture Fenevichi along the left bank of the Zdvizh River.

The 30th Rifle Corps (121st, 141st and 75th Guards rifle divisions and the 59th Tank Regiment), with its main group of forces along the right flank, received orders to break through the enemy's defense and, while attacking toward Dymer, to capture it by the close of the operation's first day and reach the front height 143.7—Dymer—Kozarovichi. By the close of the third day all of the corps' forces were to reach the line Felitsialovka—Buda Babinskaya—Balanovka, and by the close of the fourth day the line Felitsialovka—Buda Babinskaya—Mikulichi—Kozintsy, where it was to establish contact with the 38th Army's 23rd Rifle Corps.

The 3rd Guards Airborne and 322nd Rifle divisions and the 129th Tank Brigade constituted the army's second echelon.

The decision by the 3rd Guards Tank Army commander. The army was to be committed into the breach on the second day of the operation upon the infantry's reaching the line height 158.5—the northern outskirts of Priorka. The army's combat formation was organized into two echelons. The 6th and 7th guards tank corps were to attack in the first echelon and the 9th Mechanized and 1st Guards Cavalry corps in the second. By the close of the operation's second day the tank corps were to reach the line Bobritsa—Malyutyanka—Glevakha, the mechanized corps the area of Svyatoshino village, and the cavalry corps the woods west of the village. By the close of the third day the army's tank corps were supposed to capture the railroad junction of Fastov and the inhabited locale of Grebenka. The mechanized corps had the task of continuing to attack in the army's second echelon in readiness, in conjunction with the 6th Guards Tank Corps, to capture Fastov or repulse counterattacks by the enemy's reserves along the boundary between the 6th and 7th guards tank corps; the corps was to reach the Mar'yanovka—Ksaverovka area by the close of the day. The 1st Guards Cavalry Corps was ordered to operate either along the Zhitomir paved road to the west, forcing the Irpen' River, or in conjunction with the 6th Guards Tank Corps in the direction of Fastov along the right bank of the Irpen' River. Throughout the fourth and fifth days of the operation the corps were to continue developing the success in the southern and southwestern directions, depending on the situation.

In the event of the failure of the 38th Army's offensive to the south, the headquarters of the 3rd Guards Tank Army was instructed by the *front* commander to draw up a second variation for employing the army. According to this variation, the tank army and the cavalry corps were to force the Irpen' River on the first day of the operation north and south of Rakovka and, taking advantage of the 60th Army's success, on the operation's second day launch an attack from the line Filippovichi—Mirotskoye with all its forces to the south and cut the Kiev—Zhitomir paved road. Upon arriving at the paved road, part of the army's forces was to force the Irpen' River from west to east, with the mission of preventing the withdrawal of the enemy's Kiev group of forces along the paved road to the west. In the operation's subsequent days the army had the assignment of developing the success to the south and southwest and to capture the town of Fastov.

The decision by the commanders of the 40th and 27th armies. The 40th Army was to launch its main attack with the forces of five of the 47th Rifle Corps'[7] divisions and two tank corps (there were only 34 tanks and self-propelled guns in service) along the 11-kilometer front Khodorov—Romashki. Two of the 52nd Rifle Corps' divisions were to launch a supporting attack from the Shchuchinka area.

The 27th Army, in close cooperation with the 40th Army's shock group, was to launch an attack along its right flank along a 6-kilometer front. Four rifle divisions were to take part in the offensive, of which one was in the second echelon.[8] The army was to defend along the remainder of the front with the forces of two divisions.[9]

The Pace of the Operation

The following offensive paces were planned along the axes of the main attacks.

38th Army: the 50th and 51st rifle corps were to advance 11 kilometers on the operation's first day, ten kilometers on the second day, ten kilometers on the third day, and 14 kilometers on the fourth day, for a total of 45 kilometers over four days.

The 60th Army was to advance four kilometers on the offensive's first day and 36 kilometers over all four days of the operation, for an average of nine kilometers per day.

The 3rd Guards Tank Army was to advance 25 kilometers on the first day, following its commitment into the breach, ten kilometers on the second day and 43 kilometers on the third day. In all, the army was to advance about 80 kilometers over three days of attacking.

The 40th and 27th armies' rifle formations were to advance 15 kilometers over the operation's four days, and the mobile formations 40 kilometers.

The Organization of the Combat Formations of the Front's Forces

The 13th Army, which was to defend along its sector during the operation's first stage, had all of its divisions in the first line of defense, while on the army's right wing the 28th Rifle Corps occupied an average of 12 kilometers of defensive front per division and nine kilometers per division in the 15th Rifle Corps on the left wing.

The 60th Army had along its right flank the 17th Guards Rifle Corps, which was carrying out defensive tasks; two of the corps' divisions were operating in the first echelon along a 12-kilometer front. The 18th Guards Rifle Corps, which was also carrying out defensive tasks, had two divisions in a single echelon along a 16-kilometer front. The remaining corps, while carrying out offensive tasks, were organized as follows: the 77th Rifle Corps had two divisions (143rd and 132nd) in the first echelon along a 7-kilometer front and one division (280th) on the defensive along the corps' right wing; the 24th Rifle Corps had all of its forces in a single echelon;[10] the 30th Rifle Corps had two divisions and a tank regiment in the first echelon and one division in the second echelon.[11] Two rifle divisions were in the army's second echelon.[12]

---

7   253rd, 16th, 1st, 42nd Guards, 237th and 337th rifle divisions.
8   241st, 147th, 100th, and 38th rifle divisions.
9   155th and 206th rifle divisions.
10 248th Rifle Brigade, 226th and 112th rifle divisions, and the 150th Tank Brigade.
11 75th Guards, 121st and 141st rifle divisions and the 59th Tank Regiment.
12 322nd Rifle and 3rd Guards Airborne divisions.

The 38th Army had three rifle divisions (340th and 74th rifle divisions and the 71st Rifle Division, minus one regiment) along its right flank, which were carrying out defensive tasks along a 23-kilometer front. The 50th Rifle Corps organized three divisions and one tank regiment in a single echelon along a 7-kilometer front for the offensive.[13] The 51st Rifle Corps had all three of its divisions in the first echelon along a 7-kilometer front;[14] the 5th Guards Tank Corps was to support the 51st Rifle Corps' infantry with two tank brigades; the Czechoslovak 1st Brigade was marching to the 51st Rifle Corps' area and was supposed to attack in its second echelon. The 23rd Rifle Corps was in the army's second echelon behind the 50th Rifle Corps. The 21st Rifle Corps had two divisions which were on the march and which were supposed to arrive at the army's attack sector by the start of the operation and comprise its second echelon. Individual units were defending along the remaining 62 kilometers of front opposite Kiev and to the south along the eastern bank of the Dnepr River.

The 3rd Guards Tank Army, along with the 1st Guards Cavalry Corps (the *front's* mobile group) was organized as follows: the 6th and 7th guards tank corps were in the army's first echelon and the 9th Mechanized Corps in the second echelon along the western bank of the Dnepr River, behind the 38th Army's shock group. The 1st Guards Cavalry Corps, which also constituted the army's second echelon, was on the eastern bank of the Dnepr River in the Svarom'ye area.

40th Army: the 52nd Rifle Corps had along the eastern bank of the Dnepr one rifle regiment from the 237th Rifle Division defending along a 20-kilometer front; two of the corps' divisions were in one echelon on the Shchuchinka bridgehead along a 9-kilometer front and were to carry out a supporting assignment in the offensive. The 47th Rifle Corps, along with two tank corps, was to launch the main attack and had five divisions in a single echelon along an 11-kilometer front.

The 27th Army was to attack with three rifle divisions and one tank brigade along a 6-kilometer front; one rifle division was in the army's second echelon and two divisions were defending along the army's left wing along a 14-kilometer front.

The rifle formation's density in the 38th Army's offensive sector was 2.3 kilometers of front per rifle division and about three kilometers per division in the 60th Army. In the 40th and 27th armies along the secondary axis, the density was 2.6 kilometers per division. Along the axes of the armies' main attacks the density increased and reached 1.5 kilometers per division in the 38th Army.

Planning the Artillery Offensive

The artillery's distribution and concentration. The employment of the artillery was planned simultaneously with the drawing up of the operation's overall plan. At the heart of the planning was the principle of maximally massing artillery equipment along the front of the main attack. Taking into account that the 38th Army would launch the main attack, the largest amount of artillery equipment was to be concentrated along the latter's sector. By the start of the operation the 7th Breakthrough Artillery Corps, consisting of the 13th and 17th breakthrough artillery divisions, the 12th Mortar Brigade, the 24th Cannon Artillery Brigade, the 28th and 9th Guards anti-tank artillery brigades, and the 3rd Guards Mortar Division had been attached to the 38th Army.

Aside from this, the 38th Army had two cannon, two howitzer and six anti-tank artillery regiments, two mortar regiments, and five guards mortar regiments (RS). The 1st Guards Artillery Division, consisting of three brigades, the 7th Guards Anti-Tank Artillery Brigade, one cannon,

---

13 163rd, 232nd and 167th rifle divisions and the 39th Tank Regiment.
14 136th, 240th and 180th rifle divisions.

and three anti-tank artillery regiments, three mortar regiments, and two guards mortar regiments were attached to the 60th Army.

The 40th and 27th armies had been reinforced with the 33rd Heavy Cannon Artillery Brigade, the 25th Guards Howitzer Heavy Artillery Brigade, the 8th Guards and 32nd anti-tank artillery brigades, two cannon, two howitzer and six anti-tank artillery regiments, four mortar regiments, three guards mortar regiments, and one guards mortar battalion (RS).

Given this distribution of reinforcement artillery, a high density of artillery was achieved along the main breakthrough sector.

An army breakthrough group was created in the 38th Army, consisting of the 7th Breakthrough Artillery Corps. The corps commander was appointed to command the group. This group was divided into two subgroups: the 17th Artillery Division was part of the 50th Rifle Corps' subgroup and the 13th Artillery Division was part of the 51st Rifle Corps' subgroup.

The tasks of the army's artillery group were as follows:

a) to support the breakthrough of the enemy's defense in the 50th and 51st rifle corps' sectors;
b) to support the attack and to accompany these corps' infantry with massed fire and to repulse possible enemy counterattacks;
c) to support the commitment of the 3rd Guards Tank Army into the breach;
d) to prepare the fire of the 17th Artillery Division's main forces (in the event the 38th Army's offensive to the south was delayed) and supporting the 23rd Rifle Corps' attack from the line of the Irpen' River along the Sinyak—Rakovka sector; the army artillery group was supposed to be employed to support the troops storming Kiev.

Table 2.1 The Saturation of the First Ukrainian Front's Armies with Artillery by the Start of the November Offensive

Unit	Breakthrough Sector		Secondary Offensive Sector		Average Along the Entire Offensive Sector	
	Km	Tubes per km	km	Tubes per km	Km	Tubes per km
38th Army	6	347.5	8	31	14	166.7
38th Army's 50th Rifle Corps	3	383.3	4	26	7	179
38th Army's 51st Rifle Corps	3	311.7	4	36	7	154.1
60th Army	6.5	97.9	3	53.3	9.5	83.8
60th Army's 24th Rifle Corps	4	93.5	–	–	–	–
60th Army's 30th Rifle Corps	2.5	105	–	–	–	–
60th Army's 77th Rifle Corps	3	53.3	–	–	–	–
40th and 27th armies	17	59	9	26	26	49.3

The control of the counterbattery fight was also entrusted to the commander of the 7th Breakthrough Artillery Corps. For this purpose a long-range group was created in the 50th Rifle Corps, consisting of the 39th Cannon Artillery Brigade, the 108th Heavy Howitzer Artillery Brigade, the 3rd Observation Balloon Detachment, and the 624th Independent Artillery Reconnaissance Battalion. The 51st Rifle Corps' long-range group consisted of the 24th Cannon Artillery Brigade, two battalions from the 101st Heavy Howitzer Artillery Brigade and the 12th Guards Independent Artillery Reconnaissance Battalion.

The fight against the enemy's mortars was entrusted to the commanders of the artillery divisions, who were the commander of the corps breakthrough subgroups.

An army artillery group was not created in the 60th Army. All of the reinforcement artillery was part of the infantry support groups. Long-range groups were created in the 24th and 30th rifle corps for combating the enemy's artillery, repulsing his possible counterattacks and for suppressing defensive targets in the depth.

In the 40th and 27th armies, where there was little reinforcement artillery, it was entirely in the infantry support groups.

An anti-tank army reserve was created only in the 38th Army and consisted of the 9th Anti-Tank Brigade and the 139th Anti-Tank Rifle Battalion. Anti-tank reserves were created in the rifle corps from attached anti-tank units.

The organization of artillery reconnaissance. The reconnoitering of the enemy's defensive structures was chiefly carried out visually from observation posts. Observation was broadly organized to discover targets.

Adjustment aviation played a major role in reconnoitering the enemy. The wooded terrain in the Kiev area limited the opportunities for visual artillery reconnaissance from ground observation posts. In these conditions aerial reconnaissance and aerial photography played a large role and to a significant degree helped to unearth the enemy's defensive system, particularly in its depth. 16 sorties were carried out during the preparation for the operation for carrying out artillery reconnaissance assignments. Poor fighter cover of adjustment aviation made its work very difficult.

The reconnoitering of the enemy's batteries was conducted by reconnaissance artillery battalions, of which three were deployed along the axis of the main attack and of which one began working on 20 October and the other two from 29 October. The reconnaissance battalions unearthed the majority of the enemy's artillery and mortar batteries.

The organization of reconnaissance through employing all available means and the close coordination of the latter enabled us to unearth the enemy's entire defensive system and enabled us to correctly plan our artillery fire.

The topographical tying in of the artillery's combat formations was carried out in a timely manner and sufficiently completely. The meteorological service worked normally and delivered information on time to the artillery units.

Planning the Artillery Offensive

In the 38th and 60th armies the unearthed wood and earthen firing points were to be destroyed by individual guns on the eve of the offensive. The duration of the artillery preparation was set at 40 minutes and was subdivided into the following periods:

a) a fire onslaught by all of the artillery against the forward edge of the defense, headquarters, communications centers, and batteries for three minutes;
b) the suppression and destruction of targets and centers of resistance and making passages in the minefields through deliberate fire for 34 minutes;
c) a fire onslaught by all artillery against the forward edge of the enemy's defense for three minutes.

It was planned to carry out the accompaniment of the attack in the 50th Rifle Corps with a rolling barrage to a depth of 1.2-2 kilometers. The lines of the rolling barrage were set at 200 meters from each other. A feature of the rolling barrage was that fire was to be opened simultaneously against 3-4 lines and be conducted until the arrival of our infantry to each of them. In order to economize on munitions, the fire regime was established according to standing barrage norms. In the 51st Rifle Corps the attack was to be accompanied by the method of the consecutive concentration of fire. In both corps it was planned to suppress the enemy's artillery to a depth of 3.5-4 kilometers during the accompaniment period.

FIRST UKRAINIAN FRONT'S NOVEMBER OFFENSIVE OPERATION

In order to support the battle in the depth of the enemy's defense and along the axes of the enemy's likely counterattacks, it was planned to concentrate fire against individual targets. The artillery of the 7th Breakthrough Artillery Corps was to be brought in to conduct such fire. Concentrated fire by the entire breakthrough artillery corps was planned against the most important sectors, with the simultaneously inclusion of the rifle corps' artillery. The concentration of such a large mass of artillery fire against targets in the depth of the enemy's defense was supposed to secure their reliable suppression and the successful advance of our infantry and tanks.

The artillery support for the commitment of the tank army into the battle was entrusted to an army breakthrough group and it was planned to carry it out by the method of consecutively concentrating fire. Units had been previously designated for this and a fire system worked out. In all, five artillery brigades from the army group were allotted for supporting the commitment of the tank army.

The suppression of the enemy's artillery and mortar batteries was to be carried out in three fire onslaughts of five minutes each. Fire observation was planned during the intervals between the onslaughts. The first fire onslaught was to be carried out upon the start of the artillery preparation, and the last upon the start of the attack. Fire observation was planned for 25 minutes following the third fire onslaught. In light of the shortage of 152mm shells, heavy howitzer brigades were to be brought in for the counterbattery fight.

Artillery control was centralized at all levels. The movement of the artillery's combat formations was planned beforehand. All units received their movement plans, on the basis which they were to operate in the battle, in time. The uninterrupted support of the infantry and tanks with artillery fire was foreseen in planning the movement.

The following expenditure of artillery munitions was planned for the first day of the fighting:

Table 2.2 Planned Artillery Expenditure

Weapon (in combat loads)	Total	Including for the Artillery Preparation
82mm mortars	1.5	1.15
120mm mortars	1.0	0.6
76mm shells for regimental artillery	0.7	–
76mm shells for divisional artillery	0.7	0.6
122mm shells	0.7	0.6
152mm shells	1.2	0.6

The delivery of munitions to the troops proceeded slowly. The following reserves were available on 31 October (in combat loads).

Planning the Air Offensive

As opposed to the period of the first battles along the line of the Dnepr, the flight crews and units of the 2nd Air Army were well acquainted with the operations area and had acquired additional and significant combat experience.

The headquarters of the 2nd Air Army and the headquarters of the air formations carried out a number of measures in preparing for the operation. A plan for the combat employment of the aviation was drawn up; the aviation's cooperation with the combined-arms and tank armies was organized; the control of air formations and units during the forthcoming operation was also organized.

In accordance with the operational idea, the employment of all of the air army's forces along the axis of the main attack north of Kiev in conjunction with the forces of the 38th and 3rd Guards

Tank armies was foreseen. A small part of the *shturmoviks*[15] and fighters was allotted for cooperating with the 40th and 27th armies' forces on the Bukrin bridgehead. 600 sorties were planned to support these two armies on the first day.

The Organization of the Aviation's Cooperation with the Ground Forces

At the heart of the aviation's cooperation with the ground forces was the principle of supporting them with all of the air army's forces, while cooperation with the tank army was to be carried out by operationally subordinating the 5th Assault Air Corps to the commander of the tank army.

Table 2.3 Artillery Supplies (in Combat Loads)

Types of Munitions	With the Troops and at Army Bases	En Route to the Army Bases	At *Front* Depots	Total
37mm Anti-Aircraft Shells	2.1	0.2	0.9	3.2
85mm Anti-Aircraft Shells	1.5	0.1	0.6	2.2
76mm Shells for regimental artillery	0.7	0.1	0.4	1.2
76mm Shells for divisional artillery	0.3	0.1	0.1	0.5
122mm Howitzer Shells	0.8	0.1	0.3	1.2
152mm Shells for Cannon-Howitzers	1.0	–	0.2	1.2
82mm Mortar Rounds	1.1	0.1	0.5	1.7
120mm Mortar Rounds	1.2	0.2	0.1	1.5

Five stages were called for in the 2nd Air Army's cooperation plan with the 38th Army.

1) a preparatory phase involving the troops' occupation of their jumping-off positions on the eve of the offensive;
2) the artillery preparation;
3) the attack;
4) the battle within the enemy's defense;
5) the development of the success.

Throughout the preparatory period, light night bombers were to exhaust the enemy's men, suppress his fire means and disrupt his troop control and communications in the Goryanka—Dachi Pushcha-Voditsa—the children's sanitarium area. 180 Po-2 sorties were planned for this purpose.

During the period of the artillery preparation (H-30 minutes to H-five minutes) our aviation was to suppress and destroy the strong points in the first position of the enemy's defense, suppress his troops and fire system to a depth of two kilometers from the forward edge. 63 sorties by Pe-2s,[16] 42 Il-2s and 50 by fighters were planned for this purpose.

---

15 Editor's note. *Shturmovik* was the popular name for the Il-2 dive bomber, which first entered service in 1941 and quickly became one of the most popular aircraft of the war. The aircraft carried a two-man crew and had a top speed of 414 kilometers per hour. One version was armed with two 23mm cannons, two 7.62mm machine guns, and a single 12.7mm machine gun. The aircraft could carry up to 600 kilograms of bombs and several rockets.
16 Editor's note. The Pe-2 was a twin-engine Soviet medium bomber that first entered service in 1941. One model had a crew of three, a maximum speed of 580 km/hr and a range of 1,160 kilometers. It was armed with four 7.62mm machine gunsand could carry up to 1,600 kilograms of bombs.

FIRST UKRAINIAN FRONT'S NOVEMBER OFFENSIVE OPERATION

During the infantry attack (H+ 30 minutes-H+2:20 hrs) the aviation was to suppress strong points and artillery in the depth of the enemy's defensive zone. 110 sorties by Il-2s and 50 by fighters were planned for this purpose.

During the fighting in the depth of the defense and the infantry's arrival at the front Goryanka—the northern outskirts of Dachi Pushcha-Voditsa, the following approximate missions were planned: to support the troops in capturing the southeastern outskirts of Dachi Pushcha-Voditsa and the subsequent offensive to the south; to suppress the enemy's strong points, men and fire system in the second defensive position, and; to delay the arrival of the enemy's reserves and tanks. 54 Pe-2 sorties, 130 Il-2 sorties and 82 fighter sorties were planned for this purpose.

During the development of the success the *front's* aviation was to: support the ground forces in repulsing enemy counterattacks while capturing the village of Svyatoshino; support the commitment of the mobile forces into the breach and the development of the success and to cover them against the Germans' air attacks during the commitment into the breach. 120 sorties by Il-2s and 302 by fighters were planned for this purpose. Besides this, the plan foresaw the maintenance of a reserve of 54 Pe-2 aircraft and 23 fighters, which could be employed according to additional instructions by the commanders of the 2nd Air Army and the 38th Army.

In all, 1,250 sorties (180 by Po-2 night bombers, 171 by day bombers, 400 by assault aircraft, and 499 by fighters) were planned for cooperating with the 38th Army and supporting the mobile group's commitment into the breach. The cooperation plan for the 5th Assault Air Corps with the 3rd Guards Tank Army was drawn up in two variations. The first (main) foresaw air operations during the tank army's commitment into the breach to the south, while the second (likely) foresaw them while breaking through the enemy's front to the west in the Rakovka area.

The assault air corps' missions were planned by days, indicating the areas and objects of attack, depending upon what lines the 3rd Guards Tank Army reached.

On 1 November 1943 the commander of the 2nd Air Army assigned combat missions to his air formations on the basis of the plan for the combat employment of aviation and plans for cooperating with the 38th and 3rd Guards Tank armies.

Four concentrated strikes were planned throughout the first day:

> the first, from 0930 to 1040, with the forces of 295 planes (63 bombers, 140 *shturmoviks* and 92 fighters) against the enemy's centers of resistance and troops to a depth of up to seven kilometers from the forward edge of his defense;

> the second, from 1200 to 1300, with the forces of 266 planes (54 bombers, 130 *shturmoviks* and 82 fighters), with the same tasks;

> the third, from 1430 to 1530, with the forces of 253 planes (54 bombers, 120 *shturmoviks* and 79 fighters).

> As regards the fourth strike, only the operational time (1630 to 1700) was indicated and the number of aircraft (90 *shturmoviks*); the targets and operational areas were to be determined by an additional order.

The task of covering the group of forces on the Lyutezh bridgehead throughout the first day of the operation was assigned to the 5th Fighter Corps. One fighter regiment was left in the air army commander's reserve at the Semipolki airfield. A squadron of fighters was at this airfield to conduct reconnaissance of the battlefield.

Control of aviation during the first stage of the operation up to the beginning of the commitment of the tank army into the breach was based on the principle of centralizing it in the hands of the air army commander.

The air army commander's command post for controlling the aviation over the battlefield in the breakthrough sector was organized at the observation post of the commander of the 38th Army. The commander of the air army, the commanders of the assault air and fighter corps and officer-representatives from the 291st Assault Air and 202nd Bomber divisions were supposed to be here on the day of the breakthrough. Radio equipment for supporting their control of the aviation in the air and for calling it from the airfields was at the disposal of the air commanders. Wire communications with the air formations was carried out over the communications center of the air army's headquarters.

From the time of the commitment of the tank army into the breach, the commander of the 5th Assault Air Corps, along with his operational group and the necessary communications equipment, was to be located with the commander of the tank army.

The 2nd Air Army's basing remained unchanged.

The Troops' Combat Training

A great deal of work in assigning and studying the missions was carried out by the commanders of formations, units and subunits and their staffs, as well as the entire work of organizing troop cooperation, as a rule, on site. Playing out the course of combat activities according to plan was widely practiced. For example, on 30 October such a game was conducted with the 3rd Guards Tank army's command element down to brigade commander inclusively.

A great deal of training of the rank and file (taking into account the amount of time available) was carried out in the other combat arms. Exercises along the following themes were carried out with artillery commanders at all levels: "the control of corps (division) artillery in the offensive" with corps and division artillery commanders; "support of the rifle regiment in the attack" with commanders of artillery regiments; "the actions of a battalion (battery) in supporting a rifle battalion (company) in the attack" with the commanders of artillery battalions and batteries, and; "planning the artillery offensive" with the artillery staffs. The exercises were conducted together with the commanders of the rifle units and subunits and all missions and problems of cooperation were refined here. Exercises with junior officers, artillery scouts and gun crews were also conducted.

The Organization and Conduct of Intelligence

The *front's* October battles showed that the officer complement did not always know the enemy's group of forces and the condition of his forces. Thus in the days preceding the November operation measures were adopted to improve all aspects of the intelligence work and officer observation, particularly along the axis of the 38th Army's main attack.

The main task of the *front's* aviation during this period was aerial reconnaissance for the purpose of refining the enemy's defense, the distribution of his forces along the main defensive zone, and the location and movement of his operational reserves.

Aerial reconnaissance was conducted uninterruptedly during this period: during the day by the aircraft of the 2nd Air Army's reconnaissance regiment, which conducted an average of 9-10 sorties per day, as well as by the air corps' reconnaissance squadrons; at night by R-5[17] aircraft from the night bomber division.

---

17 Editor's note. The R-5 was a Soviet reconnaissance/bomber biplane, which first appeared in 1928. It carried a crew of two and had a maximum speed of 228 kilometers per hour. It was armed with two 7.62mm machine guns and could carry 250 kilograms of bombs.

FIRST UKRAINIAN FRONT'S NOVEMBER OFFENSIVE OPERATION

The reconnaissance regiment chiefly carried out operational reconnaissance, examining the most important axes and defensive lines opposite the *front's* right wing as far as the line Ovruch—Korosten'—Zhitomir—Berdichev—Vinnitsa—Uman', and in the center as far as the line Novograd-Volynskii—Shepetovka. Night reconnaissance was conducted in the Kiev area as far as the line Fastov—Belaya Tserkov'.

Engineer Support

A great deal of engineer preparation for conducting the operation was carried out, particularly a great deal of work in preparing the jumping-off position for the offensive, as well as for outfitting a broad network of observation and command posts. An observation post was prepared for the *front* commander on the right bank of the Dnepr in the area of Novo-Petrovtsy.

Measures were adopted to increase the supplies of anti-tank and anti-personnel mines among the troops, which were to be used during the operation for repulsing enemy counterattacks and consolidating captured lines. All of the troop sapper units were relieved of servicing the crossings over the Dnepr and prepared for operations with the troops upon the start of the operation. Aside from masking measures, which were carried out on the *front's* left wing for the purpose of concealing the troops' regrouping from the enemy, measures were also taken in the 13th Army's sector for creating a false troop concentration area. 200 dummy tanks and an equal number of dummy motor vehicles were set up east of Chernobyl' in the area between the Dnepr and Pripyat' rivers, for the purpose of creating an impression with the enemy of preparations for an offensive along the Chernobyl' axis. The area of the false concentration was made livelier by the movement of elements of the 129th Tank Brigade. The work of radio stations for imitating the headquarters of a tank corps in this area was unfolded. Officer reconnaissance of the banks of the Pripyat' River was conducted and the delivery of construction materials to the river bank was carried out, and false rumors concerning the preparation of an offensive along this axis were spread.

By the close of October bridges had been constructed over the Dnepr, which together with the ferry crossings, essentially satisfied the troops' needs. However, the Lyutezh bridgehead was, as before, poorly supplied with crossings and by the time of the 3rd Guards Tank Army's concentration near Svarom'ye it was necessary to remove part of the crossing equipment from the area of the Bukrin bend and move it to the 38th Army's sector The presence of crossings over the Dnepr by 1 November is shown in the following table.

Table 2.4 The First Ukrainian Front's Bridge Capacity

Types of Crossings	13th Army	60th Army	38th Army	40th Army	27th Army	Total
Bridges with a capacity of 60 tons	2	–	–	–	–	2
Bridges with a capacity of 30 tons	2	3	1	1	1	8
Bridges with a capacity of 16 tons	5	3	2	1	1	12
Bridges with a capacity of 6 tons	–	3	–	–	–	3
Bridges with a capacity of 3 tons	–	–	1	–	–	1
Ferries with a capacity of 60 tons	–	–	1	1	–	2
Ferries with a capacity of 50 tons	–	2	1	–	–	3
Ferries with a capacity of 30 tons	–	10	4	–	2	16
Ferries with a capacity of 16-18 tons	1	–	–	3	–	4
Ferries with a capacity of less than 16 tons	6	8	10	9	8	41
Landing Crossings	4	3	3	4	7	21

The Organization of Anti-Aircraft Defense

The *front* disposed of six anti-aircraft divisions, six independent anti-aircraft regiments and two independent anti-aircraft battalions. In all, these units disposed of 596 anti-aircraft guns. During the October fighting half of all the anti-aircraft artillery (23 regiments)covered the crossings and the troops' combat formations on the bridgeheads on the *front's* left wing (the Rzhishchev—Kanev sector) and 13 regiments were located north of Kiev; the remaining anti-aircraft artillery was covering airfields and the most important rear targets.

During the preparation for the November offensive the 21st Anti-Aircraft Division was transferred from the Bukrin bridgehead to the 38th Army. By 1 November the distribution of anti-aircraft units along the front was as follows: the 13th Army had the 10th Anti-Aircraft Artillery Division's 802nd and 975th anti-aircraft artillery regiments and the 1287th Army Anti-Aircraft Artillery Regiment, for a total of three regiments; the 60th Army had the 25th Anti-Aircraft Artillery Division, the 10th Anti-Aircraft Artillery Division's 984th Anti-Aircraft Regiment and the 217th Army Anti-Aircraft Artillery Regiment, for a total of six regiments; the 38th Army had the 8th and 21st anti-aircraft artillery divisions, the 10th Anti-Aircraft Artillery Division's 994th Anti-Aircraft Artillery Regiment, and the 1288th Army Anti-Aircraft Artillery Regiment, for a total of ten regiments; the 40th Army had the 9th Anti-Aircraft Artillery Division, for a total of four regiments; the 27th Army had the 23rd Anti-Aircraft Division, for a total of four regiments; and; the 3rd Guards Tank Army had the 1381st and 1394th army anti-aircraft artillery regiments, for a total of two regiments. Thus 62 percent of all the *front's* anti-aircraft artillery was supporting the offensive by the group of forces resolving the main task.

The *front's* fighter aviation's main task during 25 October-2 November was to cover the troops' regrouping and concentration. The fighters waged a very intensive struggle with the enemy air force, which was attempting to bomb our forces and crossings. The German air force was particularly active on 26, 28-29 October, carrying out 400-500 and more sorties per day. During this period the fighters carried out 90-160 sorties each day for the purpose of covering the troops and crossings.

The Organization of Communications and Troop Control

The preparation of an operation on the basis of a new operational idea and the regrouping of forces required a new organization of communications. In spite of the short deadlines, by the start of the operation the communications troops managed to secure reliable communications. A branched and smoothly working system of wire communications, which had been organized and improved throughout October, as well as the proximity of the *front* headquarters to the troops, enabled us to rapidly organized communications and troop control, proceeding from the new missions.

On 31 October 1943 a *front* auxiliary command post (VPU) was organized in the Lebedev Khutor area. Aside from this, the *front* commander ordered that an observation post be outfitted for him, from which it would be possible to view the battlefield along the axis of the 38th Army's main attack. Such an observation post was outfitted in the immediate vicinity of the observation post for the commander of the 38th Army, which was located in the Staro-Petrovtsy area, as well as the observation posts of the commander of the 51st Rifle Corps in Novo-Petrovtsy, and that of the commander of the 50th Rifle Corps in Yablonka.

The *front* headquarters disposed of the following communications units: one communications regiment, one radio battalion, three *front* and army communications battalions, two cable-pole companies, four telegraph construction companies, nine telegraph exploitation companies, one station-exploitation telegraph-telephone company, and one air regiment.

While organizing communications and planning to employ communications equipment during the operation, a great deal of attention was devoted to the securing of reliable radio communications. The *front* headquarters reinforced the headquarters of the 38th and 60th armies and the 1st Guards Cavalry Corps with its own equipment. One RLF-1, RSB-1 and RB-1 radio station apiece was allotted to the 38th Army, with one RAF-1 station for the 60th Army and one RSB-3 radio station for the 1st Guards Cavalry Corps. A reserve of radio stations was foreseen for carrying out special tasks by officers from the *front's* headquarters during their trips to the front line during the operation. As before, a shortage of radio stations and spare parts for them, radio lamps and plate supply was felt at the division-regiment-battalion level.

In planning communications, a significant place was reserved for the work of mobile communications equipment, particularly aircraft. The *front's* and armies' communications units experienced a significant shortage of mobile communications equipment and the existing vehicle park was worn out and needed repair.

Rear Organization and the Operation's Materiel Supply

On 28 October 1943 the *front's* military council confirmed a plan for organizing the rear and the troops' materiel supply for the forthcoming operation.

The armies' basing remained essentially as before, in accordance with the *front* rear directive of 11 October, with the exception of the 3rd Guards Tank Army, which from 28 October started to be based on the Nosovka—Kobyzhcha railroad sector, with the Novo-Bykovskaya branch line. The tank armies rear establishments moved by marching, while its supplies moved by railroad.

By 3 November the *front's* staging station—*front* regulating station No. 10—was created near Darnitsa station. A second regulating station (No. 9) remained in Bakhmach. The *front* was based on the same railroad sectors as in October.

The routes of the armies' supply remained as before, with the exception of the 38th and 3rd Guards Tank armies, whose supply routes from the supply stations reached the Desna River near Letki and Pukhovka and then reached the Lyutezh bridgehead over the crossings near Svarom'ye and Starosel'ye.

The *front* commander laid down a strict task for the supply troops and rear organs for accumulating ammunition and fuels and lubricants by the start of the operation. The enemy continued his local attacks along various sectors of the front until our forces' offensive and this led to a situation in which munitions were expended to repel the attacks that were being accumulated for the offensive. Throughout the 25 October-1 November period a strict limit of 0.2 combat loads was established for expending ammunition. It was also ordered not to call up High Command Reserve artillery fire without extreme need and to more broadly employ the fire from 45mm and 76mm regimental guns and 82mm mortars. The decision was made to accumulate no less than two combat loads of ammunition, 2-3 refills of fuels and lubricants and to create a 15-day constant supply of food and forage by the close of 1 November.

The *front's* hospital base exceeded by two times the anticipated losses in the operation according to the number of beds. However, there were difficulties with medical transport. For example, there was a shortage of horses of 15 percent in the medical subunits and units, while the shortage of medical auto transport exceeded 20 percent. Things were particularly bad in the 38th and 27th armies, where the shortage of medical motor vehicles reached 35-40 percent. During the operation's preparatory stage, the armies' and *front's* hospital bases were unloaded by evacuating the wounded into the interior of the country. Hospital bases were moved closer to the troops.

In October the *front's* railroad troops had essentially completed the restoration of the railroads along the left bank of the Dnepr. However, the railroads' capacity remained low; for example, it amounted to 7-8 pairs of trains per day along the Nezhin—Bobrovitsa sector. This was also influenced by disorganization in the work to unload transports, which were arriving at the army's supply stations. By 20 October 80 percent of the working boxcar park was in a loaded condition. Many transports sat around for several days. Due to this, it often happened that trains arriving with materiel supplies from the depths of the country were unable to arrive at the supply stations because the latter were filled up with unloaded trains. On 20 October seven trains—687 cars—had accumulated at the Bakhmach junction. It was the fault of the *front's* rear staff that one and the same transport was redirected two and even three times, particularly in that these redirections occurred after the trains were already broken up. This happened most often with transports of fuels and lubricants.

On 31 October the *front's* auto fuel reserves amounted to 1.5 refills, although there were only 0.5 refills immediately with the troops. The October plan for delivering transports with auto fuel was fulfilled only by 50 percent. The accumulation of a constant reserve of food and forage proceeded slowly.

The overall availability of an auto park at the disposal of the *front* and armies by the beginning of the operation was 3,389 various truck models with a carrying capacity of 6,140 tons. The condition of the roads in the last ten days of October was satisfactory and there was no precipitation, but auto transport worked very intensively, due to a shortage of vehicles.

The beginning of the operation was postponed by a day due to the slow accumulation of ammunition. By 30 November, thanks to the attention which the *front's* military council had been devoting to rear area problems and the intensive work of the rear service organs, the available materiel supplies made it possible to begin a decisive operation by the *front's* forces to capture Kiev. However, it was necessary to foresee due to the absence of sufficient reserves for developing the operation an extremely high level of intensity and organization would be required of the rear services during the course of the offensive.

The Organization of Party-Political Work During the Preparation for the Offensive

Due to the tight schedule for preparing the operation, the political organs were supposed to ensure the expansion of party-political work without the leading workers being separated from the troops. However, the armies' political sections—particularly the 38th Army—were unable to avoid frequent summonses of the political workers from their units. During the most intense days of preparing the operation, this army's political section would summon the chiefs of the corps and division political section chiefs and political workers from the units to meetings.

The conduct of party-political work was made more difficult due to the fact that the *front's* forces had been waging unsuccessful battles on the captured bridgeheads for more than a month. It was necessary to make it clear to the soldiers and officers that the command was organizing a new offensive operation with a decisive goal and to sow among the troops the sure confidence that the enemy would be defeated as a result of our attack.

As before, the main slogan around which all the work swirled, was the slogan to liberate as quickly as possible from the German aggressors Kiev, the capital of the Ukrainian Soviet Republic. The soldiers and officers of the *front's* forces, who were located along the sectors closest to Kiev, observed the destruction of Kiev by the German fascists. Fires could be seen and explosions heard from positions along the Lyutezh bridgehead and from the left bank of the Dnepr. The Germans were carrying out the methodical destruction of the city and were removing equipment from the few enterprises still working in Kiev, as well as material valuables in the city. Property was being stolen no matter where it was, whether in the buildings of state and social organizations or in citizens' apartments. A large number of the city's inhabitants were brought in to do defensive work and the mass resettlement of Kievans from the city was going on, as was the driving of part of them into German hard labor. Thus the agitation and propaganda, which inculcated hatred for

FIRST UKRAINIAN FRONT'S NOVEMBER OFFENSIVE OPERATION

the enemy, was of a specific type and was based upon fresh examples. The facts of the Germans' destruction of the city, the mockery and violence perpetrated against Soviet people in Kiev became common knowledge throughout all the *front's* forces.

During the preparatory period for the operation, the political organs and party organizations put a lot of effort into helping the unit and formation commanders prepare people for carrying out their combat assignment and to help the careful organizational and materiel preparation for the fighting. Everything was directed toward the fact that every soldier, sergeant and officer should firmly know his mission and find the best means of carrying it out. Alongside this specific work, the heroes of forcing the Dnepr and the experience of the first battles on the bridgeheads were popularized with each man individually.

On the eve of the offensive, a few hours before the start of the artillery preparation and attack, the troops were informed of the order by the *front's* military council about going over to a decisive offensive and the storming of Kiev. The order was signed by generals Vatutin and Khrushchev and was read aloud before the assembled troops in all subunits and units of the *front's* forces which were slated to attack on the morning of 3 November, after which short meetings took place. In these meetings were many emotional speeches by soldiers and officers calling on their comrades to carry out the order by the *front's* military council. This form addressing and calling upon the troops, such as the order before the battle, had been repeatedly tested in the Soviet army's history, and this time had very great significance for the operation's success.

The Correlation of Forces

By the start of the offensive the *front* had 47 rifle divisions, two rifle brigades, three cavalry divisions, 675 tanks and self-propelled guns, and 684 planes along an overall front of 324 kilometers. The enemy had 24 infantry divisions, two motorized divisions, 390-410 tanks, and 665 aircraft. Thus the *front's* forces had a two-fold superiority in rifle formations and more than 1 ½ in tanks; the number of aircraft was equal.

Table 2.5 The Correlation of Forces Along the First Ukrainian Front

	The Correlation of Forces in the *Front's* Sector by the Beginning of the Operation (An Overall Front of 324 Kilometers)						
	Number						
Forces	Rifle Divs, Rifle Bdes, Infantry Divs	Tank Corps, Panzer Divs	Mechanized Corps Motorized Divs	Cavalry Divs	Guns & Mortars (76mm and greater)	Tanks & Self-Propelled Guns (Assault guns)	Planes
Soviet	49	5	1	3	6,437	675	684
German	about 24	7	2	–	3,607	390-410	665
Correlation	2:1	0.7:1	1:2	–	1.8:1	1.7:1	1:1

A decisive superiority of forces had been created along the axis of the main attack through the bold regrouping of forces carried out according to the instructions of the Supreme High Command. For example, Soviet forces had a three-fold superiority in rifle formations, nine times in tanks and 4 ½ in artillery along the 38th Army's breakthrough sector. Along the 60th Army's main attack sector our superiority in rifle formations was almost threefold.

Table 2.6 The Correlation of Forces Along the 38th Army's Offensive Sector (Attack Front of 14 Kilometers)

Forces	Rifle Divs, Rifle Bdes, Infantry Divs	Tank Corps, Panzer Divs	Mechanized Corps Motorized Divs	Cavalry Divs	Guns & Mortars (76mm and greater)	Tanks & Self-Propelled Guns (Assault guns)
Soviet	12	3	1	3	167	550
German	about 4	2	1	–	37	60
Correlation	3:1	1.5:1	1:1	–	4.6:1	9.1:1

Note. The average number of tubes is indicated in the subheading guns and mortars (76mm and greater)

Table 2.7 The Correlation of Forces Along the 60th Army's Offensive Sector (Attack Front of 20 Kilometers)

Forces	Rifle Divs, Rifle Bdes, Infantry Divs	Tank Divs, Tank Bdes	Guns & Mortars (76mm and greater)	Tanks & Self-Propelled Guns (Assault guns)
Soviet	10	2	934	78
German	4	–	225	–
Correlation	2.5:1	–	4.1:1	–

Table 2.8 The Correlation of Forces Along the 40th and 27th Armies' Offensive Sector (Attack Front of 17 Kilometers)

Forces	Rifle Divs, Infantry Divs	Tank Corps, Panzer Divs Tank Bdes	Mechanized Corps Motorized Divs	Guns & Mortars (76mm and greater)	Tanks & Self-Propelled Guns (Assault guns)
Soviet	8	3	–	1,467	47
German	4	3	1	1,021	200-220
Correlation	2:1	1:1	–	1.4:1	1:4.5

The Course of Combat Activities During the Preparation of the Operation

During the regrouping of the forces and the preparation for the operation both sides carried out active reconnaissance all along the front. This was expressed in the conduct of combat reconnaissance, both night and day, by company and battalion-size detachments. Beginning on 31 October reinforced combat reconnaissance was waged in the 38th and 60th armies' offensive sector.

The Germans, in turn, acted extremely carefully throughout this period, sharply increased all kinds of intelligence, particularly reconnaissance in strength, while attempting to uncover the Soviet command's further intentions following the cessation of the offensive from the Bukrin bridgehead. The Germans' aerial reconnaissance yielded the Germans information regarding increased activity which had begun along the lateral roads along the left bank of the Dnepr. Following the first days of quiet in the Bukrin area, the German command was able to assume here the possible regrouping of Soviet forces, but the enemy was unable to uncover its meaning for several days. Thus from 25 October the Germans began to carry out increased reconnaissance in force along the entire front from Chernobyl' to Kanev. On 25 October powerful German reconnaissance groups crossed to the left bank of the Dnepr along the boundary between the 38th and 40th armies in the Kailov area along the 40th Army's left wing. Subsequently, up to 31 October, the enemy repeatedly threw reconnaissance detachments across the Dnepr in this area, as well as near Trukhanov Island, immediately opposite Kiev, which after a short fight crossed back to the right bank. On 26 October, during such a fight near Kailov, the Germans concentrated up to a regiment of infantry immediately near the river along the right bank. On 29 October they undertook an attack with the forces of an infantry division, supported by 60 tanks, along the boundary between the 40th and 27th armies, in the direction of Romashki, Khodorov and Bukrin. The fighting continued all day, but all of the enemy's attacks were successfully repulsed.

During this period the enemy attempted to encircle and destroy in the woods southwest of Kanev the 5th Guards Airborne Brigade, which had been disrupting the normal work of the German rear. However, the brigade, which had withstood heavy fighting with the Germans for two days, broke out of encirclement and continued its diversions in the enemy's rear.

Conclusions on the Regrouping of Forces and the Planning and Preparation of the Operation

The First Ukrainian Front's November offensive operation was organized according to direct instructions from the Supreme High Command and on the basis of a new operational idea, which was indicated to the *front* by the *Stavka*. The *Stavka* demanded the creation of a decisive superiority of forces along a narrow breakthrough sector. The enemy did not have operational reserves along the Kiev axis, thus the task consisted of crushing the enemy's defense through a decisive attack along a narrow front and defeating his group of forces in the Kiev area before he could manage to bring up forces from Western Europe or remove them from other sectors of the Soviet-German front.

Operational surprise could not be achieved through the shift of the main attack from the Bukrin bridgehead to the Lyutezh bridgehead alone, because the *front's* forces conducted an offensive north of Kiev in October. However, during the course of the October fighting the enemy became convinced that the Soviet forces did not have a sufficient superiority along this sector and thus the hidden concentration of forces and the launching of a powerful attack represented a form of operational surprise. The element of surprise was significantly increased by the rapid preparation of the operation and the designation of the start of the operation along the main axis as early as 3 November. For example, by the start of the operation the enemy had determined that the 3rd Guards Tank Army was still along the left bank of the Dnepr, while at this time it was actually already on the bridgehead in readiness to being the offensive. The creation of a false area for concentrating forces in the 13th Army's sector did not have the required effect due to the insufficient scope of the work carried out.

The main goal of the operation during its first stage was the defeat of the enemy's Kiev group of forces and the liberation of Kiev. The Lyutezh bridgehead, from which the *front's* main attack was to be launched, hung over Kiev from the north. The axis of the attack by the *front's* main shock group—the 38th and 3rd Guards Tank armies and the 1st Guards Cavalry Corps—was planned not to the west, but due south, to outflank Kiev from the west.

The successful realization of this maneuver was supposed to create a hopeless situation for the Germans' Kiev group of forces and also lead to the "rolling up" of the enemy's defense along the entire right bank of the Dnepr to the south.

Such a task was entrusted to the 60th Army. Having no fewer forces than the 38th Army, but more weakly supported by artillery and tanks, the 60th Army was also supposed to try and break through the enemy's front with an attack to the south and during the operation's first stage attack between the Irpen' and Zdvizh rivers and reach the Kiev—Korosten' railroad, thus securing the Kiev axis against any enemy attempts to launch a counterblow from the west. Besides this, the 38th Army, having a deep formation for its rifle corps (the 21st and 23rd rifle corps were in the second echelon), could in the operation's first days deploy the corps from the second echelon to the southwest and west. Thus the operational plan called for the reliable securing of the main shock group's activities by the 60th Army's activities and those of the 38th Army's second echelon.

However, the cooperation between the 38th and 60th armies noted above guaranteed against an enemy counterblow toward Kiev only during the operation's first days. The further the operation developed the more realistic would become the threat of the Germans' counterblow. Upon capturing Kiev, it would be necessary to exclude any possibility of a successful counteroffensive by the Germans on Kiev, upon which all of the First Ukrainian Front's activities would rely. Although the southwestern axis (Kazatin and Zhmerinka) was the most favorable for the *front's* operations, because it would radically change the entire operational and even strategic situation on the Ukrainian right bank, nevertheless one could not forget about the western axis toward Zhitomir and Novograd-Volynskii. The interests of the operational securing of the *front's* activities to the southwest demanded this.

This task, following the capture of Kiev, was to be decided by the development of the offensive by the 38th Army's right wing toward Zhitomir, the 60th Army toward Korosten', and the 13th Army toward Ovruch. An offensive along all these axes, especially along the Zhitomir and Korosten' axes, was the correct and necessary solution. However, one should note that the *front* dispersed its right-wing forces along a too broad sector, while it was planned to employ the 60th and 13th armies for operations in the wooded areas of the southern Poles'ye, where the presence of large enemy forces or the subsequent concentration of such forces for a counterblow was unlikely. At the same time, the 38th Army would find itself immediately after the capture of Kiev in a very difficult situation, because its forces would be scattered along two entirely independent and non-supporting operational axes: the southern (Fastov and Belaya Tserkov') and western (Zhitomir). This would result both in the sharp reduction in the density of the army's combat formations and in the creation of great difficulties in organizing the control of the army's forces. As a result of the decision adopted, the *front's* main axis would receive the smaller number of forces during the operation's second stage.

An analysis of the possible development of events following the liberation of Kiev dictated the dispatch of the 60th and 13th armies' main forces to the south, with the employment of only part of the forces for an offensive along the Korosten' and Ovruch axes.

The planned offensive pace was realistic and fully corresponded to the situation and the objectives of the *front's* forces.

In planning the operation, the *front* command correctly employed all combat arms for the achievement of a single objective. The tank army and cavalry corps were to be committed into the breach on the operation's second day and develop the success following the breakthrough of the entire tactical depth of the enemy's defense north of Kiev, and then, while bypassing Kiev, vigorously attack to the south and southwest. This fully corresponded to the situation. It was clear that the enemy would not consent to the loss of Kiev without a fight and would put all of his efforts into the most rapid organization of a powerful counterblow. Because the Germans did not dispose of free operational reserves in the Kiev area, they would have to be transferred by railroad. Thus the vigorous development of the offensive by the tanks and cavalry and the rapid capture of such important railroad junctions as Fastov, Kazatin and Zhitomir would worsen the conditions for the enemy's railroad maneuver and would force him to significantly remove the areas for the concentration of his reserves to the south and southwest.

The employment of aviation and particularly of the artillery was also correct. For the first time during the Great Patriotic War an enormous density of artillery was created along the breakthrough sector—more than 300 tubes per kilometer of front. This guaranteed the secure suppression and destruction of the enemy's forces and entire fire system immediately to a great depth and would enable us to reduce the time for the artillery preparation.

It is necessary to point out that the materiel supplies secured combat actions only through the first two days of the operation. This particularly concerned fuel and ammunition. The rear organs were to keep in mind this serious shortage and put forward the maximum energy and organizational skills for the uninterrupted supply of the troops during the course of the operation's development. Otherwise, the threat might arise of the offensive's dying out following the first successes.

The Breakthrough of the German Defense North of Kiev and the Liberation of Kiev (3-6 November). The Fighting Along the *Front's* Left Wing on the Bukrin Bridgehead

As was pointed out earlier, the beginning of the offensive north of Kiev was moved from 2 to 3 November by a decision of the *front* commander, due to the overall lack of readiness of the troops and especially the slow delivery and accumulation of ammunition. It was decided to begin the offensive from the Bukrin bridgehead on 1 November. The beginning of the offensive along the secondary axis two days before the main attack pursued the goal of tying down major enemy forces, particularly his panzer divisions, and to prevent him from employing them for countering the *front's* main shock group in the Kiev area.

The 40th and 27th Armies' Combat Activities on the Bukrin and Shchuchinka Bridgeheads During 1-6 November

The fighting on 1 November. At 1000 on 1 November the 40th and 27th armies' artillery and the 2nd Air Army's planes began their artillery and aviation preparation. At 1040 the infantry and infantry-support tanks went over to the attack. Intensive fighting went on for the entire day. The enemy put up powerful fire resistance and repeatedly counterattacked with his tactical reserves (six counterattacks in one or two-battalion strength, with 18-20 tanks apiece). As a result of the day's fighting, both armies failed to carry out their assignments for the day and were only able to advance 0.2-1.5 kilometers along individual sectors. The 40th Army's 52nd Rifle Corps, which was attacking from the Shchuchinka bridgehead, captured the first and, in places, the second line of enemy trenches. The 40th Army's 47th Rifle Corps, which was attacking from the Bukrin bridgehead, occupied the inhabited locale of Kanada. Units of the 27th Army broke into the Germans' first trench along individual sectors.

On 1 November the 2nd Air Army's planes began combat operations upon the start of the artillery preparation and continued them throughout the entire day, but as a result of the unfavorable weather their activity was limited. Combat sorties were conducted only by the best single crews and in groups of 4-6 planes. 311 sorties were carried out during the day, of which 210 were by *shturmoviks* and bombers, 89 by fighters covering the *shturmoviks*, and 12 for reconnaissance. The *shturmoviks* launched strikes against the enemy artillery in its firing positions and the bombers against the railroad stations of Fastov, Polyanichentsy, Ustinovka, Gai, Karapyshi, and Mironovka and against automobile columns along the Vintsetovka—Belaya Tserkov' road. On the night of 31 October-1 November our aviation did not work due to the bad weather. The enemy's fighters only sometimes made weak attempts in individual pairs to counter the Soviet aviation. The Germans' anti-aircraft artillery actively fought against our aviation.

Throughout the first day of fighting 30 men were captured. During interrogation the prisoners basically confirmed the same enemy group of forces that had been on the eve of the offensive. Troop observation and aerial reconnaissance unearthed more than 170 enemy tanks, which were concentrated in different places opposite the Bukrin bridgehead.

The 5th Guards Airborne Brigade was actively operating in the enemy rear. On 1 November it destroyed two enemy radio stations, five motor vehicles with ammunition, 50 soldiers, and captured 25 prisoners.

The *front* commander ordered both armies to consolidate the success achieved along individual sectors and to continue the offensive with specially allotted detachments to seize individual locales in order to improve their situation during the night of 1-2 November. It was ordered to begin the reconnaissance detachments' activities on the morning of 2 November and to renew the offensive by the main forces at 1000.

The fighting on 2 November. At 1030 on 2 November, following a fire onslaught, both armies attacked. Just as was the case on the first day, the enemy put up powerful fire resistance. The enemy's counterattacks became even fiercer. Five enemy counterattacks were repulsed in the 40th Army's offensive sector and eight in the 27th Army's sector, each in strength up to an infantry battalion, supported by tanks. As a result, the forces of both armies again failed to achieve a success in a day of fighting and by evening were fighting along their previous positions.

Our aviation did not work throughout the first half of 2 November, because of the bad weather. With the improvement in the weather during 1400-1700 the 2nd Air Army's *shturmoviks*, in groups of 15-18 planes and covered by fighters, supported the attacking troops and launched strikes against the combat formations of the enemy's infantry and his guns. In all, 102 *shturmovik* sorties were carried out and 128 fighter sorties.

In the evening the *front* commander ordered both armies to continue operations at night with individual detachments, and at 1000 on 3 November to renew the offensive with all forces.

The fighting on 3 November. At 1030 on 3 November, following an artillery onslaught against the enemy's combat formations, both armies again attacked, but as before, had no success and by the close of the day remained in their previous lines. On this day six enemy counterattacks were repulsed in the 40th Army's sector in up to a battalion in strength and supported by 3-5 tanks apiece, as well as eight counterattacks in the 27th Army's sector.

During the course of the 2-3 November fighting the enemy along the Khodorov—Romashki sector committed into the fighting the *Das Reich* SS Panzer Division, which had been pulled into the reserve on the eve of the offensive, and also reinforced his forces operating opposite the Bukrin bridgehead with an infantry division from the 168th Infantry Division and the 223rd Infantry Division, which had been transferred from a passive sector of the front southeast of Cherkassy.

The fighting on 4 November. Following a short fire onslaught, the armies once again attacked at 1300 on 4 November. Having encountered the enemy's powerful fire resistance and counterattacks, the troops once again remained along their previous lines.

The fighting on 5 November. On 5 November the armies waged battle with reinforced detachments along individual sectors in order to improve their positions. On this day the *front* commander issued an order to transfer the 38th and 337th rifle divisions from the 40th and 27th armies to the 38th Army. However, the withdrawal of these divisions from the bridgehead was delayed for a time due to the 40th and 27th armies receiving new combat assignments on 6 November. With the development of the success in the Kiev area, the *front* commander ordered the 40th and 27th armies to renew a decisive offensive on the morning of 6 November and to break through the enemy's defense.

The fighting on 6 November. At 1200 on 6 November the armies attacked, but once again had no success. On this day the enemy began to remove the *Das Reich* SS Panzer Division from its ranks and to concentrate it in the area of the village of Kagarlyk. The full complement of the 168th Infantry Division continued to operate opposite the Bukrin bridgehead.

After this, as a result of the unsuccessful fighting of 1-2 November, it became clear that the 40th and 27th armies' offensive would not yield any kind of significant success, because there remained insufficient means in these armies for subsequent active operations, the *front* commander decided, without ceasing the attempts to attack from the Bukrin bridgehead, to create the impression with the enemy that the Soviet group of forces in this area was being reinforced by means of new transfers to the Bukrin bridgehead. In accordance with instructions from the *front* commander, the headquarters of the 40th and 27th armies drew up plans for measures which called for creating false troop concentration areas along both banks of the Dnepr and on the bridgehead during 3-5 November.

The 27th Army headquarters drew up a plan for these measures comparatively quickly, all the way to moving troops over the roads, artillery registration and the troops' active reconnaissance. On the other hand, the 40th Army's headquarters treated this matter formally and limited itself to only one measure—the emplacement of dummy tanks. The idea of demonstrating a concentration of tanks on the Bukrin bridgehead on 3-5 November was correct. However, this time it was carried out without the necessary breadth and scope and consideration of the necessary details required in these cases.

Combat Operations North of Kiev

The fighting on 3 November. At 0800 on 3 November the forces of the 60th and 38th armies began an artillery preparation. At 0840 the infantry and direct infantry-support tanks attacked. Despite the enemy's fierce fire resistance and his savage counterattacks, both armies' forces broke through the enemy's defense and advanced 5-12 kilometers.

The 60th Army, along the sectors of the 17th and 18th guards rifle corps, was engaged in local fighting to improve its positions. The army's 77th Rifle Corps broke through the enemy's defense along a 3-kilometer front and occupied the inhabited locale of Sychevka and advanced four kilometers to the west. The 24th and 30th rifle corps, which launched the main attack, broke through the enemy's defense along an 18-kilometer front and occupied the inhabited locales of Fedorovka, Rovy, Rostesno, and Glebovka and by the close of the day, were engaged in fighting near the northern outskirts of Dymer. During the second half of the day the 30th Rifle Corps committed its second echelon—the 141st Rifle Division—into the fighting.

The 38th Army broke through the enemy's defense along the sector of the 50th Rifle Corps and the right flank of the 51st Rifle Corps, along a 10-kilometer front. Upon advancing seven kilometers, the army's formations captured the village of Dachi Pushcha-Voditsa. In the center and along the 51st Rifle Corps' left flank, particularly in the Vyshgorod area, the enemy was putting up stubborn resistance and holding our units' attack. Thus the army's formations broke through only the enemy's first defensive position along a narrow front and were involved in fighting along the second position in the area of Dachi Pushcha-Voditsa.

The attack's artillery preparation in both armies (particularly in the 38th) along the axes of the main attack was extremely powerful and effective. During the first hours following the artillery preparation, only individual enemy guns and mortars were firing. The attacking infantry covered the first two kilometers without encountering particular resistance. The Germans' organized artillery fire began only during the second half of the day.

Due to the heavily wooded terrain in the area, operations throughout the entire day in both armies' sectors primarily took the shape of forest fighting. This complicated the offensive to a significant degree. For example, in the woods near Fedorovka and Rostesno the enemy placed snipers with automatic rifles in the trees, who held up our infantry's advance. Batteries of small-caliber anti-aircraft artillery, anti-tank guns and anti-aircraft machine guns were employed to comb through the woods.

The shifting of fire positions took place simultaneously by one-third of all the artillery. In the 60th Army part of the artillery began to switch its firing points immediately following the artillery preparation and moved up to the areas of the artillery observation posts. These batteries helped a great deal in resolving fire tasks which arose with the beginning of the infantry attack.

The 7th Breakthrough Artillery Corps accompanied the infantry with wheeled transport in only two composite brigades (one per rifle corps). The composite brigades were composed of battalions and regiments with guns of various calibers. One composite brigade consisted of two battalions of 152mm howitzers, two battalions of 122mm howitzers, a battalion of 203mm howitzers, and a regiment of 120mm mortars. The other brigade included two battalions of 152mm howitzers, a regiment of 122mm howitzers, a regiment of 76mm guns, and a regiment of 120mm mortars. The allotment of such improvised brigades was brought about by the necessity of having various artillery calibers for accompanying the infantry and tanks and the lack of towing equipment in the artillery corps. The main mass of the artillery supported the infantry attack from the main firing positions. As a typical example, one should note the concentration of the entire artillery corps' fire against single areas. Such a concentration of fire was carried out twice against enemy centers of resistance during our infantry's fighting in the depth of the defense. In the first case, the fire was concentrated against the southern outskirts of Dachi Pushcha-Voditsa, and in the second against height 153.8, southeast of Dachi Pushcha-Voditsa. The enemy's resistance in these areas was quickly crushed as the result of powerful fire strikes.

On the first day of the offensive the 60th and 38th armies repulsed five enemy infantry and tank counterattacks along various axes, which he undertook with the forces of his tactical reserves. As a result of the day's fighting, the enemy suffered heavy losses, a large amount of combat equipment and 550 men were captured, among which were several officers. Interrogation of the prisoners and a study of captured documents confirmed the enemy's previous grouping in this area.

On the offensive's first day the enemy began to hurriedly bring up to the breakthrough area his reserves and units that had been removed from other sectors. The *front's* aerial reconnaissance discovered the movement of columns of tanks and motor vehicles (in all, 215 tanks and assault guns and up to 400 motor vehicles) from south to north from the areas of Belaya Tserkov' and Korsun'-Shevchenkovskii. On the offensive's first day the enemy committed into the fighting in the 38th Army's sector units of the 20th Motorized Division and brought up the 8th Panzer Division to the Dymer area.

On the operation's first day the 2nd Air Army operated intensively. Light night bombers carried out 207 sorties preceding the offensive on the Lyutezh bridgehead on the night of 2-3 November, for the purpose of destroying the enemy's forces in the Goryanka and Dachi Pushcha-Voditsa areas. Due to the thick morning fog, which covered the area east of the Dnepr, where our airfields were located, the *front's* aviation was not engaged in combat before 1000. The first fighter sorties for covering the troops began at 1020 and the assault aircrafts' activities at 1040. Subsequently, the activities of the *front's* aviation were quite intense throughout the entire day. 938 sorties were carried out during the day, of which assault aircraft and bombers carried out 545 and the fighters carried out 174 sorties for troop cover and 212 sorties for assault air and bomber escort, while the remaining sorties were for reconnaissance purposes.

The *shturmoviks* operated in groups of 6-22 planes and the bombers in groups of 14-24 planes. The groups' sorties were conducted at 5-10 minute intervals. In all, 26 groups of *shturmoviks* and five groups of bombers operated. The strike by the aviation's first echelon was carried out between 1100 and 1230, the second between 1350 and 1440, and the third between 1550 and 1700. 171 *shturmoviks*, covered by 66 fighters, operated in the first echelon, 151 *shturmoviks*, 58 bombers and 59 fighters in the second, and 133 *shturmoviks*, 32 bombers and 48 fighters in the third. The strikes were launched both against the enemy's infantry in his combat formations and on the march, against artillery in its firing positions, and against tanks in the areas of the villages of Goryanka, Dachi Pushcha-Voditsa and Priorka.

Following the appearance of the first echelon of *shturmoviks* and fighters over the battlefield, the enemy sharply increased the number of his fighters in the breakthrough sector. The fighters accompanying our *shturmoviks* and bombers were repeatedly drawn into air battles.

Throughout the day the enemy's bomber aviation bombed our units on the Lyutezh bridgehead in groups of 3-37 planes. During the day 287 overflights by all types of enemy aviation were noted. On this day the 2nd Air Army's fighters were covering the ground forces on the Lyutezh bridgehead. 2-3 groups of 8-10 planes apiece were simultaneously over the patrol area. The patrolling was uninterrupted from 1020 to 1745.

Throughout the day the troop-cover fighters and fighters for accompanying *shturmoviks* and bombers carried out 36 air battles, in which 31 enemy aircraft—13 bombers, 16 fighters and two reconnaissance planes—were shot down.

The 60th and 38th armies did not carry out their assignments fully. This created the danger of the operation becoming prolonged. The presence of the enemy's 7th and 8th panzer and 20th Motorized divisions in the immediate reserve meant that the fighting along the approaches to Kiev might become extremely bitter and that the 38th Army's infantry, which was poorly supported by infantry-support tanks, would encounter great difficulties. Throughout the day the *front* commander insistently demanded that the 60th Army increase the pace of its attack and carry out its assignment for the day at any cost. The success of the 38th Army's operations along the Kiev axis depended to a great extent on this army's success.

The control of the battle at the corps-division level was insufficiently precise on the first day of the operation, particularly due to the unreliable work of communications. For example, upon the start of the attack, following the first shift of the command and observation posts, wire communications from the regiment to the corps were not restored during the first 24 hours.

The *Stavka* of the Supreme High Command attached great significance to the operation in the Kiev area. On its first day a telegram (coded telegram No. 125485) was dispatched to the *front* commander, in which the *Stavka* ordered that the operation, which had begun along the *front's* right wing, not be drawn out, as each additional day would be of advantage only to the enemy, enabling him to concentrate his forces here and take advantage of the good roads, while the roads destroyed by the Germans in our lines made maneuver difficult and constrained. The *Stavka* demanded the cutting of the Kiev—Korosten' railroad east or west of the Irpen' River no later than 5 November, depending on the situation, and that Kiev be taken no later than 5-6 November. The *Stavka* pointed out that the Kiev bridgehead was the most important and favorable of the bridgeheads along the right bank of the Dnepr River and that it had great significance for expelling the Germans from the Ukrainian right bank.

At dawn on 4 November the *front* commander refined the tasks of the shock group's armies.

The 60th Army was assigned the following task: to continue a vigorous attack on the morning of 4 November, to commit the 3rd Guards Airborne Division into the fighting, and by the close of the day reach the front Manuil'sk—Osikovo—Vladimirovka—Rudnya Dymerskaya—Katyuzhanka—Nikol'skii—Tarasovshchina—Sinyak; by the close of 5 November the army's formations were to reach the front Katyuzhanka—Filippovichi—excluding Novaya Greblya—Dachi Klavdievo—Dachi Kicheeva—Irpen'.

The 38th Army was order to do the following: to operationally subordinate the 3rd Guards Tank Army's 6th Guards Tank Corps, and to commit the 23rd Rifle Corps, along with the 39th Tank Regiment and 6th Guards Tank Corps, into the fighting, employing the latter for supporting the 50th Rifle Corps' infantry. By the close of 4 November the 50th Rifle Corps' formations were to reach the front Mostishche—Shevchenko—Bobritsa—Malyutyanka—Yankovichi. At the same time, the 51st Rifle Corps' formations were to liberate Kiev and reach the front Yankovichi—Khodosovka—excluding Kazachii Island by the close of 5 November.

The 3rd Guards Tank Army received orders to reach the area Boyarka—Budaevka—Veta Pochtovaya—Khotov—Zhulyany by the close of 4 November and the area Plesetskoye—Vasil'kov—Glevakha by the close of 5 November. The 6th Guards Tank Corps was to be returned to the army on 5 November.

On 4 November the *front* commander dispatched a telegram directly to the 3rd Guards Tank Army's corps commanders and the commander of the 5th Guards Tank Corps, with an evaluation of the overall situation in the Kiev areas as of 4 November. Among other things, the telegram contained the following instructions:

> The successful accomplishment of the mission depends, in the first instance, on the vigor, boldness and decisiveness of your actions. Your mission is to carry out your assigned tasks as rapidly as possible, so that, without fearing to break free of the infantry, to vigorously advance, boldly destroy individual enemy pockets of resistance, and to spread panic within the enemy's forces. They are to be vigorously pursued so that by the morning of 5.11.1943 we take Kiev. The commanders at all levels should be with their units and personally lead them to carry out their mission.

The fighting on 4 November. On this day the 60th and 38th armies renewed the offensive. The 60th Army began the fighting with the 77th Rifle Corps' left-flank units and along the entire front of the 24th and 30th rifle corps. By the close of the day the army had advanced 2-6 kilometers, captured the villages of Manuil'sk, Alekseevka, Dymer, and Kozarovichi. The enemy, having brought up new forces, often counterattacked. During the second half of the day the 60th Army repulsed the enemy's numerous attempts to restore the situation in the Dymer area. The Germans' 8th Panzer Division took part in the counterattacks along this axis, along with five battalions of infantry.

The 38th Army renewed the offensive at 1000 on 4 November. Elements of the Germans' 7th Panzer Division appeared along its sector. Throughout the day the army's formations, having repulsed four enemy counterattacks, advanced five kilometers, captured the inhabited locales of Berkovets and Vyshgorod and reached the outskirts of Priorka (a suburb of Kiev). The 60th Army's success in the Dymer and Kozarovichi area enabled the commander of the 38th Army to remove the 340th Rifle Division from the army's right flank and dispatch it to the Dachi Pushcha-Voditsa area, in order to reinforce the shock group. Only a screen was left in the division's sector.

On this day the enemy launched his most powerful counterattacks in the 38th Army's sector in the southern part of Dachi Pushcha-Voditsa. Here he managed in the beginning to capture the area of the children's sanitarium, where the 5th Guards Tank Corps' 20th Guards Tank Brigade and a regiment from the 136th Rifle Division were fighting in conditions of semi-encirclement.

Due to the enemy's powerful resistance, on this day the commander of the 38th Army committed the entire strength of the 5th Guards Tank Corps into the fighting.

At 1030 the 3rd Guards Tank Army began to move up to its jumping-off position for commitment into the breach. The army's combat formation was organized in the following manner. The 9th Mechanized Corps was attacking in the army's first echelon, with the task of, upon overtaking the infantry, to capture the Shevchenko—Korytishchi, Dal'nii Yar area by the close of the day. The 6th Guards Tank Corps, having detached the 52nd and 53rd guards tank brigades to the commanders of the 167th and 136th rifle divisions for operating with the infantry as direct infantry-support tanks, while the remaining forces were to also attack in the army's first echelon with the task of overtaking the infantry and by the close of the day capturing the Zabor'ye—Malyutyanka—Boyarka-Budaevka area. The 7th Guards Tank Corps, which was to capture by the end of the day the villages of Glevakha, Markhalevka and Veta Pochtovaya, was to attack behind it. The 1st Guards Cavalry Corps received orders to capture the Yurova area along the Zhitomir paved road by the close of the day (eight kilometers southwest of Makarov), which would radically alter its initial task—of attacking along the right bank of the Irpen' River toward Fastov. The mission assigned to the tank army was not carried out. The 6th and 7th guards tank corps were drawn into the fighting and were completing the breakthrough of the enemy's defense along with the infantry.

FIRST UKRAINIAN FRONT'S NOVEMBER OFFENSIVE OPERATION

At first, only the 6th Guards Tank Corps, the tanks of which were operating within the 167th and 137th rifle divisions' infantry's ranks, took part in the fighting. The 7th Guards Tank Corps overtook its combat formations and captured Berkovets at 1330. By 2300 on 4 November individual elements of the 7th Guards Tank Corps reached the northern outskirts of Svyatoshino and the Kiev—Zhitomir paved road, where it fought the entire night against the enemy. During the second half of the day on 4 November the 1st Guards Cavalry Corps completed its crossing over the Dnepr and was concentrating in the woods east of Rakovka. Due to the bad weather, the *front's* aviation continued flying only in single aircraft.

The *front's* attacking soldiers and officers saw in Kiev the glow from fires. Inspired by the desire to tear the capital of Soviet Ukraine from the hands of the fascist aggressors and to prevent the enemy from destroying the city, the *front's* forces carried out offensive battles uninterruptedly during the night of 4-5 November, throughout the entire day of 5 November, and into the night of 5-6 November.

The enemy was falling back to the west and southwest, stubbornly clinging to each favorable line. The *front's* aerial reconnaissance reported a stream of vehicles from Kiev heading west and southwest. The enemy counterattacked along several sectors in up to an infantry regiment in strength, supported by several tens of tanks.

The operational plan called for the forcing of the Dnepr south of Kiev with the forces of a single rifle division. At 2046 on 2 November, the *Stavka* representative, Marshal G.K. Zhukov, recommended in a telegraph message to the *front* commander, that due to the failure of the 40th and 27th armies and the 38th Army's success, to remove two divisions from the 40th and 27th armies and cross over to the right bank of the Dnepr south of Kiev not one, but three divisions, thus assisting the 38th Army to more rapidly capture Kiev.

As a result of the operation's first day, the forces of the 60th, 38th and 3rd Guards Tank armies failed to carry out their missions. As a result of the enemy's committing reserves into the battle, the fighting became extremely bitter. One of the chief reasons for the 38th Army's slow advance was the circumstance that the army commander, upon encountering the enemy's powerful resistance, poorly augmented the attack, although he had two rifle corps in his second echelon. On 4 November the *front* commander demanded the commitment of the 23rd Rifle Corps into the battle. However, the corps was moving up from the second echelon, deployed very slowly and essentially took no part in the fighting that day.

The fighting on 5 November. On the morning of 5 November the enemy's withdrawal from Kiev to the southwest became completely clear. Columns of up to 1,000 motor vehicles, guns and tanks were moving from Kiev to Vasil'kov. The movement of enemy columns from the area of Boyarka-Budaevka to the southwest was noted. Simultaneously, the enemy began to remove forces from the area of the Bukrin bridgehead, taking advantage of the fact that the Soviet forces' offensive there had not been developed, and to shift them to the Kiev area.

During the day's fighting on 5 November the 60th Army advanced 20 kilometers along its left wing and occupied 17 inhabited locales, including Katyuzhanka, Tarasovshchina, Sinyak, Lubyanka, and Ozery. The 24th Rifle Corps was fighting along its right flank with the forces of the 248th Rifle Brigade without particular success, but advanced significantly along its left flank. The 30th Rifle Corps' offensive was developing successfully. The 17th and 18th rifle corps along the army's right wing were not engaged in active operations. During the night of 5-6 November the 70th Guards Rifle Division was removed from the 17th Guards Rifle Corps' combat formations, by expanding the neighboring division's combat formations, in order to strengthen the army's left wing. The 77th Rifle Corps' 280th and 143rd rifle divisions were not engaged in fighting, while the 132nd Rifle Division was engaged in unsuccessful fighting to the west of Manuil'sk. The enemy opposite the 60th Army's right flank removed the remnants of the 339th, 183rd and 217th infantry divisions from its combat formations in order to bring them up to strength.

Throughout 5 November the 38th Army was fighting in the central blocks of Kiev and southwest of the city. During the day the army's forces advanced 25 kilometers. By the close of the day the 23rd Rifle Corps, which had been committed into the fighting from the army's second echelon, had its 74th Rifle Division along the northeastern outskirts of Bucha; two of the corps' divisions (30th and 23rd rifle) were approaching the Irpen' River with the task of forcing it and developing the subsequent success to the west. The 50th Rifle Corps reached the line Zhulyany—Nikol'skaya-Borshchagovka—the western outskirts of Kiev. One of the corps' divisions (167th), along with the 51st Rifle Corps, was fighting in the center of Kiev. All of the 51st Rifle Corps' formations, including the Czechoslovak 1st Brigade, which had been committed into the fighting that day, were fighting in the city itself. The 21st Rifle Corps, while remaining in the army's second echelon, was moving from the Vyshgorod to the south. The 71st Division's 367th Rifle Regiment and an army screening detachment crossed from Kazachii Island to the right bank of the Dnepr south of Kiev and they were now fighting along the eastern outskirts of the village of Vita Litovskaya.

On 5 November the 3rd Guards Tank Army was fighting to destroy the enemy's strong points in the area of Belichi and Svyatoshino. By the close of the day its main forces had been concentrated in these locales, while the forward units were south of the paved road along the line Shevchenko—Zhulyany. As an example of a characteristic episode, it is necessary to note the 7th Guards Tank Corps' night attack in the Svyatoshino area with the attacking tanks' headlights turned on.

The 1st Guards Cavalry Corps had the mission of attacking in the direction of Rakovka and Yurov (eight kilometers southwest of the village of Makarov). Taking advantage of the 60th Army's success, the corps attacked on 5 November. By the close of the day the 1st and 7th guards cavalry divisions were fighting in the Rakovka area and to the south. The 2nd Guards Cavalry Division remained in the corps' second echelon along the eastern bank of the Irpen' River.

During the night of 4-5 November the aviation was not engaged in combat due to the bad weather.

The 2nd Air Army was assigned the following objectives for 5 November in order to support the offensive by the 38th Army and the 3rd Guards Tank Army, which had been committed into the breach that morning.

- to destroy the enemy's personnel and firepower along the immediate approaches to Kiev;
- to destroy the enemy's automobile columns moving along the roads from Kiev to Fastov and Vasil'kov;
- to destroy trains at their stations and stages west of Kiev.

The weather on 5 November proved to be not quite favorable for air operations. It allowed for *shturmovik* activities, but constrained to a significant degree the activities of the bombers, which could operate only singly or in flights.

The first strike against the enemy along the northern and northwestern outskirts of Kiev for the purpose of supporting the 38th Army was launched by *shturmoviks*, from 0920 to 1000. 139 Il-2 aircraft took off to carry out the assignment, flying in nine groups, each of which consisted of six to 22 planes. The *shturmoviks* were to launch preemptive strikes southwest and south of Kiev for the purpose of suppressing the enemy along the path of the 3rd Guards Tank Army's corps' movements. 34 groups of *shturmoviks* took off during the day and 444 sorties were carried out during the day. Throughout the entire day the *shturmoviks*, operating in echelon formation, launched strikes against the enemy ahead of the attacking troops.

The bombers performed only 26 sorties, while operating against German automobile columns along the Kiev—Zhitomir and Kiev—Plesetskoye and Kiev—Vasil'kov roads and against the enemy's trains. Our fighter aviation covered the troops operating in the Kiev area.

FIRST UKRAINIAN FRONT'S NOVEMBER OFFENSIVE OPERATION 117

The enemy's aviation was not active, which was due to its rebasing to rear airfields. Only single reconnaissance planes and pairs of fighters appeared which attempted to counter the Soviet planes. In all, 22 enemy flights were noted. Four enemy planes were shot down in air battles and five Ju-88s[18] were damaged at the Zabolot' airfield west of Kiev.

During the night of 5-6 November Po-2 light night bombers, while continuing the operations of daylight aviation in pursuing the retreating enemy, carried out 244 sorties to bomb the enemy's columns along the roads south of Kiev. On 5 November, in order to reinforce the *front's* shock group in the Kiev area, the *front* commander issued the following order: the 211th and 336th rifle divisions were to be removed from the 13th Army and transferred to the 60th Army by the morning of 8 November, and the commander of the 27th Army was to cross the 38th Rifle Division to the eastern bank of the Dnepr by the morning of 6 November and direct it along the route Borispol'—Brovary—Vyshgorod. Upon arriving at Borispol', the division was to be subordinated to the commander of the 38th Army and by the morning of 10 November was to reach the Vyshgorod area. By the morning of 6 November the commander of the 40th Army was also to pull back one rifle division (337th) to the eastern bank of the Dnepr and dispatch it along the route Brovary—Vyshgorod, where it was to become part of the 38th Army on the morning of 10 November.

As a result of the fighting on 5 November, the 60th Army successfully carried out the mission refined by the *front* commander on 3 November. The army had essentially taken up the pursuit of the enemy to the south, along its left wing. The 38th and 3rd Guards Tank armies were continuing stubborn fighting west of Kiev and in the city itself. These armies did not carry out their mission for the day, the enemy's resistance had not been completely crushed, and Kiev had not yet been completely liberated, but it had become clear that only hours remained before the complete cleansing of the city of German troops. The 3rd Guards Tank Army was unable to begin the pursuit of the enemy on this day.

The fighting on 6 November. On 6 November the 60th Army, while continuing to attack, advanced 12 kilometers along its left flank. The 17th and 18th guards rifle corps and the 77th Rifle Corps occupied their previous positions and were not engaged in active operations. The 24th Rifle Corps advanced somewhat along both flanks and was beating off enemy counterattacks in the center. The 30th Rifle Corps, which had advanced insignificantly along the right flank of its 141st Rifle Division, was successfully attacking with the remainder of its forces to the southwest and by the close of the day had reached the front Felitsialovka—Buda Babinskaya—Mikulichi—Dachi Nemeshaevo—Mikhailovka—Rubezhovka. The corps' 322nd Division was in the army commander's reserve and had been concentrated with two regiments in Dymer and one regiment in Rovy.

By 0400 the 38th Army had completely eliminated the enemy's resistance in Kiev. At 0500 on 6 November Marshal of the Soviet Union Zhukov and generals Vatutin and Khrushchev sent comrade Stalin the following telegram:

> With the greatest joy we can report to you that the mission assigned by you to capture our beautiful city of Kiev, the capital of Ukraine, has been carried out by the forces of the First Ukrainian Front. The city of Kiev has been completed cleansed of German occupiers.
>
> The forces of the First Ukrainian Front are continuing to carry out the mission assigned to them.

---

18 Editor's note. The Ju-88 was a twin-engine combat aircraft that appeared in 1939. One model carried a crew of four, with a maximum speed of 510 km/hr and a range of 2,430 kilometers. It was armed with five 7.92mm machine guns and could carry up to 3,000 kilograms of bombs.

On this day the capital of our motherland, Moscow, saluted the valorous troops of the First Ukrainian Front with 24 salvos, by order of the Supreme Commander-in-Chief. Many of the *front's* formations and units, which had particularly distinguished themselves in the fighting for Kiev, had the name "Kiev" accorded to them and were awarded with combat orders.

The Germans caused a great deal of damage to Kiev and the city's population experience severe deprivations, which increased several times during the enemy's final days in Kiev, during the German occupation. Comrade Khrushchev, member of the *front's* military council and secretary of the Central Committee of the CP(b)U,[19] painted a complete picture of the situation in Kiev in his telegram to comrade Stalin of 8 November 1943.

> 8 November 1943
> To comrade Stalin
> The situation in Kiev

At dawn on 6 November 1943 the troops of the First Ukrainian Front liberated the city of Kiev from the German occupiers. The leading workers of the city party and soviet organizations arrived in the city along with the forward units.

One should note the good organization of artillery fire carried out by our artillery troops. The enemy's artillery was immediately suppressed by our accurate and extremely powerful artillery fire, which enabled us to develop the vigorous offensive by our infantry and tanks. The Germans, fearing complete encirclement in Kiev, ran away from the city in panic and did not have time to burn and blow up the city of Kiev, as was the case with Poltava and other cities on the Ukrainian left bank. Nevertheless, the enemy was able to blow up and burn several significant sites. Burned were Kiev University, the defense house, the city public library, and electric stations (KRES, TsES), two shops in the "Bolshevik" factory were blown up, as were the bread factory, the water pipe system, all of the bridges and overpasses, and a number of large apartment buildings. Almost all of the city's theaters survived. The circus, the Red Army Theater, the "Young Viewer" Theater and all of the movie theaters located in the central part of the city burned earlier.

The Germans looted almost all the buildings in the city and from some of them (the buildings of the Central Committee of the CP(b)U and Supreme Soviet of the Ukrainian SSR) even the door handles have been hauled away, with the window sills, doors, window frames and parquet stolen and marble slabs blown up.

The Germans attempted to drive out the entire population of the city. They sought out inhabitants, employing dogs specially trained to track people down. The inhabitants of Kiev sought to find any means to avoid these round-ups. They hid in sewage and water wells, bricked each other up in the basements of buildings and covered themselves with junk in the attics. The Kiev doctor Pashkov told me in a conversation that in order to throw the bloodhounds off the scent, he decided to hide in the basement, and on his way there greased the soles of his shoes with *Unguentum Ichthyoli* and soaked the area where he hid with kerosene. There were many instances of suicide in Kiev during these round-ups. Professor Lozinskii, hearing that gendarmes were entering his apartment, took poison, followed by his wife and daughter. The Germans carried out mass executions of people hiding from being driven away. They found the corpses of many residents who had sought to hide from the Germans on Podval'naya Street and Mikhailovskii and Fruktovyi lanes. The Germans would shoot them

---

19 Editor's note. This was the abbreviation for the Communist Party of Ukraine (Bolshevik), the Ukrainian branch of the Communist Party of the Soviet Union.

FIRST UKRAINIAN FRONT'S NOVEMBER OFFENSIVE OPERATION

and burn them. They managed to drive a significant majority of the population out of the city. Kiev has the aspect of a dead city.

Now the residents of Kiev are returning in large groups from the neighboring forests, swamps, gullies and cemetery burial vaults. They create a sad impression from the horrors, humiliations and deprivations endured. The city's residents greet the soldiers of the Red Army with emotion that cannot be expressed.

We are now engaged in restoring order in the city, taking stock of the remaining property and the restoration of the most important aspects of the urban economy.

We will be able to restore the water pipes, which were partially blown up by the Germans, within a few days, and then we can furnish the city with water. The electrical equipment that survived in the factories will give us the opportunity to deliver about 1,000 kilowatts of electrical energy within a few days, which will be for the first stage of the water system and illumination. Some equipment was preserved in the bread factories and several ovens. Besides this, about 50 small bakeries will be employed. All of this will enable us to organize the baking of bread within a few days.

We are taking all measures to as to build a railroad bridge over the Dnepr River as soon as possible.

While in Kiev on 6-7 November I spoke with many of the city's residents, who while crying told me about the horrors of German occupation.

Everywhere I was, the residents of Kiev asked me to personally relay to you their deepest and heartfelt gratitude for the liberation of their native city and for saving the residents of Kiev from death.

N. Khrushchev

Throughout 6 November the 38th Army's formations developed the offensive to the south and advanced 20 kilometers. Simultaneously, units of the 23rd and 21st rifle corps were moving west and southwest. The 23rd Rifle Corps crossed the Irpen' River and by the close of the day had its units along the line Irpen'—Kapitanovka—Gorenichi. The 21st Rifle Corps, which had been committed into the fighting, reached the line Belgorodka—Bobritsa—Zabor'ye with units of the 202nd Rifle Division, while the 135th Rifle Division reached the Malyutyanka area. the 50th Rifle and 5th Guards Tank corps reached the front Glevakha—Markhalevka—Khodosovka. The 51st Rifle Corps was slowly advancing from Kiev to the south, out of contact with the enemy.

The 3rd Guards Tank Army, having begun to pursue the enemy, advanced 30-40 kilometers throughout 6 November and reached the Kazennaya Motovilovka area with its 6th guards Tank Corps and the area of the settlement of Vasil'kov with its 7th Guards Tank Corps. The army's forward detachment (91st Tank Brigade) reached the eastern outskirts of Fastov. By the close of the day the 9th Mechanized Corps was attacking along the Irpen' River toward Fastov, while its forward units were approaching Plesetskoye.

By the close of 6 November the 1st Guards Cavalry Corps had reached the front Dachi Klavdievo, Dachi Nemeshaevo—Dachi Kicheeva.

During 3-6 November the 13th Army was not involved in fighting and was engaged in improving its positions and in reconnoitering the enemy. During the night of 4-5 November the 28th Rifle Corps' 336th Rifle Division and the 15th Rifle Corps' 211th Rifle Division had been pulled out of the first defensive line by means of broadening the neighboring divisions' defensive sectors. On the same day both divisions were transferred to the 60th Army, on orders of the *front* commander, and at 1900 began to move south. A detachment of the 8th Rifle Division, which had been in the enemy's rear since the October fighting, was operating with local partisans. Upon the beginning of the offensive by the *front's* forces in the Ovruch area, the partisans disrupted the enemy's movements along the roads: they blew up enemy trains and destroyed his personnel and transport.

The 2nd Air Army, which was supporting the ground forces in defeating the enemy's forces resisting along certain sectors and pursuing his retreating forces, carried out 618 sorties throughout the day. *Shturmoviks* and bombers carried out 321 sorties and fighters 125 for covering the troops and 177 for accompanying the *shturmoviks* and bombers. The aviation's chief targets were the enemy's troop columns, which were falling back to the west, southwest and south of Kiev, as well as his trains at the Vasil'kov, Motovilovka and Fastov stations.

The Germans' fighter aviation put up significant resistance and their bombers bombed the *front's* forces on the march and in their combat formations in groups of eight to 36 planes. 152 enemy sorties were noted during the day.

Throughout 6 November the enemy twice carried out massed strikes against crossings over the Dnepr River, but thanks to timely placed smoke screens the bombing was without result.

The 2nd Air Army's fighters shot down 14 enemy planes (six bombers, six fighters, one reconnaissance plane, and on transport aircraft) in 14 air battles.

As a result of the fighting on 6 November the German forces in the 60th Army's offensive zone were falling back to the Zdvizh River. The Germans' 8th Panzer Division fell back to the left bank of the Zdvizh River, following unsuccessful counterattacks near Dymer and Volchkov and had concentrated in Makarov for covering the Kiev—Zhitomir paved road. Units of the routed 68th, 75th, 88th, and 323rd infantry and 20th Motorized divisions fell back to the left bank of the Irpen' River for the purpose of covering the Zhitomir paved road. Part of the 7th Panzer Division's forces fell back to Fastov. The 75th and 82n infantry and 213th Security divisions were falling back to the south to the line of the Stugna River along the Vasil'kov—Tripol'ye sector. The Germans' 25th Panzer Division, which had arrived from Norway, was unloading at Berdichev station. The division had 240 tanks, of which 100 were "Tiger" tanks.[20] Following unloading, parts of the division weres concentrating by march in the area of Belaya Tserkov'.

Throughout 6 November the *front* commander issued an order to transfer part of the anti-aircraft equipment from the 27th and 40th armies to the 38th Army. The 9th and 23rd anti-aircraft artillery divisions (each minus one regiment) were to be removed from the Bukrin bridgehead and by the morning of 8 November transferred to Kiev. On orders from the *Stavka* of the Supreme High Command, the *front* was to be reinforced by additional anti-aircraft equipment—four anti-aircraft regiments, two anti-aircraft machine gun battalions, one battalion and one independent searchlight company, two regiments of fighter aviation, and one regiment of air warning troops. All of this together (minus the 9th and 23rd anti-aircraft divisions) amounted to 160 85mm anti-aircraft guns, 110 37mm anti-aircraft guns, 54 anti-aircraft machine guns, and 78 searchlights.

Thus as the result of the fighting on 6 November, the 60th Army carried out its mission for the day and had advanced significantly to the south, cutting the Kiev—Korosten' railroad. However, the right bank of the Zdvizh River had not yet been completely cleared of the enemy, which required additional efforts on the part of the army's forces.

The 38th Army, having captured Kiev, failed to carry out its task for the day of reaching the line of the Stugna River to the south and the Motyzhin area to the west, although favorable conditions were arising for this, because the enemy group of forces had been routed and split into pieces and was falling back with exposed flanks to the west, southwest and south. On 6 November the 50th and 51st rifle corps had basically lost contact with the enemy, and despite this were advancing insufficiently rapidly. The 23rd and 21st rifle corps, which had been brought up from the army's second echelon, were slowly increasing the pace of the offensive, although the 23rd Rifle Corps

---

20 Editor's note. The Panzer VI ("Tiger") was a German heavy tank which first appeared in 1943. One model weighed 54 tons and carried a crew of five. It was armed with an 88mm gun and two 7.92 machine guns.

was faced only by defeated units of the enemy's Kiev group of forces, while the 21st Rifle Corps had no enemy at all facing it. The main reason for this was poor troop control at all levels of the 38th Army.

The 3rd Guards Tank Army also failed to carry out its mission for the day, although it had the opportunity to go over to the pursuit of the enemy as early as the evening of 5 November. Given firmer troop control (both on the part of the army commander and the corps commanders), the army enjoyed all conditions for reaching the area of Fastov and Belaya Tserkov', because only part of the forces of the Germans' defeated 7th Panzer Division were retreating along the Kiev—Fastov railroad.

The Results of the First Ukrainian Front's Offensive During 3-6 November

As a result of the fighting during 3-6 November the forces of the *front's* shock group carried out their chief assigned tasks: they routed the Germans' Kiev group of forces and liberated the capital of Ukraine, Kiev, from the German-Fascist aggressors. The 60th Army fully carried out the tasks assigned to it and in four days of fighting in difficult, wooded terrain, advanced 40 kilometers, which was even somewhat more than the planned offensive pace. The 38th Army met particularly powerful resistance along the approaches to Kiev and covered 35 kilometers in four days. The 3rd Guards Tank Army first supported the 38th Army's infantry with part of its forces in completing the breakthrough of the entire depth of the Germans' defense northwest and west of Kiev and began to pursue the enemy only from the morning of 6 November. On the first day of pursuing the enemy, the army advanced 30-40 kilometers, captured the Vasil'kov area and reached the outskirts of Fastov.

The 40th and 27th armies were unable to break through the enemy's defense in the area of the Bukrin bridgehead, because the enemy had significant forces here, including tanks and artillery. The armies' artillery was unable to suppress the fire system of the enemy's defense and the small number of tank units in this area prevented them from rendering sufficient help to the infantry in its attack. One should consider an important result of the 40th and 27th armies' offensive battles the circumstance that from the start of our forces' offensive north of Kiev the enemy was unable to carry out a major regrouping of forces and remove a large number of tanks and artillery in order to move them to the Kiev area.

The successful offensive by the forces of the First Ukrainian Front around Kiev could not but influence the course of events along other sectors of the Soviet-German front.

Even before the start of the First Ukrainian Front's Kiev operation the Germans were bringing up fresh tank divisions to the Kirovograd area. The enemy's plan was to launch a counteroffensive against the forces of the Second Ukrainian Front, which had broken through the German defense in October along the Kirovograd axis and had seized a large and operationally important bridgehead along the right bank of the Dnepr. In the beginning of November the leading echelons of the 1st Panzer Division, which was being transferred from France, the SS *Adolph Hitler* Panzer Division and the 16th Panzer Division, which were being dispatched from Italy, began to arrive in the Kirovograd area. The 25th Panzer Division was en route from France to Kirovograd. Due to the major success of the Soviet forces in the Kiev area, the German command was forced to turn the 25th Panzer Division toward Kiev. On 6 November the latter began to unload in Berdichev and then move to the area of Fastov and Belaya Tserkov' in march formation. The trains carrying the SS *Adolph Hitler* Panzer Division were delayed and unloaded in Kazatin. All of this made the subsequent operations of the Second Ukrainian Front significantly easier. During the first three days of the operation the *front's* forces in the Kiev area defeated nine infantry divisions (68th, 75th, 82nd, 88th, 183rd, 217th, 323rd, 327th, and 340th), two panzer divisions (7th and 8th) and the 20th Motorized Division, for a total of 12

German divisions. These divisions lost up to 60-70 percent of their rank and file and a large part of their combat equipment. About 10,000 enemy soldiers and officers were killed in the four days of fighting, with about 3,000 captured. Our forces also captured a great deal of the enemy's various combat equipment. On 4 November the headquarters of the Fourth Panzer Army moved from Makarov to Radomyshl'.

The German troops were stunned by the force of the First Ukrainian Front's attack. Numerous prisoner interrogations testify to this.

The headquarters of the high command of the German army's ground forces issued the following evaluation of the situation in the Kiev area by the close of 6 November 1943:

> The present situation in the Kiev area testifies to the beginning of a major enemy breakthrough operation, which will have decisive significance for the entire eastern front. The center of the main danger is Army Group South's sector in the Kiev area.

A serious shortcoming in the operations of the 38th and 3rd Guards Tank armies' forces were the low pace of the offensive and pursuit of the retreating enemy. The reason for this was the too slow commitment of the 38th Army's second-echelon rifle corps and the slow pace of their attack. One should note the same thing in regard to the 3rd Guards Tank Army and the 1st Guards Cavalry Corps. The weakness of command and control at all levels also told on the troops' activities. Both wire and radio communications in the 38th and 3rd Guards Tank armies worked poorly. The headquarters often did not know their own forces' situation and that of the enemy on the battlefield, while orders and instructions were delivered slowly and arrived late.

By 6 November the troops were already poorly supplied with ammunition and fuel. For example, there was only 0.8 of a refill in the *front* and only 0.5 of a refill with the troops. On this day the 38th and 60th armies had the following ammunition on hand (in combat loads):

Table 2.9 The 38th and 60th Armies' Ammunition Supply

	38th Army	60th Army
82mm mortar rounds	1.8	0.9
120mm mortar rounds	0.7	0.7
76mm shells for regimental artillery	1.3	0.4
76mm shells for divisional artillery	1.0	0.8
122mm shells	0.1	0.7
152mm shells	1.1	0.4

However, even these reserves were not among the troops, but at army bases on the left bank of the Dnepr.

The Subsequent Development of the Offensive During 7-12 November. The Capture of the Cities of Fastov and Zhitomir

The missions of the *front's* armies following the liberation of Kiev. On 6 and 7 November the *front* commander issued operational directives nos. 0056/op, 0058/op and 0059/op, by which the tasks for the *front's* armies for the immediate future were defined.

The 38th Army received orders to continue the vigorous pursuit of the enemy day and night. It was ordered to form an army mobile group, consisting of the 5th Guards Tank Corps, which before this had been operating jointly with the 50th Rifle Corps, and the 1st Guards Cavalry Corps, which upon arriving in the Motyzhin area, was to be subordinated to the commander of the 38th Army, to develop the offensive along the Zhitomir axis. The commander of the 5th Guards Tank Corps, Lieutenant General Kravchenko,[21] was appointed commander of the army's mobile group.

The mobile group was to reach the area Yurov—Brusilov by the close of 7 November, the Korostyshev by the close of 8 November, and to capture Zhitomir by the close of 9 November.

The 38th Army's 23rd Rifle Corps received orders to develop the success along the paved road to Zhitomir, while the army's remaining formations had the task of attacking to the south.

By the close of 7 November the army's forces were supposed to reach the line Makarov—Fastov—Grebenki—Makeevka and to capture Kagarlyk and Belaya Tserkov' with powerful mobile detachments; by the close of 8 November they were to reach the line Stavishche—Brusilov—Kozhanka. The *front* commander directed that the army pay attention to securing its left flank.

The 3rd Guards Tank Army was to operate in the center of the 38th Army's combat formation, while developing the offensive to the southwest toward Fastov and Kazatin. The army received orders to capture the Popel'nya area by the close of 7 November, while part of its forces was to cut the Belaya Tserkov'—Kazatin paved road in the area of the village of Krivosheintsy. Besides this, the army was instructed to allot a mobile detachment, which was to occupy Fursy, six kilometers west of Belaya Tserkov', and assist the 38th Army in capturing the latter. By the close of 9 November the tank army was to capture the areas of Kazatin and Berdichev. The attention of the army commander was also directed to the necessity of securing his left flank.

The 40th and 27th armies were ordered to attack in the general direction of Kagarlyk, to break through the enemy's front and, while developing the success, reach the following: the front Rzhishchev—Makedony by the morning of 9 November; the line Makeevka—Shubovka—Rossava by the close of 10 November, and; the line Veliko-Polovetskoe—Yablonovka—Koshevatoe by the close of 12 November.

Both armies were supposed to concentrate their main forces for breaking through along a narrow sector of the front and to create here an artillery and mortar density of no less than 200 tubes per kilometer of front. The start of these armies' offensive was set for 1230 on 8 November.

By 1200 on 8 November the 13th Army was to get from the 60th Army the 18th Guards Rifle Corps (6th Guards Rifle and 2nd and 4th guards airborne divisions), along with their sectors of the front. From this moment the following boundary was to be established between the 13th and 60th armies: Chemer—Morovsk—the mouth of the Teterev River—the Teterev River as far as Priborsk—Termakhovka—Bazar—Vas'kovka—Luginy (all locales inclusively for the 13th Army). Two rifle divisions, with reinforcements, were to secretly concentrate no later than the morning of 10 November in the area of Staryi Osov and the woods to the southwest and during the night of 10-11 November launch an attack in the direction of Staryi Osov and Rossokha. The 18th Guards Rifle Corps' formations had the task of simultaneously attacking in the direction of Rudnya-Veresnya and Rossokha, with the mission of defeating the enemy's units between the Uzh and Teterev rivers and by the close of 12 November reach the front Uzh River—Rossokha and then to the south as far as the army's left boundary. The army was to subsequently launch its main attack in the direction of Krasilovka and Ignatpol' and, with the forces of not less than one rifle divisions from the Rudnya-Veresnya area in the direction of Burakovka.

---

21 Editor's note. Andrei Grigor'evich Kravchenko (1899-1963) joined the Red Army in 1918 and fought in the civil war and the Soviet-Finnish War. During the Great Patriotic War he commanded a tank brigade and a tank corps, and then a tank army in Europe and the Far East. Following the war, Kravchenko commanded an army and retired in 1955.

By the close of 15 November the army's forces were to reach the front Burakovka and the Uzh River as far as Vas'kovka. Upon reaching this line, it was planned to launch attacks along the following axes: Ignatpol'—Ovruch and Burakovka—Ovruch, with a supporting attack toward Denisovichi. It was planned to capture the town of Ovruch on 18 November and to reach the front Vepry—Mukhoedy—Nagoryany—Luginy. Upon capturing the town of Ovruch an attack was to be made in the direction of Ovruch and Mozyr'. The army's forces received orders to capture Mozyr' by the close of 22 November and reach the front Mozyr'—Nagroyany, with the army's main group of forces in the Ovruch—Luginy—Ignatpol' area. The artillery density along the breakthrough sectors was set at 150 tubes per kilometer of front.

The 60th Army was supposed to continue a vigorous offensive and by the close of 9 November reach the line of the Teterev River, seizing bridgeheads along the western bank of this river in the areas of Ivankov, Kukhary and Radomyshl'. It was ordered to have the main group of forces, including the 17th Guards Rifle Corps,[22] along the army's left flank for attacking toward Radomyshl'. Subsequently, while launching its main attack in the direction of Radomyshl' and Chernyakhov and supporting attacks in the directions of Malin—Korosten' and Ivankov—Korosten', the army was supposed to defeat the opposing enemy and by the close of 12 November capture Malin and Chernyakhov and reach the front Termakhovka—Sidorovichi—Novye Vorob'i—Malin—Potievka—Brazhinka—Novopol'—Vil'sk. After this, the army was assigned to launch an attack in the direction of Chernyakhov and Korosten' and by the close of 15 November capture Korosten', and by the close of 16 November reach the front Davidki—Ushomir—Volodarsk-Volynskii—Novopol'—Vil'sk, with its main group of forces in the Korosten' area.

Thus the armies' tasks significantly expanded the overall front of the offensive. The 13th Army was to being the offensive south of the mouth of the Uzh and Pripyat' rivers, along the Ovruch axis. The *front's* left-flank armies (40th and 27th) again received active missions along the Belaya Tserkov' axis. The 60th Army was supposed to develop the offensive not to the southwest, but to the west, along the Korosten' axis. The 38th Army was to continue to operate along two diverging axes: the western, toward Zhitomir, and the southern, toward Belaya Tserkov' and Kagarlyk.

The fighting on 7 November. Throughout 7 November the enemy made a series of attempts to hold our forces' offensive, which was developing successfully to the west, southwest and south from Kiev. The *front's* aerial reconnaissance established the approach of the enemy's new automobile columns and artillery to the Belaya Tserkov' area. On this day aerial photography fixed the presence of up to 800 enemy planes on his airfields, which testified to the reinforcement of the Germans' aviation along the Kiev axis.

The enemy was hurriedly reinforcing the Belaya Tserkov' and Kazatin axes with troops, because an enormous gap had formed here during the past two days that threatened the Germans with serious consequences. The main forces of the 25th Panzer Division had concentrated in the Belaya Tserkov' area and to the northwest. A regiment from the 198th Infantry Division, which had been taken from the Kremenchug area, was arriving here by railroad. The *Das Reich* SS Panzer Division, which had been transferred from the Bukrin area, was concentrating in the Grebenki—Ustinovka area. Special trains from the *Adolph Hitler* SS Panzer Division were unloading at Popel'nya station. This division's forward elements had reached the Kozhanka area.

The Germans' 1st Panzer Division, just as was the case with the 25th Panzer Division, had been designated for operations against the Second Ukrainian Front and half of its strength was already concentrated east of Kirovograd. However, the remaining trains had been turned en route to the Kiev axis. On 7 November the headquarters of the Germans' XLVIII Panzer Corps, which had

---

22 At this time the 17th Guards Rifle Corps consisted of the 70th Guards and 211th rifle divisions. The 211th Rifle Division had been transferred to the 13th Army from the 60th Army.

been entrusted with the task of unifying the actions of the arriving units and the troops falling back to the south from the Kiev area, appeared in the Belaya Tserkov' area.

On 7 November the 13th Army was not engaged in combat operations and was preparing to carry out new tasks.

The 60th Army was engaged in successful offensive fighting. By the close of the day the army's forces in the center and along the left wing reached the eastern bank of the Zdvizh River and seized bridgeheads on the western bank south of Fenevichi, west and southwest of Abramovka, and in the area of Andreevka. On this day the army had three rifle divisions (121st, 211th and 70th Guards) in its corps' second echelons and in the reserve.

The *front* commander attached great significance to the capture of the major railroad junction of Fastov, the capture of which would yield a number of advantages. In the combat orders issued on 6 November to the commanders of the 3rd Guards Tank and 38th armies, the *front* commander categorically demanded of the tank troops the most rapid capture of Fastov and of the 38th Army the acceleration of the rifle troops to this area and its secure consolidation. The capture of Belaya Tserkov' could bring about a turning point in the fighting in the area of the Bukrin bridgehead and speed up the 40th and 27th armies carrying out their assignments. Thus on 7 November the *front* commander demanded that the 38th Army speed up its offensive on Belaya Tserkov'.

In the second half of the day on 7 November the *front* commander issued instructions to keep the 5th Guards Tank Corps for operations in the Belaya Tserkov' area and the task of capturing Zhitomir was entrusted to the 1st Guards Cavalry Corps. In order to ease the latter's operations during the first stage, the 38th Army was ordered to launch an attack with one rifle division in the direction of Zvonkovaya and Motyzhin; this was supposed to result in the encirclement of the enemy's group of forces operating opposite the 23rd Rifle Corps along the Zhitomir paved road.

The decision to transfer the 337th and 38th rifle divisions from the 40th and 27th armies to the 38th Army and their concentration in the Vishenka area was also confirmed. These divisions were to be crossed over the Dnepr south of Kiev.

On this day the 38th Army advanced 6-12 kilometers in the center and along its left flank.

The 23rd Rifle Corps, slowly developing the offensive, advanced insignificantly along the Zhitomir paved road to the west.

The 21st Rifle Corps reached the line Knyazhichi—Zvonkovaya—Plesetskoye. The 50th Rifle Corps reached the Vasil'kov area and the 51st Rifle Corps reached the line Kopachevskaya Sloboda—Neshcherov with two divisions.

On this day the 1st Guards Cavalry Corps broke away from the infantry and, having advanced 14-18 kilometers, reached the Gavronshchina—Motyzhin—Kolonshchina area. Thus the Zhitomir paved road was cut in the rear of the enemy group of forces putting up resistance to the 23rd Rifle Corps. The Germans suffered heavy casualties. The cavalry corps took more than 300 prisoners and destroyed a large amount of equipment, especially during a night attack by the corps' self-propelled artillery in the area of the village of Makovishche. The corps itself suffered almost no losses on this day.

The 3rd Guards Tank Army, captured the Fastov—Kadlubitsa—Zarech'ye area and was fighting for Potievka with the forces of the 6th Guards Tank Corps and the 91st Tank Brigade. The 7th Guards Tank Corps captured the Mar'yanovka—Ksaverovka area. On the morning of 7 November the 9th Mechanized Corps began to move out of Plesetskoye in the direction of Fastov to develop the success.

Throughout the entire day the 40th and 27th armies were fighting along individual sectors.

During the night of 6-7 November Po-2 light night bombers carried out only 29 sorties with single crews, due to the bad weather, destroying the enemy forces falling back along the Grebenki—Belaya Tserkov' road.

During the day of 7 November the weather was very bad and as a result the 2nd Air Army's planes carried out only 32 sorties to reconnoiter the enemy in the areas of Fastov, Belaya Tserkov' and Rzhishchev and to strafe the enemy's withdrawing forces. However, due to the bad weather, 17 crews did not carry out their assignments. Only five enemy sorties were noted.

As a result of the day's fighting, the *front's* forces along the main axis (38th and 3rd Guards Tank armies) fell far short of carrying out their assignments. The pursuit of the retreating enemy took place slowly, even in those cases when our units were out of contact with them, as was the case, for example, with the 21st and 51st rifle corps and the tank army's formations.

For this reason, on 7 November the *front* commander was forced to point out to the army commanders their insufficiently firm troop control and demanded the elimination of shortcomings in carrying out assignments by the troops.

The fighting on 8 November. The enemy continued withdrawing along the previous axes throughout the day.

The 13th Army began attacking along its left wing with the forces of the 18th Guards Rifle Corps. By this time the situation opposite the 13th Army's left flank had changed. Due to the success of the 60th and 38th armies, the enemy had removed part of his forces opposite the 13th Army. Active operations by the army's forces were required in the area between the Uzh and Teterev rivers. The offensive by the 18th Guards Rifle Corps was supposed to secure the 60th Army's left-wing forces, which by this time had forced the Zdvizh River and were approaching the Teterev River along the Ivankovka axis. Thus the 13th Army's operational plan began to be realized 2-3 days before the time initially indicated by the *front* commander. The corps occupied Gornostaipol' in the day's fighting and advanced 15 kilometers along its left flank. By the close of the day the corps reached the line Yampol'—Blistyu—Dityatki—Orannoye.

The 60th Army advanced up to ten kilometers along individual axes in the day's fighting and forced the Zdvizh River along the entire front. The army had the 70th Rifle Corps (70th Guards and 211th rifle divisions) in its second echelon, which was moving behind the army's center.

By the close of the day the army's forces reached the line Staryi Osov—Lyubydva—Belyi Bereg—Koblitskii Woods—Nebrod—Borodyanka—Vablya—Lipovka.

The 1st Guards Cavalry Corps was developing the offensive along the Zhitomir paved road to the west. Having advanced 15-20 kilometers, the corps' units occupied Makarov and Yurov and reached the front Nalivaikovka—Yurov.

The 38th Army was pursuing the enemy to the west and south and was moving part of its forces to the southwest behind the 3rd Guards Tank Army. The 23rd Rifle Corps (74th, 30th, 23rd, and 218th rifle divisions), taking advantage of the cavalry corps' success, advanced 32 kilometers to the west along the Zhitomir paved road and by the close of the day reached the line Makarov—Yurov—excluding Gruzkoye. The 21st Rifle Corps reached the line Gruzkoye—Vol'shka—the Yaroshovka Collective Farm—Drogintsy—the northeastern outskirts of Fastov. Units of the corps repelled three enemy counterattacks in up to a battalion in strength, with 10-15 tanks apiece, from the Yurovka area. The 50th Rifle Corps, having advanced 14-24 kilometers, reached the front excluding Fastov—Fastovets—Mar'yanovka—Yatski—Germanovka. The 5th Guards Tank Corps, which had occupied Germanovka with its 21st Guards Tank Brigade and which was attacking with its remaining forces in the direction of Ksaverovka and Grebenki, was attacking in the 50th Rifle Corps' operational zone. By the close of the day the corps' units were fighting the enemy's infantry and tanks, which were counterattacking in the direction of Germanovka and Ksaverovka. The 51st Rifle Corps reached the front excluding Germanovka—Dolina—Zhukovtsy—Vitachev, covering 12 kilometers that day.

During the day the 3rd Guards Tank Army made a fighting advance of 30 kilometers. The 9th Mechanized Corps' 69th Motorized Rifle Brigade captured Kozhanka in fighting, advancing 14 kilometers; following a fight with the enemy's infantry and assault guns, two of the 6th Guards Tank Corps' brigades captured Bertinki and Chervona, while the motorized infantry was clearing the woods southwest of Fastov of small enemy groups. The 7th Guards Tank Corps destroyed up to a battalion of enemy infantry and 16 tanks in the Palyanichentsy area and two of its brigades reached the Maloye Polovetskoye area.

Part of the 40th and 27th armies' forces continued their offensive battles on the bridgeheads, but were unable to advance.

As a result of the day's fighting, the left wing of the 13th Army, the 60th Army and the right wing of the 38th Army achieved a significant success along the Korosten' and Zhitomir axes, where the enemy was putting up weak resistance. The situation was somewhat different along the Kazatin and Belaya Tserkov' axes. On 8 November units of the 3rd Guards Tank Army ran into the first counterattacks by units of the 25th Panzer and *Das Reich* SS panzer divisions. As a result of the Germans' increased resistance, the 3rd Guards Tank Army was unable to carry out its assignment for the day. The situation was further complicated by the fact that the 38th Army's 50th Rifle Corps, due to the lack of sufficient organization of its activities, was still unable to reach the Fastov area, to relieve here units of the tank army and to free them up for operations along the southwestern axis.

The fighting on 9 November. The enemy continued to fall back along the Korosten' and Zhitomir axes throughout 9 November. Fierce fighting began in the Fastov area with the counterattacking units of the 25th Panzer Division and the *Das Reich* SS Panzer Division. On this day units of the 198th Infantry Division, which was being transferred from the Kremenchug area to the area of Belaya Tserkov', took part in the fighting.

The 10th Motorized Division and up to half of the 3rd Panzer Division were pulled out of the fighting, in which they were involved in the area of the Bukrin bridgehead, and were hurriedly concentrating opposite the 38th Army's left flank northwest of Rzhishchev. All the units of the 1st Panzer Division and the *Adolph Hitler* Panzer Division, which were designated for operations in the Kirovograd area, were moving north to the Belaya Tserkov' area.

Throughout the day the *front's* forces continued to develop the offensive along a front from the Uzh River to Fastov and from Grebenki to the Dnepr. In the Fastov area they were fighting off insistent enemy counterattacks. The 40th Army continued to fight with part of its forces along individual sectors in order to improve its position.

The 13th Army's 18th Guards Rifle Corps, having destroyed a number of individual enemy strong points, advanced 12-14 kilometers and by the close of the day reached the line Rudnya-Veresnya—Kovalevka—Rusaki.

During the battle the *front* commander demanded that the 13th Army create as strong a group of forces as possible along its left wing, paying attention to increasing the pace of the offensive with the task of capturing all of the enemy's equipment which he, in falling back in the wooded area, could remove only with difficulty.

The 60th Army, having forced the Teterev River along its right wing, reached the line Fedorovka—Ivankov—Kolentsy—Blitcha—Potashnya—Novomirovka—Nezhilovichi by the close of the day. The 226th Rifle Division, together with the 150th Tank Brigade defeated an enemy group numbering up to 1,500 men in the Blitcha area, with more than 300 corpses of enemy soldiers and officers, 30 guns and many carts with supplies remaining on the battlefield. The 112th Rifle Division destroyed up to two enemy infantry battalions, including artillery and mortars, southwest of the Koblitskii Woods. During the day's fighting the army's formations captured over 100 prisoners and a great deal of combat equipment abandoned by the enemy.

The 1st Guards Cavalry Corps, while overcoming the enemy's resistance, advanced 14 kilometers by 1700 on 9 November and was fighting along the line Komarovka—Yuzefovka.

The *front* commander ordered the 60th Army and 1st Guards Cavalry Corps to encircle and destroy the Germans' 291st Infantry Division, which was falling back to the west, in the area west and northwest of Borodyanka. However, as a result of the fact that our troops were continuing to attack toward the west in a straight line, the maneuver to encircle part of the enemy's 291st Infantry Division's forces was not accomplished.

At dawn on 9 November the *front* commander refined the 38th and 3rd Guards Tank armies' tasks (combat order No. 22636/sh of 0420 on 9 November and combat order No. 22629/sh of 0500 on 9 November).

The 38th Army along the Zhitomir axis was to capture Zhitomir by the close of 12 November and with its rifle formations reach the front Vil'sk—Al'binovka—Guiva River—Andrushevka—Brovki—Kamenka, and the cavalry corps the Marievka—Deneshi area. The army had the assignment along the Belaya Tserkov' axis of defeating the enemy's tank group of forces with the forces of the 5th Guards Tank Corps, in conjunction with the 3rd Guards Tank Army, by the close of 9 November and capturing Belaya Tserkov'. By the close of 10 November the army was supposed to reach the front Maloye Polovetskoye—Belaya Tserkov'—Peschanoye—Losyatin. The army's left-wing formations were ordered to capture Rzhishchev by the close of 9 November and link up with the forces operating from the Shchuchinka bridgehead, and by the close of 10 November reach the front Germanovka—Kagarlyk.

The 3rd Guards Tank Army received orders to defeat the enemy tank group (25th Panzer and *Das Reich* SS Panzer divisions) in conjunction with the 38th Army south and southeast of Fastov and occupy Belaya Tserkov' on 9 November; part of its forces were to capture Popel'nya and Skvira and then attack toward Kazatin.

During the 9 November fighting the *front* commander focused the attention of the commanders of the 38th and 3rd Guards Tank armies on the infantry's slowness in consolidating the Fastov area and the enemy's increasing activity in this area. Personal responsibility for securing the defense of Fastov was entrusted to the commanders of these armies.

Throughout the day the 38th Army continued to develop the offensive. The 23rd Rifle Corps, having covered 16-18 kilometers in a day, reached the front Stavishche—Vysokoye. The 21st Rifle Corps, which was attacking along a 44-kilometer front, made the greatest advance along the Brusilov axis (up to 14 kilometers) and reached the front Zhmurovka—Khomutets—Dedovshchina—Veprik. Two of the 50th Rifle Corps' divisions (232nd and 340th), along with units of the 3rd Guards Tank Army, fought off the enemy's tank and motorized infantry counterattacks in the Fastovets area. Having lost 13 tanks burned, the enemy was nevertheless able to capture Fastovets by the close of the day. The corps' other two rifle divisions (167th and 180th) reached the line Pinchuki—Vasilevo. Thus the 50th Rifle Corps' attack front increased significantly and reached 60 kilometers. By the close of the day the 51st Rifle Corps was fighting on the line Germanovka—Dolina—Chernyakhov—Staiki.

In accordance with the instructions from the commander of the 3rd Guards Tank Army, the 9th Mechanized Corps was to capture Popel'nya during 9 November and the 7th Guards Tank Corps capture Pavoloch'. The 6th Guards Tank Corps had the task of destroying the enemy in the Palyanichentsy area (southeast of Fastov) and attacking in the army's second echelon behind the 7th Guards Tank Corps.

However, on 9 November only two of the 7th Guards Tank Corps' brigades, which had reached the Dunaika area, were able to advance and here they repulsed three enemy motorized infantry and tank attacks. The 9th Mechanized Corps was engaged in stubborn fighting all day, repelling the Germans' insistent counterattacks along the front Dmitrovka—Kozhanka—excluding Bertniki. The 6th Guards Tank Corps remained in the Potievka—Bertniki and Chervona area; its 22nd Motorized Rifle Brigade and 50th Motorcycle Regiment were fighting in the Fastovets area. The 91st Tank Brigade was in Fastov.

FIRST UKRAINIAN FRONT'S NOVEMBER OFFENSIVE OPERATION

During the day the *front* commander issued an order to transfer the 8th and 32nd anti-tank brigades, two anti-tank regiments and one guards mortar regiment from the Bukrin bridgehead to the 38th Army.

On the night of 8-9 November the 40th Army was ordered to pull the 337th and 42nd Guards rifle divisions from the Bukrin bridgehead to the left bank of the Dnepr and by the morning of 10 November to concentrate them along the western bank of the river in the Kailov area, with the mission of launching an attack on Kagarlyk. With the arrival of the 38th Army's left-wing formations in the Rzhishchev area the 40th Army was also to launch an attack from the Rzhishchev area on Kagarlyk. By the morning of 10 November the 8th Guards and 10th tank corps were to be pulled from the Bukrin bridgehead to the Darnitsa area and the *front* reserve; the battle-ready tanks were to be organized into a single company and remain to take part in combat operations on the Bukrin bridgehead.

During the course of the fighting, at 1620 on 9 November the *front* commander signed operational directive No. 0059/op, in which he pointed out that the enemy was continuing to remove forces from the Bukrin area and shift them to the north and ordered the 40th and 27th armies to attack along the western and northwestern axes.

Besides this, as early as 9 November the *front* commander warned of the possibility of the enemy's massed employment of tanks and demanded that the anti-tank formations, units and subunits be as well trained as possible for repelling possible enemy tank attacks. It was ordered to replenish these units with guns and towing equipment as soon as possible and to organize all free time for training and knocking together the gun crews, to supply them with fuel and check their readiness for maneuver. All the headquarters were told to pay attention to shortcomings in their location during the fighting and their vulnerability to enemy air attacks.

As a result of the evaluation of the situation that had arisen by the close of the day opposite the 3rd Guards Tank Army's front, at 2140 on 9 November the army commander issued combat order No. 0041/op, according to which all of the corps were assigned new objectives for 10 November: to prevent the enemy from developing the success he achieved the previous day, having captured Fastovets, to fight off all his counterattacks and to securely hold Fastov. For this, each corps was to leave the motorized infantry and part of its tanks in the first defensive line and to create shock groups of tanks and self-propelled guns.

Insofar as the 38th Army's 232nd Rifle Division, which was temporarily subordinated to the 3rd Guards Tank Army, had reached the Fastov area by the close of 9 November, it was given the task of occupying defensive positions east and southeast of the town. This division had only 200 troops and arrived at Fastov without its artillery.

Thus throughout 9 November the *front's* forces, while successfully pursuing the enemy along the Korosten' and Zhitomir axes, once again failed to achieve success along the Kazatin and Belaya Tserkov' axes, where they continued fighting along their previous line. The enemy was concentrating his reserves along these axes and not only halted the Soviet forces' offensive, but himself had gone over to active operations. On 9 November the *front* commander assigned the troops along these axes tasks beyond their strength, which they could not carry out due to a shortage of forces. The situation more and more insistently demanded the adoption of measures for reinforcing the *front's* forces operating along the Kazatin and Belaya Tserkov' axes at the expense of secondary axes.

The troops' attack front had increased sharply. If on 3 November the 60th Army had begun the offensive along a sector 20 kilometers wide, and the 38th Army along a 14-kilometer sector, by the close of 9 November these armies' attack front was 220 kilometers, with the same amount of men and materiel. The offensive was moving along diverging axes and leading to the rapid thinning out of the troops' combat formations. The pace of the troops' offensive during 7-9 November is shown in the table below.

Table 2.10 The Maximum Advance of the *Front's* Forces During 7-9 November (in km)

Formations	7 November	8 November	9 November	Average
60th Army:				
77th Rifle Corps	12	8	8	9.3
24th Rifle Corps	10	10	10	10
30th Rifle Corps	16	4	18	12.8
38th Army:				
1st Guards Cavalry Corps	18	20	14	17.3
23rd Rifle Corps	8	32	18	19.3
21st Rifle Corps	12	22	14	16
50th Rifle Corps	10	24	8	13.3
5th Guards Tank Corps	14	12	6	11.3
51st Rifle Corps	10	14	12	12
3rd Guards Tank Army:	18	30	8	18.8

The fighting on 10 November. Throughout the day the enemy's resistance between the Uzh River and the Kiev—Zhitomir paved road was finally crushed. A solid front no longer existed here and the fighting was only for individual inhabited locales. The Germans in the Chernobyl' area pulled part of the 4th Panzer Division out of the fighting and into the reserve. The German 291st Infantry Division was falling back on Korosten' in individual groups. The 208th, 340th and 327th infantry divisions had organized into columns and, while attempting to break away from the 60th Army's forces pursuing them, were falling back to the southwest toward Zhitomir. The 68th, 88th and 233rd infantry, 7th Panzer and 20th Motorized divisions continued to fall back to the southwest toward Andrushevka. Units of the 25th Panzer Division, which had completed its concentration, and the leading elements of the *Adolph Hitler* SS Panzer Division, which was committing its units into the fighting as they arrived in the area of combat operations, were carrying out intensive counterattacks in the Fastov area. The *Das Reich* SS Panzer Division, with the 75th Infantry Division and part of the 198th Infantry Division, the 82nd Infantry Division, 10th Motorized Division, half of the 3rd Panzer Division's forces, and the 34th Infantry Division's left-flank forces, which had abandoned Tripol'ye, were operating east of Fastov. The 1st Panzer Division and the remaining units of the *Adolph Hitler* SS Panzer Division continued to move from the Kirovograd area north by combined march.

On this day the trains of the Germans' 1st Panzer Division, which had not managed to detrain in the Kirovograd area and were turned from the march to the Kiev axis, were unloading at Chernorudka station (18 kilometers northeast of Kazatin).

The 13th Army was engaged in combat with the forces of the 15th Rifle Corps' 8th Rifle Division. This division was attempting to cross over the Uzh River along the 6th Guards Rifle Division's sector southwest of Chernobyl'; however, due to the enemy's powerful resistance, it had no success. The 6th Guards Rifle Division in the Rudnya-Veresnya area crossed three battalions over to the northern bank of the Uzh River. The 18th Rifle Corps captured Rossokha, but could advance no further. The 6th Guards Rifle Division became part of the 15th Rifle Corps along its sector and the 336th Rifle Division on the army's right flank was marching to the 18th Rifle Corps' sector and became part of it.

The 60th Army was engaged in fighting with its right-flank formations in the area of the town of Ivankov on the western bank of the Teterev River and reached the eastern bank of this river along the rest of its front.

The 1st Guards Cavalry Corps advanced another 30 kilometers, forcing the Teterev River and occupied Radomyshl' with the forces of the 7th Guards Cavalry Division, preventing the Germans here from destroying the crossings over the Teterev River. The 2nd Guards Cavalry Division reached the area southwest of Radomyshl' and the 1st Guards Cavalry Division, moving along the paved road, reached the Tsarevka—Lazarevka area. The 38th Army's formations along the Zhitomir axis advanced ten kilometers along the paved road. The 23rd Rifle Corps reached the line of the eastern outskirts of Zabeloch'ye—the eastern outskirts of Kocherovo—Privorot'ye. The 21st Rifle Corps repelled counterattacks by a German tank group all day and, having been pressed back somewhat by the enemy, by the close of the day was fighting along the front Yastrebenka—Vil'shka—Deminovskie—the eastern part of Prishival'na.

The 50th Rifle Corps advanced 20 kilometers along its right flank and the 163rd Rifle Division occupied Kornin and Mokhnachka. The 232nd and 340th rifle divisions, together with units of the 3rd Guards Tank Army, were engaged in heavy fighting to restore the situation in the Fastov area and were repelling powerful enemy counterattacks toward Fastov.

The 51st Rifle Corps was fighting along the line Makeevka—Mirovka—Chernyakhov—Vitachev.

The 3rd Guards Tank Army captured the village of Popel'nya with a brigade (7th) from the 9th Mechanized Corps and the village of Pavoloch' with two of the 7th Guards Tank Corps' tank brigades. One of the 9th Mechanized Corps' brigades remained in the Kozhanka area, while the other was approaching the 232rd Rifle Division's sector in the Fastov area. The 6th Guards Tank Corps had one brigade in the woods south of Fastov and one brigade east of Fastov, while another brigade was fighting along the western outskirts of the village of Fastovets. Part of the 7th Guards Tank Corps' forces, along with the 50th Motorcycle Regiment, was defending along the southern outskirts of Bol'shaya Snetinka. The 91st Tank Brigade remained in Fastov.

Thus the brigades of all the tank army's corps had become mixed up and as a result the organization of the battle and troop control were made more difficult.

The 40th and 27th armies' attempts to attack from the Bukrin bridgehead were unsuccessful.

During the second half of the day on 10 November the *front* commander issued an order to shift the 40th Army's main efforts from the Bukrin bridgehead to the Chernyakhov area. The army commander was ordered to unite the operations of the troops, which had been transferred to the Kailov area from the Bukrin bridgehead and the forces operating on the 38th Army's left wing.[23] The 27th Army's 241st Rifle Division and the 40th Army's 147th Rifle Division were to be pulled into the Kailov area in order to cross them over to the right bank of the Dnepr in this area. Besides this, it was also planned to shift the 68th Guards Rifle Division from the Bukrin bridgehead to the Kailov area. The 40th Army's headquarters set about preparing a command post in the Obukhov area. the 2nd Air Army was not engaged in combat on this day, due to the poor weather.

Thus the offensive by the *front's* forces along the main axis had essentially been halted. The *front's* main shock force—the 3rd Guards Tank Army—was tied down in fighting the enemy reserves that had arrived and was forced to defend the Fastov area. The offensive along the southern axis on Belaya Tserkov', for the purpose of bringing about a turning point in the fighting on the Bukrin bridgehead, was also not developed. In such a situation a new decision was required from the *front* commander. However, he attempted to resolve the task of developing the subsequent offensive on Kazatin with his previous forces and in their previous disposition.

The overall evaluation of the situation and the idea of the *front* commander's subsequent actions are evident from the orders issued to the commander of the 3rd Guards Tank Army on 10 November.

---

23 The 40th Army's 42nd Guards, 337th and 38th rifle divisions and the 38th Army's 51st Rifle Corps.

10 November 1943
To comrade Rybalko personally

1. The enemy has pulled out the following: the 25th Panzer Division to the area south of Fastov; the *Das Reich* Panzer Division (the 6th Panzer Division, according to your report) to the Grebenki—Vinitskie Stavy area; has begun to pull out the 3rd Panzer Division from the Bukrin bridgehead. One of its radio sets was noted yesterday in Kagarlyk. No other enemy units opposite you have been noted. It is evidently the enemy's intention to seize the Fastov railroad junction, which is very important for him.
2. All of the forces north of you are continuing to attack, while capturing a great deal of equipment:
    a) Pukhov[24] has advanced about 40 kilometers.
    b) Chernyakhovskii[25] has fully reached the Teterev River and has forced it in many places. Chernyakhovskii is capturing a lot of equipment. The enemy's 7th and 8th panzer divisions, which have been left without fuel, are damaging their tanks and abandoning them.
    c) This morning Moskalenko[26] began to advance from the line Stavishche—Brusilov—Veprik, pursuing the enemy. Moskalenko occupied Mirovka and Chernyakhov and is attacking toward Kagarlyk.
    In the Fastov area Moskalenko has the task of reaching the front Kozhanka—Chervona—Grebenki.
    d) Zhmachenko[27] occupied Ul'yaniki and Veselaya Dubrova and is continuing to attack.
    e) Our neighbors to the left are renewing active operations in the immediate future.
3. Without halting the offensives by Pukhov, Chernyakhovskii and Moskalenko, I have decided to defeat the enemy in the Fastov—Belaya Tserkov' area in the near future and push Zhmachenko and Trofimenko[28] forward at all costs.
    It is very important to do this. I have brought in Moskalenko's entire southern flank and you. In doing this, I have only distracted you for a short time from your chief task—to attack toward Kazatin. This temporary distraction must in no way last for a long time, and I anticipate moving Zhmachenko from his position.
    You have not yet carried out the assignments entrusted to you in the Fastov area and have thus worsened the overall situation. Thus I have been hurrying Moskalenko to arrive in the Fastov area and have ordered his 163rd, 232nd, 340th, and 167th rifle divisions to reach the line Romanovka—Kozhanka—Bertniki—Chervona—Kovalevka—Grebenka—Trostyanskaya—Novoselitsa today and to consolidate along this line, taking up the defense of Fastov and the Vasil'kov axis. Today Moskalenko should bring up his artillery to the troops and his second echelon (38th Rifle Division) to the line Borovaya—Mytnitsa and the 74th Rifle Division should arrive in the Fastov area. A lot of anti-tank artillery has been dispatched to the Fastov area. I am counting on all of this being accomplished by evening today. After this, your task from 11.11.1943 is to renew a vigorous offensive toward Kazatin, which is to be securely occupied no later than 13-14 November. I will confirm this to you in a directive.

---

24 The commander of the 13th Army.
25 The commander of the 60th Army.
26 The commander of the 38th Army.
27 The commander of the 40th Army.
28 The commander of the 27th Army.

The Popel'nya—Pavoloch' area, which has been occupied by you, is to be held and reconnoitered further. I order you to report the situation to me this evening over the wire.

I am ordering comrade Grechko[29] to very carefully organize the 38th Army's defensive front for the purpose of securely holding the Fastov area and freeing Rybalko from this task.

I order you, comrade Rybalko, to immediately eliminate major shortcomings in troop control. Your headquarters are becoming separated from their troops. You don't know your neighbors' situation and know the enemy poorly. You are looking back and pulled back your headquarters into the rear today without need. This should be immediately corrected.

In operations on Kazatin, I demand decisiveness and vigor; otherwise the infantry will overtake you.

Report to me on measures taken and copies of orders issued today. Acquaint comrade Grechko with this letter.

Vatutin

Despite the fact that the *front* commander demanded decisive actions, it was obvious that there were insufficient forces to defeat the enemy's reserves south of Kiev, while at the same time the 13th and 60th armies were attacking with significant forces, faced by a weak enemy.

The fighting on 11 November. Taking into account the growing enemy resistance and the expansion of the latter's counterattack front, the *front* commander issued combat assignments to the 8th Guards and 10th tank corps at dawn on 11 November. These corps were being pulled from the Bukrin bridgehead to the *front* reserve in the Darnitsa area for replenishing them with men and materiel.

The 10th Tank Corps was ordered to cross over to the right bank of the Dnepr and by the close of 12 November concentrate in the Boyarka-Budaevka area and organize a defense, covering Kiev from the south. The 8th Guards Tank Corps was also to cross over to the right bank of the Dnepr and by the close of 12 November organize a defense along the right bank of the Irpen' River. It was ordered to pay particular attention to the Zhitomir—Kiev paved road. Both corps, in carrying out their task of organizing the defense of Kiev, were to at the same time replenish themselves with men and materiel, carry out combat training and to knock together their crews and subunits.

Throughout 11 November the enemy continued to fall back, waging stubborn rearguard battles along a front from the Uzh River to the Brusilov area. The capture of prisoners in the Chernobyl' area along the 13th Army's front established the presence of the 421st and 679th road construction battalions in the first line, which testified that the enemy had removed his main combat units from the secondary sectors and replaced them with rear elements.

The enemy continued his insistent counterattacks with tank units in the Fastov area and opposite the 38th Army's left wing. On this day the lead units of the Germans' 1st Panzer Division began to arrive in the Belaya Tserkov' area. Beginning 3 November, 20-25 trains with tanks and infantry were moving daily from west to east through Rovno and Novograd-Volynskii.

On 11 November the 13th Army broadened its attack front to the north. The 15th Rifle Corps, which had crossed over the Pripyat' River with part of its forces, began to attack along the Karpilovka sector and had begun fighting for Kopachi. The 8th Rifle Division forced the Uzh River and captured Malyi Chervach. The 6th Guards Rifle Division continued to fight along the northern bank of the Uzh River for Novoselki. The enemy was putting up extremely stubborn

---

29 General Grechko, the assistant *front* commander.

resistance to units of the 15th Rifle Corps and was attempting to prevent the crossing of our forces over the Pripyat' and Uzh rivers and was insistently attacking the crossed units with his infantry and tanks. The 18th Guards Rifle Corps, having committed into the fighting the 336th Rifle Division, which had joined it, advanced 10-15 kilometers along its left flank in the day's fighting. The corps' divisions reached the front Cheremoshen'—Novye Sokoly—Stalin farm—Pataleevka—the eastern outskirts of Termakhovka.

The 60th Army forced the Teterev River along the entire front and, having advanced 10-25 kilometers in the day's fighting, captured more than 200 prisoners and a large amount of equipment.

By the close of the day the army reached the front Obukhovichi—Stanishevka—Zhereva—Khanev—Sloboda Kukharskaya—Belyi Bereg—Fedorovka—Mircha—Dorogun'—Teklyanovka—the eastern outskirts of Torchin—Smykovka—the eastern outskirts of Gumenniki. The 17th Guards Rifle Corps continued to remain in the army's second echelon and had concentrated in the Mircha—Kotovka—Zabolot' area.

The 1st Guards Cavalry Corps, while developing the offensive on Zhitomir, was repelling powerful enemy counterattacks. By the close of 11 November the 23rd Rifle Corps had advanced 25 kilometers and reached the front Berezovka—Tesnovka—Korostyshev—Shakhvorostivka.

By the close of the day the 21st Rifle Corps reached the line Karabachin—Khomutets—Velikie Golyaki—east of Skragilevka.

The 50th Rifle Corps captured Zhovtnevo with the forces of the 163rd Rifle Division. The 232nd and 340th rifle divisions, together with units of the 3rd Guards Tank Army, were engaged in defensive battles with the enemy in the Fastovets area; the 167th Rifle Division was defending in the area of the town of Vinitskie Stavy.

The 51st Rifle Corps was repulsing enemy counterattacks along the front Makeevka—Germanovka—Dolina. The 5th Guards Tank Corps was fighting along the 167th Rifle Division's sector.

The 3rd Guards Tank Army was engaged in stubborn fighting with the enemy along the entire front. The 9th Mechanized Corps' 71st Motorized Rifle Brigade abandoned Popel'nya under enemy pressure and fell back on Savertsy. Up to 40 enemy tanks broke through from the Popel'nya area toward Fastov, but were halted six kilometers southwest of Fastov, near the railroad. The 9th Mechanized Corps' remaining brigades were defending south and east of Fastov. The 6th Guards Tank Corps was defending Fastov south, southeast and east of the town, while the 7th Guards Tank Corps was holding Pavoloch' with two brigades, with its remaining units in defense along the southern outskirts of Bol'shie Snetinki.

The 40th Army, having crossed the 42nd Guards and 337th rifle divisions to the right bank of the Dnepr in the Kailov area, was fighting with German tanks in the following areas: the 42nd Guards Rifle Division in Chernyakhov and the 337th Rifle Division in Vitachev. The enemy captured Zhukovtsy and was 500 meters south of Tripol'ye. The 38th Rifle Division, which had earlier been crossed south of Kiev in the Vishenko area and detached from the 27th Army, was fighting here.

Thus along with powerful counterattacks in the Fastov area, the enemy was making desperate attempts to break through along the banks of the Dnepr, reach the Kiev area and get into the rear of our forces attacking to the west and southwest.

On 11 November our aviation worked very little, because there was a cloud cover at an altitude of 100-200 meters and poor visibility (1-2 kilometers). Only the best *shturmovik* and reconnaissance crews flew. The *shturmoviks* carried out 30 sorties for the purpose of destroying the enemy's forces in the Belaya Tserkov' area and along the Pii—Belaya Tserkov' road. Five sorties were carried out for reconnaissance purposes.

The German aviation bombed our forces' combat formations in groups of 2-3 planes and conducted reconnaissance of our rear areas and communications with single aircraft. 21 sorties were observed throughout the day.

FIRST UKRAINIAN FRONT'S NOVEMBER OFFENSIVE OPERATION

The bitterness of the fighting in the Fastov area grew more and more. The enemy managed to halt the Soviet forces' offensive to the southwest and south of Kiev at the cost of heavy losses. As before, the *front* commander did not adopt any new decisions. Partial decisions to reinforce the Fastov area with artillery and engineer equipment were unable to change the overall situation and were more calculated for passive defense than active operations to defeat the enemy's arriving reserves.

The fighting on 12 November. The enemy was making a fighting withdrawal to the west along the 13th and 60th armies' offensive sector and that of the 38th Army's right wing, while he continued to launch powerful counterattacks with tanks and infantry along the Khodorkov—Fastov—Chernyakhov sector, striving at all costs to capture Fastov and break through to Kiev along the right bank of the Dnepr. Here the Germans were continuing to reinforce their group of forces, which now included the 7th, 25th and 3rd panzer divisions and the *Das Reich* and *Adolph Hitler* SS panzer divisions.

The *front's* forces, while continuing the offensive along the Ovruch, Korosten' and Zhitomir axes, were fending off enemy counterattacks in the areas of Kornin, Fastov and Tripol'ye.

Throughout the day the 13th Army fought to expand the bridgehead along the right bank of the Uzh River with the 15th Rifle Corps' 8th and 6th guards rifle divisions. The 18th Guards Rifle Corps, having advanced 10-15 kilometers, was fighting along the line Fedorovka—Veresnya—Buda Polidarovskaya.

The 60th Army's left wing advanced 25 kilometers during the day's fighting and occupied 95 inhabited locales, among which were the major district centers of Rozvazhev, Malin, Potievka, and Chernyakhov. By the close of the day the army reached the front Zhmiivka—Borovsk—Staraya Guta—Buda, Malinovka, Malin—the Stalin Collective Farm—Nyanevka—Budy—Gorodishche—Nerazh—Annopol'—Styrty—Chernyakhov—Bol'shaya Gorbasha—Vysoko-Cheskoe. The 17th Guards Rifle Corps was moving to the south and by the close of the day had reached the 38th Army's sector in the Stavetskaya Sloboda—Potashnya—Kocherovo area.

By 1500 on 12 November the 1st Guards Cavalry Corps was fighting in Zhitomir, clearing it of the enemy. By 1700 the enemy in the city had been destroyed and Zhitomir was completely liberated. By this time two regiments of the 23rd Rifle Division, which were attacking in the sector of the paved road, reached the eastern outskirts of the city, while the cavalry corps began to move out to the west, southwest and south of the city to the line Yanushevichi—Pryazhev—Bystry.

The 38th Army continued to attack along its right wing throughout 12 November. The 23rd Rifle Corps was approaching the Zhitomir area. The 21st Rifle Corps, while pursuing the enemy, had reached the line Ivnitsa—Khodorkov—Krivoye by morning. Opposite the corps' front were the same units of the enemy's 68th, 88th and 323rd infantry, 20th Motorized and 7th Panzer divisions, which were falling back from the Kiev area. The corps continued to attack along a broad 40-kilometer front.

The divisions' artillery had fallen behind and there was little ammunition with the troops. The corps' headquarters and the headquarters of the divisions poorly controlled their forces and had an unclear picture of the enemy's forces and their condition. As a result of this, when at 1000 on 12 November the enemy counterattacked, with a group of 20-25 tanks from the 7th Panzer Division, the 71st Rifle Division along the Khodorkov—Krivoye sector, the division's units did not manifest the proper steadiness and rapidly fell back to the north, exposing the flank and rear of the 135th Rifle Division, which was fighting along the approaches to Kotlyarka and Koilovka. The division also fell back to the northeast. Thus the indiscriminate advance by the 21st Rifle Corps' units, lacking firm control, without reconnoitering the enemy, the poor organization of anti-tank defense, a shortage of artillery and ammunition, led to a situation that following the first counterattack by a numerically inferior enemy the corps fell back from the line reached in a disorganized fashion.

As a result of the uninterrupted counterattacks, the Germans threw units of the 50th Rifle Corps' 163rd Rifle Division out of Mokhnachki. The corps' remaining divisions, the same as the entire 51st Rifle Corps, continued to fight along their former positions.

The 3rd Guards Tank Army was occupying its previous lines (except for the 7th Guards Tank Corps) and repulsed four enemy counterattacks in the areas of Bertniki and Chervona. The 9th Mechanized Corps' 71st Mechanized Brigade reached the woods east of Volitsy from the Savertsy area and the 7th Guards Tank Corps' 54th and 55th guards tank brigades were falling back from the Pavoloch' area on Fastov. The corps' 56th Guards Tank and 23rd Guards Motorized Rifle brigades occupied a defensive line west of Fastov.

During the night of 11-12 November the *front* commander issued a directive to withdraw the 40th Army's 253rd and 68th Guards rifle divisions and the headquarters of the 47th Rifle Corps from the Bukrin bridgehead to the eastern bank of the Dnepr River, in order to cross them again to the right bank of the Dnepr to the Kailov area.

The 40th Army's 309th, 237th and 161st rifle divisions, which remained on the Bukrin bridgehead, were to be transferred to the 52nd Rifle Corps, which, in turn, was to be transferred to the 27th Army.

Thus the 40th Army retained only the combat sector in the Tripol'ye area, which significantly eased the organization and control of the battle. The army included seven rifle divisions (38th, 42nd Guards, 337th, 147th, 241st, 68th Guards, and the 253rd) and the headquarters of the 47th Rifle Corps.

The 40th Army was fighting with the counterattacking enemy south of Tripol'ye throughout the day.

On 12 November the weather improved. On this day the 2nd Air Army, while supporting the 38th and 3rd Guards Tank armies in repelling enemy counterattacks, destroyed his tanks, artillery and personnel in the areas of Fastovets, Vinitskie Stavy, in the woods near Kozhanka, and opposite the Bukrin bridgehead. *Shturmoviks* carried out 157 sorties and the fighters 61 for covering the 38th Army's forces and 65 sorties to cover the *shturmoviks*. In all, the *front's* aviation carried out 289 sorties on 12 November. The enemy's aviation operated in single planes and in groups of up to eight planes along the Kiev—Zhitomir and Kiev—Vasil'kov roads. 32 enemy flights were noted.

Thus as a result of the day's fighting the *front's* forces achieved a major success, captured Zhitomir and continued to successfully develop the offensive along the Korosten' axis. At the same time, the *front's* forces were forced to repulse the enemy's fierce and increasingly powerful counterattacks in the Fastov area and along the Kazatin axis, while in a number of cases poorly commanded troops failed to exhibit sufficient steadfastness and abandoned their positions.

Despite the constant shifting of the command posts, the *front* headquarters during the offensive had reliable wire and radio communications with the armies' headquarters. The timely arrival of reserve communications equipment to the right bank of the Dnepr enabled us as early as 8 November to organize a *front* auxiliary command post (VPU) in Svyatoshino, in direct proximity to the troops. With the shift of the *front's* VPU to Svyatoshino the organization of troop control became easier and improved. The armies' headquarters also followed behind their forces in a timely manner and by 12 November were located as follows: the 60th Army's headquarters was in Peskovka, the 38th Army's headquarters in Boyarka-Budaevka, with an auxiliary command post in Rozhev, while the 3rd Guards Tank Army's headquarters was in Plesetskoye, with an auxiliary command post in Fastov. During the course of the offensive battles measures were adopted to increase the number of cable and air crossings over the Dnepr. Four tower crossings (20 wires) were outfitted in the Kiev area. Besides this, an underwater cable consisting of 28 strands, which had been laid across the river before the war by organs of the People's Commissariat for Communications, was located and used. All of this significantly increased the reliability of the *front's* cable communications. In all, there were ten tower crossings (36 wires), 16 cable crossings and two multi-strand cables over the Dnepr.

It should be noted that by the beginning of the 38th and 3rd Guards Tank armies' bitter fighting against the Germans' counterattacking units, troop control at the army-corps-division level was organized in an unsatisfactory manner.

Upon the beginning of the troops' rapid advance to the west and southwest, communications worked poorly. Wire communications failed to keep up with the troops and radio communications was poorly organized and insufficiently supported technically. The shifting of command posts was not regulated by the higher-ranking headquarters. The corps' and divisions' headquarters knew their troops' situation poorly, as well as the location of lower headquarters. Communications and troop control were particularly poorly organized in the 38th Army's rifle corps. There often remained only one means to clear up the situation and refine the troops' situation—the travel by senior officers directly to the troops. For example, on the night of 12-13 November the commander of the 38th Army personally ordered the commander of the 50th Rifle Corps to travel to the troops to clear up the situation in the Kornin area, because neither the commanders or the staffs of the 21st and 50th rifle corps, along the boundary of which Kornin was located, knew what was actually going on here following a German tank counterattack during the day of 12 November.

As the offensive developed, the headquarters of the 38th Army would lose communications with its corps. From 5 November, when the 1st Guards Cavalry Corps was operationally subordinated to the army, up until 12 November the army headquarters was unable to organize radio communications with it.

The *Stavka* of the Supreme High Command, having evaluated the situation that had developed by 12 November in the Zhitomir and Fastov area, demanded from the *front* commander that he quit advancing without consolidating the captured area, stressed the threat which was arising along the *front's* left wing, and demanded the adoption of emergency measures to eliminate this threat.

The following was contained in the directive of the *Stavka* of the Supreme High Command.

To the commander of the First Ukrainian Front
12.11.1943, 1800
No. 30245

The rapid advance by the right wing and center of the First Ukrainian Front to the west and the simultaneous stubbornness by the enemy and his counterattacks along the Fastov—Tripol'ye front and the concentration here of the Germans' main tank group of forces speaks to the fact that the enemy, by allowing us to advance to the west, is gathering forces for an attack at its base, in the direction of Fastov and Kiev. Taking account of the developing situation, the *Stavka* of the Supreme High Command orders the following:

1. The First Ukrainian Front is to temporarily halt the advance by its center to the west.
2. The *front* is to reinforce the 38th Army's left wing along the front Fastov—Tripol'ye in every way with artillery, tanks and engineer units and in no way allow the enemy to break through here.
3. The divisions being removed from the Shchuchinka and Bukrin bridgeheads are to be concentrated as quickly as possible to the Vasil'kov—Fastov area. 5-6 rifle divisions from Chernyakhovskii's 60th Army and the right wing of Moskalenko's 38th Army are to be dispatched here.
4. Upon the completion of this regrouping and with the arrival of the 1st Guards Army and the 25th Tank Corps, the *front's* most important and main task is to defeat the enemy's Belaya Tserkov' group of forces and to capture Popel'nya, Belaya Tserkov' and Kagarlyk

with the *front's* left wing, after which you are again to force the offensive along the Kazatin axis.

Stavka of the Supreme High Command
I. Stalin, Antonov

On the instructions of the *Stavka* of the 25th Tank Corps and the 1st Guards Army, which were to detrain during 11-26 November at Brovary and Darnitsa stations, were to be subordinated to the First Ukrainian Front, in order to reinforce it.

The 1st Guars Army consisted of nine rifle divisions: the 94th Rifle Corps (99th, 127th and 271st rifle divisions), the 107th Rifle Corps (350th, 351st and 323rd rifle divisions) and the 74th Rifle Corps (305th, 107th and 328th rifle divisions).

Throughout 12 November the *front* commander adopted a series of measures for strengthening the 38th Army and raising its readiness to repulse even more powerful counterblows by the Germans, which could be expected in connection with the continuing arrival of new enemy forces in the areas of Chernyakhov, Fastov and Kornin.

It was ordered to concentrate the entire 7th Breakthrough Artillery Corps along the Vasil'kov—Fastov and Vasil'kov—Grebenki axes.

The tasks of the 10th and 8th Guards tank corps were refined. The latter were to occupy a defensive line along the Stugna River, with their front facing south along the following sectors: Zdorovka—Khambikov for the 10th Tank Corps and Kopachevskaya Sloboda—Bezradichi—Plyuty for the 8th Guards Tank Corps. Both corps were to employ all of their artillery and that of their motorized infantry, as well as unrepaired tanks as immobile firing points, with the mission, should the Germans reach the Stugna River from the south, to halt the enemy with a stubborn defense of this line and to prevent him from spreading further to the north.

It was ordered to create obstacle sectors by the forces of the engineer troops west of Fastov and along the following lines:

a) Chernogorodka—Koshchievka—Velikaya Motovilovka—Zdorovka;
b) Bol'shaya Snetinka—Mar'yanovka.

The 7th Guards Anti-Tank Artillery Brigade was transferred from the 60th Army to the 38th Army. In the same fashion, the 17th Guards Rifle Corps, consisting of the 211th and 70th Guards rifle divisions, was to be transferred from the 60th Army to the 38th Army, by shifting it to the Vil'shka—Velikie Golyaki—Dedovshchina area.

By the decision of the *front* commander, the 1st Guards Army's arriving forces were to be immediately moved to the western bank of the Dnepr River, without waiting of their complete concentration, to the areas west and southwest of Kiev.

The Results of the First Ukrainian Front's Offensive During 7-12 November

During 7-12 November the *front's* left-wing forces successfully pursued the enemy, occupied Malin and advanced to the operationally important railroad junction of Korosten' in the southern Poles'ye and also, while unremittingly pursuing the enemy along the Kiev—Zhitomir paved road, liberated the very important railroad junction and Ukrainian oblast' center of Zhitomir from the Germans.

The enemy's routed forces were unable to hold the Soviet forces' vigorous advance. In six days of fighting in wooded and swampy terrain, the 60th Army advanced 65 kilometers and the 1st

Guards Cavalry Corps and the 38th Army's 23rd and 21st rifle corps made a fighting advance of 120 kilometers along the Zhitomir axis.

The offensive by the 38th Army's left wing along the front Fastov—Tripol'ye was halted. The 50th and 51st rifle corps' broad front and the resulting insufficient operational density of our forces kept us from developing the offensive to the southwest. The offensive front continued to broaden. The offensive was not being conducted along individual axes; the gaps between the corps and even the divisions, particularly in the 38th Army's 23rd Rifle Corps, grew rapidly. In this regard, a particularly difficult situation developed in the 38th Army's center. The army's 23rd Rifle Corps was tied down in the Fastov area, as a result of which the gap between the flanks of the 23rd and 21st rifle corps by the close of 12 November reached 16 kilometers, while the gap between the 21st Rifle Corps' 202nd and 71st rifle divisions reached 14 kilometers. In the event of a further broadening of the enemy's counterattacks to the west, this threatened us with an enemy breakthrough to the paved road into the rear of our Zhitomir group of forces.

The enemy, in turn, sought to launch a powerful counterblow with his tank divisions in the direction of Fastov, Vasil'kov and Kiev in order to force the *front's* forces to halt their offensive to the west and, if lucky, to reach the Kiev area and thus immediately deprive the Soviet forces of those results achieved during the course of the offensive. The first counterattacks by the enemy's tanks in the Fastov area did not yield him the expected results, after which the front of the German counterattacks began to broaden to the east, from Fastov to the Dnepr, due to the arrival of new formations. The German command, in striving to halt the Soviet forces' offensive, adopted all measures to strengthen its group of forces along the Fastov—Belaya Tserkov' axis by shifting forces from the Bukrin bridgehead there, as well as by removing reserves from other sectors of the front. Between 1-12 November 127 rail trains passed through Rovno to Shepetovka alone, of which 23 carried tanks, motor vehicles and motorcycles; 30 carried troops; 17 carried artillery, medical motor vehicles and carts, and; 67 trains carried fuel, ammunition and food.

By the close of 12 November the enemy group of forces opposite the First Ukrainian Front was as follows. The 4th Panzer Division, a combat group from the 292nd Infantry Division and the 8th Light Infantry Division were defending in the Chernobyl' area. The 291st Infantry Division was falling back on Korosten' along a broad front from the Uzh River to Malinovka. There were no enemy forces along the sector Malin—Chernyakhov. The defeated units of the 208th, 340th and 327th infantry divisions, which had broken contact with the 60th Army's pursuing forces, were falling back on Chervonoarmeisk and were arriving from this area at the paved road, while turning to the east toward Zhitomir.

Following the abandonment of Zhitomir, the 8th Panzer Division, the Cavalry Regiment "South" and various composite detachments covered the axis to the south and southwest of the city. Units of the 68th, 88th and 323rd infantry, 20th Motorized and 7th Panzer divisions had fallen back to the Andrushevka area. All the German units operating along the Zhitomir—Kornin sector had been unified into a group under General Mattenklott. Part of the *Adolph Hitler* SS Panzer Division's forces was fighting in the Kornin area and the 1st Panzer Division was approaching Pavoloch'. The 25th Panzer Division, the *Das Reich* SS Panzer Division, the 198th, 75th and 82nd infantry divisions, and the 10th Motorized and 3rd Panzer divisions were operating from Volitsy (southwest of Fastov) and to the east as far as the Dnepr.

One may consider the First Ukrainian Front's Kiev offensive operation to have ended with the fighting on 12 November. Subsequently, in connection with the arrival of powerful enemy reserves and the launching of a counteroffensive in the area of Brusilov and Zhitomir, it grew into a defensive operation.

Overall Results and Conclusions from the First Ukrainian *Front's* November Offensive Operation

The First Ukrainian Front's November offensive operation was conducted according to the plan by the *Stavka* of the Supreme High Command and pursued the goal of creating a large bridgehead on the right bank of the Dnepr in the Kiev area. The *Stavka* assigned strict deadlines for the preparation and conduct of this operation, proceeding from the overall situation along the southern wing of the Soviet-German front. The *Stavka* took into account the fact that the enemy had no significant reserves in the Kiev area and that it was not expedient to allow him a lengthy breathing space, during which he would be able to strengthen his defense. The plan by the *Stavka* of the Supreme High Command proceeded from a realistic evaluation of the situation. The major Kiev bridgehead, which was seized as a result of the conduct of this operation, played a major role in the conduct of subsequent operations along the Ukrainian right bank. During the course of this operation the enemy was forced to expend part of his strategic reserves, which he was transferring from Western Europe and which were designated for operations in the Kirovograd area.

The operation offers instructive experience, thanks to a number of characteristic features. These features, are as follows: the difficulty of deploying large forces of infantry, tanks and artillery on comparatively small bridgeheads 10-15 kilometers deep; the possibility of the enemy's uninterrupted attacks against our forces' crossings over the Dnepr during the concentration of the shock group and in the beginning phase of the operation, given the simultaneous presence of a network of good roads in the enemy's rear, which offered him the opportunity for broad maneuver; the vigor of the *front's* offensive actions, which enabled us to broaden the bridgehead in the Kiev area to 230 kilometers in breadth (counting along the line of the Dnepr) and 145 kilometers in depth (along the Zhitomir axis) in just a few days; the typical form of the *front's* maneuver following the breakthrough of the enemy's defense and the taking of Kiev was a fan-like offensive in the northwest (Korosten', Ovruch), west (Zhitomir), southwest and south (Fastov, Belaya Tserkov') directions.

A feature of the operation is the bold and decisive concentration of men and materiel for attacking along narrow sectors and the retention of minimal forces for defense along a broad front. 67 percent of the combined-arms formations (31 rifle divisions and two rifle brigades of the available 47 rifle divisions and two rifle brigades), 100 percent of the tanks and cavalry (five tank and one mechanized corps and three cavalry divisions) and 100 percent of the reinforcement artillery were concentrated along the 60th, 38th, 40th, and 27th armies' 61-kilometer attack front. 16 rifle divisions remained along the other 263 kilometers of the front. 11 rifle divisions and one rifle brigade, three cavalry divisions, three tank corps, one mechanized corps, and a large part of the reinforcement artillery was concentrated along the *front's* main attack axis (the 38th Army's 14-kilometer attack sector) to break through and develop the success. A decisive and overwhelming superiority over the enemy in men and materiel was created here.

It is necessary to note the skill with which the *front* carried out the regrouping of forces from the left wing to the Lyutezh bridgehead north of Kiev. The tight deadlines, the shortage of automobile transport, the necessity of crossing troops over the Dnepr and Desna rivers three times, the absence of roads with stone surface, and enemy air attacks against the crossings all created extreme difficulties both in the planning and organization and in the conduct of the march by the troops. The regrouping was carried out in the allotted time, along with measures designed to keep the enemy from uncovering the meaning of the maneuver beforehand.

The offensive by the *front's* main shock group north of Kiev was reliably supported along its right turning flank by the operations of the 60th Army, which, while developing the attack to the southwest during the first stage of the operation, reliably covered the 38th Army's operations in the Kiev area from the west.

FIRST UKRAINIAN FRONT'S NOVEMBER OFFENSIVE OPERATION

During the war with the German-Fascist aggressors, the Soviet army often had to begin an offensive from bridgeheads seized along the banks of major rivers, which were employed by the enemy for defense. The difficulty in such operations is the placing of the shock group's forces on limited bridgeheads. The 38th Army's Lyutezh bridgehead had the following maximum size: 14 kilometers from east to west in its deepest southern part, and 16 kilometers from north to south. The northern part of the bridgehead could not be used for stationing the shock group, because it was only 4-5 kilometers deep. The stationing of the rifle formations' second echelons, a major artillery group of forces and a tank army on a small bridgehead required the complete and careful employment of all natural terrain coverings, the conduct of a great deal of work to hid personnel and combat equipment, a powerful anti-aircraft defense, and strict order in the placement of units along the roads and crossings over the Dnepr.

The enemy expected the Soviet forces' decisive operations in the Kiev area. The following circumstances testify to this: the initiative was in the hands of the Soviet forces, the bridgeheads north and south of Kiev (Lyutezh and Bukrin) created favorable jumping-off positions for launching attacks in the Kiev area and, finally, the enormous significance of Kiev for the further unfolding of the struggle along the Ukrainian right bank. The enemy understood that all of this would lead to the new resumption of combat activities in this area in the near future. It follows that one could not count on the operation's complete surprise. It is necessary to add to this the difficulty of regrouping forces from the Bukrin bridgehead, which could not but be noticed by the Germans. The enemy, while expecting a repetition of the attacks from the Bukrin bridgehead and new attacks from the Lyutezh bridgehead, had his main group of forces in this area and was exhibiting heightened vigilance. Surprise in the operation's opening stage was achieved by the power of an attack by a large amount of artillery and tanks, because the enemy was not counting on such a large mass of men and materiel on a small bridgehead in a short time. The second element of surprise was operations along a narrow sector of the breakthrough front. All of this led to us winning time; the enemy was able to bring up new forces to the breakthrough sector only after the loss of Kiev and Fastov and the advance by the *front's* forces 70-75 kilometers to the south and 130 kilometers to the west.

The 38th Army carried out the *front's* main task. It attacked along a 14-kilometer sector and launched its main attack along a 6-kilometer sector. The army captured Kiev and, together with the 3rd Guards Tank Army and the 1st Guards Cavalry Corps, developed the offensive to the south, southwest and south. The 60th Army carried out the task of covering the right, exterior flank of the *front's* shock group and because this group was attacking at first to the south and southwest, the army's offensive developed to the southwest in the area between the Zdvizh and Irpen' rivers. The reliably covering of the shock group's right wing was secured by the 60th Army's sufficiently powerful makeup and the deep tasks assigned it. The cooperation between the 40th and 27th armies, which attacked on the Bukrin bridgehead, with the *front's* shock group was expressed in the fact that they were to tie down the enemy's forces on the Bukrin bridgehead and prevent them from maneuvering to the north.

How were the tasks assigned to the *front's* forces carried out? The enemy's front was pierced by a powerful attack by artillery, aviation and infantry, 12 German divisions were routed and the capital of Ukraine, the city of Kiev, was liberated. After this the enemy began to vigorously fall back to the west and southwest and the breakthrough front quickly expanded.

The 38th Army's infantry, together with the 5th Guards Tank Corps, was supposed to break through two lines of the enemy's defense and partially break through a third by the close of the first day, creating the opportunity for committing the tank army into the breach. The Germans put up stubborn resistance, employing the advantages of the terrain (the wooded nature of the sector). The breakthrough of the enemy's entire defense and the defeat of the 7th Panzer and 20th Motorized divisions, which had been committed into the fighting, were completed only on the operation's third day, 5 November, following the bringing in of part of the tank army.

Having destroyed in the Belichi—Svyatoshino area and having repelled his counterattacks from the Priorka area, the 51st Rifle Corps was fighting in Kiev itself. The timely commitment of part of the 3rd Guards Tank Army's forces to "finish the breakthrough" of the Germans' defense north of Kiev, eliminating the threat that the operation would be drawn out and led to the successful completion of its first-stage missions. However, it should be noted that in the fighting to "finish the breakthrough" of the entire depth of the enemy's defense as far as the line Belichi—Svyatoshino and even as far as the line Borshchagovka—Zhulyany, not only did the 6th Guards Tank Corps, which had been attached to the 38th Army for this task, take part, but also the 7th Guards Tank Corps, which had also been drawn into the fighting from the Berkovets area.

The 60th Army's successful offensive and the complete accomplishment of its missions by days lifted the threat to the 38th Army's right flank and enabled us to employ forces from this sector to reinforce its shock group.

The 3rd Guards Tank Army began pursuing the enemy on the morning of 6 November; that is, only the fourth day of the operation. The 1st Guards Cavalry Corps was at first fighting together with the infantry on the 60th Army's left wing in difficult, wooded terrain and could only break away from the infantry to pursue the enemy on 7 November.

The 40th and 27th armies were able to carry out the task of tying down the enemy's forces on the Bukrin bridgehead only by breaking through his defense. The employment of the enemy's tank and motorized and part of his infantry divisions against the 38th Army was only somewhat delayed because this mission was not carried out. Moreover, the 40th and 27th armies' unsuccessful offensive, which was begun before the offensive north of Kiev, enabled the enemy to remove divisions from the Bukrin bridgehead and transfer them to the areas of Fastov and Tripol'ye.

The Germans' withdrawal from the Kiev area along radial axes led to the rapid expansion of the 38th Army's offensive front and to the formation of two completely independent operational axes along which the pursuit of the enemy by the 38th Army was carried out: the Zhitomir and Belaya Tserkov' axes. This made troop control significantly more difficult for the commander and staff of the 38th Army. By this time the army contained four rifle, one cavalry and one tank corps. The troops' rapid advance broadened the front and slowed the pace of the attack and rendered its combat formation vulnerable to enemy counterattacks. The further development of the offensive could continue only given the presence of large reserves of infantry and tanks within the First Ukrainian Front and the creation of 1-2 new army headquarters in the 38th Army's offensive sector. However, it should be mentioned that the *front* failed to make use of all of its internal possibilities, having tied down a significant part of its forces along secondary axes (13th and 60th armies).

The 3rd Guards Tank Army, following the arrival of its main forces in the Fastov area and that of its forward units in the areas of Popel'nya and Pavoloch', was also unable to make use of the favorably developing situation to develop the offensive along the Berdichev—Kazatin axis. The reason for this was the fighting with the enemy's arriving tank reserves near Fastov. The 3rd Guards Tank Army was unable to break free of the Germans near Fastov and reach the Kornin—Andrushevka area and begin operations along the Andrushevka—Berdichev or Andrushevka—Kazatin axes, where one might expect weak enemy resistance, because the 38th Army's infantry was moving slowly into the Fastov area. One could not leave such an operationally-important railroad junction as Fastov, which was also only a short distance from Kiev, without a defense. By this time the 3rd Guards Tank Army had suffered significant losses in tanks. The army's motorized infantry was short of auto transport and often operated on foot. All of this weakened the army's shock power and its maneuver opportunities.

At the same time the *front* failed to make use of the opportunities at hand for reinforcing the group of forces which was attacking along the main, Kazatin axis. The 13th and 60th armies, which contained 21 rifle divisions, were attacking a weak enemy, while distributing their forces equally along the front.

If at the start of the operation there were eight German infantry and three panzer divisions in the 13th and 60th armies' attack sector, the number of divisions diminished significantly during the fighting and by 12 November there were only five infantry and two panzer divisions, of which four infantry divisions had been bled white in the fighting. Forces were timidly removed from the Bukrin bridgehead, where it was already quite obvious that one could not count on success following the offensive of 1-2 November. During the operation the *front* commander attempted to concentrate the 60th Army's main forces along its left flank, but this was done indecisively. Thus the *front* was not able to ensure a favorable correlation of forces along the main axis before the end of the operation.

The *Stavka* of the Supreme High Command, while attentively continuing to follow the course of the operation in the Kiev area, helped the *front* to correctly evaluate the situation, which had arisen following the capture of the towns of Fastov and Zhitomir, in time, and to determine the beginning of the increasing force of the German tank counterattacks near Fastov and to the east. Taking into account the continuing arrival of the enemy's reserves to the areas of Kazatin and Belaya Tserkov', as well as the condition of the 38th and 3rd Guards Tank armies' forces, the *Stavka* ordered that the offensive be halted along these axes and the achieved success consolidated and to defeat the enemy's group of forces in the Belaya Tserkov' area. The further advance by the First Ukrainian Front's forces in these conditions could only be of an unrestrained character and would have threatened the *front* with serious consequences.

There were serious shortcomings in the organization of troop control in the development of the operation. The troops' objectives changed often (an example is the authorization to employ the 5th Guards Tank Corps along the Zhitomir axis). There were cases when the 40th and 27th armies were assigned offensive tasks with decisive goals while at the same time part of their forces were being transferred to other sectors. The army, corps and division headquarters controlled the troops poorly and reconnoitered the enemy insufficiently. The most blatant examples of this was the case of the unsteadiness of the 21st Rifle Corps' forces during the Germans' counterattack of 12 November, as well as the slow and unorganized movement of the 38th Army's combined-arms formations to the Fastov area.

The rear organs worked very unsatisfactorily following the capture of Kiev on 6 November, when the troops took up the pursuit of the enemy. The *front* had sufficient instructive experience in organizing the rear service in the offensive along the left bank of the Dnepr in September. However, the same mistakes were repeated in the November operation. The rear became extended and the troops remained without fuel and ammunition. Alongside other reasons, this led to a situation in which the *front's* forces were essentially unable to continue the offensive.

3

The First Ukrainian Front's Defensive Battles in the Areas of Kornin, Zhitomir and Brusilov During 13-30 November. The Offensive by the *Front's* Right Flank Along the Korosten' and Ovruch Axes

Having failed to achieve success in the area of Fastov and Tripol'ye, the Germans concentrated a large group of tank forces in the areas of Kornin and Zhitomir and on 15 November counterattacked here with the decisive aim of defeating the Soviet Kiev group of forces, capturing Kiev and eliminating our bridgehead on the right bank of the Dnepr in the Kiev area. The German attack was launched against the 38th Army's right wing. Fierce fighting was waged throughout the entire second half of November in the areas of Kornin, Zhitomir and Brusilov, in which eight tank and seven infantry divisions took part on the enemy side and on the Soviet side a large part of the 38th, 60th and 3rd Guards Tank armies and part of the 1st Guards Army.

As a result of these battles, the Germans managed, at the cost of great losses, to again briefly seize Zhitomir and approach within 60 kilometers of Kiev. However, the enemy was unable to develop the success and achieve his assigned objective. Met by the stubborn resistance of the First Ukrainian Front's forces and having suffered heavy losses in the course of two weeks of fierce fighting, the German tank divisions were bled white and at the end of November were forced to halt their offensive in order to regroup their forces and put them in order.

Simultaneous with the intensive fighting, which the *front's* forces were engaged in during the second half of November along the western approaches to Kiev, the 13th Army's forces continued to develop a successful offensive along the Ovruch axis and the 60th Army's right-flank forces along the Korosten' axis. Both of these important railroad junctions in the southern Poles'ye had been occupied by Soviet forces. As a result of subsequent counterattacks, the Germans captured Korosten' for a brief time. There was no fighting along the *front's* left wing, on the Bukrin bridgehead, during the period under study.

The First Ukrainian Front's Defensive Battles in the Area of Kornin, Zhitomir and Brusilov

On the basis of instructions by the *Stavka* of the Supreme High Command, the *front* commander assigned objectives to the 38th, 40th and 3rd Guards Tank armies on 12-13 November for the defense of the southern face of the bridgehead that had formed on the right bank of the Dnepr along the front Zhitomir—Fastov—Tripol'ye.

The 38th Army had the task of taking up a static defense with the forces of the 1st Guards Cavalry and the 23rd and 21st rifle corps along the line Kamenka—the Guiva River as far as Volosov—Ivnitsa—Skochishche—Kornin—Volitsa station. Units of the 50th and 51st rifle corps were to defend along the line reached further to the east as far as the inhabited locale of Dolina. The defense of the Fastov area was entrusted to the 3rd Guards Tank Army, whose commander had subordinated to him the 38th Army's rifle formations operating in this area. The 38th and 3rd Guards Tank armies' main task was to prevent the enemy from breaking through to the north and northeast.

The 40th Army was to capture the inhabited locales of Zhukovtsy and Staiki, south and southeast of Tripol'ye, with the forces of the 47th Rifle Corps (36th, 42nd Guards and 337th rifle divisions) and take up a static defense along the sector Dolina—Zhukovtsy—Staiki. The 52nd Rifle Corps, the headquarters of which was being transferred from the Bukrin bridgehead, was employed for defending the approaches to Kiev from the south. This corps' 147th Rifle Division was concentrating in Vasil'kov; the remaining divisions (241st, 68th Guards and 253rd), following their transfer from the Bukrin bridgehead, had the task of occupying the second defensive line along the line Koshchievka—Borovaya and then along the northern bank of the Stugna River as far as Bezradichi. In a change to previously issued orders, the army headquarters was ordered to move to Vasil'kov by 14 November and to establish direct communications with the headquarters of the 38th and 3rd Guards Tank armies and the 50th and 51st rifle and 5th Guards Tank corps.

The *front* commander paid particular attention to the necessity of organizing the reliable defense of the Fastov area, as well as in the sectors of the Fastov—Kiev railroad, the Belaya Tserkov'—Kiev paved road and the Germanovka—Kiev and Chernyakhov—Obukhov—Kiev axes.

The fighting on 13 November. The Germans, upon encountering the stubborn defense of the *front's* forces in the Fastov area and to the east, began to shift the center of their efforts to the west, taking advantage of the unsteadiness of the 21st Rifle Corps' units, which had become evident in the preceding fighting. The enemy, having thrown back on 12 November units of the 71st and 135th rifle divisions, which were operating west and southwest of Kornin, occupied Kornin, which had not yet been occupied by our forces, without a fight on the night of 12-13 November and began to spread to the north on the morning of 13 November. Half of the *Adolph Hitler* Panzer Division and individual units of the Germans' arriving 1st Panzer Division were operating in the Kornin area on this day. A group of German forces, which had been falling back from the Kiev area, the remnants of the 68th, 323rd and 88th infantry divisions, the 20th Motorized Division, and the 7th Panzer Division, which had been reinforced by this time, were fighting in the Khodorkov area and to the west.

During the second half of the day on 13 November, the enemy, supported by aviation, began powerful counterattacks from the areas of Kornin and Khodorkov to the north toward Brusilov. The Germans managed to break through the front of the 21st Rifle Corps, which was defending here, which made significantly more difficult troop control by the corps commander and staff.

The enemy's advance along the Brusilov axis was creating a serious threat to the First Ukrainian Front's forces. With the arrival of German tanks at Brusilov and then at the Kiev—Zhitomir paved road, the 38th Army's front would be split into two parts; the enemy would have the opportunity to operate against the rear areas of the Fastov and Zhitomir groups of forces.

In order to parry the enemy's attacks along the Brusilov axis, the *front* commander adopted a series of energetic measures. The 21st Rifle Corps was quickly reinforced with anti-tank artillery; the 13th Artillery Division from the 7th Breakthrough Artillery Corps, from the High Command Reserve, which had been operating earlier as part of the 23rd Rifle Corps, was transferred to the breakthrough area. A tank group under the command of Major General Suleikov from the 3rd Guards Tank Army, which included the tank brigades of the 6th and 7th guards tank corps. This group included 59 tanks. At 1800 on 13 November the newly formed group began to move from the Fastov area to the Solov'yovka—Turbovka area (south and southwest of Brusilov) and arrived there by dawn on 14 November. The 60th Army was ordered, aside from the 17th Guards Rifle Corps (70th Guards and 211 rifle divisions), which had been pulled into the *front* reserve in the

Kocherovo area, to pull yet two more divisions (75th Guards Rifle and the 3rd Guards Airborne divisions) into the reserve. The 129th Tank Brigade was also being shifted to the Kocherovo area from the 60th Army's right wing.

The enemy did not carry out active operations along the remainder of the 38th Army's front during 13 November and only attacked units of the 180th Rifle Division in the Shevchenkivka area in a group of 20 tanks.

During the night of 13-14 November the *front* commander issued operational directive No. 61/op and a series of local orders, the instructions of which to a significant degree established order in troop control and strengthened the Brusilov axis.

The 38th Army transferred its 50th and 51st rifle corps and their occupied sectors of Mokhnachka—Fastov—Makeevka—Dolina to the 3rd Guards Tank and 40th armies. The army retained the 23rd Rifle Corps (30th, 23rd and 218th rifle divisions), 21st Rifle Corps (71st, 135th and 202nd rifle divisions), the 17th Guards Rifle Corps (70th Guards and 211th rifle divisions), the 1st Guards Cavalry Corps, and the 17th Artillery Division.

The 60th Army was to transfer the 1st Breakthrough Artillery Division and two rifle divisions (3rd Guards Airborne and the 75th Guards Rifle divisions). At 0600 on 15 November the 38th Army's boundary line on the left was established along the line Zhornovka—the Irpen' River as far as Belki—Belki, with all locales for the 38th Army. The army commander was ordered to pull the 1st Guards Cavalry Corps into the army reserve no later than 15 November.

The 50th Rifle Corps (163rd, 74th, 232nd, and 340th rifle divisions) was subordinated to the 3rd Guards Tank Army.

The 40th Army was to take on the 51st Rifle Corps (167th, 180th, 240th, and 136th rifle divisions and the Czechoslovak Brigade), the 5th Guards Tank Corps and the 13th Artillery Division. The army was also reinforced by the 8th Guards and 10th tank corps. The boundary line on the left was established as Staiki—Stritovka—Kagarlyk.

The fighting on 14 November. The Germans' *Adolph Hitler* SS Panzer and the 1st Panzer divisions were completing their concentration in the Kornin area during 14 November.

The enemy attacked our forces along the front Ivnitsa—Khodorkov—Kornin, as a result of which the 71st Rifle Division abandoned the inhabited locales of Sobolevka and Korolevka.

The German command was strengthening its Zhitomir group of forces, having concentrated west of Zhitomir the 208th, 340th and 327th infantry divisions, which before this had been following back opposite the 60th Army's left-wing forces.

Throughout the day the 7th Guards Artillery Division beat off the enemy's insistent attacks along the Yanushevichi—Al'binovka sector.

The fighting on 15 November. By the morning of 15 November the the situation of the 38th Army's forces along the Zhitomir—Fastov sector was as follows. The 1st Guards Cavalry Corps was defending Zhitomir. Its 7th Guards Cavalry Division occupied the line Yanushevichi—Al'binovka; the 2nd Guards Cavalry Division was concentrated in the area of Psyshchi; the 1st Guards Cavalry Division was marching to the Kocherovo area, by order of the *front* commander, with the task of occupying a defensive line along the Viliya River. The 23rd Rifle Corps was regrouping for the purpose of occupying the line Al'binovka—Grada: the 218th Rifle Division was to defend along the front excluding Al'binovka and then along the northern bank of the Guiva River as far as Peski; the 23rd Rifle Division was along the front Mlinishche—Tulin; the 30th Rifle Division north of Turovets and Grada. The 3rd Guards Airborne Division, which was completing its concentration in the Smolovka area, had been subordinated to the corps.

The 21st Rifle Corps was defending along the line Ivnitsa—Volitsa, with its 202nd Rifle Division along a front north and northeast of Ivnitsa, the 71st Rifle Division along the front Ozera—excluding Gnilets, and the 135th Rifle Division in the Luchin—Mokhnachka area. The 50th Rifle Corps' 163rd Rifle Division was defending along the edge of the woods north of Volitsa station.

The 3rd Guards Tank Army's tank group, having thrown the enemy out of Lisovka, took up a defense along the sector Gnilets—excluding Luchin, with its front facing south. Thus the gap along the 21st Rifle Corps' front was filled by units of the 3rd Guards Tank Army.

The 17th Guards Rifle Corps was organizing a defense along the following line: the 75th Guards Rifle Division along the line Strutsevka—Grubskoye, the 211th Rifle Division along the line Zapadnya—Gnilets, and the 70th Guards Rifle Division along the line excluding Gnilets—Lisovka—Turbovka.

By the morning of 15 November the 38th Army's defense was still not fully ready. For example, two of the 23rd Corps' divisions (23rd and 30th) had still not occupied their defensive lines and had not managed to organize a fire system. There were large gaps between the 21st Corps' divisions.

Among the shortcomings of the 38th Army's defense along the sector from Zhitomir to Fastov was the poor organization of control among the troops of the 23rd and 21st rifle corps, as well as the poorly organized rear-area services. The troops experienced a shortage of ammunition and fuel and lubricants for their combat vehicles and auto transport.

The 38th Army's neighbor on the right—the 60th Army's 30th Rifle Corps—was consolidating with its 141st and 121st rifle divisions along the line Vorov—Mokrenshchina—Klitishche—Kamenka.

The 38th Army's neighbor on the left—the 3rd Guards Tank Army—was defending with the forces of the 50th Rifle (163rd, 232nd, 340th, and 74th rifle divisions) and the 9th Mechanized corps along the line Volitsa station—Chervona—Fastovets—Mar'yanovka 1st. The 3rd Guards Tank Army's 6th and 7th tank corps continued to transfer their units to the Brusilov area. The 40th Army, consisting of the 51st Rifle Corps (167th, 180th, 240th, and 136th rifle divisions and the Czechoslovak brigade) and the 47th Rifle Corps (38th, 42nd Guards and 337th rifle divisions) was defending further to the east as far as the Dnepr. The 40th Army's 52nd Rifle Corps (147th, 241st, 253rd, and 68th Guards rifle divisions) was crossing over the Dnepr in the Kailov area with the task of organizing a second defensive zone along the northern bank of the Stugna River.

At 0150 on 15 November the *front* commander issued the following order to the 38th Army:

- to strengthen and fortify the defense of Zhitomir; forward detachments are to be moved to the line Berezovka—Perlovka—Velikii Shumsk—Singuri—Gorodishche;
- to destroy the enemy in the areas of Ivnitsa, Kornin and Korolevka by the morning of 15 November and restore the situation in these areas;
- to create a continuous defensive front by the morning of 15 November, secure the boundaries between units and formations and to organize active reconnaissance.

Responsibility for the boundary between the 38th and 60th armies was entrusted to the commander of the 60th Army. The 8th Guards Tank Corps was to be concentrating in the Korostyshev area by 1500 on 15 November and was to be transferred to the 38th Army.

However, the troops were not able to carry out this order by the deadline established. For example, the 23rd Rifle Corps' formations did not reach the Guiva River and the Popel'nya—Zhitomir paved road along the northern bank of the Guiva River remained in German hands.

The enemy, having established during the fighting of 12-14 November that the 38th Army's defense was weak along the 21st Rifle Corps' sector, shifted, as indicated above, the center of gravity of its operations to the Kornin—Brusilov axis. Having resolved to launch an attack here with the forces of the 1st Panzer Division and the *Adolph Hitler* SS Panzer Division, the Germans simultaneously planned a supporting attack southeast of Zhitomir in the direction of Levkov, for the purpose of outflanking the *front's* Zhitomir group of forces from the east.

By the morning of 15 November the group of German forces was as follows: the 208th Infantry Division, the 8th Panzer Division along with the "South" Cavalry Regiment, the remnants of the

88th Infantry Division, which had been reinforced with a reserve battalion, and the 7th Panzer Division, which had been transferred on the previous evening from the Ivnitsa area, were operating west, south and southeast of Zhitomir. The 20th Motorized Division was operating in the area Turovets—Grada. The 68th and 323rd infantry divisions were operating in the area Ivnitsa—excluding Khodorkov, while the 1st Panzer and *Adolph Hitler* SS panzer divisions were in the Kornin area. The 25th Panzer Division was fighting further, as far as Palyanichentsy. The 340th and 327th infantry divisions were concentrating west of Zhitomir. The 1st and 25th panzer and *Adolph Hitler* SS Panzer divisions were part of the Fourth Panzer Army's XLVIII Panzer Corps, while the remaining forces were part of General Mattenklott's army group.

At dawn on 15 November the enemy renewed active operations in the Kornin area and southeast of Zhitomir.

In the Kornin area the Germans attacked with the forces of the 1st Panzer Division and the *Adolph Hitler* SS Panzer Division on Solov'yovka and Brusilov. As a result of the fierce fighting, which lasted the entire day, the enemy managed to capture Solov'yovka in the evening. The 3rd Guards Tank Army's tank group and the 17th Guards Rifle Corps were forced to fall back to the north. The 21st Rifle Corps' 71st Rifle Division, while putting up weak resistance to the enemy, fell back behind the 17th Guards Rifle Corps' combat formations and was putting its units in order in the Yuzefovka area.

Southeast of Zhitomir, at dawn on 15 November the German 7th Panzer Division, which numbered no less than 75 tanks, attacked units of the 23rd Rifle Division, which were arriving at their sector in the areas of Tarasovka and Mlinishche and the 218th Rifle Division's left-flank units in the Peski area. Having encircled and destroyed individual elements of the 23rd Rifle Division, the Germans attempted to develop the offensive on Zhitomir and to break into it from the southeast. However, as a result of the stout resistance by the 23rd Rifle Division's main forces and counterattacks by the corps reserve and units of the 30th Rifle Division, the enemy offensive was halted. The insistent attacks by units of the 23rd Rifle Corps, which were undertaken throughout the entire day of 15 November and the night of 15-16 November for the purpose of defeating the Germans' 7th Panzer Division and arriving at the corps' designated defensive line, were not successful. The 218th Rifle Division, having abandoned Peski, pulled back its left-flank units to the northern bank of the Teterev River to the Sloboda Selets area. The 23rd Rifle Division was fighting along the line Bystry—excluding Tarasovka. The 30th Rifle Division remained along its designated line.

Throughout 15 November units of the 3rd Guards Tank Army were turning over their defense of the Fastov area to the 50th Rifle Corps.

During 15 November the *front* commander adopted a number of additional measures to strengthen the defense along the Brusilov axis and in the Zhitomir area. The most important measure was the decision to regroup the 132nd and 141st rifle divisions and the headquarters of the 60th Army's 30th Rifle Corps to the Zhitomir area. The *front* commander personally ordered the 30th Rifle Corps, consisting of the forces already indicated, to take up the defense along the northern bank of the Teterev River and to prevent the enemy from breaking through to the north and outflanking Zhitomir from the east. The 141st Rifle Division was to take up defensive positions along the sector the eastern outskirts of Zhitomir—Levkov and the 132nd Rifle Division along the sector excluding Levkov—Korostyshev. The corps was to remain operationally subordinated to the 60th Army. The *front* commander demanded that the 38th Army hold Zhitomir at all costs.

In order to strengthen the Brusilov axis, the commander of the 40th Army was ordered to transfer the 241st Rifle Division to the 38th Army and to concentrate it no later than 2300 on 15 November in the Brusilov area. The 100th and 237th rifle divisions were to be transferred from the 27th Army to the 40th Army.

At 0415 on 16 November the *front* commander issued the following orders to the 38th Army: to defeat the enemy's Kornin group of forces during 16-17 November and to restore the situation.

The fighting on 16 November. The enemy, having seized the initiative in the 15 November fighting, continued to carry out insistent attacks throughout the following day, both near Brusilov and east of Zhitomir.

On 16 November the 1st Panzer and *Adolph Hitler* SS Panzer divisions once again attempted to break through to Brusilov. However, due to our troops' stubborn resistance, the Germans were only able to capture the inhabited locale of Divin by the close of the day, having forced units of the 70th Guards Rifle Division and General Suleikov's group to fall back to the area of the village of Vil'shka. Having suffered a setback in their attempts to capture Brusilov by head-on attacks from the south, the enemy began attacking in the direction of Vodotyi and Vil'nya during the second half of the day along the sector of the 211th Rifle Division, which began a fighting withdrawal to the north. By the close of the day German tanks broke into the Vil'nya area. The threat arose that the Germans might reach the rear of the 75th Guards and 202nd rifle divisions.

As a result of the 16 November fighting, the Germans achieved a significant success east of Zhitomir. The 7th Panzer Division, together with the 20th Motorized Divison, which had been transferred during the night from the Turovets—Grada area, forced the Teterev River and by the close of the day captured the inhabited locale of Levkov. At the same time, the 88th Infantry Division, which was attacking toward Zhitomir from the south, also forced the Teterev River and, having pressed back units of the 218th Rifle Division, reached the southern outskirts of Zhitomir and the area south of Vats'kov. The threat arose that the enemy would reach the Zhitomir—Kiev paved road east of the city. By the close of the day the 23rd Rifle Corps was fighting along the line southern outskirts of Zhitomir—Sloboda Selets—Vats'kov—the northeastern outskirts of Levkov—Turovets—Grada.

During 15-16 November the enemy pulled the *Das Reich* SS Panzer Division, which was located along the sector of the front east of Fastov, into the reserve and concentrated it in the Grebenki area, as well as the 19th Panzer Division from the sector opposite the Bukrin bridgehead. One could assume that the enemy was employing these divisions to strengthen its attacks near Brusilov and Zhitomir.

In connection with the increasing complexity of the situation in the areas of Brusilov and Zhitomir, the *front* commander once again adopted measures to strengthen the 38th Army with units and formations at the expense of the *front's* other armies. On this day the 52nd Rifle Corps (147th, 42nd Guard and 253rd rifle divisions), the 5th Guards Tank Corps and the 37th Light Artillery and 9th Anti-Tank Artillery brigades were transferred from the 40th Army to the 38th, as well as an anti-tank artillery regiment from the 13th Army. All of these forces were dispatched from strengthening the defense along the Brusilov axis. The 93rd Tank Brigade was removed from the 27th Army and dispatched to the *front* reserve in the Svyatoshino area.

On 16 November changes were also made to the armies' composition and tasks and the boundary lines between them altered. The 1st Guards Cavalry Corps (2nd and 7th guards cavalry divisions), the 23rd Rifle (218th, 23rd and 30th rifle divisions) and the 3rd Guards Airborne Division was to be subordinated to the 60th Army. The army was to securely defend the line occupied by its forces, devoting its main attention to the defense of Zhitomir. From 2400 on 16 November the army's boundary line on the left was established along the following line: Rakovichi—Lenino—the Teterev River—Korostyshev—Ivnitsa (all locales, except for Rakovichi, were for the 60th Army).

Thus the defense of Zhitomir was entrusted to the forces of the 60th Army. The commander of the 60th Army, upon taking over the Zhitomir sector of the front, as early as 2040 on 16 November issued to the commander of the 1st Guards Cavalry Corps a short and categorical order: "Defend the city of Zhitomir to the last man!"

At 1800 the *front* commander assigned a new objective to the 30th Rifle Corps (141st and 132nd rifle divisions and a rifle brigade). The corps was to organize a defense along the Teterev River along the sector Kharitonovka—Korostyshev—Kozievka—Lenino, with its front facing the east and southeast.

The 38th Army was ordered to do the following with the forces of its newly-arrived 52nd Rifle Corps:

- to organize a defense along the Zdvizh River along the sector Fasovochka—Yurov—Bol'shoi Karashin—Lazarevka, with its front facing northwest;
- to occupy defensive positions with one of the corps' divisions along the sector Stavshie—Kostoedy, with its front facing west and southwest;
- to move up the 5th and 6th guards tank corps and the 9th Anti-Tank Brigade to the line Kocherovo—Ozeryany—Osovtsy—Kostoedy;
- the 21st Rifle Corps' 202nd Rifle Division was authorized to pull back on the night of 16-17 November to the line Grabovka—Yelizavetivka—Berezovyi Gai, and the 75th Guards Rifle Division to the line excluding Berezovyi Gai—Voitashivka—Antonovka.

The 3rd Guards Tank Army was to transfer the 50th Rifle Corps (163rd, 232nd, 340th, and 74th rifle divisions) and the 91st Tank Brigade to the 40th Army, along with their defensive sectors.[1] The 3rd Guards Tank Army was assigned the task, in conjunction with the 38th Army, of preventing the enemy from reaching the Kiev—Zhitomir paved road and also from breaking through along the paved road to Kiev.

By the close of 16 November the 7th Guards Tank Corps, along with the 70th Guards Rifle Division, continued fighting in the Vil'shka area, while the 6th Guards Tank Corps was moving north of Brusilov to the Ozeryany area, and the 9th Mechanized Corps was moving to the Vil'shka—Dedovshchina area.

At 1800 on 16 November, following the transfer of the 50th Rifle Corps to the 40th Army, the following boundary line was established between the 38th and 40th armies: Zhornovka—the Irpen' River as far as Belki and then to Pavoloch', with all locales for the 40th Army.

The fighting on 17 November. Throughout 17 November the situation in the areas of Zhitomir and Brusilov continued to worsen. The regrouping of the *front's* forces, which began on 16 November for the purpose of increasing the depth of the defense, had not been completed by the morning of 17 November. The enemy, who had broken through the previous evening to the Vil'nya area, had concentrated the main forces of the 1st Panzer and *Adolph Hitler* SS Panzer divisions here and launched attacks to the north and northwest. The 38th and 3rd Guards Tank armies' forces were engaged in bitter fighting all day and inflicted significant losses on the enemy. However, by the close of the day the tanks of the *Adolph Hitler* SS Division managed to break through Voitashivka to the Zhitomir—Kiev paved road, from which they turned to the east. Bitter fighting broke out near Kocherovo.

The Germans' 1st Panzer Division, which was attacking to the northwest from the Vil'nya area, also broke through to the paved road in the Korostyshev area and captured the latter. The Germans' offensive was less successful east of Zhitomir. However, units of the 7th Panzer and 20th Motorized divisions managed to capture the inhabited locale of Vats'kov and reach the Zhitomir—Kiev paved road.

The Germans were bringing up to the attack area additional reserves to develop the success. The 19th Panzer Division was being moved up through Kagarlyk and Belaya Tserkov' from the sector

---

1 The army included its main formations, the 6th and 7th tank and 9th Mechanized corps.

THE FIRST UKRAINIAN FRONT'S DEFENSIVE BATTLES

of the front opposite the Bukrin bridgehead to the Skviry area. Units of the 2nd Air Field Division, which had arrived by railroad, were being unloaded at the Berdichev and Popel'nya stations.

In his turn, the *front* commander was also continuing to reinforce the 38th Army with new units. On 17 November the 315th and 1070th anti-tank artillery regiments were transferred from the 40th and 27th armies to the 38th Army. Covering detachments were organized with the assignment, in the event of the enemy developing the offensive, to mine the following axes: Stavishche—Kiev; Vasil'kov—Kiev; Kopachi—Gvozdov—Kiev, and; Fastov—Plesetskoye—Kiev.

In order to mislead the enemy, the 27th Army was ordered to carry out measures on the Bukrin bridgehead during 17-30 November, enabling us to hide from the Germans the withdrawal from there of a significant part of the troops and to create the impression among the enemy that the concentration of a large group of Soviet forces was taking place on the bridgehead and that preparations were underfoot for it to go over to the offensive.

The fighting on 18 November. On 18 November the enemy launched a concentric attack on Veresy with the forces of the 8th Panzer Division from the Vil'sk area north of Zhitomir, and with the forces of the 7th Panzer and 20th Motorized divisions from the Vats'kov area. As a result of this attack, our Zhitomir group of forces (2nd and 7th guards cavalry divisions, part of the forces of the 121st, 141st and 218th rifle divisions) was encircled by the enemy. At the same time, the enemy's 1st Panzer Division pushed back units of the 23rd Rifle Corps to the north of the paved road. The *Adolph Hitler* SS Panzer Division was engaged in bitter fighting in Kocherovo, although it was unable to break through along the paved road to the east during the day.

With the start of the fighting on 18 November the *front* commander categorically demanded, in a telegram to the commander of the 1st Guards Cavalry Corps, that he hold Zhitomir at any cost.

The Soviet forces' situation along the Zhitomir—Brusilov sector was as follows by the close of 18 November. The 1st Guards Cavalry Corps (2nd and 7th guards cavalry divisions), a regiment each from the 121st and 141st rifle divisions, and the 218th Rifle Division were fighting in encirclement in Zhitomir. The 121st and 141st rifle divisions' main forces had fallen back to the north of Zhitomir and were fighting there: the 121st Rifle Division along the line Chernyakhov—Bol'shaya Gorbasha—Trokovichi, with its front facing west and southwest. The 141st Rifle Division was in the Veresy area. The 322nd Rifle Division, which had been pulled out of the 24th Rifle Corps' combat formation on 17 November and transferred to the Korostyshev area, was fighting in conjunction with the 3rd Guards Airborne Division along the line Gorodishche—Studenitsa—the northwestern outskirts of Korostyshev. The remnants of the 23rd and 30th rifle divisions had fallen back to the Tesnovka area, where they were being put in order. The 132nd Rifle Division was defending along the sector Kozievka—excluding Gorods'k, and the 248th Rifle Brigade was along the Gorods'k—Lenino sector.

In order to secure the boundary with the 38th Army in the area northeast of Korostyshev, where the *Adolph Hitler* SS Panzer Division was attacking, at 0200 on 18 November the commander of the 60th Army ordered the 1st Guards Cavalry Division to organize a stable defense along the line Chashcha—Potashnya, with its front facing south and southwest. The division arrived at the indicated line throughout the day and was organizing it for defense.

The 280th Rifle Division, which had been removed from the 77th Rifle Corps on 17 November, was concentrating in the Radomyshl' area. the 2nd Guards Airborne Division, which had been transferred by order of the *front* commander from the 13th Army to the 60th Army, was approaching the Rakovichi area. Due to the complex situation and the ongoing regrouping, the control of the army's forces along the Chernyakhov—Korostyshev sector was poorly organized. Units of various corps and even divisions were mixed up and the headquarters of the 23rd and 30th rifle corps had no communications with their troops or knew the situation poorly.

It was only on 18 November that the 38th Army put the control of its forces in order, having precisely determined the composition of the rifle corps and their defensive sectors. The 17th

Guards Rifle Corps (75th Guards, 211th and 70th Guards rifle divisions) were engaged in defensive fighting along the front Tsarevka—Kocherovo—Privorot'ye—Karabachin—Morozovka. The 21st Rifle Corps (241st and 135th rifle divisions) were defending along the line excluding Morozovka—Vil'shka—Luchin—Stavni. The 52nd Rifle Corps (42nd Guards, 147th and 68th Guards rifle divisions) occupied defensive positions along the front Fasovochka—Lazarevka, and the corps' 253rd Rifle Division, along with the 211th Rifle Division, was engaged in fighting in the Kocherovo area. The 10th Tank Corps was defending along the southern outskirts of Brusilov. The 8th Guards Tank Corps was concentrated in Osovtsy.

On 18 November the 68th Guards Rifle and 13th Artillery divisions were transferred from the 40th Army to the 38th Army.

The 3rd Guards Tank Army's 6th Guards Tank Corps was preparing a defense north of Ozeryany, with its front facing west; the 9th Mechanized Corps was defending along the line of the southern outskirts of Brusilov—Yastreben'ka, and the 7th Guards Tank Corps along the line Vil'shka—Luchin.

The 40th Army, consisting of the 50th, 51st and 47th rifle corps, continued to defend along its previous line of Fastov—Tripol'ye; it was quiet along its sector. On 18 November the 155th Rifle Division was transferred from the 27th Army to the 40th Army.

During the night of 18-19 November the *front* commander made the decision for the 1st Guards Cavalry Corps and the 218th Rifle Division and individual units of the 121st and 142t rifle divisions to get out of the encirclement in the Zhitomir area. The escape was to unfold according to the following plan by the commander of the 60th Army. The encircled group of forces' main forces (2nd and 7th guards cavalry divisions) were to concentrate along the northern outskirts of Zhitomir, from where they were to launch an attack to the north, along the railroad. The rifle units were to cover the retreat of the cavalry divisions. Simultaneously, the 30th Rifle Corps was to launch an attack on Zhitomir from the north, assisting the 1st Guards Cavalry Corps in breaking out of the encirclement.

All of the 60th Army's remaining forces were to stubbornly defend along their lines. The 280th Rifle Division, which had arrived in Radomyshl', was to occupy defensive positions along the Starosel'tsy—Ivanovka sector following a brief rest. On 19 November, the 6th Guards Rifle Division, the 874th Anti-Tank Artillery Regiment and the 323rd Guards Mortar Regiment were transferred from the 13th Army to the 60th Army by order of the *front* commander.

On the night of 18-19 November the *front* commander also issued a combat order to the 38th Army to launch a counteroffensive. The main attack was to be launched in the direction of Brusilov, Vodotyi and Khodorkov, and supporting attacks in the directions of Privorot'ye, Krapivnya and Luchin, and Kornin.

The start of the offensive was set for 21 November. By the close of this day the army's forces were to reach the front Gorodetskaya—Voitashivka—Vil'nya—Vodotyi—Solov'yovka—Turbovka—Sushchanka and by the close of 23 November the front excluding Korostyshev—Shakhvorostivka—Yaropovichi—Krivoye—excluding Mokhnachka. The troops had the task of consolidating along this sector. It was ordered to concentrate no less than 200 artillery pieces and mortars per kilometer of front along the main attack sector.

The 3rd Guards Tank Army was ordered to support the 38th Army with fire and be ready to develop its success. The 2nd Air Army was to support the 38th Army with all of its forces and also cover the forces of the 38th and 3rd Guards Tank armies against enemy air attacks.

The fighting on 19 November. There was fighting only along individual sectors throughout 19 November and the sides' situation did not change substantially. The 60th Army's forces repelled the enemy's attacks along the 30th Rifle Corps' sector south of Chernyakhov and were fighting in the center of Korostyshev. A large part of the army's Zhitomir group of forces broke through out of the encirclement on 19 November and reached the Vysoko-Cheshskoye—Zabrod'ye area. The army's remaining forces were consolidating along their lines and putting themselves in order.

The 38th Army's forces were fighting in the area of Kocherovo and Morozovka. By the close of the day Morozovka was abandoned by our forces.

The 3rd Guards Tank Army remained along its previous lines and was fighting in the Morozovka—Luchin area with part of its forces, together with the 38th Army's formations. Reserves were created in the army's corps along the lines of one brigade per corps. Due to a shortage of equipment among the troops, these brigades were weak. For example, in the 6th Guards Tank Corps the reserve consisted of eight tanks and four in the 7th Guards Tank Corps' reserve, while only the 9th Mechanized Corps' reserve had 25 tanks.

Throughout the day, the enemy, while attacking along individual sectors, regrouped. The 19th Panzer Division was pulled out of the fighting in the Solov'yovka area. The 25th Panzer Division continued to operate to the south. The *Adolph Hitler* SS Panzer Division was fighting in the Vil'nya—Vodotyi area. the 7th Panzer Division was operating in the Veresy area. The 8th Panzer Division was concentrated in Zhitomir. This testified to the fact that the enemy in the Brusilov area was preparing a powerful attack with the forces of 3-4 panzer divisions for the purpose of breaking through to Kiev. On this day the Germans began to pull the *Das Reich* SS Panzer Division out of the line in the Belaya Tserkov' area.

The fighting on 20 November. The 38th Army was unable to launch active operations on 20 November, because the enemy was engaged in powerful attacks in the Kocherovo area with the forces of the 1st Panzer Division. At the same time, the Germans launched a second attack with the forces of the 7th Panzer and 20 Motorized divisions in the direction of Studenitsa and Radomyshl'. Units of the 60th Army's 23rd Rifle Corps, unable to withstand the blow, began to fall back to the northeast.

On this day the *front* commander resubordinated the 47th Rifle Corps (337th, 38th and 136th rifle divisions) to the 27th Army and ordered the army's command post to be moved to Obukhov. Only an auxiliary command post was left on the Bukrin bridgehead. As of 2400 on 21 November the boundary line between the 40th and 27th armies was to run along the line Malye Dmitrovichi—Kopachi—Germanovka—Rozaleevka (all locales, except for Malye Dmitrovichi, were for the 40th Army inclusively). Both armies had their previous task of securely holding their position.

In his local instructions, the *front* commander transferred the 202nd Rifle Division from the 38th Army to the 60th Army, and the 28th Anti-Tank Artillery Brigade from the 40th Army to the 60th Army.

On this day the 60th Army's 15th Rifle Division (336th Rifle, 2nd Guards Airborne divisions and the 248th Rifle Brigade) reached the Radomyshl' area. It was ordered to organize a defense along the northern bank of the Bystreevka River along the sector Filippovichi—the southern outskirts of Radomyshl', with its front facing south. The 3rd Guards Tank Army's 91st Tank Brigade, which had been operationally subordinated to the 60th Army by the *front* commander, was also moving to the Radomyshl' area. During the night of 20-21 November the 7th Guards Tank Corps (which had at this time only 19 tanks in the line) also began marching to the Radomyshl' area.

The fighting on 21 November. On the morning of 21 November the enemy attacked in the direction of Rudnya, Kocherovo, Vodotyi and Divin with the forces of the 19th Panzer, *Adolph Hitler* SS Panzer and 1st Panzer divisions, and following fierce fighting pushed back the 38th Army's units along the paved road 2-3 kilometers east of Kocherovo. The army's forces abandoned Vil'shka southeast of Brusilov. The enemy was developing the attack toward Radomyshl' in the 60th Army's sector and began an attack with the forces of the 8th Panzer Division on Chernyakhov. In the Radomyshl' area the Germans reached the southern bank of the Bystreevka River and units of the 7th Panzer Division forced the Teterev River south of Radomyshl'.

On the evening of 21 November the *front* commander ordered the 1st Guards Army, which by this time was arriving at the front from the *Stavka* of the Supreme High Command reserve and which was concentrating along the right bank of the Dnepr west of Kiev, to occupy by 0800 on 22 November with the forces of the 74th Rifle Corps (three rifle divisions) defensive positions along the lline Nizhilovichi—Sitnyaki—Gruzkoye—Kozichanka—Sosnovka, with its front facing west.

On the night of 21-22 November the commander of the 60th Army moved the 132nd and 202nd rifle divisions to the Teterev River with the mission of organizing a defense along the sector Malaya Racha—Lutovka, with its front facing northeast. At the same time, the 23rd Rifle Corps was moving east of the Teterev River with the task of organizing a defense along the sector Raevka—Borovka, with its front facing south and southwest.

According to the *front* commander's order, the 1st Guards Cavalry Division was to be transferred that day from the 38th Army to the 60th Army and returned to its corps.

Throughout 21 November the Germans were concentrating the *Das Reich* SS Panzer and the 3rd Panzer divisions in the Kornin area.

The fighting on 22 November. On 22 November the enemy waged offensive actions in the 60th Army's sector in the direction of Chernyakhov and by the close of the day captured this major inhabited locale. In the 38th Army's sector the Germans' 7th Panzer Division attacked along the paved road to the east and by the close of the day occupied Yuzefovka and Stavishche. At the same time, the enemy was attempting to encircle our Brusilov group of forces, for which the 1st Panzer Division launched an attack from the Kocherovo area in the direction of Kostovtsy and Lazarevka and captured Kostovtsy.

The 19th Panzer Division, along with part of the *Adolph Hitler* SS Panzer Division's forces, attacked from the Divin area toward Yastrebenka and also captured this locale. By the close of 22 November the real threat of encirclement had arisen for the 38th Army's Brusilov group of forces.

The fighting on this day was especially bitter. The weather during all of the days of the enemy's counteroffensive, from 14 through 21 November, prevented the *front's* aviation from effectively attacking the enemy's combat formations on the battlefield. It was only on 22 November that the weather sharply improved and the 2nd Air Army's aviation carried out 681 sorties during the day. Our aviation's entire attention was concentrated on repelling the enemy's attacks in the Brusilov area. The 2nd Air Army's *shturmoviks* and bombers destroyed the Germans' tanks and motorized infantry in the areas of Kocherovo, Yuzefovka, Tsarevka, Morozovka, Solov'yovka, Divin, and Vil'shka, as well as along the Zhitomir—Kocherovo paved road. Individual bomber crews carried out strikes against the Zhitomir—Berdichev and Belaya Tserkov'—Ustanovka railroad sectors. The enemy's aviation was not very active on this day and only individual fighters and reconnaissance planes flew. Nine enemy planes were shot down this day in air battles.

The fighting on 23 November. On 23 November the enemy attacked only in the Brusilov area and following bitter fighting captured the town by the close of the day. Part of the 60th Army's left-wing forces on this day were engaged in offensive activities with the mission of launching an attack against the flank of the German group of forces attacking along the paved road to the east. However, due to the weakness of the divisions and their shortage of ammunition, the offensive's success was not significant. This can be explained by the still weak organization of troop control and cooperation among the troops. A substantial role was also played by the circumstance that on this day the German command committed into the fighting the *Das Reich* SS Panzer Division, which deployed along the sector Zabolot'ye—Stavishche, with its front facing north, and which was covering the northern wing of its Brusilov group of forces. The army commander made the decision to transfer the headquarters of the 23rd Rifle Corps to Komarovki to organize the control of the battle by the 3rd Guards Airborne, 75th Guards and the 23rd and 30th rifle divisions along their sectors. The corps' task consisted in launching a counterblow in the direction of Zabolot'ye and Kocherovo.

Thus the counterblow, planned by the 38th Army's forces from the Brusilov area to the southwest during 20-23 November was not carried out, due to the fact that the enemy, maneuvering his available panzer divisions along the front Zhitomir—Fastov—Tripol'ye and continued to launch powerful attacks and did not let the initiative fall from its hands. Upon capturing Zhitomir, the Germans put all their efforts into crushing the 38th Army's resistance and to break through with their panzer divisions along the paved road to Kiev. However, despite a significant superiority in tanks, the enemy advanced slowly and suffered heavy losses in bitter fighting.

On 23 November the *front* commander made a new decision: on 25 November part of the forces of the 60th and 1st Guards armies were to launch an attack from the area east of Radomyshl' to the south against the flank of the enemy's attacking Brusilov group of forces.

According to the *front* commander's plan, the 1st Guards Army was to attack with its shock group, consisting of the 94th Rifle Corps (9th, 127th and 350th rifle divisions), the 111th Guards and 1950th artillery regiments, and the 12th Mechanized and 93rd Tank brigades, from the Raevka—Borovka area in the direction of Rakovichi and Brusilov and by the close of 25 November cut the Kiev—Zhitomir paved road. The 1st Guards Army's boundary was established as follows: on the right, with the 60th Army, Raevka—Ozeryany—Vodotyi (all locales for the 1st Guards Army inclusively); on the left, with the 38th Army, Borovka—Stavishche—Mestechko—Khomutets (all locales, except for Mestechko and Khomutets, were for the 1st Guards Army inclusively). The 74th and 107th rifle corps had the task of preparing a defense of the line Nezhilovichi—Sitnyaki—Gruzkoye—Sosnovka and then along the Irpen' River.

The 60th Army had the task of creating a shock group in the area east and southeast of Radomyshl' and to continue the offensive in the direction of Kocherovo and Vodotyi. At the same time, the army was ordered to restore the situation in the Chernyakhov area.

The 38th Army was to attack along its right flank toward Stavishche and subsequently, while developing the success of the 94th Rifle Corps, was to attack with the forces of the 52nd and 17th Guards rifle corps in the direction of Yastrebnya and Vil'shka.

The 3rd Guards Tank Army and the 25th Tank Corps were ordered to develop the 94th Rifle Corps' success to the south.

During the course of the planned offensive, the *front's* forces were to successively capture the following lines: Tsarevka—Kocherovo—Vysokoye by the close of 25 November; Tsarevka—Voitashivka—Vil'nya—Zdvizhka—Vodotyi—Vil'shka and to securely consolidate along this line by the close of 27 November, and; on 28-29 November to continue the offensive and reach the front Slobodka—Starobel'tsy—Korostyshev—Ivnitsa—Khodorkov—Krivoye—Mokhnachka.

The fighting on 24 November. On 24 November the 60th Army attacked in the direction of Chernyakhov with the forces of the 30th Rifle Corps, as well as along its left wing east of the Teterev River. Units of the 30th Rifle Corps' 141st Rifle Division once again captured Chernyakhov as a result of the successful offensive. The enemy, having committed the 8th Panzer Division's main forces into the fighting south of Chernyakhov, halted the corps' further advance. The 23rd Rifle Corps' offensive east of the Teterev River in the general direction of Kocherovo was not successful.

The Germans continued to attack east of Brusilov, while attempting to break through to Byshev. However, all of the enemy's attacks in this area were beaten back.

The fighting during 25-29 November. On 25 November the forces of the 60th, 1st Guards and 38th armies were not ready to attack. There was a shortage of ammunition, not all the units had been able to occupy their jumping-off positions by the appointed time, and the organization of cooperation had not been completed. The *front* commander decided to move the start of the offensive to 26 November. The intensity of the fighting slacked off on 25 November. The enemy was losing hope for a success with the forces available to him and actively attacked only along the Lazarevka—Yastreben'ka sector, but even here he was unsuccessful. Along the remainder of the front both sides carried out combat reconnaissance and limited themselves to local attacks for improving their tactical situation.

On 23-24 November the weather was not conducive to flying and the aviation of both sides was not active. An insignificant improvement in the weather set in on 25 November and the 2nd Air

Army carried out 123 sorties, launching strikes chiefly against the German forces' combat formations in the Brusilov area. The enemy air force carried out only ten sorties.

By the close of 25 November the sides' situation along the sector Chernyakhov—Radomyshl'—Brusilov—Kornin was as follows.

The 60th Army's left-wing forces (30th Rifle, 1st Guards Cavalry and the 15th and 23rd rifle corps) were operating along the front Chernyakhov—the northern outskirts of Devochki—Golovin—Slipchitsy—Kamennyi Brod—the northern bank of the Bystrievka River—the southwestern outskirts of Radomyshl'—Mar'yanovka. The enemy had the following forces along this sector: the 208th Infantry Division, with the "South" Cavalry Regiment, the 340th Infantry, 213th Security, 68th and 323rd infantry, and 8th Panzer divisions.

The 1st Guards Army's 94th Rifle Corps deployed along the line Raevka—the northern outskirts of Rakovichi—Stroevka. The *Das Reich* SS Panzer Division was facing it.

The 38th Army (52nd, 17th Guards and 21st rifle corps) was defending along the front Stroevka—the eastern outskirts of Stavishche—Malyi Karashin—Staritskaya—Yastrebnya—Yurokva—Velikie Golyaki—the eastern part of Luchin—Stavni. The enemy's 7th Panzer, 20th Motorized, 1st Panzer, *Adolph Hitler* SS, and the 19th and 25th panzer divisions were opposite the army.

The 3rd Guards Tank Army was fighting with all of its forces, in conjunction with the 38th Army's forces, along the sector Malyi Karashin—Yurovka.

On this day the Germans' 3rd Panzer Division, which had been concentrated before this in the Kornin area and intended for reinforcing the Germans' Brusilov group of forces, left through Belaya Tserkov' for Cherkassy, where the offensive by the Second Ukrainian Front's 52nd Army had begun.

At 1000 on 26 November the 60th Army's 23rd Rifle Corps, the 1st Guards Army's 94th Rifle Corps, and the right flank of the 38th Army's 52nd Rifle Corps went over to the attack, which, however, was not successful. The troops' situation by the close of the day was as before. By the end of the day the enemy began move the *Adolph Hitler* SS Panzer Division to the Zabeloch'ye area, attempting in this way to reinforce the left wing of its Brusilov group of forces.

On the morning of 27 November the *front* commander ordered the continuation of the offensive with only the forces of the 94th Rifle Corps. The 60th and 38th armies' forces were so exhausted by the preceding fighting that one could not count on their success. Besides this, it was more expedient to employ the limited amount of arriving ammunition among the newly-arrived troops.

On 27 November the enemy himself attacked the 23rd and 94th rifle corps with the forces of the *Das Reich* and *Adolph Hitler* panzer divisions and part of the 1st Panzer Division. During 27-30 November there was bitter fighting along the sector Zabeloch'ye—Stavishche. Both sides attacked, although the front line remained unchanged until the end of November.

On the evening of 28 November the *front* commander ordered a halt to the offensive and to go over to the defensive along the lines occupied. On 29 November he issued operational directive No. 0062, which defined in detail the troops' tasks in defense. At the same time, this directive demanded that the army commanders step up work to bring their troops up to strength and to knock together their units for the purpose of preparing for forthcoming offensive activities.

Throughout 28-29 November the enemy carried out local and unsuccessful attacks along the sectors of the 60th Army's 23rd Rifle Corps and the 1st Guards Army's 94th Rifle Corps.

By 30 November the front had temporarily stabilized along the line Chernyakhov—Slipchintsy—Filippovichi—the southern outskirts of Radomyshl'—the northern part of Rakovichi—Stroevka—the eastern part of Stavishche—Malyi Karashin—Yastrebnya—Yurovka—Luchin.

The Offensive by the 60th Army's Right Wing Along the Korosten' Axis

On 13 November the *front* commander made the decision for the 13th and 60th armies to go over to the offensive following their arrival at the line Fedorovka—Bober—Bazar—Chepovichi—Chernyakhov. This decision did not flow from the situation that had arisen in these armies' sector and did not in essence correspond to the directive by the *Stavka* of the Supreme High Command No. 30245 of 12 November. This directive demanded that the *front* commander temporarily halt the advance to the west and in the center of the front; that is, in the Zhitomir area and to the southeast, and the all-round strengthening of his group of forces in these areas and preventing the enemy's breakthrough toward Kiev, in the event his counterattacks increased.

The Germans' 291st Infantry Division was falling back in the sector between the Uzh River and the Kiev—Korosten' railroad along a broad front opposite the 13th Army's 18th Guards Rifle Corps and the 60th Army's 77th and 24th rifle corps (in all, about ten divisions). There were no enemy forces at all in the attack sector of the 60th Army's 30th Rifle Corps (four divisions) between the Kiev—Korosten' railroad and the Kiev—Zhitomir paved road.

Thus the *front* commander made the decision to assume the defense along a front from the Uzh River to Zhitomir, in a situation when the Soviet forces were superior in strength to the enemy by 13-14 times. Only two rifle divisions had been pulled into the *front* reserve to strengthen the center.

However, despite the command's decision, the troops, not encountering particular resistance from the enemy, continued to advance to the west even after 13 November. On 14 November the *front* commander issued a series of local orders, by which the forces were given tasks to continue the offensive and to capture Korosten'.

By the close of 17 November the 60th Army's forces captured Korosten'. The 77th Rifle Corps, consisting of the single 143rd Rifle Division, was consolidating along the 16-kilometer Vas'kovichi—Bekhi sector. The 24th Rifle Corps' 226th Rifle Division, which was defending along a 10-kilometer front, occupied Korosten', while the 112th Rifle Division was stretched out along a broad 40-kilometer front from Kholosno to Pekarshchina. The 112th Rifle Division's forward detachments occupied Volodarsk-Volynskii and Chervonoarmeisk. The 6th Guards Rifle Division was concentrated in the Brazhinka—Vydybor area, comprising the 24th Corps' second echelon. The 226th Rifle Division defending Korosten' had been reinforced by the 150th Tank Brigade.

Up until 24 November both corps remained along the lines reached, with all their forces stretched out in a line along a broad front north and south of Korosten'.

The Germans' 291st Infantry Division, continued to operate in the Korosten' area, and following a hasty withdrawal had put itself in order by 23 November and had been reinforced by a regiment from the 147th Reserve Division,[2] composite detachment "C" from the LIX Army Corps and one battalion of assault guns.

On 24 November the enemy launched an attack with his available forces in the Korosten' area against the 226th Infantry Division's flanks and encircled it. On this day the army commander issued a categorical order to the commander of the 226th Division: to hold the town at all costs during 24-25 November until the arrival of the 6th Guards Rifle Division in the Korosten' area. At the same time, fearing that the enemy might develop the offensive along the railroad to Malin, on the evening of 24 November the army commander ordered the commander of the 280th Rifle Division, which was in the army reserve in the Radomyshl' area, to move to the Chepovichi area, where it was to occupy defensive positions facing west.

---

2 The German army's reserve divisions had the task of training reinforcements for the active units and were, consequently, training centers. These divisions did not have their own, organic artillery.

The *Stavka* of the Supreme High Command demanded the restoration of the situation in the Korosten' area, which was an important railroad junction. For this purpose, the *front* commander transferred the 8th and 18th rifle divisions from the 13th Army to reinforce the 60th Army and ordered the army commander to personally organize and direct the fighting for Korosten'. The fighting in the Korosten' area raged until the end of November, although the army's forces were unable to take Korosten' again. The encircled forces of the 226th Division got out of the encirclement during the fighting here.

The enemy's success in the Korosten' area is explained by the fact that the 60th Army carried out reconnaissance of the enemy poorly, the army commander stretched out all of his forces in a line and lacked powerful shock groups in the offensive or ready reserves following the assumption of the defensive. Having put the 291st Infantry Division, which had been worn down in the fighting, in order and reinforced it somewhat, the Germans unexpectedly launched a counterblow against the flanks of the weak 226th Rifle Division, which by this time numbered only 3,500 men and which was defending along a 10-kilometer front.

The bringing up of reserves to the Korosten' area following its capture by the Germans took place slowly, which enabled the enemy to organize his defense here. The 60th Army's offensive operations around Korosten' resembled head-on attacks, without any attempts to outflank the open flanks of the enemy group of forces and to get into the latter's rear. The partisans operating in this area, who well knew the fighting conditions in the areas of the southern Poles'ye, were not employed for this purpose.

The 13th Army's Offensive Along the Ovruch Axis

As early as 8 November the 18th Guards Rifle Corps, which was operating along the 13th Army's left wing, attacked along the southern bank of the Uzh River. This attack turned into the pursuit of the Germans' 291st Infantry Division, which was falling back along a broad front. On 10 November, due to the 28th Corps' attack, the army's offensive front began to broaden to the north, and on this day fighting began in the Chernobyl' area. However, due to the Germans' bitter resistance, the 13th Army's forces attacking north of the Uzh River enjoyed only insignificant success before 16 November.

By the close of 13 November the 18th Guards Rifle Corps had reached the line Fedorovka—Bober—Mezheliska and, while continuing to attack, by 17 November it had reached the line Tarasy—Narodichi—Sarnovichi. The Germans abandoned Chernobyl' on 16 November.

A composite detachment from the enemy's LVI Panzer Corps, the 5th Panzer and the 292nd Infantry divisions were defending opposite the 28the Corps in the sector between the Dnepr and Pripyat' rivers. The main forces of the enemy's 4th Panzer and 8th Light Infantry divisions were defending in the Chernobyl' area. Due to the Belorussian Front's successful offensive in the areas of Loyev and Rechitsa, the Germans were forced to pull the 4th and 5th panzer, 292nd Infantry and 8th Light Infantry divisions out of the fighting and transfer them to the north for operations against the Belorussian Front's 65th Army, which was attacking along the Kalinkovichi axis. Thus by 17 November only the LVI Panzer Corps' composite detachment remained opposite the 13th Army's right wing, while individual elements of the 4th Panzer Division were falling back along the right bank of the Pripyat' River.

Despite the absolute superiority in force over the enemy, the army's actions were not very active. For example, throughout 17-18 November the 18th Guards Rifle Corps, despite the absence of the enemy opposite, did not attack with its main forces. Only a single regiment from the 4th Guards Airborne Division reached the area of the town of Ovruch, after the town's German garrison had been defeated by the partisan detachment of Hero of the Soviet Union Major General Saburov.

THE FIRST UKRAINIAN FRONT'S DEFENSIVE BATTLES

The 336th Rifle Division, which was operating along the army's left wing, was transferred on orders from the *front* to the 60th Army and began to march to the south to the Radomyshl' area.

On 19 November a detachment from the 8th and 148th rifle divisions, which had got into an encirclement in the Karpilovka bridgehead (northwest of Chernobyl') in the October fighting and which had retreated into the forests to link up with the partisans, joined the 13th Army's forces in the area of the town of Kaganovich. The detachment contained 1,832 men and their light infantry weapons.

During 11-22 November the 28th Rifle Corps did not attack and it was only after the enemy began to fall back to the northwest that the corps took up the pursuit along both banks of the Pripyat' River. By 30 November the 415th Rifle Division, upon reaching the Yurevichi area, crossed to the right bank of the river and attempted to attack toward Yel'sk. The 4th Guards Airborne Division, with its main forces in Ovruch, attacked with one rifle regiment, in conjunction with General Saburov's partisan detachment, to the north along the railroad and on 27 November captured the town of Yel'sk. Two days later, as a result of powerful counterattacks by the enemy's units that had arrived from the north, our forces abandoned Yel'sk.

As a result of the transfer of the greater part of the 13th Army to other sectors of the front, its subsequent offensive was halted.

Rear Organization and Materiel Support

The rapid advance by the First Ukrainian Front's forces in the center to the west, southwest and south during 7-12 November once again led to the extension of the troop and army rear establishments. A shortage of auto transport in the *front* and armies, the large percentage of motor vehicles undergoing repairs, and the poor condition of the roads made the situation more complex in the second half of November and slowed down the pace of delivering ammunition and fuel to the troops, which were engaged in heavy fighting. By the start of the defensive battles all of the army bases were still on the left bank of the Dnepr and by the close of 12 November were located at the following distances from the front: 200-250 kilometers for the 60th Army, 150-200 kilometers for the 38th Army, and 220 kilometers for the 3rd Guards Tank Army.

The armies had very limited stocks of ammunition and fuel. For example, on 13 November the 60th Army had from 0.56 to 0.84 combat loads of shells and rounds ranging from 76mm-122mm. There were actually fewer shells and rounds with the troops, because the figure above includes everything that was located at the army depots or was en route. The same constrained situation with ammunition was in the 38th and 3rd Guards Tank armies as well.

The rapid transfer of the army bases to the right bank of the Dnepr could only be carried out after completing the construction of a railroad bridge in the Kiev area, as well as bridges for auto transport. The construction of bridges over such a broad water barrier as the Dnepr demanded great efforts and a significant amount of time. The correct organization of construction work, a deep consciousness of one's soldierly duty by the officers and soldiers of the railroad and bridge-construction units, enabled us to complete the construction of bridges in record time, and on 17 November movement began over a 994-meter low-water, two-lane bridge for auto transports. By the close of 20 November, when the intensity of the fighting in the Zhitomir and Brusilov areas was at its height, movement opened over a temporary rail bridge.

The construction of bridges in the Kiev area enabled us to move the army bases to the right bank of the Dnepr. On 15 November rear area directive No. 001362 was signed, which established the new organization of the *front* rear.[3]

---

3   It is necessary to make the reservation that the rebasing of the *front* rear establishments, in accordance with

It is necessary to say that in organizing their counteroffensive along the Kiev axis, the Germans miscalculated that the Soviet forces could manage to so quickly construct a sufficient number of permanent crossings over the Dnepr. They supposed that the Soviet forces on the right bank of the Dnepr were worn down and could not receive reinforcement and munitions in time. The heroic labor of the restorers of the railroad bridge and of the pontoon units guaranteed the *front's* forces' reliable communications with the left bank of the Dnepr, where all of the materiel supplies were concentrated, and the subsequent transfer of the army and *front* bases to the right bank of the Dnepr.

The *front's* rear-area boundary remained as before. The boundary lines of the armies to the left were established as follows:

- for the 38th Army, Bakhmach—Verkievka—Chemer—Morovsk—Priborsk—Termakhovka—Bazar—Vas'kovichi—Luginy (all locales, except for Bakhmach, were for the 13th Army, inclusively);
- for the 60th Army, Ichnya—Semipolki—Velikaya Dubechnya—Borki—Vorzel'—Lipovka—Berezovka (all locales, except for Borki, Vorzel' and Lipovka were for the 60th Army, inclusively);
- for the 38th Army, Zhuravka—Yagotin—Skoptsy—Zhulyany—Zhornovka—the Ipren' River—Vcheraishe (all locales, except for Skoptsy, were for the 38th Army, inclusively);
- for the 3rd Guards Tank Army, Zhulyany—Mar'yanovka—Grebenki (all locales, for the 3rd Guards Tank Army, inclusively);
- for the 40th Army, Kulazhentsy—Kozintsy—Stritovka—Kagarlyk (all locales, except for Kozintsy and Kagarlyk, were for the 40th Army, inclusively);
- for the 27th Army, the *front's* left boundary.

The armies' rear area boundary was established along the line Baturin—Bakhmach—Priluki—Grebenka—Zolotnosha (all locales exclusively for the armies).

The *front's* railroad regulating stations were as befor—Bakhmach and Darnitsa.

The armies' basing was established as follows:

- the 13th Army's supply station remained as before—Anisovka (five kilometers south of Chernigov);
- the 60th Army's supply station was Brovary, with a mobile unit at the Nikol'skii passing track near Vygurovshchina station; following the restoration of the railroad bridge over the Dnepr, the supply station moved to Teterev station;
- the 38th Army's supply station was Darnitsa, and after the restoration of the bridge it was planned to shift it to Vasil'kov station; however, the change in the situation due to the beginning of the Germans' counteroffensive near Zhitomir forced us to open a station for the 38th Army at Svyatoshino station;
- the 3rd Guards Tank Army's supply stations were in Borispol' and Bortnichi, and in Vasil'kov following the restoration of the bridge;
- the 40th Army's supply station was in Yagotin, with a mobile units at Borispol' station and, following the restoration of the bridge, at Boyarka;
- the 27th Army's supply station was in Grebenka, with a mobile unit at Berezan' station.

Army supply and evacuation routes were established as follows: Anisovo—Chernigov—Kuibyshev—Pakul'—Gden'—Parishchev for the 13th Army; following the capture of Chernobyl', the army supply route ran through Chernobyl' and Kaganovich as far as Ovruch;

---

the rear-area directive of 11 October, was completed only by 11 November.

- Brovary—Staro-Petrovtsy—Gostomel'—Borodyanka—Malin and then to Korosten', for the 60th Army;
- Darnitsa—Kiev—Glevakha—Plesetskoye—Byshev—Brusilov for the 38th Army;
- Borispol'—Bortnichi—Darnitsa—Kiev—Plesetskoye—Fastov for the 3rd Guards Tank Army;
- Borispol'—Vishenki—Podgortsy—Glevakha—Vasil'kov, and a second route of Borispol'—Kailov—Vasil'kov for the 40th Army;
- Mar'yanovka—Glemyazovo—Leplyavo—Reshetki, and a second route of Berezan'—Semenovka—Pereyaslav-Khmel'nitskii—Traktomirov for the 27th Army; after the 27th Army was assigned a new defensive sector in the Tripol'ye area, an additional supply and evacuation route was established for it of Berezan'—Kailov.

The directive demanded the deployment of first-line field mobile hospitals and army evacuation veterinary clinics on the right bank of the Dnepr.

Even before the restoration of the railroad bridge over the Dnepr near Kiev, the railroad troops had set about restoring the Kiev—Fastov and Kiev—Teterev railroad sectors. A great deal of rolling stock had been captured at the railroad junction of Fastov. Because Fastov was being subjected to strikes by German aviation and bombardment by his artillery, energetic measures were adopted to remove the captured rolling stock as quickly as possible. As early as 12 November the movement of Western European-gauge trains began along this sector. By 26 November movement on the Kiev—Teterev sector had begun.

The *front's* railroads worked very intensively. This intensity increased in the second half of November in connection with the start of the shipments of major reserves, which the *Stavka* of the Supreme High Command allotted the First Ukrainian Front (1st Guards Army, 18th Army and the 25th Tank Corps, plus a number of independent artillery units). A large number of empty vehicles were accumulating at the unloading stations, which were putting a strain on the poorly developed station ways. This overloading of the stations was caused by a number of factors: the poor technical outfitting of the unloading stations, a shortage of work force for loading and unloading work, the inefficiency of the rear-area organs—the recipients of the freight. There were cases of unnecessary shipments. For example, potatoes were delivered from the depths of the country, when they could be procured in sufficient amounts on site.

The condition of the dirt roads during the second half of November was unfavorable. The autumn rains ruined the roads and made them difficult for all types of wheeled transport. On some sectors two tractors each had to be used to pull artillery guns.

Taking into account the great elongation of the army and *front* rear and the poor condition of the dirt roads, it is necessary to point out the fact that the *front* and armies had an insufficient auto transport park. By 16 November there were 3,294 motor vehicles in the army and *front* reserve. However, a significant part of this reserve (526 vehicles, or 16 percent of the entire auto park reserve) was out of condition and was undergoing repairs. 2,768 motor vehicles of various types were running, having an overall capacity of 5,142 tons. Due to the overall intensity of the auto transport's work and the poor condition of the roads, the vehicles in the *front* and army auto park quickly broke down. By 26 November there were only 3,109 motor vehicles in reserve (a reduction of 5.7 percent), of which 735, or 23.7 percent, were out of condition and undergoing repairs. On 26 November the commander of the 60th Army was reporting to the *front's* military council that there were only 143 working motor vehicles in the army's transport units and he requested allotting 300 vehicles for three races from the *front* reserve for delivering emergency supplies (mainly munitions) to the troops. The *front* commander could only spare 50 motor vehicles for the army.

Throughout the second half of November the *front's* forces experienced a shortage of ammunition and fuels and lubricants. For example, on 23 November the 60th Army had an average of

0.75 combat loads and 0.58 of a refill, and on 26 November 0.1-0.5 of a combat load. There was a similar situation in the 38th and 3rd Guards Tank armies. Those armies that were not engaged in active defensive operations almost failed to receive ammunition. There were no artillery deliveries by rail at all to the 27th Army during 15-29 November. The *Stavka* of the Supreme High Command issued instructions for employing all existing opportunities for increasing the delivery of munitions to the *front*. Just as in October, there were cases of delivering munitions by auto transport and transport planes to the *front* directly from Moscow.

Results and Conclusions From the First Ukrainian Front's Defensive Fighting During the Second Half of November 1943

The forces of the First Ukrainian Front repelled the German forces' counteroffensive, which was undertaken by eight panzer and motorized and seven infantry divisions[4] in stubborn and bloody fighting in the areas of Zhitomir, Brusilov and Radomyshl' during the second half of November 1943.

The enemy believed that the heart of the main danger in Army Group South's sector was in the Kiev area. To eliminate the Kiev bridgehead, the Germans concentrated along the Kiev axis all the forces they could remove from the front opposite the Bukrin bridgehead and also dispatched to the Kiev area the tank divisions moving from Western Europe to the Kirovograd area for operations against the Second Ukrainian Front. To judge from the German forces' operations, it was clear that they were striving to break through to the Kiev area, to cut the Soviet forces off from the main crossings over the Dnepr, to defeat the First Ukrainian Front's forces, and to restore their defensive line along the Kiev axis along the right bank of the Dnepr.

The Germans were nevertheless unable to achieve such far-reaching goals. Having advanced 40 kilometers to the northeast and east from the Khodorkov area and 35 kilometers from the Zhitomir area, the Germans created a serious threat to Kiev, but lacked the forces for a subsequent development of the attack on Kiev. As a result of the stout defense by Soviet forces, the Germans' panzer divisions were worn out and bled white in stubborn fighting and before long were forced to call off the offensive. The average pace of advance of the German panzer divisions was miniscule and did not exceed 2-2.5 kilometers per day throughout the 13-21 November period. At the same time, the losses suffered by the Germans around Kiev were enormous. During 1-21 November these losses reached 54,953 killed and taken prisoner.

Besides this, during this time the Soviet forces destroyed and captured 1,223 tanks, 906 assault guns and armored cars, and 1,666 various guns and mortars.

During the course of the operation the enemy employed some methods, which the *front's* forces encountered for the first time and were forced to look for ways to oppose the elements of surprise in the Germans' tactics. Alongside powerful daytime attacks by a large number of tanks, the enemy often practiced night attacks in groups of 6-10 tanks, particularly against inhabited locales. Widely employing incendiary shells, the tanks set fire to structures on the outskirts of an inhabited locale and thus created difficult conditions for the infantry and especially for those guns firing over open sights that were defending the given inhabited locale. The capture of an inhabited locale at night by a small group of tanks usually meant the development of this success by more significant forces at dawn. This German method required us to shift the defense of inhabited locales beyond their confines. The enemy did not always reckon with losses by his tanks in the minefields and,

---

4   25th, 19th, 1st, 7th, and 8th panzer divisions, the *Das Reich* and *Adolph Hitler* panzer divisions, the 20th Motorized, 68th, 323rd, 340th, 327th, 208th and 88th infantry divisions, and the 213th Security Division.

while striving to achieve at all costs, insistently continued the attacks in the same direction. This required more precise fire support of minefields laid down by our sappers.

The *Stavka* of the Supreme High Command attentively followed the development of events in the Kiev area, guided the First Ukrainian Front's operations and rendered it assistance in carrying out its assigned tasks. On 12 November the *Stavka* ordered the *front* to temporarily halt its offensive to the west and southwest and to consolidate the success achieved and to defeat the enemy if he should attempt to launch a counteroffensive, thus creating favorable conditions for the *front's* subsequent launching of a further offensive.

The *Stavka* of the Supreme High Command demanded that the *front* commander eliminate the Germans' counteroffensive with the *front's* own forces, which were quite sufficient for this purpose, provided they were employed correctly.

Of the large reserves from the *Stavka* of the Supreme High Command (1st Guards and 18th armies, the 1st Tank Army, the 25th Tank Corps, the 4th Guards Tank Corps, and a number of artillery units) which arrived at the First Ukrainian Front during the second half of November, the *Stavka* authorized the *front* commander to employ for defensive needs only the 1st Guards Army's 94th Rifle Corps for the purpose of launching a counterblow against the Germans' Brusilov group of forces. All the remaining reserves, according to the *Stavka's* plan, were designated for the First Ukrainian Front's powerful offensive during the winter campaign of 1943-44, after which the enemy's offensive élan in the Kiev area would die out and the German forces would be exhausted and bled white in the fighting. Active offensive operations by other *fronts*, conducted according to the instructions of the *Stavka* of the Supreme High Command in November 1943, complicated the overall situation for the Germans and prevented them from carrying out the transfer of reserves to the Kiev axis from other sectors of the Soviet-German front, rendered no small assistance to the First Ukrainian Front's forces. For example, as early as 10 November the Belorussian Front began a major offensive in the Gomel' area, and the Second Ukrainian Front in the Cherkassy area on 13 November. On 20 November a major offensive by the Second and Third Ukrainian fronts began along the Kirovograd axis.

Insofar as the parrying of the Germans' counteroffensive was realized, for the most part, by the First Ukrainian Front's own forces, without bringing in reserves from the *Stavka* of the Supreme High Command, with the exception of a single corps, the *front* commander was required to carry out a series of regroupings during the defensive fighting for the purpose of creating along the axes of the enemy's attacks an amount of forces that could halt the German offensive. This regrouping was carried out by removing forces from inactive sectors of the front. By the close of 12 November a total of seven rifle and three cavalry divisions (30th and 23rd rifle and the 1st Guards Cavalry corps) belonging to the 38th Army were operating along the front Zhitomir—Kornin. During the defensive fighting the *front* commander concentrated significant forces along this axis from secondary axes. From the table below it is clear that 53 percent of the rifle divisions, 100 percent of the cavalry divisions, tank corps and breakthrough artillery divisions were concentrated along the 105-kilometer Zhitomir—Kornin sector, given an overall length of front of 470 kilometers.

As early as the planning of the November offensive operation, an excessively large number of troops were tied down on the secondary Ovruch and Korosten' axes. The *front* commander also employed the forces concentrated on the Bukrin bridgehead with insufficient decisiveness, after the major success of the offensive along the Kiev axis and the failure of the offensive from the Bukrin bridgehead were made clear.

Due to this reason, the *front* commander, lacking reserves along the main axis, was unable to rapidly create the necessary group of forces at the start of the German counteroffensive for parrying the enemy attacks. From the very beginning of the enemy counteroffensive, the transfer of forces from other sectors of the front to the threatened axis was carried out with insufficient decisiveness and intensity. The *front* commander made decisions almost each day to reinforce the

164   THE BATTLE OF THE DNEPR

38th Army and, later, the 60th Army's left wing, with 1-2 divisions. Thus the reserves arrived in the area of the enemy breakthrough in individual formations and were unable to rapidly bring about a decisive shift in the situation. Aside from this, the formations that were arriving to the 38th Amy during the defensive fighting from the Ovruch and Korosten' axis, as well as from the 40th and 27th armies, were thrown into the fighting from the march, having no time to bring up their artillery and rear establishments.

Table 3.1 The Distribution of the *Front's* Forces By Axes and Sectors

Axes and Sectors	12 November				29 November			
	Rifle Divs	Cavalry Divs	Tank & Mechanized Corps	Artillery Divs	Rifle Divs	Cavalry Divs	Tank & Mechanized Corps	Artillery Divs
Ovruch Axis	8	–	–	–	2	–	–	–
Korosten' Axis	13	–	–	1	5	–	–	–
Zhitomir—Kornin Sector	7	3	–	1	29	3	6	3
Fastov—Tripol'ye Sector	11	–	6	1	12	–	–	–
Bukrin Bridgehead	7	–	–	–	2	–	–	–

Note: This does note include forces arriving from the *Stavka* of the Supreme High Command reserve, except for the 94th Rifle Corps, which was already taking part in the defensive fighting.

Troop Control and the Organization of Communications

The unfolding of the defensive fighting in the 38th and 60th armies' sector placed increased demands on the organization of troop control. The control of the defensive fighting was carried out from an auxiliary *front* command post in Svyatoshino and *front* headquarters, that remained along the left bank of the Dnepr in Trebukhovo.

By the start of the operation the *front* had steady wire communications with the armies' headquarters, despite the fact that the latter changed their command posts several times. The developed network of wire communications, which had been organized along the right bank of the Dnepr during the period of the offensive during 3-12 November, enabled us to rapidly establish communications with the armies' headquarters during their shifts and to maintain these communications with each army along no less than two axes.

The communications of the armies and corps' with the troops, particularly at the start of the defensive fighting, was weak. The insufficient organization in shifting the formations' headquarters that was observed during the offensive continued during the course of the defensive battle as well. The formations' headquarters did not always try to obtain permission from the superior headquarters to move to new command posts, which were often not outfitted with communications equipment and delayed reporting their new location.

Throughout November the *front's* communications troops continued their intensive work to build and restore permanent communications lines. In all, 246 kilometers of new lines were built during the month, and 993 kilometers of wire were strung; 460 kilometers of wire were hung along existing lines; 1,019 kilometers of lines were restored, with 4,810 kilometers of wire hung.

The *front* headquarter's radio communications with the armies also worked reliably. During the course of the defensive fighting, the *front's* headquarters reinforced the 38th Army's headquarters with two RAF radio stations, the 60th Army's headquarters with one RAF radio station, and the 1st Guards Cavalry Corps with one RSV radio station.

The army headquarters' radio communications with formations and within formations often remained the single means of communications during the most intensive days of the defensive fighting. However, equipment losses during the fighting, the overall shortage of radio stations, spare parts and current for them led to a situation in which radio communications from the armies' headquarters down was organized unsatisfactorily. During the defensive fighting the *front* chief of staff was repeatedly forced to focus the attention of the 38th and 60th armies' headquarters on their poor troop control and, in particular, the insufficient employment of radio communications.

A major shortcoming at the beginning of the defensive fighting was the poor troop control on the part of the 38th and 60th armies' and the rifle corps' headquarters. On 12 November the headquarters of the 21st Rifle Corps lost control of its subordinate divisions and did not fully know the situation and could not rapidly take efficacious measures to organize the repulse of the enemy, due to the unsteadiness exhibited by units of the 71st Rifle Division. The 38th Army's headquarters also knew the situation insufficiently and, in turn, was unable to realize the precise control of its subordinate forces. The 60th Army's headquarters, while carrying out a regrouping of its rifle formations from its right wing and center to the Chernyakhov—Radomyshl' sector, and having taken on new formations from its neighbors, we unable to rapidly establish communications with them and organize control. The army's headquarters underestimated the role of the corps' headquarters and took upon itself the excessive task of organizing and controlling the fighting of a large number of formations in a difficult situation. It was only on 18 November in the 38th Army and 23 November in the 60th Army that the rifle corps' defense sectors and zones were precisely defined and control at the army and corps level began to sort itself out.

As a result of the unclear and rapidly changing situation and unreliable communications with the troops, the commanders at all levels, all the way up to the deputy *front* commander, were often forced to travel directly to the troops in order to ascertain the situation and to issue orders to the troops on site. The dispatch of responsible representatives—commanders and chiefs of staff at all levels—to the troops with the same tasks was widely practiced.

The Employment of Artillery

Artillery played an extremely important role during the course of the defensive battle. The artillery operated in a complex and rapidly changing situation, with a great extension of the formations' and units' fronts and the presence of unoccupied gaps between them. The artillery units often took upon themselves attacks by enemy tanks and the entire weight of the fighting and inflicted heavy losses on the enemy through its accurate fire.

A contribution by the *front* commander is that he issued timely instructions for the rapid concentration of reinforcement artillery units—anti-tank artillery and breakthrough artillery divisions—along the main axis of the Germans' attack. The RGK[5] 7th Breakthrough Artillery Corps and the RGK 1st Breakthrough Artillery Division, as well as a number of formations and units of anti-tank artillery, guards mortars and others were moved to the threatened sector.

---

5 Editor's note. The RGK (*Rezerv Glavnogo Komandovaniya*) was the acronym for the High Command Reserve.

Table 3.2 The Saturation of the 38th, 60th and 3rd Guards Tank Armies' Combat Formations with Artillery Along the Front Zhitomir—Kornin During the Defensive Fighting in the Second Half of November 1943

Artillery Units	15.11	20.11	25.11
Breakthrough Artillery Divisions	1	3	3
Cannon Artillery Brigades	1	1	–
Howitzer Artillery Regiments	2	2	1
Cannon Artillery Regiments	2	1	4
Army Mortar Regiments	4	4	–
Anti-Tank Artillery Brigades	2	4	5
Anti-Tank Artillery Regiments	10	15	28
Guards Mortar Regiments	8	10	10

It is clear from the table above that significant amounts of artillery equipment were concentrated along the German tank group of forces' main offensive axis. The amount of anti-tank artillery increased particularly sharply, by almost three times.

The expedient organization of anti-tank defense in conditions of fighting a major tank group of forces acquired particular importance.

The anti-tank defensive system relied on anti-tank strong points and centers of resistance. The artillery headquarters at all levels coped with their tasks in the intense situation in the second half of November. However, there were shortcomings in the work of the artillery headquarters that substantially influenced the course of the fighting. The chief shortcoming was the poor cooperation in the mobile defensive fighting between the infantry and the artillery, in which the combined-arms headquarters were equally guilty. Experience showed that the anti-tank artillery units coped with their tasks of battling the enemy's tanks better if they were not broken up by battery, but were given tasks along a single 2-3 kilometer sector. The anti-tank artillery units were in need of machine guns (mainly light ones) for repelling the enemy's infantry (automatic riflemen) that had infiltrated, because our own infantry was often absent in the combat areas.

It was necessary to organize within the anti-tank centers more precise fire control from our anti-tank guns, and also to cover these centers with artillery fire from hidden positions. As an example of the poor organization of cooperation, one may cite the following case. The anti-tank center in the Stavishche—Vysokoye area (along the Zhitomir paved road) had 119 anti-tank guns, which yielded a density of 20 guns per kilometer of front. During the fighting it was necessary to remove one anti-tank regiment from this center's right flank. Despite the fact that there was sufficient time, the maneuver within the center was not organized, nor was the cover of this sector by artillery fire from hidden positions carried out, and the powerful anti-tank center did not carry out its assignment during a German tank attack.

Artillery officers would get into their combat tanks in order to better correct the fire from their own artillery. However, because the combat tanks in which the artillery observers were located continued to carry out their assignments, it was not always possible to carry out fire correction. It follows that special tanks, which would be used only for correcting artillery fire, were necessary.

Employing the Tank Troops

In the beginning of the defensive fighting near Fastov, and then south of Brusilov, the 3rd Guards Tank Army's formations and the 5th Guards Tank Corps had their independent combat sectors, and upon the arrival of the rifle formations often continued to operate along the same sectors as they. This was caused by the complex situation, because the weak and poorly led 21st Rifle Corps in the Kornin area was unable to hold, as early as 12 November, attacks by German tanks. The arrival of a composite tank detachment in the area north of Kornin enabled us to hold off the pressure from the German tanks for a time and to organize a defense with the forces of rifle formations and artillery. The tank and combined-arms formations, while carrying out the same combat tasks along the very same combat sectors, were controlled from different army headquarters (38th and 3rd Guards Tank armies). Naturally, this made the organization of the battle extremely complicated. Insofar as the tank corps and brigades were not subordinated to the commanders of the combined-arms formations in the sectors where they were defending, the problem of organizing cooperation, which was carried out only on the basis of an "agreement" (as the report from the headquarters of the 3rd Guards Tank Army notes), became very acute.

Table 3.3 The Tank Formations' Provisioning With Combat Equipment in the Second Half of November 1943

Formations	Date	Number of Tanks	Self-Propelled Guns		Weapons			
					Artillery		Mortars	
			122mm	85mm	76mm	76mm	45mm	120mm	82mm
6th Guards Tank Corps	10.11	38	–	15	9	19	22	27	31
	15.11	38	–	–	25	–	6	3	28
	20.11	35	–	–	21	–	19	23	27
	25.11	32	–	7	9	–	21	23	27
7th Guards Tank Corps	10.11	61	–	11	4	21	22	36	50
	15.11	63	9	5	20	–	22	35	45
	20.11	37	–	1	11	–	20	26	31
	25.11	36	–	–	11	–	20	23	35
9th Mechanized Corps	10.11	95	14	–	–	35	45	51	65
	15.11	60	9	–	18	–	25	9	50
	20.11	21	4	–	14	–	34	40	46
	25.11	57	5	–	10	–	18	39	34
5th Guards Tank Corps	10.11	91	1	–	–	8	17	23	16
	15.11	65	1	–	–	7	2	13	2
	20.11	13	–	–	5	–	–	23	22
	25.11	7	–	–	8	–	1	23	19

However, despite these shortcomings, the 3rd Guards Tank Army and the 5th Guards Tank Corps played a major role during the first stag of the defensive battle. During the first days of fighting they blocked the path of the German panzer divisions along the most important sectors of the front south of Brusilov and in the Stavishche area. Being weakened following the offensive fighting in the areas of Kiev and Fastov, the tank formations inflicted heavy losses on the enemy with fire along favorable terrain lines and from ambushes and foiled his attempts to achieve operational freedom by means of vigorous attacks by large armored fists. The first days of the 3rd Guards Tank Army's defensive battles south of Brusilov already showed that despite the small numbers of equipment (tanks), the tank corps commander, having been assigned a defensive sector, should not put all his available tanks along the first defensive line, but should strive to keep in his hands as powerful a tank reserve as possible and to maneuver it during the course of the fighting. The absence of such reserves during the first days of the defensive fighting lowered the steadiness of the tank formations in the defense.

It is necessary to note that the tank formations in the second half of November were very short of equipment and that the motorized infantry, lacking auto transport, moved on foot. The table above gives a picture of the condition of the tank formations during the defensive fighting.

Aviation Employment

The *front's* air force could only operate episodically, due to the weather conditions, and for the most part in very limited numbers, which could not but tell on the pace of eliminating the enemy's counteroffensive. However, those operations which the 2nd Air Army's aviation carried out played no small role in repelling this counteroffensive. During this period the 2nd Air Army was employed purposefully, chiefly against enemy tanks and along the main axes of his offensive. Our aviation carried out its tasks over the battlefield or in the Germans' immediate rear in close tactical cooperation with the grond forces, which fully corresponded to the situation and gave us the opportunity to halt the enemy's attacks as rapidly as possible.

The Employment of Engineer Troops

During the time of the defense fighting the engineer troops were employed chiefly for mining the terrain and blowing up bridges along axes along which there was a danger of the enemy's tanks appearing. Such axes were, first of all, paved roads and through routes leading to Kiev from the west, southwest and south. However, due to the insignificant supply of mines and their equal distribution along all sectors of the front during the first part of the German armored counterattack, mining was carried out on an insignificant scale and thus minefields were not a substantial barrier for the enemy.

The *front's* engineer troops were distributed equally between the armies and only upon the start of the enemy's counteroffensive were measures taken to reinforce the 38th and 3rd Guards Tank armies with engineer troops and the number of mines issued increased. During the 11-20 November time period the engineer troops laid 12,000 anti-tank and 3,400 anti-personnel mines in the *front's* sector. However, 60 percent of the mines were placed along secondary axes where active combat operations were not being conducted. It was only on 19 November that the pace of laying mines along the axis of the German forces' attack increased somewhat, although it nevertheless remained insufficient; on this day 2,500 mines were laid. The reason for this was the overall shortage of mines with the troops, their equal distribution between active and passive sectors of the front, and the inability to redistribute the available mines in order to reinforce the 38th Army. In all, during 11-21 November 75 enemy tanks were blown up on minefields laid down by the *front's* engineer troops.

During 21-30 November the pace of mine-obstacle work began to rapidly increase. For example, on 26 November alone more than 15,000 mines were laid and 75,000 anti-tank and 21,000 anti-personnel mines over ten days. This significantly helped the troops to successfully fend off the enemy's tank attacks. Overall, 118 enemy tanks, 58 armored cars and tows and seven guns were blown up in ten days on mine obstacles.

The engineer troops' second important task was to maintain the bridge crossings over the Dnepr and the construction of new crossings. On the whole, the engineer troops coped with this task.

The chemical troops available with the *front* were chiefly employed for covering the crossings over the Dnepr with smoke. During 12 October-15 November ten crossing sectors were covered with smoke. During this period the enemy's air force carried out 132 strikes against the covered crossings, in which 370 planes took part. However, the timely laying down of smoke screens reduced the air bombardment of the crossings to insignificant results. During the entire period only five direct hits, which cause insignificant damage, were noted.

Rear Area Organization and Materiel Support

Despite the great deal of experience in organizing the rear service and materiel-technical support in rapidly developing offensive paces (the *front's* offensive battles along the Kursk and Khar'kov axes in January-March 1943, and particularly the September 1943 offensive to the Dnepr), the previous mistakes were made again. The chief shortcomings were the great extension of the army and troop rear establishments and the equal distribution of available materiel supplies along all axes (main and secondary) of the troops' operations. The poor condition of the roads in the second half of November, due to the autumn rains, and the shortage of auto transport cannot serve as a justification for the poor supply of the troops and only emphasize the necessity of concentrating the available limited materiel supplies and efforts along the main axes of the troops' operations.

An important factor was the construction of a temporary railroad bridge over the Dnepr near Kiev in record time. When this bridge came into use there arose the opportunity to shift the army bases and the forward *front* depots to the right bank of the Dnepr.

Conclusions

The offensive by the forces of the First Ukrainian (Voronezh) Front along the Kiev axis lasted three months and concluded in the brilliant victory of the Soviet forces. Having reached the Dnepr along a broad front in the second half of September 1943, our forces forced the Dnepr from the march, on the heels of the hurriedly retreaing enemy north and south of Kiev. They seized a number of bridgeheads along the right bank of the river and repelled all of the Germans' attempts to throw the Soviet units back into the river and to restore their defense along its right bank. Upon regrouping its forces, the First Ukrainian Front inflicted a severe defeat on the German Fourth Panzer Army in November, captured Kiev and created a very important and very valuable bridgehead on the right bank of the Dnepr, which had great significance for driving the Germans from the Ukrainian right bank. In November the *front's* forces successfully repelled a counteroffensive by a large German group of armored forces in the Zhitomir—Brusilov area and once again inflicted heavy losses on him.

As a result of the successful operations by five Soviet *fronts* (Belorussian, First, Second, Third, and Fourth Ukrainian), the Germans' defense along the Dnepr was crushed and with this their dream of sitting it out behind the "East Wall" was finally buried. Favorable prerequisites were created for new offensive operations by Soviet forces in the winter months of 1943-44 and for driving the Germans from the territory of the Ukrainian right bank.

During the course of the 1943-44 winter campaign, the Soviet army eliminated the Germans' powerful defense along the entire length of the Dnepr from Zhlobin to Kherson and won the historic battle of the Dnepr and the Ukrainian right bank.

The actions of the First Ukrainian (Voronezh) Front in this period are characterized by the extreme diversity of the types of combat activities. The *front's* forces carried out a vigorous offensive and pursuit of the enemy on the left bank of the Dnepr, forced a major water barrier on the heels of the retreating enemy, conducted offensive battles from the captured bridgeheads on the right bank of the river. The rapid regrouping of mobile forces and artillery was carried out during the operation in difficult conditions (crossing the Dnepr and Desna three times) from one sector of the front to another. The *front's* forces broke through the enemy's defense north of Kiev and developed the success up to 145 kilometers in depth, and repelled a counteroffensive by a powerful German tank group of forces.

The Kiev operation is of great interest for study by the Soviet army's generals and officers, precisely due to those complex conditions in which it occurred and the multiplicity of operational forms in which the combat actions of the *front's* forces expressed themselves.

Charactistic features of the *front's* combat activities along the Kiev axis worthy of close attention are as follows: the skillful organization and conduct of the regrouping of large forces in difficult conditions during the operation from one operational axis to another, hidden from the enemy and quickly carried out; the launching of a crushing surprise attack against the enemy by large forces from bridgeheads of limited size; the skillful unfolding of the *front's* offensive along several axes following the breakthrough of the enemy's defense along one of them, which completely corresponded to the task of forming a broad and strategically important bridgehead.

The well-organized, secretly and rapidly conducted regrouping of the First Ukrainian Front's forces from the Bukrin bridgehead to the Lyutezh bridgehead at the end of October ensured operational surprise in the November offensive operation north of Kiev and resulted in the successful resolution of the mission assigned by the *Stavka* of the Supreme High Command. The tight timetable and difficult conditions in which the regrouping was carried out testify to the organizing capabilities in the troops' actions and a high level of efficiency in the matter of troop control.

The preparation and unfolding of the offensive north of Kiev from a bridgehead of limited size presented great difficulties and demanded precise organization, as well as the proper training of the troops. The concentration and deployment of a major shock group of forces (14 rifle divisions, a breakthrough artillery corps and four tank and mechanized corps) on a small bridgehead was achieved in a limited amount of time, while carrying out all measures to guarantee the launching of a powerful and surprise attack on the enemy. All the difficulties of organizing delivery and evacuation in the formations of the *front's* shock group on the Lyutezh bridgehead were overcome. The difficulties consisted of the fact that there were two major water barriers (the Dnepr and Desna) in the rear of this group of forces, the crossings over which were not only being subjected to enemy air strikes, but were also withing range of his artillery fire.

The *front's* forces successfully resolved the task, despite the difficult conditions they found themselves in during the first four days of the operation, when the movement of reserves and artillery and the delivery of combat supplies became extremely difficult. During this time the enemy enjoyed favorable conditions for the maneuver of men and materiel, because he disposed of good roads and a sufficient number of supply bases in the immediate rear.

The distinctive form of the conduct of the November offensive operation consisted of launching a concentrated and crushing attack from the bridgehead north of Kiev in the general direction of Fastov, outflanking Kiev from the west. This was to result in rolling up the enemy's defense to the south along the Dnepr, along with the simultaneous development of the breakthrough in the directions of Korosten' and Zhitomir and completed corresponded to the situation and the mission assigned to the *front's* forces.

As a result of the successful conduct of the operation in a very short time, a streategically important bridgehead was created in the Kiev area, which played an enormous role in the unfolding of subsequent offensive operations to liberate the Ukrainian right bank from the German-Fascist aggressors.

In repelling the enemy's counteroffensive in the second half of November, an important condition for the success by our forces was the skillful maneuver of men and materiel. By the start of this counteroffensive the *front's* forces had instructions to halt the offensive and go over to the defensive, although they did not have time during the course of two days to fully regroup, to close the gaps between the troops that had developed during the offensive, to carry out the most necessary engineer work, and to reorganize the rear services. In conditions in which the enemy achieved several tactical successes along the shortest route to Kiev, the *front* commander adopted energetic measures to concentrate artillery and tanks along the threatened axes, to make the rifle troops' combat formations denser, and to create a deep defense. The defense's activity and our forces' powerful counterblow led to a situation in which the enemy's armored group of forces was bled white and forced to halt its offensive.

The enemy, while taking advantage of the excellent road network, had concentrated by the start of his counteroffensive powerful reserves and calculated not only on changing the operational situation in the Kiev area, but also altering the entire strategic situation along the line of the Dnepr. However, thanks to the skill of the Soviet command, which skillfully organized a rebuff to the enemy, and the trooops' training and heroism, the German-Fascist forces' counteroffensive collapsed completely.

In the difficult conditions of the fall of 1943 the *front's* forces were supplied in the operation's decisive moments with sufficient materiel supplies for resolving important operational missions. This became possible as a result of the popular support for the *front*, the selfless work of Soviet people in enterprises and factories, in mines and quarries, in transport, and in agriculture. 1943 was a turning point not only for military operations, but in the work of our rear. As a result of this turning point, the enemy's former superiority in the number of tanks, planes and mortars was eliminated and our army no longer experienced shortages in weaponry, munitions, equipment, and food.

In the fighting along the Dnepr in the Kiev area, the *front's* soldiers and officers displayed mass heroism, which testified to the unbroken growth and strengthening of the Soviet army's moral spirit.

Concrete assistance and control of the First Ukrainian (Voronezh) Front's operations on the part of the Supreme Commander-in-Chief, comrade Stalin, was the basis for the *front's* success in forming a major bridgehead of strategic significance in the Kiev area.

SUPPLEMENTS

Supplement 1.1 The Voronezh Front's Combat Strength by 20 September 1943[1]

Formations and Units	Men	Mortars		Guns	
		81mm	120mm	76mm (rgt artillery)	76mm (div artillery)
		38th Army			
71st Rifle Div	3,755	28	14	9	12
136th Rifle Div	5,376	73	19	11	20
163rd Rifle Div	5,045	25	15	5	16
167th Rifle Div	8,488	66	17	16	12
180th Rifle Div	8,517	71	20	16	12
232nd Rifle Div	7,138	28	14	10	19
240th Rifle Div	8,442	70	19	13	19
340th Rifle Div	5,404	45	18	16	12
3rd Gds Tank Corps*	5,881	57	15	–	12
39th Tank Rgt	432	–	–	–	–
1930th Gun Artillery Rgt	779	–	–	–	–
895th Gun Artillery Rgt	517	–	–	–	–
27th Anti-Tank Artillery Bde	1,157	–	–	36	–
222nd Anti-Tank Artillery Rgt	468	–	–	–	20
868th Anti-Tank Artillery Rgt	437	–	–	–	24
1660th Anti-Tank Artillery Rgt	412	–	–	16	–
491st Mortar Rgt	654	–	34	–	–
492nd Mortar Rgt	570	–	33	–	–
16th Gds Mortar Rgt	668	–	–	–	–
6th Gds Mortar Rgt	674	–	–	–	–
324th Gds Mortar Rgt	218	–	–	–	–
8th Anti-Aircraft Artillery Div	1,071	–	–	–	–
1288th Anti-Aircraft Artillery Rgt	385	–	–	–	–
Total	66,787	463	218	148	178

Formations and Units	Guns				
	105mm	107mm	122mm	152mm	203mm
	38th Army				
71st Rifle Div	–	–	9	–	–
136th Rifle Div	–	–	12	–	–
163rd Rifle Div	–	–	8	–	–
167th Rifle Div	1	–	9	–	–
180th Rifle Div	7	–	8	–	–
232nd Rifle Div	1	–	10	–	–
240th Rifle Div	3	–	10	–	–
340th Rifle Div	2	–	6	–	–
3rd Gds Tank Corps	–	–	–	–	–

---

1 Editor's note. Any mathematical errors contained in the original are retained here.

174 THE BATTLE OF THE DNEPR

Formations and Units	Guns				
	105mm	107mm	122mm	152mm	203mm
39th Tank Rgt	–	–	–	–	–
1930th Gun Artillery Rgt	–	–	–	18	–
895th Gun Artillery Rgt	–	–	19	–	–
27th Anti-Tank Artillery Bde	–	–	–	–	–
222nd Anti-Tank Artillery Rgt	–	–	–	–	–
868th Anti-Tank Artillery Rgt	–	–	–	–	–
1660th Anti-Tank Artillery Rgt	–	–	–	–	–
491st Mortar Rgt	–	–	–	–	–
492nd Mortar Rgt	–	–	–	–	–
16th Gds Mortar Rgt	–	–	–	–	–
6th Gds Mortar Rgt	–	–	–	–	–
324th Gds Mortar Rgt	–	–	–	–	–
8th Anti-Aircraft Artillery Div	–	–	–	–	–
1288th Anti-Aircraft Artillery Rgt	–	–	–	–	–
Total	14	–	91	18	–

Formations and Units	Total Guns	Total Guns and Mortars	Rocket Artillery Platforms	Anti-Aircraft Guns	Tanks and Self-Propelled Guns
		38th Army			
71st Rifle Div	30	72	–	–	–
136th Rifle Div	43	135	–	–	–
163rd Rifle Div	29	69	–	–	–
167th Rifle Div	38	121	–	–	–
180th Rifle Div	43	134	–	–	–
232nd Rifle Div	40	82	–	–	–
240th Rifle Div	45	134	–	–	–
340th Rifle Div	36	99	–	–	–
3rd Gds Tank Corps	12	84	–	–	70
39th Tank Rgt	–	–	–	–	11
1930th Gun Artillery Rgt	18	18	–	–	–
895th Gun Artillery Rgt	19	19	–	–	–
27th Anti-Tank Artillery Bde	36	36	–	–	–
222nd Anti-Tank Artillery Rgt	20	20	–	–	–
868th Anti-Tank Artillery Rgt	24	24	–	–	–
1660th Anti-Tank Artillery Rgt	16	16	–	–	–
491st Mortar Rgt	–	34	–	–	–
492nd Mortar Rgt	–	33	–	–	–
16th Gds Mortar Rgt	–	–	17	–	–
6th Gds Mortar Rgt	–	–	17	–	–
324th Gds Mortar Rgt	–	–	5	5	–
8th Anti-Aircraft Artillery Div	–	–	–	42	–
1288th Anti-Aircraft Artillery Rgt	–	–	–	16	–
Total	449	1,130	39	58	81

*Information as of 10 September 1943.
Note: This table was compiled based on materials from the Voronezh Front headquarters' replacement section.

SUPPLEMENTS 175

Formations and Units	Men	Mortars		Guns	
		81mm	120mm	76mm (rgt artillery)	76mm (div artillery)
40th Army					
42nd Gds Rifle Div	4,676	63	22	7	22
68th Gds Rifle Div	4,418	62	20	8	17
38th Rifle Div	4,613	33	18	12	19
161st Rifle Div	5,417	44	12	7	14
237th Rifle Div	5,340	48	14	12	14
253rd Rifle Div	5,035	55	19	10	19
309th Rifle Div	4,888	10	31	8	11
337th Rifle Div	3,768	23	16	7	17
8th Gds Tank Corps	3,918	–	–	–	–
10th Tank Corps	4,118	22	2	1	12
1450th Self-Propelled Artillery Rgt	201	–	–	–	–
76th Gds Gun Artillery Rgt	866	–	–	–	–
112th Gun Artillery Rgt	942	–	–	–	–
111th Howitzer Artillery Rgt	772	–	–	–	–
839th Howitzer Artillery Rgt	614	–	–	–	–
32nd Anti-Tank Artillery Bde	962	–	–	47	–
27th Anti-Tank Artillery Bde	1,070	–	–	–	31
4th Gds Anti-Tank Artillery Rgt	453	–	–	–	18
611th Anti-Tank Artillery Rgt	495	–	–	–	24
727th Anti-Tank Artillery Rgt	187	–	–	–	6
1663rd Anti-Tank Artillery Rgt	431	–	–	–	16
9th Mortar Rgt	559	–	34	–	–
10th Mortar Rgt	541	–	31	–	–
270th Mortar Rgt	492	–	12	–	–
287th Mortar Rgt	486	–	19	–	–
493rd Mortar Rgt	565	–	34	–	–
494th Mortar Rgt	634	–	34	–	–
5th Gds Mortar Rgt	662	–	–	–	–
314th Gds Mortar Rgt	660	–	–	–	–
9th Anti-Aircraft Artillery Div	1,495	–	–	–	–
148th Ant-Aircraft Artillery Rgt	385	–	–	–	–
1693rd Anti-Aircraft Artillery Rgt	328	–	–	–	–
1698th Anit-Aircraft Artillery Rgt	326	–	–	–	–
Total	60,317	360	318	112	240

Formations and Units	Guns				
	105mm	107mm	122mm	152mm	203mm
			40th Army		
42nd Gds Rifle Div	–	–	12	–	–
68th Gds Rifle Div	–	–	12	–	–
38th Rifle Div	–	–	12	–	–
161st Rifle Div	–	–	8	–	–
237th Rifle Div	–	–	19	–	–
253rd Rifle Div	–	–	12	–	–
309th Rifle Div	–	–	8	–	–
337th Rifle Div	–	–	11	–	–
8th Gds Tank Corps	–	–	–	–	–
10th Tank Corps	–	–	–	–	–
1450th Self-Propelled Artillery Rgt	–	–	–	–	–
76th Gds Gun Artillery Rgt	–	–	–	18	–
112th Gun Artillery Rgt	–	–	15	–	–
111th Howitzer Artillery Rgt	–	–	24	–	–
839th Howitzer Artillery Rgt	–	–	24	–	–
32nd Anti-Tank Artillery Bde	–	–	–	–	–
27th Anti-Tank Artillery Bde	–	–	–	–	–
4th Gds Anti-Tank Artillery Rgt	–	–	–	–	–
611th Anti-Tank Artillery Rgt	–	–	–	–	–
727th Anti-Tank Artillery Rgt	–	–	–	–	–
1663rd Anti-Tank Artillery Rgt	–	–	–	–	–
9th Mortar Rgt	–	–	–	–	–
10th Mortar Rgt	–	–	–	–	–
270th Mortar Rgt	–	–	–	–	–
287th Mortar Rgt	–	–	–	–	–
493rd Mortar Rgt	–	–	–	–	–
494th Mortar Rgt	–	–	–	–	–
5th Gds Mortar Rgt	–	–	–	–	–
314th Gds Mortar Rgt	–	–	–	–	–
9th Anti-Aircraft Artillery Div	–	–	–	–	–
148th Ant-Aircraft Artillery Rgt	–	–	–	–	–
1693rd Anti-Aircraft Artillery Rgt	–	–	–	–	–
1698th Anit-Aircraft Artillery Rgt	–	–	–	–	–
Total	–	–	157	18	–

SUPPLEMENTS

Formations and Units	Total Guns	Total Guns and Mortars	Rocket Artillery Platforms	Anti-Aircraft Guns	Tanks and Self-Propelled Guns
		40th Army			
42nd Gds Rifle Div	41	126	–	–	–
68th Gds Rifle Div	37	119	–	–	–
38th Rifle Div	43	94	–	–	–
161st Rifle Div	29	85	–	–	–
237th Rifle Div	45	107	–	–	–
253rd Rifle Div	41	115	–	–	–
309th Rifle Div	27	68	–	–	–
337th Rifle Div	35	74	–	–	–
8th Gds Tank Corps	–	–	–	–	52
10th Tank Corps	13	27	–	–	19
1450th Self-Propelled Artillery Rgt	–	–	–	–	8
76th Gds Gun Artillery Rgt	18	18	–	–	–
112th Gun Artillery Rgt	15	15	–	–	–
111th Howitzer Artillery Rgt	24	24	–	–	–
839th Howitzer Artillery Rgt	24	24	–	–	–
32nd Anti-Tank Artillery Bde	47	47	–	–	–
27th Anti-Tank Artillery Bde	31	31	–	–	–
4th Gds Anti-Tank Artillery Rgt	18	18	–	–	–
611th Anti-Tank Artillery Rgt	24	24	–	–	–
727th Anti-Tank Artillery Rgt	6	6	–	–	–
1663rd Anti-Tank Artillery Rgt	16	16	–	–	–
9th Mortar Rgt	–	34	–	–	–
10th Mortar Rgt	–	31	–	–	–
270th Mortar Rgt	–	12	–	–	–
287th Mortar Rgt	–	19	–	–	–
493rd Mortar Rgt	–	34	–	–	–
494th Mortar Rgt	–	34	–	–	–
5th Gds Mortar Rgt	–	–	20	–	–
314th Gds Mortar Rgt	–	–	16	–	–
9th Anti-Aircraft Artillery Div	–	–	–	59	–
148th Ant-Aircraft Artillery Rgt	–	–	–	16	–
1693rd Anti-Aircraft Artillery Rgt	–	–	–	12	–
1698th Anit-Aircraft Artillery Rgt	–	–	–	12	–
Total	534	1,222	36	102	79

Formations and Units	Men	Mortars		Guns	
		81mm	120mm	76mm (rgt artillery)	76mm (div artillery)
		47th Army			
23rd Rifle Div	3,266	37	16	10	19
30th Rifle Div	3,815	33	11	11	17
206th Rifle Div	3,504	22	13	6	18
218th Rifle Div	3,755	32	16	12	15
3rd Gds Mechanized Corps	6,517	49	15	–	24
1831st Self-Propelled Artillery Rgt	233	–	–	–	–
88th Howitzer Artilley Bde	1,210	–	–	–	–
29th Anti-Tank Artillery Bde	907	–	–	–	31
269th Anti-Tank Artillery Rgt	117	–	–	–	21
1593rd Anti-Tank Artillery Rgt	465	–	–	–	24
129th Mortar Rgt	467	–	29	–	–
460th Mortar Rgt	482	–	28	–	–
83rd Gds Mortar Rgt	617	–	–	–	–
33rd Gds Mortar Bn	213	–	–	–	–
21st Anti-Aircraft Artillery Div	1,488	–	–	–	–
1075th Anti-Aircraft Artillery Rgt	291	–	–	–	–
Total	27,077	173	128	39	169

Formations and Units	Guns				
	105mm	107mm	122mm	152mm	203mm
		47th Army			
23rd Rifle Div	–	–	12	–	–
30th Rifle Div	–	–	11	–	–
206th Rifle Div	–	–	12	–	–
218th Rifle Div	–	–	11	–	–
3rd Gds Mechanized Corps	–	–	–	–	–
1831st Self-Propelled Artillery Rgt	–	–	–	–	–
88th Howitzer Artilley Bde	–	–	–	31	–
29th Anti-Tank Artillery Bde	–	–	–	–	–
269th Anti-Tank Artillery Rgt	–	–	–	–	–
1593rd Anti-Tank Artillery Rgt	–	–	–	–	–
129th Mortar Rgt	–	–	–	–	–
460th Mortar Rgt	–	–	–	–	–
83rd Gds Mortar Rgt	–	–	–	–	–
33rd Gds Mortar Bn	–	–	–	–	–
21st Anti-Aircraft Artillery Div	–	–	–	–	–
1075th Anti-Aircraft Artillery Rgt	–	–	–	–	–
Total	–	–	46	31	–

SUPPLEMENTS

Formations and Units	Total Guns	Total Guns and Mortars	Rocket Artillery Platforms	Anti-Aircraft Guns	Tanks and Self-Propelled Guns
		47th Army			
23rd Rifle Div	41	94	–	–	–
30th Rifle Div	39	83	–	–	–
206th Rifle Div	36	71	–	–	–
218th Rifle Div	38	86	–	–	–
3rd Gds Mechanized Corps	24	88	–	–	15
1831st Self-Propelled Artillery Rgt	–	–	–	–	1
88th Howitzer Artilley Bde	31	31	–	–	–
29th Anti-Tank Artillery Bde	31	31	–	–	–
269th Anti-Tank Artillery Rgt	21	21	–	–	–
1593rd Anti-Tank Artillery Rgt	24	24	–	–	–
129th Mortar Rgt	–	29	–	–	–
460th Mortar Rgt	–	28	–	–	–
83rd Gds Mortar Rgt	–	–	24	–	–
33rd Gds Mortar Bn	–	–	5	2	–
21st Anti-Aircraft Artillery Div	–	–	–	61	–
1075th Anti-Aircraft Artillery Rgt	–	–	–	15	–
Total	285	586	29	78	16

Formations and Units	Men	Mortars		Guns	
		81mm	120mm	76mm (rgt artillery)	76mm (div artillery)
		52nd Army			
93rd Rifle Div	5,023	77	21	12	20
138th Rifle Div	4,514	73	18	46	20
254th Rifle Div	4,651	79	17	7	20
294th Rifle Div	4,639	68	21	12	20
373rd Rifle Div	4,193	71	18	11	20
259th Tank Rgt	373	–	–	–	–
1817th Self-Propelled Artillery Rgt	192	–	–	–	–
37th Light Artillery Bde	1,356	–	–	–	63
50th Light Artillery Bde	1,824	–	–	–	–
39th Gun Artillery Bde	1,601	–	–	–	–
92nd Howitzer Artillery Bde	1,210	–	–	–	–
108th Heavy Caliber Howitzer Artillery Bde	1,291	–	–	–	–
568th Gun Artillery Bde	769	–	–	–	–
14th Anti-Tank Artillery Bde	1,065	–	–	–	44
438th Anti-Tank Artilllery Rgt	473	–	–	–	24
444th Anti-Tank Artillery Rgt	464	–	–	–	24

Formations and Units	Men	Mortars		Guns	
		81mm	120mm	76mm (rgt artillery)	76mm (div artillery)
869th Anti-Tank Artillery Rgt	496	–	–	–	24
1689th Anti-Tank Artillery Rgt	478	–	–	–	14
22nd Mortar Bde	1,399	–	89	–	–
490th Mortar Rgt	582	–	36	–	–
15th Gds Mortar Bde	1,007	–	–	–	–
17th Gds Mortar Rgt	670	–	–	–	–
38th Anti-Aircraft Artillery Div	1,758	–	–	–	–
1712th Anti-Aircraft Artillery Rgt	372	–	–	–	–
Total	40,400	368	220	88	293

Formations and Units	Guns				
	105mm	107mm	122mm	152mm	203mm
		52nd Army			
93rd Rifle Div	–	–	12	–	–
138th Rifle Div	–	–	12	–	–
254th Rifle Div	–	–	17	–	–
294th Rifle Div	–	–	12	–	–
373rd Rifle Div	–	–	12	–	–
259th Tank Rgt	–	–	–	–	–
1817th Self-Propelled Artillery Rgt	–	–	–	–	–
37th Light Artillery Bde	–	–	–	–	–
50th Light Artillery Bde	–	–	73	–	–
39th Gun Artillery Bde	–	–	–	36	–
92nd Howitzer Artillery Bde	–	–	–	25	–
108th Heavy Caliber Howitzer Artillery Bde	–	–	–	–	24
568th Gun Artillery Bde	–	–	–	18	–
14th Anti-Tank Artillery Bde	–	–	–	–	–
438th Anti-Tank Artilllery Rgt	–	–	–	–	–
444th Anti-Tank Artillery Rgt	–	–	–	–	–
869th Anti-Tank Artillery Rgt	–	–	–	–	–
1689th Anti-Tank Artillery Rgt	–	–	–	–	–
22nd Mortar Bde	–	–	–	–	–
490th Mortar Rgt	–	–	–	–	–
15th Gds Mortar Bde	–	–	–	–	–
17th Gds Mortar Rgt	–	–	–	–	–
38th Anti-Aircraft Artillery Div	–	–	–	–	–
1712th Anti-Aircraft Artillery Rgt	–	–	–	–	–
Total	–	–	138	79	24

Formations and Units	Total Guns	Total Guns and Mortars	Rocket Artillery Platforms	Anti-Aircraft Guns	Tanks and Self-Propelled Guns
		52nd Army			
93rd Rifle Div	44	142	–	–	–
138th Rifle Div	78	169	–	–	–
254th Rifle Div	44	140	–	–	–
294th Rifle Div	44	133	–	–	–
373rd Rifle Div	43	132	–	–	–
259th Tank Rgt	–	–	–	–	6
1817th Self-Propelled Artillery Rgt	–	–	–	–	12
37th Light Artillery Bde	63	63	–	–	–
50th Light Artillery Bde	73	73	–	–	–
39th Gun Artillery Bde	36	36	–	–	–
92nd Howitzer Artillery Bde	25	25	–	–	–
108th Heavy Caliber Howitzer Artillery Bde	24	24	–	–	–
568th Gun Artillery Bde	18	18	–	–	–
14th Anti-Tank Artillery Bde	44	44	–	–	–
438th Anti-Tank Artilllery Rgt	24	24	–	–	–
444th Anti-Tank Artillery Rgt	24	24	–	–	–
869th Anti-Tank Artillery Rgt	24	24	–	–	–
1689th Anti-Tank Artillery Rgt	14	14	–	–	–
22nd Mortar Bde	–	89	–	–	–
490th Mortar Rgt	–	36	–	–	–
15th Gds Mortar Bde	–	–	143	–	–
17th Gds Mortar Rgt	–	–	24	–	–
38th Anti-Aircraft Artillery Div	–	–	–	16	–
1712th Anti-Aircraft Artillery Rgt	–	–	–	16	–
Total	622	1,210	167	32	18

Formations and Units	Men	Mortars		Guns	
		81mm	120mm	76mm (rgt artillery)	76mm (div artillery)
4th Gds Army					
69th Gds Rifle Div	5,048	59	22	22	10
80th Gds Rifle Div	4,991	64	23	20	11
166th Rifle Div	3,991	37	11	6	5
5th Gds Airborne Div	4,773	54	21	21	6
7th Gds Airborne Div	5,138	63	17	23	10
8th Gds Airborne Div	4,268	71	22	21	8
153rd Howitzer Artillery Bde	595	–	–	–	–
1528th Howitzer Artillerty Rgt	613	–	–	–	–
123rd Heavy Caliber Howitzer Artillery Bde	1,298	–	–	–	–
12th Mortar Bde	2,025	–	103	–	–
466th Mortar Rgt	573	–	35	–	–
18th Gds Mortar Bde	973	–	–	–	–
19th Gds Mortar Bde	970	–	–	–	–
96th Gds Mortar Rgt	655	–	–	–	–
27th Anti-Aircraft Artillery Div	1,559	–	–	–	–
Total	37,470	348	254	116	50

Formations and Units	Guns				
	105mm	107mm	122mm	152mm	203mm
4th Gds Army					
69th Gds Rifle Div	–	–	12	–	–
80th Gds Rifle Div	–	–	12	–	–
166th Rifle Div	–	–	5	–	–
5th Gds Airborne Div	–	–	12	–	–
7th Gds Airborne Div	–	–	11	–	–
8th Gds Airborne Div	–	–	12	–	–
153rd Howitzer Artillery Bde	–	–	23	–	–
1528th Howitzer Artillerty Rgt	–	–	23	–	–
123rd Heavy Caliber Howitzer Artillery Bde	–	–	–	–	24
12th Mortar Bde	–	–	–	–	–
466th Mortar Rgt	–	–	–	–	–
18th Gds Mortar Bde	–	–	–	–	–
19th Gds Mortar Bde	–	–	–	–	–
96th Gds Mortar Rgt	–	–	–	–	–
27th Anti-Aircraft Artillery Div	–	–	–	–	–
Total	–	–	110	–	24

SUPPLEMENTS

Formations and Units	Total Guns	Total Guns and Mortars	Rocket Artillery Platforms	Anti-Aircraft Guns	Tanks and Self-Propelled Guns
4th Gds Army					
69th Gds Rifle Div	44	125	–	–	–
80th Gds Rifle Div	43	130	–	–	–
166th Rifle Div	16	64	–	–	–
5th Gds Airborne Div	42	117	–	–	–
7th Gds Airborne Div	44	124	–	–	–
8th Gds Airborne Div	41	134	–	–	–
153rd Howitzer Artillery Bde	23	23	–	–	–
1528th Howitzer Artillerty Rgt	23	23	–	–	–
123rd Heavy Caliber Howitzer Artillery Bde	24	24	–	–	–
12th Mortar Bde	–	103	–	–	–
466th Mortar Rgt	–	35	–	–	–
18th Gds Mortar Bde	–	–	144	–	–
19th Gds Mortar Bde	–	–	149	–	–
96th Gds Mortar Rgt	–	–	21	–	–
27th Anti-Aircraft Artillery Div	–	–	–	62	–
Total	300	902	314	62	–

| Formations and Units | Men | Mortars | | Guns | |
		81mm	120mm	76mm (rgt artillery)	76mm (div artillery)
6th Gds Army					
51st Gds Rifle Div	4,064	34	9	8	15
52nd Gds Rifle Div	4,977	31	–	7	18
67th Gds Rifle Div	4,103	25	10	5	20
71st Gds Rifle Div	5,451	57	12	11	23
90th Gds Rifle Div	4,651	29	8	3	21
59th Tank Rgt	341	–	–	–	–
628th Artillery Rgt	777	–	–	–	–
1240th Anti-Tank Artillery Rgt	473	–	–	–	24
295th Mortar Rgt	605	–	33	–	–
36th Gds Mortar Rgt	652	–	–	–	–
1487th Anti-Aircraft Artillery Rgt	40	–	–	–	–
Total	26,494	176	78	34	121

Formations and Units	Guns				
	105mm	107mm	122mm	152mm	203mm
6th Gds Army					
51st Gds Rifle Div	–	–	6	–	–
52nd Gds Rifle Div	–	–	6	–	–
67th Gds Rifle Div	–	–	6	–	–
71st Gds Rifle Div	–	–	9	–	–
90th Gds Rifle Div	–	–	5	–	–
59th Tank Rgt	–	–	–	–	–
628th Artillery Rgt	–	–	18	–	–
1240th Anti-Tank Artillery Rgt	–	–	–	–	–
295th Mortar Rgt	–	–	–	–	–
36th Gds Mortar Rgt	–	–	–	–	–
1487th Anti-Aircraft Artillery Rgt	–	–	–	–	–
Total	–	–	50	–	–

Formations and Units	Total Guns	Total Guns and Mortars	Rocket Artillery Platforms	Anti-Aircraft Guns	Tanks and Self-Propelled Guns
6th Gds Army					
51st Gds Rifle Div	29	72	–	–	–
52nd Gds Rifle Div	31	68	–	–	–
67th Gds Rifle Div	31	66	–	–	–
71st Gds Rifle Div	43	112	–	–	–
90th Gds Rifle Div	29	66	–	–	–
59th Tank Rgt	–	–	–	–	12
628th Artillery Rgt	18	18	–	–	–
1240th Anti-Tank Artillery Rgt	24	24	–	–	–
295th Mortar Rgt	–	33	–	–	–
36th Gds Mortar Rgt	–	–	23	3	–
1487th Anti-Aircraft Artillery Rgt	–	–	–	12	–
Total	205	459	23	15	12

Formations and Units	Men	Mortars		Guns	
		81mm	120mm	76mm (rgt artillery)	76mm (div artillery)
27th Army					
100th Rifle Div	3,921	35	14	7	13
147th Rifle Div	3,631	61	14	11	15
155th Rifle Div	4,618	37	12	10	20
241st Rifle Div	3,651	24	13	4	11
93rd Tank Bde	816	2	–	–	–
1832nd Self-Propelled Artillery Rgt	202	–	–	–	–
408th Heavy Anti-Tank Artillery Rgt	346	–	–	–	8
483rd Anti-Tank Artillery Rgt	371	–	–	–	11
680th Anti-Tank Artillery Rgt	341	–	–	–	15
1070th Anti-Tank Artillery Rgt	360	–	–	–	20
1075th Anti-Tank Artillery Rgt	301	–	–	–	5
1667th Anti-Tank Artillery Rgt	443	–	–	–	8
480th Mortar Rgt	553	–	21	–	–
47th Gds Mortar Rgt	613	–	–	–	–
23rd Anti-Aircraft Artillery Div	1,610	–	–	–	–
Total	21,837	159	74	32	127

Formations and Units	Guns				
	105mm	107mm	122mm	152mm	203mm
27th Army					
100th Rifle Div	–	–	9	–	–
147th Rifle Div	–	–	8	–	–
155th Rifle Div	–	–	11	–	–
241st Rifle Div	–	–	10	–	–
93rd Tank Bde	–	–	–	–	1
1832nd Self-Propelled Artillery Rgt	–	–	–	–	–
408th Heavy Anti-Tank Artillery Rgt	–	–	–	–	–
483rd Anti-Tank Artillery Rgt	–	–	–	–	–
680th Anti-Tank Artillery Rgt	–	–	–	–	–
1070th Anti-Tank Artillery Rgt	–	–	–	–	–
1075th Anti-Tank Artillery Rgt	–	–	–	–	–
1667th Anti-Tank Artillery Rgt	–	–	–	–	–
480th Mortar Rgt	–	–	–	–	–
47th Gds Mortar Rgt	–	–	–	–	–
23rd Anti-Aircraft Artillery Div	–	–	–	–	–
Total	–	–	38	–	1

186 THE BATTLE OF THE DNEPR

Formations and Units	Total Guns	Total Guns and Mortars	Rocket Artillery Platforms	Anti-Aircraft Guns	Tanks and Self-Propelled Guns
		27th Army			
100th Rifle Div	29	78	–	–	–
147th Rifle Div	34	109	–	–	–
155th Rifle Div	41	90	–	–	–
241st Rifle Div	25	62	–	–	–
93rd Tank Bde	3	3	–	–	24
1832nd Self-Propelled Artillery Rgt	–	–	–	–	8
408th Heavy Anti-Tank Artillery Rgt	8	8	–	–	–
483rd Anti-Tank Artillery Rgt	11	11	–	–	–
680th Anti-Tank Artillery Rgt	15	15	–	–	–
1070th Anti-Tank Artillery Rgt	20	20	–	–	–
1075th Anti-Tank Artillery Rgt	5	5	–	–	–
1667th Anti-Tank Artillery Rgt	8	8	–	–	–
480th Mortar Rgt	–	21	–	–	–
47th Gds Mortar Rgt	–	–	19	–	–
23rd Anti-Aircraft Artillery Div	–	–	–	52	–
Total	197	430	19	52	32

| Formations and Units | Men | Mortars | | Guns | |
		81mm	120mm	76mm (rgt artillery)	76mm (div artillery)
		3rd Gds Tank Army			
6th Gds Tank Corps	6,695	29	6	–	12
7th Gds Tank Corps	6,672	53	6	–	20
9th Mechanized Corps	10,799	90	18	–	36
91st Tank Bde	1,160	6	–	–	2
1893rd Self-Propelled Artillery Rgt	210	–	–	–	–
1894th Self-Propelled Artillery Rgt	242	–	–	–	–
1835th Self-Propelled Artillery Rgt	250	–	–	–	–
1836th Self-Propelled Artillery Rgt	247	–	–	–	–
148th Anti-Tank Artillery Rgt	493	–	–	20	–
272nd Mortar Rgt	670	–	36	–	–
467th Mortar Rgt	493	–	36	–	–
1st Gds Mortar Rgt	317	–	–	–	–
91st Gds Mortar Rgt	660	–	–	–	–
286th Gds Anti-Aircraft Artillery Rgt	399	–	–	–	–
287th Gds Anti-Aircraft Artillery Rgt	370	–	–	–	–
1381st Anti-Aircraft Artillery Rgt	361	–	–	–	–
1394th Anti-Aircraft Artillery Rgt	377	–	–	–	–
Total	30,445	78	102	20	70

SUPPLEMENTS

Formations and Units	Guns					Total Guns	Total Guns and Mortars	Rocket Artillery Platforms	Anti-Aircraft Guns	Tanks and Self-Propelled Guns
	105mm	107mm	122mm	152mm	203mm					
3rd Gds Tank Army										
6th Gds Tank Corps	–	–	–	–	–	12	47	–	–	159
7th Gds Tank Corps	–	–	–	–	–	20	79	–	–	159
9th Mechanized Corps	–	–	–	–	–	36	144	–	–	182
91st Tank Bde	–	–	–	–	–	2	8	–	–	53
1893rd Self-Propelled Artillery Rgt	–	–	–	–	–	–	–	–	–	21
1894th Self-Propelled Artillery Rgt	–	–	–	–	–	–	–	–	–	21
1835th Self-Propelled Artillery Rgt	–	–	–	–	–	–	–	–	–	13
1836th Self-Propelled Artillery Rgt	–	–	–	–	–	–	–	–	–	13
148th Anti-Tank Artillery Rgt	–	–	–	–	–	20	20	–	–	–
272nd Mortar Rgt	–	–	–	–	–	–	36	–	–	–
467th Mortar Rgt	–	–	–	–	–	–	36	–	–	–
1st Gds Mortar Rgt	–	–	–	–	–	–	–	12	–	–
91st Gds Mortar Rgt	–	–	–	–	–	–	–	24	–	–
286th Gds Anti-Aircraft Artillery Rgt	–	–	–	–	–	–	–	–	11	–
287th Gds Anti-Aircraft Artillery Rgt	–	–	–	–	–	–	–	–	16	–
1381st Anti-Aircraft Artillery Rgt	–	–	–	–	–	–	–	–	16	–
1394th Anti-Aircraft Artillery Rgt						–	–	–	16	–
Total	–	–	–	–	–	90	370	36	59	624

Formations and Units	Men	Mortars		Guns	
		81mm	120mm	76mm (rgt artillery)	76mm (div artillery)
1st Gds Cavalry Corps					
1st Gds Cavalry Div	5,562	37	6	8	12
2nd Gds Cavalry Div	5,687	36	6	8	12
7th Gds Cavalry Div	5,456	36	6	8	12
Total	16,705	109	18	24	36

Formations and Units	Guns				
	105mm	107mm	122mm	152mm	203mm
1st Gds Cavalry Corps					
1st Gds Cavalry Div	–	–	8	–	–
2nd Gds Cavalry Div	–	–	8	–	–
7th Gds Cavalry Div	–	–	6	–	–
Total	–	–	22	–	–

Formations and Units	Total Guns	Total Guns and Mortars	Rocket Artillery Platforms	Anti-Aircraft Guns	Tanks and Self-Propelled Guns
1st Gds Cavalry Corps					
1st Gds Cavalry Div	28	71	–	6	–
2nd Gds Cavalry Div	28	70	–	6	–
7th Gds Cavalry Div	26	68	–	6	–
Total	82	209	–	18	–

SUPPLEMENTS

Formations and Units	Men	Mortars		Guns	
		81mm	120mm	76mm (rgt artillery)	76mm (div artillery)
	Forces Subordinated to the *Front*				
5th Gds Tank Corps	3,888	19	3	16	–
3rd Gds Mortar Div	No Information				
13th Breakthrough Artillery Div	No Information				
17th Breakthrough Artillery Div	No Information				
93rd Gun Artillery Bde	1,073	–	–	–	–
36th Heavy Gun Artillery Bde	1,039	–	–	–	–
101st Heavy Caliber Howitzer Bde	1,317	–	–	–	–
1528th Howitzer Artillery Rgt	654	–	–	–	–
496th Anti-Tank Artillery Rgt	208	–	–	–	2
1322nd Anti-Tank Artillery Rgt	468	–	–	–	24
1496th Anti-Tank Artillery Rgt	271	–	–	–	20
1672nd Anti-Tank Artillery Rgt	370	–	–	–	24
266th Mortar Rgt	695	–	34	–	–
454th Mortar Rgt	575	–	23	–	–
Total	10,588	19	60	16	70
Total for the *Front*	338,780	2,353	1,470	636	1,354

Formations and Units	Guns				
	105mm	107mm	122mm	152mm	203mm
	Forces Subordinated to the *Front*				
5th Gds Tank Corps	–	–	–	–	–
3rd Gds Mortar Div	No Information				
13th Breakthrough Artillery Div	No Information				
17th Breakthrough Artillery Div	No Information				
93rd Gun Artillery Bde	–	–	–	34	–
36th Heavy Gun Artillery Bde	–	–	–	35	–
101st Heavy Caliber Howitzer Bde	–	–	–	–	24
1528th Howitzer Artillery Rgt	–	–	19	–	–
496th Anti-Tank Artillery Rgt	–	–	–	–	–
1322nd Anti-Tank Artillery Rgt	–	–	–	–	–
1496th Anti-Tank Artillery Rgt	–	–	–	–	–
1672nd Anti-Tank Artillery Rgt	–	–	–	–	–
266th Mortar Rgt	–	–	–	–	–
454th Mortar Rgt	–	–	–	–	–
Total	–	–	19	69	24
Total for the *Front*	–	–	–	215	72

THE BATTLE OF THE DNEPR

Formations and Units	Total Guns	Total Guns and Mortars	Rocket Artillery Platforms	Anti-Aircraft Guns	Tanks and Self-Propelled Guns
		Forces Subordinated to the *Front*			
5th Gds Tank Corps	16	38	–	–	49
3rd Gds Mortar Div	No Information				
13th Breakthrough Artillery Div	No Information				
17th Breakthrough Artillery Div	No Information				
93rd Gun Artillery Bde	34	34	–	–	–
36th Heavy Gun Artillery Bde	35	35	–	–	–
101st Heavy Caliber Howitzer Bde	24	24	–	–	–
1528th Howitzer Artillery Rgt	19	19	–	–	–
496th Anti-Tank Artillery Rgt	2	2	–	–	–
1322nd Anti-Tank Artillery Rgt	21	21	–	–	–
1496th Anti-Tank Artillery Rgt	20	20	–	–	–
1672nd Anti-Tank Artillery Rgt	24	24	–	–	–
266th Mortar Rgt	–	34	–	–	–
454th Mortar Rgt	–	23	–	–	–
Total	198	277	–	–	49
Total for the *Front*	2,962	6,785	663	476	908

Supplement 1.2 The Voronezh Front's Combat Strength by 10 October 1943

Formations and Units	Men	Mortars		Guns	
		81mm	120mm	76mm (rgt artillery)	76mm (div artillery)
		13th Army			
8th Rifle Div	6,205	51	18	12	18
74th Rifle Div	5,903	56	14	6	15
148th Rifle Div	4,616	52	18	10	15
181st Rifle Div	6,419	60	20	9	12
211th Rifle Div	7,259	30	9	6	18
322nd Rifle Div	4,962	33	16	10	15
129th Tank Bde	1,432	6	–	–	4
19th Gds Gun Artillery Rgt	921	–	–	–	–
874th Anti-Tank Artillery Rgt	495	–	–	–	21
476th Mortar Rgt	592	–	35	–	–
477th Mortar Rgt	635	–	28	–	–
10th Anti-Aircraft Artillery Div	1,557	–	–	–	–
1287th Anti-Aircraft Artillery Rgt	400	–	–	–	–
Total	41,396	288	158	53	118

SUPPLEMENTS

Formations and Units	Guns				
	105mm	107mm	122mm	152mm	203mm
		13th Army			
8th Rifle Div	–	–	10	–	–
74th Rifle Div	–	–	6	–	–
148th Rifle Div	–	9	–	–	–
181st Rifle Div	–	10	–	–	–
211th Rifle Div	–	–	8	–	–
322nd Rifle Div	–	–	6	–	–
129th Tank Bde	–	–	–	–	–
19th Gds Gun Artillery Rgt	–	–	10	4	–
874th Anti-Tank Artillery Rgt	–	–	–	–	–
476th Mortar Rgt	–	–	–	–	–
477th Mortar Rgt	–	–	–	–	–
10th Anti-Aircraft Artillery Div	–	–	–	–	–
1287th Anti-Aircraft Artillery Rgt	–	–	–	–	–
Total	–	–	59	4	–

Formations and Units	Total Guns	Total Guns and Mortars	Rocket Artillery Platforms	Anti-Aircraft Guns	Tanks and Self-Propelled Guns
		13th Army			
8th Rifle Div	40	109	–	–	–
74th Rifle Div	27	97	–	–	–
148th Rifle Div	34	104	–	–	–
181st Rifle Div	31	111	–	–	–
211th Rifle Div	32	71	–	–	–
322nd Rifle Div	31	80	–	–	–
129th Tank Bde	4	10	–	4	20
19th Gds Gun Artillery Rgt	14	14	–	–	–
874th Anti-Tank Artillery Rgt	21	21	–	–	–
476th Mortar Rgt	–	35	–	–	–
477th Mortar Rgt	–	28	–	–	–
10th Anti-Aircraft Artillery Div	–	–	–	62	–
1287th Anti-Aircraft Artillery Rgt	–	–	–	15	–
Total	234	680	–	81	20

192   THE BATTLE OF THE DNEPR

Formations and Units	Men	Mortars		Guns	
		81mm	120mm	76mm (rgt artillery)	76mm (div artillery)
60th Army					
6th Gds Rifle Div	5,422	55	16	8	10
70th Gds Rifle Div	4,534	25	16	5	13
75th Gds Rifle Div	4,269	32	15	6	21
112th Rifle Div	6,211	46	16	10	19
121st Rifle Div	6,370	60	18	12	14
132nd Rifle Div	3,194	26	4	4	18
141st Rifle Div	6,183	66	16	11	20
143rd Rifle Div	3,045	26	9	7	19
226th Rifle Div	6,652	22	12	8	20
280th Rifle Div	3,570	22	9	10	17
2nd Gds Airborne Div	5,000	20	13	5	15
3rd Gds Airborne Div	4,281	14	10	6	23
4th Gds Airborne Div	3,607	16	8	6	22
248th Rifle Bde	3,734	20	11	4	10
7th Gds Mechanized Corps	5,562	39	15	9	–
150th Tank Bde	1,176	5	–	2	–
1st Gds Breakthrough Artillery Div	5,384	–	–	–	56
1156th Gun Artillery Rgt	825	–	–	–	–
130th Anti-Tank Artillery Rgt	446	–	–	–	15
493rd Anti-Tank Artillery Rgt	472	–	–	–	11
1178th Anti-Tank Artillery Rgt	335	–	–	–	7
128th Mortar Rgt	432	–	27	–	–
138th Mortar Rgt	491	–	18	–	–
468th Mortar Rgt	531	–	19	–	–
497th Mortar Rgt	507	–	29	–	–
65th Gds Mortar Rgt	636	–	–	–	–
98th Gds Mortar Rgt	633	–	–	–	–
410th Gds Mortar Bn	213	–	–	–	–
217th Anti-Aircraft Artillery Rgt	399	–	–	–	–
238th Anti-Aircraft Artillery Rgt	349	–	–	–	–
Total	74,363	494	281	113	330

Formations and Units	Guns				
	105mm	107mm	122mm	152mm	203mm
60th Army					
6th Gds Rifle Div	–	–	6	–	–
70th Gds Rifle Div	–	–	8	–	–
75th Gds Rifle Div	–	–	8	–	–
112th Rifle Div	–	–	10	–	–
121st Rifle Div	–	–	10	–	–
132nd Rifle Div	–	–	11	–	–
141st Rifle Div	–	–	9	–	–
143rd Rifle Div	–	–	12	–	–
226th Rifle Div	–	–	8	–	–
280th Rifle Div	–	–	4	–	–
2nd Gds Airborne Div	–	–	10	–	–
3rd Gds Airborne Div	–	–	12	–	–
4th Gds Airborne Div	–	–	12	–	–
248th Rifle Bde	–	–	–	–	–
7th Gds Mechanized Corps	–	–	–	–	–
150th Tank Bde	–	–	–	–	–
1st Gds Breakthrough Artillery Div	–	–	36	51	–
1156th Gun Artillery Rgt	–	–	–	18	–
130th Anti-Tank Artillery Rgt	–	–	–	–	–
493rd Anti-Tank Artillery Rgt	–	–	–	–	–
1178th Anti-Tank Artillery Rgt	–	–	–	–	–
128th Mortar Rgt	–	–	–	–	–
138th Mortar Rgt	–	–	–	–	–
468th Mortar Rgt	–	–	–	–	–
497th Mortar Rgt	–	–	–	–	–
65th Gds Mortar Rgt	–	–	–	–	–
98th Gds Mortar Rgt	–	–	–	–	–
410th Gds Mortar Bn	–	–	–	–	–
217th Anti-Aircraft Artillery Rgt	–	–	–	–	–
238th Anti-Aircraft Artillery Rgt	–	–	–	–	–
Total	–	–	156	69	–

194 THE BATTLE OF THE DNEPR

Formations and Units	Total Guns	Total Guns and Mortars	Rocket Artillery Platforms	Anti-Aircraft Guns	Tanks and Self-Propelled Guns
		60th Army			
6th Gds Rifle Div	24	95	–	–	–
70th Gds Rifle Div	26	67	–	–	–
75th Gds Rifle Div	35	82	–	–	–
112th Rifle Div	39	101	–	–	–
121st Rifle Div	36	114	–	–	–
132nd Rifle Div	33	63	–	–	–
141st Rifle Div	40	122	–	–	–
143rd Rifle Div	38	74	–	–	–
226th Rifle Div	36	70	–	–	–
280th Rifle Div	31	62	–	–	–
2nd Gds Airborne Div	30	63	–	–	–
3rd Gds Airborne Div	41	65	–	–	–
4th Gds Airborne Div	40	64	–	–	–
248th Rifle Bde	14	45	–	–	–
7th Gds Mechanized Corps	9	63	12	–	8
150th Tank Bde	2	7	–	4	4
1st Gds Breakthrough Artillery Div	143	143	–	–	–
1156th Gun Artillery Rgt	18	18	–	–	–
130th Anti-Tank Artillery Rgt	15	15	–	–	–
493rd Anti-Tank Artillery Rgt	11	11	–	–	–
1178th Anti-Tank Artillery Rgt	7	7	–	–	–
128th Mortar Rgt	–	27	–	–	–
138th Mortar Rgt	–	18	–	–	–
468th Mortar Rgt	–	19	–	–	–
497th Mortar Rgt	–	29	–	–	–
65th Gds Mortar Rgt	–	–	25	–	–
98th Gds Mortar Rgt	–	–	24	–	–
410th Gds Mortar Bn	–	–	7	2	–
217th Anti-Aircraft Artillery Rgt	–	–	–	16	–
238th Anti-Aircraft Artillery Rgt	–	–	–	13	–
Total	668	1,443	68	35	12

SUPPLEMENTS

Formations and Units	Men	Mortars		Guns	
		81mm	120mm	76mm (rgt artillery)	76mm (div artillery)
1st Gds Cavalry Corps					
1st Gds Cavalry Div	5,712	37	6	12	8
2nd Gds Cavalry Div	5,641	36	6	12	–
7th Gds Cavalry Div	5,855	36	6	12	8
143rd Anti-Tank Artillery Rgt	486	–	–	–	20
1461st Self-Propelled Artillery Rgt	242	–	–	–	–
1st Gds Mortar Bn	313	–	–	–	–
319th Anti-Aircraft Artillery Rgt	409	–	–	–	–
Total	18,658	109	18	36	36

The 1st Gds Cavalry Corps was evidently subordinated to the 60th Army, so there combined strengths are also included here. To indicate this, the following should be done.
1. The solid line immediately beneath the word Total should be moved down a space to create room for another entry
2. Create beneath the word Total the following entry: Total for the 60th Army
3. The following numbers should then be place under the headings (men, 81mm, etc.) to the right: 93,021, 603, 299, 149, 366

Formations and Units	Guns				
	105mm	107mm	122mm	152mm	203mm
1st Gds Cavalry Corps					
1st Gds Cavalry Div	–	–	8	–	–
2nd Gds Cavalry Div	–	–	8	–	–
7th Gds Cavalry Div	–	–	6	–	–
143rd Anti-Tank Artillery Rgt	–	–	–	–	–
1461st Self-Propelled Artillery Rgt	–	–	–	–	–
1st Gds Mortar Bn	–	–	–	–	–
319th Anti-Aircraft Artillery Rgt	–	–	–	–	–
Total	–	–	22	–	–

See instructions for steps 1 and 2 in the note immediately above.
3. The entries for the entire army should have dashed lines for the entries 105mm and 107mm, 178 for 122mm, 69 for 152mm, and a dashed line for 203mm

Formations and Units	Total Guns	Total Guns and Mortars	Rocket Artillery Platforms	Anti-Aircraft Guns	Tanks and Self-Propelled Guns
1st Gds Cavalry Corps					
1st Gds Cavalry Div	28	71	–	6	–
2nd Gds Cavalry Div	20	62	–	6	–
7th Gds Cavalry Div	26	58	–	6	–
143rd Anti-Tank Artillery Rgt	20	20	–	–	20
1461st Self-Propelled Artillery Rgt	–	–	–	–	13
1st Gds Mortar Bn	–	–	11	–	–

Formations and Units	Total Guns	Total Guns and Mortars	Rocket Artillery Platforms	Anti-Aircraft Guns	Tanks and Self-Propelled Guns
319th Anti-Aircraft Artillery Rgt	–	–	–	16	–
Total	94	211	11	34	13

Repeat steps 1 and 2, as shown in the previous entries for this unit.
3. The total for the entire army should read from left to right (total guns, etc.) as follows: 762, 1,654, 79, 69, 25

Formations and Units	Men	Mortars		Guns	
		81mm	120mm	76mm (rgt artillery)	76mm (div artillery)
38th Army					
71st Rifle Div	6,434	27	15	5	16
136th Rifle Div	8,774	46	15	9	20
163rd Rifle Div	7,809	24	12	5	15
167th Rifle Div	7,976	66	17	15	11
180th Rifle Div	8,875	68	20	14	12
232nd Rifle Div	10,974	52	14	9	17
240th Rifle Div	9,189	41	18	3	17
340th Rifle Div	8,465	40	18	11	12
3rd Gds Tank Corps	6,354	39	39	–	12
5th Gds Tank Corps	6,577	21	34	1	11
39th Tank Rgt	454	–	–	1	–
1436th Self-Propelled Artillery Rgt	263	–	–	–	–
112th Gds Gun Artillery Rgt	967	–	–	–	–
1950th Gun Artillery Rgt	776	–	–	–	–
839th Howitzer Artillery Rgt	562	–	–	–	–
895th Gun Artillery Rgt	587	–	–	–	–
28th Anti-Tank Artillery Bde	1,122	–	–	–	10
4th Gds Anti-Tank Artillery Rgt	496	–	–	–	18
222nd Anti-Tank Artillery Rgt	475	–	–	–	20
644th Anti-Tank Artillery Rgt	484	–	–	–	21
868th Anti-Tank Artillery Rgt	475	–	–	–	22
1075th Anti-Tank Artillery Rgt	430	–	–	–	18
1490th Anti-Tank Artillery Rgt	261	–	–	–	19
1660th Anti-Tank Artillery Rgt	474	–	–	–	15
491st Mortar Rgt	680	–	34	–	–
492nd Mortar Rgt	629	–	22	–	–
18th Gds Mortar Bde	969	–	–	–	–
16th Gds Mortar Rgt	667	–	–	–	–
66th Gds Mortar Rgt	651	–	–	–	–
6th Gds Mortar Rgt	662	–	–	–	–
8th Anti-Aircraft Artillery Div	1,438	–	–	–	–
1696th Anti-Aircraft Artillery Rgt	325	–	–	–	–
1701st Anti-Aircraft Artillery Rgt	400	–	–	–	–
Total	95,584	424	258	73	319

Formations and Units	Guns				
	105mm	107mm	122mm	152mm	203mm
		38th Army			
71st Rifle Div	–	–	9	–	–
136th Rifle Div	–	–	12	–	–
163rd Rifle Div	–	–	6	–	–
167th Rifle Div	2	–	9	–	–
180th Rifle Div	–	–	8	–	–
232nd Rifle Div	–	–	10	–	–
240th Rifle Div	3	–	10	–	–
340th Rifle Div	–	–	8	2	–
3rd Gds Tank Corps	–	–	–	–	–
5th Gds Tank Corps	–	–	–	3	–
39th Tank Rgt	–	–	–	–	–
1436th Self-Propelled Artillery Rgt	–	–	–	–	–
112th Gds Gun Artillery Rgt	–	–	–	18	–
1950th Gun Artillery Rgt	–	–	–	18	–
839th Howitzer Artillery Rgt	–	–	23	–	–
895th Gun Artillery Rgt	–	–	19	–	–
28th Anti-Tank Artillery Bde	–	–	–	–	–
4th Gds Anti-Tank Artillery Rgt	–	–	–	–	–
222nd Anti-Tank Artillery Rgt	–	–	–	–	–
644th Anti-Tank Artillery Rgt	–	–	–	–	–
868th Anti-Tank Artillery Rgt	–	–	–	–	–
1075th Anti-Tank Artillery Rgt	–	–	–	–	–
1490th Anti-Tank Artillery Rgt	–	–	–	–	–
1660th Anti-Tank Artillery Rgt	–	–	–	–	–
491st Mortar Rgt	–	–	–	–	–
492nd Mortar Rgt	–	–	–	–	–
18th Gds Mortar Bde	–	–	–	–	–
16th Gds Mortar Rgt	–	–	–	–	–
66th Gds Mortar Rgt	–	–	–	–	–
6th Gds Mortar Rgt	–	–	–	–	–
8th Anti-Aircraft Artillery Div	–	–	–	–	–
1696th Anti-Aircraft Artillery Rgt	–	–	–	–	–
1701st Anti-Aircraft Artillery Rgt	–	–	–	–	–
Total	9	–	114	41	–

198 THE BATTLE OF THE DNEPR

Formations and Units	Total Guns	Total Guns and Mortars	Rocket Artillery Platforms	Anti-Aircraft Guns	Tanks and Self-Propelled Guns
		38th Army			
71st Rifle Div	30	72	–	–	–
136th Rifle Div	41	102	–	–	–
163rd Rifle Div	26	62	–	–	–
167th Rifle Div	37	120	–	–	–
180th Rifle Div	38	126	–	–	–
232nd Rifle Div	36	102	–	–	–
240th Rifle Div	33	92	–	–	–
340th Rifle Div	33	91	–	–	–
3rd Gds Tank Corps	12	90	8	6	17
5th Gds Tank Corps	15	70	–	–	145
39th Tank Rgt	1	1	–	–	33
1436th Self-Propelled Artillery Rgt	–	–	–	–	8
112th Gds Gun Artillery Rgt	18	18	–	–	–
1950th Gun Artillery Rgt	18	18	–	–	–
839th Howitzer Artillery Rgt	23	23	–	–	–
895th Gun Artillery Rgt	19	19	–	–	–
28th Anti-Tank Artillery Bde	40	40	–	–	–
4th Gds Anti-Tank Artillery Rgt	18	18	–	–	–
222nd Anti-Tank Artillery Rgt	20	20	–	–	–
644th Anti-Tank Artillery Rgt	24	24	–	–	–
868th Anti-Tank Artillery Rgt	22	22	–	–	–
1075th Anti-Tank Artillery Rgt	18	18	–	–	–
1490th Anti-Tank Artillery Rgt	19	19	–	–	–
1660th Anti-Tank Artillery Rgt	15	15	–	–	–
491st Mortar Rgt	–	34	–	–	–
492nd Mortar Rgt	–	22	–	–	–
18th Gds Mortar Bde	–	–	144	–	–
16th Gds Mortar Rgt	–	–	24	–	–
66th Gds Mortar Rgt	–	23	23	–	–
6th Gds Mortar Rgt	–	–	24	–	–
8th Anti-Aircraft Artillery Div	–	–	–	48	–
1696th Anti-Aircraft Artillery Rgt	–	–	–	7	–
1701st Anti-Aircraft Artillery Rgt	–	–	–	15	–
Total	556	1,238	223	76	203

SUPPLEMENTS

Formations and Units	Men	Mortars		Guns	
		81mm	120mm	76mm (rgt artillery)	76mm (div artillery)
40th Army					
42nd Gds Rifle Div	5,121	17	14	3	14
68th Gds Rifle Div	4,750	28	20	7	18
161st Rifle Div	6,056	37	12	6	14
237th Rifle Div	4,019	33	9	–	13
253rd Rifle Div	4,830	56	14	10	18
309th Rifle Div	4,830	28	7	9	10
337th Rifle Div	5,473	16	11	5	17
8th Gds Tank Corps	5,383	21	19	–	9
10th Tank Corps	5,162	22	19	–	18
17th Breakthrough Artillery Div	8,463	–	77	–	62
76th Gds Gun Artillery Rgt	837	–	–	–	–
111th Gds Howitzer Artillery Rgt	772	–	–	–	–
27th Anti-Tank Artillery Bde	1,070	–	–	–	34
32nd Anti-Tank Artillery Bde	950	–	–	–	30
611th Anti-Tank Artillery Rgt	474	–	–	–	24
1076th Anti-Tank Artillery Rgt	422	–	–	–	14
1661st Anti-Tank Artillery Rgt	416	–	–	–	12
9th Mortar Rgt	557	–	33	–	–
10th Mortar Rgt	538	–	31	–	–
241st Mortar Rgt	437	–	19	–	–
242nd Mortar Rgt	316	–	11	–	–
233rd Mortar Rgt	539	–	32	–	–
245th Mortar Rgt	479	–	36	–	–
493rd Mortar Rgt	513	–	29	–	–
494th Mortar Rgt	634	–	34	–	–
36th Gds Mortar Rgt	669	–	–	–	–
314th Gds Mortar Rgt	677	–	–	–	–
316th Gds Mortar Rgt	670	–	–	–	–
9th Anti-Aircraft Artillery Div	1,516	–	–	–	–
27th Ant-Aircraft Artillery Div	1,962	–	–	–	–
Total	68,835	258	438	40	307

THE BATTLE OF THE DNEPR

Formations and Units	Guns				
	105mm	107mm	122mm	152mm	203mm
40th Army					
42nd Gds Rifle Div	–	–	8	–	–
68th Gds Rifle Div	–	–	12	–	–
161st Rifle Div	–	–	8	–	–
237th Rifle Div	–	–	8	–	–
253rd Rifle Div	–	–	10	–	–
309th Rifle Div	–	–	8	–	–
337th Rifle Div	–	–	11	–	–
8th Gds Tank Corps	–	–	–	–	–
10th Tank Corps	–	–	–	–	–
17th Breakthrough Artillery Div	–	–	75	36	49
76th Gds Gun Artillery Rgt	–	–	–	17	–
111th Gds Howitzer Artillery Rgt	–	–	24	–	–
27th Anti-Tank Artillery Bde	–	–	–	–	–
32nd Anti-Tank Artillery Bde	–	–	–	–	–
611th Anti-Tank Artillery Rgt	–	–	–	–	–
1076th Anti-Tank Artillery Rgt	–	–	–	–	–
1661st Anti-Tank Artillery Rgt	–	–	–	–	–
9th Mortar Rgt	–	–	–	–	–
10th Mortar Rgt	–	–	–	–	–
241st Mortar Rgt	–	–	–	–	–
242nd Mortar Rgt	–	–	–	–	–
233rd Mortar Rgt	–	–	–	–	–
245th Mortar Rgt	–	–	–	–	–
493rd Mortar Rgt	–	–	–	–	–
494th Mortar Rgt	–	–	–	–	–
36th Gds Mortar Rgt	–	–	–	–	–
314th Gds Mortar Rgt	–	–	–	–	–
316th Gds Mortar Rgt	–	–	–	–	–
9th Anti-Aircraft Artillery Div	–	–	–	–	–
27th Ant-Aircraft Artillery Div	–	–	–	–	–
Total	–	–	161	53	49

SUPPLEMENTS

Formations and Units	Total Guns	Total Guns and Mortars	Rocket Artillery Platforms	Anti-Aircraft Guns	Tanks and Self-Propelled Guns
		40th Army			
42nd Gds Rifle Div	25	56	–	–	–
68th Gds Rifle Div	37	85	–	–	–
161st Rifle Div	28	77	–	–	–
237th Rifle Div	21	63	–	–	–
253rd Rifle Div	38	108	–	–	–
309th Rifle Div	27	62	–	–	–
337th Rifle Div	33	60	–	–	–
8th Gds Tank Corps	9	49	–	14	21
10th Tank Corps	18	59	–	14	29
17th Breakthrough Artillery Div	222	229	–	–	–
76th Gds Gun Artillery Rgt	17	17	–	–	–
111th Gds Howitzer Artillery Rgt	24	24	–	–	–
27th Anti-Tank Artillery Bde	34	34	–	–	–
32nd Anti-Tank Artillery Bde	30	30	–	–	–
611th Anti-Tank Artillery Rgt	24	24	–	–	–
1076th Anti-Tank Artillery Rgt	14	14	–	–	–
1661st Anti-Tank Artillery Rgt	12	12	–	–	–
9th Mortar Rgt	–	33	–	–	–
10th Mortar Rgt	–	31	–	–	–
241st Mortar Rgt	–	19	–	–	–
242nd Mortar Rgt	–	22	–	–	–
233rd Mortar Rgt	–	32	–	–	–
245th Mortar Rgt	–	36	–	–	–
493rd Mortar Rgt	–	29	–	–	–
494th Mortar Rgt	–	34	–	–	–
36th Gds Mortar Rgt	–	–	24	3	–
314th Gds Mortar Rgt	–	–	26	–	–
316th Gds Mortar Rgt	–	–	28	–	–
9th Anti-Aircraft Artillery Div	–	–	–	58	–
27th Ant-Aircraft Artillery Div	–	–	–	76	–
Total	613	1,309	78	165	50

202 THE BATTLE OF THE DNEPR

Formations and Units	Men	Mortars		Guns	
		81mm	120mm	76mm (rgt artillery)	76mm (div artillery)
27th Army					
38th Rifle Div	3,767	23	16	11	20
100th Rifle Div	5,221	37	12	8	13
147th Rifle Div	4,975	57	13	11	15
155th Rifle Div	5,039	32	12	10	20
241st Rifle Div	6,058	22	13	4	11
93rd Tank Bde	810	2	–	–	1
1832nd Self-Propelled Artillery Rgt	220	–	–	–	–
13th Breakthrough Artillery Div	8,726	–	100	–	70
36th Heavy Gun Artillery Bde	1,070	–	–	–	–
122nd Heavy Caliber Howitzer Artillery Bde	1,297	–	–	–	–
1528th Howitzer Artillery Rgt	614	–	–	–	–
408th Heavy Anti-Tank Artillery Rgt	366	–	–	–	–
483rd Anti-Tank Artillery Rgt	432	–	–	–	20
680th Anti-Tank Artillery Rgt	331	–	–	–	16
1070th Anti-Tank Artillery Rgt	353	–	–	–	20
1667th Anti-Tank Artillery Rgt	421	–	–	–	16
480th Mortar Rgt	544	–	24	–	–
3rd Gds Mortar Div	2,006	–	–	–	–
47th Gds Mortar Rgt	671	–	–	–	–
23rd Anti-Aircraft Artillery Div	1,044	–	–	–	–
Total	44,565	173	190	44	222

SUPPLEMENTS

Formations and Units	Guns				
	105mm	107mm	122mm	152mm	203mm
			27th Army		
38th Rifle Div	–	–	12	–	–
100th Rifle Div	–	–	9	–	–
147th Rifle Div	–	–	8	–	–
155th Rifle Div	–	–	11	–	–
241st Rifle Div	–	–	10	–	–
93rd Tank Bde	–	–	–	–	–
1832nd Self-Propelled Artillery Rgt	–	–	–	–	–
13th Breakthrough Artillery Div	–	–	103	62	24
36th Heavy Gun Artillery Bde	–	–	–	35	–
122nd Heavy Caliber Howitzer Artillery Bde	–	–	–	–	24
1528th Howitzer Artillery Rgt	–	–	23	–	–
408th Heavy Anti-Tank Artillery Rgt	–	8	–	–	–
483rd Anti-Tank Artillery Rgt	–	–	–	–	–
680th Anti-Tank Artillery Rgt	–	–	–	–	–
1070th Anti-Tank Artillery Rgt	–	–	–	–	–
1667th Anti-Tank Artillery Rgt	–	–	–	–	–
480th Mortar Rgt	–	–	–	–	–
3rd Gds Mortar Div	–	–	–	–	–
47th Gds Mortar Rgt	–	–	–	–	–
23rd Anti-Aircraft Artillery Div	–	–	–	–	–
Total	–	8	176	97	48

Formations and Units	Total Guns	Total Guns and Mortars	Rocket Artillery Platforms	Anti-Aircraft Guns	Tanks and Self-Propelled Guns
27th Army					
38th Rifle Div	43	82	–	–	–
100th Rifle Div	30	79	–	–	–
147th Rifle Div	34	104	–	–	–
155th Rifle Div	41	85	–	–	–
241st Rifle Div	25	60	–	–	–
93rd Tank Bde	1	3	–	–	–
1832nd Self-Propelled Artillery Rgt	–	–	–	–	21
13th Breakthrough Artillery Div	259	259	–	–	5
36th Heavy Gun Artillery Bde	35	35	–	–	–
122nd Heavy Caliber Howitzer Artillery Bde	24	24	–	–	–
1528th Howitzer Artillery Rgt	23	23	–	–	–
408th Heavy Anti-Tank Artillery Rgt	8	8	–	–	–
483rd Anti-Tank Artillery Rgt	20	20	–	–	–
680th Anti-Tank Artillery Rgt	16	16	–	–	–
1070th Anti-Tank Artillery Rgt	20	20	–	–	–
1667th Anti-Tank Artillery Rgt	16	16	–	–	–
480th Mortar Rgt	–	24	–	–	–
3rd Gds Mortar Div	–	–	301	–	–
47th Gds Mortar Rgt	–	–	21	–	–
23rd Anti-Aircraft Artillery Div	–	–	–	52	–
Total	595	958	322	52	26

SUPPLEMENTS

Formations and Units	Men	Mortars		Guns	
		81mm	120mm	76mm (rgt artillery)	76mm (div artillery)
47th Army					
23rd Rifle Div	4,857	30	12	10	14
30th Rifle Div	5,320	33	14	10	17
206th Rifle Div	4,878	23	13	6	18
218th Rifle Div	5,010	17	16	11	15
3rd Gds Mechanized Corps	7,630	40	13	–	33
1831st Self-Propelled Artillery Rgt	229	–	–	–	–
14th Anti-Tank Artillery Bde	1,273	–	–	–	57
29th Anti-Tank Artillery Bde	1,104	–	–	–	35
869th Anti-Tank Artillery Rgt	473	–	–	–	23
1672nd Anti-Tank Artillery Rgt	467	–	–	–	24
33rd Heavy Gun Artillery Rgt	1,074	–	–	–	–
628th Gun Artillery Rgt	798	–	–	–	–
129th Mortar Rgt	447	–	30	–	–
460th Mortar Rgt	499	–	28	–	–
83rd Gds Mortar Rgt	581	–	–	–	–
334th Gds Mortar Bn	213	–	–	–	–
21st Anti-Aircraft Artillery Div	1,488	–	–	–	–
Total	36,341	143	126	37	241

Formations and Units	Guns				
	105mm	107mm	122mm	152mm	203mm
47th Army					
23rd Rifle Div	–	–	12	–	–
30th Rifle Div	–	–	11	–	–
206th Rifle Div	–	–	12	–	–
218th Rifle Div	–	–	11	–	–
3rd Gds Mechanized Corps	–	–	–	–	–
1831st Self-Propelled Artillery Rgt	–	–	–	–	–
14th Anti-Tank Artillery Bde	–	–	–	–	–
29th Anti-Tank Artillery Bde	–	–	–	–	–
869th Anti-Tank Artillery Rgt	–	–	–	–	–
1672nd Anti-Tank Artillery Rgt	–	–	–	–	–
33rd Heavy Gun Artillery Rgt	–	–	–	35	–
628th Gun Artillery Rgt	–	–	–	18	–
129th Mortar Rgt	–	–	–	–	–
460th Mortar Rgt	–	–	–	–	–
83rd Gds Mortar Rgt	–	–	–	–	–
334th Gds Mortar Bn	–	–	–	–	–
21st Anti-Aircraft Artillery Div	–	–	–	–	–
Total	–	–	46	53	–

Formations and Units	Total Guns	Total Guns and Mortars	Rocket Artillery Platforms	Anti-Aircraft Guns	Tanks and Self-Propelled Guns
		47th Army			
23rd Rifle Div	41	83	–	–	–
30th Rifle Div	38	85	–	–	–
206th Rifle Div	36	72	–	–	–
218th Rifle Div	37	70	–	–	–
3rd Gds Mechanized Corps	33	86	–	15	19
1831st Self-Propelled Artillery Rgt	–	–	–	–	1
14th Anti-Tank Artillery Bde	57	57	–	–	–
29th Anti-Tank Artillery Bde	35	35	–	–	–
869th Anti-Tank Artillery Rgt	23	23	–	–	–
1672nd Anti-Tank Artillery Rgt	24	24	–	–	–
33rd Heavy Gun Artillery Rgt	35	35	–	–	–
628th Gun Artillery Rgt	18	18	–	–	–
129th Mortar Rgt	–	30	–	–	–
460th Mortar Rgt	–	28	–	–	–
83rd Gds Mortar Rgt	–	–	24	–	–
334th Gds Mortar Bn	–	–	8	–	–
21st Anti-Aircraft Artillery Div	–	–	–	62	–
Total	377	646	32	77	20

Formations and Units	Men	Mortars		Guns	
		81mm	120mm	76mm (rgt artillery)	76mm (div artillery)
		3rd Gds Tank Army			
6th Gds Tank Corps	5,944	37	31	–	19
7th Gds Tank Corps	6,853	86	6	–	21
9th Mechanized Corps	9,862	109	18	–	42
91st Tank Bde	1,148	6	–	–	2
50th Motorcycle Rgt	1,139	12	–	–	4
1835th Self-Propelled Artillery Rgt	257	–	–	–	–
1836th Self-Propelled Artillery Rgt	246	–	–	–	–
1893rd Self-Propelled Artillery Rgt	227	–	–	–	–
91st Gds Mortar Rgt	664	–	–	–	–
1381st Anti-Aircraft Artillery Rgt	367	–	–	–	–
1394th Anti-Aircraft Artillery Rgt	381	–	–	–	–
Total	27,088	250	55	–	88

SUPPLEMENTS

Formations and Units	Guns				
	105mm	107mm	122mm	152mm	203mm
3rd Gds Tank Army					
6th Gds Tank Corps	–	–	–	–	–
7th Gds Tank Corps	–	–	–	–	–
9th Mechanized Corps	–	–	–	–	–
91st Tank Bde	–	–	–	–	–
50th Motorcycle Rgt	–	–	–	–	–
1835th Self-Propelled Artillery Rgt	–	–	–	–	–
1836th Self-Propelled Artillery Rgt	–	–	–	–	–
1893rd Self-Propelled Artillery Rgt	–	–	–	–	–
91st Gds Mortar Rgt	–	–	–	–	–
1381st Anti-Aircraft Artillery Rgt	–	–	–	–	–
1394th Anti-Aircraft Artillery Rgt	–	–	–	–	–
Total	–	–	–	–	–

Formations and Units	Total Guns	Total Guns and Mortars	Rocket Artillery Platforms	Anti-Aircraft Guns	Tanks and Self-Propelled Guns
3rd Gds Tank Army					
6th Gds Tank Corps	19	87	–	14	135
7th Gds Tank Corps	21	113	–	16	157
9th Mechanized Corps	42	169	–	20	208
91st Tank Bde	2	8	–	–	52
50th Motorcycle Rgt	4	16	–	–	–
1835th Self-Propelled Artillery Rgt	–	–	–	–	13
1836th Self-Propelled Artillery Rgt	–	–	–	–	13
1893rd Self-Propelled Artillery Rgt	–	–	–	–	20
91st Gds Mortar Rgt	–	–	20	–	–
1381st Anti-Aircraft Artillery Rgt	–	–	–	15	–
1394th Anti-Aircraft Artillery Rgt	–	–	–	16	–
Total	88	395	20	81	598

Formations and Units	Men	Mortars		Guns	
		81mm	120mm	76mm (rgt artillery)	76mm (div artillery)
Forces Subordinated to the Front					
12th Mortar Bde	2,178	–	103	–	–
22nd Mortar Bde	1,399	–	89	–	–
307th Gds Mortar Bn	193	–	–	–	–
1954th Anti-Aircraft Artillery Rgt	378	–	–	–	–
22nd Gds Anti-Aircraft Artillery Bn	349	–	–	–	–
332nd Anti-Aircraft Artillery Bn	359	–	–	–	–
Total	4,856	–	192	–	–
Total for the *Front*	411,686	2,139	1,716	396	1,661

Formations and Units	Guns				
	105mm	107mm	122mm	152mm	203mm
Forces Subordinated to the Front					
12th Mortar Bde	–	–	–	–	–
22nd Mortar Bde	–	–	–	–	–
307th Gds Mortar Bn	–	–	–	–	–
1954th Anti-Aircraft Artillery Rgt	–	–	–	–	–
22nd Gds Anti-Aircraft Artillery Bn	–	–	–	–	–
332nd Anti-Aircraft Artillery Bn	–	–	–	–	–
Total	–	–	–	–	–
Total for the *Front*	9	8	737	317	97

Formations and Units	Total Guns	Total Guns and Mortars	Rocket Artillery Platforms	Anti-Aircraft Guns	Tanks and Self-Propelled Guns
Forces Subordinated to the Front					
12th Mortar Bde*	–	103	–	–	–
22nd Mortar Bde	–	89	–	–	–
307th Gds Mortar Bn	–	–	8	–	–
1954th Anti-Aircraft Artillery Rgt	–	–	–	16	–
22nd Gds Anti-Aircraft Artillery Bn	–	–	–	12	–
332nd Anti-Aircraft Artillery Bn	–	–	–	17	–
Total	–	192	8	43	–
Total for the *Front*	3,225	7,080	762	646	942

* As of 5 October 1943.

Supplement 1.3 The Voronezh Front's Combat Strength by 31 October 1943

Formations and Units	Men	Mortars		Guns	
		81mm	120mm	76mm (rgt artillery)	76mm (div artillery)
13th Army					
8th Rifle Div	5,415	25	12	2	1
148th Rifle Div	4,772	22	84	4	–
181st Rifle Div	6,397	55	21	9	9
211th Rifle Div	7,567	35	10	9	17
336th Rifle Div	5,623	53	12	11	17
415th Rifle Div	5,464	42	13	11	20
19th Gds Gun Artillery Rgt	787	–	–	–	–
874th Anti-Tank Artillery Rgt	402	–	–	–	13
476th Mortar Rgt	624	–	35	–	–
477th Mortar Rgt	573	–	24	–	–
323rd Gds Mortar Rgt	667	–	–	–	–
10th Anti-Aircraft Artillery Div	1,563	–	–	–	–
1287th Anti-Aircraft Artillery Rgt	400	–	–	–	–
Total	40,254	232	135	46	81

Formations and Units	Guns				
	105mm	107mm	122mm	152mm	203mm
13th Army					
8th Rifle Div	–	–	10	–	–
148th Rifle Div	–	–	9	–	17
181st Rifle Div	–	–	12	–	–
211th Rifle Div	–	–	7	–	–
336th Rifle Div	–	–	12	–	–
415th Rifle Div	–	–	12	–	–
19th Gds Gun Artillery Rgt	–	–	10	4	–
874th Anti-Tank Artillery Rgt	–	–	–	–	–
476th Mortar Rgt	–	–	–	–	–
477th Mortar Rgt	–	–	–	–	–
323rd Gds Mortar Rgt	–	–	–	–	–
10th Anti-Aircraft Artillery Div	–	–	–	–	–
1287th Anti-Aircraft Artillery Rgt	–	–	–	–	–
Total	–	–	72	4	17

THE BATTLE OF THE DNEPR

Formations and Units	Total Guns	Total Guns and Mortars	Rocket Artillery Platforms	Anti-Aircraft Guns	Tanks and Self-Propelled Guns
		13th Army			
8th Rifle Div	13	50	–	–	–
148th Rifle Div	47	–	–	–	–
181st Rifle Div	30	106	–	–	–
211th Rifle Div	33	78	–	–	–
336th Rifle Div	40	105	–	–	–
415th Rifle Div	43	98	–	–	–
19th Gds Gun Artillery Rgt	14	14	–	–	–
874th Anti-Tank Artillery Rgt	13	13	–	–	–
476th Mortar Rgt	–	35	–	–	–
477th Mortar Rgt	–	24	–	–	–
323rd Gds Mortar Rgt	–	–	17	–	–
10th Anti-Aircraft Artillery Div	–	–	–	61	–
1287th Anti-Aircraft Artillery Rgt	–	–	–	15	–
Total	203	570	17	76	–

Formations and Units	Men	Mortars		Guns	
		81mm	120mm	76mm (rgt artillery)	76mm (div artillery)
		60th Army			
112th Rifle Div	5,506	33	16	10	18
121st Rifle Div	6,044	62	18	12	16
132nd Rifle Div	6,142	16	5	20	–
141st Rifle Div	5,970	55	16	10	20
143rd Rifle Div	6,729	41	17	7	21
226th Rifle Div	4,465	24	13	9	14
280th Rifle Div	5,859	33	11	5	19
322nd Rifle Div	6,368	22	15	11	12
6th Gds Rifle Div	4,754	50	16	3	27
70th Gds Rifle Div	4,428	31	16	5	17
75th Gds Rifle Div	4,004	37	35	7	21
2nd Gds Airborne Div	3,926	33	14	9	15
3rd Gds Airborne Div	3,648	7	10	5	12
4th Gds Airborne Div	3,555	15	86	20	–
248th Rifle Bde	2,865	16	12	4	7
129th Tank Bde	1,268	6	–	4	–
150th Tank Bde	1,048	6	–	4	–
59th Tank Rgt	400	–	–	–	–
1st Gds Breakthrough Artillery Div	2,662	–	–	–	54
1156th Gun Artillery Rgt	810	–	–	–	–
128th Mortar Rgt	430	–	27	–	–
138th Mortar Rgt	502	–	18	–	–

SUPPLEMENTS

Formations and Units	Men	Mortars		Guns	
		81mm	120mm	76mm (rgt artillery)	76mm (div artillery)
497th Mortar Rgt	379	–	27	–	–
7th Gds Anti-Tank Artillery Bde	935	–	–	–	49
130th Anti-Tank Artillery Rgt	445	–	–	–	24
493rd Anti-Tank Artillery Rgt	454	–	–	–	11
1178th Anti-Tank Artillery Rgt	363	–	–	–	14
65th Gds Mortar Rgt	675	–	–	–	–
98th Gds Mortar Rgt	682	–	–	–	–
25th Anti-Aircraft Artillery Div	1,580	–	–	–	–
217th Anti-Aircraft Artillery Rgt	385	–	–	–	–
Total	86,281	487	294	111	411

Formations and Units	Guns				
	105mm	107mm	122mm	152mm	203mm
			60th Army		
112th Rifle Div	–	–	10	–	–
121st Rifle Div	–	–	10	–	–
132nd Rifle Div	–	–	10	–	–
141st Rifle Div	–	–	10	–	–
143rd Rifle Div	–	–	12	–	–
226th Rifle Div	–	–	8	–	–
280th Rifle Div	–	–	10	–	–
322nd Rifle Div	–	–	7	–	–
6th Gds Rifle Div	–	–	6	–	–
70th Gds Rifle Div	–	–	8	–	–
75th Gds Rifle Div	–	–	8	–	–
2nd Gds Airborne Div	–	–	12	–	–
3rd Gds Airborne Div	–	–	12	–	–
4th Gds Airborne Div	–	–	12	–	–
248th Rifle Bde	–	–	–	–	–
129th Tank Bde	–	–	–	–	–
150th Tank Bde	–	–	–	–	–
59th Tank Rgt	–	–	–	–	–
1st Gds Breakthrough Artillery Div	–	–	–	36	–
1156th Gun Artillery Rgt	–	–	–	18	–
128th Mortar Rgt	–	–	–	–	–
138th Mortar Rgt	–	–	–	–	–
497th Mortar Rgt	–	–	–	–	–
7th Gds Anti-Tank Artillery Bde	–	–	–	–	–
130th Anti-Tank Artillery Rgt	–	–	–	–	–
493rd Anti-Tank Artillery Rgt	–	–	–	–	–
1178th Anti-Tank Artillery Rgt	–	–	–	–	–
65th Gds Mortar Rgt	–	–	–	–	–

THE BATTLE OF THE DNEPR

Formations and Units	Guns				
	105mm	107mm	122mm	152mm	203mm
98th Gds Mortar Rgt	–	–	–	–	–
25th Anti-Aircraft Artillery Div	–	–	–	–	–
217th Anti-Aircraft Artillery Rgt	–	–	–	–	–
Total	–	–	135	54	–

Formations and Units	Total Guns	Total Guns and Mortars	Rocket Artillery Platforms	Anti-Aircraft Guns	Tanks and Self-Propelled Guns
		60th Army			
112th Rifle Div	38	87	–	–	–
121st Rifle Div	38	118	–	–	–
132nd Rifle Div	30	51	–	–	–
141st Rifle Div	40	111	–	–	–
143rd Rifle Div	40	98	–	–	–
226th Rifle Div	31	68	–	–	–
280th Rifle Div	34	78	–	–	–
322nd Rifle Div	30	67	–	–	–
6th Gds Rifle Div	36	102	–	–	–
70th Gds Rifle Div	30	77	–	–	–
75th Gds Rifle Div	36	108	–	–	–
2nd Gds Airborne Div	36	83	–	–	–
3rd Gds Airborne Div	29	46	–	–	–
4th Gds Airborne Div	32	133	–	–	–
248th Rifle Bde	11	39	–	–	–
129th Tank Bde	4	10	–	–	31
150th Tank Bde	4	10	–	–	15
59th Tank Rgt	–	–	–	–	32
1st Gds Breakthrough Artillery Div	90	90	–	–	–
1156th Gun Artillery Rgt	18	18	–	–	–
128th Mortar Rgt	–	27	–	–	–
138th Mortar Rgt	–	18	–	–	–
497th Mortar Rgt	–	27	–	–	–
7th Gds Anti-Tank Artillery Bde	49	49	–	–	–
130th Anti-Tank Artillery Rgt	24	24	–	–	–
493rd Anti-Tank Artillery Rgt	11	11	–	–	–
1178th Anti-Tank Artillery Rgt	14	14	–	–	–
65th Gds Mortar Rgt	–	–	13	–	–
98th Gds Mortar Rgt	–	–	14	–	–
25th Anti-Aircraft Artillery Div	–	–	–	63	–
217th Anti-Aircraft Artillery Rgt	–	–	–	16	–
Total	711	1,492	27	79	78

SUPPLEMENTS 213

Formations and Units	Men	Mortars		Guns	
		81mm	120mm	76mm (rgt artillery)	76mm (div artillery)
38th Army					
23rd Rifle Div	4,602	20	11	10	18
30th Rifle Div	4,681	19	14	10	16
71st Rifle Div	6,557	25	14	5	16
74th Rifle Div	6,274	38	16	8	19
136th Rifle Div	6,843	36	14	9	20
163rd Rifle Div	6,901	22	12	9	15
167th Rifle Div	6,821	40	16	12	2
180th Rifle Div	6,984	54	19	15	12
218th Rifle Div	5,044	6	14	9	14
232nd Rifle Div	7,370	55	13	8	17
240th Rifle Div	8,011	62	18	12	7
340th Rifle Div	8,931	49	17	11	3
1st Czechoslovak Bde	3,281	12	–	12	–
5th Gds Tank Corps	6,022	17	23	8	–
39th Tank Rgt	406	–	1	–	–
13th Breakthrough Artillery Div	8,479	–	99	–	70
17th Breakthrough Artillery Div	8,661	–	90	–	62
24th Gds Gun Artillery Bde	1,069	–	–	–	–
112th Gds Gun Artillery Rgt	885	–	–	–	–
1950th Gun Artillery Rgt	777	–	–	–	–
805th Howitzer Artillery Rgt	577	–	–	–	–
839th Howitzer Artillery Rgt	581	–	–	–	–
9th Gds Anti-Tank Artillery Bde	876	–	–	–	32
28th Anti-Tank Artillery Bde	1,040	–	–	–	40
4th Gds Anti-Tank Artillery Rgt	448	–	–	–	16
224th Anti-Tank Artillery Rgt	466	–	–	–	20
316th Gds Anti-Tank Artillery Rgt	460	–	–	–	21
868th Anti-Tank Artillery Rgt	436	–	–	–	15
1075th Anti-Tank Artillery Rgt	389	–	–	–	15
1600th Anti-Tank Artillery Rgt	457	–	–	–	12
12th Mortar Bde	2,137	–	82	–	–
491st Mortar Rgt	637	–	34	–	–
492nd Mortar Rgt	646	–	32	–	–
3rd Gds Mortar Div	3,125	–	–	–	–
1st Gds Mortar Rgt	328	–	–	–	–
5th Mortar Rgt	677	–	10	–	–
16th Mortar Rgt	683	–	16	–	–
66th Mortar Rgt	650	–	20	–	–
83rd Mortar Rgt	665	–	18	–	–
8th Anti-Aircraft Artillery Div	1,465	–	–	–	–
21st Anti-Aircraft Artillery Div	1,485	–	–	–	–
1288th Anti-Aircraft Artillery Rgt	396	–	–	–	–
Total	127,226	455	527	142	480

Formations and Units	Guns				
	105mm	107mm	122mm	152mm	203mm
38th Army					
23rd Rifle Div	–	–	12	–	–
30th Rifle Div	–	–	11	–	–
71st Rifle Div	–	–	9	–	–
74th Rifle Div	–	–	6	–	–
136th Rifle Div	–	–	12	–	–
163rd Rifle Div	–	–	6	–	–
167th Rifle Div	–	–	14	–	–
180th Rifle Div	4	–	9	–	–
218th Rifle Div	–	–	11	–	–
232nd Rifle Div	3	–	10	–	–
240th Rifle Div	3	–	9	–	–
340th Rifle Div	3	–	8	–	–
1st Czechoslovak Bde	–	–	5	–	–
5th Gds Tank Corps	–	–	–	–	–
39th Tank Rgt	–	–	–	–	–
13th Breakthrough Artillery Div	–	–	78	62	23
17th Breakthrough Artillery Div	–	–	73	61	24
24th Gds Gun Artillery Bde	–	–	–	35	–
112th Gds Gun Artillery Rgt	–	–	–	18	–
1950th Gun Artillery Rgt	–	–	–	18	–
805th Howitzer Artillery Rgt	–	–	19	–	–
839th Howitzer Artillery Rgt	–	–	24	–	–
9th Gds Anti-Tank Artillery Bde	–	–	–	–	–
28th Anti-Tank Artillery Bde	–	–	–	–	–
4th Gds Anti-Tank Artillery Rgt	–	–	–	–	–
224th Anti-Tank Artillery Rgt	–	–	–	–	–
316th Gds Anti-Tank Artillery Rgt	–	–	–	–	–
868th Anti-Tank Artillery Rgt	–	–	–	–	–
1075th Anti-Tank Artillery Rgt	–	–	–	–	–
1600th Anti-Tank Artillery Rgt	–	–	–	–	–
12th Mortar Bde	–	–	–	–	–
491st Mortar Rgt	–	–	–	–	–
492nd Mortar Rgt	–	–	–	–	–
3rd Gds Mortar Div	–	–	–	–	–
1st Gds Mortar Rgt	–	–	–	–	–
5th Mortar Rgt	–	–	–	–	–
16th Mortar Rgt	–	–	–	–	–
66th Mortar Rgt	–	–	–	–	–
83rd Mortar Rgt	–	–	–	–	–
8th Anti-Aircraft Artillery Div	–	–	–	–	–
21st Anti-Aircraft Artillery Div	–	–	–	–	–
1288th Anti-Aircraft Artillery Rgt	–	–	–	–	–
Total	15	–	311	194	47

Formations and Units	Total Guns	Total Guns and Mortars	Rocket Artillery Platforms	Anti-Aircraft Guns	Tanks and Self-Propelled Guns
		38th Army			
23rd Rifle Div	40	71	–	–	–
30th Rifle Div	37	70	–	–	–
71st Rifle Div	30	69	–	–	–
74th Rifle Div	33	87	–	–	–
136th Rifle Div	41	91	–	–	–
163rd Rifle Div	30	64	–	–	–
167th Rifle Div	39	84	–	–	–
180th Rifle Div	40	113	–	–	–
218th Rifle Div	34	54	–	–	–
232nd Rifle Div	38	106	–	–	–
240th Rifle Div	31	111	–	–	–
340th Rifle Div	32	98	–	–	–
1st Czechoslovak Bde	17	29	–	4	20
5th Gds Tank Corps	8	48	–	6	73
39th Tank Rgt	1	1	–	–	15
13th Breakthrough Artillery Div	233	332	–	–	–
17th Breakthrough Artillery Div	220	310	–	–	–
24th Gds Gun Artillery Bde	35	35	–	–	–
112th Gds Gun Artillery Rgt	18	18	–	–	–
1950th Gun Artillery Rgt	18	18	–	–	–
805th Howitzer Artillery Rgt	19	19	–	–	–
839th Howitzer Artillery Rgt	24	24	–	–	–
9th Gds Anti-Tank Artillery Bde	32	32	–	–	–
28th Anti-Tank Artillery Bde	40	40	–	–	–
4th Gds Anti-Tank Artillery Rgt	16	16	–	–	–
224th Anti-Tank Artillery Rgt	20	20	–	–	–
316th Gds Anti-Tank Artillery Rgt	21	21	–	–	–
868th Anti-Tank Artillery Rgt	15	15	–	–	–
1075th Anti-Tank Artillery Rgt	15	15	–	–	–
1600th Anti-Tank Artillery Rgt	12	12	–	–	–
12th Mortar Bde	–	82	–	–	–
491st Mortar Rgt	–	34	–	–	–
492nd Mortar Rgt	–	32	–	–	–
3rd Gds Mortar Div	–	–	422	–	–
1st Gds Mortar Rgt	–	–	11	–	–
5th Mortar Rgt	–	–	10	–	–
16th Mortar Rgt	–	16	–	–	–
66th Mortar Rgt	–	20	–	–	–
83rd Mortar Rgt	–	18	–	–	–
8th Anti-Aircraft Artillery Div	–	–	60	–	–
21st Anti-Aircraft Artillery Div	–	–	61	–	–
1288th Anti-Aircraft Artillery Rgt	–	–	16	–	–
Total	1,189	2,171	197	147	108

Formations and Units	Men	Mortars		Guns	
		81mm	120mm	76mm (rgt artillery)	76mm (div artillery)
40th Army					
42nd Gds Rifle Div	5,144	35	23	6	10
68th Gds Rifle Div	4,293	53	22	6	10
161st Rifle Div	4,777	36	12	6	12
237th Rifle Div	5,424	25	13	10	13
253rd Rifle Div	4,223	25	98	14	–
309th Rifle Div	5,234	29	10	8	18
337th Rifle Div	4,587	11	10	5	15
8th Gds Tank Corps	4,915	17	19	–	2
10th Tank Corps	4,611	24	13	–	–
25th Gds Heavy Caliber Howitzer Bde	1,278	–	–	–	–
33rd Heavy Gun Artillery Rgt	1,060	–	–	–	–
76th Gds Gun Artillery Rgt	837	–	–	–	–
111th Howitzer Artillery Rgt	772	–	–	–	–
8th Gds Anti-Tank Artillery Bde	1,070	–	–	–	29
32nd Anti-Tank Artillery Bde	995	–	–	–	34
12th Anti-Tank Artillery Rgt	360	–	–	–	18
315th Gds Anti-Tank Artillery Rgt	465	–	–	–	24
1663rd Anti-Tank Artillery Rgt	416	–	–	–	12
9th Mortar Rgt	543	–	35	–	–
10th Mortar Rgt	515	–	31	–	–
493rd Mortar Rgt	461	–	22	–	–
314th Gds Mortar Rgt	674	–	–	–	–
316th Gds Mortar Rgt	669	–	–	–	–
307th Gds Mortar Bn	194	–	–	–	–
9th Anti-Aircraft Artillery Div	1,534	–	–	–	–
Total	55,050	255	219	49	228

SUPPLEMENTS

Formations and Units	Guns				
	105mm	107mm	122mm	152mm	203mm
			40th Army		
42nd Gds Rifle Div	–	–	8	–	–
68th Gds Rifle Div	–	–	12	–	–
161st Rifle Div	–	–	7	–	–
237th Rifle Div	–	–	9	–	–
253rd Rifle Div	–	–	8	–	–
309th Rifle Div	3	–	8	–	–
337th Rifle Div	–	–	11	–	–
8th Gds Tank Corps	–	–	–	–	–
10th Tank Corps	–	–	1	–	–
25th Gds Heavy Caliber Howitzer Bde	–	–	–	–	24
33rd Heavy Gun Artillery Rgt	–	–	–	35	–
76th Gds Gun Artillery Rgt	–	–	–	17	–
111th Howitzer Artillery Rgt	–	–	24	–	–
8th Gds Anti-Tank Artillery Bde	–	–	–	–	–
32nd Anti-Tank Artillery Bde	–	–	–	–	–
12th Anti-Tank Artillery Rgt	–	–	–	–	–
315th Gds Anti-Tank Artillery Rgt	–	–	–	–	–
1663rd Anti-Tank Artillery Rgt	–	–	–	–	–
9th Mortar Rgt	–	–	–	–	–
10th Mortar Rgt	–	–	–	–	–
493rd Mortar Rgt	–	–	–	–	–
314th Gds Mortar Rgt	–	–	–	–	–
316th Gds Mortar Rgt	–	–	–	–	–
307th Gds Mortar Bn	–	–	–	–	–
9th Anti-Aircraft Artillery Div	–	–	–	–	–
Total	3	–	88	52	24

Formations and Units	Total Guns	Total Guns and Mortars	Rocket Artillery Platforms	Anti-Aircraft Guns	Tanks and Self-Propelled Guns
		40th Army			
42nd Gds Rifle Div	24	82	–	–	–
68th Gds Rifle Div	28	103	–	–	–
161st Rifle Div	25	73	–	–	–
237th Rifle Div	32	70	–	–	–
253rd Rifle Div	30	64	–	–	–
309th Rifle Div	37	76	–	–	–
337th Rifle Div	31	52	–	–	–
8th Gds Tank Corps	2	38	–	13	19
10th Tank Corps	18	55	–	12	10
25th Gds Heavy Caliber Howitzer Bde	24	24	–	–	–
33rd Heavy Gun Artillery Rgt	35	35	–	–	–
76th Gds Gun Artillery Rgt	17	17	–	–	–
111th Howitzer Artillery Rgt	24	24	–	–	–
8th Gds Anti-Tank Artillery Bde	29	29	–	–	–
32nd Anti-Tank Artillery Bde	34	34	–	–	–
12th Anti-Tank Artillery Rgt	18	18	–	–	–
315th Gds Anti-Tank Artillery Rgt	24	24	–	–	–
1663rd Anti-Tank Artillery Rgt	12	12	–	–	–
9th Mortar Rgt	–	35	–	–	–
10th Mortar Rgt	–	31	–	–	–
493rd Mortar Rgt	–	22	–	–	–
314th Gds Mortar Rgt	–	–	17	–	–
316th Gds Mortar Rgt	–	–	18	–	–
307th Gds Mortar Bn	–	–	8	2	–
9th Anti-Aircraft Artillery Div	–	–	–	58	–
Total	444	918	43	85	29

SUPPLEMENTS

Formations and Units	Men	Mortars		Guns	
		81mm	120mm	76mm (rgt artillery)	76mm (div artillery)
		27th Army			
38th Rifle Div	3,699	18	14	8	20
100th Rifle Div	4,830	33	11	8	12
147th Rifle Div	3,828	46	13	11	15
155th Rifle Div	4,665	28	12	10	18
206th Rifle Div	6,078	29	13	10	10
241st Rifle Div	5,275	26	13	3	11
93rd Tank Bde	787	2	–	–	1
1832nd Self-Propelled Artillery Rgt	210	–	–	–	–
628th Gun Artillery Rgt	791	–	–	–	–
1528th Howitzer Artillery Rgt605	605	–	–	–	–
408th Heavy Anti-Tank Artillery Rgt	361	–	–	–	–
312th Gds Anti-Tank Artillery Rgt	412	–	–	–	20
1070th Anti-Tank Artillery Rgt	365	–	–	–	24
1667th Anti-Tank Artillery Rgt	427	–	–	–	15
480th Mortar Rgt	511	–	24	–	–
47th Gds Mortar Rgt	667	–	–	–	–
23rd Anti-Aircraft Artillery Div	1,497	–	–	–	–
Total	45,008	182	100	50	146

Formations and Units	Guns				
	105mm	107mm	122mm	152mm	203mm
		27th Army			
38th Rifle Div	–	–	12	–	–
100th Rifle Div	–	–	9	–	–
147th Rifle Div	–	–	8	–	–
155th Rifle Div	–	–	11	–	–
206th Rifle Div	–	–	12	–	–
241st Rifle Div	–	–	9	–	–
93rd Tank Bde	–	–	–	–	–
1832nd Self-Propelled Artillery Rgt	–	–	–	–	–
628th Gun Artillery Rgt	–	–	–	18	–
1528th Howitzer Artillery Rgt	–	–	23	–	–
408th Heavy Anti-Tank Artillery Rgt	–	7	–	–	–
312th Gds Anti-Tank Artillery Rgt	–	–	–	–	–
1070th Anti-Tank Artillery Rgt	–	–	–	–	–
1667th Anti-Tank Artillery Rgt	–	–	–	–	–
480th Mortar Rgt	–	–	–	–	–
47th Gds Mortar Rgt	–	–	–	–	–
23rd Anti-Aircraft Artillery Div	–	–	–	–	–
Total	–	7	84	18	–

220 THE BATTLE OF THE DNEPR

Formations and Units	Total Guns	Total Guns and Mortars	Rocket Artillery Platforms	Anti-Aircraft Guns	Tanks and Self-Propelled Guns
		27th Army			
38th Rifle Div	40	72	–	–	–
100th Rifle Div	29	73	–	–	–
147th Rifle Div	34	93	–	–	–
155th Rifle Div	39	79	–	–	–
206th Rifle Div	32	74	–	–	–
241st Rifle Div	23	62	–	–	–
93rd Tank Bde	1	3	–	–	13
1832nd Self-Propelled Artillery Rgt	–	–	–	–	5
628th Gun Artillery Rgt	18	18	–	–	–
1528th Howitzer Artillery Rgt	23	23	–	–	–
408th Heavy Anti-Tank Artillery Rgt	7	7	–	–	–
312th Gds Anti-Tank Artillery Rgt	20	20	–	–	–
1070th Anti-Tank Artillery Rgt	24	24	–	–	–
1667th Anti-Tank Artillery Rgt	15	15	–	–	–
480th Mortar Rgt	–	24	–	–	–
47th Gds Mortar Rgt	–	–	15	–	–
23rd Anti-Aircraft Artillery Div	–	–	–	51	–
Total	305	587	15	51	18

Formations and Units	Men	Mortars		Guns	
		81mm	120mm	76mm (rgt artillery)	76mm (div artillery)
		3rd Gds Tank Army			
6th Gds Tank Corps	5,642	30	26	–	14
7th Gds Tank Corps	5,818	56	42	–	28
9th Mechanized Corps	8,925	65	51	–	35
91st Tank Bde	1,151	6	–	–	2
50th Motorcycle Rgt	1,180	12	–	–	4
1835th Self-Propelled Artillery Rgt	217	–	–	–	–
1836th Self-Propelled Artillery Rgt	235	–	–	–	–
36th Gds Mortar Rgt	678	–	–	–	–
91st Gds Mortar Rgt	682	–	–	–	–
1381st Anti-Aircraft Artillery Rgt	372	–	–	–	–
1394th Anti-Aircraft Artillery Rgt	382	–	–	–	–
Total	25,282	169	119	–	83

SUPPLEMENTS

Formations and Units	Guns				
	105mm	107mm	122mm	152mm	203mm
3rd Gds Tank Army					
6th Gds Tank Corps	–	–	–	–	–
7th Gds Tank Corps	–	–	–	–	–
9th Mechanized Corps	–	–	–	–	–
91st Tank Bde	–	–	–	–	–
50th Motorcycle Rgt	–	–	–	–	–
1835th Self-Propelled Artillery Rgt	–	–	–	–	–
1836th Self-Propelled Artillery Rgt	–	–	–	–	–
36th Gds Mortar Rgt	–	–	–	–	–
91st Gds Mortar Rgt	–	–	–	–	–
1381st Anti-Aircraft Artillery Rgt	–	–	–	–	–
1394th Anti-Aircraft Artillery Rgt	–	–	–	–	–
Total	–	–	–	–	–

Formations and Units	Total Guns	Total Guns and Mortars	Rocket Artillery Platforms	Anti-Aircraft Guns	Tanks and Self-Propelled Guns
3rd Gds Tank Army					
6th Gds Tank Corps	14	70	–	12	75
7th Gds Tank Corps	28	126	–	16	81
9th Mechanized Corps	35	151	–	20	116
91st Tank Bde	2	8	–	–	51
50th Motorcycle Rgt	4	16	–	–	10
1835th Self-Propelled Artillery Rgt	–	–	–	–	8
1836th Self-Propelled Artillery Rgt	–	–	–	–	11
36th Gds Mortar Rgt	–	–	20	3	–
91st Gds Mortar Rgt	–	–	18	–	–
1381st Anti-Aircraft Artillery Rgt	–	–	–	15	–
1394th Anti-Aircraft Artillery Rgt	–	–	–	16	–
Total	83	371	38	82	352

Formations and Units	Men	Mortars		Guns	
		81mm	120mm	76mm (rgt artillery)	76mm (div artillery)
1st Gds Cavalry Corps					
1st Gds Cavalry Div	4,921	37	6	12	–
2nd Gds Cavalry Div	4,980	34	6	8	–
7th Gds Cavalry Div	5,299	32	6	8	–
1461st Self-Propelled Artillery Rgt	236	–	–	–	–
143rd Anti-Tank Artillery Rgt	481	–	–	–	20
319th Anti-Aircraft Artillery Rgt	379	–	–	–	–
Total	16,296	103	18	28	20

Formations and Units	Guns				
	105mm	107mm	122mm	152mm	203mm
1st Gds Cavalry Corps					
1st Gds Cavalry Div	–	–	8	–	–
2nd Gds Cavalry Div	–	–	8	–	–
7th Gds Cavalry Div	–	–	8	–	–
1461st Self-Propelled Artillery Rgt	–	–	–	–	–
143rd Anti-Tank Artillery Rgt	–	–	–	–	–
319th Anti-Aircraft Artillery Rgt	–	–	–	–	–
Total	–	–	24	–	–

Formations and Units	Total Guns	Total Guns and Mortars	Rocket Artillery Platforms	Anti-Aircraft Guns	Tanks and Self-Propelled Guns
1st Gds Cavalry Corps					
1st Gds Cavalry Div	27	70	–	6	28
2nd Gds Cavalry Div	28	68	–	6	16
7th Gds Cavalry Div	27	65	–	5	25
1461st Self-Propelled Artillery Rgt	–	–	–	–	21
143rd Anti-Tank Artillery Rgt	20	20	–	–	–
319th Anti-Aircraft Artillery Rgt	–	–	–	15	–
Total	102	223	–	32	90

Formations and Units	Men	Mortars		Guns	
		81mm	120mm	76mm (rgt artillery)	76mm (div artillery)
Forces Subordinated to the *Front*					
630th Anti-Tank Artillery Rgt	400	–	–	–	11
317th Gds Anti-Tank Artillery Rgt	468	–	–	–	23
1593rd Anti-Tank Artillery Rgt	492	–	–	–	23
1672nd Anti-Tank Artillery Rgt	417	–	–	–	24
334th Gds Mortar Bn	212	–	–	–	–
424th Gds Mortar Bn	218	–	–	–	–
1954th Anti-Aircraft Artillery Rgt	376	–	–	–	–
22nd Gds Anti-Aircraft Artillery Bn	351	–	–	–	–
332nd Anti-Aircraft Artillery Bn	351	–	–	–	–
Total	3,285	–	–	–	81
Total for the *Front*	398,682	1,883	1,412	428	1,558

SUPPLEMENTS

Formations and Units	Guns				
	105mm	107mm	122mm	152mm	203mm
Forces Subordinated to the *Front*					
630th Anti-Tank Artillery Rgt	–	–	–	–	–
317th Gds Anti-Tank Artillery Rgt	–	–	–	–	–
1593rd Anti-Tank Artillery Rgt	–	–	–	–	–
1672nd Anti-Tank Artillery Rgt	–	–	–	–	–
334th Gds Mortar Bn	–	–	–	–	–
424th Gds Mortar Bn	–	–	–	–	–
1954th Anti-Aircraft Artillery Rgt	–	–	–	–	–
22nd Gds Anti-Aircraft Artillery Bn	–	–	–	–	–
332nd Anti-Aircraft Artillery Bn	–	–	–	–	–
Total	–	–	–	–	–
Total for the *Front*	18	7	714	322	71

Formations and Units	Total Guns	Total Guns and Mortars	Rocket Artillery Platforms	Anti-Aircraft Guns	Tanks and Self-Propelled Guns
Forces Subordinated to the *Front*					
630th Anti-Tank Artillery Rgt	11	11	–	–	–
317th Gds Anti-Tank Artillery Rgt	23	23	–	–	–
1593rd Anti-Tank Artillery Rgt	23	23	–	–	–
1672nd Anti-Tank Artillery Rgt	24	24	–	–	–
334th Gds Mortar Bn	–	–	6	2	–
424th Gds Mortar Bn	–	–	8	–	–
1954th Anti-Aircraft Artillery Rgt	–	–	–	16	–
22nd Gds Anti-Aircraft Artillery Bn	–	–	–	12	–
332nd Anti-Aircraft Artillery Bn	–	–	–	15	–
Total	81	81	14	45	–
Total for the *Front*	3,118	6,413	651	597	675

Supplement 1.4 The Voronezh Front's Combat Strength by 15 November 1943

Formations and Units	Men	Mortars		Guns	
		81mm	120mm	76mm (rgt artillery)	76mm (div artillery)
		13th Army			
6th Gds Rifle Div	4,309	48	15	3	15
8th Rifle Div	5,062	50	12	4	16
148th Rifle Div	5,079	36	14	4	4
181st Rifle Div	6,908	59	21	9	12
336th Rifle Div	6,370	53	11	11	17
415th Rifle Div	5,655	33	13	11	20
2nd Gds Airborne Div	3,820	34	14	9	15
4th Gds Airborne Div	3,518	15	8	6	20
19th Gds Gun Artillery Rgt	787	–	–	–	–
493rd Anti-Tank Artillery Rgt	447	–	–	–	8
874th Anti-Tank Artillery Rgt	485	–	–	–	14
476th Mortar Rgt	651	–	34	–	–
477th Mortar Rgt	621	–	27	–	–
323rd Gds Mortar Rgt	675	–	–	–	–
10th Anti-Aircraft Artillery Div	1,563	–	–	–	–
1287th Anti-Aircraft Artillery Rgt	400	–	–	–	–
Total	46,350	328	169	57	141

Formations and Units	Guns				
	105mm	107mm	122mm	152mm	203mm
		13th Army			
6th Gds Rifle Div	–	–	6	–	–
8th Rifle Div	–	–	10	–	–
148th Rifle Div	–	–	9	–	–
181st Rifle Div	–	–	10	–	–
336th Rifle Div	–	–	12	–	–
415th Rifle Div	–	–	12	–	–
2nd Gds Airborne Div	–	–	12	–	–
4th Gds Airborne Div	–	–	12	–	–
19th Gds Gun Artillery Rgt	–	–	–	4	–
493rd Anti-Tank Artillery Rgt	–	–	–	–	–
874th Anti-Tank Artillery Rgt	–	–	–	–	–
476th Mortar Rgt	–	–	–	–	–
477th Mortar Rgt	–	–	–	–	–
323rd Gds Mortar Rgt	–	–	–	–	–
10th Anti-Aircraft Artillery Div	–	–	–	–	–
1287th Anti-Aircraft Artillery Rgt	–	–	–	–	–
Total	–	–	83	4	–

SUPPLEMENTS 225

Formations and Units	Total Guns	Total Guns and Mortars	Rocket Artillery Platforms	Anti-Aircraft Guns	Tanks and Self-Propelled Guns
		13th Army			
6th Gds Rifle Div	24	87	–	–	–
8th Rifle Div	30	92	–	–	–
148th Rifle Div	17	67	–	–	–
181st Rifle Div	31	111	–	–	–
336th Rifle Div	40	104	–	–	–
415th Rifle Div	43	89	–	–	–
2nd Gds Airborne Div	36	84	–	–	–
4th Gds Airborne Div	38	61	–	–	–
19th Gds Gun Artillery Rgt	4	4	–	–	–
493rd Anti-Tank Artillery Rgt	8	8	–	–	–
874th Anti-Tank Artillery Rgt	14	14	–	–	–
476th Mortar Rgt	–	34	–	–	–
477th Mortar Rgt	–	27	–	–	–
323rd Gds Mortar Rgt	–	–	17	–	–
10th Anti-Aircraft Artillery Div	–	–	–	61	–
1287th Anti-Aircraft Artillery Rgt	–	–	–	15	–
Total	285	782	17	76	–

Formations and Units	Men	Mortars		Guns	
		81mm	120mm	76mm (rgt artillery)	76mm (div artillery)
		60th Army			
70th Gds Rifle Div	3,793	36	16	5	17
75th Gds Rifle Div	3,355	37	35	7	21
112th Rifle Div	4,898	32	4	7	17
121st Rifle Div	4,981	62	18	12	16
132nd Rifle Div	4,613	21	5	–	18
141st Rifle Div	4,926	55	22	10	20
143rd Rifle Div	5,111	35	10	7	20
11th Rifle Div	7,514	34	11	8	18
226th Rifle Div	3,838	21	11	10	16
280th Rifle Div	5,984	33	13	8	19
322nd Rifle Div	6,514	22	15	–	12
3rd Gds Airborne Div	3,181	9	–	5	12
248th Rifle Bde	2,577	19	12	–	10
129th Tank Bde	1,189	6	–	–	5
150th Tank Bde	1,039	–	–	–	3
59th Tank Rgt	361	–	–	–	–
1st Gds Breakthrough Artillery Div	2,647	–	–	–	51
1156th Gun Artillery Rgt	815	–	–	–	–
7th Gds Anti-Tank Artillery Bde	1,147	–	–	–	48
12th Anti-Tank Artillery Rgt	360	–	–	–	18

226   THE BATTLE OF THE DNEPR

Formations and Units	Men	Mortars		Guns	
		81mm	120mm	76mm (rgt artillery)	76mm (div artillery)
130th Anti-Tank Artillery Rgt	450	–	–	–	24
1178th Anti-Tank Artillery Rgt	506	–	–	–	15
138th Mortar Rgt	486	–	21	–	–
497th Mortar Rgt	380	–	25	–	–
65th Gds Mortar Rgt	883	–	–	–	–
98th Gds Mortar Rgt	679	–	–	–	–
316th Gds Mortar Rgt	680	–	–	–	–
25th Anti-Tank Artillery Div	1,554	–	–	–	–
217th Anti-Aircraft Artillery Rgt	384	–	–	–	–
Total	74,845	425	218	79	380

Formations and Units	Guns				
	105mm	107mm	122mm	152mm	203mm
		60th Army			
70th Gds Rifle Div	–	–	8	–	–
75th Gds Rifle Div	–	–	8	–	–
112th Rifle Div	–	–	10	–	–
121st Rifle Div	–	–	10	–	–
132nd Rifle Div	–	–	10	–	–
141st Rifle Div	–	–	10	–	–
143rd Rifle Div	–	–	12	–	–
11th Rifle Div	–	–	7	–	–
226th Rifle Div	–	–	8	–	–
280th Rifle Div	–	–	10	–	–
322nd Rifle Div	–	–	8	–	–
3rd Gds Airborne Div	–	–	12	–	–
248th Rifle Bde	–	–	–	–	–
129th Tank Bde	–	–	–	–	–
150th Tank Bde	–	–	–	–	–
59th Tank Rgt	–	–	–	–	–
1st Gds Breakthrough Artillery Div	–	–	–	36	–
1156th Gun Artillery Rgt	–	–	–	18	–
7th Gds Anti-Tank Artillery Bde	–	–	–	–	–
12th Anti-Tank Artillery Rgt	–	–	–	–	–
130th Anti-Tank Artillery Rgt	–	–	–	–	–
1178th Anti-Tank Artillery Rgt	–	–	–	–	–
138th Mortar Rgt	–	–	–	–	–
497th Mortar Rgt	–	–	–	–	–
65th Gds Mortar Rgt	–	–	–	–	–
98th Gds Mortar Rgt	–	–	–	–	–
316th Gds Mortar Rgt	–	–	–	–	–
25th Anti-Tank Artillery Div	–	–	–	–	–
217th Anti-Aircraft Artillery Rgt	–	–	–	–	–
Total	–	–	113	54	–

Formations and Units	Total Guns	Total Guns and Mortars	Rocket Artillery Platforms	Anti-Aircraft Guns	Tanks and Self-Propelled Guns
		60th Army*			
70th Gds Rifle Div	30	82	–	–	–
75th Gds Rifle Div	36	108	–	–	–
112th Rifle Div	34	70	–	–	–
121st Rifle Div	38	118	–	–	–
132nd Rifle Div	28	54	–	–	–
141st Rifle Div	40	117	–	–	–
143rd Rifle Div	39	84	–	–	–
11th Rifle Div	33	78	–	–	–
226th Rifle Div	34	66	–	–	–
280th Rifle Div	37	83	–	–	–
322nd Rifle Div	20	57	–	–	–
3rd Gds Airborne Div	29	38	–	–	–
248th Rifle Bde	10	41	–	–	6
129th Tank Bde	5	14	–	8	10
150th Tank Bde	3	3	–	4	4
59th Tank Rgt	–	–	–	–	–
1st Gds Breakthrough Artillery Div	87	87	–	–	–
1156th Gun Artillery Rgt	18	18	–	–	–
7th Gds Anti-Tank Artillery Bde	48	48	–	–	–
12th Anti-Tank Artillery Rgt	18	18	–	–	–
130th Anti-Tank Artillery Rgt	24	24	–	–	–
1178th Anti-Tank Artillery Rgt	15	15	–	–	–
138th Mortar Rgt	–	21	–	–	–
497th Mortar Rgt	–	25	–	–	–
65th Gds Mortar Rgt	–	–	16	–	–
98th Gds Mortar Rgt	–	–	12	–	–
316th Gds Mortar Rgt	–	–	19	–	–
25th Anti-Tank Artillery Div	–	–	–	63	–
217th Anti-Aircraft Artillery Rgt	–	–	–	16	–
Total	626	1,269	47	91	20

* The figures for the 60th Army are as of 10 November 1943.

Formations and Units	Men	Mortars		Guns	
		81mm	120mm	76mm (rgt artillery)	76mm (div artillery)
		38th Army			
70th Gds Rifle Div	2,768	36	16	–	17
75th Gds Rifle Div	3,355	37	35	7	21
23rd Rifle Div	3,217	18	11	8	18
30th Rifle Div	3,677	18	14	11	16
71st Rifle Div	6,920	25	14	5	16
74th Rifle Div	5,759	28	14	8	18
136th Rifle Div	3,601	42	10	3	9
163rd Rifle Div	4,382	24	12	9	15
202nd Rifle Div	4,442	15	15	12	18
211th Rifle Div	7,514	35	11	8	19
218th Rifle Div	4,454	7	13	7	14
232nd Rifle Div	5,573	47	11	7	13
241st Rifle Div	4,624	35	13	3	11
310th Rifle Div	3,455	36	17	13	10
5th Gds Tank Corps	5,831	12	2	4	–
39th Tank Rgt	433	–	–	–	1
13th Breakthrough Artillery Div	8,875	–	99	–	70
17th Breakthrough Artillery Div	8,838	–	90	–	62
24th Gun Artillery Bde	1,069	–	–	–	–
112th Gds Gun Artillery Rgt	863	–	–	–	–
1950th Gun Artillery Rgt	775	–	–	–	–
805th Howitzer Artillery Rgt	552	–	–	–	–
839th Howitzer Artillery Rgt	581	–	–	–	–
7th Gds Anti-Tank Artillery Bde	1,138	–	–	–	48
9th Gds Anti-Tank Artillery Bde	1,051	–	–	–	39
28th Anti-Tank Artillery Bde	986	–	–	–	39
32nd Anti-Tank Artillery Bde	1,181	–	–	–	33
4th Gds Anti-Tank Artillery Rgt	448	–	–	–	16
312th Gds Anti-Tank Artillery Rgt	473	–	–	–	20
317th Gds Anti-Tank Artillery Rgt	464	–	–	–	21
12th Anti-Tank Artillery Rgt	485	–	–	–	18
222nd Anti-Tank Artillery Rgt	404	–	–	–	18
316th Gds Anti-Tank Artillery Rgt	453	–	–	–	21
868th Anti-Tank Artillery Rgt	418	–	–	–	19
1075th Anti-Tank Artillery Rgt	410	–	–	–	14
491st Mortar Rgt	629	–	34	–	–
492nd Mortar Rgt	654	–	32	–	–
454th Mortar Rgt	600	–	21	–	–
3rd Gds Mortar Div	3,089	–	–	–	–
1st Gds Mortar Rgt	328	–	–	–	–
5th Gds Mortar Rgt	670	–	–	–	–
16th Gds Mortar Rgt	675	–	–	–	–
47th Gds Mortar Rgt	680	–	–	–	–
65th Gds Mortar Rgt	679	–	–	–	–
66th Gds Mortar Rgt	677	–	–	–	–
83rd Gds Mortar Rgt	654	–	–	–	–
314th Gds Mortar Rgt	669	–	–	–	–
8th Anti-Aircraft Artillery Div	1,481	–	–	–	–
21st Anti-Aircraft Artillery Div	1,477	–	–	–	–
Total	112,401	415	415	484	654

Formations and Units	Guns				
	105mm	107mm	122mm	152mm	203mm
38th Army					
70th Gds Rifle Div	–	–	8	–	–
75th Gds Rifle Div	–	–	8	–	–
23rd Rifle Div	–	–	12	–	–
30th Rifle Div	–	–	11	–	–
71st Rifle Div	–	–	9	–	–
74th Rifle Div	–	–	6	–	–
136th Rifle Div	–	–	6	–	–
163rd Rifle Div	–	–	7	–	–
202nd Rifle Div	–	–	12	–	–
211th Rifle Div	–	–	7	–	–
218th Rifle Div	–	–	11	–	–
232nd Rifle Div	3	–	10	–	–
241st Rifle Div	–	–	9	–	–
310th Rifle Div	–	–	8	–	–
5th Gds Tank Corps	–	–	1	–	–
39th Tank Rgt	–	–	–	–	–
13th Breakthrough Artillery Div	–	–	78	62	23
17th Breakthrough Artillery Div	–	–	–	135	24
24th Gun Artillery Bde	–	–	–	35	–
112th Gds Gun Artillery Rgt	–	–	–	15	–
1950th Gun Artillery Rgt	–	–	–	18	–
805th Howitzer Artillery Rgt	–	–	22	–	–
839th Howitzer Artillery Rgt	–	–	24	–	–
7th Gds Anti-Tank Artillery Bde	–	–	–	–	–
9th Gds Anti-Tank Artillery Bde	–	–	–	–	–
28th Anti-Tank Artillery Bde	–	–	–	–	–
32nd Anti-Tank Artillery Bde	–	–	–	–	–
4th Gds Anti-Tank Artillery Rgt	–	–	–	–	–
312th Gds Anti-Tank Artillery Rgt	–	–	–	–	–
317th Gds Anti-Tank Artillery Rgt	–	–	–	–	–
12th Anti-Tank Artillery Rgt	–	–	–	–	–
222nd Anti-Tank Artillery Rgt	–	–	–	–	–
316th Gds Anti-Tank Artillery Rgt	–	–	–	–	–
868th Anti-Tank Artillery Rgt	–	–	–	–	–
1075th Anti-Tank Artillery Rgt	–	–	–	–	–
491st Mortar Rgt	–	–	–	–	–
492nd Mortar Rgt	–	–	–	–	–
454th Mortar Rgt	–	–	–	–	–
3rd Gds Mortar Div	–	–	–	–	–
1st Gds Mortar Rgt	–	–	–	–	–
5th Gds Mortar Rgt	–	–	–	–	–
16th Gds Mortar Rgt	–	–	–	–	–
47th Gds Mortar Rgt	–	–	–	–	–
65th Gds Mortar Rgt	–	–	–	–	–
66th Gds Mortar Rgt	–	–	–	–	–
83rd Gds Mortar Rgt	–	–	–	–	–
314th Gds Mortar Rgt	–	–	–	–	–
8th Anti-Aircraft Artillery Div	–	–	–	–	–
21st Anti-Aircraft Artillery Div	–	–	–	–	–
Total	3	–	249	265	47

Formations and Units	Total Guns	Total Guns and Mortars	Rocket Artillery Platforms	Anti-Aircraft Guns	Tanks and Self-Propelled Guns
		38th Army			
70th Gds Rifle Div	30	82	–	–	–
75th Gds Rifle Div	36	108	–	–	–
23rd Rifle Div	38	67	–	–	–
30th Rifle Div	38	70	–	–	–
71st Rifle Div	30	69	–	–	–
74th Rifle Div	32	74	–	–	–
136th Rifle Div	18	70	–	–	–
163rd Rifle Div	31	67	–	–	–
202nd Rifle Div	42	72	–	–	–
211th Rifle Div	34	80	–	–	–
218th Rifle Div	32	52	–	–	–
232nd Rifle Div	33	91	–	–	–
241st Rifle Div	23	71	–	–	–
310th Rifle Div	31	84	–	–	–
5th Gds Tank Corps	5	19	–	16	65
39th Tank Rgt	1	1	–	–	20
13th Breakthrough Artillery Div	233	332	–	–	–
17th Breakthrough Artillery Div	221	311	–	–	–
24th Gun Artillery Bde	35	35	–	–	–
112th Gds Gun Artillery Rgt	15	15	–	–	–
1950th Gun Artillery Rgt	18	18	–	–	–
805th Howitzer Artillery Rgt	22	22	–	–	–
839th Howitzer Artillery Rgt	24	24	–	–	–
7th Gds Anti-Tank Artillery Bde	48	48	–	–	–
9th Gds Anti-Tank Artillery Bde	39	39	–	–	–
28th Anti-Tank Artillery Bde	39	39	–	–	–
32nd Anti-Tank Artillery Bde	33	33	–	–	–
4th Gds Anti-Tank Artillery Rgt	16	16	–	–	–
312th Gds Anti-Tank Artillery Rgt	20	20	–	–	–
317th Gds Anti-Tank Artillery Rgt	21	21	–	–	–
12th Anti-Tank Artillery Rgt	18	18	–	–	–
222nd Anti-Tank Artillery Rgt	18	18	–	–	–
316th Gds Anti-Tank Artillery Rgt	21	21	–	–	–
868th Anti-Tank Artillery Rgt	19	19	–	–	–
1075th Anti-Tank Artillery Rgt	14	14	–	–	–
491st Mortar Rgt	–	34	–	–	–
492nd Mortar Rgt	–	32	–	–	–
454th Mortar Rgt	–	21	–	–	–
3rd Gds Mortar Div	–	–	422	–	–
1st Gds Mortar Rgt	–	–	12	–	–
5th Gds Mortar Rgt	–	–	24	–	–
16th Gds Mortar Rgt	–	–	23	–	–
47th Gds Mortar Rgt	–	–	21	–	–
65th Gds Mortar Rgt	–	–	25	–	–
66th Gds Mortar Rgt	–	–	24	–	–
83rd Gds Mortar Rgt	–	–	24	–	–
314th Gds Mortar Rgt	–	–	24	–	–
8th Anti-Aircraft Artillery Div	–	–	–	61	–
21st Anti-Aircraft Artillery Div	–	–	–	61	–
Total	1,328	2,227	599	138	85

Formations and Units	Men	Mortars		Guns	
		81mm	120mm	76mm (rgt artillery)	76mm (div artillery)
40th Army					
42nd Gds Rifle Div	3,716	28	23	6	15
68th Gds Rifle Div	3,540	35	18	6	19
136th Rifle Div	6,303	43	14	9	20
147th Rifle Div	4,151	35	13	7	18
167th Rifle Div	7,603	50	14	16	11
180th Rifle Div	7,202	54	19	–	12
240th Rifle Div	6,640	61	18	13	17
253rd Rifle Div	3,908	35	13	7	18
337th Rifle Div	3,468	11	10	6	16
380th Rifle Div	3,061	20	14	8	20
1st Czechoslovak Bde	3,270	12	–	12	–
33rd Artillery Bde	1,060	–	–	–	–
25th Gds Heavy Caliber Howitzer Bde	1,280	–	–	–	–
76th Gds Artillery Rgt	810	–	–	–	–
111th Howitzer Artillery Rgt	640	–	–	–	–
1663rd Anti-Tank Artillery Rgt	456	–	–	–	20
9th Mortar Rgt	557	–	35	–	–
10th Mortar Rgt	482	–	28	–	–
493rd Mortar Rgt	582	–	36	–	–
315th Gds Anti-Tank Artillery Rgt	465	–	–	–	24
9th Anti-Aircraft Artillery Div	1,538	–	–	–	–
Total	60,732	384	255	90	210

Formations and Units	Guns				
	105mm	107mm	122mm	152mm	203mm
40th Army					
42nd Gds Rifle Div	–	–	9	–	–
68th Gds Rifle Div	–	–	11	–	–
136th Rifle Div	–	–	12	–	–
147th Rifle Div	–	–	7	–	–
167th Rifle Div	2	–	9	–	–
180th Rifle Div	–	–	9	–	–
240th Rifle Div	3	–	9	–	–
253rd Rifle Div	–	–	7	–	–
337th Rifle Div	–	–	11	–	–
380th Rifle Div	–	–	12	–	–
1st Czechoslovak Bde	–	–	5	–	–
33rd Artillery Bde	–	–	–	35	–
25th Gds Heavy Caliber Howitzer Bde	–	–	–	–	24
76th Gds Artillery Rgt	–	–	–	17	–
111th Howitzer Artillery Rgt	–	–	–	23	–
1663rd Anti-Tank Artillery Rgt	–	–	–	–	–
9th Mortar Rgt	–	–	–	–	–
10th Mortar Rgt	–	–	–	–	–
493rd Mortar Rgt	–	–	–	–	–
315th Gds Anti-Tank Artillery Rgt	–	–	–	–	–
9th Anti-Aircraft Artillery Div	–	–	–	–	–
Total	5	–	101	75	24

Formations and Units	Total Guns	Total Guns and Mortars	Rocket Artillery Platforms	Anti-Aircraft Guns	Tanks and Self-Propelled Guns
		40th Army			
42nd Gds Rifle Div	30	81	–	–	–
68th Gds Rifle Div	36	89	–	–	–
136th Rifle Div	41	98	–	–	–
147th Rifle Div	32	80	–	–	–
167th Rifle Div	38	102	–	–	–
180th Rifle Div	21	94	–	–	–
240th Rifle Div	42	121	–	–	–
253rd Rifle Div	32	80	–	–	–
337th Rifle Div	33	54	–	–	–
380th Rifle Div	40	74	–	–	–
1st Czechoslovak Bde	17	29	–	–	–
33rd Artillery Bde	35	35	–	–	–
25th Gds Heavy Caliber Howitzer Bde	24	24	–	–	–
76th Gds Artillery Rgt	17	17	–	–	–
111th Howitzer Artillery Rgt	23	23	–	–	–
1663rd Anti-Tank Artillery Rgt	20	20	–	–	–
9th Mortar Rgt	–	35	–	–	–
10th Mortar Rgt	–	28	–	–	–
493rd Mortar Rgt	–	36	–	–	–
315th Gds Anti-Tank Artillery Rgt	24	24	–	–	–
9th Anti-Aircraft Artillery Div	–	–	–	47	–
Total	505	1,144	–	51	20

Formations and Units	Men	Mortars		Guns	
		81mm	120mm	76mm (rgt artillery)	76mm (div artillery)
		27th Army			
100th Rifle Div	4,380	38	10	7	12
155th Rifle Div	1,520	30	10	9	20
16th Rifle Div	4,428	35	12	11	10
206th Rifle Div	6,220	49	13	8	17
237th Rifle Div	3,409	11	9	9	10
309th Rifle Div	4,393	32	10	8	18
93rd Tank Bde	934	6	–	–	1
1831st Self-Propelled Artillery Rgt	235	–	–	–	–
1832nd Self-Propelled Artillery Rgt	208	–	–	–	–
628th Gun Artillery Rgt	789	–	–	–	–
1528th Howitzer Artillery Rgt	605	–	–	–	–
408th Heavy Anti-Tank Artillery Rgt	382	–	–	–	–
1070th Anti-Tank Artillery Rgt	388	–	–	–	22
1593rd Anti-Tank Artillery Rgt	496	–	–	–	24
1667th Anti-Tank Artillery Rgt	414	–	–	–	15
1672nd Anti-Tank Artillery Rgt	417	–	–	–	24
480th Mortar Rgt	535	–	21	–	–
23rd Anti-Aircraft Artillery Div	1,487	–	–	–	–
Total	31,240	201	85	52	173

SUPPLEMENTS

Formations and Units	Guns				
	105mm	107mm	122mm	152mm	203mm
		27th Army			
100th Rifle Div	–	–	9	–	–
155th Rifle Div	–	–	11	–	–
16th Rifle Div	–	–	7	–	–
206th Rifle Div	–	–	12	–	–
237th Rifle Div	–	–	9	–	–
309th Rifle Div	–	–	8	–	–
93rd Tank Bde	–	–	–	–	–
1831st Self-Propelled Artillery Rgt	–	–	–	–	–
1832nd Self-Propelled Artillery Rgt	–	–	–	–	–
628th Gun Artillery Rgt	–	–	–	18	–
1528th Howitzer Artillery Rgt	–	–	23	–	–
408th Heavy Anti-Tank Artillery Rgt	–	7	–	–	–
1070th Anti-Tank Artillery Rgt	–	–	–	–	–
1593rd Anti-Tank Artillery Rgt	–	–	–	–	–
1667th Anti-Tank Artillery Rgt	–	–	–	–	–
1672nd Anti-Tank Artillery Rgt	–	–	–	–	–
480th Mortar Rgt	–	–	–	–	–
23rd Anti-Aircraft Artillery Div	–	–	–	–	–
Total	–	7	79	18	–

Formations and Units	Total Guns	Total Guns and Mortars	Rocket Artillery Platforms	Anti-Aircraft Guns	Tanks and Self-Propelled Guns
		27th Army			
100th Rifle Div	28	76	–	–	–
155th Rifle Div	40	80	–	–	–
16th Rifle Div	28	75	–	–	–
206th Rifle Div	37	99	–	–	–
237th Rifle Div	28	48	–	–	–
309th Rifle Div	34	76	–	–	–
93rd Tank Bde	1	7	–	–	3
1831st Self-Propelled Artillery Rgt	–	–	–	–	14
1832nd Self-Propelled Artillery Rgt	–	–	–	–	7
628th Gun Artillery Rgt	18	18	–	–	–
1528th Howitzer Artillery Rgt	23	23	–	–	–
408th Heavy Anti-Tank Artillery Rgt	7	7	–	–	–
1070th Anti-Tank Artillery Rgt	22	22	–	–	–
1593rd Anti-Tank Artillery Rgt	24	24	–	–	–
1667th Anti-Tank Artillery Rgt	15	15	–	–	–
1672nd Anti-Tank Artillery Rgt	24	24	–	–	–
480th Mortar Rgt	–	21	–	–	–
23rd Anti-Aircraft Artillery Div	–	–	–	61	–
Total	329	615	–	61	24

Formations and Units	Men	Mortars		Guns	
		81mm	120mm	76mm (rgt artillery)	76mm (div artillery)
1st Gds Cavalry Corps					
1st Gds Cavalry Div	5,154	24	6	7	11
2nd Gds Cavalry Div	4,649	34	6	12	8
7th Gds Cavalry Div	5,337	30	6	10	8
1461st Self-Propelled Artillery Rgt	235	–	–	–	–
143rd Anti-Tank Artillery Rgt	472	–	–	–	20
Total	15,847	88	18	29	47

Formations and Units	Guns				
	105mm	107mm	122mm	152mm	203mm
1st Gds Cavalry Corps					
1st Gds Cavalry Div	–	–	8	–	–
2nd Gds Cavalry Div	–	–	8	–	–
7th Gds Cavalry Div	–	–	6	–	–
1461st Self-Propelled Artillery Rgt	–	–	–	–	–
143rd Anti-Tank Artillery Rgt	–	–	–	–	–
Total	–	–	22	–	–

Formations and Units	Total Guns	Total Guns and Mortars	Rocket Artillery Platforms	Anti-Aircraft Guns	Tanks and Self-Propelled Guns
1st Gds Cavalry Corps					
1st Gds Cavalry Div	26	56	–	6	7
2nd Gds Cavalry Div	28	68	–	6	17
7th Gds Cavalry Div	24	60	–	5	8
1461st Self-Propelled Artillery Rgt	–	–	–	–	20
143rd Anti-Tank Artillery Rgt	20	20	–	–	–
Total	98	204	–	17	52

Formations and Units	Men	Mortars		Guns	
		81mm	120mm	76mm (rgt artillery)	76mm (div artillery)
3rd Gds Tank Army					
6th Gds Tank Corps	5,688	28	23	–	13
7th Gds Tank Corps	6,701	45	35	–	20
9th Mechanized Corps	7,754	50	42	–	18
91st Tank Bde	971	6	–	–	1
50th Motorcycle Rgt	1,180	12	–	–	4
1835th Self-Propelled Artillery Rgt	195	–	–	–	–
1836th Self-Propelled Artillery Rgt	237	–	–	–	–
1451st Self-Propelled Artillery Rgt	233	–	–	–	–
36th Gds Mortar Rgt	665	–	–	–	–
91st Gds Mortar Rgt	665	–	–	–	–
1381st Anti-Aircraft Artillery Rgt	372	–	–	–	–
1391st Anti-Aircraft Artillery Rgt	400	–	–	–	–
Total	25,061	141	100	–	56

Formations and Units	Guns				
	105mm	107mm	122mm	152mm	203mm
3rd Gds Tank Army					
6th Gds Tank Corps	–	–	–	–	–
7th Gds Tank Corps	–	–	–	–	–
9th Mechanized Corps	–	–	–	–	–
91st Tank Bde	–	–	–	–	–
50th Motorcycle Rgt	–	–	–	–	–
1835th Self-Propelled Artillery Rgt	–	–	–	–	–
1836th Self-Propelled Artillery Rgt	–	–	–	–	–
1451st Self-Propelled Artillery Rgt	–	–	–	–	–
36th Gds Mortar Rgt	–	–	–	–	–
91st Gds Mortar Rgt	–	–	–	–	–
1381st Anti-Aircraft Artillery Rgt	–	–	–	–	–
1391st Anti-Aircraft Artillery Rgt	–	–	–	–	–
Total	–	–	–	–	–

238   THE BATTLE OF THE DNEPR

Formations and Units	Total Guns	Total Guns and Mortars	Rocket Artillery Platforms	Anti-Aircraft Guns	Tanks and Self-Propelled Guns
3rd Gds Tank Army					
6th Gds Tank Corps	13	61	–	9	50
7th Gds Tank Corps	20	100	–	14	77
9th Mechanized Corps	18	110	–	20	69
91st Tank Bde	1	7	–	–	32
50th Motorcycle Rgt*	4	16	–	–	10
1835th Self-Propelled Artillery Rgt	–	–	–	–	3
1836th Self-Propelled Artillery Rgt	–	–	–	–	2
1451st Self-Propelled Artillery Rgt	–	–	–	–	12
36th Gds Mortar Rgt	–	–	17	–	–
91st Gds Mortar Rgt	–	–	19	–	–
1381st Anti-Aircraft Artillery Rgt	–	–	–	14	–
1391st Anti-Aircraft Artillery Rgt	–	–	–	16	–
Total	56	297	36	43	255

* Information as of 10 November 1943

Formations and Units	Men	Mortars		Guns	
		81mm	120mm	76mm (rgt artillery)	76mm (div artillery)
Forces Subordinated to the *Front*					
8th Gds Tank Corps	4,302	18	–	–	2
10th Tank Corps	4,064	20	–	–	10
2nd Anti-Tank Artillery Bde	1,097	–	–	–	–
287th Mortar Rgt	463	–	17	–	–
269th Anti-Tank Artillery Rgt	483	–	–	–	–
563rd Anti-Tank Artillery Rgt	453	–	–	–	2
680th Anti-Tank Artillery Rgt	433	–	–	–	–
1954th Anti-Aircraft Artillery Rgt	390	–	–	–	–
22nd Gds Anti-Aircraft Artillery Bn	350	–	–	–	–
332nd Anti-Aircraft Artillery Bn	352	–	–	–	–
Total	12,387	38	17	–	16
Total for the *Front*	381,893	2,020	1,346	417	1,677

SUPPLEMENTS

Formations and Units	Guns				
	105mm	107mm	122mm	152mm	203mm
	Forces Subordinated to the *Front*				
8th Gds Tank Corps	–	–	–	–	–
10th Tank Corps	–	–	–	–	–
2nd Anti-Tank Artillery Bde	–	–	–	–	–
287th Mortar Rgt	–	–	–	–	–
269th Anti-Tank Artillery Rgt	–	–	–	–	–
563rd Anti-Tank Artillery Rgt	–	–	–	–	–
680th Anti-Tank Artillery Rgt	–	–	–	–	–
1954th Anti-Aircraft Artillery Rgt	–	–	–	–	–
22nd Gds Anti-Aircraft Artillery Bn	–	–	–	–	–
332nd Anti-Aircraft Artillery Bn	–	–	–	–	–
Total	–	–	–	–	–
Total for the *Front*	8	7	647	416	71

Formations and Units	Total Guns	Total Guns and Mortars	Rocket Artillery Platforms	Anti-Aircraft Guns	Tanks and Self-Propelled Guns
	Forces Subordinated to the *Front*				
8th Gds Tank Corps	2	20	–	3	10
10th Tank Corps	10	30	–	9	–
2nd Anti-Tank Artillery Bde	–	–	–	–	–
287th Mortar Rgt	–	17	–	–	–
269th Anti-Tank Artillery Rgt	–	–	–	–	–
563rd Anti-Tank Artillery Rgt	2	2	–	–	–
680th Anti-Tank Artillery Rgt	2	–	–	–	–
1954th Anti-Aircraft Artillery Rgt	–	–	–	16	–
22nd Gds Anti-Aircraft Artillery Bn	–	–	–	12	–
332nd Anti-Aircraft Artillery Bn	–	–	–	12	–
Total	16	71	–	52	10
Total for the *Front*	3,243	6,609	699	529	466

Part II
The Second Ukrainian Front's Operations in September-December 1943

1

The Forcing of the Dnepr by the 37th Army in the Kremenchug Area (September-October 1943)

Introduction

One of the Soviet army's greatest victories in the 1943 summer campaign was the rout of the German-Fascist forces in the battle of the Dnepr, which was accomplished under the direct leadership of the *Stavka* of the Supreme High Command. In this battle, which unfolded in the second half of 1943, five *fronts* were directly involved: Central, Voronezh, Steppe, Southwestern, and Southern.

As a result of the fierce fighting, Soviet forces defeated a major enemy group of forces along the Ukrainian left bank, forced the Dnepr on the march along its middle and lower course along a front of more than 700 kilometers and seized bridgeheads along its western bank, from which they subsequently launched major offensive operations along the Ukrainian right bank.

The Steppe Front's offensive operation to reach the Dnepr and force it unfolded in an extremely complex situation. Throughout August and the first part of September the *front's* forces advanced 200-300 kilometers in heavy fighting. The materiel-technical supply of the troops became more difficult due to the *front's* rapid advance to the west, the extensive destruction of the railroads and the significant lagging behind of the *front* and army supply bases. As a rule, the delivery of ammunition, fuel, food, and crossing equipment was carried out by auto transport, of which there was a shortage in the *front*. The complexity of the troops' materiel-technical and engineer supply told significantly on the operations of our forces while forcing the Dnepr and in the fighting for the bridgeheads along the right bank of the river. Despite this, the *front's* forces successfully resolved the task of defeating the enemy along the Kremenchug and Dnepropetrovsk axes, forced the powerful water barrier of the Dnepr from the march and consolidated important bridgeheads along its right bank.

The offensive operation of the Steppe Front's 37th Army, along with its forcing of the Dnepr River, is a part of this grandiose battle. The army began its offensive operation on 24 September 1943 along the approaches to the Dnepr and concluded it on 11 October by the seizure of a major bridgehead on the other side of the river. The 37th Army's forcing of the Dnepr was accomplished in close coordination with the forces of the neighboring 53rd and 7th Guards armies. The forces of the Steppe Front then carried out offensive operations along the Kirovograd and Krivoi Rog axes from the captured bridgeheads.

It should be especially emphasized that questions of materiel-technical and engineer support for this operation are of particular interest and may be the subject of a special study.

In this article only the main problems of the 37th Army's offensive operation and forcing of the Dnepr are illuminated. Questions of employing the combat arms and troops' materiel-technical and engineer support are highlighted in the article only to the degree necessary for elucidating an army operation with the forcing of a river from the march.

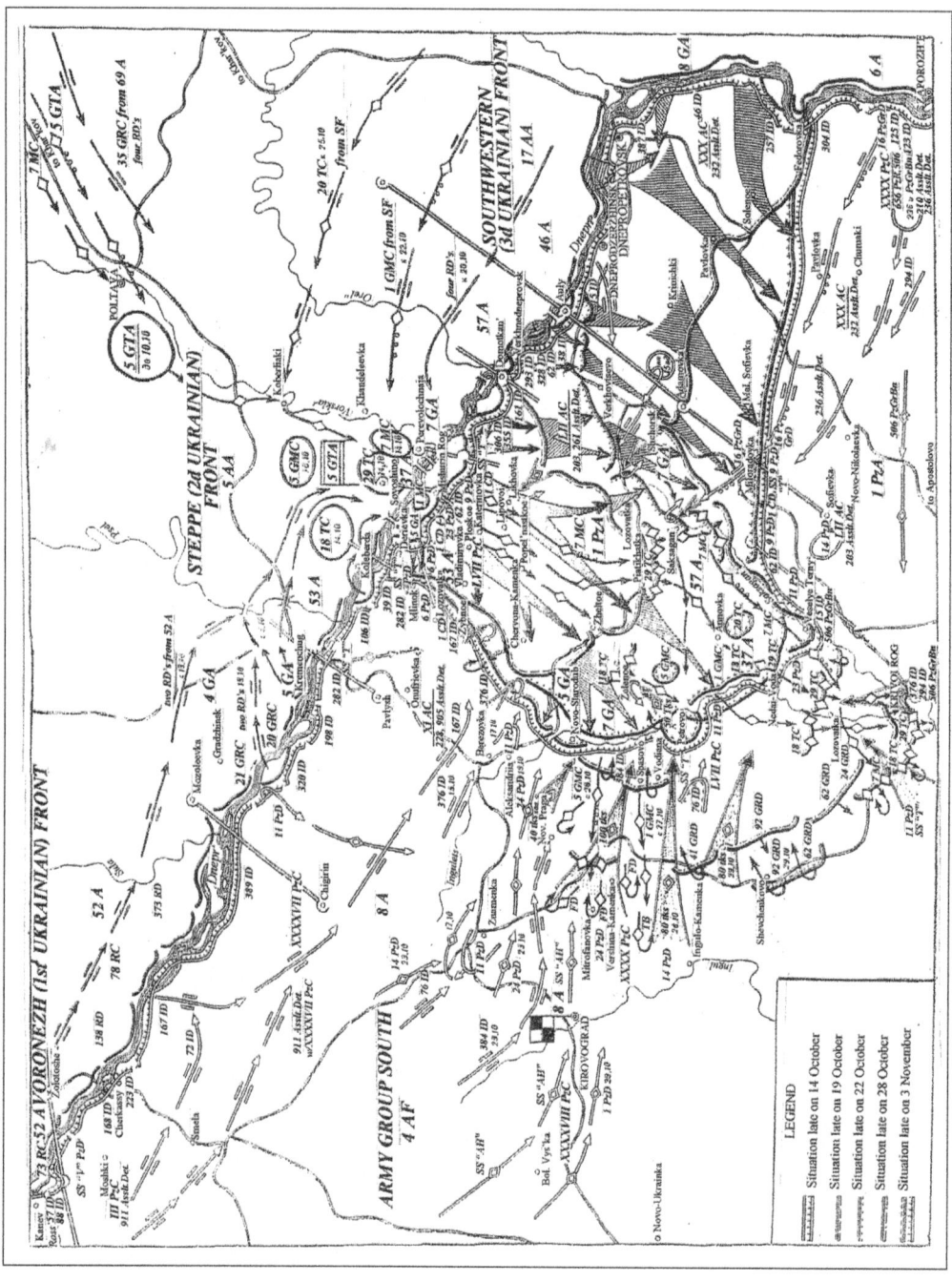

Map 3 The Steppe (2nd Ukrainian) Front's Operations along the Krivoi Rog Axis, 15 October-3 November 1943.

The Situation in the Steppe Front's Sector During the Second Half of September 1943

Following the defeat of the enemy's Orel and Belgorod—Khar'kov groups of forces, the enemy's troops, lacking the strength to withhold the Soviet army's mighty offensive, began to fall back to the Dnepr along the entire front in the beginning of September.

The Steppe Front's forces[1] (*front* commander—I.S. Konev, member of the military council—Lieutenant General of Tank Troops I.Z. Susaikov,[2] and the chief of staff—Lieutenant General M.V. Zakharov[3]), consisting of 44 rifle divisions and one mechanized corps, while pursuing the retreating enemy in the *front's* offensive sector, by 20 September had reached the line Miloradovo—Vasil'yevka—Mikhailovka—Pereshchepino and was 70-130 kilometers from the Dnepr. While continuing to develop the offensive, the *front's* right-wing forces (5th Guards and 53rd armies) were outflanking Poltava from the north and south, with the task of capturing it. The 69th and 7th Guards armies were attacking in the center of the front, in the general direction of Kobelyaki. Along the *front's* left wing, the forces of the 57th and 46th armies were pursuing the enemy in the general direction of Petrikovka and Verkhovtsevo.

The 37th Army (commander—Lieutenant General M.N. Sharokhin,[4] member of the military council—Colonel A.S. Bagnyuk and chief of staff—Colonel A.K. Blazhei), which had been transferred to the *front* from the *Stavka* reserve, comprised the *front's* second echelon and by 20 September had concentrated in the Nagornaya—Pervomaiskoye—Kamyshevatoye area. This area was 45 kilometers from the *front's* forward units and 150 kilometers from the Dnepr. The army's formations and units had by this time been replenished with men and weaponry.

The enemy's Eighth and part of the First Panzer Army, consisting of 15 divisions and combat groups, including three panzer divisions, which had been significantly weakened in the preceding fighting, continued to fall back before the Steppe Front's forces. The enemy was hurriedly withdrawing the 11th and 3rd panzer and 72nd Infantry divisions through Reshetilovka toward Kremenchug for occupy and organize a defense on the right bank of the Dnepr.

The strength of the divisions and combat groups did not exceed 2,500-4,000 men. No more than 40-60 tanks remained in the panzer divisions.

The enemy had no prepared defense along the approaches to the Dnepr. His forces could only employ the wooded areas east of Poltava and the Vorskla, Psyol and Kobelyachka rivers as favorable lines.

The German-Fascist command placed particular hopes on organizing a defense along the right bank of the Dnepr, to which it was striving to pull back its forces and to halt the Soviet army's offensive here.

One should take into account that by 20 September the Steppe Front's forces considerably outnumbered the enemy in men and combat materiel. In the developing situation, the *front's* forces would have to capture Poltava, vigorously arrive at the Dnepr, force it, seize bridgeheads along the

---

1   5th Guards, 53rd, 69th, 7th Guards, 57th, 46th, and 37th armies, and the 1st Mechanized Corps.
2   Editor's note. Ivan Zakharovich Susaikov (1903-62) joined the Red Army in 1924 and served in its political apparatus. During the Great Patriotic War he served on the military council of various *fronts* as the chief political officer. Following the war, he continued in political posts at home and abroad. Susaikov retired in 1960.
3   Editor's note. Matvei Vasil'evich Zakharov (1898-1972) joined the Red Army in 1918 and fought in the civil war. During the Great Patriotic War he served as chief of staff on several *fronts* in Europe and the Far East. Following the war, Zakharov high positions in the central military apparatus and was chief of the General Staff during 1960-63 and 1964-71.
4   Editor's note. Mikhail Nikolaevich Sharokhin (1898-1974) joined the Red Army in 1918 and fought in the civil war. During the Great Patriotic War he was chief of staff of an army and two *fronts* and also commanded armies. Following the war, he served in the central military apparatus. Sharokhin retired in 1960.

river's right bank, and create the necessary conditions for the development of the offensive along the Ukrainian right bank.

The resolution of these tasks required that the *front* and army commands devote particular attention to the organization and preparation of the troops for forcing the Dnepr from the march during the course of the pursuit.

A Short Description of the Area of Military Activities

The Vorskla, Kobelyachka and Psyol rivers flow from north to south in the left-bank part of the area adjacent to the Dnepr. The most significant obstacle for troops is the Vorskla River. This river is 40-60 meters wide and 0.9 to 2.5 meters deep; its rate of flow is as much as 1.2 meters per second and its bottom is, for the most part, made of clay. The terrain in this area is plain, with an average height of up to 100-180 meters above sea level. The presence of rivers and swampy sectors in the offensive's sector made the arrival of our forces at the Dnepr more difficult. The enemy destroyed all of the bridges and crossings during his withdrawal.

The terrain is open along the approaches to the Dnepr. At the same time, the presence of inhabited locales, as well as deep gullies, overgrown with bushes and, in places, woods, aided the disguised concentration and massing of troops.

There were insufficient roads leading directly to the Dnepr in the *front's* offensive sector. In light of this, the *front* and army commands had to devote the most serious attention to the construction and maintenance in working condition of the communications leading to the Dnepr crossings along a front from Kremenchug to Dneprodzerzhinsk. The materials necessary to repair the roads and build crossings were located 10-15 kilometers from the Dnepr.

The most important lateral routes were the Yeristovka—Ozery—Kishen'ki and Koleberda—Soloshino—Perevolochnaya roads.

A railroad , which had been destroyed by the enemy and required restoration, runs in the army's sector from Poltava to Kremenchug.

The forcing of the Dnepr by the forces of the Steppe Front was to be accomplished along the front Kremenchug—Dneprodzerzhinsk. The 37th Army had to force the Dnepr in the center of the *front's* offensive sector along the Uspenskoye—Mishurin Rog sector.

The Dnepr's width in the army's area of operations was 250-1,200 meters, while its depth, given the average level of water, varied from 1.8 to seven meters, and the speed of the current is 1.0-1.2 meters per second. The banks are primarily sandy and gently sloping, 2-4 meters above the water level. The width of the valley near Derievka and Mishurin Rog narrows to 2-3 kilometers. Both banks are heavily cut by ravines.

The presence of islands, overgrown with bushes and, in places, woods in the area northwest and east of Derievka created favorable conditions for organizing landings and ferry crossings.

The terrain to the west of the Dnepr facilitated the organization of a secure defense. The right bank here commands the left one and has a number of heights, from which the enemy had the opportunity of viewing the entire area along the opposite bank as far as the line Motrino—Ozery—Brachkovka; that is, to a depth of up to 10-12 kilometers.

The inhabited locales of Uspenskoye, Derievka and Kutsevolovka and heights 172 and 177 enabled the enemy to outfit powerful strongpoints, the secure retention of which created serious difficulties for our forces while crossing and fighting for bridgeheads.

Thus, on the whole, the terrain in the area of combat operations, particularly along the forcing sectors, favored the creation of a stout defense by the enemy and seriously hindered the activities of our attacking forces.

The meteorological conditions were favorable for offensive activities. During 25 September-15 October 1943 there was steady dry weather. Visibility reached 10-20 kilometers. Light fog, which sometimes turned into real fog, appeared at times during the night and the pre-morning hours. Visibility in the light fog fell to 2-4 kilometers and down to 50 meters in real fog.

The Training of the 37th Army's Forces for Forcing the Dnepr

The Front Commander's Decision to Force the Dnepr

On 20 September the commander of the Steppe Front adopted a decision, according to which the *front's* forces were to complete the defeat of the enemy's Eighth and First Panzer armies, which were falling back on Kremenchug and Dneprodzerzhinsk, to force the Dnepr from the march and capture during 24-28 September bridgeheads along the right bank of the Dnepr.

It was planned to have a two-echelon formation. The 5th Guards, 53rd, 69th, 7th Guards, 57th, and 46 armies, and the 1st Mechanized Corps were to attack in the first echelon. The 37th Army, the commitment of which was planned in the 69th Army's sector to seize a bridgehead southeast of Kremenchug, was in the second echelon.

In accordance with the decision adopted, the armies were assigned the following tasks:

The 5th Guards Army was to launch an attack in the direction of Reshetilovka and Frunzovka, outflanking Poltava from the north. On 24 September the army's formations were to reach the front Frunzovka—Manzheliya, while its forward detachments were to capture the crossings along the Dnepr River in the area of Taburishche and Kremenchug. The city of Kremenchug was to be captured on 25 September.

The 53rd Army was given the assignment, while outflanking Poltava from the south, of energetically developing the pursuit of the enemy in the general direction of Koshubovka, Koby and Kozel'shchina. On 24 September the army's formations were to reach the front Vasil'yevka—excluding Prigarevka, while its forward detachments were to capture crossings along the Dnepr River in the area of Sadki and Chikalovka.

The 69th Army had the mission of attacking in the direction of Veliki and Breusovka and on 24 September to capture crossings along the Dnepr River in the Derievka area.

The 7th Guards Army was ordered, while energetically developing the offensive in the direction of Livenskoe and Novyi Orlik, to capture crossings along the Dnepr River in the area of Perevalochnaya, Borodaevka and Staryi Orlik on 23 September, and on 24 September force the Dnepr River and seize a bridgehead along the sector Mishurin Rog—Annovka—Novo-Aleksandrovka.

The 57th Army received orders to develop the offensive in the direction of Pryadovka and Shul'govka and on 28 September capture crossings along the Dnepr River in the Pushkarevka—Soshinovka area, and on 24 September to force the Dnepr and seize a bridgehead along the sector Shevchenkovo—Verkhovtsevo.

The 46th Army was ordered to develop the offensive in the general direction of Pochino-Sofievka and Chaplinka and on 23 September capture crossings along the Dnepr River in the Auly—Dneprodzerzhinsk—Trituznaya area, and on 24 September to force the Dnepr and seize a bridgehead along the Mironovka—Blagoveshchenka sector.

The 37th Army, which consisted of seven rifle divisions, was to be ready to be committed into the fighting, to relieve the 69th Army and to force the Dnepr along the Uspenskoye—Kutsevolovka area; that is, in the center of the *front's* offensive sector.

The overall front for forcing the Dnepr was to reach 130 kilometers. As is clear from the decision adopted by the *front* commander, the 7th Guards, 57th and 46th armies, which were 90 kilometers from the Dnepr, were given more specific assignments. They were instructed not only as to what sectors the crossings were to be seized, but also the bridgeheads' width and depth. They were assigned a daily rate of advance of 18-20 kilometers.

As regards the *front's* right-wing armies—the 5th Guards and 53rd armies, which were still 140 kilometers from the Dnepr—they were to seize crossings with their forward detachments and hold them until the arrival of the main forces. The pace of the right-flank armies was determined at 25-35 kilometers per day. Such an offensive pace was a bit high, because the 5th Guards and 53rd armies had to force the Vorskla and Psyol rivers, capture the major towns of Poltava and Kremenchug and then force the Dnepr in the course of four days. The resolution of such a task was further complicated by the fact that it was precisely along the Kremenchug axis that the enemy's main forces were retreating.

In carrying out the assigned tasks, the armies of the Steppe Front were pursuing the retreating enemy to the southwest.

On 23 September the 5th Guards and 53rd armies captured Poltava. By the close of 24 September the forces of the 5th Guards, 53rd and 69th armies had reached the line excluding Glubokii—Yatsenki—excluding Kobelyaki and were 40-70 kilometers from the Dnepr. By this time the forces of the 7th Guards, 57th and 46th armies had arrived directly at the Dnepr along the front Perevolochnaya—Nikolaevka—Goryanovskie. Thus the average daily pace of the advance by the *front's* formations was 15-20 kilometers.

By the close of 24 September the *front's* second echelon—the 37th Army—was in the Bogdanovka—Karlovka—Tishinovka—Maksimovka area, at a distance of 60-70 kilometers from the 69th Army's forward detachments and 110 kilometers from the Dnepr; that is, three or four days' march.

In order to interfere with the enemy's crossing to the right bank of the Dnepr, the 5th Air Army's aviation carried out strikes against troops and bridges. On 24 September the air force was able to destroy the bridge near Kremenchug. As a result of this, five of the enemy's infantry and about two of his panzer divisions, which had been falling back to the Kremenchug area, were forced to cross with their organic crossing equipment, which slowed down extremely the arrival of these forces to occupy defenses along the right bank of the Dnepr.

The retreat of the enemy's left-bank group of forces along diverging axes favored the rapid arrival of our troops at the Dnepr in the area between the Psyol and Vorskla rivers, and the Marshevka—Kustolovo-Kushchi—Kutsevolovka acquired particular importance in the developing situation, because the enemy had no significant forces here to speak of and had not had time to prepare and occupy a defense along the opposite bank of the Dnepr. The German-Fascist command, evidently believing that the 69th Army, which had been weakened in the previous fighting, was operating here and did not attach particular significance to this axis, while assuming that this army would not be able to force such a powerful water barrier. Besides this, the forcing of the Dnepr by the 7th Guards, 57th and 46th armies, which had begun as early as 24 September, had already attracted the significant enemy forces that had crossed over to the right bank of the river.

In the developing situation, the *front* commander decided to commit the 37th Army in the 69th Army's sector to complete the defeat of the enemy's retreating units, to force the Dnepr from the march and to seize a bridgehead along its right bank.

During the second half of 24 September the *front* commander made the decision to commit the 37th Army. The army was ordered to reach by forced march the area of the 69th Army's forward detachments by 2400 on 25 September. Upon relieving the 69th Army's forces here, it was to develop the offensive, to force the Dnepr from the march and on 27 September to capture a bridgehead along the sector Uspenskoye—Mishurin Rog.

For the purpose of organizing the uninterrupted control of the 37th Army's forces during the relief and their arrival at the Dnepr, the *front* commander ordered the commander of the 69th Army to leave all his active communications equipment at the disposal of the 37th Army's headquarters before the morning of 27 September. The presence of operating communications created conditions for the timely and successful resolution of the tasks facing the 37th Army's forces.

THE FORCING OF THE DNEPR BY THE 37TH ARMY

For the resolution of the assigned tasks, the 37th Army was reinforced during 24-26 September with the 89th Guards Rifle Division from the 69th Army, and the 27th Gun Artillery Brigade, 90th Heavy Howitzer Artillery Brigade, the 31st Anti-Tank Artillery Brigade (minus one regiment), the 324th and 1658th anti-tank artillery regiments, the 381st Gun Artillery Regiment, 562nd Mortar Regiment, the 80th, 302nd and 315th guards mortar regiments, the 11th, 26th and 35th anti-aircraft artillery divisions, the 6th and 19th independent mechanized pontoon-bridge battalions, the 69th and 328th engineer-sapper battalions, and the 8th Engineer-Sapper Brigade.

In order to carry out the assigned tasks, the 37th Army's forces had to carry out a 60-70 kilometer march in three and a half days, to relieve the 69th Army's forces, complete the rout of the enemy's retreating forces, and to force the Dnepr River. Slowness and insufficient energy by the troops and lack of organization in such a situation could have meant that the enemy would be able to put his worn-out formations in order and put up resistance to our forces while forcing the Dnepr.

Simultaneously, the *front* commander adopted all measures to speed up the arrival of the 5th Guards and 53rd armies' forces at the Dnepr and to seize bridgeheads in the Kremenchug area and to the south, as well as to speed up the forcing of the Dnepr by the forces of the 7th Guards, 57th and 46th armies. The *front's* aviation was assigned the task of launching uninterrupted bomber and strafing attacks against the bridges and crossings in the Kremenchug area in order to prevent the crossing of the enemy's forces.

The Decision by the Commander of the 37th Army on Forcing the Dnepr

By the time of the receipt of the task to force the Dnepr, the 37th Army was located in the Bogdanovka—Karlovka—Tishinovka—Maksimovka area.

The army's strength is show in Tables 1.1 and 1.2.

Table 1.1 The 37th Army's Strength as of 25 September 1943

Units and Formations	Men	Machine Guns		Mortars		Guns			Tanks
		Light	Heavy	82mm	120mm	45mm	76mm	122mm	
57th Rifle Corps									
62nd Guards Rifle Division	8,368	491	166	85	24	41	36	12	–
92nd Guards Rifle Division	8,472	499	166	85	24	48	36	12	–
110th Guards Rifle Division	8,818	490	171	75	16	40	32	12	–
82nd Rifle Corps									
1st Guards Airborne Division	8,256	499	166	85	24	48	36	12	–
10th Guards Airborne Division	7,818	493	166	75	24	45	36	12	–
188th Rifle Division	7,044	444	111	83	21	45	32	12	–
89th Guards Rifle Division	3,864	197	51	48	14	21	26	2	–
43rd Tank Regiment	364	2	–	–	–	–	–	–	30
Total	53,004	3,115	997	536	147	288	234	74	30*

* Including ten light tanks.

As can be seen from Table 1.1, the army's six divisions were sufficiently up to strength and numbered from 7,000 to 8,500 men, and only the 89th Guards Rifle Division, which had been transferred from the 69th Army, had only 3,864 men.

The army was poorly supplied with crossing equipment. In all, the army's formations had 16 small inflatable boats, ten wet suits and five A-3 boats. The *front* commander's decision called for the army to be reinforced with two mechanized pontoon-bridge battalions (two parks of bow half-pontoons and a "V" park), an RVK engineer-sapper brigade (UVSA-3 park) and 48 wooden boats. By the time the army received its assignment, this crossing equipment had not yet arrived. The rear establishments and a significant part of the artillery were also overextended, due to a shortage of fuel and were lagging behind the troops.

In light of the fact that on 24 September the 37th Army was still in the Karlovka—Tishinkovka—Maksimovka area, or 60-70 kilometers from the 69th Army's forces and 110 kilometers from the Dnepr, the most important task was the movement of the army's forces as close as possible to the *front's* first-echelon forces. At the same time, the army's forces had to carry out preparations for forcing the Dnepr during the march.

Thus in conditions of restricted time, a great shortage of crossing equipment and the overextension of the rear organs and the artillery during the pursuit, as well as the continuing resistance by the enemy's rearguards, the troops and staffs set about preparing for the forcing en route. Naturally, in such a situation one could not count on the detailed and thorough planning of the operation. The loss of time in such conditions would only have made more difficult an already complex task.

Thus at 2100 on 24 September the commander of the 37th Army issued an order to the commander of the 57th Rifle Corps to begin immediately moving the corps' formations to the Kustolovo-Kushchi—Komarovka—Chapaevo area and to relieve the 69th Army's formations in this area by the morning of 26 September and to then pursue the enemy in the direction of Kobelyaki and Ozery. The 82nd Rifle Corps was to concentrate by the morning of 27 September in the area Maloye Pereshchepino—Drabinovka—Petrovka.

While carrying out these orders, the army's forces carried out a 60-kilometer march during 25 September and by the close of the day had reached the areas indicated for them. However, the units of the 57th Rifle Corps were unable to relieve the 69th Army's formations west of the Vorskla River, because the latter had advanced another 20-25 kilometers during that day.

At 2245 on 25 September the commander of the 37th Army made the decision to reach the Dnepr and to force it along the sector Uspenskoye—Mishurin Rog. In forcing the river, it was planned to concentrate the main forces along the sector excluding Derievka—Mishurin Rog.

It was planned to have the army's operation formation in two echelons: the 57th Rifle Corps and the 89th Guards Rifle Division were to be in the first echelon and the 82nd Rifle Corps in the second. Thus the army's first echelon contained four rifle divisions and the second two airborne and one rifle divisions.

It was planned to relieve the 69th Army's forces during the subsequent pursuit of the enemy during the approach to the Dnepr.

Taking into account the fact that the enemy had not yet managed to create an organized defense along the right bank of the Dnepr, the army commander planned to begin the forcing and seizure of bridgeheads from the march.

In accordance with the decision adopted for forcing the Dnepr, on 25 September the commander of the 37th Army issued orders to his troops. In view of the fact that the corps headquarters had only just been formed and lacked sufficient experience in troop control, the army commander, on the basis of the *front* commander's instructions, assigned tasks directly to the commanders of the first-echelon divisions. The underestimation of the corps level essentially led to the removal of the corps commanders and their headquarters from the control of the troops and relieved them of responsibility for the combat activities of their subordinate divisions. The army commander and his staff, by bypassing the corps level, were not always able to exercise firm leadership of the divisions' combat activities. In such a situation, it would have been more expedient to bring in the corps headquarters more actively into the organization and control of the battle, while at the same time rendering them timely and necessary assistance.

THE FORCING OF THE DNEPR BY THE 37TH ARMY

The army's first-echelon formations—the 89th, 92nd, 62nd, and 110th guards rifle divisions—were to vigorously try to reach the Dnepr, to force it from the march and to seize bridgeheads along the right bank of the river in their sectors. In order to speed up the arrival at the river and the rapid seizure of bridgeheads, each division was ordered to detail forward detachments. These detachments were to reach the river as quickly as possible, without getting tied down in fighting with the enemy's units covering his withdrawal, to force it and seize bridgeheads and hold them until the arrival of the division's main forces. As they approached the river, the divisions' main forces were to attempt to cross over to the bridgeheads seized by the forward detachments and, in conjunction with the neighboring divisions, unite these bridgeheads into one, overall army bridgehead, to which the army's second echelon and attached reinforcements were to then cross over.

The 89th Guards Rifle Division received orders to continue pursuing the retreating enemy in the general direction of Aleksandrovka and Pavlovka and by the close of 26 September reach the Dnepr. This division's forward detachments were to force the river by the morning of 27 September and seize bridgeheads in the area northeast of the village of Uspenskoye.

The 92nd Guards Rifle Division, which by the close of 25 September was located 50 kilometers from the Dnepr, was to relieve the 69th Army's 94th Guards Rifle Division and, while pursuing the enemy in the direction of Breusovka and Derievka, was to reach with its main forces the line Motrino—Ozery by the close of 26 September, while the forward detachments were to force the Dnepr by the morning of 27 September and to seize and consolidate a bridgehead in the Derievka area.

The 62nd Guards Rifle Division, which was located 45 kilometers from the Dnepr by the close of 25 September, was to relieve units of the 69th Army's 93rd Guards Rifle Division and by the close of 26 September reach the line Ozery—Prosyanikovka, while its forward detachments were to force the Dnepr and seize a bridgehead along the western bank of the river along the sector Lake Liman—height 172.

The 10th Guards Rifle Division, which comprised the 57th Rifle Corps' second echelon, was ordered to concentrate in the Baranniki—Zabegailovka—Kovalenki area by 1600 on 27 September, with the task of being ready to force the Dnepr.

According to the army commander's instructions, in each of the 37th Army's first echelon rifle divisions a rifle battalion each was to be detached, which was reinforced by an artillery battalion two batteries of anti-tank artillery and a sapper platoon, to form the forward detachments. The forward detachments were supported by auto transport. Due to the absence of crossing equipment in the army, the forward detachments were to force the Dnepr using local means and items gathered on the bank.

It was planned to cross over the first-echelon divisions' main forces, artillery, tank, and other equipment using organic equipment, which was expected from the *front* reserve.

The crossing equipment which was supposed to arrive at the army was not to be distributed, but rather employed as it arrived and in accordance with the situation.

Each first-echelon division was to have one to three artillery regiments and from one to two guards mortar battalions attached to it. In light of the paucity of artillery and the army commander's striving to directly influence the course of the forcing and the seizure and expansion of the bridgehead, corps artillery groups were not to be created. It was planned to create an army artillery group, consisting of a gun artillery brigade and one gun artillery regiment. The army artillery group was designated for combat operations along the army's main attack axis.

As can be seem from this, the decision by the army commander, on the whole corresponded to the *front* commander's idea for the forcing of the Dnepr as the situation had developed by this time.

The army commander made the decision to force the Dnepr and issued orders to his forces located 50-70 kilometers from the river. The army's first-echelon formations, having received orders, were to immediately move from their concentration area into their assigned sectors, without carrying out any additional regroupings. It was planned to carry out the relief of the 69th Army's forces and the preparations for the forcing during the ongoing pursuit.

Insofar as the troops, the command and staffs did not dispose of the necessary time, detailed plan for the artillery and air offensive, as well as plans for engineer and materiel support in the army were not compiled. All of the necessary measures for preparing for the forcing were reflected in individual orders, calculations and oral instructions, issued by the army commander and the chiefs of the combat arms and troop and headquarters services.

One should note that very difficult conditions were to arise as a result of the untimely arrival of crossing equipment from the *front* reserve for conducting the forcing of the Dnepr.

The Arrival of the 37th Army's Forces at the Dnepr

On the morning of 26 September the division's of the 37th Army's 57th Rifle Corps left the Novye Senzhary—Kustolovo-Kushchi—Velikie Solontsy area in order to relieve the 69th Army's forces. The latter, upon encountering weak enemy resistance in the center and along the left flank, was rapidly approaching the Dnepr. The 69th Army's units were relieved by the 57th Rifle Corps' divisions only along the line Dobinevka—Ozery.

The enemy, while striving to support the crossing of its units in the Kremenchug area, was continuing to put up stubborn resistance to the 53rd Army's forces and the right flank of the 37th Army's forces. Thus the 37th Army's first-echelon formations arrived at the Dnepr at different times.

While continuing the pursuit during the night of 26-27 September, the 37th Army's first-echelon rifle divisions reached by morning the line Prishib—Karpovka—Botsuly—Soloshino. The 92nd and 62nd guards rifle divisions' forward detachments, which had reached the Dnepr as early as 0200 on 27 September, were unable to immediately set about forcing the river due to the absence of crossing equipment and were forced to begin gathering various materials at hand along the bank. The 110th Guards Rifle Division—the 57th Rifle Corps' second echelon—was on the march northeast of Ozery, 15-20 kilometers from the Dnepr. The 82nd Rifle Corps was located in its previous concentration area: Maloye Pereshchepino—Drabinovka—Petrovka, at a distance of 70 kilometers from the Dnepr. The 90th Heavy Howitzer Artillery Brigade, which had been attached to the army, and the 302nd and 80th guards mortar divisions were located in the area Kalinin—Zelenovka—Solomki, awaiting the delivery of fuel.

By this time the commander of the 37th Army, along with a group of staff officers, had arrived at Ozery, where an auxiliary command post was organized. The army headquarters was located in Breusovka.

The 53rd Army was fighting along the line Suki—Romanyukhi—Pas'ki. Its neighbor to the left—the 7th Guards Army—which had begun to force the river on 25 September, had by the morning of 27 September seized a small bridgehead in the area of the village of Domotkan', as well as a number of islands in the Dnepr.[5]

By this time the remnants of two enemy infantry divisions were operating in the 37th Army's offensive sector. The combat groups of the German Eighth Army's 106th and 39th infantry divisions continued to fall back opposite the army's right flank. Covered by rear guards, these groups were crossing over the Dnepr in the area of the village of Koleberda and taking up defensive positions along the sector Kamenno-Pototskoe—Derievka, along a front of about 25 kilometers. These groups numbered about 4,500 soldiers and officers, up to 200 machine guns, and up to 160 guns and mortars. Upon crossing

---

5 The 127th and 128th engineer-sapper battalions and the 43rd Light Crossing Park.

all of these enemy elements, the following average tactical density might be created per kilometer of front: 0.2 battalions, up to eight machine guns and up to 6-7 guns and mortars.

Elements of an SS cavalry division continued to operate along the front from Derievka to Borodaevka.

The Organization of the Artillery Offensive While Forcing the Dnepr

As was shown earlier, the *front* commander, in committing the 37th Army into the battle, reinforced it with one gun artillery brigade, one heavy howitzer artillery brigade, one anti-tank artillery brigade (minus one regiment), one gun artillery regiment, two anti-tank artillery regiments, one mortar regiment, three guards mortar regiments, and three anti-aircraft artillery divisions.

The strength of the 37th Army's artillery as of 27 September is shown in Table 1.2.

From the table it is clear that in all the army had 1,204 guns and mortars. Such an amount of artillery, given a forcing sector with a width of 29 kilometers, enabled us to have a density of 41.5 guns and mortars per kilometer of front.

Due to the rapid arrival of the 37th Army's forces at the Dnepr and the shortage of fuel, a significant part of the artillery had fallen behind. For example, the 90th Heavy Howitzer Artillery Brigade and the 80th and 302nd guards mortar regiments were located 50-60 kilometers from the Dnepr by the beginning of the forcing.

The distribution of the artillery among the army's first-echelon divisions at the beginning of the forcing is shown in Table 1.3.

From the table it is clear that the corps' artillery and the army artillery group, which numbered about 655 guns and mortars, could take part in the forcing by the 57th Rifle Corps' main forces, which would create an average density per kilometer of front of about 23 guns and mortars. The forcing by the forward detachments could be supported by the artillery fire of two of the 57th Rifle Corps' first-echelon rifle divisions and the army artillery group.

The artillery's main tasks were: the destruction of the enemy's weapons and personnel in the most important strongpoints along the western bank of the river and the prevention of the enemy's counterattacks from the direction of Kutsevolovka and Mishurin Rog and the suppression of his artillery and mortar batteries. Besides this, following the seizure of a bridgehead, our artillery was to be in constant readiness to repel the enemy's infantry and tank counterattacks.

In accordance with the orders received and the presence of artillery, infantry-support groups were to be created in the first-echelon rifle regiments, consisting of three to five artillery battalions in the 57th Rifle Corps' first-echelon divisions by the time of the forcing. For example, in the 62nd Guards Rifle Division, which was operating along the axis of the corps' main attack, the 1st and 3rd battalions of the 131st Guards Artillery Regiment and the 1658th Anti-Tank Artillery Regiment comprised the 182nd Guards Rifle Regiment's infantry-support group, while that of the 184th Guards Rifle Regiment consisted of the 131st Guards Artillery Regiment's 2nd Artillery Battalion and the 417th Anti-Tank Artillery Regiment. At the same time, anti-tank artillery regiments were to be included as parts of the infantry-support groups only during the forcing of the Dnepr. A battalion of rocket artillery was at the disposal of the division commander. An army artillery group was created, consisting of the 27th Gun Artillery Brigade and the 381st Gun Artillery Regiment.

In order to support the forcing of the river by the forward detachments and the rifle divisions' first echelons and their fight for a bridgehead, a part of the army's first-echelon formations' artillery was positioned on open firing positions for waging fire over open sights. For this purpose, all of the rifle regiments' artillery, a part of the gun batteries from division artillery, and also part of the anti-tank artillery regiments' batteries were brought in. In all, by the beginning of the forcing, 54 guns had been positioned on open positions for firing over open sights. The firing positions for

Table 1.2 The 37th Army's Artillery Strength on 27 September 1943

Units and Formations	Mortars		Guns						M-13 and M-8 Launchers	Total Guns and Mortars*
	82mm	120mm	45mm	76mm	122mm	152mm	Anti-Aircraft			
Rifle Divisions' Artillery	536	147	288	234	74	–	–	–	991	
27th Gun Artillery Bde	–	–	–	–	16**	18	–	–	34	
90th Heavy Howitzer Bde	–	–	–	–	–	31***	–	–	31	
31st Anti-Tank Artillery Bde	–	–	–	28	–	–	–	–	28	
324th Anti-Tank Artillery Rgt	–	–	–	24	–	–	–	–	24	
417th Anti-Tank Artillery Rgt	–	–	–	24	–	–	–	–	24	
381st Gun Artillery Rgt	–	–	–	–	–	18	–	–	18	
1658th Anti-Tank Artillery Rgt	–	–	–	18	–	–	–	–	18	
562nd Mortar Rgt	–	36	–	–	–	–	–	–	36	
80th Guards Mortar Rgt	–	–	–	–	–	–	–	26	–	
302nd Guards Mortar Rgt	–	–	–	–	–	–	–	24	–	
315th Guards Mortar Rgt	–	–	–	–	–	–	–	22	–	
26th Anti-Aircraft Div	–	–	–	–	–	–	58	–	–	
11th Anti-Aircraft Div	–	–	–	–	–	–	62	–	–	
35th Anti-Aircraft Div	–	–	–	–	–	–	60	–	–	
Total	536	183	288	328	90	67	180	72	1,204	

* Not counting anti-aircraft artillery, 45mm guns and guard mortar platforms.
** 122mm guns.
*** 152mm howitzers.

these guns were chosen and outfitted by the very bank, based on the calculation that they could wage flanking and oblique fire. Each gun was assigned 1-2 previously reconnoitered targets. These guns were to take up their firing positions on 27 September, with the onset of darkness.

One battalion each of reinforcement artillery and two batteries each of division artillery were made part of the forward detachments to support their activities on the right bank of the Dnepr. Due to the fact that according to the army commander's decision, the forcing of the Dnepr was to be carried out at night and unexpectedly for the enemy, an artillery preparation preceding the forcing was not planned. However, the artillery was to be in readiness to immediately suppress the enemy's weapons in case he should open fire against our crossing forces.

Table 1.3 The Presence of Artillery and Mortars in the First-Echelon Rifle Divisions and in the Army Artillery Group by the Start of the Forcing

Units and Formations	Mortars 82mm	Mortars 120mm	Guns 76mm (regiment)	Guns 76mm (division)	Guns 122mm (1938)	122mm Guns	152mm Gun-Howitzers	Total Guns and Mortars*	M-13 and M-8 Launchers
89th Guards Rifle Div	—	10	9	16	2	—	—	63	—
1851st Anti-Tank Artillery Rgt	—	—	—	17	—	—	—	17	—
One bn of rocket artillery	—	—	—	—	—	—	—	—	6
Total	26	10	9	33	2	—	—	80	6
57th Rifle Corps:									
92nd Guards Rifle Div	85	24	12	24	12	—	—	157	—
324th Anti-Tank Artillery Rgt	—	—	—	24	—	—	—	24	—
One bn of rocket artillery	—	—	—	—	—	—	—	—	6
Total	85	24	12	48	12	—	—	181	6
62nd Guards Rifle Div	85	24	12	24	12	—	—	157	—
417th Anti-Tank Artillery Rgt	—	—	—	24	—	—	—	24	—
1658th Anti-Tank Artillery Rgt	—	—	—	8	—	—	—	8	—
One bn of rocket artillery	—	—	—	—	—	—	—	—	8
Total	85	24	12	56	12	—	—	189	8
10th Guards Rifle Div	78	20	11	24	9	—	—	142	—
1849th Anti-Tank Artillery Rgt	—	—	—	11	—	—	—	11	—
One bn of rocket artillery	—	—	—	—	—	—	—	—	5
Total	78	20	11	35	9	—	—	153	5
Army Artillery Group: 27th Gun Artillery Bde	—	—	—	—	—	16	18	34	—
381st Gun Artillery Rgt	—	—	—	—	—	—	18	18	—
Total	—	—	—	—	—	16	36	52	—
Grand Total	274	78	44	172	35	16	36	655	25

* Not counting anti-aircraft artillery, 45mm guns and guards mortar platforms.

It was planned to carry out the artillery support and accompaniment of the troops during the fighting for the bridgehead through the method of the consecutive concentration of fire.

The order of crossing the artillery to the Dnepr's right bank was established as follows. The battalion and regimental artillery and that of a company of 82mm mortars were to cross along with the rifle divisions' first-echelon regiments on organic equipment and means at hand. It was planned to cross the division 76mm guns and the regiments' anti-tank guns behind the infantry over ferries built from organic equipment, which were arriving from the *front*. It was planned to cross 122mm and 152mm guns over heavy crossing equipment, which were supposed to arrive during the forcing. All of the artillery and mortars were supposed to support the activities of the crossed-over units from firing positions along the left bank before the seizure of a bridgehead by the first echelon.

The battery commanders were to have forward observation posts along the right bank of the river, among the combat formations of the units and subunits being supported by them, for the reliable cooperation between the artillery and infantry.

The aviation offensive during the forcing of the Dnepr was planned on the *front* scale. Our aviation's main tasks came down to covering and supporting the troops while forcing the Dnepr and during the fighting for a bridgehead along the opposite bank. The air cover of the 37th Army's forces was entrusted to the 4th and 7th fighter corps, and their support to the 5th Air Army's 1st Assault Air Corps.

The enemy's air activity increased with the arrival of the Steppe Front's forces at the Dnepr. The German-Fascist command sought through strikes against our forces in their concentration areas and along the crossings, to prevent their forcing the Dnepr. In this situation, the anti-aircraft defense's main efforts came down to covering the troops in their concentration areas, during the crossings and along the captured bridgeheads. The covering of the troops by fighter aviation was planned by the *front* headquarters. The army had three anti-aircraft divisions (11th, 26th and 35th), for combating enemy aircraft, which numbered 180 anti-aircraft guns. The presence of anti-aircraft equipment and its simultaneous deployment in the army's sector (29 kilometers) enabled us to create a density of more than six guns per kilometer of front. In the areas of the villages of Soloshino and Perevolochnaya, where it was planned to cross the troops, the density of anti-aircraft equipment could be raised to 10-20 guns per kilometer of front. It was planned to carry out the crossing of anti-aircraft artillery to the right bank simultaneously with the first-echelon divisions' main forces. However, due to the absence of fuel, the anti-aircraft equipment did not arrive at the Dnepr in a timely manner. By the close of 27 September only a battery from the 987th and three batteries from the 276th artillery regiments (11th Anti-Aircraft Division), or a total of 16 guns, had arrived. The task of covering our forces from the sky during their forcing of the Dnepr was at first entrusted to them.

The remaining anti-aircraft equipment arrived at the forcing area during the period from 29 September through 2 October. The 35th Anti-Aircraft Artillery Division deployed in the area excluding Koleberga—Semenki—Grigoro-Brigadirovka; the 26th Anti-Aircraft Artillery Division deployed in the Soloshino area and to the south, and; the 11th Anti-Aircraft Artillery Division deployed in the Perevolochnaya area and to the west.

Engineer Support for the Forcing of the Dnepr

The successful fulfillment of the tasks for forcing the Dnepr and seizing a bridgehead by our forces depending chiefly on the presence of crossing equipment and their skillful employment during the forcing. By the time orders were received to commit the army into the fighting, the latter had almost no crossing equipment. It was stated above that there were only 16 small inflatable boats, five A-3 boats and ten diving suits in the army's divisions. This amount of crossing equipment could in no way satisfy even the minimal requirements of the forward detachments.

The capabilities of the crossing equipment attached to the army are shown in Table 1.4.

As is clear from the table, the crossing equipment being attached by the *front* were capable of crossing the 57th Rifle Corps' forward detachments in 2-3 trips and the 92nd and 62nd guards rifle divisions' main forces in a single day. However, at the moment the 37th Army's forces arrived at the Dnepr, the engineer-sapper units and subunits being attached by the *front* to the army, had not yet arrived. The 6th Independent Mechanized Pontoon-Bridge Battalion was in the Karlovka area; that is, more than 110 kilometers from the Dnepr. Meanwhile, the battalion's transport equipment was capable of simultaneously lifting up to 50 percent of the crossing equipment in the battalion.

The 19th Independent Mechanized Pontoon-Bridge Battalion was in the Komarovka area at a distance of about 45 kilometers from the Dnepr. The 43rd Army's UVSA-3 crossing park from the Supreme High Command Reserve's 8th Engineer-Sapper Brigade was at Belomost'ye station, 300 kilometers from the Dnepr.

The engineer-sapper units and subunits, which had been transferred from the 69th Army, could not be employed for supporting the forcing on 27 September. The 69th Army Engineer-Sapper Battalion had put all of its crossing equipment into laying a bridge over the Vorskla River in the Kustolovo-Kushchi area. The 328th Independent Engineer-Sapper Battalion had begun the completion of a permanent bridge over the Vorskla River in the same area.

The army's 112th and 116th engineer-sapper battalions were occupied repairing roads and restoring bridges destroyed by the enemy.

In this situation, a particular concern of the army commander, his headquarters and the headquarters of the of the engineer troops was the adoption of immediate measures for organizing the gathering of local crossing equipment and various materials at hand, as well as bringing up the 6th and 19th mechanized engineer-pontoon battalions.

Despite all exertions, we were not able to resolve this task during the course of 27 September. The available crossing equipment had either been driven off by the enemy, or destroyed. The shortage of transportation and fuel kept us from speeding up the arrival of the 19th and 6th mechanized pontoon-bridge battalions at the river. By the close of 27 September; that is, by the actual start of the forcing, only six pontoons from a bow half-pontoon park had arrived of the crossing equipment attached to the army. We managed to gather eight small fishing boats on the shore and build 20 small rafts from materials at hand. The remaining crossing equipment was on the move to the Dnepr and was stretched in depth to more than 200 kilometers.

The available crossing equipment could lift up to 300 men and six 76mm guns, with their limbers, or 12 guns without their limbers, at the same time. Given this overall lift capability of the crossing equipment, the forward detachments could be thrown over to the right bank, not taking into account possible losses, in 5-6 trips; that is, in 4-6 hours.

The army commander decided to employ all of the available crossing equipment for supporting the forcing of the river by the forward detachments. At the same time, he was taking all measures to maximally speed up the arrival of the crossing equipment at the Dnepr. The crossing equipment which was supposed to arrive at the forcing area was not to be distributed beforehand. It was planned to use them as they arrive, in accordance with the specific situation.

At the same time, one should note that the army's engineer troops' 112th and 116th engineer-sapper battalions were nonetheless not employed to build and prepare crossing equipment from local materials and those at hand. Almost to the completion of the crossing by the first-echelon divisions' main forces, they were employed repairing roads and restoring bridges on the left bank of the Dnepr, which reduced the army's capabilities for supporting the river's forcing.

The organic crossing equipment was distributed between the divisions in the following manner. The 92nd Guards Rifle Division, which was to force the Dnepr in the Semenki area, was allotted

258 THE BATTLE OF THE DNEPR

Table 1.4 Crossing Equipment with the 37th Army

Units and Types of Crossing Equipment	Number of Half-Pontoons	Launches	Assault Boats	A-3 Boats	Small Inflatable Boats	Bow Half-Pontoon Parks	UVSA-3
6th Independent Mechanized Pontoon-Bridge Battalion (a Captured "V" Type Park)	33	2	9	–	–	–	–
19th Independent Mechanized Pontoon-Bridge Battalion (2/3 of a bow half-pontoon park)	–	2	–	–	–	16	–
43rd Light Crossing Park (UVSA-3)	–	–	–	–	–	–	25
69th Army Engineer Battalion (UVSA-3)	–	–	–	–	–	–	16
With the divisions and the army's depot	–	–	–	5	16	–	–
Total	33	4	9	5	16	16	41

Units and Types of Crossing Equipment	Capabilities for Building Ferries or Laying Down Bridges				Ferry Capacity	
	Ferries			Length of 14-16 Ton Bridges (in meters)	Men	Regimental and Division Guns
	6-Ton	9-Ton	16-Ton			
6th Independent Mechanized Pontoon-Bridge Battalion (a Captured "V" Type Park)	–	8	–	102	480	8-12
19th Independent Mechanized Pontoon-Bridge Battalion (2/3 of a bow half-pontoon park)	–	–	–	110	–	10
43rd Light Crossing Park (UVSA-3)	10	5	4	80	300	10
69th Army Engineer Battalion (Army Military Construction Dirctorate-3)	6	4	2	50	180	6
With the divisions and the army's depot	–	–	–	–	164	5
Total	16	18	6	342	1,124	39-43

three bow half-pontoons. The 62nd Guards Rifle Division, which was to force the river in the Soloshino—Perevalochnaya area, was allotted three bow half-pontoons and five boats. It was ordered to use materials at hand in those divisions where they had been prepared.

In order to achieve a higher forcing pace, the army commander decided to employ the available crossing equipment in a centralized manner. As early as the second half of 28 September the control of all crossing equipment and the crossing of the troops were being carried out by the crossing staff, which was led by the deputy army commander. The chief of staff of the army's engineer troops was appointed his deputy. This staff included officers from the operational section, the headquarters of the engineer troops, the headquarters of the artillery, armored, and mechanized forces, and that of the rear services, representatives from the chief of the chemical service and messenger officers.

The crossing staff was entrusted with the following duties: controlling the crossing of the troops and materiel-technical equipment, controlling provost service and keeping track of the units crossing. It is necessary to note that the creation of a crossing staff was not expedient, because such a control organization for crossing the troops divorced the army and corps' headquarters and that of the chief of the engineer troops from their direct responsibilities.

The conduct of engineer reconnaissance and obstacle clearance on the right bank of the Dnepr was entrusted to the sapper platoons, which were part of the forward detachments.

The engineer support of the divisions' main forces on the right bank of the Dnepr was to be carried out by the forces of the rifle divisions' sapper battalions. These battalions were entrusted with carrying out engineer reconnaissance, laying down routes of march and roads along the western bank of the Dnepr, road repair, and the outfitting of command and observation posts. Mobile obstacle detachments, in strength from a platoon to a company, were allotted in each division, but in view of the army's shortage of anti-tank mines, they were used in a very restricted manner.

Thus, because of the untimely arrival of organic crossing equipment to the army from the *front*, the 37th Army's forces were placed in extremely unfavorable conditions. First of all, the crossing of the forward detachments over the Dnepr was drawn out over a long time. The army commander and his headquarters were deprived of the opportunity of planning and organizing the crossing of the main forces in the designated times.

The Organization of Control and Communications

Troop control was organized in accordance with the decision adopted by the army commander as early as 25 September. Subsequently, as they moved ahead and received new information about the situation, the divisions would receive additional instructions. On 27 September a combat order was issued, in which the formations' tasks were refined and detailed.

With the arrival of the first-echelon rifle divisions at the Dnepr, the 37th Army's command posts were located as follows: the command post was in Breusovka (28-30 miles from the Dnepr River, and a auxiliary command post in Soloshino (3-4 kilometers from the Dnepr River). The army commander and the chiefs of the combat arms and services, with a group of staff officers, were at the auxiliary command post. During the forcing the army's command post was shifted by 30 September to Ozery, and then to Soloshino.

The command posts of the formation commanders were located in the areas of Botsuly and Soloshino (1-2 kilometers from the Dnepr). The observation posts of the division commanders were located right along the left bank of the Dnepr. It was planned to shift the command posts to the bridgehead in the following sequence: the regimental commanders' command posts with the regiment's first echelon, the division commanders' command posts following the crossing of the division's first echelon, and the corps commander's command post following the crossing of the corps' first echelon. Officers from the divisions' and corps' headquarters, with communications and observation equipment, were to cross with the first echelons in order to organize control on the opposite bank. The army's command post was to remain on the left bank of the river, in Soloshino, during the forcing and fighting to expand and hold the bridgehead.

Wire communications with the corps was organized by axes. It was planned to augment the axis direction of the army's communications, which it was planned to lay down from Kustolovo—Kushchi, through Breusovka and Ozery as far as Soloshino, behind the attacking troops.

By the time of the first-echelon troops' arrival at the Dnepr, the army headquarters had wire communications with the rifle corps and with the first-echelon rifle divisions. A permanent communications line was brought forward as far as Soloshino. It was planned to lay down an army communications axis in the direction of Yasinovatka. A great deal of attention was devoted to the organization of reliable communications with the commandants of the crossings.

The army commander, who was in Soloshino, had reliable communications with the crossing staff (Dvornikovka) and the crossing points in Koleberda, Botsuly, marker 57 and Perevolochnaya. Wire communications across the Dnepr were being prepared. Upon the start of the forcing and the seizure of a bridgehead north of Kutsevolovka, wire communications were laid down over the island at marker 63.0. The span's length reached 350 meters.

Alongside this, wire communications were being laid down over the Dnepr River in the area of the island south of Soloshino. The laying down of wire communications began immediately, as soon as the forward detachments forced the river.

Radio communications was organized in order to support troop control, both during the forcing and during the fighting for the bridgehead. Great significance was attached to the organization of radio communications with the units and subunits forcing the river in the first echelon. Radio communications were organized from both the command and observation posts of the army and formations. A network was organized for the crossing staff, which included the radio set of the crossing chief of staff and of the crossing sector commandants.

On the whole, an organized communications system secured reliable troop control in the jumping-off position for the forcing, as well as during the forcing and the fighting for the bridgehead.

Political Support for the Operation

The army, while comprising the *front's* second echelon, was in motion almost the entire time and in readiness to be committed into the battle to resolve an important mission at the concluding stage of the *front* offensive operation. This made heightened demands on the organization and conduct of party-political work.

The liberation on 23 August of Khar'kov by the forces of the Steppe Front, of Krasnograd on 18 September, and Poltava on 23 September, inspired the soldiers, sergeants and officers to accomplish new feats for the greater glory of their beloved motherland and for overcoming any difficulties and obstacles.

The *Stavka* of the High Command's directive No. 30187 of 9 September 1943 played a great role in the success of forcing water obstacles and in raising the troops' combat spirit and offensive élan. The following was stated in this directive, which was addressed to the military councils of the *fronts and* armies:

> During the course of combat operations, the Red Army's forces will have to overcome many water obstacles. The rapid and decisive forcing of rivers, especially major ones, such as the Desna and Dnepr rivers, will have great significance for our troops' subsequent successes.

For this reason, the *Stavka* of the Supreme High Command believes it necessary to inform the commanders of the armies, corps, divisions, brigades, regiments, and engineer battalions that the commanders of the above-named formations and units will be recommended for the highest state decorations for the successful forcing of major river obstacles and the consolidation of a bridgehead for the subsequent development of the offensive.

This directive called forth an enormous uplift among the troops. Before departing for the jumping-off position for the forcing, brief meetings were held in the companies, during which the battalion commander, his deputy for political affairs and party organizers spoke. The text of the military oath was read out following these meetings.

The combat spirit of the army's troops was extremely high. Inspired by the brilliant victories over the forces of Hitlerite Germany, Soviet soldiers and officers strained to get into the fighting in order to carry out as quickly as possible the task laid down before the Soviet army by the Supreme High Command—to liberate our Soviet motherland from the Hitlerite aggressors.

The Operation's Materiel Support

With the 37th Army's arrival at the Dnepr, it experienced significant difficulties with the supply of ammunition and fuel for auto transport. Food supplies were also restricted.

In all, among the troops and in army depots there were the following: 0.3 combat loads of 82mm mortar rounds; 0.4 combat loads of 120mm mortar rounds; 0.5 combat loads of 45mm gun shells; 0.8 combat loads of 76mm gun shells; 0.6 combat loads of 122mm howitzer shells, and; there was only 0.1 combat loads of shells for 1909/30 152mm guns. There were no more than 0.2-0.3 refills of fuel for auto transport. There were rations for 1-3 days with the troops. There was no flour, groats, fats, or meat at all in the army depots.

The *front* command released the necessary amount of ammunition, fuel and food for the 37th Army, but their delivery was made more difficult by the great remove of the army's supply station, which had been deployed in Kovyagi, 170-180 kilometers from the division depots. The restoration of the railroads, as a result of their heavy destruction by the enemy, fell significantly behind the pace of the troops' advance.

By the start of the forcing of the Dnepr River, there were a total of 135 functioning motor vehicles in the army, which could be employed for delivering materiel supplies to the troops. Besides this, there were 168 functioning cars in the divisions.

In conditions of the army's low provisioning with all kinds of supplies, it was necessary to deliver no less than 500 tons of ammunition, up to 75 tons of fuel and lubricants and up to 50 tons of food daily; that is, in all, about 625 tons. The army's auto transport lift capability did not exceed 300 tons. Given the extension of the delivery routes up to 170-80 kilometers and the poor condition of the roads, the army's auto transport could deliver no more than 200 tons per day, or about 30 percent of the necessary freights.

In this situation, almost all of the troop auto transport was brought in for delivering all kinds of supplies from the army depots to the regimental ones, inclusively, by decision of the army commander. Besides this, a strictly prescribed order for delivering kinds of supplies and a prescribed order for supplying formations was established. First of all, ammunition was to be brought up and those formations were to be supplied which were operating in the army's first echelon and which were getting ready for the forcing. Fuels and lubricants were allotted particularly for the artillery units and formations and the auto transport busy with deliveries of crossing equipment and ammunition.

Nevertheless, despite the measures adopted, the difficult situation with the delivery and provisioning of ammunition and fuel was not fully eliminated. The troops had already reached the

Dnepr on 27 September and were supposed to begin the forcing, but by this time, as before, there was an extremely limited amount of ammunition and other kinds of supplies with the troops.

The low level of provisioning of the army's units and formations with ammunition and their poor delivery due to the great lagging of the rear establishments and the shortage of fuel for the auto transport put the troops in a very difficult situation in forcing the Dnepr and in the fighting for the bridgehead.

Reconnaissance and Refining the 37th Army Commander's Decision on Forcing the Dnepr

As was noted earlier, by the morning of 27 September the forward detachments reached the Dnepr, but they were unable to force the river because of the absence of crossing equipment.

Throughout 27 September the main efforts of the army commander, army headquarters and those of the unit and formation commanders were directed toward preparing the forcing. The bringing up of crossing equipment, the refining of data about the enemy and the reconnoitering of forcing sectors and crossing points acquired great significance.

The collection of data about the enemy and the preparation for the forcing of the Dnepr were begun as early as the pursuit of the enemy. On instructions of the army commander, the army headquarters and the headquarters of the engineer troops studied the forcing sector by maps and guidebooks, by questioning local residents, prisoners, and information from partisans. Aerial photography of the Dnepr and the adjacent area was carried out. Descriptions of the river were compiled on the basis of this work and sent out to the troops. New data about the enemy's group forces and the character of his defense on the right bank of the Dnepr was gathered during the pursuit. The forward detachments were supposed to carry out the reconnaissance of the opposite bank and the Dnepr and the enemy's defense. However, with the forward detachments' arrival at the Dnepr, they were forced to wait on the left bank, due to the absence of crossing equipment, and were unable to carry out their missions for refining data about the enemy's defense and the character of the river's right bank.

From the morning of 27 September the formation and unit commanders organized an engineer reconnaissance. The engineer reconnaissance was organized throughout the 37th Army's entire offensive sector. By the moment of refining the decision, reconnaissance had yielded initial data about the forcing sectors, crossing points, convenient approaches to the river, and jumping-off areas, etc. Engineer reconnaissance failed to provide necessary data about the right bank due to the absence of crossing equipment.

The reconnaissance of the enemy on 27 September was mostly carried out through observation and the questioning of prisoners and local residents. In order to get the fullest possible data about the enemy, a broad network of commanders' observation posts and engineer observation posts was organized.

Defining the depth of the river's old channel in the area of the island south of Soloshino was of particular importance. We received information from local residents that the river's old channel was not deep and could be forded.

During the second part of the day on 27 September the army commander carried out a reconnaissance, in which the artillery commander, the chief of the engineer troops and officers from the army's operational and intelligence sections took part, as well as the commander of the 57th Rifle Corps, the commander of the 62nd and the deputy commander of the 92nd guards rifle divisions. During the reconnaissance forcing sectors and places for crossings were refined, the decisions of the formation commanders were heard and confirmed, and the order of forcing the river was established. These questions were worked out with particular thoroughness in the 62nd Guards Rifle Division, which was designated for operations along the axis of the 57th Rifle Corps' main attack.

Following this reconnaissance, the army commander refined his decision on forcing the Dnepr.

The army commander decided to force the Dnepr on the night of 27-28 September along the Moldavan Island—Soloshino—Perevolochnaya sector, while launching his main attack in the general direction of Kutsevolovka and Popel'nastoye. As was shown above, it was planned to have the army's operational formation in two echelons: the 57th Rifle Corps and the 89th Guards Rifle Division in the first echelon and the 82nd Rifle Corps in the second. The choice of the forcing sector of Moldavan Island—Soloshino—Perevolochnaya was conditioned by the presence of islands south of Botsuly, southwest of Soloshino, as well as inhabited locales, ravines and bushes, which facilitated the hidden approach and concentration of the troops. The right and left banks along this sector were convenient for the organization of landing and ferry crossing points.

In accordance with this decision, the missions of the army's first-echelon divisions, which were assigned as early as 25 September, were refined.

The 89th Guards Rifle Division was to clear the enemy from the left bank and by the close of 28 September to reach the Dnepr along the Gaponovka—Koleberda sector, where it was to force it. The division was to be reinforced with two tank companies from the 43rd Tank Regiment, the 1851st Anti-Tank Artillery Regiment and one battalion of guards mortars.

The 57th Rifle Corps was to force the Dnepr on the night of 27-28 September and to seize a bridgehead along the front excluding Uspenskoye—Kutsevolovka—Mishurin Rog.

The corps' 92nd Guards Rifle Division was ordered to force the Dnepr along the sector excluding Uspenskoye—the island south of Botsuly and seize a bridgehead with a forward detachment along the line of the northern outskirts of Uspenskoye—the northern outskirts of Derievka; the corps' main forces were to force the river behind the forward detachment and occupy the line height 155.0—Derievka. The width of the forcing sector would reach 12 kilometers. The depth of the division's bridgehead was defined as being 3-5 kilometers. The division was to be reinforced with the 304th Anti-Tank Artillery Regiment and a battalion of guards mortars.

The 62nd Guards Rifle Division was given the assignement of forcing the Dnepr along the sector of the island southwest of Soloshino—Mishurin Rog and to occupy the line of the northeastern outskirts of Kutsevolovka—height 172.0 with its forward detachments. The division's main forces were to cross behind the forward detachments and take Kutsevolovka and height 177.0. The width of the forcing sector was 12 kilometers and the depth of the mission was five kilometers. The division was reinforced with the 417th and 1658th anti-tank artillery regiments, the 562nd Mortar Regiment and two battalions of guards mortars during the forcing.

Three places were planned for the landing crossing: the Botsuly area and over the island northeast of Derievka for the 92nd Guards Rifle Division, the Soloshino area and over the island southwest of Soloshino and in the Perevolochnaya area over the sandbank on the right bank of the Dnepr for the 62nd Guards Rifle Division. False crossing points were not organized due to the shortage of crossing equipment.

The army commander, proceeding from the developing situation, established the following order for the forcing. With the onset of darkness and by observing masking measures, the forward detachments and first-echelon divisions' regiments were to move into their jumping-off areas for the forcing. From 0400 to 0600 on 28 September the forward detachments were supposed to cross to the opposite bank and seize bridgeheads in their designated areas, after which the first-echelon regiments would begin their crossing, followed by the divisions' main forces and reinforcement units.

During the forcing period and the forward detachments' fighting along the opposite bank, artillery support was to be carried out by all the first-echelon rifle divisions' artillery and mortars. The artillery's readiness to open fire was set for 0200 on 28 September. At the same time, the artillery was to open fire only if summoned and only in case the enemy discovered our crossing.

The army commander ordered the formation commanders to carry out the covering of the crossing with smoke screens during the day. The army was also to occupy firing positions with the onset of darkness.

Thus the forced one-day halt by the 37th Army's forces opposite the Dnepr, due to the absence of crossing equipment, was employed by the command and troops for preparing a forcing. The army commander personally conducted a reconnaissance, refined his decision and the troops' tasks, defined the crossing points, and established the order of the crossing.

The Forcing of the Dnepr and the Seizure of Bridgeheads Along its Right Bank

The 37th Army's offensive operation continued from 24 September through 11 October 1943.

During 24-27 September the army's forces were committed into the battle, reached the Dnepr and carried out preparations for forcing the river.

On 28 September the forward detachments, having forced the Dnepr, seized bridgeheads along the opposite bank. The main forces of the first-echelon divisions' regiments were crossed over to the bridgeheads which had been seized by the forward detachments.

Throughout 29-30 September the army's forces threw the remnants of the enemy across the Dnepr. During this time the 57th Rifle Corps' main forces were crossing to the right bank of the Dnepr and during fierce fighting with the enemy linked up the isolated bridgeheads, which had been seized by the forward detachments on 28 September, into a single overall bridgehead of operational significance.

During 1-11 October the crossing of the army's second-echelon divisions to the bridgehead was completed, the growing enemy counterattacks were repulsed, and the captured bridgehead was somewhat widened and consolidated.

The Forcing of the Dnepr by the Forward Detachments on 28 September

With the onset of darkness on 27 September the 92nd and 62nd guards rifle divisions' forward detachments began their movement to the jumping-off line, and these divisions' main forces to their jumping-off areas for the forcing.

The 92nd Guards Rifle Division's forward detachment, which was to force the river in the direction of the island at marker 60.8, reached the water line in the area south of Botsuly. The 92nd Guards Rifle Division's right-flank regiment was still continuing to fight with the retreating enemy in the area east of Pavlovka. The division's main forces were moving to the jumping-off area in readiness to force the river behind the forward detachment.

The 62nd Guards Rifle Division's forward detachment (the 182nd Guards Rifle Regiment's 2nd Battalion) reached the river bank in the area southwest of marker 60.8. The 182nd Guards Rifle Regiment's main forces had concentrated in the area marker 60.8—excluding marker 59.0, in readiness to force the Dnepr for the purpose of developing the forward detachment's success. The 62nd Guards Rifle Division's second forward detachment (the 184th Guards Rifle Regiment's 3rd Battalion), which had the task of seizing a bridgehead in the area of marker 172.6, had concentrated in the area of marker 57.6, in readiness to force the river. The regiment's main forces occupied a jumping-off area directly behind the forward detachment.

In accordance with the army commander's decision, the forcing was to have begun at 0200 on 28 September, but by this time the reconnaissance, which had been sent out by the 62nd Guards Rifle Division to the river's right bank in the area south of the island with marker 63.0, had not yet returned and thus the deadline for the beginning of the forcing was shifted to 0400. Actually, the reconnaissance party became disoriented in the dark and went around the island, landed on its own bank and failed to carry out its assignment.

THE FORCING OF THE DNEPR BY THE 37TH ARMY

At 0400 on 28 September a landing by the 92nd Guards Rifle Division's forward detachment, having 50 men apiece on each of three bow half-pontoon pontoons, set out for the northern bank of the island with the marker 60.8. The enemy discovered the movement of the pontoons and opened artillery and mortar fire on the landing party. As a result of the enemy's artillery fire, two pontoons were sunk and the third was forced to return to its own bank. Subsequent attempts to force the Dnepr along this sector were not successful. The enemy's powerful artillery, mortar and machine gun fire prevented us from lowering other crossing equipment into the water. The 92nd Guards Rifle Division's artillery attempted to suppress the enemy's weapons, but without success. The crossing's surprise had been lost and the troops suffered unjustified losses. Thus the army commander ordered the commander of the 92nd Guards Rifle Division to temporarily halt the forcing.

Events developed differently in the 62nd Guards Rifle Division's sector. Here the enemy had on the right bank of the river only separate subunits from an SS cavalry division, which was defending along a broad front.

The landing by the 182nd Guards Rifle Regiment's 2nd Battalion, with 50 men apiece on three bow half-pontoon pontoons, set out for the northern bank of the island with the marker 63.0 at 0400. Simultaneously, a second landing by the 184th Guards Rifle Regiment's forward detachment on five A-3 boats (20 men in each boat) set out for the jetty north of the village of Mishurin Rog, which was nine kilometers downstream.

Both forward detachments' landings, which were not detected by the enemy, carried out a landing on the island with marker 63.0 and in the area of the jetty. However, because the enemy had combat security on the island, it immediately got into a fight with it. As a result of a brief fight, the enemy's detachment was destroyed and the island seized. The enemy managed to detect the forcing in the 62nd Guards Rifle Division's sector only after the landing by forward elements on the island and the right bank of the Dnepr in the area of the jetty.

The division's artillery opened fire in a timely manner against the enemy's artillery and mortar batteries and against his other positions, while supporting the subunits forcing the river.

The forcing of the river by the forward detachments' remaining subunits began behind the first landings. A part of the pontoons were shifted from oars to motors in order to speed up the movement. The forward detachments' rank and file displayed amazing resourcefulness and mass heroism, while crossing the river not only on pontoons and A-3 boats and fishing boats, but also on rafts, boards, logs, and fuel barrels, etc. By 0800 on 28 September the 62nd Guards Rifle Division's right-flank forward detachment (the 182nd Guards Rifle Regiment's 2nd Battalion) crossed the channel dividing the right bank from the island, completely crossed the Dnepr and seized a bridgehead two kilometers wide and up to a kilometer in depth. The 182nd Guards Rifle Regiment's 3rd Battalion crossed behind it without any kind of pause.

By 1300 the 182nd Guards Rifle Regiment's 2nd and 3rd battalions had crossed to the river's right bank and, having beaten off three enemy counterattacks, reached the line of the southeastern bank of Lake Liman—marker 72.0—the Koshikov ravine.

By 0800 on 28 September the 3rd Battalion's 7th Rifle Regiment (184th Guards Rifle Regiment) had crossed with five heavy machine guns and seized a small bridgehead on the western bank of the Dnepr River northeast of Mishurin Rog.

The soldiers and officers demonstrated models of heroic action during the forcing. Despite the enemy's artillery and mortar fire, while employing various materials at hand and by swimming across, the crossed to the right bank of the Dnepr and began fighting the enemy from the march.

By the middle of the day on 28 September elements of the 127th Engineer-Sapper Battalion began to arrive in the Perevolochnaya area with UVSA-3 park. Upon the arrival of the crossing equipment, six landing boats and one three-boat ferry were lowered into the water, which sped up the crossing of the infantry and the battalion and regimental artillery.

By 1300 the 184th Guards Rifle Regiment's 3rd Battalion had completed its forcing, had repelled an enemy infantry counterattack, in strength up to a company, from the northern outskirts of Mishurin Rog, and had expanded the captured bridgehead along the front and in depth.

The enemy, having by this time brought up his artillery and mortars to the forcing sector, had increased his fire against the crossed subunits and crossing points. As a result of the enemy's artillery and mortar fire, a significant part of the 182nd Guards Rifle Regiment's crossing equipment was put out of action, while all the A-3 boats in the 184th Guards Rifle Regiment were put out of action. The knocking out of a significant amount of crossing equipment seriously delayed the further crossing of the division's units. During 1300-1700 the 182nd Guards Rifle Regiment was unable to cross a man more in addition to the two battalions that had already crossed the river, while only two of the 2nd Battalion's companies from the 184th Guards Rifle Regiment crossed.

In view of the fact that the crossing points had been discovered by the enemy and were being subjected to heavy fire from his artillery and mortars, the army commander decided to carry out a maneuver with his crossing equipment. He ordered that the landing points be shifted to areas not under enemy observation and to continue the forcing. The previous crossing points were to remain as false ones. Demonstration activities were carried out unceasingly at the false crossings. Boats were lowered into the water and the noise of troop activities was imitated, etc.

After 1700, due to the arrival of crossing equipment, the forcing of the Dnepr in the 62nd Guards Rifle Division's sector was sped up. The crossed subunits of both of the 62nd Guards Rifle Division's regiments continued to expand the captured bridgeheads. By the close of 28 September the 182nd Guards Rifle Regiment's 2nd and 3rd battalions expanded the bridgehead as far as the village of Kutsevolovka and the bridgehead was now 4-6 kilometers deep and up to 5-6 kilometers wide. The 3rd Battalion and two companies from the 184th Guards Rifle Regiment's 2nd Battalion captured a bridgehead up to 1.5 kilometers deep and up to two kilometers in width. 16 guns from battalion and regimental artillery were crossed together with the 182nd and 184th guards rifle regiments' infantry.

It was only in the 92nd Guards Rifle Division's attack sector that we were unable to force the Dnepr on this day.

Throughout 28 September various crossing equipment arrived with the army. In all, on this day there arrived 21 half-pontoons of various types and 67 boats (A-3, small inflatable boats, and collapsible landing boats). However, the newly arrived crossing equipment was still insufficient for continuing the forcing at a higher rate of speed. A significant part of the equipment could only make up for the losses suffered during the forcing on this day.

One should note that while the forward detachments were forcing the Dnepr, local materials and those at hand, which were gathered directly along the bank, as well as light organic crossing equipment, which by this time had arrived with the army and had been brought up to the river, were primarily employed. Crossing materials at hand, due to their slowness and the difficulty of controlling them in the water (the river's rate of flow was 1-1.2 meters per second), also proved to be vulnerable to enemy fire and were quickly put out of action. Besides this, they were quickly carried away by the river's swift current, as a result of which the subunits were unable to land at their appointed places and were forced to spend time gathering in their assigned areas and suffered significant casualties from enemy fire.

The experience of forcing the Dnepr by forward detachments showed how important it was that the forward detachments be supplied in time with the necessary organic crossing equipment. Upon arriving at the Dnepr on the morning of 27 September, the 37th Army's forward detachments were forced to organize the gathering of local materials and those at hand along the bank and lost an entire day. It was only thanks to the fact that the enemy's defense along the western bank was occupied by the SS cavalry' division's insignificant forces, which were operating along a broad front, that the 62nd Guards Rifle Division's forward detachments were able to seize two small bridgeheads.

By the close of 28 September the 37th Army's situation was as follows.

The 89th Guards Rifle Division (82nd Rifle Corps), while overcoming the enemy's resistance, captured the village of Prishib and was fighting along the line Makhnovka—Mikhailenki.

The 92nd Guards Rifle Division's (57th Rifle Corps) right-flank regiment captured Pavlovka. The division's remaining forces were preparing to force the Dnepr.

The corps' 62nd Guards Rifle Division, while holding the captured bridgeheads in the area northeast of Kutsevolovka and northeast of Mishurin Rog, still had its main forces on the left bank of the Dnepr.

The 57th Rifle Corps' 110th Rifle Division was in the second echelon.

By 2400 the 82nd Rifle Corps' main forces (1st and 10th guards airborne and the 188th Rifle divisions) had concentrated in the Ulinovka—Shabel'niki—Khmarina area.

To the right, by the close of the day the 53rd Army's right-flank units were fighting for the crossings over the Psyol River and along its right flank had reached the eastern bank of the Dnepr with its main forces along the sector between the mouth of the Psyol River and the village of Drobetskovka.

To the left, the 7th Guards Army was fighting to expand the bridgehead captured by the morning of 27 September along the right bank of the Dnepr in the area of the villages of Borodaevka and Domotkan'. The commander of the 7th Guards Army made the decision to attack on the morning of 29 September, launching its main attack in the general direction of Borodaevskii Island and Odinets, with the task of defeating the opposing enemy and by the end of the day reaching the line Mikhailovka—Zapolichki—Odinets.

The enemy, while striving to prevent the forcing of the Dnepr, as well as to eliminate the bridgeheads seized by the forces of the 37th and 7th Guards armies, began to hurriedly bring up his men and materiel. Subunits from the *Grossdeutschland* Panzer Division were arriving in the Mlinok area and subunits from the 23rd Panzer Division to the area southeast of Mishurin Rog. Simultaneously, the enemy command was taking measures to hurry up the crossing of the remnants of the 106th and 39th infantry divisions (from the 89th Guards Rifle Division's sector) to the Dnepr's right bank in the Koleberda area.

By the close of 28 September the enemy directly opposite the 37th Army's front occupied the following position. The remnants of the 106th and 37th infantry divisions were completing their crossing to the western bank of the Dnepr and were hurriedly occupying defensive positions along the sector Chikalovka—Derievka. As before, units of the SS cavalry division were defending along the line excluding Derievka—Kutsevolovka—Mishurin Rog and then along the right bank of the Dnepr.

The Forcing of the Dnepr by the Army's First-Echelon Main Forces and the Unification of the Individual Bridgeheads into a Single Bridgehead (29-30 September)

The main efforts of the 37th Army's command and troops on 29-30 September were directed at expanding the captured bridgeheads and uniting them into one, as well as to repel the increasingly powerful enemy counterattacks. The main forces of the 57th Rifle Corps were employed to resolve these tasks. On the night of 28-29 September the 37th Army commander made the decision to commit the 57th Rifle Corps' second echelon—the 110th Guards Rifle Division—into the battle for the purpose of expanding the captured bridgehead. At the same time, the army commander planned to clear the left bank of the Dnepr of the remnants of the enemy in the Koleberda area and to force the Dnepr with the forces of the 89th and 92nd guards rifle divisions along the Uspenskoye—Derievka sector.

In accordance with the decision adopted, the following tasks were assigned to the army's forces.

The 89th Guards Rifle Division was ordered to defeat the enemy on the left bank of the Dnepr and to force it in the Konoplyanka—Koleberda area and to occupy the line Uspenskoye—height 140.3 by the close of the day.

The 57th Rifle Corps was to continue forcing the Dnepr along the Koleberda—Perevolochnaya sector and by the close of the day occupy the line "Pershe Travnya" Collective Farm—"Partisan" State Farm—height 151.0—Yasinovatka—Mishurin Rog.

The corps' 92nd Guards Rifle Division, together with the 324th Anti-Tank Artillery Regiment, was to force the Dnepr on the night of 28-29 September along the sector Moldavan Island—the island at marker 60.8 and by the close of the day occupy the line "Pershe Travnya" Collective Farm—"Partisan" State Farm—Derievka.

The 62nd Guards Rifle Division, together with the 417th and 1658th anti-tank artillery regiments, received orders to complete the crossing of the division's main forces by the morning of 29 September and, having gone over to the offensive, to occupy the line height 168.0—Mishurin Rog by the close of the day.

The 110th Guards Rifle Division (the corps' second echelon) received orders to cross the Dnepr along the sector marker 73.8—marker 57.1 and, while launching its main attack on Kutsevolovka and Ustimovka, to occupy the line height 158.4—Yasinovatka and to subsequently attack toward Ustimovka.

The 82nd Rifle Corps—the army's second echelon—was to concentrate to the Kolisniki—Brachkovka—Baranniki area by 0300 on 30 September, in readiness to cross over to the right bank of the Dnepr along the front Koleberda—Perevolochnaya.

In view of the absence of heavy crossing equipment, the 43rd Tank Regiment remained in the army commander's reserve and was to complete its concentration to the Grigoro-Brigadirovka area by the morning of 29 September.

The army commander decided to complete the crossing of all four divisions in the army's first echelon during the course of 29 September and to capture a bridgehead more than 30 kilometers along the front and up to ten kilometers in depth. According to the army commander's decision, the 89th Guards Rifle Division was to complete the elimination of the enemy group of forces along the left bank of the Dnepr during the day and to force the river north of Koleberda and seize a bridgehead up to six kilometers along the front and in depth. The 92nd Guards Rifle Division was to force the Dnepr, capture the major strongpoint of Derievka and to seize a bridgehead more than ten kilometers across and up to five kilometers deep. The 6nd and 110th guards rifle divisions received similar assignments.

Naturally, in this situation not one of the divisions, even given the maximum exertion of its forces, could carry out the task assigned to it.

During the second half of 29 September the army headquarters received an order from the commander of the Steppe Front, in which it was ordered: "To energetically develop the offensive along the right bank of the Dnepr River and by the close of 29 September occupy the line Uspenskoye—Mlinok—Malaya Kushkovka." This task was significantly deeper than the task assigned by the army commander.

In examining the *front* and army commanders' decisions, one should note that unrealistic tasks were assigned to the troops, without taking into account the specific situation as it had arisen. The army's forces, as was shown earlier, were experiencing a great shortage of crossing equipment. All of the army's available crossing equipment, in the best case, allowed for crossing only one division per day.

On the night of 28-29 and throughout the entire day, the army's forces sought to carry out the tasks assigned by the army and *front* commanders.

By the morning of 29 September the 89th Guards Rifle Division had eliminated the enemy remnants in the Stognoevka—Konoplyanka—Koleberda area and had arrived at the shore of the

Dnepr. Throughout the day the division's units were unable to set about forcing the river. They were preparing to cross and were carrying out reconnaissance. By the close of the day the crossing points in the areas of Konoplyanka and Koleberda had been defined and reconnoitered.

There were only three A-3 boats and four small inflatable boats of crossing equipment with the division. Besides this, before the beginning of the forcing the division's units found and delivered to the crossing points four fishing boats and prepared 18 rafts from local materials. All of the division's available crossing, even in the most favorable conditions, could lift no more than two platoons with weapons in one trip. Armed with this equipment, the division set about forcing the river at 2000.

The 89th Guards Rifle Division's forward detachment (a battalion from the 267th Guards Rifle Regiment) secretly reached the river's right bank and seized a bridgehead in the area of Lake Chervyakovo-Rechitse. By 2400 we managed to concentrate only two rifle companies on this bridgehead. The remaining subunits were located in their jumping-off positions in readiness to force the river.

The 92nd Guards Rifle Division, having resumed the forcing on the night of 28-29 September, was able to capture Moldavan Island with a battalion from the 280th Guards Rifle Regiment and cross to the river's right bank to the Limany area with two rifle companies from this regiment. One rifle company managed to seize the island at marker 60.8.

While forcing the Dnepr, the soldiers and officers of the 280th Guards Rifle Division exhibited resourcefulness, bravery and valor.

For example, the commander of the 1st Battalion, Guards Captain Zvezdin, noticed as early as the reconnoitering, four boats on the shore occupied by the enemy. As soon as darkness set, several soldiers, led by section commander Sergeant Goryachev, swam unnoticed to the opposite bank of the Dnepr, unexpectedly seized the four boats from the enemy and delivered them to their shore. The battalion, without losing time, set about crossing its subunits. When organic crossing equipment arrived at the battalion, it was necessary to outfit a jetty as quickly as possible on the opposite shore for the successful crossing of the artillery. The accomplishment of this task was entrusted to Senior Lieutenant Bogachev. When the enemy discovered that a small group of soldiers was working on the shore and launched a counterattack, Senior Lieutenant Bogachev, along with sappers Kostyakov, Sedov, Gavaziev, and Danil'chenko from his platoon, quickly occupied the firing line and repelled the enemy's counterattack with fire from their automatic rifles. In this manner the uninterrupted work of the ferries was assured.

During the night of 28-29 September the 62nd Guards Rifle Division continued to cross troops over to the right bank of the Dnepr. By the morning of 29 September all of the rifle regiments and a large part of the regimental artillery had been crossed. As before, due to the absence of crossing equipment, division and attached artillery remained on the right bank and continued to support the attacking troops from its previous firing positions.

However, from the morning of 29 September the division's units, having gone over to the offensive, were unable to carry out the task assigned by the army commander. While repelling the enemy's infantry and tank counterattacks from the area of the villages of Yasinovatka and Nezamozhnik, they continued to fight to broaden the captured bridgehead. By the close of the day the divisin's units occupied the following positions. The 182nd Guards Rifle Regiment was fighting for Kutsevolovka. The 186th Guards Rifle Regiment captured height 156.9. The 184th Guards Rifle Regiment reached the northern slopes of height 177.6, having captured the northern part of the village of Mishurin Rog.

It should be noted that on 29 September the sappers were working with particular intensity. For example, Senior Sergeant Shezhoev, of the 8th Engineer-Sapper Brigade, made 30 trips in the course of one day's work with his crew and crossed more than 650 men with their weapons. Sergeants Bekedin and Andrianov of this brigade made 36 trips in shifts in the course of the day and crossed more than 900 men and the 184th Guards Rifle Regiment's regimental artillery.

In light of the fact that all of the crossing equipment had been taken by units of the 62nd Guards Rifle Division, the 110th Guards Rifle Division (the corps' second echelon) began crossing the Dnepr only at 1700; that is, well behind schedule. By the close of the day the division had crossed to the bridgehead occupied by the 62nd Guards Rifle Division two battalions from the 310th Guards Rifle Regiment and all of the 313th Guards Rifle Regiment, which concentrated in the Koshikov ravine and along the northern outskirts of Mishurin Rog, along the 62nd Guards Rifle Division's right flank. The 307th Guards Rifle Regiment and the artillery remained on the left bank of the Dnepr in its jumping-off area.

The 82nd Rifle Corps was marching to the Kolisiniki—Brachkovka—Baranniki area and was preparing to cross the Dnepr River.

Throughout 29 September we manged to cross a total of 58 guns from regimental and battalion artillery to the bridgehead.

Despite significant losses, the amount of crossing equipment with the army's troops increased somewhat through the arrival of 25 bow half-pontoons and 35 various boats.

Upstream, during 29 September the 53rd Army captured the city of Kremenchug and its right-flank formations reached the eastern bank of the Dnepr. The army's left-flank units captured Kryachok Island and the island at marker 65.7 and 60.9. Downstream, during 29 September the 7th Guards Army widened its bridgehead to up to 20 kilometers along the front and up to eight kilometers in depth.

There were no particular changes in the enemy's group of forces on this day. Remnants of the 106th and 39th infantry divisions were defending along the Uspenskoye—Derievka sector. The same elements of the SS cavalry division were defending along the Kutsevolovka—Mishurin Rog sector. Units of the 23rd Panzer Division were operating in the Mishurin Rog area, while elements of the *Grossdeutschland* Panzer Division continued to move from the Mlinok—Lozovatka area to the area north of Likhovka. Elements of the *Totenkopf* Panzer Division were concentrating toward the Derievka area. In concentrating his reserves north of Likhovka and in the southeastern part of Mishurin Rog, the enemy intended not only to prevent the unification of the 37th and 7th Guards armies' bridgeheads, but to eliminate the bridgeheads seized by our forces.

On the basis of instructions by the *front* commander on 29 September, the army commander demanded that during 30 September the troops carry out their previous tasks and simultaneously take measures to speed up the crossing of men and equipment to the bridgehead. Alongside this, the army commander, taking into account the real threat of an enemy counterblow, ordered his formation commanders to immediately set about consolidating the lines seized, placing especial attention on the organization of anti-tank defense on the bridgehead. The division commanders were ordered to deploy in positions one anti-tank artillery regiment each along the likely Uspenskoye—Kutsevolovka, Yasinovatka—Kutsevolovka and Likhovka—Mishurin Rog axes of attack and to also prepare screening fire along the approaches to Kutsevolovka. It was ordered to create anti-tank reserves in the divisions and regiments to repel the enemy's tank counterattacks, as well as mobile obstacle detachments with a supply of anti-tank and anti-personnel mines.

Alongside measures for organizing an anti-tank defense on the bridgehead, the army commander demanded the speeding up of the crossing of division and anti-tank artillery to the right bank of the Dnepr. On instructions of the army commander, an army artillery group was moving to firing positions closer to the Dnepr, in the Soloshino area.

In the developing situation it was becoming obvious that on 30 September there would be a difficult and stubborn fight to widen and hold the captured bridgeheads. The success of this struggle depended, first of all, on the pace of the troops' crossing and the creation of the necessary superiority of men and materiel over the enemy on the opposite bank. However, the pace of the crossing on 29 September was still low. The arriving crossing equipment was unable to support the rapid crossing of the army's forces to the captured bridgehead to create a decisive superiority over the enemy.

On the night of 29-30 September and all of the next day events in the 37th Army's offensive sector developed in the following manner.

By the morning of 30 September the 89th Guards Rifle Division had crossed the main forces of its rifle regiments to the right bank of the Dnepr. The crossing was halted at dawn, in view of the enemy's powerful artillery fire bombing strikes. As a result of this, division artillery was not crossed and was forced to support the attack by the division's units from the left bank. During the day the division's units, having successfully repelled the enemy's counterattacks, advanced 500-1,000 meters and reached the line with markers 84.4 and 63.4

The following were crossed in the 92nd Guards Rifle Division by the morning of 30 September: the 276th Guards Rifle Regiment in the Koleberda area (the 89th Guards Rifle Division's bridgehead), and the 282nd Guards Rifle Regiment in the area east of Derievka (the 62nd Guards Rifle Division's bridgehead), with regimental and battalion artillery. At dawn both regiments attacked. The 276th Guards Rifle Regiment encountered powerful enemy resistance from the area of the "Pershne Travnya" Collective Farm and, having repelled a counterattack by up to a battalion of infantry, supported by tanks, advanced a total of 500 meters. The 282nd Guards Rifle Regiment reached the northeastern outskirts of Derievka, where it encountered the enemy's powerful resistance and could advance no further. The entirety of the 280th Guards Rifle Regiment concentrated in the center of the division's front on Moldavan Island. Due to the shortage of crossing equipment, division and attached artillery remained on the left bank.

By the morning of 30 September the 62nd Guards Rifle Division had completed the crossing of all of its forces to the western bank of the Dnepr, except for division artillery. Fierce fighting unfolded at dawn along this division's bridgehead.

The enemy, having brought up units of the 23rd Panzer Division, was seeking to eliminate the bridgehead seized by the division's units. From 0500 to 0600 up to a battalion of enemy infantry, supported by 20 tanks, twice counterattacked the division's units from the Nezamozhnik area, but all of the counterattacks were beaten off by artillery and machine gun fire. At 1100 the enemy once again counterattacked with units of the 23rd Panzer Division from the Kaluzhino area in the direction of Mishurin Rog. As a result of the counterattack, the enemy managed to break through, with the forces of 15 tanks and 11 armored transports with infantry, to the area of height 127.5. The enemy was thrown out of the area of height 127.5 by a decisive attack by the division's units and subunits. In all, the enemy undertook eight powerful counterattacks with the forces of the 23rd Panzer Division's forces during 30 September.

The situation in the 62nd Guards Rifle Division's sector continued to be intense. The division's broad front (about 15 kilometers), the insufficient amount of anti-tank artillery in the combat formations and the significant losses prevented us from creating a solid anti-tank defense and supporting the retention of the positions occupied. As a result of the continuing enemy counterattacks, the division's units along individual sectors were forced to fall back and by the close of the day were fighting along the line marker 72.0—marker 70.4—height 177.3—excluding marker 58.5.

The 110th Guards Rifle Division (without division artillery) was crossed to the 62nd Guards Rifle Division's bridgehead during the first half of the day on 30 September. However, in view of the fact that it was committed into the fighting piecemeal and along different axes and without the necessary artillery support, its commitment did not have a serious effect on changing the situation on the bridgehead. Two of the division's regiments reached Lake Liman and got into a fight with the enemy in Derievka and to the east. On orders from the army commander, the 313th Guards Rifle Regiment was moved up to the area of the northeastern outskirts of Mishurin Rog to secure the army's flank.

Despite the complex situation, on 30 September; that is, by the close of the third day of the forcing, the crossing of the army's first-echelon rifle units, along with their organic artillery, had essentially been accomplished. The crossed units, in spite of the shortage of ammunition and anti-tank artillery in the combat formations, repelled a series of fierce enemy counterattacks and held the bridgeheads seized earlier. In the 89th and 92nd and along the left flank of the 62nd guards rifle divisions the bridgeheads had even been broadened somewhat.

It is necessary to note that the accumulation of forces on the bridgehead was being accomplished too slowly, because of the shortage of crossing equipment, the weak anti-aircraft defense and insufficiently strong troop control. The crossing of the rifle division's main forces, which had begun on 28 September, was completed only on 30 September. The troops' crossing was mainly conducted at night, because during the daytime the enemy's aircraft launched bombing strikes against the crossing troops and put the crossing equipment out of action.

Due to the late approach of the engineer equipment, which had been attached to the army by the *front*, a significant part of the rifle divisions' reinforcement artillery remained uncrossed and continued to support the crossed units from their firing positions along the Dnepr's left bank.

It should be emphasized in particular that the ammunition situation among the troops (both on 29 and 30 September) was extremely tight. On 30 September there were only 0.3-0.8 of a combat load for mortar rounds, 0.2-0.3 regimental artillery shells and no more than 0.5-0.8 shells for division artillery.

These circumstances were the chief reasons for the troops failing to carry out their assigned tasks on 29 and 30 September.

The course of combat operations on 30 September confirmed with complete clarity that the troops' tasks, which had been assigned by the army commander on 30 September, were just as unrealistic as those assigned on 29 September. The slow pace of the crossing in conditions of the enemy's increasing infantry and tank counterattacks, forced the formation commanders to commit the crossing troops into the fighting piecemeal, without the proper training and without proper artillery support. Aviation support was also insufficient. On 30 September the 5th Air Army carried out only 206 sorties throughout the *front's* entire combat sector. The crossing units entered the fighting against the counterattacking enemy from the march and, at best, were able to unite the previously seized bridgeheads in the Kutsevolovka—Mishurin Rog area and to hold them.

The absence of firm troop control on the part of the formation commanders, who on 30 September continued to remain on the left bank, had a negative effect on the fighting along the right bank of the Dnepr.

By the close of 30 September, as a result of three days of fighting, the bridgehead in the 62nd Guards Rifle Division's sector had been expanded to 15 kilometers in width and up to 5-6 kilometers in depth. In the 89th and 92nd guards rifle divisions' offensive sector the bridgehead in the area of the village of Uspenskoye did not exceed 5-6 kilometers in breadth and 3-4 kilometers in depth.

In the developing situation it was necessary to take all measures in order to speed up the crossing of the artillery and tanks to the bridgehead and to expand the captured bridgehead to such an extent that would secure the crossings against enemy artillery fire and the deployment of a group of forces significantly larger than the enemy's.

The delay in crossing the troops, and particularly of the artillery and tanks, enabled the enemy to securely consolidate and, upon bringing up his reserves, to launch a counterblow for the purpose of defeating the army's forces on the right bank of the river and eliminating the captured bridgehead.

The *front* commander, having correctly evaluated the situation, demanded from the commander of the 37th Army that he maximally speed up the pace of the troops' crossing to the bridgehead and that he carry out the previously assigned tasks. On 30 September the 1st Mechanized Corps (19th, 36th and 37th mechanized and 19th Tank brigades, the 32nd Independent Armored

Battalion, and the 67th Motorcycle Regiment), which was concentrated in the Motrino—Grigoro-Brigadirovka—Ozery area, was subordinated to the commander of the 37th Army. However, the corps contained only 36 tanks, including six light ones.

The Crossing of the Army's Second-Echelon Divisions to the Bridgehead and the Fighting to Expand the Consolidate the Bridgehead (1-11 October)

By 1 October the 37th Army's forces still continued to experience a great shortage of crossing equipment, particularly heavy equipment, upon which we could cross tanks and artillery. In conditions in which the enemy was striving to consolidate as quickly as possible on the right bank of the Dnepr and to throw the army's forces from the bridgehead through counterattacks by panzer divisions brought up from other sectors of the front, the timely crossing of tanks and artillery acquired particular importance. A change in the correlation of forces in favor of the enemy could only lead to a sharp worsening of the situation and an extended struggle on the bridgehead.

As early as the close of 30 September the enemy opposite the 37th Army disposed of the remnants of the 106th and 39th infantry divisions, which had been organized into combat groups, elements of the SS cavalry division, the 23rd Panzer Division, and part of the *Totenkopf* Panzer Division's forces, while the *Grossdeutschland* Panzer Division was completing its concentration toward the area southeast of Mishurin Rog. The enemy had 100-130 tanks here and 130 guns (without mortars). By this time the 37th Army's forces, which were operating along the right bank of the Dnepr along the Kutsevolovka—Mishurin Rog sector, had 21 rifle battalions, 199 guns of various types and only nine tanks.

The enemy's absolute superiority in tanks gave him great advantages in fighting the army's forces on the bridgehead. If one also takes into account the fact that the enemy occupied a number of commanding heights (155.7, 191.6 and 165.8) and the major inhabited locales of Derievka, Kutsevolovka and the southeastern part of Mishurin Rog, then it will become all the more obvious that the 37th Army's forces would be forced to wage stubborn and intensive fighting in order to carry out the tasks previously assigned to them.

The army's situation was still further complicated by the fact that, as before, there was a serious shortage of ammunition. By 1 October the troops disposed of, on the average, 0.3-0.6 combat loads of mortar rounds and 0.9-1.1 combat loads of shells for regimental and division artillery and 0.1 combat load for High Command Reserve Artillery. Naturally, such an amount of ammunition could not support the needs of the troops, who were faced with resolving the task of expanding the bridgehead in a complex and intense situation.

By the close of 30 September there were 41 bow half-pontoon, 12 "V" half-pontoons, 40 collapsible wooden boats, 39 wooden boats, and 45 inflatable A-3 boats. This equipment, taking into account possible losses, enabled us to cross about 700 men with their weapons, ten division artillery guns with their tractors, and no more than four tanks to the bridgehead in a single trip. Given conditions of this equipment's continuous work, up to a single rifle division could be crossed in the space of a single day. However, even with the arrival of the 19th Independent Mechanized Pontoon Battalion for assembling ferries capable of freights of 12, 16 and 30 tons, there were not enough pontoons. Also, the slow speed of the ferries across the Dnepr often enabled the enemy's aviation and artillery to put them out of action. There were only four tugs, which could in no way satisfy our needs.

Taking into account the developing situation, by the close of 30 September the army commander made the decision to commit into the fighting the army's second echelon—the 82nd Rifle Corps, which was concentrated in the Baranniki—Prosyanikovka—Brachkovka area.

In his decision, the army commander also called for the seizure of the Derievka strongpoint and the elimination of the enemy there, the unification of the bridgeheads into a single one and its expansion as far as the line "Pershe Travnya" Collective Farm—Petrovka—Ploskoye. The forces of the 57th Rifle Corps were to carry out these tasks, along with the formations of the 82nd Guards Rifle Corps (10th and 1st airborne and 188th Rifle divisions), which were being committed into the battle. There was no crossing equipment in the 82nd Corps and thus it supposed to cross on the 57th Rifle Corps' crossing equipment.

In accordance with the decision taken, the army's forces were assigned the following objectives. The 89th Guards Rifle Division was to capture Uspenskoye. The 92nd and 110th guards rifle divisions received orders to capture Derievka and reach the line "Pershe Travnya" Collective Farm—Petrovka—Ploskoye. The 62nd Guards Rifle Division had the task of destroying the enemy who had broken through in the Mishurin Rog area and to expand the bridgehead as far as the line Ustimovka—Mikhailovka. The 82nd Corps' 10th Guards Airborne Division was supposed to cross the Dnepr and concentrate in the area southeast of the village of Mishurin Rog and the village of Kaluzhino.

The 43rd Tank Regiment received orders to cross to the right bank of the Dnepr on the night of 30 September-1 October and to operate with the 110th Guards Rifle Division to expand the bridgehead.

Thus one may consider timely and appropriate to the developing situation the army commander's decision to continue the troops' crossing to the right bank of the Dnepr along the entire front from Uspenskoye to Mishurin Rog, the capture of Derievka and the linking up of two bridgeheads into one. It's quite clear that the continuation of the crossing by the army's forces along a broad front and their active operations on the bridgehead would tie down significant enemy forces and would thus prevent him from concentrating reserves along a narrow sector of the front for launching a powerful counterblow.

On 1 October the army's first-echelon forces were engaged in heavy fighting along the western bank of the river, while striving to expand and unite the captured bridgeheads.

On the morning of 1 October the 89th Guards Rifle Division attacked toward Uspenskoye. Upon encountering the enemy's stubborn resistance, the division's units were unable to advance and were forced to repel enemy counterattacks along their previous line. The crossing of artillery to the Dnepr's western bank continuing all day in the division.

On the morning of 1 October the 57th Rifle Corps' formations repelled fierce enemy counterattacks and, upon attacking, were only able to expand slightly the captured bridgehead during the second half of the day.

Throughout the day the 92nd Guards Rifle Division attacked the enemy, who was defending in the Derievka strongpoint, several times, but encountering the enemy's stubborn resistance, was unable to capture it and by the close of the day was holding its former line.

It was only by the morning of 1 October that the 110th Guards Rifle Division fully completed its crossing to the western bank, and two of its regiments were fighting for the southern part of Derievka and Kutsevolovka. By the close of the day the division captured the southeastern part of Derievka, height 167.8 and Kutsevolovka.

On 1 October the 62nd Guards Rifle Division completed crossing all of its division and anti-tank artillery. Throughout the day, the division's units, having repelled six enemy counterattacks, were fighting along the line height 156.9—height 122.7—the southwestern part of Mishurin Rog.

On 1 October the enemy reinforced his group of forces in the area of the village of Mishurin Rog with units from the 62nd Infantry Division, which had been transferred from the Dnepropetrovsk area. The enemy forces along the entire front were putting up stubborn resistance to the 62nd Guards Rifle Division's units. Throughout the entire day, the enemy air force, operating in single planes and groups, launched strikes against the crossings over the river and our troops' combat formations.

THE FORCING OF THE DNEPR BY THE 37TH ARMY

The 43rd Tank Regiment began crossing at 2130 on 30 September on three 30-ton ferries. However, by the morning of 1 October we had managed to cross only nine T-34[6] tanks, which after crossing to the right bank immediately entered the fighting in support of the 110th Guards Rifle Division's units. In view of the losses suffered in crossing equipment, the crossing of the tank regiment became extended. Given the presence of the single, remaining 30-ton ferry, we were unable to completely cross the tank regiment on 1 October without towing equipment.

The 10th Guards Airborne Division's 30th Guards Regiment, in conjunction with the 110th Guards Rifle Division's 313th Guards Rifle Regiment, cleared the enemy out of Mishurin Rog and reached the southern outskirts of this inhabited locale.

Meanwhile, due to the absence of crossing equipment, by the close of 1 October the 82nd Rifle Corps (minus the 30th Guards Airborne Regiment) was in its previous concentration area, in readiness to cross. Throughout 1 October, despite efforts by the troops and the army command, the troops were nevertheless unable to decisively change the situation on the bridgehead in their favor. The fighting across the Dnepr was taking on an increasingly intense and prolonged form.

To the right of the 37th Army, on the night of 30 September-1 October the 53rd Army forced the Dnepr with units from two rifle divisions, seized a small bridgehead in the area southeast of Chikalovka and throughout the day was engaged in fighting for this inhabited locale. To the left, the 7th Guards Army, while repelling counterattacks by a significant group of tank forces (more than 100 tanks) throughout the day , fell back to the line Pogrebnaya—Odinets in its 25th Rifle Corps' sector.

The 5th Air Army supported the ground forces throughout the day and carried out 213 sorties.

Thus the tasks of expanding the bridgehead to a depth of up to 20 kilometers, and 30-35 kilometers along the front, proved to be too much for our troops. Not one of the army's divisions was able to in any way significantly advance and expand the captured bridgehead. The enemy was putting up stubborn resistance to the army's forces and was continuously counterattacking with the forces of the *Totenkopf, Grossdeutschland* and 23rd panzer divisions, supported by bomber aviation. The enemy still had superiority in tanks and aircraft. Also, the shortage of ammunition among the army's forces prevented us from carrying out a powerful artillery preparation for the purpose of suppressing the enemy's personnel and weapons. Thus as soon as the army's forces attacked they would be met with powerful fire from all of the enemy's weapons and suffered significant losses.

The situation was further complicated by the fact that the neighboring armies were repelling heavy enemy counterattacks and were unable to offer tangible assistance to the 37th Army. Finally, the shortage of crossing equipment prevented the army command from rapidly concentrating its second echelon on the bridgehead and to speed up the crossing of the artillery and tanks and to then launch an attack, in conjunction with the neighboring armies, for the purpose of defeating the enemy and carrying out the assigned tasks.

At 1040 on 2 October the army's first-echelon formations resumed the offensive for the purpose of carrying out their previous tasks. While overcoming the enemy's powerful resistance and repelling his continuous counterattacks, the troops were only able to advance to a depth of no more than two kilometers along individual axes.

The 89th Guards Rifle Division, having encountered the enemy's powerful resistance, continued fighting for Uspenskoye.

The 57th Rifle Corps' divisions, while overcoming the enemy's powerful resistance, had advanced up to two kilometers by the end of the day along individual axes. The corps' 92nd Guards Rifle

---

6 Editor's note. The T-34 was the Red Army's outstanding medium tank during the Great Patriotic War and beyond. One model weighed 26.5 tons, carried a crew of four and was armed with a 76.2mm gun and two 7.62mm machine guns. A later model carried a crew of five and was armed with an 85mm gun.

Division, having repelled three enemy counterattacks, was fighting by the end of the day along the eastern outskirts of Derievka, with its front facing west.

The 110th Guards Rifle Division, along with the 43rd Tank Regiment, which had finished crossing only by 1400 on 2 October, repelled two powerful enemy counterattacks and, having advanced up to one kilometer, captured the line of heights 179.9—192.7.

The 62nd Guards Rifle Division captured the village of Nezamozhnik.

Two of the 10th Guards Airborne Division's regiments (10th and 30th) cleared Mishurin Rog of enemy groups that had penetrated along the boundary with the 7th Guards Army, capturing height 122.2 and the village of Kaluzhino. The 82nd Rifle Corps' main forces continued to be located along the eastern bank of the Dnepr, in expectation of crossing equipment.

On this day the 53rd Army was fighting along its previous line. The 7th Guards Army repelled enemy infantry and tank counterattacks throughout the day. By the close of the day up to 40 enemy tanks, along with assault guns and infantry, penetrated into the army's defense and captured Borodaevka (western). The enemy's seizure of Borodaevka made the 37th Army's situation even more complex.

The intensive fighting during 29 September-2 October showed that the enemy was striving to hold at any cost the strongpoints of Uspenskoye and Derievka, which directly abutted the Dnepr and divided the 37th Army's forces into two isolated groups of forces. Simultaneously, through counterattacks by tank units along the flanks, the enemy was seeking to prevent the expansion of the captured bridgeheads. The enemy was seeking to interfere by air strikes against our crossings and troops with their further crossing to the bridgehead. Finally, the German-Fascist command was striving to throw our forces off the bridgeheads into the Dnepr. The enemy was also applying all his efforts in the neighboring armies' sectors to split up their forces and destroy them in detail.

In the developing situation, coordinated and decisive actions by all the armies that were forcing the river were necessary, particularly from the 37th and 7th Guards armies, against which the enemy was concentrating his main efforts.

Taking into account the necessity of eliminating the crisis on the 7th Guards Army's right flank, the commander of the Steppe Front did not confirm the 37th Army commander's decision for 3 October, which called for the concentration of the army's main efforts along its right flank for the purpose of unifying the 57th Rifle Corps' and 89th Guards Rifle Division's bridgeheads and the arrival of the army's forces at the line "Pershe Travnya" Collective Farm—the "Partisan" State Farm—Yasinovatka—Nezamozhnik.

At 0500 on 3 October the *front* commander assigned the 37th Army the following task. Part of the army's forces along its right flank was to temporarily take up the defensive. The army's main forces (no less than three divisions), along with all of the 1st Mechanized Corps' and 43rd Tank Regiment's crossed tanks, were to be concentrated along the left flank and were to attack in the direction of Annovka and height 177.0 and, together with the 7th Guards Army, defeat and destroy the enemy's group of forces in the Annovka—Borodaevka—height 177.0 area.

The 5th Air Army was given the task of supporting the 37th and 7th Guards armies with bomber and assault air attacks against the enemy in the Annovka—Borodaevka—height 177.0 area to destroy the enemy here.

In carrying out the *front* commander's order, the commander of the 37th Army decided, without halting combat operations throughout the army's entire sector, to launch his main attack in the direction of Annovka and height 177.0 for the purpose of linking up with the 7th Guards Army's main forces and to attack with the forces of the 62nd Guards Rifle Division toward Likhovka.

Proceeding from this decision, the troops were assigned the following tasks. The 10th Guards Airborne Division, together with the 43rd Tank Regiment, was to attack in the direction of

Kaluzhino, Annovka and height 177.0. The 62nd Guards Rifle Division received orders to launch an attack in the direction of Vasil'yevka farm and Likhovka. The attack was set for 1000 on 3 October.

By 3 October the situation along the 37th Army's left flank had changed sharply. The enemy had reinforced his group of forces in the area south of Mishurin Rog with units from the 6th Panzer Division, which had been transferred from the Novo-Georgievsk area. Having carried out up to ten counterattacks, he put up stubborn resistance to the 37th Army's forces. Units of the 10th Guards Airborne and 62nd Guards Rifle divisions were unable to carry out their assignment on this day. The 10th Guards Airborne Division, which had been reinforced with the 1st Mechanized Corps' 219th Tank Brigade, was able to advance 1-3 kilometers in day's heavy fighting and had begun fighting for Annovka. There were no significant changes along the army's right flank and in the center. The 89th Guards Rifle Division was fighting along the previous line following an unsuccessful attack in the direction of Uspenskoye.

Units of the 57th Rifle Corps, having renewed the offensive, advanced only 500-700 meters along individual axes. By the close of the day the corps' forces were fighting along the line of the northeastern outskirts of Derievka—Derievka—height 179.9—height 192.76—height 158.4—height 177.3—Nezamozhnik.

Throughout 3 October the 82nd Rifle Corps continued its crossing over the Dnepr.

The 1st Mechanized Corps, on instructions from the army commander, set about crossing to the bridgehead and began to concentrate in the Mishurin Rog—Kaluzhino area.

As before, the 53rd Army was occupying a very limited bridgehead in the Chikalovka area and continued to cross its forces over the Dnepr to the bridgehead. The 7th Guards Army was engaged in heavy fighting with large enemy tank and infantry forces throughout the day along its right flank. Particularly bitter fighting unfolded on 3 October in the area of Borodaevka (western) and Tarasovka, where more than 70 enemy tanks had broken through. Units of the 7th Guards army's 213th and 15th guards rifle divisions, which had been cut off from the army's main forces, operated jointly with the 37th Army's left-flank formations in the subsequent fighting.

The attack carried out on 3 October with the forces of two divisions along the Annovka and height 177.0 and Nezamozhnik axes showed that given the enemy's significant superiority in tanks and, the forces allotted were obviously insufficient. At the same time, the attack by the 62nd Guard Rifle Division, which had been weakened in the previous fighting, in the direction of Likhovka, as called for by the army commander's decision, led only to the undesirable dispersion of the army's force. It would have been more expedient to also direct its efforts in the direction of Annovka and height 177.0. It was necessary to entrust the support of the shock group's left flank against Likhovka to the 57th Rifle Corps.

Besides this, there were serious shortcomings in troop control. The unit and formation commanders' observation posts were located at a great distance from the troops. This led to a situation in which they were unable to observe the battlefield and react in a timely manner to all changes in the situation.

The absence of a well organized system of observation prevented us from discovering in time the enemy's weapons. As a result, the formation, unit and subunit commanders were unable to assign specific tasks to the artillery and aviation.

At the same time, one must note that the 5th Air Army's aviation was unable to render effective support to the 37th Army's forces because of the distance of the airfields and the shortage of fuel and ammunition.

On 3 October the *front* commander pointed out these shortcomings to the army command and demanded that they be eliminated. He ordered that the division commanders' observation posts be located on the right bank of the Dnepr, no more than 1-1.5 kilometers from the troops and in places which would enable them to observe the battlefield. The battery commanders were to have their observers directly in the infantry's combat formations. The commander of the army artillery group was also ordered to have an observation post on the right bank of the Dnepr, with forward observation posts, along with communications equipment, along the army's flanks.

Upon evaluating the situation that had arisen by the close of 3 October, the commander of the 37th Army undertook measures to speed up the crossing by the second echelon—the 82nd Rifle Corps' divisions and units of the 1st Mechanized Corps—in order to create a decisive superiority over the enemy and then, in conjunction with the 7th Guards Army, defeat the enemy group of forces operating in this area and to expand the bridgehead.

The army's available crossing equipment enabled us during the night of 3-4 October and during 4 October to begin crossing units of the 1st Mechanized Corps to the bridgehead and to complete the crossing of the 82nd Rifle Corps' 188th Rifle Division, which was concentrating in the Mishurin Rog area. Only the corps' 1st Guards Airborne Division still remained along the Dnepr's left bank.

On 4 October all of the 89th Guards Rifle Division, the 57th Rifle Corps (92nd, 110th and 62nd Guards rifle divisions), the 82nd Rifle Corps (minus the 1st Guards Airborne Division) and the 1st Mechanized Corps' main forces were located on the right bank of the Dnepr; that is, five rifle divisions, three mechanized and one tank brigades, a tank regiment, 538 guns of various types, and 63 tanks.

By this time the enemy had the 106th and 39th infantry divisions' combat groups, elements of the SS cavalry divisions, one-third of the *Totenkopf* Panzer Division, the 23rd Panzer Division, up to half of the *Grossdeutschland* Panzer Division, combat groups from the 62nd Infantry Division, and part of the 6th Panzer Division's forces opposite the 37th Army; that is, up to two infantry and three panzer divisions, with reinforcements. There were about 150 tanks in the enemy's panzer divisions.

The army commander managed to create an overall superiority of nearly two to one over the enemy in men and artillery. However, the enemy still maintained a nearly 2.5:1 superiority in tanks.

On the morning of 4 October the forces of the 57th and 82nd rifle corps renewed the offensive, but were unable to achieve a decisive success. The enemy put up fierce resistance and did not cease his tank and infantry counterattacks. Stubborn fighting raged all day on the bridgehead. The enemy undertook numerous counterattacks in the 57th Rifle Corps' sector, in strength from a company to a regiment of infantry, with 9-20 tanks, while striving to throw our units back to the Dnepr. Units of the 110th Guards Rifle Division were involved in particularly heavy fighting.

Only units of the 82nd Rifle Corps' 10th Guards Airborne Division were able to advance slightly in the day's fighting in the direction of Annovka. However, despite all the troops' efforts, they were unable to link up with the 7th Guards Army's main forces (25th Rifle Corps) on this day.

By the close of 4 October, thanks to the measures adopted to provide crossing equipment in the army's sector, four ferry crossing were already operating regularly. This enabled us to significantly speed up the augmentation of men and materiel along the right bank of the Dnepr—particularly tanks, artillery and ammunition. For example, about 20,000 men, 145 guns, 28 tanks, and 186 motor vehicles were crossed during 3-4 October. The size of the bridgehead, which had been broadened up to 20-25 kilometers in width and up to eight kilometers, prevented the enemy from waging aimed fire against our crossings in the areas south of Soloshino, Mishurin Rog and other places.

The crossing of men and materiel could be carried out both night and day. Measures had been adopted to strengthen anti-aircraft defense in the crossing areas. The regiments of all three anti-aircraft artillery divisions occupied firing positions in the areas of Botsuly, Soloshino and Perevolochnaya. The activity of the 5th Air Army's fighter aviation increased. All of this was creating favorable conditions for the rapid crossing of men and materiel to the bridgehead.

At this time the question arose of reconsidering the 89th and 92nd guards rifle divisions' tasks. These divisions' bridgeheads were kept under fire throughout not only by artillery and mortar fire, but by that of machine guns as well. The task of tying down the enemy's forces at the beginning of the forcing had already been accomplished by them. During 1-4 October they tied down the 106th and 39th infantry divisions' and elements of the *Totenkopf* SS Panzer Division through active operations, thus preventing the enemy from freely maneuvering. Besides this, it was becoming all the more obvious that the continuation of the fighting for the powerful strongpoints of Uspenskoye and Derievka was becoming inexpedient. The struggle for these strongpoints did not hold out the promise of tangible results and could only lead to unjustified losses.

The commander of the 37th Army, having fully and critically evaluated the events that took place during the final days of the bitter fighting on the bridgehead, came to the correct conclusion as to the necessity of regrouping two rifle divisions from the secondary axis to the main one and, having created a powerful group of forces along his left flank, to defeat the enemy along the boundary with the 7th Guards Army and to expand the bridgehead.

It was planned to carry out the regrouping in two nights. The 92nd Guards Rifle Division was to regroup on the night of 4-5 October and the 89th Guards Rifle Division on the night of 5-6 October. The divisions were to leave behind a small covering force on their bridgeheads and cross their main forces to the eastern bank of the Dnepr and then concentrate them on the bridgehead in the Mishurin Rog area. At the same time, the village of Uspenskoye was transferred to the 53rd Army's sector. Subsequently, when the army, as the *front's* shock group, went over to the attack, the timely accomplished regrouping played a significant role in securing the operation's success.

In order to continue the offensive in the direction of Annovka and height 177.0, by the close of 4 October the commander of the 37th Army had fully concentrated along the army's left flank the 82nd Rifle Corps' 10th Guards Airborne and 188th Rifle divisions, the 1st Mechanized Corps' main forces and most of the reinforcement equipment. Besides this, the 89th and 92nd guards rifle divisions were also moving along to this axis. The commander of the 37th Army had in his reserve the 1st Guards Airborne Division on the left bank of the Dnepr, in the Botsuly—Dvornikovka area.

Thus from the morning of 5 October up to two divisions and the 1st Mechanized Corps' main forces could be employed for carrying out the task assigned by the *front* commander, to defeat the enemy's group of forces in the Annovka—Borodaevka and height 177.0 area, as early as 3 October. It was necessary to quickly organize coordination and take all measures for supplying the troops with ammunition, which they were painfully short of. Contrary to the *front* commander's instructions, on the night of 4-5 October the army commander made the decision to attack in the direction of Annovka and height 177.0 with only the forces of the 10th Guards Airborne Division, while he directed the 188th Rifle Division toward Mikhailovka, while he decided to carry out a deep maneuver with the 1st Mechanized Corps to outflank the enemy group of forces operating opposite the 57th Rifle Corps.

Proceeding from this decision, the army commander assigned the following tasks to the troops. The 10th Guards Airborne Division, together with the 219th Tank Brigade, received orders to continue the offensive in the direction of height 177.0 and, to encircle and destroy the enemy in the Borodaevka—Annovka—Pogrebnaya area by the morning of 5 October in conjunction with units of the 7th Guards Army. The 188th Rifle Division was ordered to attack the enemy along the Mikhailovka axis. By the morning of 5 October the 1st Mechanized Corps was to complete its concentration in the Annovka area and, in conjunction with the 188th Rifle and 10th Guards Airborne divisions, launch an attack in the general direction of Lipovyi farm and Chervono-Praporovka against the flank and rear of the enemy operating against the 57th Rifle Corps. By the close of the day the corps was to reach the Tomakovka—Novo-Troitskoe—Chervono-Praporovka area.

Thus according to the army commander's decision, the efforts of the army's shock group were to be once again dispersed along two opposite axes. At the same time, the lesser part of the shock group's forces was to be directed toward resolving the main task—the destruction of the enemy group of forces operating in the area of the villages of Annovka and Borodaevka and height 177.0. Such a decision corresponded neither to the conditions of the situation nor to the *front* commander's instructions.

On 5 October combat operations in the army's sector developed in the following manner. On the night of 4-5 October the 110th Guards Rifle Division made an attack and occupied the line height 118.1—height 105.2—height 177.0. Despite the enemy's stubborn resistance, powerful artillery and mortar fire, and his counterattacks, the guards soldiers and officers acted boldly and decisively in the night's fighting. Having broken into the trench, the guards troops killed 20 Hitlerites in hand-to-hand fighting and captured a gun. Lieutenant Maslya, the platoon commander, turned the weapon on the enemy, opened fire and forced the enemy to fall back. The brave officer was wounded in this battle, but continued to command the platoon.

The 188th Rifle Division, which had been committed into the fighting as early as the night of 4 October between the 62nd Guards Rifle and the 10th Guards Airborne divisions, repelled the enemy's vicious infantry and tank attacks throughout 5 October and was fighting along the line excluding height 106.7—height 122.2. The 10th Guards Airborne Division also undertook a night attack. It captured the northern part of Annovka, but was unable to advance further.

The 1st Mechanized Corps also failed to carry out its assignment.

The 92nd Guards Rifle Division, which had begun it regrouping on the night of 4-5 October, had concentrated two of its regiments in the Koshikova ravine—Pochikalovka area.

As is clear, stubborn and intense fighting continued along the 37th Army's entire front on 5 October. However, on this day, as on 3 and 4 October, the main events developed along the army's left flank in the area of Zelenyi farm—Annovka and Tarasovka. The enemy fully committed the *Grossdeutschland* Panzer Division, the 23rd Panzer Division, part of the 6th Panzer Division's forces, and the 262nd Infantry Division's combat group in this area. The enemy, having broken through to the Dnepr in the Borodaevka area, was applying all his efforts to widening the gap between the 37th and 7th Guards armies and eliminating the bridgeheads seized by them. At the same time, the enemy's was concentrating his main forces against the 7th Guards Army, the bridgehead of which did not exceed 14-15 kilometers in width and 10-12 kilometers in depth and which was completely enfiladed by artillery fire. The situation here was particularly intense and threatening.

On this day the enemy strengthened his resistance along other sectors. In the day's fighting our forces repelled up to ten enemy counterattacks in force from two companies to regiment of infantry, with 30-40 tanks. The enemy's aviation, operating with single aircraft and groups of 25-40 planes, launched uninterrupted strikes against our forces' combat formations. Our forces repelled all of the enemy's counterattacks in intensive fighting and held their positions, but were unable to advance further. The situation remained approximately the same as it had been by the close of 4 October.

Throughout 5 October the 53rd Army was fighting along its previous lines. The 7th Guards Army was engaged in fierce fighting along its right flank with the enemy's tanks and infantry. The enemy, having committed fresh tank units into the fighting, captured the western outskirts of Borodaevka following stubborn fighting.

On 5 October, as during the previous days, the 5th Air Army was unable to render effective support to the *front's* and 37th Army's forces due to inclement weather. Only 200 sorties were carried out during the day, while about 400 enemy flights were noted in the *front's* offensive sector.

Thus on 5 October not a single one of the 37th Army's divisions managed to carry out its assignment. Operating along separate axes and without the necessary preparation and supply, they were unable to overcome the enemy's increasing resistance.

THE FORCING OF THE DNEPR BY THE 37TH ARMY

On 5 October four ferry crossings were operating in the army's sector: one 9-ton ferry made from A-3 boats in the area of Koleberda village; one 30-ton ferry from a bow half-pontoon park and a 16-ton ferry from a "V" park in the Derievka area; a 30-ton ferry from a bow half-pontoon park, two 12-ton ferries from a bow half-pontoon park and two 5-ton ferries from A-3 boats in the area of the island at marker 63.0, and; a 16-ton ferry from a bow half-pontoon park and two 9-ton ferries from A-3 boats in the Mishurin Rog area. The presence of four crossings with ferries carrying weights of nine to 30 tons enabled us to cross to the right bank of the Dnepr all kinds of equipment present in the army and to support the attack by units and formations with the necessary amount of ammunition and other kinds of supplies.

Having evaluated the situation by the close of 5 October, the army commander made the decision to concentrate the army's main forces along a single axis and, with an attack on Annovka and Odinets, link up with the 7th Guards Army's forces on 6 October.

In accordance with the decision adopted, the army commander assigned the following tasks to the troops. The 57th Rifle Corps received orders to securely hold its bridgehead and to active operations in the Kutsevolovka and Yasinovatka area prevent the enemy from maneuvering his men and materiel in the direction of the army's main attack.

The 82nd Rifle and 1st Mechanized corps were ordered to attack in the direction of the northern outskirts of Annovka, height 177.0, Popov, and Odinets and, in conjunction with the 7th Guards Army, to destroy the enemy group of forces in the area Tarasovka—Borodaevka—excluding Pogrebnaya.

The 92nd Guards Rifle Division, having completed its concentration on the bridgehead, was to be resubordinated to the commander of the 82nd Rifle Corps.

At 1100 on 6 October the army's shock group attacked. Upon encountering the enemy's stubborn resistance and counterattacks by his infantry and tanks, supported by aviation, the troops were unable to overcome the enemy's resistance and were fighting along their previous lines.

Nor was the task assigned by the army commander carried out on this day either. The main reason for this was the unsatisfactory organization of the offensive in the units and formations. In light of the shortage of ammunition and the great remove of a significant part of the reinforcement artillery, which was still located on the left bank of the Dnepr, an artillery preparation was not conducted. The infantry, which was being supported by a small number of tanks,[7] attacked without artillery support. The 5th Air Army's operations were quite limited. On this day, while intense fighting raged in the 37th and 7th Guards armies' sectors, the 5th Air Army carried out only 270 sorties. One must add to all of this that the armies' units and formations had suffered significant casualties in several days of fighting to broaden and retain the bridgehead, as a result of which their offensive capabilities fell sharply.

On 6 October a 16-ton bridge was erected near Perevolochnaya. The intensive crossing of the artillery remaining on the left bank of the Dnepr, particularly division artillery, began along this bridge on the night of 6-7 October.

Due to the fact that the tasks assigned to the army's forces for 6 October had not been carried out, the army commander ordered that they be fulfilled on 7 October.

During 7-10 October stubborn fighting continued along the 37th Army's front. The 37th Army's forces repeatedly attempted to attack in order to link up with the 7th Guards Army.

The German-Fascist command, while striving to prevent the further widening of the bridgehead by the 37th Army's forces, continued to reinforce its group of forces. On 7 October up to one-third of the 282nd Infantry Division, which had been transferred from the area south of Kremenchug,

---

[7] Editor's note. The 1st Mechanized Corps had only 42 tanks and operated as a combined-arms formation.

was brought up to the Uspenskoye and Kutsevolovka area. the 6th Panzer Division's main forces had concentrated to the area south of Mishurin Rog.

The most intensive fighting unfolded on 8-9 October. These days passed in continuous mutual attacks. The 37th Army's forces, having renewed the offensive on 8 October in the direction of Annovka, height 177.0 and the village of Odinets, only captured the road from Annovka to Borodaevka, but were halted by the enemy's powerful resistance, which often turned into counterattacks.

The fighting was particularly fierce on this day. The guards units' and formations' rank and file manifested extreme stubbornness in repelling the enemy's counterattacks and in the attack. The soldiers and officers of the 10th Guards Airborne Division's 24th Guards Airborne Regiment captured Annovka following a stubborn battle. In order to win back this inhabited locale, the enemy undertook a series of vicious counterattacks. He threw in up to a battalion of infantry and seven tanks during the first counterattack. When the enemy approached closely he was met with the guards troops' powerful fire from all kinds of weapons. Then the deputy regimental commander for political affairs, Captain Shapkin, shouted "For Stalin, for Soviet Ukraine, forward!" and rushed the enemy, taking the regiment's rank and file with him. The enemy could not withstand the guards troops' vigorous attack and fell back in panic. Four tanks were knocked out and up to 150 soldiers and offices were killed in this battle.

After some time, the enemy launched a second counterattack with the support of 15 tanks and began to outflank the battalions commanded by captains Portnoi and Litvinov. These battalions' rank and file manifested stoutness and valor and once again beat off the enemy's counterattack. This time, 450 enemy soldiers and officers were killed and seven tanks knocked out. Guards Private Yershov especially distinguished himself in this fighting. While repelling the German counterattack, he was on the battalion's left flank. Six enemy tanks were bearing down on him, but Yershov did not waver. He knocked out three enemy tanks with accurate shots from an anti-tank rifle and the remainder turned back. During the counterattack Guards anti-tank rifleman Sergeant Asharakhmetov was cut off from his subunit. Remaining at his firing position, he knocked out the lead tank with two shots from an anti-tank rifle. The tanks halted and continued to fire. Taking advantage of this moment, Asharakhmetov knocked out another two tanks.

By the close of 8 October the laying down of a second 16-ton bridge near Soloshino had been completed. The ferry crossings continued to operate simultaneously with the bridges. By this time a significant amount of crossing equipment had arrived with the army: two bow half-pontoon parks, three UVSA-3 parks, two division bridge parks, and 16 Hungarian half-pontoons. With the activation of these two bridges in the army's sector, the situation with the crossing of troops, reinforcement units and freight improved sharply and this told positively on the troops' actions in the succeeding days.

At the same time, one should note the heroic work of the engineer units' and subunits' rank and file, who secured the troops' crossing to the Dnepr's right bank. Without halting the crossing of the troops either day or night, in conditions of the uninterrupted shelling of the enemy's artillery and air strikes, the ferry crews and bridge construction teams did not abandon their posts. They continued working in the cold water to save personnel and military shipments.

The soldiers and officers of the 12th Independent Engineer Battalion's 1st Engineer Company exhibited extreme hardiness. They crossed over men and materiel without rest over the course of three days. In order to speed up the crossing of the artillery to the right bank of the Dnepr, the company's soldiers, working up to their chests in the cold water, towed the pontoons from the left to the right bank of the Dnepr with ropes. The 12th Independent Engineer Battalion's 2nd and 3rd companies successfully supported the crossing in the Soloshino area. The following example shows how intensively the crews of these companies operated. On the night of 7-8 October, the crews crossed about 2,500 men with their weapons, 600 boxes of ammunition and a good deal of food in six hours, while working on three A-3 boats, a wooden sapper boat and a single ferry. Some crews made 19-20 trips apiece.

On 9 October the enemy continued to attack for the purpose of breaking through the 37th Army's front. The fighting was particularly intense in the sector of the 57th Rifle Corps' 110th Guards Rifle Division, where the enemy undertook eight counterattacks in strength of one to two battalions of infantry, supported by 8-12 tanks. As a result of the bitter fighting, the enemy, at the cost of heavy losses, managed to insignificantly push back the division's units along individual sectors. One may judge the intensity of the fighting by the 307th Guards Rifle Division's combat activities. During the night of 8-9 October, the 307th Guards Rifle Regiment was pushed back by the enemy to the area of height 177.0. Height 177.0 was occupied by the enemy only when all of the soldiers defending it died the death of the brave. The fighting for the height did not cease throughout the night. By the morning of 9 October, having inflicted heavy losses on the enemy, a company of scouts and sappers from the 307th Guards Rifle Regiment once again took the height. It was only during the second half of the day, when the enemy brought up his forces and once again undertook rabid attacks with his infantry and tanks and managed to finally capture height 177.0, at the cost of heavy casualties.

Heavy fighting unfolded on this day along the army's left flank. The enemy, while striving to defeat the 24th Guards Airborne Regiment, threw up to 70 tanks into the counterattack. The rank and file of a platoon of anti-tank guns displayed extreme heroism in repelling this attack. The artillerists of Utkin's platoon knocked out 15 tanks with accurate fire over open sights. The entire rank and file of the platoon perished in this unequal fight and the guns were put out of action. Utkin knocked out another three tanks, while remaining alone at his firing position. The 24th Guards Airborne Regiment, along with the 1658th Anti-Tank Artillery Regiment, which had just arrived, beat off this enemy attack as well.

By the close of 9 October no sort of significant changes in the 37th Army's situation had taken place. The troops were fighting along the same lines they had reached as early as 4-5 October. The 1st Guards Airborne Division, having begun the crossing to the right bank of the Dnepr, had concentrated in the area of marker 56.2—Lake Ustup. By 0500 the 89th Guards Rifle Division had also crossed the Dnepr and had concentrated in the area of Koshikov ravine—marker 144.1—Pertsev ravine.

Thus by the close of 9 October the crossing of all the army's combined-arms formations had been completed. Only part of the army and attached artillery remained on the left bank of the Dnepr.

On 10 October the enemy had been finally worn out; the shock force of the enemy's battered tank divisions had dried up. On this day the enemy limited himself to artillery and mortar fire against our troops' combat formations and undertook several counterattacks of up to a battalion of infantry in force, supported by 8-13 tanks and aviation.

The army's forces, while holding their occupied lines along the right flank and in the center, resumed the offensive in the direction of Borodaevka and advanced 0.5 to five kilometers along the bank.

By the close of 10 October the 82nd Rifle Corps' formations occupied the following position: the 188th Rifle Division was holding the line Nezamozhnik—height 122.2 (south); the 92nd Guards Rifle Division the line of the northern outskirts of Annovka—the burial mound with the marker +1.5; the 10th Guards Airborne Division, along with individual units of the 7th Guards Army's 213th and 15th guards rifle divisions, was holding the line excluding the burial mound with the marker +1.5—height 147.4.

The units and subunits of the 1st Mechanized Corps, in which there remained only 12 tanks, were operating with the 10th Guards Airborne Division and the 7th Guards Army's 213th and 15th guards rifle divisions.

The 1st Guards Airborne and 89th Guards Rifle divisions were in their previous concentration areas.

As a result of the fighting on 10 October, the army's forces were able to slightly broaden the bridgehead and on the left flank reach Borodaevka (western), but they were nonetheless unable to link up with the 7th Guards Army. However, the enemy, who had been battered and bled white in the preceding fighting, was also forced to give up continuing active operations and went over to the defensive along the entire front.

The correlation of forces, which by this time had changed in our forces' favor (see Table 1.5), as well as the insignificant results achieved by the troops in the latest fighting, insistently demanded the organization and conduct of a new offensive operation with more decisive aims.

Table 1.5 The Correlation of Forces Opposite the 37th Army's Front on 10 October

The Enemy	Correlation of Forces	37th Army
Infantry Battalions—14	1:5	Rifle Battalions—70
Tanks—147	6:1	Tanks—26
Guns and Mortars—403	1:4	Guns and Mortars—1,496

The intense and stubborn fighting during 5-10 October concluded with a significant broadening of the bridgehead along the right bank of the Dnepr up to 35 kilometers in width and up to 6-12 kilometers in depth. The presence of two bridge and four ferry crossings in the army's sector gave us the opportunity to rapidly concentrate the necessary men and materiel on the bridgehead.

On 10 October the commander of the Steppe Front decided to concentrate the 5th Guards Army to the bridgehead for the purpose of carrying out a new offensive operation. The 37th and 5th Guards armies were to break through the enemy's front by their joint efforts, destroy his group of forces in the Nezamozhnik—Katerinovka—Likhovka area and create the conditions for the commitment of the 5th Guards Tank Army from the line of Katerinovka and Likhovka to develop the success in the direction of Pyatikhatka.

Brief Results and Conclusions

The 37th Army's combat activities to force the Dnepr and to seize and widen a bridgehead lasted 17 days—from 24 September through 11 October 1943. During this time the army's forces inflicted significant losses on the enemy in its offensive zone, reached the Dnepr, forced the river from the march along a broad front, and seized a bridgehead of operational significance on its right bank.

During the operation the 37th Army's forces, in conjunction with those of the 7th Guards Army, routed two infantry divisions and an SS cavalry division from the German Eighth Army. Four enemy tank and one infantry divisions suffered a serious defeat.

The forcing of the Dnepr and the 37th Army's intense fighting with the enemy's reserves on the captured bridgehead for the purpose of seizing and holding it, occupy an important place in the Steppe Front's offensive operation.

The *front's* combat operations, particularly those of its 37th Army in the battle for the Dnepr, had great significance in foiling the German-Fascist command's plan for organizing a defense along the Dnepr and halting the Soviet forces' further offensive along this important strategic line.

During the second half of October 1943, the forces of the Steppe Front (it was renamed the Second Ukrainian Front by a *Stavka* directive of 20 October), in close coordination with the Southwestern Front, carried out a new offensive operation from the bridgehead which had been

THE FORCING OF THE DNEPR BY THE 37TH ARMY

seized and held by the 37th Army, along the Kirovograd and Krivoi Rog axes. With the Soviet forces' offensive along these axes, as well as with the offensive by the First Ukrainian Front's forces, the liberation of the Ukrainian right bank from the Hitlerite aggressors began.

The Soviet army's experience of offensive operations in the Great Patriotic War showed that the combined-arms armies allotted to the *front's* second echelon were employed for the resolution of the most diverse missions during the course of a *front* offensive operation. The most characteristic of these was the development of the first-echelon armies' success along the axis of the main attack following the breakthrough of the tactical depth of the enemy's defense, the widening of the breakthrough toward the flank of the *front's* shock group, the completion of the encirclement and destruction of the enemy's encircled groups of forces, and the repulse of powerful enemy counterblows or securing the flank.

The Steppe Front's 37th Army, comprising its second echelon, was committed into the battle in September 1943 during the course of the vigorous pursuit of the enemy forces. The army had the task of forcing the Dnepr from the march and seizing a bridgehead along its right bank, which would secure the further development of operations along the Ukrainian right bank. The commitment of an combined-arms army into the battle with the task of forcing a river from the march and seizing a major bridgehead is one of the most instructive examples of such an employment of a *front's* second echelon.

By the time the *front* commander made the decision to commit the second echelon into the battle, the *front's* right wing and center had fallen significantly behind the left-wing armies. This required the timely augmentation of efforts in the center of the *front* in order to simultaneously bring the troops to the Dnepr at a high speed and along a broad front, to force it from the march and to seize a bridgehead of such size that would enable us to deploy the *front's* shock group for the subsequent operation. One must add to this that the 69th Army, which was attacking in the center of the front and in its first echelon, had been significantly weakened and tied down in fighting the enemy falling back to the crossings in the Kremenchug area. This army would not have been in a condition by itself to force the Dnepr from the march along a broad front and to seize an important bridgehead. Thus the commitment of fresh forces—the *front's* second echelon—was extremely important.

The commitment of the *front's* second echelon in the 69th Army's sector was conditioned to a significant degree by enemy's group of forces and the character of his actions. The German-Fascist command was pulling back the main forces of the Eighth and First Panzer armies along two divergent axes—toward Kremenchug and Dnepropetrovsk. The enemy was taking advantage of the permanent bridge crossings over the river in the Kremenchug and Dnepropetrovsk areas, while striving to pull back his forces behind the Dnepr as quickly as possible and to organize a defense, while only the remnants of two enemy infantry divisions were falling back along the axis of the 37th Army's planned commitment. These features of the situation had been correctly accounted for by the *front* commander in making the decision to force the river. In such a situation, a delay in making the decision to commit the second echelon into the battle would have enabled the enemy to conduct an organized retreat behind the Dnepr, to occupy a defensive position along its right bank from Kremenchug to Dneprodzerzhinsk and to prevent our forces from forcing the river along this sector of the front.

The commander of the 37th Army, while taking the situation that had arisen by the time he made his decision, correctly determined the axis of the main attack and the forcing sector, along which the army's main men and materiel were to concentrate. The main attack was to be launched in the direction of Kutsevolovka and Popel'nastoye, while concentrating the main efforts along the sector excluding Derievka—Mishurin Rog. This was conditioned, first of all, by the fact that the enemy's defense along the right bank along this sector was the most weakly held, the character of the Dnepr's banks and the presence on it of major islands, which favored the organization of landing and ferry crossing points. The successful actions of the neighboring 7th Guards Army, which forced the river three days earlier and which had drawn the enemy's reserves to itself, facilitated the 37th Army's success to a great extent.

At the same time, it is necessary to note that the army commander, in foreseeing the forcing of the Dnepr, did not adopt all of the necessary measures to provision at least the forward detachments, which had been allotted from the first-echelon rifle divisions, with crossing equipment. As a result of this, the forward detachments, having reached the Dnepr and lacking crossing equipment, were forced to organize the collection of local and available crossing materials on the bank and lost about a day doing this.

As was already noted above, with the commitment of the 37th Army into the battle it was planned to reinforce it with four parks of various types. This crossing equipment had not arrived by the time the army's forces reached the river. Crossing equipment from the *front* to the army arrived extremely slowly—over the course of 14 days. The constant shortage of crossing equipment led to a situation in which the transfer of men and materiel to the bridgehead was carried out over the course of an extended time and was very late. For example, the 110th Guards Rifle Division (the 57th Rifle Corps' second echelon) crossed to the bridgehead over the course of two days. Four days were need to cross two divisions from the army's second echelon.

It's quite obvious that if this crossing equipment had arrived at the army by the beginning of the forcing or during the operation's first days, then the results might have been completely different. The army could have more quickly crossed its men and materiel to the right bank of the Dnepr and achieved greater results with fewer losses.

As is clear from the crossing of the 37th Army's force, between 28 September and through 3 October, mostly light organic, local and stray crossing equipment arrived with the troops and was employed, which enabled us to cross over the Dnepr rifle subunits with their personal weaponry, battalion, regimental, and anti-tank artillery, plus a small amount of divisional artillery, as well as individual tanks. In light of the fact that there was not a sufficient amount of heavy crossing equipment with the troops, the army and formation commanders were unable to organize the crossing of artillery and tanks behind the forward detachments. The latter, while engaged in stubborn fighting with the enemy's counterattacking infantry and tanks, was desperately in need of reinforcement and support by artillery and tanks. The reinforcement artillery, which was firing from the left bank of the Dnepr at maximum range, was unable to render the necessary support to the troops.

Heavy organic crossing equipment began to arrive at the army mainly only from 5 October, which enabled us to sharply speed up the crossing of troops and equipment to the bridgehead and significantly improve the situation. As regards bridge crossings, they were erected in the army's sector with a great deal of delay (6-8 October) and did not have a significant influence on changing the results achieved by the troops by this time. All of this led to a situation in which only by the end of the operation; that is, following two weeks of fierce fighting, was the army able to change the correlation of forces on the bridgehead in its favor, not only in infantry, but in artillery as well.

The maneuver of crossing equipment has very great significance while forcing. However, in light of its severe shortage and the high percentage of losses, the army, unit and formation commanders did not have the opportunity of creating even minimal reserves. As a result of this, the maneuver of crossing equipment from the reserve or by transferring it from other axes was limited among the army's forces. The arriving crossing equipment only made up for losses along the active crossing points and supported their non-stop work.

The slow pace of crossing the troops (and particularly of artillery and tanks during the first days) enabled the enemy to rapidly regroup from other axes the combat groups of three infantry divisions and four tank divisions and to create a significant superiority in tanks and to sharply complicate the situation for our forces on the bridgehead. The density of artillery and direct infantry-support tanks among the army's forces on the bridgehead was very low, which failed to secure superiority over the enemy and the reliable support of the attacking troops.

Counterattacks by the enemy's infantry and tanks, with the support of significant forces from bomber aviation, against the 37th Army's forces on the bridgehead demanded the organization of a powerful anti-tank and anti-aircraft defense from the commanders at all levels. However, the slow pace of the crossing of artillery prevented us from quickly organizing a reliable anti-tank and anti-aircraft defense for the troops on the bridgehead. As a result of this, the infantry was forced to battle the enemy tanks with only its organic weapons, as a result of which it suffered significant losses and failed to carry out its tasks, while along some axes it was thrown back by the enemy from its previously captured lines.

Weak anti-aircraft defense, particularly our troops' cover by fighter aviation, enabled the enemy air force to launch strikes against the troops and crossings during the first days of the forcing. The cover of the troops and crossings was also poorly organized from the air. The troops began to force the Dnepr almost without any kind of anti-aircraft cover. By the beginning of the forcing there were only six ant-aircraft guns in the army. Anti-aircraft equipment arrived at the Dnepr extremely slowly and it was only on the sixth day of the operation that we managed to completely bring up our anti-aircraft weapons and organize an anti-aircraft defense. Serious shortcomings in the organization of anti-aircraft defense slowed down the crossing of troops and resulted in losses among the rank and file and weapons, as well as to putting crossing equipment out of action.

One of the typical features of the troops' combat activities on the opposite bank was their high level of activity—both on the part of the 37th Army's units and formations and on the part of the enemy.

Constant counterattacks by enemy infantry and tanks from the first days of the forcing often forced the army and formation commanders to commit their second echelons in detail, as they crossed to the opposite bank, given the weak artillery and air support, which resulted in prolonged and unsuccessful fighting on the bridgehead. No less important reasons for the prolonged nature of the fighting on the opposite bank and the troops failure, in a number of cases, to carry out their assignment to expand the bridgehead were: the poor reinforcement of the army's forces with direct infantry-support tanks, the absence of proper support for the attacking troops by *front* aviation, the insufficiently precise organization of cooperation between the combat arms, chiefly between the infantry, artillery and aviation, as well as the low provisioning of the troops with ammunition. Upon entering the battle and over the course of the entire operation, the army experienced a critical shortage of ammunition. At times the provisioning of the artillery and mortars with ammunition did not exceed 0.3 combat loads, while individual batteries and battalions lacked them altogether.

The operation's experience emphasizes with special force that the great gap in time between the forcing of the river by the rifle units and the crossing of the artillery and tanks leads to a sharp worsening of the situation for the troops on the opposite bank. Even given a numerical superiority in infantry, the troops' offensive opportunities and their ability to withstand powerful enemy infantry and tank attacks fall rapidly. The untimely development of the success achieved by the first echelons and the insufficient support for the troops by artillery and aviation while repelling enemy infantry and tank counterattacks on the opposite bank leads to the loss of the initial surprise achieved enables the enemy to seize the initiative and complicates the fulfillment of the tasks assigned to the troops.

The 37th Army's operation to force the Dnepr is instructive in the skillfully conducted maneuver of two rifle divisions from a secondary axis during the operation to the main attack axis for the purpose of repelling the enemy's powerful counterattacks and defeating the enemy group of forces that had broken through to the Dnepr along the boundary with the neighboring 7th Guards Army.

The moment was fortunately chosen for realizing the planned maneuver. When the attempts by the 89th and 92nd guards rifle divisions to expand the captured bridgeheads had been repulsed by the enemy and the further crossing over the Dnepr was linked to heavy losses in men and materiel and crossing equipment, the army commander decided to secretly regroup these divisions over two nights to the left flank, where the troops had achieved a significantly greater success and where the threat of the enemy's breakthrough to the Dnepr was forming. A small covering force was left in these divisions' former zone of operations and the crossings were employed as demonstration ones.

The regrouping of the two divisions to a new axis also had great significance for the creation of the army's shock group for the purpose of carrying out a subsequent offensive operation by the *front* on the Ukrainian right bank.

Alongside this, one should note that the prolonged nature of the fighting to retain and expand the bridgehead was to a certain extent linked with the desire to simultaneously resolve several tasks, as a result of which the army's efforts were dispersed along a broad front. In accordance with the *front* commander's order of 3 October, the army's main task was to destroy, in conjunction with the 7th Guards Army's forces, the enemy group of forces in the Annovka—Borodaevka—height 177.0 area. The defeat of the enemy's group of forces in this area would have led to the unification of two army bridgeheads into a single overall bridgehead. The army's chief efforts should have been directed toward resolving this task. Alongside the resolution of this task, the army commander sought at the same time to resolve another task—to expand the army's bridgehead west of Mishurin Rog by an attack by a single rifle division and the mechanized corps' main forces from the Annovka area in the general direction of Tomakovka. The simultaneous resolution of the two tasks did not conform to the specific situation that had arisen by this time and resulted in the dispersal of men and materiel along a broad front; as a result, neither of the tasks assigned to the troops was resolved.

Serious miscalculations in troop control were also committed. The assignment of excessive tasks to the troops was noted. The command and observation posts for the unit and formation commanders following the crossing of men and materiel to the right bank of the Dnepr continued to remain on the left bank of the river for several days. Insufficient attention was paid to the employment of radio equipment for troop control.

The operation's experience once again confirms that troop control during the forcing and combat activities on the opposite bank must be as flexible as possible and as close to the troops as possible and should foresee the employment of all communications means. The nearness of the command posts increases the troops' steadiness while repelling powerful enemy counterattacks on the opposite bank and secures unbroken control even when a significant amount of communications equipment is put out of action. The commanders' personal interaction with their subordinates acquires great importance. This enables them to constantly on top of the situation and to rapidly react to all its changes and influence the course of combat activities.

In trying to achieve unbroken troop control, it is also necessary that the observation and command posts be moved behind the main forces of the units and formations that have crossed over.

A broad river with a rapid current seriously complicates the organization of wire communications and communications by mobile means with troops fighting on the opposite bank. Thus radio communications acquires particular importance while forcing a river, and is the chief means of control during this period.

Despite the unfavorably developing situation on the opposite bank, the troops fought with great stubbornness and persistence, exhibiting personal valor and mass heroism in carrying out their military duty. Suffice it to say that 17,618 men were decorated for heroism and valor among the 37th Army's forces, including 213 who were awarded the highest government medal—the Hero of the Soviet Union.

THE FORCING OF THE DNEPR BY THE 37TH ARMY

From all that has been said above, it follows that the most instructive moments in the 37th Army's combat activities are the following: the commitment of the *front's* second-echelon army with the task of forcing the river and seizing a bridgehead from the march; the army's forcing of the Dnepr with a limited amount of crossing equipment and with poor materiel provisioning for the troops, and; the maneuver of men and materiel during the forcing of the Dnepr and the struggle to expand and hold the captured bridgehead.

Supplement 1.1 The Arrival of Crossing Equipment to the 37th Army in September-October 1943

Type	September				October										Total
	27	28	29	30	1	2	3	4	5	6	7	8	9	10	
Division Bridge Park-42 (pontoons)	–	–	–	–	–	–	–	–	80	–	–	–	–	80	160
Division Bridge Park-41	–	–	–	–	–	–	–	–	–	–	–	40	–	–	40
Launches	–	2	1	–	1	–	–	1	–	–	1	1	–	1	8
"V" Half-Pontoons	–	12	–	–	21	–	–	–	–	–	–	–	–	–	33
Bow Half-Pontoons	12	9	20	–	–	–	–	48	–	–	–	48	–	–	137
Wooden Boats	8	21	–	10	–	–	–	–	–	–	–	–	–	–	–
Collapsible Landing Boats	–	22	18	–	–	3	–	–	–	–	–	–	–	–	39
Small Inflatable Boats	–	2	–	–	–	10	–	–	–	–	–	–	–	–	12
A-3	6	22	17	–	5	18	7	–	–	–	–	–	–	–	75

Supplement 1.2 The Crossing of the 37th Army's Forces From 28 September To 11 October 1943

Type	September			October									
	28	29	30	1	2	3	4	5	6	7	8	9	10
Guns	16	58	125	103	91	81	64	116	171	68	151	249	191
Rank and File	6,201	17,025	7,177	11,726	8,270	9,497	10,557	6,182	14,406	10,902	9,160	4,646	9,181
Tanks	–	–	9	2	24	22	5	5	9	3	–	12	2
Carts, Kitchens	10	89	58	405	274	328	165	142	114	160	244	750	866
Horses	55	115	240	1,067	712	761	280	410	270	506	672	515	278

Note. The table shows the number of men and equipment which was crossed and counted by the engineer troops. Actually, far more were crossed.

2

The Forcing of the Dnepr by the 52nd Army in the Cherkassy Area (November-December 1943)

Introduction

The Cherkassy operation with the forcing of the Dnepr, which was conducted by the troops of the Second Ukrainian Front's 52nd Army during 13 November-14 December 1943, is a component part of the battle for the Dnepr. As a result of this operation, the 52nd Army's forces captured a major economic center in Ukraine—the city of Cherkassy, and important center of the enemy's defense along the Dnepr and formed a bridgehead of operational significance along its right bank.

The 52nd Army in this operation attacked along the *front's* secondary axis for the purpose of distracting the enemy's forces from the Second Ukrainian Front's main attack axis—Krivoi Rog and Kirovograd. Its purpose was to capture the city of Cherkassy and the railroad junction of Smela.

The army's forces forced the Dnepr and created on its right bank a bridgehead of operational significance, which was subsequently used in routing the enemy's Korsun-Shevchenkovskii group of forces. Aside from this, as a result of the Cherkassy operation, the unhindered work of the Belaya Tserkov'—Smela—Krivoi Rog lateral railroad, which was the main artery used by the enemy for operational and supply shipments, was disrupted. The operation tied down significant enemy forces along its front for an extended time, which facilitated the success of the First Ukrainian Front's combat operations in the areas of Zhitomir and Fastov, as well as the unfolding of the Second Ukrainian Front's offensive along the Krivoi Rog and Kirovograd axes.

Despite a number of substantial shortcomings, which were committed by the army command and formation commanders, the Cherkassy operation is instructive as an army offensive operation conducted along a *front's* secondary axis, with the forcing of a major water obstacle and the capture of the city of Cherkassy through the combined efforts of a combined-arms army with partisan detachments and airborne elements operating in the enemy rear. This operation was carried out in conditions of the significant remove of the army's forces from the *front's* main group of forces. During the offensive the 52nd Army's units and formations demonstrated their ability for force major water obstacles, to wage night battles in inhabited locales, to encircle enemy forces, and to themselves fight in encirclement and organize an escape from it.

The Situation by the Start of the Operation's Preparation

Following the defeat of the Hitlerite forces on the Ukrainian left bank, the forces of the First, Second and Third Ukrainian fronts developed a successful offensive and at the end of September 1943 reached the Dnepr, having seized at the same time a number of important bridgeheads along its right bank.

During the first half of November 1943 the First Ukrainian Front's forces carried out the Kiev offensive operation. By 6 November the enemy's defense north of Kiev had been penetrated and

THE FORCING OF THE DNEPR BY THE 52ND ARMY

the front's forces captured Kiev. While pursuing the enemy in the direction of Korosten', Zhitomir and Belaya Tserkov', by 12 November our forces reached the line Radenke—Zhitomir—Fastov, having formed a major bridgehead west of Kiev. On instructions from the *Stavka* of the Supreme High Command, from 12 November the First Ukrainian Front temporarily halted its offensive along the line reached, in order to prepare a new offensive.

The forces of the Second Ukrainian Front developed their offensive in close coordination with the forces of the First Ukrainian Front. Having undertaken an offensive along the Krivoi Rog and Kirovograd axes in the middle of October from the bridgeheads seized along the right bank of the Dnepr, the *front's* forces got into fighting along the approaches to the city of Krivoi Rog and captured the major rail center of Pyatikhatka. Having repelled powerful enemy counterattacks along its left wing at the end of October and the beginning of November, the Second Ukrainian Front's forces securely occupied the line Prokhorovka—Chigirin Dubrova—Kremenchug—Derievka—Novo-Starodub—Iskrovka—Sergeevka.

Of the seven combined-arms and one tank armies in the Second Ukrainian Front, the 57th, 37th and part of the 53rd armies and the 5th Guards Tank Army were on the bridgehead in the Dneprodzerzhinsk area. The 52nd and 4th Guards armies and part of the 53rd Army's forces were defending on the left bank of the Dnepr along the front Prokhorovka—Yeremeevka—Kremenchug—Derievka. To the left, the Third Ukrainian Front's right-wing forces were holding a bridgehead along the front Malaya Sofievka—Fedorovka.

By the start of November 1943 the German Eighth Army and part of the German First Panzer Army were defending opposite the Second Ukrainian Front. Overall, by this time the *front* was faced by 14 infantry, six panzer and one mechanized divisions and six combat groups, which had been formed from the remnants of the previously routed infantry and tank divisions. The enemy had concentrated up to 70 percent of these forces against the *front's* left-wing forces. The III and XLVII panzer and XI Army corps were defending against the 52nd, 4th Guards and 53rd armies along the right wing. In all, the enemy was holding up to eight infantry and one tank division against these armies' front.

The 52nd Army (commander Lieutenant General K.A. Koroteev,[1] member of the military council Major General A.F. Bobrov and chief of staff Major General A.N. Kolominov) was operating on the *front's* extreme right flank, in a sector 140 kilometers in length. In all, the army contained three rifle divisions,[2] two anti-tank artillery regiments, a guards mortar regiment, a gun artillery regiment, a tank and self-propelled artillery regiments, and an anti-aircraft division, as well as three engineer-sapper battalions. While occupying defensive positions along the left bank of the Dnepr along the front Koleberda—Chigirin Dubrova, the army was securely holding the bridgehead north of Kreshchatik (13 kilometers in width and 3-4 kilometers deep). Attempts by the 73rd Rifle Corps' units to expand the bridgehead were unsuccessful.

While consolidating along the lines reached, the army's forces occupied the following front. The 4th Army Screening Detachment was defending the unnamed island west of Prokhorovka. The 73rd Rifle Corps' 254th and 294th rifle divisions were on the right bank of the Dnepr, on the bridgehead north of Kreshchatik. The corps' overall defensive front was 18 kilometers. Army course units for junior lieutenants were positioned along the sector excluding Bubnovo—the mouth of Dolgun River along a 7-kilometer front. Units of the 373rd Mirgorod Rifle Division,

---

1 Editor's note. Konstantin Apollonovich Koroteev (1901-53) joined the imperial army in 1916 and the Red Army two years later. During the Great Patriotic War he commanded a number of corps and armies. Following the war, Koroteev commanded a military district.

2 The 254th and 294th rifle divisions were part of the 73rd Rifle Corps. The 78th Rifle Corps contained only the 373rd Rifle Division.

which was part of the 78th Rifle Corps, were defending along the remainder of the more than 110-kilometer front from the mouth of the Dolgun River to Chigurin Dubrova.

The 73rd Rifle Corps' divisions had gotten rich experience of fighting in wooded areas. Before this the 254th Rifle Division had fought in the Staraya Russa area and the 294th Rifle Division along the Volkhov River. Besides this, one should note that before this operation the 254th Rifle Division had already forced the Dnepr in the Kreshchatik area and had successfully captured a bridgehead on its right bank.

Thus the 73rd Rifle Corps had been trained and had good experience both in forcing a major water obstacle and in combat operations in the forests northwest of Cherkassy.

To the right of the 52nd Army were the forces of the First Ukrainian Front's 27th Army along the front Starik River—excluding Koleberda; to the left units of the Second Ukrainian Front's 4th Guards Army were defending along the front excluding Chigirin Dubrova—excluding Kremenchug.

The 52nd Army's forces were being reinforced with men and materiel. By the beginning of November 1943 the strength of the rifle divisions had been raised to 6,000-6,300 men. In all, at the beginning of November the army numbered 26,327 men, 470 guns and mortars of all calibers, and ten tanks and self-propelled guns. The army's crossing equipment consisted of 5.6 parks of various types, 96 fishing boats and 17 wooden sapper boats. Part of the crossing equipment was already in action along the crossings southwest of Sushka and south of Bubnovo. There was a 9-ton ferry consisting of three light inflatable pontoon parks, a set of flotation equipment, 27 fishing boats, and four boats from an UVSA-3 park southwest of Sushka. Two pontoons from a light inflatable pontoon park, four boats from an UVSA-3 park and seven fishing boats were at the crossing south of Bubnovo. All of this equipment enabled us to cross about 300-400 men, along with their weapons, in one trip. The remaining crossing equipment was in the army reserve.

Thus the army's main forces had been concentrated along the right flank for holding the bridgehead north of Kreshchatik. 70 percent of the army's forces were located here. Only one rifle division was defending a 110-kilometer front in the center and along the left flank. The average operational density was 46 kilometers per division and 3-4 guns and mortars per kilometer of front.

Partisan detachments and Major Sidorchuk's airborne group, consisting of elements of the 5th Guards Airborne Brigade, were operating in the enemy's rear in the woods northwest of Cherkassy. This brigade had been landed on the night of 23-24 September 1943 west of the Dnepr's Bukrin bend. Following the unsuccessful airborne landing, elements of the brigade fell back in fighting to the woods west of the city of Cherkassy. Here they were operating against the enemy's communications together with the local partisans. The overall strength of the airborne forces and the partisans operating in the enemy's rear reached 1,600-1,700 men. Of this number, approximately half consisted of the landing group under the command of Major Sidorchuk. This group disposed of 12 heavy machine guns and six anti-tank rifles, as well as rifles and automatic rifles for the entire rank and file.

The local partisans, numbering 800-900 men, operated in separate detachments. The detachments' strength varied from 60 to 300 men. The largest of these detachments numbered 300 men and was led by the secretary of the Cherkassy area's underground party organization, G.A. Ivashchenko. The partisan detachments had weapons for 50 percent of their personnel.

The 52nd Army's headquarters did not have communications with the landing group and the partisans. The 52nd Army's headquarters received the latest information about the parachutists and partisans from the First Ukrainian Front's headquarters on 27 October. According to this data, the parachutists and partisans were in two groups: one in the area of marker 173.9 (four kilometers south of Moshny) and the other in the Vasil'yevka woods. The 52nd Army's headquarters managed to establish communications with these groups only on 12 November.

Units of the 57th, 332nd, 72nd and 167th infantry divisions and the *Wiking* SS Panzer Division were defending opposite the 52nd Army. The panzer division had an insignificant amount of tanks and operated as an infantry division.

By the beginning of the preparation for the operation the enemy group of forces was as follows. The 57th Infantry Division's 217th Infantry Regiment was defending along the 6-kilometer front from Kanev to the village of Pekari, along the Dnepr. The enemy's 332nd Infantry Division was operating against the bridgehead being defended by the 52nd Army's 254th and 294th rifle divisions along the sector from Pekari to Kreshchatik. Units of the *Wiking* SS Panzer Division were defending along the front east of Kreshchatik as far as the inhabited locale of Svidovok (30 kilometers in length). The 72nd Infantry Division, along with the 167th Infantry Division's subordinated 331st Infantry Regiment, was defending the sector of the front from Svidovok to Chaplishche (up to 90 kilometers in length).

The 57th and 72nd infantry divisions consisted of three infantry regiments (each consisting of two battalions) each, one artillery regiment each and special subunits. The *Wiking* SS Panzer Division had the *Deutschland* and *Westland* motorized regiments (each consisting of three battalions), an artillery regiment, the *Wiking* Panzer Regiment, the "Narva" Motorized Battalion, and a number of specialized subunits. The strength of each of the enemy's divisions did not exceed 4,000-5,000 men.

The enemy's defense opposite the 52nd Army's front consisted of one and, in places, two lines of rifle trenches and separate strongpoints in the depth. The first line of trenches, with the exception of individual sectors, ran directly along the shoreline of the right bank of the Dnepr. The enemy had a well organized system of infantry and artillery fire along the entire front, which enabled him to enfilade the main river channel with oblique and flanking fire from different sectors.

A second line of trenches was being prepared along two sectors: west of the bridgehead and northwest of Cherkassy it ran along the western outskirts of the village of Pekari—Khmel'na farm—Novaya Guta and along the eastern edge of the grove west of Kreshchatik. The inhabited locales of Pekari, Khmel'na farm, Novaya Guta, and Kreshchatik had been prepared for a perimeter defense. All of the approaches to these inhabited locales had been mined. Trenches had also been dug along the northeastern and eastern outskirts of the inhabited locales of Lozovok, Yelizavetovka, Svidovok, Dakhnovka, Vasilitsa, and Sosnovka.

The enemy had outfitted strongpoints in the inhabited locales directly adjacent to the wooded area (Svidovok, Dakhnovka, Vasilitsa, Geronimovka, Russkaya Polyana). The enemy was trying to fortify the village of Svidovok most strongly. However, by the start of the 52nd Army's offensive the work to fortify it had not been completed. The strongpoints that had been outfitted in the Dakhnovka—Vasilitsa—Sosnovka area covered the immediate approaches to the city of Cherkassy from the northwest.

For the defense of Cherkassy, the German-Fascist command had created a system of rifle trenches and wooden and earthen pillboxes, which were located along the right bank of the Dnepr, along the northwestern and northeastern outskirts of the city, and along Frunze and Kalinin streets. The enemy built 185 earth and wooden pillboxes along the Vasilitsa—Krasnaya Sloboda sector alone. Cherkassy was less defended from the southwest. Only a single platoon strongpoint, which had been outfitted north of marker 110, was along this axis. A number of buildings in the city were employed as platoon strongpoints, linked with each other by a unified system of fire. Barbed wire obstacles had been set up on the streets, various structures had been outfitted for weapons, and sniper's nests had been built in the attics of buildings. The river bank, the outskirts of the city and the intersections of streets had been mined. A resistance center, which had been outfitted in the Zmogailovka—Krasnaya Sloboda area, covered the city of Cherkassy from the southeast.

Thus by the beginning of the preparation for the offensive operation, more than four enemy divisions were located opposite the 52nd Army's front. The enemy had his lowest density of men and materiel along the front Zmogailovka—Borovitsa, as well as along the Lozovok—Svidovok sector. A motorized battalion and a reconnaissance detachment from the *Wiking* SS Panzer Division were defending along this 12-kilometer sector. Our intelligence established the boundary line between the *Wiking* SS Panzer Division and the 72nd Infantry Division southeast of the village of Svidovok. The enemy's most developed defense was opposite our bridgehead northwest of Kreshchatik and in the Cherkassy area.

A major shortcoming in the enemy's engineer preparation was the absence of continuous trenches and the insignificant depth of the defensive sector.

A Short Description of the Area of Combat Operations

The 52nd Army's offensive unfolded in the area of the city of Cherkassy.

A steppe valley predominates along the Dnepr's left bank; the right represents a mix of forest and steppe, with large wooded areas. The commanding heights are predominantly on the right bank. The soil is loamy along almost the entire left-bank, while along the right bank it is sandy and, in places, of sandy loam.

The Dnepr's channel in the 52nd Army's offensive sector is winding, with many branches forming islands. The width of the Dnepr's channel in the Cherkassy area varies from 360 to 420 meters, the depth of the river is 3.5-7.0 meters, and the speed of the current reaches 0.65 meters per second. The bottom is sandy. The height of the banks does not exceed 2.5 meters above the water level.

The periodic change in the Dnepr's water level required the scrupulous engineer reconnaissance of the river before its forcing by the troops. During 12-23 November the water level in the river remained almost unchanged, while during 24 November through 11 December it rose 32 centimeters, and over the next four days the water level dropped sharply, which made the work the crossings more difficult as the result of the formation of sand bars. On 5 December a sparse drifting of ice had begun.

The presence of swampy sectors in the Dnepr's floodplain and lakes along certain axes made the troops' movement to the river more difficult. On the whole, the Dnepr represented a very serious obstacle along its middle course, the overcoming of which demanded the thorough and careful training of the troops.

The Irdyn' swampy sector, difficult of passage, lies in the western area of combat operations, and a small river of by the same name flows here. There were seven corduroy roads and a railroad bridge for travel through the swamp.

The Ol'shanka River, a tributary of the Dnepr, flows 20 kilometers west of the city of Cherkassy. The river's floodplain is broad, the right bank dominates the left, the channel is winding, its width is 15-20 meters, it is 0.4-2.0 meters deep, and the bottom is sandy. The terrain in the area of our forces' bridgehead north of Kreshchatik was particularly unfavorable. The Ross' River flows here. Both banks of this river are quite swampy and teem with a large number of small lakes. The terrain along the bridgehead occupied by the 52nd Army's forces represented a swampy lowland. At the same time, the terrain in the enemy's hands had plenty of favorable heights and woods. The heights in the enemy's position enabled him to view and maintain under fire the 73rd Rifle Corps' combat formations located on the bridgehead.

Precipitation in the form of rain and freezing rain fell in the first half of November. The air temperature in November varies from +10.1 to -4.8 and from +5.2 to -10.7 in December. There was a lot of black ice on 23 November. Cloudy weather with low cloud cover and fog predominated throughout the entire operation, with southeasterly winds in November and westerly winds in December. The meteorological conditions in the fall of 1943 significantly complicated our forces' combat operations, which were linked to forcing major rivers. Thick fogs, sheer low cloud cover, which sometimes reached ten degrees, and ceaseless rains, and which continued up to 23 November, made the employment of aviation by both sides difficult, both during the operation's preparatory period and during its first stage.

West of the city of Cherkassy there is a wooded area, which directly abuts the Dnepr for a distance of 15 kilometers and which changes to thickets along the shoreline. As was mentioned above, partisans and elements of the 5th Guards Airborne Brigade operated in these woods.

The inhabited locales located along the right bank of the Dnepr, around the wooded area, as well as along the banks of the Ol'shanka and Tyasmin rivers, facilitated to a sufficient degree the organization of the enemy's solid defense. The largest inhabited locale in the enemy's position was the Kiev Oblast's district center of Cherkassy, which is adjacent to the Dnepr. The city is laid out in a straight fashion. A significant part of the stone buildings, with basement and half-basement structures, could easily be configured for defense. Factories and plants were mostly located in the city's shore area and along its outskirts. There were four brick factories 1-2 kilometers southeast of Cherkassy, which could be configured for defending the immediate approaches to the city. There were large structures in a military settlement's on the city's southwestern outskirts. There were large structures in the "Sosnovka" rest home in the pine woods two kilometers southwest of Cherkassy. There were a number of heights south of the city favorable for organizing a defense. The majority of buildings in the rural inhabited locales were of wood, with straw roofs.

The main (one-track) railroad line ran through the Zolotonosha, Cherkassy and Smela stations. Smela station is a major railroad junction along the lateral main line between Belaya Tserkov' and Krivoi Rog. This main line was broadly employed by the enemy for operational shipments. The railroad bridge over the Dnepr north of Cherkassy had been blown up.

The enemy had built two narrow-gauge railroad lines of Cherkassy—Svidovok and Cherkassy—Geronimovka on the right bank of the Dnepr, aside from the existing Cherkassy—Smela rail line. A narrow-gauge railroad had also been laid in the central part of the city.

There were insufficient dirt roads on the left bank. The normal exploitation of the roads from Zolotonosha to Svidovok and from Chekhovka to Cherkassy required the construction of corduroy roads and the replacement of the majority of bridges. In light of the frequent rains, the movement of military equipment and auto transport along the country roads during the operation was made extremely difficult.

On the whole, the 52nd Army's area of combat operations represented a serious of unquestionable advantages for the defending enemy. The presence of a powerful water obstacle, large wooded areas, swamps, lakes, and a large number of inhabited locales made the enemy's organization of a powerful defense easier.

The features of the area of combat operations outlined here created numerous difficulties for the attacking troops, both during the preparation for the offensive operation, and during its course. The wooded and broken character of the terrain, in particular, made the organization of cooperation and their control more difficult, and reduced the effectiveness of artillery fire and made the employment of tanks more difficult. Besides this, the forcing of such a mighty water line as the Dnepr required the skillful organization of the forcing and made great demands on the troops' combat training.

The Operation's Preparation

The Decision by the Commander of the Second Ukrainian Front

In the beginning of November 1943, while continuing to repel the enemy's counterblows northwest of Krivoi Rog, the Second Ukrainian Front's forces set about preparing an offensive operation with the mission of defeating, in conjunction with the Third Ukrainian Front, the enemy's Krivoi Rog group of forces and capturing Krivoi Rog. The *Stavka* of the Supreme High Command, in its 5 November 1943 directive No. 30238 ordered the commander of the Second Ukrainian Front, "upon firmly consolidating on along the current line, to launch an attack with the forces of the

37th, 57th and 5th Guards Tank armies in the general direction of Lozovakta and Shirokoye and, to capture Krivoi Rog and reach the line Petrovo—Gurovka—excluding Shirokoye."

The troops' attack was set for 12-14 November. Simultaneously, the Third Ukrainian Front was to launch an attack along its right wing in the direction of Sofievka and Dolgintsevo and reach the line Shirokoye—Apostolovo, while assisting the Second Ukrainian Front in capturing Krivoi Rog.

The commander of the Second Ukrainian Front, General I.S. Konev, on the basis of the directive by the *Stavka* of the Supreme High Command, decided to concentrate his main efforts of the *front's* left-wing forces along the Krivoi Rog axis and attack with the forces of a single combined-arms army (7th Guards) in the direction of Kirovograd. On the right wing, the *front* commander called for forcing the Dnepr north of Cherkassy, with the mission of distracting part of the enemy's forces from the axis of the *front's* main attack and to capture the city of Cherkassy. The resolution of this task was to be entrusted to the 52nd Army, which was to carry it out with its available forces, without counting on reinforcements from the *front*. The army's forces were to coordinate their actions with the airborne group and local partisans. *Front* aviation was not to be set aside for supporting the 52nd Army, as it was designated for supporting the offensive by the *front's* main forces along the Krivoi Rog axis.

The Decision by the Commander of the 52nd Army

Proceeding from the assigned task and an evaluation of the situation, the commander of the 52nd Army made the following decision for the offensive operation with the forcing of the Dnepr River (combat order No. 0021 of 11 November 1943, to the army's forces). It was planned to launch the main attack with the forces of the 73rd Rifle Corps along the 8-kilometer sector Yelizavetovka—Svidovok, to force the Dnepr here and to seize a bridgehead on the river's right bank. While developing the success in the general direction of Russkaya Polyana and Smela, the army's forces were to defeat, in conjunction with Sidorchuk's airborne forces and the partisans, the enemy's Cherkassy group of forces and to capture Cherkassy on the night of 13-14 November. It was planned to force the river with two regiments from the 373rd Rifle Division in the area north of Dakhnovka and Zmogailovka to support the 73rd Rifle Corps' forces in capturing the city.

The offensive was to be carried out in a single echelon. Reserves were not allotted. The operation was planned to a depth of 17 kilometers and to last one day. The beginning of the forcing was set for 2400 on 12 November along the sectors west of Sekirna, north of the villages of Svidovok and Dakhnovka, and east of Zmogailovka. The forcing of the river was to be carried out without an artillery preparation to insure surprise.

In accordance with this decision, the army's forces were assigned the following tasks.

The 73rd Rifle Corps (254th and 294th rifle divisions, Major General P.F. Batitskii, corps commander) was to launch an attack with the forces of the 254th Rifle Division in the direction of Svidovok and Russkaya Polyana with the immediate objective of forcing the Dnepr on the night of 12-13 November, with the assistance of the airborne group and partisan detachments, north of the village of Svidovok, to seize a bridgehead along the line Yelizavetovka—Budishche—Svidovok and, while securely supporting the attacking group's right flank, to capture Russkaya Polyana. Subsequently, in conjunction with units of the 73rd Rifle Corps' 373rd Rifle Division, it was to capture the city of Cherkassy. Simultaneously, the 73rd Rifle Corps was to securely defend the captured bridgehead north of Kreshchatik with the forces of the 294th Rifle Division.

The 78th Rifle Corps (373rd Rifle Division, Major General G.A. Latyshev, corps commander) received orders to force the Dnepr along two sectors with the forces of two regiments with the immediate task of seizing a bridgehead during the night of 12-13 November along the Dakhnovka—Sosnovka sector and, while developing the offensive, capturing Cherkassy together with the 254th Rifle Division during the night of 13-14 November.

It was planned to cross the 1817th Self-Propelled Artillery and 259th Independent Tank regiments to the captured bridgehead behind the 936th Rifle Regiment (the 254th Rifle Division's second echelon) and to employ them for capturing the village of Geronimovka.

Following the establishment of radio communications with the airborne group, it was assigned the following task on 12 November: to capture Yelizavetovka and Svidovok on the night of 12-13 November, thus facilitating the army's troops in forcing the Dnepr.

On the morning of 12 November an officer from the operational section of the 52nd Army's headquarters arrived by plane at Major Sidorchuk's airborne group and confirmed the previously assigned task.

In accordance with the army commander's decision, the formation commanders made their own decisions. According to the decision by the commander of the 73rd Rifle Corps, the 294th Rifle Division, along with the 438th Anti-Tank Artillery Regiment, was to firmly defend the bridgehead north of Kreshchatik. The 254th Rifle Division, along with the 490th Mortar Regiment, a battalion from the 568th Gun Artillery Regiment, and a battalion from the 17th Guards Mortar Regiment, with its combat formation in two echelons (two regiments in the first echelon and one regiment in the second), was to force the Dnepr on the night of 12-13 November along the Yelizavetovka—Svidovok sector and, while launching its main attack in the direction of Svidovok and Russkaya Polyana, to capture a bridgehead along the line Yelizavetovka—Budishche—Svidovok and by the close of the day seize Russkaya Polyana. The division, on conjunction with the 373rd Rifle Corps, was to capture the city of Cherkassy on the night of 13-14 November.

The decision by the commander of the 73rd Rifle Corps foresaw crossing the rifle regiments' artillery and mortars to the right bank together with the first-echelon battalions.

Upon taking Svidovok, the commander of the 254th Rifle Division was ordered to cross the division artillery and the 490th Mortar Regiment to the captured bridgehead. All of the crossing equipment was to be employed for the forcing, with a small reserve left at the disposal of the division commander.

According to the decision by the commander of the 254th Rifle Division, the 929th Rifle Regiment was to force the Dnepr at crossing point No. 1, west of Sekirna and to seize a bridgehead in the Yelizavetovka—Sekirna area. The regiment was to subsequently capture the village of Budishche, thus securing the division's main forces from the west, against Moshny. The 929th Rifle Regiment received orders to force the Dnepr north of the village of Svidovok (crossing point No. 2) and capture Svidovok. The 936 Rifle Regiment was in the division's second echelon. It was planned to employ it for capturing Russkaya Polyana.

The commander of the 78th Rifle Corps ordered the commander of the 373rd Mirgorod Rifle Division to force the Dnepr along two sectors. The 1239th Rifle Regiment was to force the Dnepr south of Maloye Lipskoye and to capture a bridgehead in the Dakhnovka area. The 1235th Rifle Regiment was to force the Dnepr in the area of marker 81.0 and to capture Zmogailovka. The 373rd Rifle Division's units were to subsequently launch an attack on Cherkassy and, in conjunction with the 254th Rifle Division, to capture the city on the night of 13-14 November. The 1239th Rifle Regiment was to be supported by two artillery battalions, and the 1235th Rifle Regiment by one battalion. The 1237th Rifle Regiment was to defend the left bank of the Dnepr along the sector from the Orekhovaya River to Chigirin Dubrova (60 kilometers southeast of Cherkassy).

As is clear from the information above, of the five rifle regiments assigned to force the Dnepr and capture Cherkassy, four regiments were to simultaneously force the river along a broad front (in four areas) more than 30 kilometers in width. The army had neither a second echelon nor reserves.

The rifle corps' combat formation was in a single echelon. The 73rd Rifle Corps' 254th Rifle Division formed its combat formation in two echelons, with two regiments in the first echelon and one in the second. The 78th Rifle Corps' 373rd Rifle Division was to attack with two regiments,

298 THE BATTLE OF THE DNEPR

which were located at a significant remove from one another and which organized their combat formations into two echelons.

The Organization of the Artillery Offensive

The artillery's tasks during the forcing and seizure of a bridgehead on the right bank of the river consisted of suppressing the enemy's weapons along the forcing sectors and their flanks, as well as in preventing the concentration of the enemy's reserves and his counterattacks from the directions of Sekirna, Svidovok, Dakhnovka, the brick factories (southeast of Cherkassy), and Zmogailovka.

By the start of the offensive operation the army disposed of the following amount of artillery weapons (Table 2.1).

Thus the army disposed of 470 guns and mortars of all calibers for carrying out the assigned tasks while forcing the Dnepr and defending the bridgehead in the area north of Kreshchatik.

Table 2.1 The Combat Strength of the 52nd Army's Artillery

Units and Formations	Mortars			Guns and Rocket Artillery		
	82mm	120 mm	Total	45mm	57mm	76mm (regimental)
294th Rifle Div	39	14	53	22	–	8
254th Rifle Div	33	12	45	12	–	8
373rd Rifle Div	41	13	54	44	–	8
568th Gun Artillery Rgt	–	–	–	–	–	–
490th Mortar Rgt	–	36	36	–	–	–
438th Anti-Tank Artillery Rgt	–	–	–	–	–	–
1322nd Anti-Tank Artillery Rgt	–	–	–	–	24	–
17th Gds Mortar Rgt	–	–	–	–	–	–
Total	113	75	188	78	24	24

Units and Formations	Guns and Rocket Artillery					
	76mm (division)	122mm	152mm	M-13	Total	Total Guns and Mortars
294th Rifle Div	19	12	–	–	61	114
254th Rifle Div	19	12	–	–	51	96
373rd Rifle Div	19	12	–	–	83	137
568th Gun Artillery Rgt	–	–	18	–	18	18
490th Mortar Rgt	–	–	–	–	–	36
438th Anti-Tank Artillery Rgt	21	–	–	–	21	21
1322nd Anti-Tank Artillery Rgt	–	–	–	–	44	44
17th Gds Mortar Rgt	–	–	–	24	24	24
Total	78	36	18	24	282	470

All of the artillery of the 294th Rifle Division, two battalions of the 568th Gun Artillery Regiment, a battalion of the 17th Guards Mortar Regiment, and the 438th Anti-Tank Artillery Regiment was allotted for defending the bridgehead north of Kreshchatik. There was a total of 155 guns and mortars here, which yielded an average density of 12 guns and mortar per kilometer of front. The artillery of the 254th Rifle Division, the 490th Mortar Regiment, a battalion from the 17th Guards Mortar Regiment, and a battalion from the 568th Gun Artillery Regiment, for a total of 146 guns and mortars, of which 136 were 76mm and greater, was designated for supporting the forcing along the front Yelizavetovka—Svidovok. Such an amount of all types of artillery enabled us to have 17 guns and mortars per kilometer of front along the 8-kilometer forcing sector. Finally, in distributing the 373rd Rifle Division's artillery (137 guns and mortars), which was operating along a secondary axis, 86 units were set aside for supporting the forcing of the Dnepr by elements of the 1239th and 1235th rifle regiments, and 51 units for carrying out defensive tasks. Besides this, the 1322nd Anti-Tank Artillery Regiment (24 guns) and eight rocket platforms from the 17th Guards Mortar Regiment were in the army reserve.

As can be seen from this, the artillery density along the 254th Rifle Division's forcing sector was almost the same as the artillery density along the sectors where the army's forces were defending. The army commander committed a serious mistake, allotting 50 percent of the available artillery for carrying out defensive assignments. He corrected this mistake during the offensive, removing two battalions from the 568th Gun Artillery Regiment, the 438th Anti-Tank Artillery Regiment, two battalions from the 294th Rifle Division's 849th Artillery Regiment, and two battalions from the 17th Guards Mortar Regiment from the defensive sectors and assigning them to support the army's offensive actions.

However, the artillery's transfer to the captured bridgehead was carried out piecemeal and failed to support the successful development of combat activities to expand the bridgehead.

The 568th Gun Artillery and 17th Guards Mortar regiments were allotted to the long-range artillery group. In accordance with the army commander's decision, this group was chiefly designated for carrying out tasks for supporting the defense of the bridgehead on the right bank of the Dnepr north of Kreshchatik, as well as the boundary with the 27th Army. Only a single battalion from the 568th Gun Artillery Regiment and a battalion from the 17th Guards Mortar Regiment were brought in from the long-range artillery group for fighting the enemy's artillery in the Svidovok area; that is, along the forcing sector.

This decision to employ the long-range artillery group should not be viewed as correct. It would have been more expedient to bring in the entire group to support the forcing of the Dnepr by the units of the 254th Rifle Division.

The 1322nd Artillery Regiment was allotted to the army's anti-tank artillery reserve.

It was not planned to conduct an artillery preparation before the start of the crossing so as to achieve surprise. The artillery was assigned the task of being ready to suppress the enemy's weapons, should they open fire on our troops. Battalion and regimental artillery, as well as part of the division artillery's gun batteries were to be placed in their firing positions in the immediate vicinity of the shore for firing over open sights, for the more effective suppression of the enemy's weapons. The support and accompaniment of the infantry and tanks on the opposite bank were to be carried out through the method of the sequential concentration of fire at to the formation commanders' requests.

From two to three battalions were to be attached to the infantry support groups, depending on the importance of the tasks being carried out by the rifle divisions and regiments.

As can be seen from this, the shortage of artillery in the army was considerably exacerbated by its unfortunate distribution. A density of 17 guns and mortars per kilometer of front was clearly insufficient for supporting the forcing of the Dnepr by the army's forces.

Engineer Support for the Operation

The following engineer units were part of the army: the 366th Army Engineer Battalion and the 9th Engineer-Sapper Brigade's 133rd and 135th independent engineer-sapper battalions.

The army had 5.6 parks of various types, 17 collapsible wooden boats (SDL) and 62 fishing boats for supporting the forcing of the Dnepr River. Besides this, five pontoons from a light inflatable pontoon park, a unit of flotation equipment, eight boats from USVA-3, and 34 fishing boats were operating at the crossings southwest of Sushka and south of Bubnovo.

The names of the parks and their capabilities are shown in Table 2.2.

As can be seen from this table, one could lay down one bridge with a length of 343 meters and a carrying capacity of six tons, or a bridge 192 meters long with a carrying capacity of 16 tons, with the crossing equipment at the army's disposal, at a time when the width of the Dnepr's channel in the Cherkassy area was 360-420 meters. It was possible to cross no more than two rifle battalions and their reinforcements in a single trip while using all of the crossing equipment for ferry and landing crossings.

In this situation, the bold concentration of all the crossing equipment along the axis of the army's main attack, their skillful distribution between the units forcing the river and the crossing point's precise work acquired special significance. However, as we see from Table 2.3, the crossing equipment was almost equally distributed among the corps.

The table shows that in essence almost no distinction was made in distributing crossing equipment between the 73rd Rifle Corps, which was supposed to force the Dnepr along the army's main attack axis, and the 78th Rifle Corps, which was operating along a secondary axis.

Table 2.2 The Types of Crossing Equipment and Their Capabilities

Types of Crossing Equipment	Number of Parks or Boats (in units)	Bridge-Laying Capabilities (in meters)			Number of Ferries		
		3 Tons	5-6 Tons	14-16 Tons	3 Tons	5-6 Tons	14-16 Tons
USVA-3	1.5	–	170	120	–	15	6
MdPA-3	1	–	111	46	–	11	3
Division Bridge Park-42	0.1	–	62	26	–	–	2
Wooden Landing Park	3	–	–	–	24	–	–
Wooden Sapper Boat	17	–	–	–	–	–	–
Fishing Boats	62	–	–	–	–	–	–
Total	–	120	343	192	24	26	11

Types of Crossing Equipment	Capabilities for Crossing Men and Materiel on Ferries in One Trip		
	People Only	45mm Guns With Limbers (in units)	Larger Caliber Guns (in units)
USVA-3	450	30	15
MdPA-3	440	22	11
Division Bridge Park-42	120	6	2
Wooden Landing Park	360	24	24
Wooden Sapper Boat	170	–	–
Fishing Boats	300	–	–
Total	1,840	82	52

THE FORCING OF THE DNEPR BY THE 52ND ARMY

Table 2.3 The Distribution of Crossing Equipment by Rifle Corps y the Start of the Operation

Crossing Equipment	73rd Rifle Corps	78th Rifle Corps	Army Reserve
USVA-3	1 park	0.5 parks	–
MdPA-3	1 park	–	–
Wooden Landing Park	1 park	2 parks	–
Wooden Sapper Boat	7 units	10 units	–
Fishing Boats	–	62 units	–
Division Bridge Parks-42	–	–	0.1

Four crossing points were established according to the army commander's decision.

Point No. 1 in the Sekirna area and point No. 2 in the area of marker 80.9 (north of Svidovok) were designated for crossing units of the 254th Rifle Division.

Point No. 3 I the area of marker 78.4 (north of Dakhnovka) and point No. 4 in the area of marker 81.0 (northeast of Zmogailovka) were designated for crossing units of the 78th Rifle Corps' 373rd Rifle Division.

The distribution of equipment by crossing point shown above enabled us to cross the following (taking into account 10 percent allotted to the crossing commanders) in a single trip: up to one reinforced rifle battalion at crossing point No. 2 and from one to two reinforced rifle corps at the remaining crossing points.

Thus the 254th Rifle Division's 929th Rifle Regiment, which had forced the Dnepr in the area west of Sekirna (crossing point No. 1) was able to cross all of its men and materiel in 10-15 trips, which would have required about 24 hours. The 933rd Rifle Regiment, which was crossing north of Svidovok (crossing point No. 2) was able to force the river in 5-7 trips; that is, in the course of half a day. Two of the 373rd Rifle Division's regiments, which had forced the Dnepr at crossing points 2 and 3, were able to cross their main forces during the course of 24 hours.

Table 2.4 The Distribution of Crossing Equipment by Crossing Points

Crossing Equipment	Number of Crossing Points				Reserve	Total
	No. 1	No. 2	No. 3	No. 4		
USVA-3	–	1 park	0.5 park	–	–	1.5 parks
MdPA-3	–	1 park	–	–	--	1 park
Division Bridge Park-42	–	–	–	–	0.1 park	0.1 park
Wooden Landing Parks	1 park	–	0.5 park	1.5 parks	–	3 parks
Wooden Sapper Boats	5 units	2 units	–	10 units	--	17 units
Fishing Boats	–	–	30 units	32 units	--	62 units

As can be seen from this, the crossing equipment available in the army was poorly distributed among the formations and crossing points. There was only half of all the crossing equipment along the axis of the main attack (at crossing points 1 and 2). Their crossing capability under even the most favorable conditions enabled us to cross the 254th Rifle Division's first echelon over 24 hours. Due to this, the transfer of men and materiel to the right bank did not support the accomplishment of the assigned task in the time period set by the army commander.

Two companies from the 366th Army Engineer Battalion, a company from the 135th Independent Engineer-Sapper Battalion and division sappers were detached for servicing the 73rd Rifle Corps' crossing. A company from the 366th Army Engineer Battalion and division sappers was detached for servicing the 78th Rifle Corps' crossing points. One company from the 135th Independent Engineer-Sapper Battalion was detached to the army's anti-tank artillery reserve.

The 133rd Independent Engineer-Sapper Battalion was designated for the construction of an observation post, the procurement of materials for a bridge in the area of crossing point No. 2 and the building of mooring places for a 30-ton ferry in the area northeast of Svidovok.

On 12 November all the crossing equipment had been delivered to the designated concentration sites and put into complete readiness for employment.

The Organization of Control and Communications

The following exerted a direct influence on the organization of control and communications in the Cherkassy operation: the limited time for preparing the operation; the simultaneous resolution by the army of the tasks of forcing a major water obstacle and the defense along a broad front against an overall shortage of men and materiel in the army; the necessity of ensuring coordinated activities by the army's attacking forces from the *front* with those of the parachute group and partisan detachments in the enemy rear.

The relay of tasks to their executors was carried out by responsible army staff officers, who were also entrusted with tasks for exercising control and rendering assistance to the troops while preparing for and conducting the operation. The personal interaction of the army commander, the army chief of staff and responsible staff officers with subordinate commanders and headquarters was widely employed.

During the operation's preparation the army commander controlled his forces from his command post, which was in the village of Ol'khovka. The corps commanders' command posts were located as follows: the 73rd Rifle Corps' in Korobovka and the 78th Rifle Corps' in Skorodistika. Upon the seizure of a bridgehead by our forces on the right bank of the Dnepr an auxiliary army command post was to be organized in the village of Svidovok.

The army and formation commanders' observation posts were outfitted within 150-500 meters of the bank, which enabled them to observe the course of the forcing and to control the formations' fighting on the captured bridgehead.

A great deal of attention during the operation's preparation was devoted to questions of organizing coordination. In accordance with the army commander's decision, the army headquarters issued an order to the troops on the order of reconnoitering the crossing sectors. Particular attention was paid to the detailed working out at the site of all coordination problems between the infantry and artillery and engineer subunits while forcing the river.

The reconnoitering of the forcing sectors was conducted during 10-11 November.

During the reconnaissance of the enemy's defense along the opposite bank, the forcing sectors and crossing points, as well as the troops' combat tasks were refined on the spot. All the problems of organizing the infantry's cooperation with the artillery and engineer subunits were worked out at the site. Particular attention was paid in this to the order of employing crossing equipment and the organization of the artillery offensive.

Assignments to the artillery were issued directly on the site and were relayed to the immediate executors. A great deal of attention was paid to making sure that the battery commanders knew the forcing order, as well as to the establishment of secure communications with those rifle subunits with which they would be forcing the Dnepr. Smoke release areas for masking the troops' crossing were defined, no matter what direction the wind was blowing, and cooperation between the chemical subunits and the anti-aircraft artillery covering the crossing points was organized.

The precise organization of cooperation with the airborne group and the partisan detachments had great significance for the troops' successful completion of their tasks. However, we were able to establish direction contact with the airborne group only on the morning of 12 November; that is, less than a day before the start of the offensive. The remaining time before the start of the forcing was insufficient for the detailed working out of coordination questions between the army's formations, the airborne troops and the partisans.

On this day the airborne group was given the task of capturing the stronpoints of Svidovok and Yelizavetovka. The beginning of the attack on these strongpoints was set for 2400 on 12 November; that is, simultaneously with the beginning of the forcing of the Dnepr by the rifle regiments' first echelons. Besides this, the group commander was informed of the 254th and 373rd rifle divisions' missions. A representative from the 52nd Army's headquarters, with radio set and a radio signals table, was dispatched for coordinating actions with the airborne group.

Communications with the *front* and neighboring armies—the 27th on the right and the 4th Guards on the left—was maintained over permanent lines.

Telephone communications with the army's formations were conducted along permanent wires. The army's signal units were distributed in the following manner. The 82nd Independent Line Battalion was designated for the construction and restoration of the army communications axis. The battalion's cable-pole company serviced the communications lines to the 78th Rifle Corps. Two independent cable-pole companies were employed for building cable-pole lines to the 73rd Rifle Corps and for organizing communications along the army commander's observation posts with the formation commanders.

Permanent communications lines of six wires along the line Ol'khovka—Korobovka—marker 80.9 (north of Svidovok) were built in anticipation of the offensive and a second communications line along the Zolotonosha—Cherkassy railroad was being restored. As our forces advanced, both of these lines were to link up along the northwestern outskirts of Cherkassy and support troop control during the development of combat activities on the right bank of the Dnepr.

The 52nd Army's radio communications was organized in the following manner: along two channels with the Red Army General Staff and the Second Ukrainian Front's headquarters, with a radio station set with the 27th Army on the right, along the *front* headquarters' network with the 4th Guards Army, and along three channels with the headquarters of the 73rd and 78th rifle corps.

The army headquarters' communications with the rifle division were carried out through corps radio networks. A radio station, which maintained communications only with the army headquarters, along with operators, was attached to the headquarters of the 254th Rifle Division, which was operating along the axis of the army's main attack.

In light of the fact that we could only use radio for communications with the airborne group and the partisans, the organization of radio communications with it was given great attention. At the same time, the presence of a weak radio station with the airborne group, the audibility of which fell sharply at times, was taken into account. Thus the reception of reports from the airborne group was carried out simultaneously by two of the army headquarters' receivers, which had been set up on different places and were working on different antennas. The transmission of orders and instructions from the army headquarters to the airborne group were conducted over medium and high-power radio stations.

Radio communications worked only to receive before the start of the forcing.

Low-power radio stations were allotted to the rifle subunits and units which were to force the river in the first echelons. Troop control was carried out exclusively by radio until the construction of river cable crossings.

The army's mobile communications equipment included three communications planes, six motor vehicles, nine motorcycles, and a horse platoon. The rainy weather, the poor condition of the roads and the shortage of fuel limited the opportunities for employing auto transport for communications purposes. Of all the mobile means, messengers on horseback were most widely used in these conditions.

On the whole, the organization of communications during the operation's preparatory period enabled the army command and commanders of its units and formations to control their troops. With the beginning of the forcing, radio communications and the organization of wire communications on the right bank of the Dnepr acquired great significance.

Operational Support for the Operation

By the beginning of the operation's preparation, the army's headquarters disposed of incomplete data about the enemy's group of forces and the location of his weapons in the immediate depth of his defense. Upon the receipt of the order to attack, the task of refining the available data and getting additional information about the enemy, particularly along the forcing sectors, arose. It was necessary to refine the numeration of the enemy's units and formations, their combat and numerical strength, to determine the unoccupied gaps, flanks and boundaries in his position, to refine the fire system along the forward edge of the defense, to discover the enemy's fire system and engineer structures in the depth of his defense. The main efforts of our intelligence during the preparatory period were concentrated in the army's offensive sector along the front from Yelizavetovka to Zmogailovka. However, in order to not attract the enemy's attention to the forthcoming offensive's sectors, intelligence was carried out in the army's entire offensive sector.

The main method of conducting intelligence during this time was around-the-clock observation from the combined-arms and artillery commanders' observation posts, as well as from the special forces' observation posts. Night searches, which were conducted for the purpose of capturing prisoners, often did not enjoy success. The main difficulty in organizing and conducting reconnaissance lay in the presence of a broad water obstacle in front of the army's forces.

Artillery reconnaissance was part of the general system of troop intelligence and was conducted in cooperation with the other combat arms' intelligence. The absence of sound reconnaissance equipment in the artillery units made more difficult the discovery of the enemy's artillery and mortar batteries. Nevertheless, eight 150mm guns, 42 105mm guns, 13 75mm guns, and 44 mortars were discovered by observation from artillery observation posts.

Intelligence data arriving from various sources was generalized by the formations' and army's headquarters and immediately transmitted to the unit and formation commanders. Based on prisoner testimony and data received from partisans, it was established that the boundary between the *Wiking* SS Panzer Division and the enemy's 72nd Infantry Division was in the area southeast of the village of Svidovok. In order to not reveal the operational plan, the activities of reconnaissance groups in the Svidovok area were subsequently halted.

As a rule, intelligence activities did not reach beyond the forward edge of the enemy's defense, which was one of the serious shortcomings in the army's preparation for the offensive operation.

Headquarters at all levels carried out a great deal of work for the purpose of uncovering the enemy's measures for operational deception. In particular, on the eve of the offensive the enemy, in order to deceive our command as to the true disposition of his forces, shifted several of the *Wiking* SS Panzer Division's walky-talkies to the Krivoi Rog area and simultaneously organized a demonstration movement of auto transport in the direction of that city. The enemy's intentions were discovered in time, thanks to our scouts' vigilance.

By the start of the operation, the army's headquarters disposed of some data about the enemy's group of forces and fire systems along the forward edge, but the depth of the enemy's defense had been poorly reconnoitered. Aerial photography of the enemy's position in the army's sector was not carried out. The existing shortcomings in the organization and conduct of intelligence of the enemy's fire system had a negative influence on the course of the fighting. For example, the absence of reliable data on the enemy's fire system in the Sekirna area prevented us from suppressing it in time with our artillery fire and led to the foiling of the 929th Rifle Regiment's crossing along this sector.

In order to achieve a surprise attack, a great deal of attention was devoted among the army's forces to problems of the secret conduct of regroupings, masking the troops' position and fooling the enemy as regards the intentions of the 52nd Army command. For this purpose, a series of measures were carried out for securing the operation's secret preparation. The enemy's intelligence, as was mentioned earlier, was conducted along a broad front: it was forbidden to employ radio equipment for transmitting orders and reports regarding the offensive's preparation; officers from the army headquarters were widely employed for transmitting the army commander's orders and to their executors and seeing to their fulfillment. Finally, as a rule, all troop movements were conducted at night.

Measures were also carried out for fooling the enemy regarding the true main axis of the army's attack. The goal of these measures was to create the impression with the enemy of our forces' concentration along the front Bubnovo—Prokhorovka, for the purpose of broadening the previously captured bridgehead along the right bank of the river north of Kreshchatik and, having thus tied down his forces here, to prevent the reinforcement of the enemy's group of forces along the forcing sectors.

In order to carry out these tasks, false tank and artillery positions were outfitted in the area of Prokhorovk and Kaleberda, as well as false concentration areas for auto transport. In all, eight dummy tanks (two groups of four tanks each), eight dummy 76mm guns (two batteries), six dummy 122mm guns, two groups of dummy ZIS-5[3] motor vehicles were set up and situated directly behind the artillery's main firing positions.

As a result of carrying out measures for securing the secret preparation of the operation, up to the very start of the operation the enemy had not undertaken any king of measures for reinforcing his group of forces along the 52nd Army's forcing sectors and continued to fortify his positions in the area of our forces' bridgehead north of Kreshchatik.

The 38th Anti-Aircraft Artillery Division, consisting of one regiment of medium-caliber anti-aircraft artillery and three regiments of small-caliber anti-aircraft artillery (16 anti-aircraft guns in each regiment), was for organizing anti-aircraft defense in the army. Two regiments of the anti-aircraft artillery division's small-caliber anti-aircraft artillery and a regiment of medium-caliber anti-aircraft artillery were brought in for covering the crossing point in the area north of Svidovok, the army's command post and the most important targets in the army rear in the town of Zolotonosha. One regiment of small-caliber anti-aircraft artillery was employed for covering out troops on the bridgehead north of Kreshchatik, which was not expedient. Such a dispersal of anti-aircraft equipment weakened the anti-aircraft defense of the army's units and formations attacking along the main attack axis.

Anti-aircraft defense in the units and formations was chiefly organized using the latters' means, for which anti-aircraft machine guns and anti-tank guns, which had been adapted for firing against aerial targets, and heavy and light machine guns, as well as group fire of all kinds of infantry weapons against the enemy's low-flying aircraft.

The timely notification of danger from the air was carried out through a system of air observation, notification and communications posts. In the event of an enemy air strike, shelters for the rank and file had been outfitted in the jumping-off area. A great deal of attention was devoted to observing masking measures by the troops.

---

3   Editor's note. The ZIS-5, a product of the Stalin Automobile Factory, was a medium truck produced in the USSR during 1933-58.

Materiel Support for the Operation

The army was based on the railroad sector from Mirgorod (120 kilometers northeast of Zolotonosha) to Zolotonosha. The army's supply station was at Zolotonosha. Army depots were deployed in the area of this station.

By the start of the operation the army's average provisioning with ammunition did not exceed 2.5 combat loads. Its provisioning according to various types of ammunition was as follows: 2.5 combat loads of 82mm and 122mm mortar rounds, 4.0 combat loads of 45mm shells, 2.0 combat loads of 76mm shells, 1.3 combat loads of 122mm shells, and 0.9 combat loads of 152mm shells.

The supply of diesel fuel significantly exceeded the tanks' and self-propelled guns' requirements. There was only 1.03 of a refill of gasoline. The supplies of food and forage did not exceed 8-10 days' rations.

Due to the fact that the task of capturing the city of Cherkassy was to be completed in the course of 24 hours, as well as the fact that the *front* was concentrating its main efforts along the Krivoi Rog axis, the delivery of materiel supplies to the 52nd Army was not planned.

The delivery of supplies from the army depots to the division ones was carried out by the army automobile battalion's equipment, which disposed of 139 vehicles and 40 single-axle trailers with a carrying capacity of 1.5 tons each.

The following delivery and evacuation routes were maintained by the army's equipment: Pal'mira[4]—Zolotonosha (15 kilometers) and Zolotonosha—Irkleev—Mozoleevka (90 kilometers). Besides this, the construction of the following roads was planned: Zolotonosha—Korobovka—Geronimovka (30 kilometers) and Zolotonosha—Kedina Gora—Dakhnovka—Geronimovka (30 kilometers). The 174th Independent Road Construction and 97th Independent Road Exploitation battalions were engaged in road work, while the local population was brought in to help.

Due to the unfavorable weather and the washing away of the roads, particularly during the operation's preparatory period, corduroys made of brushwood and poles had to be built on many road sectors. Round-the-clock duty by tractors was established along difficult-to-traverse sectors for towing stuck transport. 14 commandants' offices were set up for organizing control over transport movements.

By the start of the operation eight different hospitals had been deployed in the army's sector, with a capacity of 4,300 cots. The hospitals' location (the nearest hospitals were located 9-12 kilometers from the crossing points) supported the timely treatment of the wounded with qualified medical assistance. Army sanitary transport and empty vehicles were fully employed for the evacuation of wounded from the regimental and division medical stations, which secured the rapid freeing up of the medical establishments in the troop rear.

Medical stations in the crossing areas were staffed by the men and materiel of the 254th and 373rd rifle divisions' medical-sanitary battalions.

The Operation's Political Support

Meetings and gatherings, dedicated to the 26th anniversary of the Great October Socialist Revolution, were held in all units and subunits. A great deal of work was conducted to propagandize combat experience accumulated by the army's forces in the preceding operations.

Meetings of veteran soldiers with soldiers who had just begun their military career yielded the most positive results in this work. Colonel Puteiko, the commander of the 254th Rifle Division, personally addressed the young soldiers, telling them about the soldiers who had distinguished

---

4 Northeast of Zolotonosha.

themselves while forcing the Dnepr, about the division's traditions and about the experience of the division's best anti-tank riflemen.

Upon receiving orders to force the Dnepr, they set about preparing in the units special "Glory" and "Lightning" leaflets, which were designed to be passed along the skirmish line and in the subunits that had consolidated along the opposite shore of the river.

The Troops' Regrouping and Their Occupation of the Jumping-Off Position

It was necessary for the army's troops to carry out a regrouping for the purpose of creating a shock group of forces for the attack in accordance with the decision adopted for the operation. The regrouping was to take place along the front and consisted of removing the 254th Rifle Division from the bridgehead north of Kreshchatik and concentrating it along the main axis of the army's attack in the area north of the village of Svidovok, the concentration of two of the 373rd Rifle Division's regiments in the areas north and east of Cherkassy and in the transfer to the forcing sectors of the support artillery, the main mass of which was on the army's right flank. According to the regrouping plan, two days were allowed for carrying this out.

On 10 November the 254th Rifle Division turned over its defensive sector of the bridgehead to units of the 294th Rifle Division and, upon carrying out a march following the crossing to the left bank of the Dnepr, reached its designated sector for the offensive. By the morning of 11 November it had relieved the 373rd Rifle Division's 1239th Rifle Regiment along the sector Domantov—Lipskoe. By the morning of 12 November the 373rd Rifle Division's main forces had concentrated as follows: the 1239th Rifle Regiiment in the Lipskoe area, the 1235th Rifle Regiment north of Zmogailovka.[5] The regrouping of these rifle units was carried out under the cover of darkness and with the strictest observance of all masking measures.

The partial regrouping of the artillery (490th Mortar and 568th Gun Artillery regiments), the conduct of which was planned for the night of 10-11 November, was only completed during the day of 11 November. The chief reason for the untimely arrival of the artillery units to their designated areas was the poor preparation of the routes and bridges for the movement of artillery.

During the operation's preparatory period, insufficient attention was paid to the problems of outfitting routes along which the regroupings and the delivery of material-technical equipment to the army were to be conducted. All of the roads became impassable for automobile and then horse-drawn transport following several days of constant rain, which made the delivery of everything needed for the battle to the troops more difficult and delayed the timely conduct of the artillery's regroupings.

By the close of 12 November the army's forces occupied their jumping-off position for forcing the Dnepr.

The 73rd Rifle Corps' 254th Rifle Division deployed along a front excluding Lake Buchatik—the shoreline marker 80.9.

The 78th Rifle Corps' 373rd Rifle Division's 1239th Rifle Regiment had concentrated in the area west of the village of Maloye Lipskoye and the 1235th Rifle Regiment along the left bank of the Dnepr north of Zmogailovka.

A large part of the supporting artillery occupied combat positions in the area immediately adjacent to the shore. The artillery of the second-echelon divisions' rifle regiments had been moved up to the river for firing over open sights. As a result of the troops' regrouping, the following correlation of forces had been achieved by the start of the operation.

---

5   One of this division's regiments occupied defensive positions along the front Samovitsy (north of Zmogailovka)—Chigirin Dubrova (60 kilometers southeast of Cherkassy).

As is clear from the table, the 52nd Army's forces did not have a superiority of men and materiel over the enemy in the army's entire sector.

Table 2.5 The Correlation of Men and Materiel in the 52nd Army's Sector by the Start of the Operation

	In the Army's Entire Sector (140 km)			Along the Forcing Sector (30 km)		
	Soviet	Enemy	Correlation	Soviet	Enemy	Correlation
Battalions	27	31	1.0:1.1	15	10	1.5:1.0
Guns and Mortars	419	343	1.2:1.0	220	84	2.6:1.0
Tanks and Self-Propelled Guns	10	20	1.0:2.0	10	10	1.0:1.0

In spite of this, the 52nd Army command managed to create a superiority over the enemy in the offensive sector of 1.5 times in the number of battalions and more than 2.5 times in the amount of artillery.

Thus during seven days (5-12 November) a great deal of work to prepare the offensive and to force a water obstacle was carried out among the army's forces.

It should be noted that the commander of the 52nd Army made an expedient decision about directing the main attack on Svidovok and Russkaya Polyana and about active operations along a broad front in the 373rd Rifle Division's sector, so as to disperse the enemy's efforts and to distract his attention from the army's main attack sector. The enemy had insignificant forces along the main attack axis and considered the forcing of the Dnepr along this sector unlikely. Besides this, the launching of an attack on Svidovok would enable us to resolve the task of capturing a bridgehead along the river's right bank through the joint efforts of the 52nd Army's forces and those of the airborne group and the partisans.

However, at the same time the army committed a number of serious mistakes in preparing the operation, which could not but exert a substantial influence on the course of the operation. Chief among these mistakes was the indecisive concentration of men and crossing equipment and the insufficient massing of the army's artillery along the axis of the main attack.

In the specific situation of the 52nd Army, the shock group could have been reinforced by means of a bolder weakening of the *front's* other sectors. Taking into account the enemy's passivity against the bridgehead in the Kreshchatik area, part of the 294th Rifle Division's also could have been concentrated along the axis of the army's main attack. At the same time, according to the army commander's decision, all of the men and materiel in the army were equally distributed along three axes: the 294th Rifle Division on the bridgehead north of Kreshchatik; the 254th Rifle Division along the axis of the main attack, and the 373rd Rifle Division along the secondary axis. Neither the army commander nor the commander of the 73rd Rifle Corps had any reserves.

Besides this, the successful resolution of the assigned tasks by the army's forces depended to a great degree on the correct employment of crossing equipment and the engineer support for the operation as a whole. As was noted earlier, it was planned to carry out the forcing of the Dnepr along four crossing points, which were located along a front of more than 30 kilometers. At the same time, only a little more than 50 percent of all the crossing equipment, which could support the transfer of no more than two rifle regiments to the opposite bank in the course of a day, was concentrated on the first two points, where the forcing by the army's shock force was to be carried out.

These mistakes were committed because the army commander, in creating a group of forces for the offensive, proceeding only from the most favorable prerequisites. He calculated on depriving the enemy of the opportunity to put up organized resistance through a surprise attack and to achieve the assigned task in a very short time (in 24 hours). Such a decision was correct, in principle. Given the shortage of men and materiel, the assigned task could only be carried out by the army's forces by achieving complete surprise in forcing the river and in the troops' decisive actions. However, at the same time one must note that the army commander's decision did not take into account the possibility that the enemy would transfer forces to the Cherkassy area. This underestimation resulted in a situation in which reserves were not created in the army and corps and the regrouping of men and materiel from the bridgehead in the Kreshchatik area to the axis of the army's main attack was not called for.

The Conduct of the Operation

According to the operational plan, the 52nd Army's forcing and offensive along the opposite bank was supposed to develop at a vigorous pace. Within a day following the beginning of the forcing, the army's forces were supposed to completely capture the city of Cherkassy. In reality, the offensive took on a stubborn and prolonged character and continued 31 days.

The Cherkassy operation may be divided into two clearly expressed stages, according to the course of combat activities.

The first stage embraced the 13-18 November time period. During this time the army's forces forced the Dnepr and seized a bridgehead of operational significance northwest of Cherkassy.

The second stage lasted from 19 November through 14 December. During this time the army's forces captured the city of Cherkassy as a result of intense fighting, reached the Tyasmin River, expanded the bridgehead to up to 60 kilometers in width and 30 kilometers in depth, and created favorable conditions for the launching of an attack against the flank of the enemy's Korsun'-Shevchenkovskii group of forces.

The Forcing of the Dnepr and the Capture of a Bridgehead North of Svidovok (13-18 November)

The forcing of the Dnepr began at 2400 on 12 November. The 254th Rifle Division, as was noted earlier, was to force the Dnepr along two sectors: in the area west of Sekirna and north of Svidovok. Elements of the division's 929th Rifle Regiment began to force the river northwest of Sekirna without an artillery preparation. The enemy, upon discovering the beginning of the forcing by the regiment's subunits, opened a heavy fire on the landing. As a result of this, a significant part of our crossing equipment was sunk by the enemy. Repeated attempts to force the Dnepr along the 929th Rifle Regiment's sector in the area northwest of Sekirna were unsuccessful, due to the large amount of crossing equipment being put out of action. Due to this, the army commander ordered that the forcing along this sector be halted and that the 929th Rifle Regiment be crossed to the opposite bank during the night of 13-14 November in the area north of Svidovok.

The forcing proceeded more successfully along the sector north of the village of Svidovok. The 254th Rifle Division's 933rd Rifle Regiment was to carry out the forcing in the area of crossing No. 2. At exactly 2400 on 12 November the landing pushed off from the shore on rafts and boats.

Taking advantage of the noise from the fighting at crossing No. 1, elements from the 933rd Rifle Regiment's first trip reached the opposite bank without opposition and successfully landed here. Then, having succeeded in getting a foothold on the shore, the units attempted just as silently to penetrate into the depth of the enemy position, but were discovered by his sentries. The enemy, upon opening a disorderly fire against the crossing area, undertook several counterattacks against the crossed troops. However, the 933rd Rifle Regiment's subunits, supported by fire from artillery located along the left bank of the river, threw the enemy out of his trenches in an energetic attack and seized a small bridgehead near the village of Svidovok. Having organized an anti-tank defense on the captured bridgehead, these subunits secured the crossing of the regiment's second echelon.

By 0700 on 13 November, following the completion of the crossing, the regiment reached the northeastern outskirts of the village of Svidovok and also destroyed three enemy tanks.

The 254th Rifle Division's 936th Rifle Regiment crossed on fishing boats and the ferries from a wooden landing park behind the 933rd Rifle Regiment. Due to the enemy's increased artillery and mortar fire, the regiment's crossing was carried out in small groups. By 23 on 13 November the regiment had concentrated in the woods one kilometer northeast of the village of Sekirna.

Simultaneously with the crossing by the 254th Rifle Division's units, the group of parachutists, in conjunction with partisans, attacked unexpectedly from the rear on the night of 12-13 November and broke into Lozovok, Yelizavetovka and Budishche, while part of its forces attacked the enemy along the southern outskirts of Svidovok. The actions by the airborne group and the partisans were supported by the army's artillery through signals, transmitted by radio, from the right bank of the Dnepr. However, as a result of the dispersal of the airborne group's and partisans' forces and their failure to take the necessary measures to consolidate the achieved success, all of the village listed above were later abandoned.

During the second half of the day a group of soldiers in company strength from the 254th Rifle Division's 933rd Rifle Regiment, which had managed to break through to it through the enemy's combat formations northwest of the village of Svidovok, joined the airborne group. Simultaneously, officers from the 73rd Rifle Corps' headquarters were dispatched here for refining the combat assignemtn and resolving questions of cooperation.

Throughout the day the subunits that had forced the Dnepr north of Svidovok repelled six enemy counterattacks, in which 4-13 tanks took part. During the last counterattack, which was undertaken against the 933rd Rifle Regiment from the Sekirna area, a group of enemy automatic riflemen, numbering 200 men, managed to break into the lake area east of Sekirna. The enemy automatic riflemen were destroyed by the skillful actions of the 933rd Rifle Regiment's subunits.

Our troops' crossing throughout 13 November was chiefly carried out on boats from a wooden landing park and on fishing boats. The artillery's crossing chiefly began upon completion of the assembly of 5-ton ferries. By 0700 on 13 November two such ferries were operating north of Svidovok and another two ferries began operating somewhat later. Simultaneously, the construction of landings for a 30-ton ferry, which was designated for crossing tanks and self-propelled guns, was begun by the forces of the 133rd Independent Engineer-Sapper Battalion. The assembly of this ferry was carried out by the rank and file of the 366th Army Engineer Battalion and was completed on 15 November. Besides this, the commander of the 52nd Army ordered that immediately upon the beginning of the forcing that they set about laying down a floating bridge north of Svidovok with a capacity of six tons. The 135th Independent Engineer-Sapper Battalion and part of the 133rd Independent Engineer-Sapper Battalion were designated to carry out this work.

By the close of 13 November only two rifle regiments from the 254th Rifle Division, numbering a total of 2,473 men, had been crossed to the Dnepr' right bank. These regiments' elements had 17 heavy machine guns, 46 light machine guns, 25 anti-tank rifles, four anti-tank guns, and 28 mortars. The shortage of artillery in the subunits on the right bank made the repulse of the enemy's numerous infantry and tank counterattacks more difficult and lowered the pace of these subunits' attack.

Units of the 373rd Rifle Division set about forcing the Dnepr simultaneously with the 254th Rifle Division.

The 1239th Rifle Regiment's 2nd Battalion made a landing in the area north of Dakhnovka (crossing point No. 3) on fishing boats and ferries from a wooden landing park and by 0600 had advanced a kilometer into the depth. The enemy, having hurriedly transferred up to a battalion of infantry to this sector, with tanks, from the 72nd Infantry Division's reserve, counterattacked the selflessly defending battalion four times. As a result of the counterattacks by the numerically superior enemy, the 2nd Battalion was pressed back to the shore, where it continued to engage in an unequal fight until the onset of darkness. Having suffered significant losses, the battalion's elements returned to their jumping-off position on the left bank of the Dnepr on the night of 13-14 November. We also suffered tangible losses in crossing equipment. Eight boats from USVA-3 park were smashed by enemy artillery, which put crossing point No. 3 north of Dakhnovka out of action. Because of this, the remaining crossing equipment was employed for reinforcing the crossing points in the areas north of Svidovok and Zmogailovka.

The 1235th Rifle Regiment also forced the river on boats and ferries with its 1st Battalion southeast of Cherkassy and north of Zmogailovka (crossing point No. 4). By 0600 on 13 November it captured the island on marker 80.6. At sunrise the enemy undertook a number of attacks, under the cover of artillery and mortars, through a dried-up channel of the river, destroyed crossing equipment and held off our forces' advance. The regiment's further crossing was becoming difficult as a result of the losses in crossing equipment sustained.

Thus by the close of 13 November a bridgehead had been seized only along the 254th Rifle Division's sector north of the village of Svidovok, which amounted to four kilometers in width and up to three kilometers in depth. The attempts to force the Dnepr along the other sectors proved to be unsuccessful.

The enemy, having established the direction of the attack by the 52nd Army's main group of forces, began to shift his forces from inactive sectors to the captured bridgehead. For example, the enemy removed a battalion each from the *Deutschland* and *Westland* motorized regiments and the 332nd Infantry Division's 678th Infantry Regiment from the defensive sectors northwest of the village of Moshny and concentrated them in the Moshny area. At the same time, the 57th Infantry Division's 217th Infantry Regiment was being transferred from the Kanev area (18 kilometers northwest of Kreshchatik). Besides this, the enemy sought to cut off our units from their crossings and to destroy them by an attack from the Sekirna area in the direction of Svidovok, in conjunction with units of the 72nd Infantry Division, which were operating from Dakhnovka.

The situation had become difficult. It was necessary to immediately commit new forces into the fighting in order to expand and consolidate the captured bridgehead. However, as the result of the absence of reserves at the disposal of the army and corps commanders, the immediate augmentation of forces along the axis of the main attack was excluded. Thus the commander of the 52nd Army, having evaluated the situation that had arisen by the close of 13 November, decided to reinforce the forces attacking along the axis of the main blow, by transferring units from secondary sectors in the army's offensive zone. For this purpose, the commander of the 73rd Rifle Corps was ordered to pull the 294th Rifle Division's 861st Rifle Regiment from the defensive sector north of Kreshchatik and to concentrate it on the night of 13-14 November in the Korobovka area in readiness to move to the Dnepr's right bank.

The commander of the 78th Rifle Corps received instructions from the commander of the 52nd Army to cease forcing the river in the areas north of Dakhnovka and east of Zmogailovka and cross part of the 373rd Rifle Division's forces (the 1239th Rifle Regiment and the 1235th Rifle Regiment's 2nd Battalion) over the Dnepr along the 254th Rifle Division's sector to develop the offensive on Dakhnovka. The airborne group was ordered by radio to capture the line Yelizavetovka—Budishche together with the partisans and to firmly secure from the shock group's offensive from the northwest, and to also cut off the enemy's route of retreat on Geronimovka and Dakhnovka.

The corps commanders were ordered to maximally employ the night for launching surprise and vigorous attacks against the enemy. The 929th Rifle Regiment crossed in full strength over to the Dnepr's right bank on the night of 13-14 November.

On the morning of 14 November stubborn fighting unfolded on the captured bridgehead. The enemy, while putting up powerful resistance, undertook several counterattacks from the woods south of Sekirna, Geronimovka and Dakhnovka. The enemy counterattacks, in which from a company to a battalion of infantry, along with 10-16 tanks, took part, were supported by fire from 4-6 battalions of artillery. As a result of the increased enemy opposition, our offensive to capture Sekirna and Svidovok during the first part of the day was unsuccessful. It was only by the close of 14 November that the 254th Rifle Division's 929th Rifle Regiment managed to capture the unnamed farm east of Sekirna. By this time the division's main forces, as a result of an attack from the north and northeast, supported by the airborne group and partisans attacking from the south, captured the greater part of the village of Svidovok.

Soviet soldiers displayed great heroism in this fighting. The 254th Rifle Division's soldiers and officers bravely fought off enemy counterattacks. They destroyed six tanks and held their positions in repulsing the enemy's first infantry counterattack, aided by 16 tanks, and destroyed six tanks. Puteiko, the division commander, personally led the repulse of the enemy's infantry and tank attack and with his fearlessness and valor inspired the soldiers to brave and decisive actions.

The airborne group, while operating jointly with the partisan detachments, had by the close of the day once again captured the village of Budishche and was fighting in the village of Svidovok with part of its forces. Part of the partisans' and parachutists' forces were fighting in the woods northwest of Svidovok, with the task, in conjunction with the 929th Rifle Regiment, to capture Sekirna, the garrison of which consisted of up to a regiment of infantry, 20 tanks and up to two artillery battalions.

Throughout the first half of 15 November the enemy made repeated attempts to throw the 254th Rifle Division's units out of Svidovok, but the village was securely held by our troops.

On 15 November, due to the activation of a 30-ton ferry to the right bank of the Dnepr, two T-34 tanks from the 259th Independent Tank Regiment were crossed to the right bank of the Dnepr. The tanks were placed in ambush in the area northeast of Sekirna and took part in repelling enemy counterattacks. By the morning of 16 November the crossing of the 1817th Self-Propelled Artillery Regiment, which concentrated in the area east of Svidovok, was completed. However, the situation with the crossing equipment remained intense. The losses in crossing equipment by 15 November amounted to the following: 40 boats from a wooden landing park, 18 boats collapsible wooden boats, two boats from MdPA-3 park, 12 USVA-3 boats and 62 fishing boats.

On 15 November an auxiliary army command post was organized in Svidovok for the direct control of the troops' combat activities.

By this time the divisions' command posts and the corps' observation posts were located along the northern outskirts of Sekirna and in the Svidovok area.

Thus in three days of fighting along the Cherkassy axis the army's forces managed to seize in intensive fighting with the enemy a bridgehead in the Svidovok area seven kilometers wide and five kilometers deep. The enemy continued to transfer newer and newer forces to the bridgehead. The correlation in men and materiel began to rapidly change in his favor.

In this situation the troops' main efforts during 16-18 November were directed at expanding and consolidating the captured bridgehead. The army could not count on reinforcements from the *front's* reserve or removed from other axes along the front, because at this time the main events were developing along the Kirovograd and Krivoi Rog axes. At the same time, the enemy's resistance continued to increase. Suffice it to say that the enemy also committed the 1st Battalion of the 332nd Infantry Division's 676th Infantry Regiment, the *Deutschland* Motorized Regiment from the *Wiking* SS Panzer Division, the "Narva" Motorized Battalion, a panzer battalion and up to a battalion of assault guns into the fighting in order to keep the strongpoint of Sekirna in his hands. More than a battalion of 150mm guns were transferred to the area of the village of Moshny, which bombarded the 73rd Rifle Corps' crossing in the area north of the village of Svidovok. According to data supplied by the partisans, the enemy concentrated up to two regiments of infantry in the Sosnovka area, while up to 20 medium and heavy caliber guns had been discovered in the area of markers 105.0, 94.4 and 98.4 (south of Cherkassy).

In order to support the successful battle for the bridgehead, the commander of the 52nd Army decided to once again reinforce the troops operating on the bridgehead at the expense of the secondary axes. The commander of the 73rd Rifle Corps was ordered to additionally transfer the 294th Rifle Division's 859th Rifle Regiment from the left bank of the Dnepr to the Svidovok area, leaving only one regiment on the bridgehead north of Kreshchatik, while the corps' main forces, in conjunction with the airborne group, were to capture the line Yelizavetovka—marker 86.6—Geronimovka—Sosnovka.

The 294th Rifle Division, along with the 254th Rifle Division's temporarily subordinated 929th Rifle Regiment, received orders to capture Sekirna in conjunction with this group, to clear the enemy out of the woods south of Svidovok and to reach the line Yelizavetovka—marker 86.6—Geronimovka.

The 254th Rifle Division was to seize Geronimovka on the night of 16-17 November with the forces of the 936th Rifle Regiment, in conjunction with the 259th Independent Tank and 1817th Self-Propelled Artillery regiments, after which it was to develop the offensive on Russkaya Polyana; the division's main forces were to capture the line Geronimovka—Sosnovka.

The commander of the 78th Rifle Corps was ordered to attack in the direction of the northwestern outskirts of Cherkassy with part of the 373rd Rifle Division's forces (the 1239th Rifle Regiment and the 1235th Rifle Regiment's 2nd Battalion) and to capture the inhabited locales of Dakhnovka, Vasilitsa and Sosnovka.

The airborne group, having captured the village of Budishche on the previous evening, was temporarily subordinated to the commander of the 73rd Rifle Corps and by the close of 16 November was to occupy and firmly hold the line Lyuterevka—Yelizavetovka, securing the offensive by the 73rd Rifle Corps' main forces from the northwest. At the same time, the army commander ordered that the leadership of the airborne forces and partisans be entrusted to the commander of the airborne group.

The fighting to expand the army's bridgehead on the right bank of the Dnepr during 16-18 November was distinguished by great intensity.

The enemy, while undertaking counterattacks from the areas of Sekirna, Dakhnovka and Geronimovka, was seeking to destroy the army's units that had crossed over to the bridgehead and to restore his defense along the right bank of the Dnepr. The army's units, while repelling the enemy's counterattacks, completely cleared Svidovok on 15 November and by the close of 16 November had broadened the bridgehead up to eight kilometers in width and six kilometers in depth.

The capture of the inhabited locales of Sekirna, Yelizavetovka, Geronimovka, and Sosnovka had special significance for consolidating the success of the forcing. These tasks were resolved by the army's forces during 17-18 November.

There were already about two divisions (all of the 254th Rifle Division's regiments, two of the 294th Rifle Division's regiments, and more than a regiment from the 373rd Rifle Division) on the bridgehead by the morning of 17 November. The chief task of the army's shock group on this day was the capture of Sekirna and the arrival at the line Yelizavetovka—excluding Russkaya Polyana.

On the morning of 17 November the 294th Rifle Division's main forces attacked toward Sekirna. The enemy, while repelling the attack by the division's units with fire, undertook several powerful counterattacks for the purpose of cutting elements of the 859th and 929th rifle regiments from the crossings. During the daylight hours of 17 November up to a battalion of infantry, with ten tanks and two assault guns counterattacked from the Sekirna area the right flank of the 861st Rifle Regiment, which was attacking west of Svidovok. The enemy's tanks managed to break through to the western outskirts of the village. Simultaneously, the enemy managed to break through the airborne group's combat formations by an attack through Budishche from the village of Moshny, with up to a regiment of infantry, and reach the Sekirna—Svidovok road. A direct threat of the enemy's breakthrough along the boundary between the 861st and 859th rifle regiments on Sekirna arose. The gap between the 294th Rifle Division's regiments was about a kilometer. In order to eliminate the enemy's penetration, the commander of the 294th Rifle Division ordered the 859th and 861st rifle regiments to attack the enemy's flank. At the same time, the 350th Independent Anti-Tank Battalion's 2nd Battery was moved to the area of the northwestern outskirts of the village of Svidovok. The battery, having quickly occupied its firing positions, opened fire on the enemy tanks. Four enemy tanks were destroyed during the fighting and one assault gun knocked out. The remaining tanks turned back.

With the retreat of the enemy's tanks, his infantry counterattacks ceased. Having repelled the enemy's counterattacks, the 294th Rifle Division's units resumed their attack on Sekirna and, having outflanked it from the north and southwest, captured this inhabited locale on the night of 17-18 November.

Simultaneously with the fighting west of Sekirna, the attack by the army's units on Geronimovka and Dakhnovka began.

The village of Geronimovka, which is adjacent to Russkaya Polyana from the north, formed a sort of single inhabited locale with it, which covered the exit from the eastern part of the wooded area to the city of Cherkassy. The enemy had up to two battalions of infantry and an anti-tank battalion from the 72nd Infantry Division in these inhabited locales. The defending forces were supported by the fire of up to two artillery battalions.

According to intelligence data, Geronimovka was poorly prepared for defense, in the engineer sense of the word. Having refined his data on the nature of the enemy's defense, the commander of the 73rd Rifle Corps decided to detach the 936th Rifle Regiment, seven self-propelled guns and two tanks to capture the village. A company of automatic riflemen from the 259th Independent Tank Regiment was used for a descent on tanks and self-propelled guns. The 936th Rifle Regiment received orders to attack Geronimovka from the west, while the newly formed armored group made up of tanks, self-propelled guns and a company of automatic riflemen, would attack from the north.

With the onset of darkness on 16 November the tanks and self-propelled guns with their automatic riflemen had concentrated along the southern outskirts of Svidovok. The 936th Rifle Regiment, along with experienced partisan guides and supported by regimental and battalion artillery, began its march to outflank Geronomovka from the west. Having destroyed the enemy's combat security detachment along the way, reached Geronimovka by 0400 on 17 November and by dawn had occupied its jumping-off position for the attack 200 meters west of the inhabited locale. By this time the armored group had reached the northern outskirts of Geronimovka. At 0430 on 17 November, following a short artillery fire onslaught, the enemy was simultaneously attacked by the 936th Rifle Regiment from the west and the tanks with a descent of automatic riflemen from the north. The tanks and self-propelled guns destroyed the enemy's weapons and personnel with their fire and treads. Anti-tank guns waged battle with the firing points hindering the tanks' and infantry's advance. Having been taken by surprise by the unexpected appearance of our tanks and infantry, the enemy fell back in disorder to Russkaya Polyana. While developing the success, the 936th Rifle Regiment captured Geronimovka and the northern part of Russkaya Polyana.

The German-Fascist troops, which had fallen back from Geronimovka, were able to consolidate in the southern part of Russkaya Polyana. While continuously counterattacking from the area of the woods and the height at marker 116.0, they were seeking to halt the further attack by the division's units. An entire enemy medical company was captured in the fighting for Geronimovka, as well as 30 motor vehicles, three supply depots, 43 horses, and other materiel.

The capture of Geronimovka and the seizure of the northern part of Russkaya Polyana improved our troops' situation on the bridgehead. The army's forces exited the wooded area and had the

THE FORCING OF THE DNEPR BY THE 52ND ARMY

opportunity to launch an attack on Cherkassy form the southwest, where the enemy's defense was less developed than along the other sectors.

Upon our troops' capture of the inhabited locales of Sekirna and Geronimovka, the enemy, while holding off the attack by units of the 254th Rifle Division in Russkaya Polyana, began to fall back on Budishche and Cherkassy. By the close of 18 November the 73rd Rifle Corps, with the forces of the 294th Rifle Division and the airborne group, reached the line Yelizavetovka—Budishche—marker 86.6—excluding Geronimovka. The corps' 254th Rifle Division was continuing to fight along its right flank in Russkaya Polyana, and along its center and left flank had reached the edge of the woods northwest of Cherkassy. The 78th Rifle Corps' 373rd Rifle Division captured Vasilitsa and Sosnovka.

Thus the bridgehead which had been seized by the 52nd Army's forces had been expanded by the close of 18 November to 16 kilometers in width and nine kilometers in depth. In the 13-18 November fighting the army's forces destroyed 41 enemy tanks, ten armored cars, ten machine guns, and six mortars. Our troops captured 33 machine guns, seven guns, five tanks, one armored car, 37 motor vehicles, and five quartermaster depots.

The first stage of the Cherkassy operation was essentially completed with the seizure of a significantly large bridgehead west of Cherkassy.

The fighting on the bridgehead was extremely stubborn. The 52nd Army's activities were made more difficult by the rapid augmentation of the enemy's resistance and the slow accumulation of its own forces (particularly the army's artillery equipment) along the right bank of the Dnepr. As early as 13 November the enemy had begun to rapidly gather men and materiel from different sectors to the forcing sector. At the same time, the 52nd Army command was not able to quickly create a sufficiently strong group of forces on the right bank of the Dnepr in order to crush the enemy's resistance from the march and to develop the offensive on Cherkassy.

One of the main reasons for the slow accumulation of the army's men and materiel on the right bank was the absence of the necessary amount of crossing equipment and the disruption of the crossing points' work as the result of the enemy's powerful fire against them. Suffice it to say that by the close of the operation's first day only one crossing point was operating north of the village of Svidovok in the army's offensive sector. The absence of a bridge crossing slowed down the transfer of reinforcement equipment to the captured bridgehead. Only the rifle regiments' artillery, a battalion each from the 731st and 849th artillery regiments and three batteries from the 438th Anti-Tank Artillery Regiment were crossed to the right bank of the Dnepr in six days of fighting. The slow pace of crossing the artillery was chiefly due to a shortage of organic crossing equipment. Besides this, the dispersal of the limited amount of crossing equipment along the 30-kilometer front also told. The dispersal of crossing equipment along a broad front did not only make their maneuver along the front more difficult, but prevented us from having the necessary reserve in the hands of the army commander. It would have been more expedient to organize false crossing points for carrying out demonstration actions for the purpose of creating the impression among the enemy of our troops' crossing along a broad front, while employing the crossing equipment along the axis of the main attack, with the necessary reserve.

A substantial shortcoming in the actions of the airborne group and the partisans was their poor consolidation of the lines captured. One of the chief reasons the airborne group abandoned its lines was the absence in it of anti-tank weapons, particularly anti-tank artillery.

The army's rank and file displayed skill and unbending stubbornness in repelling the enemy's numerous counterattacks, having foiled the enemy's attempts to eliminate the bridgehead captured by our forces.

The Development of the Offensive Along the Right Bank of the Dnepr and the Beginning of the Fighting for the City of Cherkassy (19-24 November)

The 52nd Army's forces, having captured a bridgehead along the right bank of the Dnepr, had created a realistic threat to the enemy's group of forces in the Cherkassy area. Concerned by our forces' successful actions, the enemy continued to thrown reinforcements to the breakthrough sector and to Cherkassy from the areas of Kanev, Kreshchatika, Novaya Guta, and Moshny. The enemy's group of forces in the Smela area was being reinforced.

This was significantly facilitated by the situation that had arisen opposite the Second and First Ukrainian fronts at the beginning of the second half of November 1943. The offensive undertaken on 14 November by the Second Ukrainian Front's left-wing forces for the purpose of defeating the enemy's Krivoi Rog group of forces was not developed. The enemy, having reinforced his forces along the Krivoi Rog axis with two tank divisions, had as early as 15 November halted the offensive by the *front's* left-wing forces through powerful counterattacks. Because of this, the *front's* forces were assigned the task of consolidating along the lines reached and to prepare for a new offensive on 20 November along the previous axes. Simultaneously, a part of the forces (53rd and 5th Guards armies) was detached for rolling up the enemy's defense along the right bank of the Dnepr west of Kremenchug.

The First Ukrainian Front's forces, having conducted the Kiev offensive operation during 1-12 November, were engaged in heavy defensive fighting from 13 November against major enemy forces which were attempting to break through to Kiev. Particularly bitter fighting was going on in the areas of Zhitomir and southwest of Fastov. With the assumption of the defense by our forces, the enemy had the opportunity to remove part of his forces from these axes and to direct them against the 52nd Army's forces. For example, units of the 57th Infantry Division were being transferred from the Kanev area toward Cherkassy. The 6th Panzer Division, which was located east of Kirovograd, was being prepared for transfer to Smela.

By the close of 19 November the enemy's group of forces defending the city of Cherkassy consisted of units of the 72nd Infantry Division, the 1st and 3rd battalions of the 167th Infantry Division's 331st Infantry Regiment, the 5th Panzer Regiment's 1st Company, elements of the *Wiking* SS Panzer Division, three motorized sapper companies and the 503rd Sapper Battalion. In the city the enemy had no less than 40 tanks and ten assault guns. In all, there was up to one and a half infantry divisions, which had been reinforced with tanks, assault guns, and sappers here. The main group of enemy artillery—up to five artillery regiments—was in firing positions in the areas of the village of Lozovok, Kirillovka farm, the city of Cherkassy, and the village of Zmogailovka. Aside from this, an armored train was maneuvering along the Cherkassy—Smela railroad.

Additional forces, which were designated for reinforcing the Cherkassy group of forces, were being transferred from Kanev and Kirovograd and were supposed to concentrate in the areas of Cherkassy, Smela, Belozer'ye, and Khatski. Simultaneously, defensive works were undertaken along the left bank of the Ol'shanka River, along the southwestern and southern banks of the Irdyn' Marsh, and then along the right bank of the Tyasmin River.

By 19 November the 52nd Army had, as before, six rifle regiments, the numerical strength of which had decreased significantly as the result of the bitter fighting with the enemy during 13-18 November, on the captured bridgehead. A large part of the army's artillery continued to remain on the left bank. Only the rifle regiments' artillery, a battalion apiece from the 254th and 294th Rifle Divisions' 791st and 849th artillery regiments and three batteries from the 438th Anti-Tank Artillery Regiment were on the bridgehead.

Taking into account the possible arrival of new enemy reserves, the army commander decided to resume the offensive on the morning of 20 November and to capture the city of Cherkassy with his available forces by the close of the day, and also to capture Belozer'ye for the purpose of preventing the movement of the enemy's reserves from the Smela area to Cherkassy. The main attack in the direction of the slaughterhouse and Cherkassy station was again to be launched by the 254th Rifle Division, which had been significantly weakened in the preceding fighting.

The 373rd Rifle Division received orders to launch an attack with the forces of the 1239th Rifle Regiment from the Sosnovka area in the direction of the northwestern outskirts of Cherkassy. The division's 1235th Rifle Regiment was to attack from the island, occupied by it southeast of Cherkassy, to the city's eastern outskirts.

It was planned to detach part of the airborne group's and partisans' forces to support the offensive by the army's forces on Cherkassy from the south and southwest. One detachment, numbering 600 men, was to capture the village of Belozer'ye on the approaches to the town of Smela, while another was assigned the task of attacking from the Russkaya Polyana area to the southeastern outskirts of Cherkassy.

The attack on Cherkassy was prepared in a hurry. The cooperation between the infantry, artillery and tanks was not organized, due to a lack of time. An artillery preparation was not planned before the start of the attack on the city. All of the available artillery equipment was designated for employment in the infantry's combat formations. Combat tasks were assigned to the units and subunits were without specificity. For example, the 254th Rifle Division's rifle battalions were only instructed in what direction they should attack when orders were issued.

After the regrouping that was carried out on 19 November, the army's forces occupied the following positions.

The 294th Rifle Division, along with the greater part of the airborne group's forces, was consolidating along the line Yelizavetovka—excluding Budishche—eastern part of Lyuterevka—northern part of Russkaya Polyana—Geronimovka. One of the division's regiments continued to defend the bridgehead north of Kreshchatik.

Two of the 254th Rifle Division's regiments were along the line excluding Geronimovka—excluding Sosnovka, while the third regiment had concentrated in the village of Svidovok.

One of the 373rd Rifle Division's regiments occupied its jumping-off position for an attack southeast of Sosnovka and its second regiment had captured the unnamed island east of Cherkassy and was fighting in the area of the sugar factory along the eastern outskirts of the city. The third regiment was defending along its previous line southeast of Cherkassy.

On 19 November the army's auxiliary command post remained in the northern part of the village of Svidovok. The rifle corps' and divisions' command posts were distributed as follows: the 73rd Rifle Corps' in the southern part of Svidovok, the 294th Rifle Division's in Dakhnovka, the 254th Rifle Division's in the woods west of Sosnovka, the 73rd Rifle Corps' in Skorodistika, and the 373rd Rifle Division's in the village of Belki.

In evaluating the situation by the beginning of the offensive on Cherkassy, one should note that it was unfavorable for the 52nd Army's forces. The commander of the 52nd Army could only oppose no more than four rifle regiments, which had been significantly weakened in the preceding fighting, to the enemy's four infantry regiments located in the Cherkassy area. If one also takes into account the offensive's poor organization and the shortage of ammunition, then it will be quite clear that the offensive on Cherkassy could not yield any kind of positive results for the 52nd Army's forces.

The attack on the city began at 0630 on 20 November. An hour later our tanks and self-propelled guns, with a descent of automatic riflemen, broke into the city from the direction of the railroad station. By 0800 their forward detachments had reached the blocks in the central part of the city. Among the first to break through to the railroad station was the self-propelled gun of First Sergeant Tarasov, the party organizer for a battery from the 1817th Self-Propelled Artillery Regiment. The crew destroyed six guns, one six-barreled mortar, nine motor vehicles, and up to 80 enemy soldiers with accurate fire. When he ran out of ammunition, Senior Sergeant Tarasov continued to destroy the enemy's personnel and equipment with his treads.

Units of the 254th Rifle Division, while taking advantage of the tanks' and self-propelled guns' success, reached the area of the tobacco factory. The 373rd Rifle Division's 1239th Rifle Regiment captured the Shevchenko Collective Farm.

At 1200 the enemy undertook a powerful counterattack in the center of the city in the direction of the railroad station and forced the 254th Rifle Division's units to abandon the area of the tobacco factory. The bitter fighting did not cease until the onset of darkness. In all, the enemy undertook four counterattacks throughout the second half of 20 November with forces ranging from a company to a battalion of infantry in size, supported by 6-15 tanks. Particularly vicious attacks were carried out by the enemy in the directions of the Shevchenko Collective Farm, the military camp and the railroad station.

As a result of the enemy's counterattacks, by the close of the day the army's units had been forced to fall back to their jumping-off position.

The unsuccessful outcome of the first storming of Cherkassy may be explained, first of all, by the bad preparation of the offensive and the poor organization of cooperation between the army's units, formations and combat arms. When evaluating the course of the 52nd Army's combat activities northwest of Cherkassy, it is necessary to keep in mind the fact that with the seizure of a bridgehead in this area, favorable conditions were created for developing the offensive on Smela for the purpose of capturing this major railroad junction.

With our forces' arrival in the Smela area, the work of the Belaya Tserkov'—Znamenka railroad would have been disrupted and the enemy prevented from maneuvering men and materiel between his Zhitomir and Kirovgrad groups of forces. However, for this it was necessary to reinforce the 52nd Army with additional men and materiel and to support the attack on Smela with aviation. At the same time, the Second Ukrainian Front command did not attach the necessary significance to the 52nd Army's active operations in the direction of Smela in time. Thus the *Stavka* of the Supreme High Command, in its directive No. 30250 of 20 November 1943, instructed the *front* commander on the necessity of capturing the important railroad junction of Smela as quickly as possible and cutting the enemy's Belaya Tserkov'—Smela—Znamenka lateral railroad.

The commander of the Second Ukrainian Front was ordered to launch an attack on Smela with the forces of the 52nd Army no later than 25-26 November, for the purpose of occupying this important railroad junction. It was suggested that the *front* commander reinforce the 52nd Army with two rifle divisions and two tank regiments, or with one tank brigade, to develop the success achieved. Further along in the directive the necessity of supporting the 52nd Army's offensive with *front* aviation, which was to launch systematic bombing strikes against the railroad junction of Smela from 20 November until the arrival there of the 52nd Army's main forces, was pointed out.

As is clear from the directive, the capture of the railroad junction of Smela had acquired prime importance for the 52nd Army in the given situation and should be its prime mission.

In accordance with the instructions from the *Stavka* of the Supreme High Command, the *front* commander decided to reinforce the 52nd Army with the 62nd Guards Rifle and 7th Guards Airborne divisions and the 173rd Independent Tank Brigade and to capture the railroad junction of Smela by the close of 26 November. He also supposed that the 52nd Army would manage to simultaneously capture the city of Cherkassy with its available forces and, while developing the offensive to the south, reach the approaches to Smela, before the arrival of these reinforcements.

Proceeding from the decision adopted in directive No. 00844 of 21 November, the 52nd Army was assigned the following tasks:

> The army is to continue to develop the offensive with its available forces in the general direction of Russkaya Polyana, Belozer'ye and Smela. The immediate task is to capture the city of Cherkassy by the close of 21.11.1943. Subsequently, having reinforced the shock group with the 7th Guards Airborne Division, the 62md Guards Rifle Division and the 173rd

Independent Tank Brigade, it is to continue the offensive and by the close of 23.11.1943 capture the railroad junction of Smela and reach the front Bereznik—Balakleya—Bol'shaya Yablonovaya—Sunki—Lomovatoye.

Simultaneously, the commander of the 5th Air Army was given the following order: to systematically launch air strikes from 20 November against the railroad junction of Smela; to cover the 52nd Army's main group of forces and its crossing over the Dnepr with fighter aviation, and to support the 52nd Army's offensive with assault aviation.

Following the unsuccessful fighting of 20 November, the 52nd Army's forces were not ready to resume the offensive on the morning of 21 November. In accordance with the *front* commander's orders, on 21 November the 52nd Army's headquarters drew of a plan "for continuing the 52nd Army's offensive operation to further expand the bridgehead on the western bank of the Dnepr River by seizing the city of Cherkassy and the railroad junction of Smela during 21-26.11.1943."

It was planned to accomplish the task for capturing Cherkassy and Smela in two stages.

As a result of the first stage, which was planned for two days (21-22 November), the army's forces were to capture the city of Cherkassy and expand the bridgehead in the wooded area as far as the line Lyuterevka—Dubievka. It was planned to launch the main attack with the forces of the 254th Rifle Division and a regiment from the 373rd Rifle Division in the direction of Geronimovka, the height with marker 109.8 and the brick factories southeast of Cherkassy. It was planned to conduct the offensive in the direction of Dubievka with the 294th Rifle Division's 861st Rifle Regiment, with Major Sidorchuk's group, to consolidate the line Geronimovka—Dubievka. The support of the forces attacking Cherkassy against the enemy's attacks from the Moshny area was entrusted to the 294th Rifle Division's 859th Rifle Regiment.

The second stage was planned for 23-26 November. During this time it was planned to seize Smela and reach the line Bereznik—Balakleya—Kovalikha—Bol'shaya Yablonovka—Sunki—Lomovatoye. The 73rd Rifle Corps, consisting of the 294th and 254th rifle and 7th Guards Airborne divisions, was to make the main attack. The 62nd Guards Rifle Division, which was late in arriving, remained in the army reserve.

However, the preceding battles had already shown that the enemy in the Cherkassy area, disposing of significant amounts of men and materiel, would put up stubborn resistance. The fighting against the enemy's superior forces in Cherkassy was becoming prolonged. The continuation of the offensive on Cherkassy was inexpedient in this situation.

For carrying out the assigned task to capture the city of Cherkassy and to reach the approaches to Smela, the commander of the 52nd Army had only two divisions at his disposal, which had moreover been significantly weakened in the preceding fighting. For example, the 254th Rifle Division numbered only 1,210 soldiers (minus the rank and file of the rear units and establishments), eight heavy machine guns, 36 light machine guns, 39 anti-tank rifles, 24 82mm mortars, 12 120mm mortars, 16 76mm division guns, and 11 122mm howitzers. The 373rd Rifle Division's units were also significantly under strength.

It was quite obvious that an offensive by such small forces along the army's main attack axis could not secure the successful fulfillment of the task for defeating the enemy's Cherkassy group of forces. It is also necessary to note that the reserves, which were designated by the *front* commander for developing the 52nd Army's offensive on Smela, were late in arriving at their concentration areas.

We should have limited ourselves to the more careful preparation of the troops for the offensive before the arrival of the reserves and the accumulation of forces for launching a decisive attack against the enemy, as well as fighting to improve our positions on the bridgehead and capturing the inhabited locales of Belozer'ye and Khatski. The capture of these inhabited locales and their secure retention was extremely important for the subsequent attack on Smela.

The attack on Cherkassy was resumed on the night of 21-22 November. According to the decision by the commander of the 254th Rifle Division, its main forces (929th and 933rd rifle regiments) were to attack Cherkassy in the direction of the railroad station and, having captured the latter, to develop the offensive toward the center of the city. The 936th Rifle Regiment, reinforced with one tank and two self-propelled guns, had the task of capturing the area of the brick factories southeast of Cherkassy.

In carrying out the assigned task, by dawn the 933rd Rifle Regiment had seized the water tower and the garden northeast of the railroad station. By 0800 on 22 November the 929th Rifle Regiment, which had left its concentration area late, had reached the area of marker 110.5. Our units' further advance was halted as a result of the stubborn enemy resistance. The units were forced to halt their attack and repel the enemy's frequent counterattacks.

Throughout 22 November the enemy undertook 12 counterattack against the 254th Rifle Division's units, in each of which there took part from a company to a battalion of infantry, supported by tanks and assault guns. During the fighting the division's units knocked out 15 enemy tanks and set fire to eight, and destroyed seven enemy guns. A large part of the enemy tanks were put out of action by the artillery in the attacking troops' combat formations and employed, as a rule, for firing over open sights. At 1800 the 254th Rifle Division's 933rd and 929th rifle regiments fell back to the area south of the slaughterhouse under pressure from superior enemy forces.

The attack by the division's 936th Rifle Regiment in the direction of the brick factories also developed unsuccessfully. By 0900 the regiment's elements had capture the area of the brick factories and had cut the Zmogailovka—Cherkassy road. The tank and two self-propelled guns that had been attached to the regiment, while moving along a separate route, got lost and reached the area of the railroad station and actually took part in the fighting with the 933rd Rifle Regiment. The enemy undertook a number of counterattacks, as a result of which the 936th Rifle Regiment was pushed back to the area of the collective farm southwest of the brick factories. Having organized a perimeter defense, the regiment continued to fight in this area in complete encirclement. By 0800 on 23 November, having suffered heavy losses and running low on ammunition, elements of the regiment broke through the encirclement front and fell back to the line the slaughterhouse—marker 112.1.

The attack by the 373rd Rifle Division's units was also unsuccessful.

Simultaneously with the attack on the city of Cherkassy, the army's forces were fighting in the Russkaya Polyana area and on 23 November they completely captured it.

Russkaya Polyana, while it was in enemy hands, enabled him to launch an attack from the rear at any time against our forces attacking the city of Cherkassy. Taking this possibility into account, the enemy fortified the inhabited locale, having concentrated up to a battalion of infantry there, reinforced with tanks and assault guns. The task of capturing Russkaya Polyana was entrusted to the 294th Rifle Division's 861st Rifle Regiment. According to the decision by the regimental commander, the village was to be taken by the forces of two battalions in a simultaneous attack from the north and west.

By the morning of 20 November the 1st Battalion had outflanked Russkaya Polyana from the west, but was discovered by the enemy and was successfully counterattacked by him from the school and graveyard. Having been deprived of the factor of surprise, the commander of the 861st Rifle Regiment made the decision to concentrate both battalions in the northern part of Russkaya Polyana for an attack against the enemy positions in the village from the north. Subsequently, however, due to the discovery of weaker sectors in the enemy's defense along the eastern outskirts of the village, the final version of the commander of the 861st Rifle Regiment's decision came down to attacking the enemy in Russkaya Polyana from the north and east.

On the night of 22-23 November the regiment's subunits attacked the enemy's positions located along the northern and eastern outskirts of the village. Our subunits' vigorous actions prevented the enemy from putting up organized resistance. By the morning of 23 November he had been forced to abandon the village. All of the enemy's subsequent infantry and tank counterattacks were successfully repulsed by the regiment's subunits.

On the evening of 23 November the enemy undertook a powerful counterattack with the support of 18 tanks. The enemy infantry was cut off by artillery fire from his tanks and forced back to its jumping-off position. Three enemy tanks were also destroyed. However, a part of the tanks broke through to the center of the village. On orders from the commander of the 73rd Rifle Corps, the 859th Rifle Regiment's 3rd Battalion and part of the 849th Artillery Regiment's anti-tank artillery were detached from the corps reserve to reinforce the 861st Rifle Regiment.

At the height of the fighting a significant part of the artillery supporting the 861st Rifle Regiment was unable to render it any assistance, because it was moving to new firing positions. There arose the real threat of our troops abandoning the inhabited locale. The commander of the 73rd Rifle Corps quickly dispatched two batteries from the 1322nd Anti-Tank Artillery Regiment and the 350th Independent Anti-Tank Battalion to Russkaya Polyana. The enemy counterattacks were beaten back not long after the arrival of the reinforcements to the 861st Rifle Regiment and all of his attempts to capture Russkaya Polyana were unsuccessful.

Thus by the close of 24 November the army's forces occupied the following lines:

The 254th Rifle Division was consolidating along the line marker 107.3—marker 112.1.

The 373rd Rifle Division's main forces were located along the line excluding marker 112.1—excluding the railroad bridge over the Dnepr, and in the area of the island at marker 81.0 (southeast of Cherkassy); one of the division's regiments was defending along its previous line on the left bank of the Dnepr along the front the Odvernitsa woods—Nalesin.

By this time elements of the airborne group and the partisans had captured the "New Path" Collective Farm and had thrown the enemy out of Dubievka. However, they were unable to consolidate this inhabited locale. The enemy, who was falling back from Russkaya Polyana, forced our troops to abandon Dubievka and fall back to the west.

The 294th Rifle Division's main forces were on the bridgehead northwest of Cherkassy, while only one battalion from the 857th Rifle Regiment remained in defense in the Kreshchatik area.

The main forces of the 7th Guards Airborne Division, which had been subordinated to the 73rd Rifle Corps and which included the 18th, 21st and 29th airborne regiments, having carried out a 124-kilometer march from the Gradizhsk area (80 kilometers southeast of Cherkassy), had concentrated in the Korobovka area only on 23 November. On 24 November the division was crossing to the right bank of the Dnepr. The division's 10th Guards Artillery Regiment and 8th Independent Anti-Tank Battalion were running even more late, due to the absence of fuel.

Because it was very short of personnel, the 62nd Guards Rifle Division, consisting of the 182nd, 184th and 186th rifle regiments, was undergoing reinforcement in the area of the town of Domantov.

The 173rd Independent Tank Brigade arrived with the army only on 27 November and by 29 November had been concentrated in Russkaya Polyana. There were seven T-34s and 13 T-70s[6] in the brigade. In light of the unfavorable meteorological conditions, the aviation that had been detached for supporting the 52nd Army's offensive, set about carrying out its tasks only on 28 November.

Thus as a result of the offensive on 22-24 November the army's forces managed to somewhat expand their bridgehead and to consolidate along some sectors directly on the outskirts of

---

6 Editor's note. The T-70 was a light Soviet tank often used for reconnaissance and infantry support. One model weighed 9.2 tons and carried a crew of two. It was armed with a 45mm gun and a 7.62mm machine gun.

Cherkassy. However, the city continued to remain in the hands of the enemy. The army's significant losses in both men and materiel told. There was a serious shortage of anti-tank artillery in the army's units and formations. The 254th Rifle Division's attempts to attack Cherkassy along two axes—from the northwest and west—had essentially played out in its units' uncoordinated actions, which made it easier for the enemy to maneuver his forces in order to eliminate our troops' success. The army commander, the unit and formation commanders and their staffs did draw lessons from the preceding attack on the city. Cooperation between the divisions and regiments and between the combat arms was not organized, and there was not firm troop control in the battle.

The Encirclement of the Enemy in the City of Cherkassy and the Capture of the Northwestern Part of the City (26-29 November)

On 20 November the troops of the Second Ukrainian Front's main group of forces renewed the offensive from the bridgehead west of Dneprodzerzhinsk. As a result of the enemy's stubborn resistance, the fighting along the Krivoi Rog axis became prolonged. At the same time, our troops' success could be discerned in the direction of Znamenka. For this reason, the *front* commander decided to concentrate his main efforts in the direction of Aleksandriya, Znamenka and Chigirin and to expand the bridgehead on the right bank of the Dnepr.

The Soviet forces' offensive in the direction of Znamenka significantly worsened the enemy's overall operational situation. For example, as early as 26 November the German command was deprived of the ability to detach the necessary men and materiel to reinforce his Cherkassy group of forces.

As was noted earlier, the 52nd Army's offensive on Cherkassy during 22-23 November was unsuccessful. The units and formations designated for reinforcing the army were still located on the left bank of the Dnepr. The 7th Guards Airborne Division was able to cross to the bridgehead no earlier than 25 November and the 62nd Guards Rifle Division only at the end of November.

During the day on 24 November the army headquarters received an order from the *front* commander. The order pointed out that the fighting for Cherkassy had become prolonged and that the plan drawn up by the army's headquarters for "the continuation of the 52nd Army's offensive operation for the further expansion of the bridgehead on the western bank of the Dnepr River and the seizure of the city of Cherkassy and the railroad junction of Smela" was not realistic. The *front* commander suggested drawing up and presenting a new plan to the *front* headquarters, which called for conducting an operation in two stages. The army was assigned the immediate objective of capturing Cherkassy, for which the 7th Guards Airborne Division was to launch an attack from the Russkaya Polyana area in the direction of the "New Plowman" Collective Farm, Kirillovka farm and the brick factory along the southeastern outskirts of Cherkassy. The securing of the offensive against possible enemy attacks from the south was to be entrusted to units of the 294th Rifle Division, which was to go over to the defensive with two regiments along the line Dubievka—Zhandarov's grave—the height at marker 92.1 and to hold it until the capture of the city of Cherkassy. The 254th and 373rd rifle divisions received orders to encircle the enemy in Cherkassy and along the immediate approaches.

The army's subsequent task was to capture the railroad junction of Smela.

As is clear from the *front* commander's instructions, as before, he considered the army's main task as the capture of the city of Cherkassy, and only afterwards was it planned to attack on Smela. At the same time, the *front* commander did not establish a deadline for capturing Cherkassy or Smela.

Thus the resolution of an the very important task of capturing the major railroad junction of Smela was placed in complete dependence on the outcome of the 52nd Army's fight for the city of Cherkassy, the fighting for which had become prolonged.

In accordance with these orders, the army commander decided to launch his main attack on 26 November with the forces of the 73rd Rifle Corps in the direction of the "New Plowman" Collective Farm, Kirillovka farm and the brick factories, in cooperation with units of the 78th Rifle Corps' 373rd Rifle Division, to encircle the enemy in Cherkassy and by the close of the day capture the city. The following were detached to reinforce the 73rd Rifle Corps: the 259th Independent Tank Regiment, 568th Gun Artillery Regiment, 490th Army Mortar Regiment, 849th Artillery Regiment, 438th and 1322nd anti-tank artillery regiments, and the 17th Guards Mortar Regiment.

In carrying out the army commander's instructions, the commander of the 73rd Rifle Corps assigned his forces the following tasks.

The 7th Guards Airborne Division, along with the 259th Independent Tank Regiment, three batteries from the 1322nd Anti-Tank Artillery Regiment and an independent anti-tank battalion from the 294th Rifle Division, was ordered to destroy the enemy in the areas of the Kirillovka, Ternovka and Danilovka farms with two regiments and, while developing the attack in the direction of the collective farm, to capture the southeastern part of the city of Cherkassy by the close of 26 November. Simultaneously with the attack by the division's main forces on Cherkassy, the 29th Guards Airborne Regiment was to reach the line Dubievka—Zhandarov's grave, securing the corps' main forces against enemy attacks from the south. The 254th Rifle Division, along with attached reinforcements (two batteries from the 438th Anti-Tank Artillery Regiment and the 490th Army Mortar Regiment's 2nd Battalion) was given the task of attacking in the direction of the railroad station and by the close of 26 November to capture the central part of the city.

The 294th Rifle Division, consisting of the 861st Rifle Regiment, two battalions from the 857th Rifle Regiment, the 373rd Rifle Division's 1239th Rifle Regiment, the 490th Army Mortar Regiment's 1st Battalion, and a battalion from the 373rd Rifle Division's artillery regiment, was to capture the northwestern part of the city, while launching its main attack in the direction of the Shevchenko Collective Farm.

The 78th Rifle Corps' 373rd Rifle Division, having transferred its 1239th Rifle Regiment to the 294th Rifle Division, was to attack with the forces of its 1235th Rifle Regiment from the island east of Cherkassy in the direction of the sugar factory, thus supporting the 73rd Rifle Corps' forces in capturing the southeastern part of the city.

The army's artillery was assigned the following tasks: to suppress the enemy's artillery in the areas of Cherkassy, Zmogailovka and Krasnaya Sloboda; to prevent the arrival of the enemy's reserves from the areas of Belozer'ye, Verguny and Zmogailovka and his infantry and tank attacks against the flanks and rear of our forces attacking Cherkassy, and; to prevent the movement of the enemy's armored train along the Smela—Cherkassy railroad sector and flanking fire from the directions of Smela and the brick factories.

The army's forces were to occupy their jumping-off position for the offensive by 0600 on 26 November. Taking into account the experience of the preceding fighting, the corps and division commanders, in their instructions for preparing the offensive, called for the creation of assault groups, to which up to a company of riflemen and a section of automatic riflemen and sappers each, 1-2 anti-tank guns and anti-tank rifles would be attached to each of them. It was demanded of the entire rank and file that it consolidate the captured buildings, streets and blocks and to carefully prepare the attacks on the subsequent objectives. Attention was paid to the continuous conduct of reconnaissance of the enemy, to supporting firm cooperation and the presence of the necessary amount of anti-tank artillery and anti-tank rifles in the troops' combat formations for waging the successful struggle against the enemy's tanks.

By the close of 25 November the correlation of men and materiel in the 52nd Army's sector was as follows.

The table shows that with the arrival of fresh forces to the army we managed to create a two-fold superiority over the enemy and a four-fold superiority in artillery and mortars along the main group of forces' attack sector. Only in the number of tanks did superiority continue to remain with the enemy.

However, in the event the enemy committed new forces, which were being concentrated in the Smela area, into the fighting, this superiority could sharply change in favor of the enemy. This circumstance demanded decisive and skillful actions by the troops and the adoption of the most serious measures for securing the attack on the city of Cherkassy from the area of Smela station.

At 0600 on 26 November, following a 50-minute artillery preparation, the army's main forces attacked.

The 7th Guards Airborne Division's 29th Airborne Regiment pushed back the enemy to the southeastern part of Dubievka as the result of fierce fighting. The enemy put up stubborn resistance. By 0100 on 26 November the enemy's resistance had been crushed and the regiment completely captured Dubievka and the inhabited locale of Brody. The 18th Regiment attacked in the direction of Kirillovka farm. Throughout the first half of the day the regiment beat off three enemy counterattacks, each of which with up to a battalion of infantry, with tanks, and by 1200 on 26 November it had reached under the cover of fog the enemy strongpoint in the direction of the "New Plowman" Collective Farm's living quarters. Following a brief fire onslaught by our artillery, the strongpoint was attacked from the front and rear and from the flanks. As a result of this attack, the regiment completely captured the strong-point, routed the 2nd Battalion of the *Wiking* SS Panzer Division's 5th Artillery Regiment and captured the following equipment: 14 guns of various calibers, two combat-ready tanks, 23 machine guns, and four depots with ammunition, as well as other equipment. The captured artillery was immediately employed to fire on the enemy. By the close of 26 November the 18th Regiment had reached the Cherkassy—Smela dirt road in the area of the "New Plowman" Collective Farm.

Table 2.6 The Correlation of Men and Materiel in the 52nd Army's Sector on 25 November 1943

Units and Weapons	Along the Army's Entire Sector (140 km)			The Attack Sector (30 km)			The Sector From Lake Rakita to Excluding the Railroad Bridge Over the Dnepr (13 km)		
	Soviet	Enemy	Correlation	Soviet	Enemy	Correlation	Soviet	Enemy	Correlation
Battalions	36	28	1.3:1.0	32	18	1.8:1.0	22	11	2.0:1.0
Guns and Mortars	572	245	2.3:1.0	516	146	3.5:1.0	440	112	4.0:1.0
Tanks and Self-Propelled Guns	12	35	1.0:3.0	12	35	1.0:3.0	12	35	1.0:30.0

Note: The table does not include the 62nd Guards Rifle Division, which was being brought up to strength, nor the enemy's men and materiel being concentrated in Smela.

The 21st Regiment's attack unfolded in a more difficult situation. Striving to prevent our troops' arrival at his main communications connecting Cherkassy with the town of Smela, the enemy counterattacked the 21st Regiment with the forces of the 57th Infantry Division's 217th Regiment and elements of the *Wiking* SS Panzer Division from the area of Kirillovka farm and pushed our subunits back to their jumping-off position.

On the following day the 21st Regiment, supported by 11 tanks from the 259th Independent Tank Regiment, once again attacked in the direction of Kirillovka farm. By the close of 27 November the 18th and 21st regiments, supported by the 259th Independent Tank Regiment, captured Kirillovka and Danilovka farms. Five strongpoints were outfitted by the forces of the 18th Regiment (minus its 3rd Battalion) in the area of these farms for covering the army's actions from the south, each of which was defended by up to a reinforced rifle company. In the fighting for Kirillovka farm our units defeated the 57th Infantry Division's 217th Regiment and the 72nd Infantry Division's reserve battalion. On 27 November the airborne group was removed from the army's control and no longer took part in its combat operations.

By 0500 on 28 November the 18th Airborne Regiment's 6th Rifle Company, with ten tanks, got across the Cherkassy—Zmogailovka road southeast of the brick factories. The 21st Regiment, which attacked along with elements of the 18th Airborne Regiment, with the support of tanks and self-propelled guns, completely captured the area of the brick factories by 1000 and blocked the enemy's Cherkassy garrison from the southeast.

By the morning of 28 November the 254th Rifle Division's units had broken through the enemy's defense along the immediate approaches to the city of Cherkassy and reached the military camp along its western outskirts.

During the night of 27-28 November the 294th Rifle Division reached the northwestern outskirts of Cherkassy and was continuing to develop the attack toward the center of the city.

By 1100 on 28 November the army's forces were blocking the enemy in the city, having formed an external encirclement front along the line Dubievka—south of Lake Rakita—Danilovka farm—marker 94.5. The distance between the internal encirclement front, which ran along the line of the nail factory as far as the railroad station and then along the southwestern and southeastern outskirts of the city, and the external front was 2-15 kilometers.

Following the completion of the encirclement of the Cherkassy garrison, the enemy soldiers were issued an ultimatum to capitulate. The German-Fascist command rejected this demand and issued an order to its forces to break through the encirclement front, without regard for losses. The encircled enemy directed his main efforts along the Cherkassy—Zmogailovka road to link up with its group of forces advancing toward it from the Zmogailovka area. Due to the fact that the 18th Airborne Regiment's units did not adopt the necessary measures to consolidate their positions southeast of the city, the enemy managed to once again occupy the area of the brick factories following a number of counterattacks from the area of Cherkassy and Zmogailovka. The situation was restored here only on the night of 28-29 November.

While repelling the enemy's counterattacks, the 52nd Army's forces set about storming the city. The activities of the army's main group of forces were to be secured from the south and southeast by the main forces of the 7th Guards Airborne Division, which occupied defensive positions along the external encirclement front. The greatest success on this day was noted in the 294th Rifle Division's attack zone. By 2100 on 28 November the division's units had occupied the northwestern part of the city. The 254th Rifle Division captured the railroad station and the military camp. The 373rd Rifle Division's 1235th Rifle Regiment was fighting in the area of the sugar factory.

It is necessary to note that that during the street fighting in the city the commanders did not devote the necessary attention to questions of intelligence and the securing of flanks and boundaries, as well as the consolidation of blocks occupied by our forces. As a result of this, there were instances of the unexpected appearance of enemy groups in the rear of our units and subunits, which forced the latter to distract their men and materiel for fighting the enemy's breakthroughs. Significant assistance was rendered to the attacking troops by units of the 5th Air Army, which on 28 November launched an assault air and bomber strike against the enemy's group of forces concentrated in the southeastern part of Cherkassy, as well as against the railroad junction of Smela.

On 29 November the fighting in the city and along the approaches to it continued with undiminished force. The enemy's air activity increased in particular. On this day, according to the testimony of prisoners captured in the area of Kirillovka farm, the arrival of the enemy's 3rd Panzer Division from Krivoi Rog to Smela on 27 November became known.

Our aviation established the concentration of enemy infantry and tanks in the areas of Smela, Belozer'ye and Stepankov. The presence here of two of the 57th Infantry Division's regiments, which had been transferred from near Kanev, elements of the 6th Panzer Division's 11th Panzer Regiment, and units of the 3rd Panzer Division became known later. It was clear that the German-Fascist command would attempt to restore the previous situation at any price.

The situation that had arisen by 29 November testified to the fact that the fighting for the city of Cherkassy was going to become even more prolonged and that the favorable conditions for an attack on Smela had been missed.

The Fighting in the City. The Repulse of the Enemy's Counterblow from Smela and the Counterattacks South and Southeast of Cherkassy (30 November-5 December)

Having concentrated its shock groups north of Smela and Zmogailovka, the German-Fascist command was determined to break through to Cherkassy and liberate the Cherkassy garrison by an attack from the Belozer'ye—Stepanki area with the forces of two divisions (including up to a panzer division) and counterattacks from the areas of Zmogailovka with the forces of a single tank and a single infantry regiments. Simultaneously, the enemy's units in Cherkassy were to launch meeting attacks along the Cherkassy—Belozer'ye—Smela and Cherkassy—Zmogailovka roads.

At 0900 on 30 November the enemy, following an air strike against our forces in the areas of Sosnovka, Ternovka farm and the brick factories in the northwestern part of Cherkassy, undertook a counterblow against the 52nd Army's forces.

Possessing numerical superiority, the enemy managed to break through the external encirclement front along the 29th Regiment's sector in the area of Kurgan grave along a 2-kilometer front and to penetrate into our forces' position. In order to halt the advance by the enemy's shock group toward the city, the commander of the 52nd Army decided to counterattack him with his reserve forces—the 173rd Independent Tank Brigade and the 182nd Rifle Regiment. These forces were to attack in the direction of marker 97.4 for the purpose of restoring the previous situation and to destroy the enemy's infantry and tanks which had broken through to the area of the "New Plowman" Collective Farm.

The counterattack was not successful. The enemy, while continuing his attack, pushed back elements of the 18th Regiment and occupied a group of buildings along the southern outskirts of Ternovka farm. Throughout the day the enemy's aviation, in groups of 5-10 planes, carried out more than 20 raids, in which up to 300 planes overall took part. Our fighter aviation was unable to offer substantial opposition to the enemy's air raids due to a shortage of forces and fuel and the great remove of its airfields from the area of combat operations.[7]

During the night of 30 November-1 December all of the 7th Guards Airborne Division's antitank artillery was brought up to the enemy's breakthrough sector. The following were stationed at firing positions for firing over open sights: ten 76mm guns northwest and west of the "New Plowman" Collective Farm, and four 76mm and 45mm guns each in the area of marker 107.3.

At 1100 on 1 December the enemy resumed his attack following an air and artillery preparation. This time his main efforts were once again concentrated along the Belozer'ye—Cherkassy road.

---

7 The 5th Air Army's 804th Short Range Bomber, 992nd Night Light Bomber and the 21st Guards Fighter air regiments and the 556th Independent Air Squadron supported the 52nd Army's offensive.

Having broken through the defense along the 18th Airborne Regiment's sector in the Lake Rakita area, the enemy's tanks reached the railroad booth east of marker 107.3, where they were met with our artillery fire. Bitter fighting broke out. The rank and file of the battery under the command of Guards Senior Lieutenant Mats particularly distinguished itself in the fighting. In a short time a handful of brave men knocked out ten enemy tanks. During the bitter fighting with the enemy's group of forces that had broken through to Cherkassy, the shortage of ammunition was keenly felt. The 254th Rifle Division's artillery subunits were forced to fight to the last shell.

Simultaneous with the enemy's attack on Cherkassy from the south, a part of the Cherkassy garrison's forces attacked from the north. Having broken through the 254th Rifle Division's combat formations, a detachment of the Cherkassy garrison was attempting to link up in the area of marker 107.3 with its group of forces attacking along the Belozer'ye—Cherkassy road.

As a result of this attack, the 7th Guards Airborne Division's 18th and 21st regiments were cut off from the army's main forces. During the subsequent fighting, the enemy repeatedly attempted to split the encircled regiments and destroy them in detail, but he was unable to achieve his goal. Experiencing a shortage of ammunition and food and undergoing a great deal of physical and moral stress, the 18th and 21st airborne regiments' rank and file valiantly and steadfastly repelled the pressure from the enemy's superior forces.

At 1430 on 2 December more than a battalion of enemy infantry, supported by 18 tanks, attacked the 18th Regiment's left flank, while striving to get into the boundary between the 18th and 21st regiments in the area north of marker 93.7. The enemy was thrown back to the northeast by the forces of the garrisons of the Danilovka farm and Dolgaya grave and the 18th Regiment's reserve. Within a day the enemy again tried to capture Kirillovka farm, having thrown a battalion of infantry and 24 tanks and assault guns into the fighting. The enemy was once again thrown back to his jumping-off position by a decisive counterattack, which was led by the commander of the 18th Regiment.

By 1700 on 3 December the enemy had concentrated up to two battalions of infantry between the railroad and Kirillovka farm and up to one infantry battalion west of Danilovka farm. At 1700 the enemy broke through with these forces along the boundary between the Kirillovka farm and Ternovka farm strong points. As a result of heavy losses in men and materiel, by order of the commander of the 52nd Army, the 18th Regiment fell back to the area of marker 105.0. It was simultaneously decided to launch an attack on the night of 3-4 December with the forces of the 184th Regiment and the 173rd Independent Tank Brigade from the area of marker 107.3 in the direction of the state farm and the brick factories, to break through the enemy's encirclement front, with the assistance of the 18th Regiment, and to link up with the 18th and 21st regiments.

In order to secure the attack from the south, the army commander ordered that upon the arrival of our forces in the area of marker 105.0, that they securely consolidate the line marker 107.3—marker 105.0. Units of the 294th and 254th rifle divisions were to meanwhile continue to attack in the city. The 373rd Rifle Division's 1235th Rifle Regiment received orders to tie down the enemy through active operations in the area of the sugar factory. The 62nd Guards Rifle Division's 186th Rifle Regiment comprised the army commander's reserve.

On the morning of 4 December our units attacked and following stubborn fighting linked up with the 18th Regiment. However, they were unable to develop the success in the direction of the brick factories. Meanwhile, the 21st Regiment, while occupying a perimeter defense in the area of the brick factories and repelling the enemy's numerous attacks, was in a very difficult situation: ammunition was running out and the enemy continued to augment his efforts.

Due to the difficult situation of the 7th Guards Airborne Division's units, the commander of the 73rd Rifle Corps, with the permission of the 52nd Army's commander, decided to pull this division's regiments back to the area of Russkaya Polyana and Geronimovka in order to put them in order. The 18th Regiment was pulled back to Geronimovka and the 21st Regiment to Russkaya Polyana.

As can be seen from the above, the commitment of the 7th Guards Airborne Division's fresh forces into the fighting enabled us to carry out the encirclement of the enemy in the city of Cherkassy on 28 November. However, our forces were unable to consolidate the success and to destroy the enemy garrison. Despite this, the 52nd Army's military council was paying particular attention to covering the Smela—Cherkassy axis, although this requirement was essentially not carried out. All measures for securing this axis came down to detaching two of the 7th Guards Airborne Division's regiments for occupying defensive positions along a broad 25-kilometer front, with an equal distribution of men and materiel.

A powerful defense capable of opposing the enemy's attacks was not created along the main axis. The strongpoints were poorly outfitted by engineer work and were not sufficiently suffused with anti-tank artillery. The artillery density per kilometer of front was 1-2 guns. Thus the axis along which the German-Fascist command was most likely to launch an attack in order to render assistance to his encircled group of forces proved to be very weakly covered. All of this gave the enemy the opportunity to concentrate significant amounts of men and materiel at the planned breakthrough sector and to create an overwhelming superiority in infantry and particularly in artillery and tanks.

The indicated shortcomings enabled the enemy not only to restore communications with the Cherkassy garrison through attacks from the south and southeast, but also to encircle the 7th Guards Airborne Division's main forces. As a result of six days of stubborn fighting, by the close of 5 December the 52nd Army's forces once again were occupying the line Dubievka—marker 111.5—"New Plowman" Collective Farm—the military camp—the city cemetery—the tobacco factory—Lenin Street—the sawmill along the northeastern outskirts of the city.

By this time the 62nd Guards Rifle Division's artillery, which was being brought up to strength, had been transferred from the left bank to the bridgehead. The concentration of the 33rd Anti-Tank Artillery Brigade, which was to be transferred to the 52nd Army, was being completed.

The partisans were operating in the woods south and southeast of Moshny, trying to prevent the enemy's movement along the forest roads.

As a result of several days of intensive fighting, the enemy's capacity for decisive actions had been significantly undermined.

The Storming and Complete Liberation of the City of Cherkassy (6-14 December)

In the beginning of December 1943 the main efforts of the Second Ukrainian Front's forces were directed at defeating the enemy's group of forces in the area of Aleksandriya. On 6 December the *front's* forces, following bitter fighting, captured the town of Aleksandriya. The enemy tried to slow down our forces' advance along the approaches to Znamenka.

Due to the successful offensive by the Second Ukrainian Front's forces along the Aleksandriya axis and the active operations of the *front's* left-wing forces along the Krivoi Rog axis, the enemy was forced to remove part of his forces from the Cherkassy axis and transfer them to strengthen his Aleksandriya group of forces. Bled-white units of the 72nd Infantry Division and part of the 3rd Panzer Division's forces, the remnants of the *Wiking* SS Panzer Division's panzer regiment, and the 57th Infantry Division's 217th Infantry Regiment were left in the 52nd Army's sector.

Taking the developing situation into account, on 6 December the commander of the 52nd Army made the decision to continue attacking, with the immediate objective of finally capturing the city of Cherkassy and only after developing the success toward Smela. The offensive was set for 9 December.

In accordance with the 52nd Army commander's order No. 0023/op of 6 December, the army's forces were supposed to, while launching their main attack from the area of marker 117.9 in the direction of the southeastern outskirts of Cherkassy, to capture the city, after which they were to develop the offensive on Smela. The resolution of the task of defeating the enemy in Cherkassy and capturing the city was entrusted to the 73rd Rifle Corps' formations. The 78th Rifle Corps was to assist the 73rd Rifle Corps' offensive, with the 373rd Rifle Division's main forces from the direction of the Dnepr. From the south the offensive by the army's shock group was to be supported by the forces of the 62nd Guards Rifle Division, which received orders to the 7th Guards Airborne Division's 29th Guards Airborne Regiment along the sector Dubievka—height 111.5, to securely defend this line and to attack along its left flank in the direction of marker 98.4 in accordance with the 7th Guards Airborne Division's advance. A battalion from the 62nd Guards Rifle Division's 186th Regiment comprised the army commander's reserve.

An army artillery group, consisting of the 568th Gun Artillery Regiment and the 17th Guards Mortar Regiment was supposed to suppress the enemy's artillery in the Kirillovka area, along the southern outskirts of Cherkassy, and in the area of Zmogailovka, and also to prevent the arrival of the enemy's reserves from the direction of Belozer'ye, Stepanki and Zmogailovka. The 33rd Anti-Tank Artillery Brigade, which comprised the army commander's anti-tank reserve, was to prepare and occupy three anti-tank areas with its main forces: in the area of the "New Plowman" Collective Farm, the second in the area of markers 115.6 and 117.9 and the former overhead covers north of marker 115.6, and the third in the area of marker 117.7 and the excavation at marker 2.3. One of the brigade's regiments was designated for creating an anti-tank area along the sector marker 110.5—marker 104.2—marker 110.3, with the task of preventing the enemy's infantry and tanks from breaking through from the area of Kirillovka farm and the brick factories.

The 5th Air Army was given the following assignment: while launching assault air raids against the enemy's troops and defensive targets, to support the 52nd Army's offensive on Cherkassy and carry out reconnaissance of the approach of the enemy's reserves. The chief targets for our bomber aviation were the enemy's personnel and guns in his strongpoints and artillery in its firing positions, as well as the most important targets in the city of Cherkassy, Smela and the Bobrinskaya railroad station.

On the whole, the *front* commander approved the decision reached by the commander of the 52nd Army. At the same time, he pointed out to the army commander in his directive of 7 December 1943 the necessity of creating a more powerful artillery grouping along the axis of the main attack.

On the basis of the army commander's order, the commander of the 73rd Rifle Corps decided to defeat the enemy's defending forces in Cherkassy and to capture the city by a simultaneous attack from three sides—from the west, northwest and east.

The 7th Guards Airborne Division, along with the attached 173rd Independent Tank Brigade, was ordered to launch an attack from the area of height 117.9 in the direction of the southeastern outskirts of Cherkassy, to capture the area of the slaughterhouse and the railroad station, and subsequently, having covered itself with a single regiment from the south along the line excluding the slaughterhouse—the barn 1.5 kilometers southwest of the railroad station, to attack with its remaining forces in the direction of block 243 along the southeastern outskirts of the city. Besides this, the commander of the 173rd Independent Tank Brigade was ordered to be ready to pursue the enemy in the directions of Smela and Zmogailovka. The 254th Rifle Division was to, while launching its main attack along the right flank in the direction of the water tower, to capture the area of the fork in the railroad near Cherkassy station in conjunction with the 7th Guards Airborne Division, and to then develop the attack in the direction of block 136. The 294th Rifle Division was assigned the task, while launching its main attack along the left flank in the direction of the cloth mill, to capture the area of the mill in conjunction with units of the 373rd Rifle Division, after which it was to develop the attack in the direction of blocks 214 and 216.

In accordance with the plan for the artillery offensive, 30 minutes were allotted for the artillery preparation of the attack, of which guns and mortars of all calibers were to take part in a fire onslaught against the forward edge of the enemy's defense in the first five minutes. In the following 15 minutes the artillery and mortars were to be brought in for waging aimed fire against previously noted and newly discovered enemy firing points and personnel. A 10-minute fire onslaught against the forward edge of the enemy's defense and the reverse slopes of the heights in the area of the enemy's strongpoints was to precede the attack. The artillery support of the attack was to be carried out by the method of the consecutive concentration of fire. A significant part of the artillery was to be detached as accompaniment guns in the infantry's and tanks' combat formations.

During 6-8 December part of the troops' forces were fighting in the city, while the main forces prepared for the decisive storming. Our aviation continued to launch strikes against the enemy's forces in the area of the railroad station, in the southeastern part of Cherkassy, and in the areas of the Kirillovka and Danilovka farms.

By the morning of 9 December the army's forces had occupied their jumping-off positions for the attack. At 0830, following a 30-minute artillery preparation, the storming of the city began.

The enemy put up stubborn resistance from the first minutes of the fighting along all sectors of our forces' attack. The fiercest fighting was in the area of the railroad station. While repelling the enemy's ferocious infantry and tank counterattacks and slowly advancing, clearing the city's blocks of the city, units of the 7th Guards Airborne Division had captured the railroads station by the close of the day, cleared the enemy soldiers out of block 137 and had begun fighting for block 138. One of the division's regiments, while pushing the enemy to the south, reached the line of the barn 1.5 kilometers southwest of the station—the excavation at marker 1.5, thus securing the army's main forces against possible enemy attacks from the south.

Units of the 254th Rifle Division were attacking directly in the city. Having cleared a number of blocks of the enemy, the division repelled two powerful enemy counterattacks during the second half of the day from the direction of block 192 and by the close of the day had reached the area of blocks 171 and 168.

The 294th and 373rd rifle divisions were fighting in the city simultaneously with the 254th Rifle Division's units. Two regiments of the 294th Rifle Division, while attacking along the streets to the southeast, cleared blocks, 143, 144, 145, and 146 of enemy troops and began fighting in blocks 163, 165 and 166.

The 373rd Rifle Division's 1239th Regiment was attacking in the direction of the station along the bank of the Dnepr. Throughout the day the regiment's subunits repelled several enemy counterattacks from the direction of the station, cleared the enemy of more than ten blocks and reached Kaganovich Prospekt. The 373rd Rifle Division's 1235th Regiment, along with elements of the 1237th Rifle Regiment, was fighting throughout all of 9 December in the area of the sugar factories along the eastern outskirts of the city, having thrown the enemy back to the line of the railroad.

Units of the 62nd Guards Rifle Division, while securing the army main group of forces attacking in the city, from the south, beat off two enemy attacks during the day from Lake Rakita and the Kirillovka farm and by the close of the day were holding their positions.

Especially heavy fighting unfolded on 10 December in the area of the railroad station. The enemy, having concentrated up to two battalions of infantry and 13 tanks against the 29th Guards Airborne Regiment, counterattacked on the morning of 10 December the regiment's elements defending along the flanks. As a result of the unexpectedness of the attack, the enemy managed to crumple the regiment's subunits along the left flank and to upset its combat formations.

Several officers were put out of action at the very start of the fighting and control of the subunits by the regimental commander and his staff was lost. In these difficult conditions the regiment's subunits fell back to the railroad station, under the pressure of superior enemy forces. A group of officers, lead by the deputy division commander for political affairs, was quickly dispatched to the regiment to restore the situation. By 1800 the regiment once again captured its previously abandoned sector.

On 10 December the units fighting in the city captured 13 blocks. On 11 December our forces occupied another 12 blocks. By the close of this day the enemy held no more than 50 blocks in the southeastern part of the city.

During the street fighting storm groups operated in the attacking forces' combat formations. As a rule, each storm group had 45mm guns, one 76mm gun apiece from regimental and division artillery, and one 122mm howitzer attached to it. The distribution of fire tasks between the attached artillery was carried out in accordance with their combat capabilities. The 45mm guns suppressed the enemy's machine guns along the flanks of a strongpoint, the 76mm regimental gun kept the second story under fire, the 76mm division gun fired to destroy a building, and the 122mm howitzer was employed for firing on the upper story for the purpose of destroying it and bury the basement structures, in which the enemy's heavy machine guns and anti-tank rifles were located, under bricks. The artillery crews' smooth work secured the rapid seizure of strongpoints and our subunits' advance.

In the street fighting our troops broadly employed smoke grenades and bottles with flammable ingredients, which were good weapons for blinding and destroying enemy weapons and his defensive structures. One should point out as one of the serious shortcomings in the army's combat activities the non-fulfillment of the demand to immediately consolidate the city's captured buildings and blocks.

On 12 December the 294th Rifle Division's left-flank elements stormed and captured the railroad station in the area of the landing. The attack by the army's units in the city had slowed down significantly. The enemy was resisting, paying no heed to his heavy losses, while intending to hold on until the arrival of his reserves from the Smela area. In these conditions, the commander of the 52nd Army decided to carry out a partial regrouping on the night of 12-13 December and, having reinforced the troops along the army's main attack axis at the expense of the 294th Rifle Division, to clear the city of the enemy by the close of 13 December.

The general attack was set for 0900 on 13 December. The dispatch of a rifle battalion from the 62nd Guards Rifle Division to the southern outskirts of Belozer'ye was planned, for the purpose of preventing the arrival of the enemy's reserves to the area of combat activities.

In accordance with the army commander's plan, the commander of the 73rd Rifle Corps decided to attack with the corps' main forces (7th Guards Airborne and 294th Rifle divisions) in the direction of the southeastern outskirts of the city, and with part of his forces (254th Rifle Division and the 373rd Rifle Division's 1239th Regiment) to securely defend the line along blocks 182, 176 and 157. In order to assist the attack by the corps' main group of forces, the 254th Rifle Division was to form a composite battalion, which, given favorable circumstances, was to immediately attack the enemy along the direction of block 213. The corps commander ordered all of the regimental and divisional artillery to be located in the attacking subunits' combat formations.

In evaluating the army commander's decision, one should point out that the regrouping of forces, which was undertaken for the purpose of reinforcing the formations attacking along the axis of the army's main attack, was already late. It is known that before this only one division had been attacking along the axis of the army's main attack, while two divisions were operating in the city. The entire course of combat operations showed that the army's main forces should have been employed for launching an attack from the south and southeast, in order, to cooperate with the units attacking in the city from the northwest, to defeat the enemy and prevent him from escaping from Cherkassy.

Throughout 11-12 December our aviation bombed the areas of the village of Lozovok, Moshny, Belozer'ye, Zmogailovka, and the southeastern outskirts of Cherkassy.

On the night of 12-13 December the army's forces completed their regrouping and occupied their jumping-off positions for the attack.

At 0900 on 13 December the army's forces began to storm the city. The 294th Rifle Division, having seized several buildings along the city's outskirts, by 1500 had pierced the depth of the enemy's defense. The infantrymen broke into the buildings and, employing grenades and automatic weapons, cleared them of the enemy. The artillery troops fired point-blank at the enemy's counterattacking tanks. The mortar troops hit the infantry following behind the tanks with accurate fire. The 7th Guards Airborne Division did not advance in the beginning. Everything that the enemy possessed along this sector was thrown in to help the Cherkassy garrison. The enemy was trying at all costs to hold on in the city. Measures were necessary that would secure the successful completion of the storming. For this purpose, the army commander entrusted to the army's artillery commander the mission of keeping concentrations of enemy forces under continuous fire. The aviation was to control the enemy's main communications. The rank and file of the rear establishments was dispatched to cover the shortages of troops in the combat subunits that had suffered heavy casualties. The army's military council called on all soldiers to honorably fulfill their assigned combat task and to completely liberate the city of Cherkassy from the German-Fascist occupiers.

While attacking the enemy, our units captured almost all of the city's major buildings.

By the close of the day the 7th Guards Airborne Division had reached the southeastern outskirts of the city and had completed clearing another four blocks of the Hitlerites. The 254th Rifle Division's composite battalion threw the enemy out of his positions along the railroad embankment and, having overcome several enemy screens, by 2200 had created favorable conditions for attacking in the 254th Rifle Division's sector.

The 373rd Rifle Division's 1235th Regiment, along with a battalion from the 1237th Rifle Regiment, beat off all of the enemy's counterattacks and captured three blocks during the day.

Having finally lost faith in the possibility of holding his positions in Cherkassy, the enemy began to pull his troops out of the city through Zmogailovka and Smela.

At 0230 on 14 December the storming of the city ended with its complete liberation from the fascist aggressors. Having consolidated in the city with part of its forces, the army's forces took up the pursuit of the enemy in the directions of Smela and Krasnaya Sloboda.

On 14 December the capital of our motherland, Moscow, congratulated with an artillery salute the troops who had liberated the city of Cherkassy.

By order of the Supreme Commander-in-Chief of 14 December, the units and formations which had distinguished themselves in the fighting to liberate the city of Cherkassy were awarded the title "Cherkassy", and thanks expressed to their rank and file.

While continuing to pursue the remnants of the enemy's defeated units, which were falling back to the south and southwest, by the close of 15 December the 52nd Army's forces had reached the line Budishche—the eastern outskirts of Bol'shoye Starosel'ye—the northern bank of the Irdyn' Marsh—the northern outskirts of Belozer'ye—Stepanki, and then along the left bank of the Tyasmin River as far as Khudoleevka (28 kilometers southeast of Cherkassy).

Our forces' attempt to force the Irdyn' Marsh and the Tyasmin River and to capture the town of Smela was not crowned with success. The enemy, having taken advantage of the delay of the 52nd Army's main forces in the Cherkassy area, was able to reinforce his forces in the Smela area and to securely strengthen this axis and to repel all attacks by the army's forward units, which later only cleared Belozer'ye and Basy of the enemy.

However, the arrival of the army's forces at the immediate approaches to Smela and Bobrinskaya, which had created conditions for our artillery's systematic shelling of these areas, made it significantly more difficult for the German-Fascist command to employ the Belaya Tserkov'—Smela—Krivoi Rog lateral railroad.

The town of Smela and Bobrinskaya station were liberated only on 3 February 1944.

The Operation's Results and Brief Conclusions

The 52nd Army's Cherkassy operation was conducted along the *front's* secondary axis and lasted 31 days. During this time the army's forces successfully forced the Dnepr, seized a major bridgehead along the right bank of the river, defeated the enemy's Cherkassy group of forces, and liberated the city of Cherkassy and more than 40 other inhabited locales. During the offensive Soviet forces once again demonstrated high moral qualities and increased military skill, achieving major successes. The 52nd Army's combat successes were noted on 14 December 1943 in an order by the Supreme Commander-in-Chief I.V. Stalin, who expressed gratitude to the army's command and troops.

The bridgehead seized by the 52nd Army's forces reached 60 kilometers in width and 30 kilometers in depth. This was the third largest bridgehead, after the Kiev and Dnepropetrovsk ones, formed by the Soviet army in the battle for the Dnepr in the autumn and winter of 1943. The Cherkassy bridgehead was employed by our forces in carrying out the Korsun'-Shevchenkovskii operation in January-February 1944. Besides this, with the arrival of our forces in the Gorodishche area and the approaches to Smela, the work of the enemy's Belaya Tserkov'—Smela—Krivoi Rog lateral railroad was disrupted.

During the stubborn fighting to expand the bridgehead and for the city of Cherkassy, the enemy's 57th and 72nd infantry and 3rd Panzer divisions were routed and a serious defeat inflicted on the *Wiking* SS Panzer Division. The 52nd Army's forces distracted the enemy's reserves (two infantry and one panzer division) from the Zhitomir and Kirovograd axes and, having tied down up to five enemy divisions for a significant amount of time, facilitated our forces' successful operations along the Kirovograd and Zhitomir axes.

One of the characteristic features of the 52nd Army's Cherkassy operation was that the army's forces operated in wider sectors and possessed significantly fewer reinforcement weapons that the forces attacking along the main axis.

A second characteristic feature of the operation is that our forces had to force a major water obstacle—the Dnepr—along a broad front and given a serious shortage of crossing equipment. This circumstance inevitably created an entire series of difficulties, both during the forcing itself and in developing the offensive along the opposite bank.

In the Cherkassy operation, the 52nd Army's forces operated in a sector more than 140 kilometers wide and had at the beginning of the operation only three rifle divisions and insignificant reinforcements. At the same time, the enemy, covering himself with a major water line, disposed of more than three infantry and one panzer division along this front.

The 52nd Army was reinforced during the operation with two divisions, while the German-Fascist command transferred up to three divisions to the army's attack sector. Finally, a characteristic feature of the 52nd Army's operation was also that the army's forces were supposed to carry out an operation in close cooperation with the partisans and elements of an airborne group, which were operating in the wooded area northwest of Cherkassy. This is one of a few examples of conducting an army offensive operation in such conditions.

The experience of the Great Patriotic War showed that the most important conditions of success in forcing with a planned-out preparation are: the correct selection of the main attack axis, the careful organization of the river's forcing, a high rate of forcing, and the rapid seizure of a bridgehead and the decisive development of the offensive along the opposite bank faster than the enemy can undertake countermeasures.

The 52nd Army's was to make its main attack in the direction of Svidovok and Russkaya Polyana. The decision to launch the main attack on Svidovok and Russkaya Polyana was quite expedient. While operating along this axis, the army's forces would have the opportunity, in cooperation with the partisans and elements of the 5th Guards Airborne Brigade, to seize a bridgehead on the right bank of the Dnepr and capture the city of Cherkassy. Given the shortage of men and materiel, the skillful concentration of the army's main efforts along the axis of the main attack by means of the bold regrouping of forces from secondary sectors of the front, the skillful organization of demonstration actions along a broad front, the rapidity of maneuvering men and materiel, as well as surprise, acquires particular significance.

However, these very important requirements were not observed in full measure, which complicated the conditions for the troops' actions from the very start of the operation. All of the army's men and materiel had been almost equally distributed along different axes. For example, only the 254th Rifle Division, along with insignificant reinforcements, was detached for the forcing and seizure of a bridgehead along the army's main attack axis. The main forces of the 373rd Rifle Division were to attack along the secondary axes. Units of the 294th Rifle Division were designated for defending the bridgehead north of Kreshchatik. At the same time, neither the army commander nor the commander of the 73rd Rifle Corps had any reserves at their disposal. All of the crossing equipment, given its limited number, was also equally distributed along all of the crossing points.

In the specific situation in which the 52nd Army was conducting its operation, it was necessary to carry out a more decisive concentration of men and materiel along the axis of the main attack, along with the simultaneous organization of demonstration actions along a broad front. We should have concentrated the main mass of crossing equipment in the army along the main attack axis, with the simultaneous organization of false crossings along a broad front. Powerful reserves should have been created in the army and the corps, which was attacking along the army's main axis, by greatly weakening the secondary sectors in the army's zone. All of this would undoubtedly have secured the forcing of the Dnepr at a faster pace, the rapid accumulation of men and materiel along the captured bridgehead and the successful struggle for its expansion.

As was pointed out earlier, the army was suffering from a serious shortage of crossing equipment for the forcing of such a major river as the Dnepr. However, this shortage was further exacerbated by the incorrect distribution of the equipment between the main and secondary axes. The equal distribution of crossing equipment along the entire forcing front led to a situation in which no more than a single battalion could be crossed in a single trip along the main attack axis. As a result of this, the accumulation of men and materiel along the opposite bank took place very slowly. The subunits which crossed in the army's first echelon had neither regimental or battalion artillery, which began to be transferred to the captured bridgehead on pontoons only during the second half of the day. By the close of the first day of the forcing there were four anti-tank guns and 28 mortars on the right bank of the Dnepr. The main mass of artillery and the tanks were crossed after 16 November over a bridge ladid down in the area north of the village of Svidovok.

The slow accumulation of men and materiel, particularly of artillery, along the right bank of the Dnepr was one of the chief reasons for the prolonged fighting, both for expanding the captured bridgehead as well as for the city of Cherkassy. The commander of the 52nd Army decided to correct the mistakes committed in the initial organization of forces during the course of the offensive. At first he refused to continue the offensive along the secondary axes and employed units of the 373rd Rifle Division along the main attack axis. Then he removed and transferred units and subunits from other defensive sectors to the bridgehead near Svidovok. On the night of 13-14 and 15-16 November two of the 294th Rifle Division's regiments were removed from the bridgehead in the Kreshchatik area and shifted to the army's main attack axis. Thus the army commander's desire to correct planning mistakes during the operation was carried out indecisively. The transfer of troops to the main attack axis was carried out too late.

The coordination of the actions of the army's forces with the partisans and parachutists was one of the conditions of the successful struggle for Cherkassy. The careful organization of the army's forces' cooperation with the partisans and airborne troops was complicated by the absence of the army headquarters' direct communications with them. Reliable communications were established only on 12 November; that is, a few hours before the forcing. Of course, we were unable to work out all the problems of cooperation between the army's formations, the airborne forces and the partisans during this time. The result of this was a lack of coordination of our actions in forcing the river and capturing a bridgehead.

One should note that the *front* failed to devote the necessary significance to rendering assistance to the 52nd Army's forces during the first seven days of the offensive, all the way up to the *Stavka* of the Supreme High Command's instructions to seize the railroad junction of Smela as quickly as possible.

With the seizure of a bridgehead northwest of Cherkassy along the right bank of the Dnepr, favorable conditions were created for developing the offensive in the direction of Smela for the purpose of cutting the enemy's Belaya Tserkov'—Smela—Znamenka lateral railroad. And it was only after the *Stavka's* direct instructions on the importance that the 52nd Army's forces attack Smela that the *front* command reinforced the army with two rifle divisions and a tank brigade and began to render the army commander more concrete assistance.

In reviewing the course of the Cherkassy offensive operation, worthy of note is the excessive desire of the *front* and army command to capture Cherkassy, although the fighting for the city had become prolonged. With the arrival of the *front* reserves to the army it would have been expedient to develop the offensive on Belozer'ye and Smela with the army's main forces. With the arrival of the army's forces at the approaches to Smela, the enemy would have been deprived of the opportunity of shifting his forces from the Smela area to the northern bank of the Irdyn' River. This would have excluded the enemy's launching of a counterblow and at the same time the capture of Cherkassy would have been speeded up significantly. The 52nd Army would have had the opportunity to uninterruptedly fire on the enemy's lateral railroad.

Being drawn into extended fighting for Cherkassy would inevitably tie down the army's main forces and prevent it from developing the offensive on Smela, in order to cut the enemy's very important Belaya Tserkov'—Znamenka lateral railroad.

There were a number of shortcomings in organizing the fighting for Cherkassy. The attack by the units and formations directly on the city was conducted along the same axes, without careful preparation and without securely consolidating the captured lines.

Besides this, during the fighting for the city the existing artillery was not always employed in accordance with the actual situation. For example, in encircling the enemy in Cherkassy, one of the most important sectors representing a danger from tanks along the Smela—Cherkassy road in the 73rd Rifle Corps' zone remained essentially uncovered by anti-tank artillery.

The artillery's maneuver possibilities were note fully taken advantage of. Reconnaissance was poorly conducted during the offensive; the enemy's appearance was unexpected for our troops. The artillery fired upon the enemy's non-observable targets. In this situation, the maneuver of artillery weapons took on special significance. However, this maneuver was carried out indecisively and far too late.

Tanks and self-propelled guns began to take part in the operation only from 16 November and were employed both for the resolution of independent tasks and as immediate infantry-support vehicles. The 259th Independent Tank Regiment's successful advance in the direction of the brick factories facilitated the rapid encirclement of the enemy's Cherkassy garrison. The 173rd Independent Tank Brigade participated independently in repelling the enemy's counterblow from the Smela area and, being subordinated to the commander of the 73rd Rifle Corps, was employed in conjunction with the corps' units in the street fighting in the city of Cherkassy.

One of the most serious shortcomings in troop control while preparing the operation and during its conduct was the poor organization of intelligence. Our intelligence did not uncover the fire system in the Sekirna area before the start of the operation, which foiled our troops' forcing in this area. In a number of cases during the course of the operation our intelligence was late in uncovering the arrival of new enemy units and formations. For example, the lateness in uncovering the enemy's group of forces and the underestimation of his men and materiel north of Smela made the army's operations more difficult while repelling the enemy's counterblow in the direction of Belozer'ye and Cherkassy.

As a result of the shortcomings in troop control, there were incidents of uncoordinated activities by units and formations in the fighting for the city of Cherkassy. This led to a situation I which the enemy, while successively employing maneuver against our formations operating in an uncoordinated manner, threw back the 52nd Army's forces to their jumping-off position.

Due to the insufficient provisioning with ammunition for the artillery and gasoline for motor vehicles, the 52nd Army's forces experienced great difficulties. The most difficult situation with ammunition arose at the end of November and in the first days of December, at a time when bitter fighting in the city had broken out and the enemy had brought up to two divisions from the Smela area and was preparing an attack on Cherkassy for the purpose of linking up with its garrison. For example, on 30 November the army had among the troops and in depots the following amounts of ammunition:

0.5 to 1.0 combat loads of mortar rounds of various calibers;
About 0.7 combat loads of 45mm shells;
0.3 to 1.0 combat loads of 76mm shells and greater.

In a number of cases, the situation with ammunition often came to a point in which the artillery batteries and battalions, in repelling the enemy's tank attacks, were firing off their last shells. The poor provisioning of the army's forces with ammunition created great difficulties in repelling enemy counterattacks, forced the command to employ extreme measures in seeking out ammunition (taking bullets and shells from units on defense) and, on the whole, led to prolonged fighting for the city. To a significant degree, these difficulties were a consequence of the fact that the *front* did not devote sufficient attention to supplying the 52nd Army's forces with ammunition.

The 52nd Army's Cherkassy operation was conducted in extremely unfavorable conditions that had arisen for our forces. However, despite the intensive fighting over many days and given the absence of an overall superiority over the enemy, the army's forces exhibited great firmness and mass heroism. This heroism was supported by purposeful work of commanders at all levels, the political organs, and the party and Komsomol[8] organizations. 1,150 men were presented with government awards for bravery and valor in the fighting to capture the city of Cherkassy and 26 soldiers were awarded the high honor of Hero of the Soviet Union.

---

8 Editor's note. The *Komsomol* (*Kommunisticheskii Soyuz Molodezhi*) was the youth auxiliary of the Communist Party.

THE FORCING OF THE DNEPR BY THE 52ND ARMY

Supplement 2.1 The 52nd Army's Combat and Numerical Strength as of 5 November 1943

Units and Formations	Numerical Strength				Tanks and Self-Propelled Guns	Armored Cars
	Officers	NCOs	Enlisted	Total		
73rd Rifle Corps						
Headquarters	123	115	509	777	–	–
254th Rifle Div	621	792	4,700	6,113	–	–
294th Rifle Div	670	865	4,712	6,247	–	–
Total	1,414	1,802	9,921	13,137	–	–
78th Rifle Corps						
Headquarters	132	105	563	800	–	–
373rd Rifle Div	688	865	4,403	5,956	–	–
Total	820	976	4,976	6,762	–	–
259th Independent Tank Rgt	86	231	177	491	2	–
1817th Self-Propelled Artillery Rgt	45	75	121	241	1/7	1
438th Anti-Tank Artillery Rgt	44	130	219	423	–	–
1322nd Anti-Tank Artillery Rgt	49	132	262	403	–	–
568th Gun Artillery Rgt	79	20	470	749	–	–
17th Gds Mortar Rgt	67	183	399	649	–	–
490th Mortar Rgt	64	182	323	569	–	–
38th Anti-Aircraft Artillery Division						
1401st Anti-Aircraft Artillery Rgt	35	132	308	475	–	–
1405th Anti-Aircraft Artillery Rgt	36	121	231	388	–	–
1409th Anti-Aircraft Artillery Rgt	36	121	222	379	–	–
1712th Anti-Aircraft Artillery Rgt	35	121	225	381	–	–
Total	142	495	986	1,623	–	–
Total Combat Forces	2,310	4,406	17,874	25,090	3/7	1

Units and Formations	Rifles	Automatic Rifles	Machine Guns			Anti-Tank Rifles
			Light	Heavy	Anti-Aircraft	
73rd Rifle Corps						
Headquarters	576	22	3	–	–	2
254th Rifle Div	3,078	947	156	34	–	65
294th Rifle Div	2,216	1,282	–	23	–	59
Total	5,900	2,251	243	57	–	126
78th Rifle Corps						
Headquarters	577	70	2	–	–	–
373rd Rifle Div	2,101	1,093	160	44	–	87
Total	2,678	1,163	162	44	–	87
259th Independent Tank Rgt	143	142	2	–	–	–
1817th Self-Propelled Artillery Rgt	64	49	–	–	–	23

338 THE BATTLE OF THE DNEPR

Units and Formations	Rifles	Automatic Rifles	Machine Guns			Anti-Tank Rifles
			Light	Heavy	Anti-Aircraft	
438th Anti-Tank Artillery Rgt	150	219	2	–	–	–
1322nd Anti-Tank Artillery Rgt	122	212	12	–	–	14
568th Gun Artillery Rgt	140	16	8	–	6	–
17th Gds Mortar Rgt	449	137	17	–	–	–
490th Mortar Rgt	406	136	–	–	6	–
38th Anti-Aircraft Artillery Division						
1401st Anti-Aircraft Artillery Rgt	257	103	–	–	–	–
1405th Anti-Aircraft Artillery Rgt	257	103	–	–	16	–
1409th Anti-Aircraft Artillery Rgt	257	103	–	–	16	–
1712th Anti-Aircraft Artillery Rgt	257	103	–	–	16	–
Total	1,028	412	–	–	48	–
Total Combat Forces	11,380	4,737	446	101	60	259

Units and Formations	Guns						
	152mm	122mm	85mm	76mm (Regimental)	45-57mm	76mm (Divisional)	37mm
73rd Rifle Corps							
Headquarters	–	–	–	–	–	–	–
254th Rifle Div	–	12	–	8	12	19	–
294th Rifle Div	–	12	–	8	22	19	–
Total	–	24	–	16	34	38	–
78th Rifle Corps							
Headquarters	–	–	–	–	–	–	–
373rd Rifle Div	–	12	–	8	44	19	–
Total	–	12	–	8	44	19	–
259th Independent Tank Rgt	–	–	–	–	–	–	–
1817th Self-Propelled Artillery Rgt	–	–	–	–	–	21	–
438th Anti-Tank Artillery Rgt	–	–	–	–	24	–	–
1322nd Anti-Tank Artillery Rgt	18	-	-	-	-	-	–
568th Gun Artillery Rgt	–	–	–	–	–	–	–
17th Gds Mortar Rgt	–	–	–	–	–	–	–
490th Mortar Rgt	–	–	16	–	–	–	–
38th Anti-Aircraft Artillery Division							
1401st Anti-Aircraft Artillery Rgt	–	–	–	–	–	–	16
1405th Anti-Aircraft Artillery Rgt	–	–	–	–	–	–	–
1409th Anti-Aircraft Artillery Rgt	–	–	–	–	–	–	16
1712th Anti-Aircraft Artillery Rgt	–	–	–	–	–	–	16
Total	–	–	16	–	–	–	48
Total Combat Forces	18	36	16	24	102	78	48

THE FORCING OF THE DNEPR BY THE 52ND ARMY

Units and Formations	Mortars			
	120mm	82mm	50mm	M-13
73rd Rifle Corps				
Headquarters	–	–	–	–
254th Rifle Div	12	33	4	–
294th Rifle Div	14	39	7	–
Total	26	72	11	–
78th Rifle Corps				
Headquarters	–	–	–	–
373rd Rifle Div	13	41	17	–
Total	13	41	17	–
259th Independent Tank Rgt	–	–	–	–
1817th Self-Propelled Artillery Rgt	–	–	–	–
438th Anti-Tank Artillery Rgt	–	–	–	–
1322nd Anti-Tank Artillery Rgt	–	–	–	–
568th Gun Artillery Rgt	36	–	–	24
17th Gds Mortar Rgt	–	–	–	–
490th Mortar Rgt	–	–	–	–
38th Anti-Aircraft Artillery Division				
1401st Anti-Aircraft Artillery Rgt	–	–	–	–
1405th Anti-Aircraft Artillery Rgt	–	–	–	–
1409th Anti-Aircraft Artillery Rgt	–	–	–	–
1712th Anti-Aircraft Artillery Rgt	–	–	–	–
Total	–	–	–	–
Total Combat Forces	75	113	29	24

Notes
1. The combat and numerical strength of the support troops and rear units and establishments are not shown here.
2. In the fifth column the numerator shows the number of tanks and the denominator the number of self-propelled guns.

Index

INDEX OF PEOPLE

Chernyakhovskii, Lieutenant General Ivan Danilovich ix, 83, 132, 137

Khrushchev, Lieutenant General Nikita Sergeevich 38, 47, 63, 82, 105, 117-119

Moskalenko, Colonel General Kirill Semyonovich 34, 90, 132, 137

Rybalko, Lieutenant General Pavel Semyonovich 34, 72, 82, 85, 132-133

Sidorchuk, Major 292, 296-297, 319

Stalin, General Iosif Vissarionovich 15-16, 38, 65, 71, 82-83, 117-118, 134-135, 138, 172, 282, 305, 333

Vatutin, General Nikolai Fedorovich i, 13, 16, 38, 47, 63, 82, 105, 117, 133

Zhukov, Marshal Georgii Konstantinovich 82, 115, 117

INDEX OF PLACES

Andrushevka 128, 130, 139, 142
Andrushi 29, 33, 62
Annovka 247, 276-283, 288

Bakhmach 19, 24, 48, 62, 77, 103-104, 160
Baranniki 251, 268, 270, 273
Bazar 123, 157, 160
Belaya Tserkov' 16, 19-21, 31, 33, 49-50, 54, 56, 70, 87, 89-90, 101, 108-109, 112, 120-121, 123-129, 131-134, 137, 139-140, 142-143, 145, 150, 153-154, 156, 290-291, 295, 318, 332-333, 335
Belgorod 13, 22, 245
Belichi 88-89, 91, 116, 142
Belki 146, 150, 317
Belozer'ye 316-319, 323, 326-327, 329, 331-332, 335-336
Berdichev 15-16, 19-20, 49-50, 59, 87, 89, 101, 120-121, 123, 142, 151, 154
Berezovka 134, 147, 160
Berkovets 88, 91, 114-115, 142
Bertniki 38, 128, 132, 136
Bezradichi 90, 138, 145
Black Sea 13, 22, 80
Bobritsa 91-92, 113, 119
Bogodukhov 32, 52, 62
Borispol' 20, 26, 42-43, 84, 117, 160-161
Borodaevka 247, 253, 267, 276-277, 279-284, 288
Borodyanka 126, 128, 161
Borshchagovka 90, 116, 142
Botsuly 252, 259-260, 263-264, 278-279
Boyarka 91, 113-115, 133, 136, 160
Brachkovka 246, 268, 270, 273
Breusovka 247, 251-252, 259-260
Brigadirovka 25, 27, 30, 256, 268, 273
Brovary 20, 26, 29, 43, 62, 84, 117, 138, 160-161
Brusilov v, 14, 49, 54, 123, 128, 132-133, 139, 144-156, 159, 161-163, 166-167, 170
Bubnovo 46, 291-292, 300, 305
Bucha 33, 91, 116
Buchak 38, 64, 72-73
Buda 92, 117, 135
Budaevka 90-91, 113-115, 133, 136
Budishche 296-297, 310-313, 315, 317, 332
Bukrin v, 15-16, 33-39, 41, 48, 50-52, 54-56, 62, 64-66, 69, 72-73, 75-78, 82-87, 89-90, 98, 101-102, 106-107, 109-111, 115, 120-121, 124-125, 127, 129, 131-133, 136-137, 139, 141-145, 149, 151, 153, 162-164, 170, 292

Cherkassy vi, ix, 16, 18-19, 23-24, 27, 30, 35-36, 38-39, 45, 71, 110, 156, 163, 290, 292-298, 300, 302-303, 306-307, 309, 311-336
Chernigov 14, 16, 19, 25, 46, 57, 62, 160
Chernobyl' 25, 59, 77, 101, 106, 130, 133, 139, 158-160
Chernyakhov 53, 65, 124, 128, 131-132, 134-135, 138-139, 145, 151-157, 165
Chervona 127-128, 132, 136, 147
Chigirin Dubrova 291-292, 297, 307
Chigirin 291-292, 297, 307, 322
Chikalovka 247, 267, 275, 277

Dachi Pushcha-Voditsa 86, 88-89, 91, 98-99, 111-112, 114
Dakhnovka 293, 296-298, 301, 306, 310-311, 313-314, 317
Darnitsa 19, 42-43, 45, 58, 103, 129, 133, 138, 160-161
Dedovshchina 128, 138, 150
Derievka 246-247, 250-253, 263, 267-268, 270-271, 273-274, 276-277, 279, 281, 285, 291
Desna River 13, 16-17, 19, 24-26, 29, 43-44, 57, 84, 103, 140, 170-171, 260
Dnepr River i, iii, v-vii, ix, 13-29, 31-63, 65, 67-70, 74-80, 84-86, 88, 90, 94, 97, 101, 103-107, 111-113, 115-117, 119-122, 125, 127, 129, 131, 133-136, 138-141, 143-144, 147, 154, 158-162, 164, 168-172, 243, 245-254, 256-257, 259-304, 307-313, 315-316, 319, 321-322, 324, 329-330, 333-335
Dneprodzerzhinsk 16, 77, 246-247, 285, 291, 322
Dnepropetrovsk 14, 16, 24, 77, 243, 274, 285, 333
Dolina 53, 126, 128, 134, 145-146
Domantov 46, 307, 321
Don River 16, 74, 133
Donbass 14, 16, 22, 24
Dubievka 319, 321-325, 328-329
Dymer 58-59, 69, 77, 89-90, 92, 111-112, 114, 117, 120

Fastov 19, 21, 49, 54, 88-90, 92-93, 101, 108-109, 114, 116, 119-123, 125-149, 151-152, 154, 161, 164, 166-167, 171, 290-291, 316
Fastovets 126, 128-129, 131, 134, 136, 147
Fedorovka 111, 127, 134-135, 157-158, 291
Filippovichi 58, 92, 113, 153, 156

Gamarnya 33, 35, 37, 65
Germanovka 126, 128, 134, 145, 153
Geronimovka 293, 295, 297, 306, 311, 313-315, 317, 319, 327
Glemyazovo 26, 29, 34, 56-57, 60, 62, 161

INDEX 341

Glevakha 87, 90, 92, 113-114, 119, 161
Gogolev 25-26, 42-43, 84
Gomel' 16, 25, 77, 163
Gornostaipol' 59, 87, 126
Gorodishche 29, 62, 135, 147, 151, 333
Goryanka 86, 91, 98-99, 112
Gostomel' 67, 86, 161
Grebeni 35, 39, 51-52
Grebenka 19, 25, 32, 62, 92, 132, 160
Grebenki 38, 54, 89-90, 123-127, 132, 138, 149, 160
Grigoro-Brigadirovka 256, 268, 273
Grigorovka 18, 25, 27, 29, 34-36, 38-40, 50-52, 55, 85
Gruzkoye 54, 126, 154-155
Guiva River 128, 144, 146-147
Gusentsy 29, 35-36, 38

Irpen' River 17-18, 33, 42-43, 47, 58-60, 67, 69, 88-92, 95, 107, 113-114, 116, 119-120, 133, 141, 146, 150, 155
Ivankov 58, 87, 124, 127, 130
Ivnitsa 135, 144, 146-149, 155

Kaganovich 18, 87, 159-160, 330
Kagarlyk 27, 33, 49, 53-54, 65, 70, 87, 89-90, 110, 123-124, 128-129, 132, 137, 146, 150, 160
Kailov 26, 42, 53, 58, 85, 106-107, 129, 131, 134, 136, 147, 161
Kal'ne 25, 29, 33
Kaluzhino 271, 274, 276-277
Kamenka 128, 144, 147
Kanev viii, 19, 24, 26-27, 29, 34-36, 38-39, 46, 48, 50, 52-53, 57, 64-66, 70-71, 75-78, 88-89, 102, 106-107, 293, 311, 316, 326
Karpilovka 59, 67, 69, 133, 159
Katyuzhanka 90, 92, 113, 115
Kazatin 19, 21, 49-50, 108, 121, 123-124, 127-133, 136, 138, 142-143
Khar'kov 13, 22, 46, 48, 169, 245, 260
Khmel'na 33-35, 37, 47, 293
Khmel'nitskii 17, 20-21, 23, 25, 27, 29-31, 34, 37, 40, 47, 55, 62, 74, 84, 161
Khodorkov 135, 145-146, 148, 152, 155, 162
Khodorov 35-36, 54-55, 64, 70-72, 85, 93, 107, 110
Khomutets 54, 128, 134, 155
Khotski 29, 38, 56, 84
Kiev i, v, vii, ix, 11, 13-17, 19-27, 29, 31, 33, 42-50, 55, 57-60, 62, 67-70, 72-78, 80-83, 85-97, 101-102, 104-105, 107-111, 113-122, 124-125, 130, 133-145, 149-151, 153-155, 157, 159-163, 167-172, 290-291, 295, 316, 333
Kirovograd 16, 71, 77, 121, 124, 127, 130, 140, 162-163, 243, 285, 290-291, 296, 312, 316, 318, 333
Kobelyaki River 245, 248, 250
Kocherovo 131, 135, 146, 150-155
Koleberda 246, 252, 260, 263, 267-269, 271, 281, 291-292
Komarovka 127, 250, 257
Kopachi 133, 151, 153
Kornin v, viii, 131, 135, 137-139, 142, 144-149, 152, 154, 156, 163-164, 166-167
Korobovka 26, 302-303, 306, 311, 321
Korosten' 14, 16, 19-21, 49-50, 59, 87, 89, 101, 107-108, 113, 120, 124, 127, 129-130, 135-136, 138-140, 144, 157-157, 161, 163-164, 171, 291
Korostyshev 18, 123, 134, 147-152, 155
Korsun'-Shevchenkovskii ix, 14, 71, 112, 309, 333
Kozarovichi 43-44, 58, 86, 90, 92, 114
Kozhanka 123-124, 126, 128, 131-132, 136
Kozintsy 29, 37, 90, 92, 160
Kremenchug i, vi, ix, 14, 16, 27, 45-47, 77, 80, 124, 127, 243, 245-249, 252, 270, 281, 285, 291-292, 316
Kreshchatik 87, 291-294, 296-299, 305, 307-309, 311, 313, 317, 321, 334

Krivoi Rog vii, 16, 71, 77, 80, 243-244, 285, 290-291, 295-296, 304, 306, 312, 316, 322, 326, 328, 332-333
Krivoye 135, 152, 155
Kursk i, 13-14, 16, 21-22, 24, 82-83, 169
Kustolovo-Kushchi 248, 250, 252, 257, 260
Kutsevolovka 246-248, 253, 260, 263, 266-270, 272-274, 281-282, 285

Lazarevka 131, 150, 152, 154-155
Letki 25, 29, 43, 60, 62, 84, 103
Likhovka 270, 276-277, 284
Liman (Lake) 251, 265, 271
Loyev 16, 77, 158
Lozovok 293, 310, 316, 331
Lubny 19-20, 25, 31, 34, 40, 48
Luchin 146-147, 152-153, 156
Lyuterevka 313, 317, 319
Lyutezh 15-16, 43-44, 57-59, 62, 67-70, 85, 87-90, 99, 101, 103-104, 107, 112-113, 140-141, 170-171

Makarov 58-59, 87, 114, 116, 120, 122-123, 126
Makedony 34-35, 37, 123
Makeevka 25, 70, 123, 131, 134, 146
Malin 124, 135, 138-139, 157, 161
Maloye Pereshchepino 25, 250, 252
Malyi Bukrin 36-37, 54-55, 64-65
Malyutyanka 92, 113-114, 119
Manuil'sk 58, 69, 90, 92, 113-115
Mar'yanovka 92, 125-126, 138, 147, 156, 160-161
Mikhailovka 117, 245, 267, 274, 279
Mikulichi 86, 92, 117
Mirgorod 291, 297, 306
Mironovka 19, 31, 50, 54, 70, 109, 247
Mishurin Rog 246-248, 250, 253, 263, 265-279, 281-282, 285, 288
Mogilev 15, 49-50, 52
Mokhnachka 131, 146, 152, 155
Moldavan Island 263, 268-269, 271
Moscow 38, 71, 118, 162, 332
Moshny 292, 297, 311-313, 316, 319, 328, 331
Motrino 246, 251, 273
Motyzhin 90-91, 120, 123, 125
Mozyr' 57, 77, 87, 124

Nezamozhnik 269, 271, 276-277, 283-284
Nezhin 16, 19, 24-25, 32, 48, 62, 77, 103
Nikolaevka 54, 65, 90-91, 248
Novograd-Volynskii 87, 101, 108, 133
Novo-Petrovtsy 44, 58, 69, 101-102

Obukhov 87, 131, 145, 153
Odinets 267, 275, 281-282
Orel 13, 22, 245
Oster 19-20, 29, 62, 84
Ovruch v, 14, 16, 19, 21, 49-50, 87, 90, 101, 108, 119, 124, 135, 140, 144, 158-160, 163-164
Ozery 33, 115, 246, 250-252, 259-260, 273
Ozeryany 150, 152, 155

Pavlovka 251, 264, 267
Pavloch' 128, 131, 133-134, 136, 139, 142, 150
Pereshchepino 25, 245, 250, 252
Perevolochnaya 246, 248, 256, 260, 263, 265, 268, 278, 281
Pereyaslav ix, 14, 17, 20-21, 23, 25, 27, 29-31, 34, 37, 40, 47, 55, 62, 74, 84, 161
Petrovka 250, 252, 274
Pii 36, 39, 89, 134
Piryatin 16, 31-32, 40, 62
Plesetskoye 90-91, 113, 116, 119, 125, 136, 151, 161

Podol'skii 15, 49-50, 52
Pogrebnaya 275, 279, 281
Poles'ye 17, 20-21, 80, 108, 138, 144, 158
Poltava i, 23-25, 27, 45-46, 48, 118, 245-248, 260
Popel'nya 123-124, 128, 131, 133-134, 137, 142, 147, 151
Potashnya 127, 135, 151
Potievka 124-125, 128, 135
Potok 54, 65, 87
Priluki 16, 19-20, 24-26, 29, 31-32, 34, 45, 62, 160
Priorka 33, 44, 58, 88, 90-92, 112, 114, 142
Pripyat' River 17-18, 50, 57-59, 67, 69, 91, 101, 124, 133-134, 158-159
Prokhorovka 46, 291, 305
Psyol 23-24, 41, 245-246, 248, 267
Pukhovka 26, 42, 44, 103
Pyatikhatka 16, 77, 80, 284, 291

Radomyshl' 49, 122, 124, 131, 151-153, 155-157, 159, 162, 165
Rakita (Lake) 324-325, 327, 330
Rakitno 38, 50, 70, 89
Rakovichi 149, 151, 155-156
Rakovka 92, 95, 99, 115-116
Rechitsa 14, 16, 158
Reshetilovka 45, 245, 247
Romashki 64-65, 70-71, 76, 93, 107, 110
Romny 23-26, 32, 45, 62
Ross River 36-38, 50, 52, 294
Rossava 54, 70, 123
Rovno 15, 21, 49, 133, 139
Rovy 69, 89-90, 92, 111, 117
Rozhny 29, 43, 84
Rudnya 84-85, 113, 123, 127, 130, 153
Russkaya Polyana 293, 296-297, 308, 313-315, 317-318, 320-322, 327, 333
Rzhishchev viii, 17-18, 23-24, 27, 30, 34-36, 38-39, 48, 50-54, 57, 64-66, 71-72, 75-77, 89, 102, 123, 126-129

Sekirna 296-298, 301, 304, 309-315, 335
Semipolki 43, 84, 99, 160
Shandra 33-35, 37-38, 47, 50, 54-55, 65
Shchuchinka 34-36, 38-41, 52, 64, 71, 76, 86-87, 93-94, 109, 128, 137
Shepetovka 87, 101, 139
Shevchenko 113-114, 116, 318, 323
Sinyak 67, 95, 113, 115
Sloboda 53, 62, 125, 134-135, 138, 148-149, 293, 323, 332
Smela 290, 295-296, 316-319, 322-326, 328-329, 331-333, 335-336
Sofievka 62, 90, 247, 291, 296
Soloshino 246, 252, 256, 259-260, 262-263, 270, 278, 282
Solov'yovka 145, 148, 152-154
Sosnovka 154-155, 293, 295-296, 312-313, 315, 317, 326
Staiki 35-36, 38, 53, 128, 145-146
Stalingrad 14, 16, 22
Starosel'ye 43, 103, 332
Stavishche 49, 54, 123, 128, 132, 151, 154-156, 166-167
Stavy 54, 90, 132, 134, 136
Stepanki 326, 329, 332
Stritovka 37, 65, 146, 160
Stugna River 120, 138, 145, 147
Sumy ix, 13, 23-25, 32, 46
Svarom'ye 43-44, 49, 59, 62, 84-85, 90, 94, 101, 103
Svidovok 293-299, 301-305, 307-315, 317, 333-334
Svyatoshino 49, 58, 91-92, 99, 115-116, 136, 142, 149, 160, 164

Tarasovka 148, 277, 280-281
Termakhovka 123-124, 134, 160

Teterev River 18, 58-59, 67, 69-71, 86, 91, 123-124, 126-127, 130-132, 134, 148-150, 153-155, 160-161
Traktomirov 35-36, 52, 85, 161
Tripol'ye 17, 39, 44, 52-53, 59, 72, 86, 120, 130, 134-137, 139, 142, 144-145, 152, 154, 161, 164
Tsarevka 131, 152, 154-155
Tsybli 29, 56, 62
Turbovka 145, 147, 152
Tyasmin River 309, 316, 332

Ukraine 14, 16, 21, 33, 38, 46, 77, 115, 117-118, 121, 141, 282, 290
Uspenskoye 246-248, 250-251, 263, 267-268, 270, 272, 274-277, 279, 282
Uzh River 17-18, 58-59, 86-87, 123-124, 126-127, 130, 133-135, 139, 157-158

Vasil'yevka 245, 247, 277, 292
Vasil'kov 20, 31, 49, 88-91, 113, 115-116, 119-121, 125, 132, 136-139, 145, 151, 160-161
Vasilitsa 293, 313, 315
Velikie Golyaki 134, 138, 156
Velikii Bukrin 36, 39, 55, 64
Veresnya 123, 127, 130, 135
Vil'nya 149-150, 152-153, 155
Vil'shka 131, 138, 149-150, 152-155
Vil'sk 124, 128, 151
Vinitskie Stavy 132, 134, 136
Vinnitsa 87, 89, 101
Vitachev 17, 126, 131, 134
Vodotyi 149, 152-153, 155
Voitashivka 150, 152, 155
Voronezh i, v, viii-ix, 13-16, 21, 23-27, 30-32, 36-37, 41, 45-50, 52-53, 57, 60-61, 63, 69-70, 74-77, 170, 172-174, 190, 209, 224, 243
Vorskla River 25, 245-246, 248, 250, 257
Vyshgorod 17, 44, 86-90, 111, 114, 116-117
Vysokoye 128, 155, 166

Yablonovka 91, 123, 319
Yagotin 25, 40, 47, 58, 62, 84, 160
Yanivka 33, 35, 37-38, 53-55, 65
Yashniki 29, 35-36, 38
Yasinovatka 260, 268-270, 276, 281
Yel'sk 16, 87, 159
Yelizavetovka 293, 296-297, 299, 303-304, 310-311, 313, 315, 317
Yerkovtsy 43, 60, 84
Yurov 58, 116, 123, 126, 150
Yurovka 91, 126, 156
Yushki 33, 35, 37, 39, 47, 50, 52, 90
Yuzefovka 65, 127, 148, 154

Zabor'ye 90, 114, 119
Zaporozh'ye 14, 19, 74, 77, 80
Zarubentsy 25, 27, 29, 34-36, 40, 52, 55
Zdvizh River 33, 58, 60, 89-90, 92, 107, 120, 125-126, 141, 150
Zhitomir i, v, viii, 14-17, 19-21, 49-50, 58, 67, 87, 89-92, 101, 108, 114-116, 120, 122-131, 133-140, 142-155, 157, 159-160, 162-164, 166, 170-171, 290-291, 316, 318, 333
Zhmerinka 21, 49, 89, 108
Zhornovka 146, 150, 160
Zhukovtsy 126, 134, 145
Zhulyany 49, 113, 116, 142, 160
Zmogailovka 293, 296-298, 301, 304, 307, 311, 316, 320, 323, 325-326, 329, 331-332
Znamenka 318, 322, 328, 335
Zolotonosha 19, 25, 27, 30, 32, 39, 45, 48, 52, 57, 62, 295, 303, 305-306

INDEX 343

INDEX OF AXIS MILITARY FORMATIONS & UNITS

Army Group South ix, 26, 122, 162

Second Army ix, 25, 77, 87
Fourth Panzer Army 26, 59, 87-89, 122, 148, 170
Eighth Army 25-27, 53, 88, 252, 284, 291

XLVIII Panzer Corps 34, 53, 124, 148

Adolph Hitler SS Panzer Division 124, 130, 139, 147-148, 151, 153-154, 156
Das Reich SS Panzer Division 86, 110, 124, 127-128, 130, 139, 149, 153-154, 156
Grossdeutschland Panzer Division 267, 270, 273, 278, 280
Wiking SS Panzer Division 292-294, 304, 312, 316, 324, 328, 333
1st Panzer Division 121, 124, 127, 130, 133, 139, 145, 147-148, 150-151, 153-154, 156
3rd Panzer Division 39, 53, 87, 127, 130, 132, 156, 326, 328
4th Panzer Division 59, 67, 130, 139, 158
6th Panzer Division 27, 132, 277-278, 280, 282, 316, 326
7th Panzer Division 27, 34, 39, 59, 68-69, 86, 114, 120-121, 130, 135, 139, 141, 145, 148-151, 153-154, 156

8th Panzer Division 59, 67, 86-87, 112-114, 120, 132, 139, 147, 151, 153, 155-156, 162
10th Motorized Division 24, 26, 34, 36, 39, 52, 86, 127, 130, 139
11th Panzer Division 64, 66, 71, 77
19th Panzer Division 27, 34, 36, 39, 52, 86, 149-150, 153-154
20th Motorized Division 34, 39, 52, 87, 112-113, 120-121, 130, 135, 139, 141, 145, 148-151, 156, 162
23rd Panzer Division 267, 270-271, 273, 278, 280
25th Panzer Division 86, 120-121, 124, 127-128, 130, 132, 139, 148, 153, 156
34th Infantry Division 27, 34, 39, 51-52, 72, 86-87, 130
57th Infantry Division 34, 53, 87-88, 293, 311, 316, 324-326, 328
72nd Infantry Division 27, 34, 39, 52, 72, 86, 245, 293-294, 304, 310-311, 314, 316, 325, 328, 333
75th Infantry Division 44, 59, 69, 86, 130
198th Infantry Division 124, 127, 130
208th Infantry Division 26, 43-44, 59, 86, 147, 156
213th Security Division 26-27, 44, 59, 86-87, 120, 156, 162
291st Infantry Division 26, 86, 128, 130, 139, 157-158

INDEX OF SOVIET MILITARY FORMATIONS & UNITS

Steppe Front i, vii, 13-14, 16-17, 23, 25, 27, 45-47, 49, 52, 61, 64, 71, 77, 80, 82, 243-248, 256, 260, 268, 276, 284-285, 294
First Ukrainian Front v, viii-ix, 11, 13, 15-16, 80, 82-83, 85-88, 95, 101, 105, 107-108, 117-118, 121-122, 137-140, 142-145, 159, 161-163, 170, 285, 290-292, 316
Second Ukrainian Front vi, ix, 13, 71, 88, 121, 124, 156, 162-163, 241, 284, 290-292, 295-296, 303, 316, 318, 322, 328
Stavka 13, 15-16, 23-25, 34, 36, 49-50, 57, 65-66, 71, 73-74, 80, 82-84, 86, 107, 113, 115, 120, 137-138, 140, 143-144, 153, 157-158, 161-164, 171, 243, 245, 260-261, 284, 291, 295-296, 318, 335

1st Guards Army 137-138, 144, 153, 155-156, 161, 163
3rd Guards Tank Army 23-25, 27, 29, 31-43, 48-51, 54-55, 62, 64-66, 70-72, 76, 78, 82-85, 89-90, 92-95, 99-103, 107, 113-114, 116-117, 119, 121-123, 125-131, 134, 136, 141-142, 145-148, 150, 152-153, 155-156, 159-161, 166-167
4th Guards Army 23, 27, 30-32, 45-46, 49, 52, 55, 57, 123, 158-159, 163, 291-292, 303
5th Guards Army 50, 57-59, 67-68, 70, 75, 89-91, 94, 107, 110, 114, 119, 122-123, 125-126, 128, 130, 134, 141, 143, 145-146, 149, 166-167, 245, 247-249, 284, 291-292, 295-296, 316, 333
7th Guards Army ix, 25, 29, 39-40, 54, 59, 65, 71-72, 76, 84, 92, 94, 114-116, 119, 125, 127-128, 131, 134, 136, 138, 142, 145-146, 149-153, 167, 243, 245, 247-249, 252, 267, 270, 275-281, 283-284, 286-288, 296, 318-319, 321-332
13th Army v, 57-60, 62, 67, 69, 77, 83-85, 90, 93, 101-102, 107-108, 117, 119, 123-127, 130, 132-133, 135, 144, 149, 151-152, 157-160, 190-191, 209-210, 224-225
27th Army 24-25, 30, 32, 34, 37-39, 42, 48-51, 54-56, 62, 64-66, 70-73, 78, 86-87, 90, 93-94, 101-102, 109-111, 117, 131-132, 134, 136, 148-149, 151-153, 160-162, 185-186, 202-204, 219-220, 234-235, 292, 299, 303
37th Army vi, viii-ix, 243, 245-254, 256-259, 261-262, 264, 266-267, 271-273, 275-289

38th Army viii-ix, 24, 27, 29, 31-33, 42-45, 47-50, 57-60, 62, 67-70, 72, 75, 79, 83-84, 86-96, 98-108, 110-117, 119-133, 135-156, 159-161, 163-165, 168, 173-174, 196-198, 213-215, 228-230
40th Army 24, 29, 31-42, 48-49, 51, 53-56, 62-66, 70-72, 84, 86-87, 90, 93-94, 101-102, 106, 109-111, 117, 127, 129, 131-132, 134, 136, 145-150, 152-153, 160-161, 175-177, 199-201, 216-218, 231-233
47th Army 24, 27, 29, 31, 34-39, 42, 45-46, 48, 50, 52-55, 61-62, 64-66, 70-72, 84, 86, 178-179, 205-206
52nd Army vi, viii-ix, 30-32, 45-46, 52, 71, 156, 179-181, 290-298, 303, 305-306, 308-311, 313, 315-319, 321-329, 331-337
53rd Army 247, 252, 267, 270, 275-277, 279-280, 291
60th Army v, viii, 45, 57-60, 62, 67-71, 84-87, 89-96, 101-103, 105-108, 111, 113-117, 119-130, 132, 134-149, 151-161, 164-165, 192-195, 210-212, 225-227
69th Army 247-252, 257-258, 285

1st Mechanized Corps 245, 247, 272, 276-281, 283
3rd Guards Mechanized Corps 29-30, 38-39, 54, 75
3rd Guards Tank Corps 27, 29, 42, 45
5th Guards Tank Corps 50, 57-59, 67-68, 70, 90-91, 94, 114, 119, 122-123, 125-126, 128, 130, 134, 141, 143, 145-146, 149, 166-167
6th Guards Tank Corps 23-25, 29, 34-35, 39, 44, 54, 92, 113-115, 119, 123, 125, 127-128, 130-131, 133-135, 142, 150, 152-153, 157, 167
7th Breakthrough Artillery Corps 30, 40, 56, 65, 72, 84-85, 89, 94-95, 97, 112, 138, 145, 165
7th Guards Tank Corps 29, 54, 65, 71-72, 76, 92, 94, 114-116, 119, 125, 127-128, 131, 134, 136, 142, 145, 150, 152-153, 167
8th Guards Tank Corps 29-30, 39, 53-54, 75, 82, 95, 129, 133, 138, 146-147, 152
9th Mechanized Corps 29, 33, 39, 54, 65, 92, 94, 114, 119, 125-126, 128, 131, 134, 136, 147, 150, 152-153, 167, 186-187, 206-207, 220-221, 237-238
10th Tank Corps 29, 36, 54, 75, 82, 129, 133, 138, 146, 152, 175-177, 199-201, 216-218, 238-239
15th Rifle Corps 93, 119, 130, 133-135

17th Guards Rifle Corps 58, 93, 115, 124, 134-135, 138, 145-148, 151, 155-156, 297-299, 323, 329
18th Guards Rifle Corps 67, 93, 111, 117, 123, 126-127, 134-135, 157-158
21st Rifle Corps 29, 39, 54, 84, 86, 91, 94, 116, 119-121, 125-126, 128, 130-131, 134-135, 139, 143-148, 150, 152, 156, 165, 167
23rd Rifle Corps 29, 39, 54, 72, 84, 86, 91-92, 94-95, 107, 113, 115-116, 119-120, 123, 125-126, 128, 130-131, 134-135, 139, 145-149, 151, 153-156
24th Rifle Corps 67, 69-70, 92-93, 95, 115, 117, 130, 151, 157
25th Tank Corps 137-138, 155, 161, 163
28th Rifle Corps 93, 119, 159
30th Rifle Corps 36, 58, 67, 92-93, 95-96, 111, 114-115, 117, 130, 146-152, 154-157, 178-179, 205-206, 213-215, 228-230
47th Rifle Corps 29, 35, 39, 51, 53-55, 64, 66, 71-72, 93-94, 109, 136, 145, 147, 152-153
50th Rifle Corps 27, 42, 57, 67, 90-91, 94-96, 102, 111, 113, 116, 119, 123, 125-128, 130-131, 134, 136-137, 146-148, 150
51st Rifle Corps 27, 42, 44-45, 57-58, 67, 90-91, 93-96, 102, 111, 113, 116, 119-120, 125-126, 128, 130-131, 134, 136, 139, 142, 144, 146-147
52nd Rifle Corps 29, 35, 38-39, 52-53, 64, 71, 93-94, 109, 136, 145, 147, 149-150, 152, 156
57th Rifle Corps 249-253, 255, 257, 262-264, 267-268, 274-279, 281, 283, 286
73rd Rifle Corps 291-292, 294, 296-297, 300-303, 307-308, 310-315, 317, 319, 321, 323, 327, 329, 331, 334-335, 337-339
77th Rifle Corps 58, 67, 69, 92-93, 95, 111, 114-115, 117, 130, 151, 157
78th Rifle Corps 291-292, 296-297, 300-303, 307, 311, 313, 315, 323, 329, 337-339
82nd Rifle Corps 249-250, 252, 263, 267-268, 270, 273, 275-279, 281, 283
94th Rifle Corps 138, 155-156, 163-164

1st Guards Airborne Division 249, 278-279, 283
1st Guards Cavalry Division ix, 23, 25, 27, 29, 34-36, 38, 50, 57-59, 67-70, 75, 82, 89-90, 92, 94, 103, 107, 114-116, 119, 122-123, 125-128, 130-131, 134-135, 137-138, 141-142, 144, 146, 149, 151-156, 161, 163, 165, 249, 278-279, 283-284
2nd Guards Cavalry Division 116, 131, 146
3rd Guards Airborne Division 92-93, 113, 146, 149, 151, 154
3rd Guards Mortar Division 30, 40, 84, 94
6th Guards Rifle Division 130, 133, 152, 157
7th Guards Airborne Division 318, 321-330, 332
10th Guards Airborne Division 249, 267, 274-280, 282-283
13th Artillery Division 40, 56, 95, 145-146
17th Artillery Division 40, 56, 95, 146
23rd Rifle Division 29, 135, 146, 148
38th Rifle Division 36, 39, 51, 72, 117, 132, 134
42nd Guards Rifle Division 29, 51, 54, 66, 93, 129, 131, 134, 136, 145, 147, 152
62nd Guards Rifle Division 249, 251-253, 255, 257, 259, 262-272, 274, 276-278, 280, 318-319, 321-322, 324, 327-331
68th Guards Rifle Division 52, 54, 131, 136, 147, 152
70th Guards Rifle Division 57-58, 115, 124-126, 138, 145-147, 149-150, 152
71st Rifle Division 45, 94, 135, 146, 148, 165
74th Rifle Division 84, 91, 116, 132
75th Guards Rifle Division 57, 92, 146-147, 150
89th Guards Rifle Division 249-251, 263, 267-269, 271, 274-279, 283
92nd Guards Rifle Division 249, 251, 257, 263-269, 271, 274-275, 279-281, 283
110th Guards Rifle Division 249, 252, 267-268, 270-271, 274-276, 278, 280, 283, 286
132nd Rifle Division 115, 148, 151
135th Rifle Division 119, 135, 146
141st Rifle Division 111, 117, 148, 151, 155
147th Rifle Division 38, 54, 131, 145
155th Rifle Division 38-39, 51, 54, 152, 185-186, 202-204, 219-220, 234-235
163rd Rifle Division 131, 134, 136, 146
188th Rifle Division 249, 267, 274, 278-280, 283
202nd Rifle Division 119, 146, 150, 153
211th Rifle Division 119, 124, 147, 149, 152
218th Rifle Division 30, 146, 148-149, 151-152
232nd Rifle Division 42, 44, 129
241st Rifle Division 54, 65, 131, 148
254th Rifle Division 292, 296-297, 299, 301, 303, 306-313, 315, 317-323, 325, 327, 329-332, 334
280th Rifle Division 92, 151-152, 157
294th Rifle Division 292, 296-299, 307-308, 311, 313-315, 317, 319-323, 325, 329-332, 334
336th Rifle Division 119, 130, 134, 159
340th Rifle Division 43-44, 58, 67, 114
373rd Rifle Division 291, 296-297, 299, 301, 307-308, 310-311, 313, 315, 317-321, 323, 325, 327, 329-332, 334

Czechoslovak Brigade 91, 146-147
5th Guards Airborne Brigade 107, 110, 292, 295, 333
7th Guards Anti-Tank Artillery Brigade 84, 94, 138
8th Engineer-Sapper Brigade 249, 257, 269
21st Guards Tank Brigade 51, 76, 126
69th Mechanized Brigade 29, 36, 76
91st Tank Brigade 119, 125, 128, 131, 150, 153
129th Tank Brigade 84, 92, 101, 146
150th Tank Brigade 92-93, 127, 157
173rd Independent Tank Brigade 318, 321, 326-327, 329, 335
248th Rifle Brigade 57, 67, 92-93, 115, 151, 153

17th Guards Mortar Regiment 297-299, 323, 329
39th Tank Regiment 91, 94, 113
43rd Tank Regiment 249, 263, 268, 274-276
182nd Guards Rifle Regiment 253, 264-266, 269
184th Guards Rifle Regiment 253, 264-266, 269-270
259th Independent Tank Regiment 297, 312-314, 323, 325, 335, 337-339
438th Anti-Tank Artillery Regiment 297-299, 315-316, 323
568th Gun Artillery Regiment 179-181, 297-299, 307, 323, 329, 337-339
849th Artillery Regiment 299, 321, 323
859th Rifle Regiment 313, 319, 321
861st Rifle Regiment 311, 313, 319-321, 323
929th Rifle Regiment 297, 301, 305, 309, 311-313, 320
933rd Rifle Regiment 301, 309-310, 320
936th Rifle Regiment 297, 310, 313-314, 320
1235th Rifle Regiment 297, 307, 311, 313, 317, 323, 325, 327
1237th Rifle Regiment 297, 330, 332
1239th Rifle Regiment 297, 307, 310-311, 313, 317-318, 323
1322nd Anti-Tank Artillery Regiment 299, 321, 323
1817th Self-Propelled Artillery Regiment 179-181, 297, 312-313, 317, 337-339

2nd Air Army 30-31, 41, 43, 48, 55, 64, 66, 78, 97-100, 109-110, 112-113, 116, 120, 126, 131, 136, 152, 154-155, 168
5th Air Army 248, 256, 272, 275-278, 280-281, 319, 325-326, 329
5th Assault Air Corps 30, 55, 98-100
5th Fighter Corps 30, 55, 99